The Untold Story Of Western Civilization

Vol. 4

The Untold Story of Western Civilization

Volume 4

Modern History

The Age of Merchant Capitalists

Chuck and Tom Paprocki

InnerWorld Publications
San Germán, Puerto Rico
www.innerworldpublications.com

Copyright 2019 by Chuck & Tom Paprocki

All rights reserved under International and Pan-American Copyright Conventions

Published in the United States by InnerWorld Publications

P.O. Box 1613, San Germán, Puerto Rico, 00683

Library of Congress Control Number
2018948333

ISBN: 978-1-881717-75-1

Cover Design: Tom Paprocki

All rights reserved. This book, or parts thereof, may not be reproduced in any form or by any means, electronic or mechanical, including photocopying, recording, without the permission of the publisher except for brief quotations.

Cover photo: J. Pierpont Morgan, the capitalist's capitalist. He organized the Morgan "money trust" that owned controlling interests in U.S. Steel, General Electric, International Mercantile Marine, International Harvester, AT&T, Aetna Life Insurance, and twenty-one railroads. He also created State Monopoly Capitalism in the United States in partnership with President Theodore Roosevelt.

Dedication

To the memory of Prabhat Rainjan Sarkar,
our spiritual guide.

Contents

Introduction	1
Chapter One: The Italian Renaissance	**7**
The Beginning of the Renaissance.	9
Secular Thought and the Modern Age	12
Sculpture	12
Painting	15
Music	16
Theatre	17
Science	19
Medicine	21
The Renaissance in Eastern Europe	21
The Polish-Lithuanian Commonwealth	22
Hungary	24
Croatia	27
Russia	28
Women in the Renaissance	29
Gender Relations	29
Women's Education	30
Women Intellectuals	31
Women Artists	31
Women Politicians	35
Literature Keeps Women in Their Place	38
Women Mystics	39
The New World and the Birth of Colonialism	39
Chapter Two: The Protestant Reformation	**46**
Precursors to the Protestant Reformation	46
John Wycliffe	46
John Huss	47
Huldrych Zwingli	48
Martin Luther: Against Church Corruption	48

King Henry's Church	50
John Calvin: Champion of the Bourgeoisie	51
Calvin the Persecutor	56
Setting the Stage for Capitalism	59
The Counter Reformation	64
The Fifth Council of the Lateran (1517)	65
Sack of Rome	66
The Council of Trent (1545 to 1563)	66
Virgin Mary Mother of God and Queen of Heaven	68
Religious Wars (1560 to 1648)	69
Protestant Religions of Western Europe	72
Anabaptists	72
Anglicans	73
Episcopalians	74
Puritans	74
Presbyterians	75
Congregationalists	76
Pietists	77
Women under Protestantism	79

Chapter Three: The Enlightenment 85

The Church after the Thirty Years War	85
The Church in North America	87
The Church in South America	87
The Absolute Monarchies of France, England, and Russia	87
France	88
England	91
Eastern Europe	92
Emancipation of the Serfs in Russia	95
The Society of Middle Class Merchants	98
Salons	99
Coffeehouses	102
Republic of Letters	104
Women in the Enlightenment	104
Women in the French Revolution	106
Women in England	109
Liberalism	116

Theological Liberalism	116
Secular Liberalism and the Birth of Modern Philosophy and Science	124
Sir Francis Bacon (1561-1626)	125
Thomas Hobbes (1588-1679)	127
Rene Descartes (1596-1650)	134
Baruch Spinoza (1632-1677)	138
John Locke (1632-1704)	140
Gottfried Liebniz (1646-1716)	143
Charles Montesquieu (1689-1755)	146
David Hume (1711-1776)	151
Jean-Jacque Rousseau (1712-1778)	154
Adam Smith (1723-1790)	158
Immanuel Kant (1724-1804)	160
Friedrich Schleiermacher (1768-1834)	169
Georg Hegel (1770-1831)	171
Arthur Schopenhauer (1788-1860)	180
John Stewart Mill (1806-1873)	185

Chapter Four: The Making of the United States 196

Native Americans	197
The Algonquian Tribes	200
Contact with the Colonists	203
Iroquois Confederation	205
The Political Structure of the Iroquois Confederation	207
Social Structure	208
Religion	210
Settlements	212
Festivals	214
Households	215
Iroquois Women	217
Relations with the Colonists	218
The Cherokee	220
Social Structure	221
Cherokee Women	223
Religious Beliefs	224

Settlements	225
Households	227
Festivals	228
Relations with the Colonists	230
The Coming of the Colonialists	**235**
The Dutch	235
The Spanish	236
The French and the English	237
The American Revolution	**243**
Sam Adams	243
Events Leading to the American Revolution	**246**
The Sugar Act	247
The Stamp Act	251
The Townshend Acts	261
The Boston Massacre	263
The Committee of Correspondence	267
The Hutchinson Scandal	268
Boston Tea Party	272
Revolution	277
George Washington	280
Hamilton vs Jefferson	284
Hamilton's Plan	285
The Opposition of Madison and Jefferson	287
The Compromise of 1790	289
Jefferson Sees the Writing on the Wall	290
The Jefferson Strategy	292
Women of the Revolution	296
Early Social Reform Movements	298
Suffrage Movement	298
Andrew Jackson (1767–1845)	300
President Andrew Jackson	305
The Spoils System	307
Federal Rights vs States Rights	308
Taking on the Bank of the United States	309
Jackson and Slavery	314
Native Americans	316
The Ladies Take Jackson Down a Peg	319
Slavery	**321**
Slavery and American Politics	325

The Slave Trade	326
Resistance	331
How the Haitian Slave Revolt Changed History	332
From Indentured Servitude to Racial Slavery	337
Slavery and Christianity	339
Abolition	342
American Religions	345
Religion of the Founding Fathers	345
Methodists	348
Baptists	350
Black Baptists	352
The Church of God in Christ	356
Summary	358

Chapter Five: A Global Capitalist Empire in the Making   360

Events Leading to the Civil War	361
The Civil War	366
An Economic Lesson	369
Reconstruction	384
Robber Barons: Laissez Faire Capitalism Reaches the United States	392
Cornelius Vanderbilt (1794 – 1877)	395
John D. Rockefeller (1839 – 1937)	401
Andrew Carnegie	404
J. P. Morgan (1837-1913)	409
J. P. Morgan Meets Theodore Roosevelt: the Rise of State Monopoly Capitalism	419
How Does State Monopoly Capitalism Work?	426
The Federal Reserve Bank	435
World War I	438
Events Leading to World War I	439
Pan-Slavism and the Bosnia Crisis	440
The Balkan League and the Balkan Wars	441
The Black Hand	444
Austria-Hungary Invades Serbia	445

The Russian Revolution	446
Lessons Learned from the Russian Communist Experiment	450
The War Rages On	451
Trench Warfare	454
Germany Surrenders	455
Religion and WWI: For God and Country	457
African Americans in the War	459
Women in World War I	461
The Economics of World War I	463
Postwar	476
The Great Depression	477
Inflation during the 1920s	479
The Stock Market Crash of 1929	481
The Next Three Years	483
Saving the Banks	487
Fireside Chats	488
The Dust Bowl and the Civilian Conservation Corps (CCC)	489
Other Recovery Programs	490
The Tennessee Valley Authority	492
The Global Impact of the Great Depression	496
Women in the Great Depression	503
Lessons Learned from the Great Depression	507
At the Government Level	507
At the Family and Community Level	508
Recovery	509
World War II	510
Fate of Jewish Refugees	515
1938 Developments Continued	516
How Hitler Built the Wehrmacht with Money from US Corporations	518
The Banks	518
The War Effort	523
IBM	523
Standard Oil	525
Ford	525
Kodak	528
Coca Cola	528

Other Corporations	528
Eugenics	530
The Course of the War	531
1939	533
1940	535
1941	541
1942	550
1943	555
1944	560
1945	568
Women in World War II	573
Religion in World War II	579
Dancing with the Devil	584
The Protestant Churches in Germany	586
The Church in the Immediate Aftermath of Germany's Surrender	591
Lessons Learned	592

Appendix A: Significant Artists of the Italian Renaissance   596

Appendix B: Significant Musicians of the Renaissance   601

Notes   603

Illustration Credits   686

Index   701

About the Authors   720

List of Figures

Fig. 4-1: Leonardo da Vinci's *Vitruvian Man*	10
Fig. 4-2: Nicolas Pisano's The Baptistery of Pisa	13
Fig. 4-3: Michaelangelo's Ceiling of the Sistine Chapel	14
Fig. 4-5: Michaelangelo's David	14
Fig. 4-4: Michaelangelo's Pieta	15
Fig. 4-6: Gentilischi's Self-Portrait as a Lute Player	32
Fig. 4-7: Gentilischi's Judith Slaying Holofernes	32
Fig. 4-8: Anguissola's Self-Portrait at Easel	32
Fig. 4-9: Anguissola's of the Artist's Family	32
Fig. 4-10: van Hemessen's Self-Portrait	33
Fig. 4-11: Beale's Self-Portrait	33
Fig. 4-12: Galizia's Still Life	34
Fig. 4-13: Galizia's Judith with Head of Holofernes	34
Fig. 4-14: Fontana's Portrait of a Lady with a Dog	34
Fig. 4-15: Fontana's Minerva Dressing	34
Fig. 4-16: Leyster's Game of Cards	35
Fig. 4-17: Leyster's Serenade	35
Fig. 4-18: Ruysch's Flowers on a Stone Slab	35
Fig. 4-19: Ruysch's Still Life with Flowers	35
Fig. 4-20: Cantino planisphere	42
Map 4-1: Map of New Russia (Novorossiya)	94
Fig. 4-21: Woman Lowering Children Down Into Coal Mine	112
Fig. 4-22: Woman Pulling Coal Tub	113
Fig. 4-23: The British East India Company	196
Map 4-2: Land of Beringia	198
Map 4-3: Native Languages of North America	199

Fig. 4-24: Iroquois Cradleboard	209
Figs. 4-25 & 4-26: Traditional Iroquois Dress	216
Fig. 4-27: Traditional Cherokee House	226
Map 4-4: Forks of the Ohio River	240
Fig. 4-28: 1772 Portrait of Sam Adams Pointing to the Massachusetts Charter	265
Map 4-5: Battle of Long Island	282
Fig. 4-29: Alexander Hamilton	288
Fig. 4-30: James Madison	288
Fig 4-31: Thomas Jefferson	288
Map 4-6: Louisiana Purchase	303
Map 4-7: United States in 1830	315
Fig. 4-32: Interior Hold of a Slave Ship	328
Map 4-8: Louisiana Purchase	334
Map 4-9: Slave Trade Routes from Africa to the Americas	336
Map 4-10: Northwest Territory in 1787	362
Map 4-11: Louisiana Purchase	364
Fig. 4-33: Value of the Stock of Slaves in the US, 1805-1860	370
Fig. 4-34: Revenues of the US Government, 1861-1865	374
Fig. 4-35: "The Robber Barons"	393
Map 4-12: WWI Military Alliances in 1914	442
Map 4-13: Treaty of Bucharest, 1913	443
Map 4-14: Trench Warfare in WWI	455
Fig. 4-36: Woman at Work in a Factory in WWI	462
Fig 4-37: Navy Recruitment Poster	464
Fig. 4-38: 1920's Flapper	478
Fig. 4-39: 1930's Dust Bowl	490
Fig. 4-40: General Butler Testifying Before the HUAC	521
Fig 4-41: Henry Ford Receiving the Grand Cross of the German	

Eagle Award	526
Fig. 4-42: Washington Post Story on GM's contribution to the German War Effort	527
Fig. 4-43: Woolworth Receives the German Designation "Adefa Zeichen"	529
Fig. 4-44: Jews Being Rounded Up by the Nazis	556
Fig. 4-45: Jews Humiliated and Murdered by Germans in WWII	557
Fig. 4-46: Warsaw Uprising	564
Map 4-15: Battle of the Bulge, 1944	568
Fig 4-47: Poster Campaign Encouraging Women to Enter the Workforce	575
Fig. 4-48: Female Pilots During WWII	576
Fig. 4-49: Photo of Klavdiya Kalugina, Young Female Soviet Sniper	579
Fig. 4-50: Illustration of Christians Bowing to the Will of the German Leaders	589

Introduction

THIS FOURTH VOLUME OF *The Untold Story of Western Civilization* covers the period of the Modern Age in Europe and the United States. The dominance of western society by the intellectual/priest class during the Middle Ages lasted for a millennium, from the time of the fall of Rome in the fifth century until the beginning of the Italian Renaissance in the fifteenth century. After centuries of crusades, inquisitions, and witch hunts, the revolt against the Church brought not only religious freedom, but it also brought a reawakening of secular thought and a return to philosophy and science that had not been present in Western Civilization since the fall of the Greek and Roman empires. Even more significant, the revolt against the Church ushered in an entirely different social psychology and the ascendance of a new ruling class. This new class was composed of merchants and capitalists. While the merchant psychology had always existed in human history in the merchants, traders, bankers, etc., such people had never before been in a position to dominate the social structure as a social class. When they did gain ascendency, however, and began to set the conditions for new social interactions, their psychology was so different from that of the intellectual/priests and the warrior/aristocracy, who had composed the ruling classes of the medieval world, that Europe went through a revolutionary upheaval in all areas of social expression, including economics, politics, law, culture, religion and class relations. With the rise of the merchant psychology, Western Civilization left the Middle Ages and entered the period of Modern History. Just as the warrior psychology had dominated Pre-history and Ancient History, and the intellectual psychology had dominated the Middles Ages, so too would the merchant/capitalist psychology come to dominate Modern History. Their institutions of power were not the army nor the church, but the banks and trade associations that evolved into the multinational corporations that today dominate the world.

This volume on Modern History continues to address the evolution of our three major themes. The first theme is that our intrinsic thirst for limitlessness continues to shape our definition of God in each era of human history by governing the way we worship and by providing the rationale for religious institutions. The second theme explores the relationship between men and women and how it affects our roles in the family and society, the nature of sexuality, and our concept of each other as human beings. The third theme looks at the relationship between social psychologies—warrior, intellectual, and merchant—and how they are affected by the given social conditions that may or may not provide opportunities for class dominance.

Our volume on the Middle Ages ended with the Witch Hunts that were initiated by the Catholic Church and then adopted by many of the Protestant churches. The period of persecution of women, in so far as it lasted for five hundred years, bridged the transition between the Middle Ages and the Modern Age and therefore also sets the conditions for gender relations within the modern age and into the present day. The persecution of women by men has continued regardless of their religion, nationality, social psychology, class, or race. Therefore, we are presented with a fundamental schism in human society that has yet to be healed and which requires a completely different set of ideas and actions from any other attempts at social revolution. So nuclear is our sense of gender to our self-identity, that without a balance between the genders, both in the household and in society at large, we can categorically say that Western Civilization will not make further progress, nor perhaps even survive in the coming days.

When men remain blind to the contribution of women within their relationships and within society at large, they exhibit their own lack of spiritual development. Unity remains unattainable and their quest for an external, perfect God, remains, in all cases, a mere figment of their imaginations. If we follow the guidelines of the experts on God-realization, who are the mystics of all faiths, who have existed throughout human history, we learn that the Divine is achieved through love, service to others, and self-sacrifice. While this message has continued as an undercurrent in human society, its fundamental principles have never been clearly articulated from a universal perspective outside the politically motivated confines and dogmas of different religions. Patriarchal institutions, in the modern age, have made even less progress in articulating a universal spiritual ideology than have those spiritualists in the past, thus making it impossible for human beings to create a united human society.

While the Protestant reform movement successfully challenged many of the abuses and stultifying dogma of the Catholic Church, it did so without raising the bar concerning spiritual theory and practice. Like the Catholic Church in its emergence, the Protestants made their gains only in the political and economic sphere, but in doing so, sacrificed any spiritual vitality that such a movement could have produced. In fact, the severe, materialist nature of the Protestant movement added to the dehumanization of Christianity by ideologically dismissing the value of serving one's neighbor. Most Protestants, strongly influenced by Calvinism, rejected the message of Christ that one could come closer to God by serving one's neighbor. The Calvinists completely ignore appeals to any form of human assistance on both theological grounds as well as social grounds. Calvin and his congregation of middle class merchants (the bourgeoisie) argued that to help others was actually a disservice to them because it inhibited them from helping themselves. This message still echoes in the speeches of right wing Protestant conservatives today.

Calvinism, which provides the theological underpinnings for most Protestant religions, unfortunately followed the Catholic Church, even while rebelling against it, by destroying the original message of Jesus Christ to love one's neighbor. We will look at how this constricted consciousness developed when we look at the rise of Protestantism and its relationship with the emerging merchant class in the days of mercantile capitalism.

The class structure that arose out of the rise of the merchant class continues to exist today and the capitalist ruling class continues to govern the social system under which we live. Leadership within a capitalist society does not depend upon valor or intelligence; it depends upon the money that one possesses.

As we begin our review of the Modern Age, we enter the time in history when the current social values of Europe and the United States gained their first expression—capitalism, separation of church and state, constitutional democracy, economic liberalism, personal freedom, etc. As we review the birth of these social values, let us be mindful of the impending social and environmental cataclysm that we face today and consider how we might use our growing knowledge to reject or modify those values that inhibit us from advancing as a human society, or to keep or modify those values that empower us to prevent social and environmental chaos. We cannot afford to move blindly into the future. It is our hope that this work of history will help us negotiate the difficult road ahead. We believe that the knowledge of history is meant to help us progress as individuals and as a human society by building a world in which we can all live in peace and prosperity with one another. To achieve such an epic task, we will need everyone to move together regardless of gender, age, race, class, religion, social psychology, or nationality.

Consider the prospects for developing a universal morality. Today human beings group themselves according to different propensities regarding their gender, race, class, religion, social psychology or nationality. In doing so, they oppose themselves to others who do not meet the requirements of their particular group. As such, one's sense of morality only extends to those in one's group, whereas those in other groups do not deserve the same treatment as human beings. This process of "dehumanizing" can be seen in nationalist wars, racial conflicts, gender dominance, etc.

Given this half-baked morality, it is no wonder that human beings have been prevented from making significant spiritual or social progress. We have never yet been able to create a true human society. We have never yet been able to achieve an understanding of the spiritual masters who tell us to love our neighbor. As such, our ability to know God, to fulfill our thirst for limitlessness and to realize our highest potential is consistently curtailed.

To achieve that which we desire at the deepest level of our being, we must first develop a universal morality; that is, a worldview that seeks the betterment of all humanity and indeed all of life. There is only one Absolute Consciousness. It exists beyond forms and yet all forms are manifestations of it. Consciousness exists in all things, whether immediately obvious or not. It is this Absolute Consciousness that people try to define in their definitions of God. Because all definitions are limited, however, people do not believe that another's definition pertains to the God of their definition.

For simplicity's sake, let us define God as the Absolute Consciousness, the Supreme Oneness. It is out of this Oneness that everything is derives and into which everything finds its conclusion. Given this definition, everything that leads to Oneness is good and everything that prevents unity is bad.

For example, sexism, ageism, racism, classism, religious exclusivism and nationalism are bad because they divide humanity and prevent us from following the charge of our spiritual masters to love our neighbor as ourselves.

It is quite difficult to relinquish our attachment to these divisive sentiments because they exist is our history and as such form the stuff of our subconscious programming. It is especially difficult for conservatives to relinquish attachment to such values because they see the solution to contemporary problems in the answers of the past. Today the most extreme conservatives struggle to keep women and racial minorities subservient, to promote capitalist values, national dominance, and religious exclusivism. Through such means they are able to elevate their social position at the expense of others.

Today the sins of the past have led us to the brink of disaster. Much of the world lives in dire poverty and is ravaged by wars for the accumulation of remaining resources. Human disrespect for the planet's natural systems is causing a widespread breakdown. Entire species are being eliminated, the soil, water, air, and atmosphere are poisoned, and weather patterns have been disrupted creating hellish conditions on earth.

Given these circumstances, the very survival of humanity, depends upon human society as a whole ascribing to a universal morality and working toward manifesting the Supreme Oneness in every thought, word, and deed.

We are, after all, one species, in a march, out of animality and headed for Divinity. In this march, we are all brothers and sisters, children of the Supreme Progenitor, and just as a loving family would not let a single member fall behind to writhe in the dust, we must also take responsibility for our larger family as well. In our service to others we define ourselves as worthy of the limitless happiness of Divine union.

Chapter One: The Italian Renaissance

AS FAR BACK AS can be remembered, merchants in Europe had established trading relations with merchants in the Middle East in order to bring luxury goods to the Christian nobility in Europe. Ptolemy's map of the World shows the Middle East as the heart of the known world. This was where the Spanish and Italian merchants went to purchase silks, spices, and ceramics, which transformed the homes and palaces of Christian Europe.

European merchants openly traded with Muslim, African, and Hindu businessmen, undeterred by religious or cultural differences. This development created the philosophy of mercantilism that was the first stage of capitalism in Western Europe and thus Western Civilization.

The merchants also learned from the Muslims new ways of doing business. As early as the twelfth century, Fibonacci, a Pisan merchant, who traded throughout the Arabic east, had learned the ability to calculate profit and loss using Arabic numerals. In his revolutionary book, *Liber abbaci* (1202), Fibonacci introduced Europe to the Arabic methods of addition, subtraction, and multiplication, explaining how he was 'marvelously instructed in the Arabic-Hindu numerals and calculation'[1] and how much this had helped him in his business.

By trading with the Arabs, Europeans had also learned a safe way to extend credit over distances. As such, they adopted the word 'cheque' from the Arabic 'sakk'. When international finance increased between the thirteenth and fifteenth centuries, Florentine merchants of the Medici bank opened offices throughout the Near East and used these cheques to secure lucrative contracts with Muslim merchants. The wealth gained by such merchants allowed for the cultural revolution that is known today as the Italian Renaissance.

As the Italian city-states became rich, their buildings became more opulent and oriental in their appearance. Merchants became patrons of the arts and drew up contracts with artists that specified the exact amounts of gold, silver, lapis lazuli, and cochineal to be used in the art they commissioned.[2]

The concentration of wealth by the merchants, not only developed secular art and culture in the fifteenth century, but it also filled the coffers of the Church. While the rich commissioned portraits and other forms of art for their homes, the Church commissioned altarpieces, frescoes, and churches.

As the taste for new wealth, aided by experimental science, generated improvements in mapping, ship design, and other technological innovations, the merchants began to seek funds from bankers and commissions from kings to explore new travel routes to distant lands.

Many historians assert that the greatest feature of early modern history was the fact that the great powers of Europe began the exploration and colonization of Africa, India, the Far East, and the Americas. This led to global trade between the "Old World" (the countries of Europe) and the "New World." The trade association in the Americas was called the Columbian Exchange[3] after Christopher Columbus. It increased European access to food crops, medicinal plants, animals, people, and goods from around the Americas. Such a profound economic revolution also led to personal, cultural, political, and environmental revolutions.[4]

As Europe began to shift away from the medieval political economy that was based upon land estates and serfs, the Church's authority, as well as that of the aristocracy, began to decline. With the new found wealth gained by banks and trading companies, regional and international economies quickly became more sophisticated. As these economies developed, the rise of money, debt, credit, and finance capital assumed a larger role and came to replace political office and land as the universal expression of wealth that had characterized the Middle Ages. Under these conditions, the merchant class rose to power. These were the men who possessed capital, understood finance, and who knew how to turn a profit from trade or the expropriation of other people's labor and material resources.

The Beginning of the Renaissance.

Otto of Freising (1114–1158), a German bishop who visited north Italy during the twelfth century, noticed that, even at this early date, a new urban society, based on merchants and commerce, was evolving and had already begun to replace the feudal structure. Italy, at the time, did not exist as a nation-state. Instead, it was composed of smaller city-states and territories. The Republic of Florence and the Papal States were at the center of the land mass. The Kingdom of Naples controlled the south; the Milanese, the north; the Genoese, the west; and the Venetians controlled the east. By the fifteenth century, Italy was one of the most urbanized areas in Europe. Many of its cities stood among the ruins of ancient Roman buildings; so it was quite natural that the classical nature of the Renaissance originated there.

This emergent society was critical of the national monarchies of the north and was also suspect of Church dogma and corruption. Holding both Church and Empire at bay, these city republics, due to their wealth, began to explore the realms of secular thought and personal liberty.

Such an environment proved fertile ground for revolution. The ideas and wealth that these cities came to possess allowed for the creation of large public and private artistic projects. Individuals also had more leisure time for study and artistic pursuits.

The Renaissance means the "rebirth" of the arts and sciences known to the ancient Greeks and Romans. Religion, which had dominated the Middle Ages, could no longer provide satisfactory freedom from the Church and aristocracy in order to explore new lands and new ideas. The merchant class was unashamed in their love of worldly values, of power, splendor, and sexuality.

The revolution of the Renaissance spread throughout Europe from the twelfth to the sixteenth century and, in so doing, influenced literature, philosophy, art, music, politics, science, religion, and education on the European mainland. The impetus for the Renaissance was quickened by the introduction of classical Greco-Roman works which were translated by secular intellectuals living within the Italian cities. The study of these ancient works and the incorporation of their knowledge into medieval society came to be known as humanism. Humanism was not so much a philosophy as it was a way of thinking that valued reason over myths and dogmas, as well as the expression of human emotions in the arts and culture.[5]

An example of this humanistic method can be seen in Leonardo da Vinci's *Vitruvian Man* that shows the correlations of ideal human proportions with geometry as described by the Roman architect Vitruvius in his *De Architectura*.[6] Vitruvius had described the human figure as being the principal source of proportion among the Classical Orders of architecture. An "order" in architecture is a way of assembling certain parts subject to uniform established proportions based on the function that each part has to perform.[7]

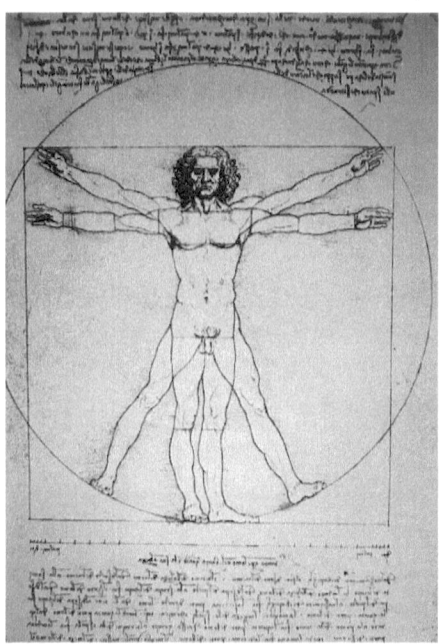

Fig. 4-1: Leonardo da Vinci's *Vitruvian Man*

Renaissance humanism was a response to the "narrow pedantry" associated with medieval Church-dominated teaching that prevailed in its universities in Europe from AD 1100 to 1700. The Church's education system, known as "scholasticism," was used to articulate and defend Church dogma. Humanists, on the other hand, wanted to create a citizenry that could speak, write, and think with clarity. They wanted a richer civic life that reflected thoughtful and virtuous action. This was to be accomplished through the study of the humanities: grammar, rhetoric, history, poetry, and moral philosophy.

Humanism became a pervasive cultural movement that was not limited to a small intellectual elite. There were important centers of humanism in Florence, Naples, Rome, Venice, Genoa, Mantua, Ferrara, and Urbino.[8]

The humanist movement began with certain intellectuals like Petrarch, Coluccio Salutati, and Poggio Bracciolini who collected antique manuscripts. Petrarch's rediscovery of Cicero's letters is often credited with initiating the Renaissance and as such Petrarch was dubbed the "Father of Humanism." Many humanists, including Petrarch, worked for the Church, while others were lawyers and chancellors of Italian cities and thus had access to book copying resources.

By the mid-fifteenth century, many members of the upper classes had received a humanist education that came to be known as the Humanities, which is still taught in American universities today.

The Renaissance spread northward to France, Germany, the Netherlands, Belgium, England, and into the countries of Eastern Europe. As this occurred, many leading churchmen became humanists who, in their writings, introduced new understandings of the Bible and other early Christian writings. This work was greatly influenced by thinkers like Erasmus and *Jacques Lefevre* d'Etaples.

Erasmus (1466 to 1536), who was a Catholic priest, social critic, teacher, and theologian, was known as the "Prince of the Humanists." As a classical scholar, he prepared new Latin and Greek editions of the New Testament. He also wrote *On Free Will, The Praise of Folly, Handbook of a Christian Knight, On Civility in Children*, and many other works.[9]

As a reformer, he raised questions that influenced and inspired the more radical Protestant reformers. Yet, while he criticized the abuses within the Church and called for reform, he kept his distance from radicals like Martin Luther and his collaborator, the theologian, Melanchthon.[10] Erasmus rejected Luther's emphasis on faith alone and supported the Catholic Church's doctrine of free will versus the doctrine of predestination that had gained support among Wycliffe, Luther, and Calvin. At the same time, he continued to criticize the abuses of the Church. His middle path gained him enemies on both sides of the emerging conflict.[11]

Jacques Lefèvre (1455 to 1536) was a French theologian and humanist who was a friend of Erasmus. While remaining a Roman Catholic all his life, he also sought to reform the Church without separating from it. Nonetheless, the Church later banned several of his books as heretical.[12]

Secular Thought and the Modern Age

While the Renaissance revolution was largely in the service of the Church, it also had the distinct effect of secularizing Western thought as well. While artists and writers created visual art, music, and different forms of literature and philosophy that exemplified Church beliefs and mythology, they also, in the process, evolved new dimensions of art, science, mathematics, and philosophy with non-religious themes that were characteristic of the Humanist movement.

Sculpture

Nicola Pisano, (1220-1284) introduced the Roman sculptural style to Medieval Italy and is therefore considered to be the founder of modern sculpture. His Pulpit in the Baptistery of Pisa, one of his masterpieces, used the orders of Roman architecture but merged them with the Gothic style that was being introduced to the Italians by the Germans in the north. Arnolfo di Cambio and Giovanni Pisano followed his lead in blending these two styles.[13]

The art and science of Sculpture advanced quickly. Sculptors from all over Europe gained inspiration from the work of these early artists and over the next two centuries, hundreds of great artists emerged. Among them Donatella, Lorenzo Ghiberti, Michelozzo, Baccio da Montelupo, Giovan Francesco Rustici, Jacopo Sansovino, Maximilian Colt, Alonso González de Berruguete, and Bartolomeo Bellano to name a few.

Michelangelo (1475 to 1564) came on the scene when sculpting was already in its golden era. He was considered to be the greatest artist of his time and even today is considered to be one of the greatest artists

Fig. 4-2: Nicolas Pisano's The Baptistery of Pisa

who ever lived. Because Michelangelo was also a painter, architect, poet, and engineer, he vies with his contemporary, Leonardo da Vinci, for the title of the archetypal Renaissance man. A number of Michelangelo's works in painting, sculpture, and architecture rank among the most famous in existence. The sheer volume of his surviving correspondence, sketches, and reminiscences also make him the best-documented artist of the sixteenth century.

Michelangelo sculpted the *Pieta* and *David* before he was thirty years old. He also created two of the most influential frescoes in the history of Western art: the scenes from Genesis on the ceiling of the Sistine Chapel in Rome and *The Last Judgment* on its altar wall.

At the age of seventy-four, he became the architect of St. Peter's Basilica. One of the qualities most admired by his contemporaries, and subsequent artists up to the present, was his sense of "awe-inspiring grandeur." The attempts by later artists to imitate his passionate and yet highly personal style resulted in Mannerism, the next major movement in Western art after the High Renaissance.[14]

Fig. 4-3: Michaelangelo's Ceiling of the Sistine Chapel

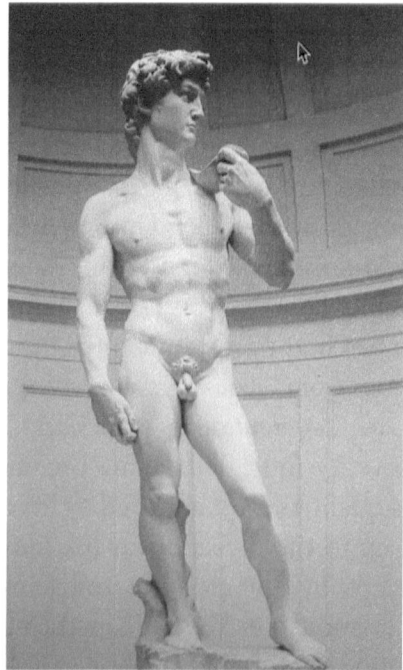

Fig. 4-5: Michaelangelo's David

Fig. 4-4: Michaelangelo's Pieta

Painting

Before the Renaissance, painting was done on wet plaster. These paintings were called *frescoes*. Artists used tempera, which was an egg-based paint, which dried quickly so that careful planning had to be taken. There was little room for error or spontaneity. The problem with this type of painting was that it required rich patrons and large walls so the market was primarily limited to the Church, kings, and the nobility.

The Renaissance artists created a revolution in painting. For one thing, they adopted the use of canvas, which was cheaper, smaller, and portable. Painting on canvas also allowed them to set up studios where they could invite models and paint still lifes, providing a much greater range of topics. Artists at this time also developed oil paints that could be mixed with each other allowing a much broader range of colors, better shading, and more spontaneity. Since oil paints dried more slowly than tempera, this invention led to more realistic and vibrant paintings. Artists could give more attention to detail and this led to the development of perspective, proportion, and the study of light and its effect on color and form.

Some of the great painters of the day are listed in Appendix A.

Music

Musicians during the Italian Renaissance created a common, unifying musical language, in particular the polyphonic style of the Franco-Flemish school. In music, polyphony is a *texture* consisting of two or more simultaneous lines of independent melody, as opposed to a musical texture with just one voice, which is called monophony.[15] Texture is how the melodic, rhythmic, and harmonic materials are combined in a composition, thus determining the overall quality of the sound in a piece. The Catholic masses had been accompanied by monophonic Gregorian chants since the eleventh and twelfth centuries. Now polyphonic pieces were introduced at the mass, allowing for harmonies. As musicians experimented with the multiple voices, however, the sacred got mixed with the secular, causing concern among the clergy. At the time that polyphony arose, the Church was going through the Western Schism in which more than one pope contested for legitimacy. The popes in Avignon, who were considered by the clergy in Rome to be the antipopes, ruled in a town that was known for its secular music making, which then came to have its impact on sacred music.

As the secular music began to merge with the sacred, it gave church music more of a humorous or light-hearted quality that challenged the solemn worship to which the clergy were accustomed. Harmony was considered "frivolous, impious, and lascivious," and an obstruction to the sound of the words. The Church banned certain instruments because of their association with secular music and pagan rites. Dissonance was labeled as evil, fueling the argument against polyphony as being the devil's music. After banishing polyphony from the Liturgy in 1322, Pope John XXII wrote in his 1324 bull *Docta Sanctorum Patrum* warning against the unbecoming elements of this musical innovation.[16]

The invention of the Gutenberg press in 1440, however, made the distribution of music and musical theory available on a wide scale. Demand for music as entertainment and as an activity for educated amateurs increased with the emergence of the merchant class. Relative political stability and prosperity in Netherlands and Belgium, along with a flourishing system of music education in the local churches and cathedrals, allowed the training of hundreds of singers and composers.

These musicians were highly sought after throughout Europe, particularly in Italy, where churches and aristocratic courts hired them as composers and teachers. By the end of the sixteenth century, Italy had absorbed the northern influences, with Venice, Rome, and other cities being centers of musical activity, reversing the situation from a hundred years earlier. Opera, which drew on Medieval and Renaissance court entertainment arose in 1639.[17]

As music became increasingly freed from medieval constraints in range, rhythm, harmony, form, and notation, it became a vehicle for new personal expression. Many familiar modern instruments, including the violin, guitar, lute, and keyboard instruments developed into new forms during the Renaissance, allowing a further evolution of musical ideas for composers and musicians to explore. Modern woodwind and brass instruments like the bassoon and trombone also appeared, extending the range of sonic color and power.

Both secular and sacred music, vocal and instrumental, survive in quantity from the Italian Renaissance era. An enormous diversity of musical styles and genres flourished during the Renaissance, which can still be heard on commercial recordings in the twenty-first century, including masses, motets, madrigals, chansons, accompanied songs, instrumental dances, and many others. Numerous early music ensembles, specializing in music of the period, give concert tours and make recordings, using a wide range of interpretive styles.

Some great musicians of the Renaissance period are included in Appendix B.

Theatre

Modern theatre also grew out of the Italian Renaissance. The humanists became familiar with the Greek comedies and tragedies. While they based their works on Greek mythology, they presented their plays from the perspective of contemporary problems. Looking back, the Romans had developed their theatre based on the Greeks. Plautus and Terence were noted for their comedies, while Seneca continued the Greek tragedies. When the Church came to power, however, these classical dramas were outlawed and forgotten. However, because the common people found

Catholic ideology unintelligible, in large part because it was presented in Latin, the Church began to embrace religious miracle plays and then morality plays to teach the people about Christianity. Traveling companies developed and presented skits on sacred themes, but also featured jugglers and singers.

During the Renaissance, the morality plays began to take on more secular themes and some even introduced comedy. In England, during the time of Henry VIII, these plays began to introduce lower class characters and ludicrous plots. After 1580, during the reigns of Henry's daughter, Queen Elizabeth, followed by James I and Charles I, permanent playhouses were built with stages and curtains. Costumes became more elaborate and their colors came to signify the social classes. Public performances were open to all classes. And for the first time, lines were spoken in blank verse rather than rhyme.

Genres of the period included the history play, which depicted English or European history. Shakespeare's plays about *Richard III* and *Henry V* belong to this category, as do Christopher Marlowe's *Edward II* and George Peele's *Famous Chronicle of King Edward the First*. History plays also dealt with more recent events like A *Larum for London* which dramatized the sack of Antwerp in 1576.

Tragedy was also a popular genre. Marlowe's tragedies, *Dr. Faustus* and *The Jew of Malta* were exceptionally popular, as was Thomas Kyd's *The Spanish Tragedy*. The four tragedies considered to be Shakespeare's greatest, *Hamlet*, *Othello*, *King Lear*, and *Macbeth*, were composed during this period, as well as many others.[18]

Comedies became popular as well. City comedies that dealt satirically with life in London like Thomas Dekker's *The Shoemaker's Holiday* and Thomas Middleton's *A Chaste Maid in Cheapside* were especially popular. So also were the biting satires of Ben Jonson, including *Volpone*, *Bartholomew Fair*, and *The Devil is an Ass*.[19]

Though marginalized by now, the old morality plays like John Fletcher's *Four Plays in One* (1608-13) could still draw a crowd. After about 1610, a new hybrid tragicomedy became popular, as did the masque, a courtly presentation involving music and dancing, singing and acting, within an elaborate stage design. These were popular during the reign of the first two Stuart kings, James I and Charles I.[20]

Science

In the beginning, the intellectual humanists favored human-centered subjects like religion, politics, art, and history over the study of nature or applied mathematics. Many of the early humanists were still under the sway of the Church that viewed the natural world as an animate spiritual creation that was not governed by laws or mathematics.[21] Nonetheless, as we have seen, science and art were very much intermingled in the Renaissance. We might say that Leonardo Da Vinci started this synthesis by setting up systematic studies of movement and aerodynamics and creating principles of the research method, achievements that led some historians to call him the "father of modern science."

The rediscovery of ancient scientific texts was accelerated after Constantinople fell to the Ottoman Empire in 1453, forcing many Greek intellectuals to migrate to Rome. The invention of the printing press, similar to the invention of the internet today, democratized learning and allowed a faster propagation of new ideas.

These developments greatly advanced the sciences, especially in the areas of astronomy, chemistry, physics, mathematics, engineering, manufacturing, and also in anatomy and geography.

Alchemy was an early expression of Renaissance science. Sometimes described as an early form of chemistry, alchemists believed that there was an essential substance from which all other substances formed, and that if you could reduce a substance to this original material, you could then construct it into another substance, like lead to gold. Medieval alchemists worked with three main elements, sulphur, mercury, and salt.[22] Although some like Paracelsus saw alchemy as a practical science to develop herbal medicine and plant remedies, others took advantage of entrepreneurial opportunities by contracting with the elite for practical purposes related to mining, medical services, and the production of chemicals, medicines, metals, and gemstones.[23]

Astronomy was another great interest to the early scientists. It was based on the geocentric model described by Claudius Ptolemy in his *Almagest*, which addressed the motion of the stars and planets. Sometime around 1450, mathematician Georg Purbach (1423–1461) began a series of lectures on astronomy at the University of Vienna that were collected by his student Regiomontanus (1436–1476) and published as *Theoricae novae planetarum* in the 1470s. This "New *Theorica*" replaced the older *theorica* as the textbook of advanced astronomy. This set the stage for a later publication published in 1496, the *Epitome of the Almagest*, that made the highest levels of Ptolemaic astronomy widely accessible to European astronomers for the first time.

These were the works that were studied by Nicolaus Copernicus (1473–1543) who, shortly before 1514, began to explore a shocking new idea that the Earth revolved around the Sun, instead of vice-versa. He spent the rest of his life attempting a mathematical proof of this phenomenon. When his treatise, *De revolutionibus orbium coelestium*, was finally published in 1543, it was initially accepted by the Catholic Church but was rejected by Protestants as heresy. Catholics eventually joined the wave of Protestant opposition and banned the book in 1616. While the Protestant churches eventually accepted Copernicus' findings after more evidence emerged to support it, the Catholic Church, continued to hold their anti-Copernican beliefs until the nineteenth century. The ban on Copernicus's views was not lifted until 1822, and the ban on his book not until 1835.[24]

Copernicus was followed in the field of astronomy by Johannes Kepler (1571–1630) a German mathematician, astronomer, and astrologer. Kepler is best known for his laws of planetary motion, based on his works *Astronomia nova*, *Harmonices Mundi*, and *Epitome of Copernican Astronomy*. These works provided one of the foundations for Isaac Newton's theory of universal gravitation.[25]

Galileo Galilei (1564–1642), a contemporary of Kepler and an Italian astronomer, physicist, engineer, philosopher, and mathematician, has been called the "father of observational astronomy," the "father of modern physics," and the "father of science." His contributions to observational astronomy include the telescopic confirmation of the phases of Venus, the discovery of the four largest satellites of Jupiter (named the Galilean moons in his honor), and the observation and analysis of sunspots. Galileo's championing of heliocentrism was controversial within his lifetime. He was investigated by the Roman Inquisition in 1615 because his *Dialogue Concerning the Two Chief World Systems* appeared to attack Pope Urban VIII. He was tried by the Inquisition, found "vehemently suspect of heresy," forced to recant, and spent the rest of his life under house arrest.[26]

Medicine

With the Italian Renaissance came an increase in experimental investigation, principally in the field of dissection and body examination, thus advancing our knowledge of human anatomy. The development of modern neurology began in the sixteenth century with Vesalius, who described the anatomy of the brain and other organs; he had little knowledge of the brain's function, thinking that it resided mainly in the ventricles.

William Harvey (1578-1657), an English physician who made original contributions in anatomy and physiology, was the first known to describe in detail the circulation and properties of blood being pumped to the brain and body by the heart, thus providing a refined and complete description of the circulatory system. His definitive work is *On the Motion of the Heart and Blood in Animals*. The most useful works in medicine at the time however, used both by students and expert physicians, were the *Materiae Medicae* and the *Pharmacopoeiae*.

While understanding of medical sciences and diagnosis improved, little direct benefit to health care occurred. Few effective drugs existed, beyond opium and quinine. In terms of health care, people still went to women for their superior knowledge of healing plants and their ability to relieve common diseases. Thus, the women witches continued to provide a challenge not only to the Church but also to the class of emerging male physicians.

The Renaissance in Eastern Europe

The Renaissance in Eastern Europe was primarily expressed in its politics and its architecture. Poland, Lithuania, Hungary, Croatia, and Russia were all strongly influenced by the Renaissance of Western Europe.

The Polish-Lithuanian Commonwealth

During the fourteenth and fifteenth centuries, Poland and Lithuania, strongly influenced by humanist ideas, experimented with joining their two countries. This resulted in an elective monarchy in 1569 with the signing of the Union of Lublin.[27] The two countries then shared a common king elected by a common senate. The Commonwealth created a large, multi-ethnic and multi-religious state that has shaped the modern identity of these two countries.

During the subsequent peace between the two states, the Renaissance in Poland and Lithuania flourished. Lasting from the late fifteenth to the late sixteenth century, it is considered to have been the Golden Age of Polish culture.

The period gave rise to the flowering of architecture, literature, and art. The Latin Culture of the Renaissance also helped to integrate this multilingual state. Latin, together with Polish, became the main media of communication among the nobility.[28]

Many Italian architects were welcomed in the country, including Francesco Fiorentino, Bartolommeo Berecci, Santi Gucci, Mateo Gucci, Bernardo Morando, and Giovanni Battista di Quadro. Thinkers, educators, and merchant families were also welcomed and most of these settled in Krakow, the Polish capital.[29] The humanist ideas concerning the dignity of man and the power of reason were much appreciated in the Commonwealth and many works from classical Latin, Greek, Hebrew, and Italian were translated into Polish.

The ááááá, one of the world's oldest universities, graduated 3,215 students in the first decade of the sixteenth century and produced many outstanding artists and scientists. Among them were Nicolaus Copernicus who, in his *De revolutionibus orbium coelestium,* presented the heliocentric theory of the universe; Maciej of Miechów, author of *Tractatus de duabus Sarmatis*, the most accurate up-to-date geographical and ethnographical account of Eastern Europe; Bernard Wapowski, a cartographer whose maps of that region appeared in Ptolemy's *Geography*; Marcin Kromer who, in his *De origine et rebus gestis Polonorum libri,* described both the history and geography of Poland; Andrzej Frycz Modrzewski, a philosopher concerned with governance; Mikolaj Rej who popularized the use of Polish language in poetry; and Jan Kochanowski, whose poems in the Polish language elevated him to the ranks of the most prominent Slavic poets.[30]

The Commonwealth refused to get involved in the Thirty Years War between the Catholics and Protestants that ravaged Western Europe in the first half of the seventeenth century. Rather, in the Commonwealth, the Reformation spread peacefully throughout the country. Living conditions improved, cities grew, and exports of agricultural products enriched the population.

Many students, who attended the twenty-five hundred schools and academies of the Commonwealth, traveled abroad to complete their education and many maintained contacts with leading European philosophers of the Renaissance, including Thomas More, Erasmus, and Philip Melanchthon. Poland not only partook in the exchange of major cultural and scientific ideas and developments of Western Europe, but also spread the Western heritage eastwards among the East Slavic nations bringing printing, the Latin language, art, and poetry to Belarus, Ukraine, and eventually Russia. The first four printed Cyrillic books in the world were published in Kraków, in 1491, by printer Szwajpolt Fiol.[31]

In 1578, the Chancellor of the Commonwealth, Jan Zamoyski, began the design of the ideal Renaissance city,[32] sponsoring the construction of Zamosc, which became an important administrative, commercial, and educational town of Renaissance Poland. Kraków and Gdansk were also sites for the development of Renaissance architecture as were other major cities in the Commonwealth.

Renaissance painting was introduced in Poland by many immigrant artists, like Lucas Cranach, Hans Dürer and Hans von Kulmbach. Portraitists became popular and found patronage among the nobility.

The center of musical culture was the royal residence at Kraków, where the royal court welcomed many foreign and local performers. The most significant works of the Renaissance in Poland include compositions, usually for lute and organs, both vocal and instrumental, from dances, through polyphonic music, to religious masses. Nicolas Cracoviensis (Mikołaj of Kraków) composed many masses, songs, dances, and preludes. Mikołaj Gomółka authored musical rendition of Kochanowski's poems (*Melodies for the Polish Psalter*). The most famous

Polish composer was Wacław Szamotulski, recognized as one of the outstanding Renaissance composers.

Literature progressed beyond religious themes. Contemporary poetry celebrated the country's nobles, expounding on the pleasures and beauty of life in the countryside, surrounded by nature. Literary forms varied, from ode, pastorals, and sonnets to elegy, satire, and romance.

Jan Łaski (religious reformer), Maciej of Miechów (writer and professor), Nicolaus Copernicus (astronomer), Wawrzyniec Grzymała Goślicki (political philosopher), Marcin Kromer (geographer), Andrzej Frycz Modrzewski (philosopher), Piotr Skarga (political reformer), and Józef Struś (doctor and scientist) were considered to be among the best intellectuals and scientists of the time.[33]

Polish Renaissance architecture is divided into three main periods.[34] The first period (1500–1550) is often called "Italian," because most of the Renaissance buildings in this time were built by Italian architects invited by Polish nobility. During the second period (1550–1600), the Renaissance style became common, and included influences from the Mannerist style created by Michelangelo. In the third period (1600–1650), Mannerism became popular, along with the first introduction of the Baroque style.[35]

Hungary

In the latter half of the fifteenth century, Christian princes all over Europe were alarmed by the successful military campaigns of the Ottoman Turks. After Constantinople, the capital of the Byzantine Empire, fell to an invading army of the Ottoman Empire in 1453, the Turks advanced north on the Balkan peninsula and within three years were standing at the gates of Belgrade, the southernmost city in Hungary. *János* (John) *Hunyadi*, a Hungarian regent and general, led the Hungarian military in a campaign against the Turks that resulted in the Turks defeat at Belgrade in 1456. In honor and gratitude for his victory, the bells of Catholic and Protestant churches were rung each day at noon to commemorate the Belgrade victory.[36] While the victory stopped the Turkish Empire's northward thrust for many years, it was Hunyadi's last feat. He died a few weeks later of a fever contracted in the camp and his son Matthias became king.

The power of the Hungarian Kingdom reached its peak under the reign of King Matthias I (1458-90). Matthias was a true Renaissance man whose capabilities included being a great soldier, diplomat, administrator, legislator, a brilliant linguist, and a discriminating patron of the arts and letters.[37] He has been remembered ever since, in popular tradition and folktales, as *Matthias the Just*. The splendor of his court surpassed anything seen in Eastern Europe at the time. He loved artistic luxuries, and the relics of classical Greece and Rome. Thanks to Matthias, the Renaissance reached Hungary at an early date. After he married Beatrix of Aragon, the daughter of the King of Naples, Italian Renaissance artists found a second home in his court.

The Renaissance style of architecture was promoted in Hungary under Matthias. The most important work of Hungarian Renaissance ecclesiastical architecture is the Bakócz Chapel in Esztergom. It was the first centrally conceived chapel outside of Italy. In 1823, the medieval church was rebuilt into the new Neo-Classical Esztergom Cathedral.[38]

The magnificent Coronation Church of Buda[39] proved that Matthias's capital was one of the most elegant cities of Europe. Buda Castle[40] was also enlarged and modernized in Renaissance style. King Matthias also built a sumptuous summer palace in Visegrad.[41] His successor, King Ulászló II, built an Italianate hunting lodge in Budanyék. Aristotile Fioravanti travelled from Hungary to Moscow where he built the Cathedral of the Dormition.[42] The Hungarian constructions were largely destroyed in the Ottoman wars, but the remains of the Visegrád Palace were partially reconstructed in the twentieth century.[43]

Matthias and his guests, the Hungarian nobility, foreign diplomats, scholars, astronomers, etc., the men of the Renaissance, indulged in spirited and witty conversations, while they were entertained by musicians, magicians, artists and poets. Unfortunately, only descriptions of his court, parts of his library, and a few architectural relics of his reign survived.

Matthias's collection of books is known as the *Corvina Library*.[44] The greater part of the collection was destroyed during the Turkish wars, but we know of several hundred surviving volumes scattered all over the world. Most of the hand written books (codices) are now housed in the Hungarian National Library, but individual volumes are to be found in the British Library in London as well as in the New York Public Library, and many more may come to light.[45]

Matthias also founded the University of Pozsony in 1467,[46] and set up a printing press in the capital, Buda, the old town of contemporary Budapest in 1472.

In 1526, after the death of Matthias in 1490, the Turks returned again to Hungary and after the Battle of Mohacs,[47] withdrew from Hungary, but kept control of Budapest the capital. The absence of the Turks in the country created a power vacuum. Ferdinand I of Hapsburg seized power in the west of Hungary, while János Szapolyai, a Hungarian nobleman, took control of the eastern part, which became known as Transylvania.[48] Szapolyai was known for murdering Hungarian peasants, who rebelled-because a Transylvanian bishop had ordered peasants to pay tithes in coin rather than in goods.[49]

When the capital city became occupied by the Ottomans in 1541, the central part of the Kingdom of Hungary became a border province of its Empire. Thus Hungary was split into three parts, becoming the buffer zone of two world powers.

Apart from political events, the Hungarian economy, society, and culture remained unified and the impact of the European trends, including the Renaissance, humanism, the Protestant Reformation, and the Catholic Counter Reformation continued to impact the people. Catholicism, Eastern Orthodox, and Judaism were all practiced. This "composite state" in the sixteenth century, developed close diplomatic relations with the Italian states, the Habsburg provinces, and the Kingdom of Poland, whereas the weakened kingdoms of the Balkan became its vassals in the late Middle Ages. The Hungarian state engaged in a flourishing trade with Venice, the southern German territories, and Poland. These connections survived well after the partition of the country.[50]

While the royal court ceased to exist, Hungarian nobles continued to build many provincial Renaissance castles in the sixteenth and seventeenth centuries. The most important of them was the Rakoczi Castle in Sarospatak.

Many significant Renaissance castles were also built in Transylvania. The palace of the Prince of Transylvania, Gabriel Bethlen, built in Gyulafehervar (now Alba Iulia in Romania) was designed by Italian architects. The Transylvanian Renaissance lasted well until the first half of the eighteenth century because of the aesthetic conservatism of the country. The vernacular architecture of Transylvania preserved Renaissance details quite late in modern history.

Croatia

The Renaissance in Croatia began at the end of the fifteenth century and lasted until the second quarter of the sixteenth century.

In the fifteenth century, Croatia had a strong relationship with the Kingdom of Hungary. Also, at the time, Dalmatia, one of the four regions of Croatia, was under the rule of the Venetian Republic. In the early sixteenth century, the Hapsburgs took control over the Croatian crown and some territory also came under Ottoman occupation. Dalmatia therefore came under the influence of Italy, the Ottomans, and the Austrians. Under such circumstances, Dalmatian religious and public architecture flourished. Three works from that period contributed to the development of the Renaissance. These were the *Cathedral of St James in Šibenik*[51], the *Chapel of Blessed John* in Trogir[52], and *Sorkočević's villa* in Dubrovnik.[53] Many Croatian renaissance sculptures are linked to its architecture, and the most beautiful one is perhaps the relief, *Flagellation of Christ,* by Juraj Dalmatinac[54] on the altar of St Staš, the cathedral of Split, Croatia's second largest city.

The most important Croatian renaissance painters were from Dubrovnik, a Croatian city on the Adriatic Sea, within the region of Dalmatia. It is a walled city that achieved a high level of development during the fifteenth and sixteenth centuries through trade and diplomacy.

Important artists included Lovro Marinov Dobričević[55], Mihajlo Hamzic,[56] Nikola Božidarević,[57] and John of Kastav[58]. They painted altar screens, introducing portraits of contemporaries, linear perspective, and still life motifs. With the threat of danger from the Ottomans in the east, the Renaissance art had only a modest influence, but the architecture of fortifications thrived. The fortified city of Karlovac in 1579[59] and the Renaissance fort *Veliki Tabor*[60] are two good examples.

Croatia also produced its share of poets, playwright and prose writers. Among them were Marko Marulić,[61] Jeronim Vidulić,[62] Hanibal Lucić,[63]

Juraj Šižgorić,[64] Janus Pannonius,[65] Petar Hektorović,[66] Marin Držić,[67] Petar Zoranić,[68] Brne Karnarutić,[69] and Dominko "Dinko" Zlatarić.[70] Some of the most popular works in Croatian literature include: *Judita* by Marko Marulić, *Fishing and Fishermen's Talk* by Petar Hektorović, *Planine* by Petar Zorani, and *Robinja* by Hanibal Lucić.[71]

Russia

The influence of the Renaissance on Russia was limited due to the large distances between Russia and the main European cultural centers and also because Russia maintained a strong adherence to their Orthodox traditions.

For example, most Russian art was made for the Orthodox Church. This art did not incorporate the humanist preoccupation with dimension, physical space, or appearance. Rather, its intent was to convey a meditative harmony rather than portray realistic or mythological scenes. Nonetheless, during the fourteenth century, icon painting did reflect a greater degree of subjectivity and personal expression.[72] Some icon artists of renown are Bogdan Saltanov,[73] Simon Ushakov,[74] Gury Nikitin,[75] and Karp Zolotaryov.[76] Nonetheless, because Russia at this time was a Mongol-Tartar Empire, it mostly missed the rebirth of the arts that had swept through Europe.

The Russians did, however, appreciate Renaissance architecture. Prince Ivan III (1440 - 1505) invited a number of architects from Italy, who brought new construction techniques and some Renaissance style elements with them. These artists were commissioned so long as they confined themselves to the traditional designs of Russian architecture. As we have mentioned, in 1475, Aristotele Fioravanti came from Hungary to rebuild the Cathedral of the Dormition in the Moscow Kremlin. He produced a design that combined the traditional Russian style with a Renaissance sense of spaciousness, proportion, and symmetry.[77]

Other Russian monuments having Renaissance features are the *Terem Palace*[78] within the Kremlin, the *Palace of Facets*,[79] the *Cathedral of the Archangel*,[80] and the *Metropolitan Peter Cathedral* in Vysokopetrovsky Monastery.[81]

The Russians were also interested in Renaissance technologies, particularly those related to warfare. Russia began casting cannons in the fifteenth century and produced the Tsar Cannon, which was the largest caliber cannon of the day.[82]

The Russians also embraced the technology that produced vodka, which has become the national drink of Russia. Apparently, an Arab inventor had created a distillation apparatus that was used by alchemists in Provence France to convert grapes into alcohol. The Genoese ambassador brought this "water of life" to Moscow and presented it to Grand Duke Dmitry Donskoy in 1386. This *aqua vitae* (alcohol) became the predecessor of all modern strong alcoholic beverages, including brandy, cognac, whisky, and schnapps.[83] Later Isidore, a Muscovite monk, used this technology to produce the first original Russian vodka, which is made from potatoes.[84]

The Russians also adopted printing from Central Europe. In the seventeenth century, printing became widespread, and woodcuts became especially popular. That led to the development of the Russian folk art called lubok printing, which persisted in Russia well into the nineteenth century.[85]

Women in the Renaissance

Gender Relations

Much of the oppression that women suffered under Roman law and Church law still existed during the Renaissance. In fact, when an ancient Roman law regarding the *pater familias* was rediscovered in the late middle ages, the Renaissance society adopted it. This meant that a father's perpetual authority over his children lasted until he either died or emancipated them through a court of law.[86]

The view of marriage changed somewhat during the Renaissance because the Black Death had eliminated so many people. Secular humanists began to stress the importance of marriage. Even love in marriage was deemed to be important because a wife could offer companionship to her husband. Nonetheless, women were still married to older men so as to continue men's control over them. However, the severe demand for celibacy among married couples began to abate.

Marriages for the elite were still arranged and women were still used to cement partnerships among the political and business elite. Dowries were still required on the part of the wife, but funds were set up to help pay these dowries. For example, the Florence Dowry Fund (Monte Delle Doti) was especially well financed.[87] Fathers could enroll their daughters when they were born by paying a small fee, and when the young maiden was married, the Fund paid the husband her dowry. Florence even borrowed from the vast dowry funds.

City women were expected to be virgins when married and they were closely chaperoned to keep them pure for marriage. In Perugia, the capital city of Umbria, a law forbade men between the ages of fifteen and forty to loiter around churches to admire women attending services. Heavy fines were given to violators. There were also laws that forbade men from following or touching women. In return, women were pressured not to look men in the eyes. Once married, husbands fretted about their wives' potential sexual indiscretions and society pressured husbands to ensure that this did not happen. If neighbors knew of an adulterous wife, they would place horns on the doorway of the cuckolded husband. Municipalities had strict laws against adultery. Male adulterers were fined; women were whipped.

While the Catholic Church retained its extreme view of abstinence and celibacy in marriage, contraception and abortion were still practiced illegally. The proverb "If you can't be good, be careful" dates from this time. *Coitus interruptus*, arduous exercises, and herbs were used and in extreme cases, infanticide. Abortion was still practiced and authorities tried various punishments as deterrents: women were buried alive, drowned, and burned at the stake.

Women's Education

As the humanist ideal spread, the idea of educating girls took hold among the elite and even the merchant class. Of course, the purpose of educating females was to teach them how to act as ladies in service to their husband. It was not to gain greater independence or to gain employment in a profession. Men suggested that women read specific books that would assist them in their given roles. In Italy, Baldassare Castiglione, in his popular book, *The Courtier*, described the attributes Renaissance women needed to become a proper lady. While the education of women was for the benefit of a man, it, nonetheless, was the first time in Western history that education became available to women. A girl's education, if desired, was usually acquired from her father or a paid tutor. As women became educated, it was not surprising that some came to exert influence in society, especially over the arts, and even politics. Lord Chancellor Thomas More was instrumental in spreading humanism education in England. His eldest daughter Margaret was educated in Latin, Greek, Logic, Philosophy, Theology, Mathematics and Astronomy. This encouraged other English nobility to also educate their daughters.

However, domestic duties were never to be neglected for educational pursuits. Most male humanists preferred that learned women remain unwed and metaphorically likened them to amazons and women warriors, i.e., oddities.[88] Women were to be ornaments, not significant contributors to scholarship.

Women Intellectuals

Even though men remained generally blind to the fact, some women did excel in the Renaissance period, competed with, and often outshined their male companions. It is to their credit that while doing so they also carried the heavy burden of constant scrutiny, discouragement, and systemic male chauvinism. Some great women intellectuals included Alessandra Scala,[89] Lucrezia Tornabuoni,[90] Marguerite de Navarre,[91] Louise Labe,[92] Vittoria Colonna,[93] and Lucrezia Borgia.[94]

Women Artists

Some women also began to excel in art. Artemisia Gentilischi[95] (1593 to 1656) was perhaps the most accomplished woman painter, considered to be of the stature of Caravaggio. In an era when women painters were not easily accepted by the artistic community, or its patrons, she was the first woman to become a member of the Accademia della Arte del Disegno in Florence. Artemisia was raped by her art tutor and spent a long time seeking justice against her rapist, even undergoing torture to prove her case. Although this overshadowed her career as an artist, she used her anger to portray strong women and women warriors in her art.

Fig. 4-6: Gentilischi's Self-Portrait as a Lute Player

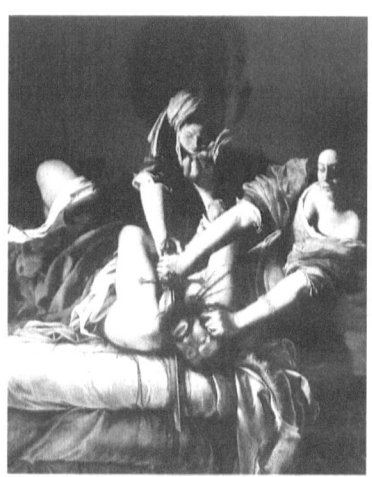
Fig. 4-7: Gentilischi's Judith Slaying Holofernes

Sofonisba Anguissola, (1535-1625), of Cremona, was a painter whom Michelangelo took special interest in. For nearly two decades, Sofonisba painted at the court of King Philip II of Spain.

Her best works are portraitures of herself and her family.[96]

Fig. 4-8: Anguissola's Self-Portrait at Easel

Fig. 4-9: Anguissola's Portrait of the Artist's Family

Levina Teerlinc (1510 to 1576) was a Flemish Renaissance miniaturist who, under the patronage of Henry VIII, served as a manuscript illuminator. It is said that Henry paid more for her work than he did for the work of painter Hans Holbein, who created a celebrated portrait of the king.[97]

Royal patronage was also bestowed on Catharina van Hemessen (1528 to 1587), a Flemish painter who enjoyed the support of Queen Mary of Hungary. A painter of introspective portraits, she is the earliest female Flemish painter for whom there is verifiable extant work. She is often cited as creating the first self-portrait of an artist of either gender seated at an easel.[98]

Fig. 4-10: van Hemessen's Self-Portrait

Mary Beale (1633-1699) was an English painter noted for her portraits. She became one of the most important portrait painters of seventeenth century England, and has been described as the first professional female English painter.[99]

Fig. 4-11: Beale's Self-Portrait

Fede Galizia (1578-1630) was an Italian Renaissance painter who pioneered the still life genre. At a young age, Galizia was already an established portrait painter handling many commissioned works. Her treatment of jewels and clothing made her a very desirable portrait painter. She was often commissioned to paint religious and secular themes as well.[100]

Fig. 4-12: Galizia's Still Life

Fig. 4-13: Galizia's Judith with Head of Holofernes

Lavinia Fontana (1552-1614) was an Italian painter and is regarded as the first woman artist who worked as a professional outside a court or convent. She was the first woman artist to paint female nudes, and was the main breadwinner of a family of thirteen.[101]

Fig. 4-14: Fontana's Portrait of a Lady with a Dog

Fig. 4-15: Fontana's Minerva Dressing

Judith Jans Leyster (1609 to 1660) was a Dutch painter of genre works, portraits, and still lifes. Her entire work was attributed to Frans Hals until 1893, when it was discovered that they were signed with her distinctive monogram 'JL*'.[102]

Fig. 4-16: Leyster's Game of Cards

Fig. 4-17: Leyster's Serenade

Rachel Ruysch (1664-1750) was a still life painter from the Northern Netherlands who specialized in flower still lifes. She invented her own style and achieved international fame in her lifetime. Due to her successful career that spanned over six decades, she became the best documented woman painter of the Dutch Golden Age.[103]

Fig. 4-18: Ruysch's Flowers on a Stone Slab

Fig. 4-19: Ruysch's Still Life with Flowers

Women Politicians

Isabella D'Este, (1474-1539) is generally considered to be a true Renaissance woman, comparable to Leonardo Da Vinci. She played a number of musical instruments and was an avid reader. She kept a library of rare books, wrote hundreds of letters, and kept a chronicle of the events and interests of her day. She was a generous patron of the arts, as well as a leader of fashion. Her innovative style was copied by women throughout Italy and at the French court. Isabella married Francesco II Gonzaga, the Marquis of Mantua, and when her husband was captured in war, she successfully ruled the Duchy in his absence. The poet Ariosto referred to her as the "liberal and magnanimous Isabella," while the author Matteo Bandello described her as having been "supreme among women." Diplomat Niccolò da Correggio went even further calling her "The First Lady of the world."[104]

Catherine de Medici (1519 to 1589) was the daughter of Lorenzo II de' Medici and Madeleine de La Tour d'Auvergne. As the wife of Henry II, she bore three sons each of whom became the king of France. Henry's death in a jousting tournament in 1559 thrust Catherine into politics as mother of the frail fifteen-year-old King Francis II. When he died in 1560, she became regent and ruled the state on behalf of her ten-year-old son King Charles IX. After Charles died in 1574, Catherine played a key role in the reign of her third son, Henry III. During her reign as wife, queen mother, and regent, France was almost in constant civil and religious war. Catherine, as a Catholic, made concessions to the rebelling Protestants, (Huguenots), but failed to grasp the theological issues that drove their movement. Later, in frustration and anger, she resorted to hardline policies against them. She was blamed for the St. Bartholomew's Day massacre of 1572, in which three thousand Huguenots were killed in Paris and throughout France.[105]

Mary I (1516 to 1558), daughter of King Henry VIII, became the queen of England. When her father broke from the Catholic Church and set up the Church of England (Anglican Church), it became the first Protestant church of the Reformation and set England on a course of civil war between the English Catholics and Protestants. When Henry died, his son, Edward VI, ascended the thrown and England became even more Protestant, but he died only six years later. This brought Mary to the throne and she reinstated Catholicism as the state religion. This action was reinforced by her marriage to Philip the King of Spain who was a strict Catholic. Philip tried to usurp Mary's power in England, but the Parliament was able to thwart his attempt to dilute Mary's power. A compromise was reached. Philip would rule in the marriage arena, but Mary would rule the state. Many Protestants at the time chose martyrdom in England and Mary gained the epithet "Bloody Mary." Yet the number of people killed for their faith in her reign paled in comparison to Elizabeth's time. Mary did not rule long. She died of a malignant tumor.[106]

Mary Queen of Scots (1542 to 1587), also known as Mary Stuart or Mary I of Scotland, was Queen of Scotland from 1542 to 1567 and Queen consort of France from 1559 to 1560. She was the great-niece of King Henry VIII of England. Six days after her birth, she became Queen of Scots when her father died, most likely from drinking contaminated water while on a campaign. Vivacious, beautiful, and clever, Mary had a promising childhood. She was sent to France at five years when the French king, Henry II, proposed a marriage between Mary and his three-year old son as a means to unite France and Scotland against the invasion of England, which also wanted control of Mary. At the French court, Mary learned to play the lute and was competent in prose, poetry, horsemanship, falconry, and needlework. She also learned to speak French, Italian, Latin, Spanish, and Greek, in addition to speaking her native language.[107]

In November 1558, when Henry VIII's elder daughter, Mary I of England, died, she was succeeded by her sibling, Elizabeth I. Elizabeth was recognized as her sister's heir, because Henry VIII's last will and testament excluded the Stuarts from succeeding to the English throne. Yet, in the eyes of many Catholics, Elizabeth was illegitimate and Mary Stuart, as the descendant of Henry VIII's elder sister, was the rightful queen of England. Henry II of France proclaimed his eldest son and daughter-in-law, king and queen of England. Mary never succeeded to the throne of England, but her claim to the English throne was a perennial sticking point between her and Elizabeth.

Elizabeth I (1558-1603 reign) oversaw the development of England as a great empirical power that lasted into the twentieth century. In the first year of her reign, she defeated the Spanish Armada, which up until that time had been the most powerful navy in the world. This victory stopped Spain's dominance of America and established England's domination. England's economy boomed, in part because Elizabeth invested in piracy along with the establishment of trading companies. Also the patronage of Shakespeare and his plays had extraordinary long-term benefits. The English Renaissance did not fully flower in England until Elizabeth's time when she was respected as the epitome of a well-educated Renaissance woman.[108]

Perhaps her wisest policy had to do with religion. As long as her subjects displayed outward conformity to the Protestant cause, she vowed not to "open windows in men's souls." Elizabeth played the violin, studied poetry, drama, painting and architecture, and her openness to the Renaissance created what became known as the Elizabethan Age.

While some Renaissance writers recognized women's ability to govern, most men were still quite reluctant to accept their authority. John Calvin, for instance, vociferously rejected government by women as an "unnatural monstrosity and such a government might be sometimes imposed on a nation by an angry God to punish the people for their sins, in which case, it should be born with patience, like any tyranny." The more famous classic statement of this view was espoused by the Presbyterian Protestant Reformer in Scotland, John Knox, in his *The First Blast of the Trumpet Against the Monstrous Regiment of Women*, in 1558, where he argued that female rule was contrary to divine and natural law.[109] As it was, while women could rule as monarchs, they still were not admitted to assemblies like Parliament at this time.

Literature Keeps Women in Their Place

Most didactic literature of the Renaissance was still being written to keep women submissive to the patriarchal structure of society. Male writers in Italy, France, and England wrote of the young and beautiful maiden Grieselda who was the patient, ideal wife. Husbands were admonished in such literature that if they did not rule their wives properly, they would turn into shrews, i.e., ill-tempered, nagging women. Shakespeare's *Taming of the Shrew* is a good example of this genre.

Leon Alberti, the famous Renaissance writer who wrote voluminously on the proper procedure for breaking in a new wife said:

> "... I often used to express my disapproval of bold and forward females who try too hard to know about things outside the house ... husbands who take counsel with

their wives . . . are madmen if they think true prudence or good counsel lies in the female brain . . . dear wife, listen to me. I shall be most pleased if you do just three things: First, see that you never want another man to share this bed but me. Second . . . take care of the household . . . Third . . . see that nothing comes wrong in the house . . . then she and I knelt down and prayed to God . . . that he might grant us the grace to live together in peace and harmony for many happy years and with many male children."[110]

Women Mystics

We have already spoken in depth in Volume 3 about the female mystics of this time. Before the Church began its systematic oppression of these women, however, they flourished during the early Renaissance period. These women inspired learned men to write about their heroic asceticism, their extreme fasts, their unselfish service, their otherworldly visions, their inner strength, and the miracles that surrounded them. The Baroque sculpture Bernini had immortalized St. Teresa of Avila in marble at the exact moment of her ecstasy and such works inspired the people to admire these great female mystics. Records show that sainthood for women greatly expanded in the Renaissance. During the early Christian centuries there were five male saints for each female saint, but after the mid fourteenth century this number was cut in half. In no other period of history were there so many female saints, even though the requirements for canonization of women were even more rigorous than that of men.[111]

The New World and the Birth of Colonialism

Europe at the time of the Renaissance was composed of many independent states that were impossible to control by any one supreme ruler. Neither the Church, the Emperor of the Holy Roman Empire, the kings of independent states, nor the nobility of these various states were able to monopolize control of Europe, nor for that matter any raw material or product. This situation was also complicated by the fact that the geography of Europe was broken up by mountains, rivers, and forests that made consolidation virtually impossible. Such conditions, along with the expansion of international trade, gave rise to a middle class that moved from state to state and promoted new ideas and technologies to those areas. The advantage that the middle class merchants brought to their states tended to be greater tolerance and less autocratic rule. The competitive spirit of capitalism was encouraged. New science and technologies permitted more sophisticated fortifications, large ships that could travel great distances, and the development of strong navies.

The improvement in shipbuilding and naval technology created what historians call the Age of Discovery. It existed from the end of the fifteenth century to the eighteenth century and was a time when European nations sent out merchant ships around the globe to explore new lands. This produced new trading partners with developed countries like India, China, and Japan and it also produced a source of slaves and raw materials from the lands of Africa, the Americas, and the islands of the Pacific Ocean.

The expropriation of wealth and slaves from these continents made Western Europe the center of the world economy and resulted in Western Europe controlling eighty-five percent of the global economy by 1900.

As we have seen, this expansion of merchant activity began with the city-states of northern Italy, but it quickly spread to other European countries. The Italians dominated the trade with the Near East and had little incentive to explore other areas. It was the Portuguese and the Spanish, therefore, who, because of their position on the Mediterranean Sea and Atlantic Ocean and their developed seaports, seized the initiative in the quest to discover new lands. They were motivated by a confluence of circumstances. Italian merchants were raising the cost of foreign goods at a time when these countries had developed navies with technologies that made it possible to sail greater distances. They longed to discover a sea route to India around Africa and trade for eastern luxuries. They were thus positioned to explore the coast of Africa and sail the Atlantic Ocean. The Portuguese were driven to Africa to find the source of Arab gold. The Spanish believed that they could reach the Far East by sailing west. They thought that the world was much smaller than it is and did not realize that the vast continents of North and South America lie between Europe and India by traveling to the west.

The Portuguese took the lead by exploring the western coast of Africa and setting up forts along the coast between 1418 and 1488. These forts would be the base for the Portuguese slave trade and establish a route around the south of Africa by which they eventually reached India. Methodical expeditions began under the sponsorship of Prince Henry the Navigator, with Bartolomeu Dias reaching the Cape of Good Hope and entering the Indian Ocean in 1488. Ten years later, Vasco da Gama led the first fleet around Africa to India, arriving in Calicut (Kozhikode) in southern India. This established a sea route from Portugal to India. The Portuguese also sailed west and discovered Brazil. Further explorations took the Portuguese to Southeast Asia and Japan by 1542. The goal of the Portuguese was to control the ancient spice trade by discovering a new and faster route to the Far East.[112] In their quest to achieve control of the spice trade, the Portuguese had to fight the Arabs who had a long history of trade with India and other countries of the Far East.

A few years after Bartholomew Dias rounded the Cape of Good Hope of southern Africa, the Spanish entered the race to control trade with the Far East. In 1492, Spain funded Christopher Columbus to sail west to find a route to India. They believed that if they traveled west, the distance between Spain and India was only thirty-five hundred miles. In reality, traveling as the crow flies, the distance is more like twenty thousand miles. Within ten years, Columbus would make four trips to the west and while he never discovered India, he did discover the Bahamas, Cuba, Haiti, Dominican Republic, the Island of Hispaniola, Guadalupe, the Antilles, Jamaica, Puerto Rico, the Virgin Islands, Trinidad, the eastern coast of South America and the eastern coast of Central America.

While it was Leif Ericson of Iceland who first discovered Canada and North America almost five hundred years before Columbus, it was Columbus, because of the current age of discovery, who was the first to create an avid interest in the New World and make it a target of colonization efforts by the Spanish, French, English, and the Dutch.[113]

It is of interest that even after all his trips, Columbus never realized that he had discovered a new land. He died believing that he had found a route to India. It was Amerigo Vespucci, an Italian, who realized that the Americas were an entirely new and undiscovered continent. Vespucci sailed with a Spanish fleet to the new land in 1499 and discovered the mouth of the Amazon River. Consequently, the Americas were named after him and not Columbus.

For the next century, the Portuguese and the Spanish continued to compete with each other in their explorations of new lands. The Portuguese explorer Pedro Álvares Cabral discovered Brazil in South America in 1500, while Gaspar Corte-Real went north and discovered Greenland, Labrador, and Newfoundland in 1502. With this new information the Portuguese created the first world map which is today called the Cantino planisphere.[114] The map is named for Alberto Cantino who stole the map from the Portuguese and brought it to Italy.

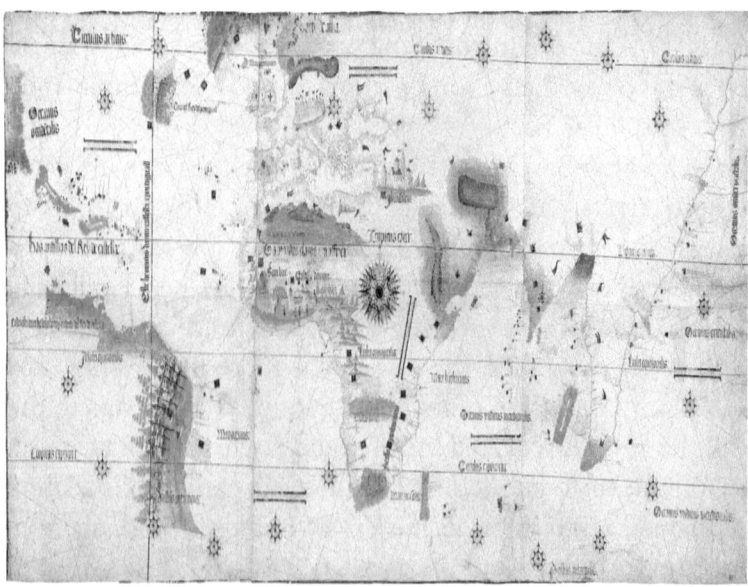

Fig. 4-20: Cantino planisphere

Despite these forays to the west, the Portuguese, for the remainder of the century, concentrated on establishing trade with the Far East by going around Africa. Once they had discovered a route to India, they continued to travel further east until they eventually reached Japan. The chart below shows the major discoveries made during the fifteenth and sixteenth centuries by European explorers:

Explorer	Country	Year (AD)	Discovery
Leif Erikson	Iceland	1000	Canada and North America
Marco Polo	Italy	1269	Central Asia and China
Prince Henry	Portugal	1418	Atlantic side of Africa
Diogo de Silves	Portugal	1427	Azores
Pedro de Sintra	Portugal	1460	Sierra Leone
Bartolomeu Dias	Portugal	1488	Cape of Good Hope, reached Indian Ocean
Christopher Columbus	Spain	1492	Caribbean Islands
Christopher Columbus	Spain	1493	Dominica, Guadalupe and the Antilles
John Cabot	England	1497-8	Northeast coast of N. America
Christopher Columbus	Spain	1498	Eastern coast of South America
Vasco Da Gama	Portugal	1498	India
Amerigo Vespucci	Italy	1499	Mouth of the Amazon river
Padro Alvares Cabral	Portugal	1500	Brazil
Diogo Dias	Portugal	1500	Madagascar
Gaspar Corte-Real	Portugal	1501	Greenland, Labrador, Newfoundland
Christopher Columbus	Spain	1502	Eastern coast of Central America - Panama, Columbia
Alberto Cantino	Portugal	1502	World Map created Cantino planisphere
Afonso de Albuquerque	Portugal	1511	Malaysia, Siam (Thailand)
Juan Ponce de Leon	Spain	1513	Florida
Jorge Álvares	Portugal	1513	China
Vasco Nunez de Balboa	Spain	1513	Isthmus of Panama and Pacific Ocean
Lorenço Gomes	Portugal	1518	Borneo
Ferdinand Magellan	Spain	1522	Sails around the world, Philippines
Pizzaro, Ponce de Leon, Cortez, de Soto	Spain	1522	Conquistadors explore the Americas
Giovanni da Verranzzano	France	1524	NE coast of N. America from Carolinas to Nova Scotia
Aleixo Garcia	Spain	1525	Paraguay and Bolivia
Jorge de Menezes	Portugal	1526	New Guinea

Jacques Cartier	France	1534	St Lawrence River to Montreal
Francisco de Coronado	Spain	1535	Explores southern United States
Fernão Mendes Pinto	Portugal	1542	Japan
Juan Rodríguez Cabrillo	Spain	1542	Coast of California
Francis Drake	England	1577	Second circumnavigation of world
António da Madalena	Portugal	1583	Cambodia

While the Portuguese went east, the Spanish continued their exploration of the New Land to the west that had been pioneered by Columbus. In 1497, the English entered the contest for discovery. King Henry VIII hired John Cabot, an Italian merchant mariner, who was living in the seaport town of Bristol England, to sail west to find a northwest passage to India. Cabot made it to Newfoundland on the eastern coast of Canada and thought he had reached the northern coast of China. In 1498, he made another voyage and sailed down the northeastern coast of North America probably reaching as far south as the Chesapeake Bay. It was these journeys of Cabot that established England's claim to North America.

The French did not enter the competition for new land until 1524 when King Francis I hired Giovanni da Verrazzano, another Italian, to explore the east coast of North America. Verrazzano charted the coast from the Carolinas to Newfoundland, including the New York Harbor. Today, the Verrazano–Narrows Bridge in New York bears his name.

During the early seventeenth century, the Dutch began their era of exploration and colonization, and soon became a world colonial power. They were motivated by lack of natural resources, a land that was below sea level, and by their knowledge of trade routes. In their efforts to reclaim land from the sea, they set up dikes, windmills, and drainage systems, which helped them become resourceful engineers, merchants, and artisans. They developed efficient and inexpensive cargo ships and advanced their foreign trade with the Scandinavian countries, Russia, and Poland. Domestically they developed textile, tobacco, munitions, soap, and sugar refineries. They also developed a prosperous banking system whose profits they employed to expand their trade for salt, slaves, spices, and grain. In no time, they had created the best naval ship building industry in Europe, causing jealousy, particularly among the French and English. Amsterdam became the center of world trade and culture during the seventeenth century.

In 1606, Willem Janszoon discovered Australia. In 1609, the Dutch hired Henry Hudson to discover a northwest passage to India. Hudson sailed up what became known as the Hudson River and set up a camp around Albany NY. In 1624, Peter Minuit, the Director of the Dutch West India Company brought a company of Walloons (French speaking Belgians) and company-owned slaves to Governors Island. He then purchased Manhattan from the Amsterdam Indians and established a colony. The colony expanded to include Brooklyn, Bronx, and Long Island.[115] In 1642, Abel Tasman discovered New Zealand for the Dutch.

In 1606, Pedro Fernandes de Queiros, had discovered North America for the Spanish. He sailed the Chesapeake Bay, the Delaware Bay, and the Hudson River up to Albany, New York. The discoveries in North America on the part of Spain, England, France, and Holland established their claim to land on this continent and set the stage for colonization and the conflict that played itself out in the wars leading to and following the American Revolution.

The wealth that began to accumulate in Europe as a result of the Age of Discovery was not without its costs. Storms at sea, the doldrums, shipwrecks, piracy, diseases on shipboard and on land, sun stroke, starvation, and being eaten by cannibals all took their toll. Very few, if any, expeditions made it back to their homeland with all their ships intact and all their crews alive. Nonetheless, these explorations established the preeminence of Europe on the world stage and set the course for the birth of capitalism in modern history.

Chapter Two: The Protestant Reformation

As European nations began to prosper and cities rose again, now dominated by middle class merchants, the economy of Europe began to radically change. Kings who had long bristled under the domination of the Church began to clash with the bishops and the popes. The Church saw its land-based rents decrease and its abuses and corruption called into focus. From 1377 to 1417, the "Great Schism" occurred in which two popes, one in Rome and one in Avignon France, each claimed to be the supreme authority. The opulence, corruption, and authoritarian rule of the Catholic Church gave rise to many calls for reform. The most strident of these reformers, those that would not be silenced, changed the call for reform to the call for revolution. This chapter looks at the Protestant Reformation and the men who brought it about.

Precursors to the Protestant Reformation

John Wycliffe

John Wycliffe (1320 to 1384) was one of the earliest reformers. He was an English philosopher, theologian, Biblical translator, and seminary professor at Oxford.[116] Wycliffe expounded three doctrines that the Roman Catholic Church condemned as subversive. First, he emphasized that one's personal interpretation of the Bible was the only viable source of religious truth, thereby denying that it was the Church and the Pope who constituted religious authority. Secondly, he rejected the Church's idea that the Sacraments were important for salvation and went so far as to declare that *transubstantiation*, the main ritual of the Catholic mass, in which bread and wine are transformed into the body and blood of Christ, was a fraud and tantamount to idol worship. Thirdly, Wycliffe declared the pope to be the Antichrist and the Catholic Church to be a corrupt institution. Wycliffe was also one of the earliest preachers to advocate the idea of predestination. This view held that God, from the beginning of time, choose some people to be saved while others to be damned. This idea would later be picked up by John Calvin and become a cornerstone of Protestant doctrine. To help reduce the power of the Church over people, Wycliffe translated the Bible into English, and distributed it.

The Lollards, who were followers of Wycliffe, began to appear at Oxford University around 1382, led by Nicholas of Hereford. They gained followers among the townspeople, merchants, gentry, and even the lower clergy. Soon several knights of the royal household also gave their support, as well as a few members of the House of Commons.[117]

When Henry IV, a strict Catholic and "soldier of Christ," became king in 1399, he attacked these "heretics," and established a law that legalized burning them alive. In 1414, a Lollard uprising, led by Sir John Oldcastle, was quickly defeated by Henry V. Driven underground, the movement spread chiefly among merchants and artisans, supported by a few clergy. About 1500, the Lollard movement began to merge with new Protestant forces. These developments facilitated the spread of Protestantism in England and set the stage for Henry VIII's seizure of church property during the English Reformation.

John Huss

Another precursor to the Protestant Reformation was John Huss (1369 to 1415).[118] Huss was a Bohemian priest, who followed the teachings of Wycliffe closely. He translated Wycliffe's *Trialogus*[119] into Czechoslovakian, and modeled the first ten chapters of his own *De Ecclesia* after Wycliffe's writings. The *Trialogus* was written as a three-way dialogue, which familiarized priests and the faithful with complex issues underlying Christian doctrine. It discussed divine power and knowledge, creation, virtues and vices, the Incarnation, redemption, and the sacraments. Huss was excommunicated in 1410, and burned at the stake for heresy in 1415. His death led to the Hussite Wars in Bohemia.[120]

Huldrych Zwingli

Huldrych Zwingli (1484 to 1531) was a reform leader in Switzerland.[121] He was drawn to the writing of Erasmus but sought a more extreme means to reform the Church. He spoke against corruption within the Church hierarchy, promoted clerical marriage, and attacked the use of art and music in churches. He also denied the custom of fasting during Lent.[122] In 1525, Zwingli introduced a new communion liturgy to replace the Mass. In his reform efforts, he sought to create a strict theocracy in Zurich. In his aggressive missionary zeal, he attempted to establish a Protestant confederation among the separate states (cantons) of Switzerland. In doing so, he triggered a war with the Swiss Catholics in which he was defeated and died.

Zwingli is considered to be one of the three leaders of the Protestant Revolution along with Luther and Calvin. He displayed a greater social consciousness than either Luther or Calvin by preaching that any community that called itself Christian should care for the poor. Zwingli also debated with Luther and Calvin over issues regarding baptism and transubstantiation, but the three found agreement in condemnation of the Catholic Church and its corrupt leadership.

Even though Zwingli's theological ideas are considered to be the first expression of Reformed theology, no church today, outside of Switzerland, counts Zwingli as its founder. His name may not be widely recognized, but his legacy survives in the founding *confessions* (principles of belief) of the Reformed church of today. Nonetheless, it was John Calvin, who is credited with founding the Reformed Church.

Martin Luther: Against Church Corruption

Martin Luther (1483-1546), a Catholic priest, is credited with beginning the Protestant Reformation by nailing his *95 Theses* to the doors of the Cathedral of Wittenberg in 1517.[123] His purpose was to protest against the nepotism, simony, usury, pluralism (a priest holding multiple Church offices at the same time), and the sale of indulgences by the Church. Luther was a populist who championed the people's cause against the corrupt dictatorship of the Catholic hierarchy. He began by disputing the Church's sale of *indulgences,*[124] which were a forgiveness of sins issued by the Church based on its claim that a person could reduce the amount of punishment for one's sins if he gave money to the church.

At the time of Luther's campaign, a priest from Rome was in Germany selling indulgences to raise money to rebuild St. Peter's Basilica. By this time, the poor resented this practice. Why should the rich be able to buy their way into heaven, while they could not afford it.

Luther, as did many others, believed that salvation could not be earned by such means. He went further, however, and claimed that salvation could not be received by taking any actions at all. Salvation only resulted from having faith in God and in Jesus Christ as the redeemer.

Luther taught that only the Bible, not the Pope and clergy, were divinely inspired and to support his claim he translated the Bible into German. Luther's radical ideas and the dissemination of the Bible created a revolution in thought across the country. For the first time, people could read for themselves the "word of God." They no longer needed the priests to act as interpreters and intercessors between them and their creator. Neither did they need the priests to forgive their sins. Luther, of course, was considered a heretic by the Church but he refused to retract his teachings. This resulted in his excommunication by the Pope and his condemnation as an outlaw by the Emperor.[125]

The dispute regarding the manner by which a sinner was able to have his or her sins forgiven became the fault line between the Catholic Church and the Protestant movement.[126] This conflict laid bare an even deeper problem of faith. The Church believed that a sinner could get his or her sins forgiven by good deeds. Protestants came to believe that salvation is possible by faith alone.

The bottom line regarding the emergence of Lutheranism is that it broke the monopoly of the Church over religious belief and set the population free from the Church's control over their minds and souls.

By challenging the Pope's authority, Lutheranism validated individual freedom in the interpretation of the word of God and, at the same time, freed people from having to confess their sins to a priest in order to receive salvation. Protestants had only to believe in Jesus to be saved. This groundbreaking revolution in thought gave rise to a host of protestant religions, but most of them evolved by way of the teachings of John Calvin, the father of the Dutch Reformed Church, who was even more radical than Luther in his theology and condemnation of the Church.

In Europe, during the days of the Renaissance, the kings and nobles were fighting among themselves for power and the Church became even more repressive of the people. Anger continued to build and it was Luther who provided a vent for the release of much of this anger. He defied the Church in its attempt to silence him by starting the Lutheran Church. The Lutheran church preached that priests are not the only ones who are sacred to God. In fact, all jobs were useful and equal in God's eyes. Because it only required faith in Jesus to be saved, the Lutheran Church consisted of all believers and not just the clergy.

King Henry's Church

In England, an entirely different dynamic gave rise to the protest against the power of the Church. It had to do with King Henry VIII's rebellion against the authority of the Pope, who would not grant Henry a right to divorce his wife.

Henry VIII (1509-1547) was a competent ruler. Under him, England grew more prosperous through trade and the introduction of humanist values. Henry's problem, however, had to do with the question of succession. The king was married to Catherine of Aragon, the aunt of the Holy Roman Emperor Charles V. Henry and Catherine had a good marriage but after five heartbreaking miscarriages, only Mary, a daughter was born. Catherine was reaching the end of her child-bearing years and Henry had no male heir. Despite his love for his daughter, he did not want to entrust the kingdom to a woman. Henry was also a womanizer. When he asked Pope Clement VII to annul his marriage so that he could marry the beautiful Anne Boleyn, Catherine's lady-in-waiting, the pope refused. This incensed Henry who then secured the passage of the Act of Supremacy by Parliament in 1534. This act ended papal authority in England and made the king the head of the English Church. Henry seized Catholic Church property within his realm. Monks and nuns were turned out of monasteries and their lands sold to members of the nobility. When Sir Thomas More, Henry's Chancellor, refused to acknowledge Henry as Head of the Church of England and refused to support the annulment, he was found guilty of treason and beheaded.[127] This act secured the support of cowering bishops for the annulment of his first marriage and his new marriage to his second wife Anne Boleyn. With his increased treasury that resulted from the confiscation of Catholic Church property, and the strong support of his grateful nobles, Henry was free to rule according to his own designs.

The Church of England, under Henry, was not fraught with Protestant harangues against Church dogma and ritual. Rather, Henry liked the theology of the Catholic Church and its rites and rituals; except for the fact that he wanted it to be ruled by Henry instead of the pope. During the remainder of Henry's reign, the Church in England remained largely untouched by the Protestant Reformation, except for the severance of ties with Rome. Following Henry's death, England split between Catholic and Protestant religious factions.

During the short reign of Edward VI (1547 to 1553), Henry's son by his third wife, Jane Seymour, the English church veered toward Calvinism, but under Mary I (1553 to 1558) ties were reestablished with Rome. Protestants were then ruthlessly persecuted and the queen earned the epithet "Bloody Mary." Many religious dissidents fled during these years, and many found their way to Geneva where they came under the influence of the stern edicts of John Calvin. Some of these people would later return to England where they became known as the Puritans.[128]

John Calvin: Champion of the Bourgeoisie

While it was Martin Luther who crashed the gates of the Catholic Church's religious hegemony, and Henry VIII, who openly rebelled against the power of the Papacy, it was John Calvin (1509-1564) who did the heavy damage and set the course for the religious wars to follow. He is credited as being the most important figure in the second generation of the Protestant Reformation.

Born in France, John Calvin was a law student at the University of Orléans when he first joined the cause of the Reformation. Upon getting his law degree, he moved to Geneva where he became involved in the Protestant revolution.

In 1536, he published the landmark text *Institutes of the Christian Religion in* an attempt to standardize the theories of Protestantism. Calvin's religious teachings emphasized the following five points, which were adopted by most of the protestant religions that followed:

Total depravity (Original Sin)
Calvin held that Adam and Eve sinned against God and as a consequence humanity fell from grace. Their fall is expressed in the inability of human beings to will any spiritual good or to seek salvation. As human being, we are averse to good and immersed in sin. Therefore, we are unable, by our own strength, to spiritually prepare ourselves or to gain salvation. We are a depraved species. The Protestants shared this belief with the Catholic Church.

Unconditional election (God's Election)
Because we are totally depraved, salvation can come only from God. But some people are saved and others are not. Because we naturally do not wish to follow God's will, preferring to follow our own will and enjoy worldly pleasures, whenever a sinner is truly regenerated, it must be God that has done it. Because God is omniscient and unchangeable he must have known from eternity his own intention to do it. This belief led to the belief in predestination and a definition of the elect and the damned. The elect were those whom Jesus touched. In the hands of John Calvin, the elect became identified with the rising bourgeoisie whose discipline and hard work were desired by God and by those who truly accepted Jesus Christ as their savior. All others were eternally damned.

Limited atonement (Particular Redemption)
This point answered the question, "Did Christ die for the elect only, or for all men?" and concludes that individual salvation (the reconciliation of a believer with his or her God) is only possible when the

believer accepts the sacrifice that Christ made. Atonement means the reconciliation of God and humanity through the sacrificial death of Jesus Christ. Yet atonement is particular and limited only to the sinner who now believes. While the act of making atonement is infinite, redemption is particular. All whom God ever intended to save in Christ will be saved. But some souls will never be saved; therefore, God never intended that these souls be saved by Christ's atonement. Those who were damned by God came to be defined as the non-believers, those of other religions, and the poor.

Irresistible grace (Effectual Calling)
In order for God's calling to be effective, however, it requires a change of behavior on the part of the sinner. It must be more than a change of purpose. It must entail a reversal of one's disposition to choose sin over godliness. A man must not only forsake selfishness for godliness, he must also love being good for its own sake. No change can be permanent which does not go this deep; nothing less is true conversion. The inward revolution of principles is called *regeneration*. The change of life, which immediately begins from the new principles, is called *conversion*. Regeneration is an initial act while conversion is a continuous process. Regeneration came to be known as "born again."

Perseverance of the Saints
This point holds that whomever God elects to be among his beloved can neither totally nor finally fall away from the state of grace, but shall persevere to the end and be eternally saved. Having said this, Protestants do not believe that all professed believers and church members will certainly persevere and reach heaven. Many are only believers in name while they actually live in sin. They will fall fatally because they never had true grace to begin with. The fact that a deluded man can live in willful sin is the strongest possible proof that he never was elected. No intelligent believer can possibly abuse this doctrine into a pretext for earthly security. It only promises *perseverance in holiness* to true believers.[129]

These five points, according to Calvin, were a synthesis of the writings of Protestant reformers. They presented a simple, self-fulfilling doctrine for all Protestants to follow. To summarize: as human beings, we are born having a sinful nature thanks to Adam and Eve. Fortunately God has elected to save human beings, well at least some of us—the elect. We can become a member of the elect if, by grace, we accept Jesus as our savior and repent for our sins and try to live a good life. Unfortunately, the idea of predestination eliminates the idea of free will or the reason for loving one's neighbor. Fortunately, if we are among the lucky elect, our salvation is guaranteed. However, backsliding is possible and we can never be sure that we will avoid temptation, so we must keep alert and follow the commandments of God.

While simple and easy to understand, there are, from a spiritual perspective, significant drawbacks to having such a belief structure. First, in Calvinist theology, God is presented as unfair, punitive, and prejudiced. Because God is not loving but punitive, he engenders fear and alienation from Divine Consciousness. Calvinism simply replaced repression by the Catholic Church with Protestant repression. Calvin and his followers thundered that we were nothing more than sinners in the hands of an angry god. This perspective denies any potential for a mystical relationship with God.

Secondly, Calvinism holds that, as a species, mankind is fundamentally depraved. This concept is based upon the myth of Adam and Eve and the idea of original sin that prevents any spiritual evolution of the individual.

Thirdly, Calvinism denies any sense of love for one's neighbor or the spiritual imperative to serve others. This is also a profound psychological impediment to spiritual growth. In the name of religion, it provides a justification for prejudice against anyone who experiences a different lifestyle or worldview. Like the Catholic Church, Calvinist dogma also keeps people locked in a static, negative mental projection concerning one's self and the Creation. Only worse, Calvin turns human charity into a sin, on the assumption that it prevents a person from standing on his own two feet. This constricted psychology still dominates Protestantism and Conservatism today.

Fourthly, Calvinism holds that only dedicated Protestants can reach Divinity, while the majority of humanity is doomed to eternal damnation, whether they are loving people or not. This extremely provincial worldview might have made sense in the Euro-centric world of the early Protestants, but in the present world, where we are able to see people worshipping the One God through many religious and non-religious paths, and where we are able to understand that mystics can become God-realized by using any of these paths, such a narrow-minded prejudice can no longer be supported. Anyone who follows another religion is not automatically damned. Any soul born before Christ's coming is not automatically damned. Anyone who has never been introduced to Christian teachings will not suffer the fires of hell for eternity. The poor of the world are not automatically damned because they are poor or do not have the time or inclination to lead a disciplined Protestant lifestyle.

Fifthly, as with the Catholic Church, Jesus Christ is not viewed as a spiritual teacher who achieves Divinity, but as someone who dies for another's sins. This is spiritually impossible. No spiritual master, of any faith, can change another's karma. Seeing Jesus from such an unrealistic vantage point stultifies human spiritual growth. It denies Jesus's message that love of God, love of neighbor, and the willingness to sacrifice for a greater good, leads to God-realization or Self-realization. It denies the truth that the kingdom of God resides within each of us.

Finally, by denying the message of Jesus, Protestant Christians absolve themselves from serving and loving their neighbors. If human beings are predetermined to be either saved or damned, there is no sense in trying to help other people, other species, or the environment. The "elect" will be raised to heaven regardless of their abuse. There is no reason within Calvinist theology to act like a compassionate human being to anyone outside the Protestant group.

The deficit of love and compassion expressed in Calvinism can be seen in the fact that just as the Catholic Church persecuted those who did not act and believe according to their dictates, so too did Calvin and his followers persecute others with the same political fervor.

The protestant movement to which Calvin gave birth has become known as the Reformed tradition, Reformed Christianity, or Reformed faith. His beliefs constitute the core values of Protestantism to this day. The leaders of his movement came from the cities and addressed their teaching, not exclusively, but primarily to those who were engaged in trade and industry. These merchants at the time were the most modern and progressive elements in Europe.[130]

When Calvin left France and moved to Geneva, his stay there was short because anti-Protestant authorities in 1538 forced him to leave. He went to Germany but was invited back again to Geneva in 1541 when the Protestants took control of the city. There, he became an important political figure. Calvin used his Protestant principles to establish an anti-Catholic, Christian state in the city of Geneva and, in 1555, he was given absolute supremacy as its leader.[131] Under his rule, Geneva became the center of Protestantism.

Calvin the Persecutor

If we believe in the Bible, especially the New Testament, as the standard against which actions are judged, then we must judge Calvin and Calvinism as being unchristian. From the very beginning, Calvin, in his *Institutes of the Christian Religion,* (1536) *advises Francis I, the* King of France, how to deal with "bad men in his realm":

> They ... ought to be punished with confiscation, exile, imprisonment, and flames, as well as exterminated by land and sea. This, I allow, is a fearful punishment which God sends on the earth; but if the wickedness of men so deserves, why do we strive to oppose the just vengeance of God?[132]

Just as the Church, sought out "heretics" and killed them, Calvin did the same. He had, for example, a great hatred for Michael Servetus (1511 to 1553), who was a Spanish Renaissance man and honored as a theologian, physician, cartographer, and humanist. Servetus, was also active in the Protestant Reformation but his "heresy" was that he developed a philosophy of Christ that was not based on the dogma of the Trinity. As such, he was condemned by both Catholics and Protestants. When he went to Geneva in 1553, at the time when Calvin served as the head of the city's governing Council, he was imprisoned, found guilty of heresy and burned at the stake. In a letter written to William Farel, a French evangelist, as early as 1546, Calvin states "If he [Servetus] comes [to Geneva], I shall never let him go out alive if my authority has weight."

In another letter written on August 20, 1553, one week after Servetus was arrested, Calvin wrote: "do not fail to rid the country of those scoundrels [Anabaptists and others], who stir up the people to revolt against us. Such monsters should be exterminated, as I have exterminated Michael Servetus the Spaniard."

In 1554, Calvin attempted to justify his self-righteous thirst for blood in his *Defense of Orthodox Faith against Prodigious Errors of the Spaniard Michael Servetus*:

> "Whoever shall now contend that it is unjust to put heretics and blasphemers to death will knowingly and willingly incur their very guilt. This is not laid down on human authority; it is God who speaks and prescribes a perpetual rule for his Church. It is not in vain that he banishes all those human affections which soften our hearts; that he commands paternal love and all the benevolent feelings between brothers, relations, and friends to cease; in a word, that he almost deprives men of their nature in order that nothing may hinder their holy zeal. Why is so implacable a severity exacted but that we may know that God is defrauded of his honor, unless the piety that is due to him be preferred to all human duties, and that when his glory is to be asserted, humanity must be almost obliterated from our memories? Many people have accused me of such ferocious cruelty that I would like to kill again the man I have destroyed. Not only am I indifferent to their comments, but I rejoice in the fact that they spit in my face."[133]

By such words, Calvin mirrors the sentiments behind the Catholic Inquisition. Claim to know the will of God and kill anyone who does not believe in what you say.

During Calvin's reign in Geneva, the *Minutes Book of the Geneva City Council, 1541-59*, reveal the complete loss of his humanity under the command of a concept of God that is stunted, vindictive, and cruel:

- "During the ravages of the pestilence in 1545 more than twenty men and women were burnt alive for witchcraft.

- From 1542 to 1546, fifty-eight judgments of death and seventy-six decrees of banishment were passed.
- During the years 1558 and 1559, the cases of various punishments for all sorts of offences amounted to four hundred and fourteen.
- One burgher smiled while attending a baptism: three days imprisonment.
- Another, tired out on a hot summer day, went to sleep during a sermon: prison.
- Two men played dice for a quarter bottle of wine: prison.
- A blind fiddler played a dance: expelled from the city.
- Another praised Castellio's translation of the Bible: expelled from Geneva.
- A girl was caught skating, a widow threw herself on the grave of her husband, a burgher offered his neighbor a pinch of snuff during divine service: they were summoned before the Consistory, exhorted, and ordered to do penance.
- A couple of peasants talked about business matters on coming out of church: prison.
- A man played cards: he was pilloried with the pack of cards hung around his neck.
- Two barge workers had a brawl: executed.
- A man who publicly protested against the reformer's doctrine of predestination was flogged at all the crossways of the city and then expelled.
- A book printer who in his columns had railed at Calvin, was sentenced to have his tongue perforated with a red-hot iron before being expelled from the city.
- Jacques Gruent was racked and then executed for calling Calvin a hypocrite.

Each offence, even the most paltry, was carefully entered in the record of the Consistory, so that the private life of every citizen could unfailingly be held up against him in evidence."[134]

In Philip Schaff's *History of the Christian Church*, Vol 8,[135] which was written in the 1880s, we find the following quotes concerning Calvin's Geneva:

> The death penalty against heresy, idolatry, and blasphemy and barbarous customs of torture were retained. Attendance at public worship was commanded on penalty of three sols. Watchmen were appointed to see that people went to church. The members of the Consistory visited every house once a year to examine the faith and morals of the family. Every unseemly word and act on the street was reported, and the offenders were cited before the Consistory to be either censured and warned, or to be handed over to the Council for severer punishment.

Barbarous customs included dancing, gambling, drinking, swearing, and wearing attractive clothes were condemned. Calvin allowed no art other than music, and even music could not involve instruments.

His teachings were spread to the rest of Europe by his pastors where they gave root to Presbyterianism in Scotland, the Puritan Movement in England, and the Reformed Church in the Netherlands.[136] His message was also carried to the big cities of the day by traveling traders and tradesmen, where it was spread among the merchants of these cities. These were the same men who would institute the iron rule of slavery and colonialism in the New World, including that of New Amsterdam, which later became New York.

Setting the Stage for Capitalism

Calvin's austere, dehumanized vision of spirituality garnered the support of the rising merchant class for several reasons, not the least of which was his belief that charity was not a virtue but a sin. It was Calvin, more than any theologian during the fifteenth and sixteenth centuries that linked Protestantism to the rise of capitalism and in so doing, established the tenets of current conservative ideology. It is this same ideology that stands, to this day, against any movement for social reform whether it seeks to ease human suffering or confront the degeneration of our natural environment.

Regarding the topic of trade and money lending, Calvin made a sharp break with the Catholic Church's double standard which permitted the Church to amass wealth through exploitation while preaching that it was reprehensible for others to be preoccupied with business interests beyond what is necessary for subsistence. While the Church condemned merchants as parasites, usurers, and thieves, Calvin praised them for their hard work, frugality, and discipline. The people, however, were already enraged by the early capitalists, not simply because money lending entailed charging interest, but because it all too often resulted in the expropriation of their property as well.

A popular pamphlet, written in Germany in 1521, brings together a peasant and a merchant in a dialogue on the question of how the merchant makes his money:

> Peasant: Tell me burgher, who gave you so much money that you spend all your time counting it.
>
> Burgher: You want to know who gave me my money. I shall tell you. A peasant comes knocking at my door and asks me to lend him ten or twenty gulden. I inquire of him whether he owns a plot of good pasture land or a nice field for plowing. He says: "Yes, burger, I have a good meadow and a fine field, worth a hundred gulden the two of them." I reply: "Excellent! Pledge your meadow and your field as collateral, and if you will undertake to pay one gulden a year as interest, you can have your loan of twenty gulden." Happy to hear the good news, the peasant replies: "I gladly give you my pledge." "But I must tell you," I rejoin, "that if ever you should fail to pay your interest on time, I will take possession of your land and make it my property." As this does not worry

the peasant, he proceeds to assign his pasture and field to me as his pledge. I lend him the money, and he pays interest punctually for a year or two; then comes a bad harvest and soon he is behind in his payments. I confiscate the land, evict him, and the meadow and the field are mine. Thus I gain both money and property. And I do this not only with peasants but with artisans as well. If a tradesman owns a good house I lend him a sum of money on it, and before long the house belongs to me. In this way I acquire much property and wealth, which is why I spend all my time counting my money.

Peasant: And I thought only the Jews practiced usury! Now I hear that Christians do it, too.

Burgher: Usury? Who is talking about usury? Nobody here practices usury. What the debtor pays is interest. Interest, not usury.[137]

Calvin supported the money-making technique of the merchants saying, "What reason is there why the income from business should not be larger than that from land-owning. Whence do the merchant's profits come, except from his own diligence and industry?" [138]

It was a marriage made in heaven. Calvin gave the merchants religious legitimacy, while the merchants spread his teachings and gave money to his church. Calvin designed his teachings to support the middle class merchants who sat in the pews of his Church in Geneva. He was the first to recognize and even applaud the *economic virtues* and include them in his religious teaching. These virtues included individual initiative, discipline, frugality, sobriety, patience, economic service, etc. It was not the accumulation of riches that was the problem for Calvin, but the misuse of such riches for ostentation and self-indulgence. An ideal Christian society, according to Calvin, is one that *seeks wealth* with the seriousness of men who are conscious of disciplining their own character by patient labor and of devoting themselves to a service acceptable to God. In other words, Calvin held that merchants were predestined to pursue profits for the good of his church. It did not take long, however, for the merchants to feel justified in seeking profits for their own self-aggrandizement.

The significance of Calvin's contribution to the rise of capitalism was that he assumed credit and debt to be a part of normal business practice and inevitable in modern society. He dismissed the Old Testament and the Church Fathers statements against usury by saying that they were irrelevant because they were designed for conditions that no longer existed. This shows that, in its infancy, Protestants realized that things change and that dogma's became irrelevant with such changes, but today, Protestant fundamentalists will fight to maintain their dogma even though the planet itself is at risk.

The acceptance and support of commercial practices by Calvin led to the belief that the capitalist's accumulation of riches was a sign of spiritual reward. By elevating the merchants to the position of paragon of Christian virtue, they quickly became the definition of the *elect*, chosen by God for salvation.

While lavishing praise on the merchants, Calvin alternately was punitive in his approach to the poor. Unlike those who saw the problem of pauperism as a problem of exploitation or unjust social administration, Calvin saw it as a lapse of an individual's character. He quoted with approval the words of St. Paul, "If a man will not work, neither shall he eat" (2 Thess. 3:10). These were certainly not the words of Jesus Christ who understood the ravages of poverty and spent his entire life in service to the poor. But Calvin even misconstrued these words of Paul. Paul was pointing out to his disciples, when he used these words, that as a Christian, he was not personally taking advantage of those with whom he found shelter and food, because he was working as well to bring them the Christian message. His words were a caution against taking advantage of others, not a license to exploit others. It was not his intention to suggest that those in need should not be helped. Nonetheless, given his constricted consciousness, Calvin condemned "indiscriminate alms giving" and urged his church authorities to annually visit every family to determine whether its members were idle, drunk, or otherwise undesirable.[139]

Calvin's dogma of predestination, in which no amount of good works or charity had any effect on one's salvation, also justified the capitalist mindset that they were not responsible for the welfare of others less fortunate than they, even if their misfortune was caused by being exploited by the capitalists themselves. In fact, the capitalist could prey on such people without mercy because they were already doomed by God. This mindset continues to justify the exploitation of others who are not of the capitalist class. According to R. H Tawney, who wrote *Religion and the Rise of Capitalism*:

> Calvin did for the bourgeoisie[140] of the sixteenth century what Marx did for the proletariat[141] of the nineteenth century, or that the doctrine of predestination satisfied the same hunger for an assurance that the forces of the universe are on the side of the elect as was to be assuaged in a different age by the theory of historical materialism. He set their virtues at their best in sharp antithesis with the vices of the established order at its worst, taught them to feel that they were a chosen people, made them conscious of their great destiny in the Providential plan and resolute to realize it.[142]

Calvin's "protestant work ethic"[143] made its way to the shores of America with the coming of the Puritans. There, it entered the main stream of American values with the mass immigration of Germanic peoples between 1800 and 1920, at the time of the industrial revolution in America.

A positive effect of Calvin's revolution was his support for laymen within the administration of his Christian state. He included elected laymen (church elders, presbyters) in his concept of government. The Huguenots (French Calvinists) added synods whose members were also elected by the congregations. The other Reformed churches took over this system of church self-government, which was essentially a representative democracy. Presbyterians, Congregationalists, Baptists, and Methodists are organized in a similar way. These denominations, along with the Anglican Church were influenced by Calvin's theology in varying degrees.[144]

Calvin's support of democracy stemmed from his desire to safeguard the rights and freedoms of the bourgeoisie middle class but his support was not unqualified. Rather, he favored a mixture of democracy and aristocracy as the best form of government. Referred to as *mixed government*, it is a form of government in which some issues are decided by the majority of the people, some other issues by the few, and some other issues by a single person. This idea is commonly treated as a forerunner of the separation of powers into a legislature, an executive, and a judiciary that is defined in the US Constitution.[145]

The Congregationalists who founded Plymouth Colony (1620) and Massachusetts Bay Colony (1628) were convinced that this democratic form of government was the will of God. Enjoying self-rule they, however, supported the separation of the powers of church and state. Rhode Island, Connecticut, and Pennsylvania, founded by Roger Williams, Thomas Hooker, and William Penn, respectively, combined democratic government with freedom of religion. These colonies became safe havens for persecuted religious minorities, including Jews.[146]

Most settlers in the American Mid-Atlantic and New England were Calvinists, including the English Puritans, the French Huguenots, the Dutch settlers of New Amsterdam (New York), and the Scotch-Irish Presbyterians of the Appalachian back country.

The Counter Reformation

As the criticism against the Church became louder and Protestant uprisings destabilized different states across Europe, the Church hunkered down to confront the onslaught. Its strategy was based on the stick and carrot approach. It initiated some reforms, but also rekindled the Inquisitions to destroy those enemies who would not be silenced. The time of this counter-reformation lasted from 1515 to 1563. It began with the Fifth Council of the Lateran and ended with the close of the Thirty Years War (1648).

Church reform did not entail questioning any of its dogma; rather it was confined to organizational matters only. It included the creation of seminaries to train priests in the theological traditions of the Church and the proper religious life. It included the reform of religious orders so as to return them to their spiritual roots and away from corrupt politics and economic matters. The reform movement also attempted to focus on a more devotional life and a personal relationship with Jesus Christ. This included the promotion of Spanish mystics like St. Teresa of Ávila, St. John of the Cross, and Ignatius of Loyola, S.J. It also included the promotion of the French School Of Spirituality led by Pierre de Berulle, Charles de Condren, Jean-Jacques Olier, Jean Eudes, and Francis de Sales.[147]

While these reforms constituted the "carrot" of the Church's reform effort, there was also the "stick" of the Roman Inquisition that was responsible for prosecuting individuals accused of Protestant heresy, sorcery, immorality, blasphemy, Judaizing (insisting that Christians follow the Old Testament rulings of Moses) and, of course, witchcraft. This part of the counter-reformation also oversaw the censorship of printed literature and secular thought that was at odds with the Church's worldview.[148] The Counter-Reformation also sought to make Catholics of the indigenous peoples of the newly colonized lands, and to bring the populations of countries like Sweden and England that had once been Catholic, back into the fold.

The Fifth Council of the Lateran (1517)

The Church's first attempt to regain control was to convene the Fifth Council of the Lateran in opposition to the King of France and his allies who were, at the time, at war with the pope. The Council was held just seven months after Luther nailed his *95 Thesis* to the Cathedral doors in Wittenberg. The Council produced several decrees, among them:

- the condemnation of the decrees of the King of France and rebel cardinals who were in revolt against the Papacy in Rome;
- the excommunication of those cardinals;
- the sanction of financial institutions that provided loans to the needy;
- the reconfirmation of Purgatory as the place where souls wait before Judgment Day;
- the confirmation of the freedom of the Church and the dignity of bishops;
- the condemnation of any philosophical propositions that contradicted the "truth of the enlightened Christian faith";

- the requirement that in order to preach, one now had to have "documented" competence; and
- the approval of levying taxes to meet the expense of a new proposed Crusade against the Turks to reclaim the Holy Land.[149]

Sack of Rome

Politics in the early sixteenth century was chaotic. The Papacy, Spain, France, the Holy Roman Emperor, protestant rebels, and warlord princes were all vying for wealth and power. Throughout the entire European land, combatants fought among themselves and even the city-states of Italy were under siege by the French. Internal conflicts and corruption also plagued the Church while the Ottoman Empire was pressuring Eastern Europe. The insanity reached its peak in 1527.

Rebel cardinals, in alliance with France and the Emperor, led an army against the Pope, pillaged St Peter's Basilica on Vatican Hill, and took control of Rome. This was followed by an attack led by Charles III, Duke of Bourbon, who led the Emperor's forces to lay siege to the city. Charles died at the beginning of the siege while mounting a ladder and his hungry troops, now leaderless and unpaid, felt free to sack the city. The murder, rape, and destruction of property ended the Renaissance splendor of Rome forever.

The Council of Trent (1545 to 1563)

By the time the Council of Trent convened, twenty years had passed since Luther nailed his *95 Theses* to the doors of the Wittenberg Castle church. The Council of Trent reaffirmed Church dogma that until this day had not been changed. Four hundred years later, when Pope John XXIII prepared the Second Vatican Council (Vatican II) in 1959, he affirmed the decrees of Trent: "What was, still is."[150]

Protestantism and political chaos had continued to flame across Europe. Under such conditions, the Church set about the task of affirming its beliefs while condemning Protestant heresies. It issued statements and clarifications of Church dogma concerning the scriptures, Biblical canon, the mass, church liturgy, veneration of saints, sacred tradition, origin sin, salvation, and the importance of the seven Church sacraments. To reinvigorate the confession of sins, which had been under caustic attack from the Protestants, the Church modified the sacrament of penance from a public community act to a private confession. It now took place in private in a confessional and its intention was changed from reconciliation with the Church to reconciliation directly with God and from emphasis on social sins of hostility to private sins. The Council met for twenty-five sessions between 1545 and 1563 and was overseen by three successive popes, Paul III, Julius III, and Pius IV.

It was at this time that the Church also settled on a version of the canonical Bible that is still used by Catholics today. It contained Jerome's translation of the Old Testament directly from the Hebrew Tanakh instead of the Greek Septuagint. The Council also standardized the Tridentine Creed, in which all men in the Church hierarchy must publically confess before being accepted into the clergy. The Roman Catechism was created and revisions of the Breviary and Missal were made. The Breviary is the official set of prayers consisting primarily of psalms, hymns, readings, and other prayers. Together with the Mass, it constitutes the official public prayers of the Church.[151] The Missal contains all instructions and texts necessary for the celebration of Mass throughout the year. These revisions led to the codification of the Mass, which remained in place until Vatican II, four hundred years later.[152]

In short, the accomplishments of the Council were to:

- Clarify the doctrines of the Catholic Church and condemn the principles and doctrines of Protestantism;
- Create reform measures within the Church to mitigate corruption;
- Establish the Church as the only valid interpreter of Scripture, the Bible, and Church tradition;
- Reconfirm that charitable works were necessary for salvation, not simply faith alone as the Protestants believed;

- Forbid the sale of indulgences but reconfirm the value of indulgences, pilgrimages, veneration of saints and relics, and the veneration of the Virgin Mary; and
- Suppress Renaissance music and religious art that the Church did not feel were acceptable.[153] Any work that might arouse "carnal desire" was inadmissible in churches, while any depiction of Christ's suffering and explicit agony was desirable and proper. This resulted in a resurgence of Baroque art.

Virgin Mary Mother of God and Queen of Heaven

The Council of Trent, in its attempt to generate a revival of religious life, also supported Catholic devotion to Mary, the virgin mother of Jesus Christ and the ascended Queen of Heaven. Mary had been, for many centuries, the only mother figure within the pantheon of the Catholic Church. She was the mythical ideal of Catholic womanhood, conceived not by man but by God himself, who impossibly remained a virgin while giving birth to Jesus. She was portrayed as quiet, humble, beautiful, and pure. Catholics, who needed a female deity to whom they could pray, were encouraged to pray to Mary who could act as an intercessor between Jesus and the supplicant.

In 1571, just eight years after the conclusion of the Council of Trent, the Church won a decisive victory[154] over the Ottomans and the victory was credited to the intervention of the Virgin Mary. This helped to create a strong resurgence of devotion to her.[155] The Jesuits founded the Colloquium Marianum[156] and the Sodality of Our Lady,[157] elite groups that honored Mary as the perfect example of a virtuous woman, free of the seven deadly sins.[158]

In 1617, Pope Paul V, and again in 1622, Gregory XV, ruled that it was heretical to state that Mary was not a virgin when she conceived Jesus. In 1661, Alexander VII declared that Mary was the only human born without original sin thanks to God's grace. When Pope Clement XI ordered the feast of the Immaculate Conception in 1708, it inspired a vast movement of prayer directed to Mary. The Feast of the Rosary was introduced in 1716 and the Feast of the Seven Sorrows in 1727. The Angelus prayer (Hail Mary) was reinforced by Pope Benedict XIII in 1724 and by Pope Benedict XIV in 1742. Popular expressions of devotion to Mary multiplied into pilgrimages, devotions, litanies, theatre plays, hymns, processions, and the formation of clubs that at the time had millions of members. Today miracles witnessed across the Catholic world continue to be attributed to the intervention of Mary in the prayers of the faithful.

Religious Wars (1560 to 1648)

Calvin's Protestant ideas and his support for the middle class merchants who congregated in the cities and towns, created a revolution against the control of the Catholic Church and the crowned heads of Europe and set Europe on a course of continuous warfare for the next eighty-eight years (1560 to 1648).

When the Church found itself unable to quell the Protestant revolution, it went to war against them, charging the rebels with heresy and burning them at the stake.

Protestantism had begun to flourish in the Holy Roman Empire because Emperor Charles V was beset with many other problems at the time. Enemies within the empire and wars abroad diverted his attention from the religious revolution being ignited right under his nose. Charles had money problems and his army was deserting on a large scale. When he was finally able to defeat the Protestants, Charles was undermined by German and French Catholic princes who feared his growing power. In 1555, a temporary peace known as the Peace of Augsburg[159] was reached between the emperor and his rebellious princes. The agreement allowed each prince to choose Catholicism or Protestantism within their realms. The emperor also had to make concessions to Spain by splitting his empire between the Austrian branch, which favored Protestantism and the Spanish branch, which under Phillip II, was fervently Catholic. Nonetheless, many princes within the Spanish-dominated region still adapted the revolutionary rhetoric of Calvinism. Calvin, himself, was forced to flee to the Netherlands and then to France where he spread the tenets of revolution.

In the Spanish Netherlands, religious unrest led to protests and riots that resulted in Spanish repression. Even so, the Protestant rebels were able to maintain their influence due to strong leadership, the seizing of seaports, and public reaction to Spanish atrocities.

In France, growing tensions between the Catholics and the Calvinists (Huguenots) led to anarchy that weakened the French government. France descended into chaos due to bitter warfare, separatism, feuds between nobles, foreign intervention, and a weakened government.

In England, religious tensions between the Anglicans and the Spanish Catholics led to England raiding Spanish ships and giving aid to the Dutch rebels fighting Spain. At this time, Philip II of Spain tried to dethrone Elizabeth I of England. He sent the Spanish navy (Armada) to destroy England in 1588, but the English, under Sir Francis Drake, with the blessings of favorable weather, destroyed the Armada and sent the remnants limping back to Spain.[160]

England also launched an attack against Catholic France and the Spanish Netherlands who were fighting the Dutch Protestants.

The English attack on Spain in the Netherlands and the military success of the Dutch Protestant rebels eventually forced Spain to grant independence to the Netherlands in 1648. The Dutch Revolt helped to continue Dutch economic dominance in the sixteenth and seventeenth centuries.

The English Protestant wars against Spain also helped to save the Protestant cause in Western Europe and set the stage for the Thirty Years War (1618 to 1648).[161] This war, actually a series of wars, which ravaged the European mainland, brought two rival camps into conflict. Largely defined by religion, it was, however, not exclusively a religious war, because political rivalries within each camp often caught fire due to power struggles. The Catholic camp was largely composed of German Catholics, Hapsburg Spain, Hapsburg Austria,[162] Poland, and the Papacy. The Protestant camp included the German Protestants, Denmark, the Dutch, English, Swedish, French, and Venice.

The political, economic, military, and religious tensions in Europe led to a war in 1618 when Bohemian Protestant rebels attacked their Catholic Austrian rulers and threw several magistrates out the window of city hall.[163] This action, known as the *Defenestrations of Prague*, triggered the involvement of countries across Europe in what became an exhaustive stalemate that neither side could win nor withdraw from, even though they watched helplessly while their resources were drained away. The

Spanish pope, Paul V, and Poland helped Austria beat the Bohemian rebels. This led to Denmark, Holland and England joining the rebels' cause but they were defeated by the combined power of Hapsburg Spain and Austria (1625 to 1629). Sweden then joined the Protestant side but it too was defeated (1630 to 1634). France entered the fray against the Hapsburg Empire but was unable to defeat it. This led to a war of attrition between 1635 and 1648.

In 1648, when everyone was completely exhausted, the major combatants signed the Treaties of Westphalia.[164] These treaties constituted a new development in European political economy. The Peace of Westphalia involved the Holy Roman Emperor Ferdinand III, the Kingdom of Spain, the Kingdom of France, the Swedish Empire, the Dutch Republic, the Princes of the Holy Roman Empire, and sovereigns of the free imperial cities. The treaties ended thirty years of war and set up a peace between the Holy Roman Empire and its opponents, France, Sweden, and their respective allies. The treaties also ended the eighty years of war between Spain and the Dutch Republic and recognized the independence of the Dutch.

While the treaties did not bring peace throughout Europe, they did create the basis for national self-determination. They set a precedent of establishing peace by a diplomatic congress and also established the concept of co-existing sovereign nation-states. National aggression was to be held in check by a balance of power and a norm was established against interference in another state's domestic affairs. As the European colonization process spread across the globe, these principles became central to international law and to the new world order.[165]

The bottom line of the Protestant Reformation was that it was not a spiritual revolution. It introduced no new spiritual theory or practice. It was largely a political movement against the Catholic Church and those kingdoms that supported the Church. As such, its effect was the further crudification of Western consciousness. Now one's love of neighbor had no consequence within the Protestant religions. At the same time, the denial of human free will led to an even greater oppression of people by authority and allowed the rising merchant capitalists to rationalize their economic exploitation of fellow humans as a legitimate means to secure personal wealth and wealth for the Protestant Church. In so doing, it set the stage for the most advanced form of material exploitation that human beings have ever been subject to in history.

Protestant Religions of Western Europe

Anabaptists

Anabaptism in Switzerland began as an offshoot of the church reforms instigated by Ulrich Zwingli. Zwingli had gathered a group of reform-minded men around him with whom he studied classical literature and the scriptures. However, some of these men believed that Zwingli was not moving fast enough in his reform efforts. To Zwingli, the reforms depended upon the deliberations of the city's Council. To the more radical reformers, the Council had no right to make religious decisions. Rather, it was the Bible that constituted the final authority over church reform. Feeling frustrated, some of them began to meet on their own for Bible study. As early as 1523, William Reublin began to preach against infant baptism in villages surrounding Zurich. He encouraged parents not to baptize their children as infants because they did not have the consciousness to choose to be a Christian.

A Council meeting was held to address the issue of baptism and it was ruled at this meeting that all who continued to refuse to baptize their infants should be expelled from Zurich if they did not have their children baptized within one week of birth. At a subsequent meeting of the radical reformers, in 1525, it was recorded that:

> After prayer, George of the House of Jacob [George Blaurock] stood up and besought Conrad Grebel for God's sake to baptize him with the true Christian baptism upon his faith and knowledge. And when he knelt down with such a request and desire, Conrad baptized him, since at that time there was no ordained minister to perform such work.[166]

After Blaurock was baptized, he, in turn, baptized others at the meeting. These baptisms marked the first re-baptisms of those who had been baptized as infants and thus, technically, Swiss Anabaptism was born on that day.

The Amish, Hutterites, and Mennonites are direct descendants of the movement. Schwarzenau Brethren, Bruderhof, and the Apostolic Christian Church are considered later developments among the Anabaptists.

The name *Anabaptist*, meaning "one who baptizes again," was given them by their persecutors. The early members of this movement did not accept the name *Anabaptist*, claiming that since infant baptism was unscriptural and null and void, the baptizing of believers was not a re-baptism, but in fact their first real baptism. Balthasar Hubmaier, who was one of the earliest leaders of the movement, wrote:

> I have never taught Anabaptism . . . But the right baptism of Christ, which is preceded by teaching and oral confession of faith, I teach, and say that infant baptism is a robbery of the right baptism of Christ. . . .[167]

As a result of their views, Anabaptists were heavily persecuted during the sixteenth century and into the seventeenth century by both Magisterial Protestants[168] like Zwingli and Calvin, as well as by Roman Catholics.

Anglicans

In 1534, King Henry VIII separated the English Church from Rome. Even while dismantling the Catholic Church in England and seizing its wealth, Henry maintained a preference for traditional Catholic dogma and liturgy and persecuted any Protestant reformers. He also persecuted Catholics if they opposed him. The bloodbath that Henry caused was ameliorated somewhat by Queen Elizabeth I (from 1558) who took a middle path that changed the character of the Church of England (Anglican Church). It accepted some Reformed doctrines but also emphasized continuity with the Catholic and Apostolic traditions of the Church Fathers. Elizabeth also established the Anglican Church as part of the English constitution and made the head of state the supreme governor of the Church.

As the British Empire expanded, British colonists and colonial administrators took the established church doctrines and practices, together with its ordained ministry, and formed overseas branches of the Church of England. In colonial America, the English Tories constituted the ruling class and the Anglican Church was their religion. Most of the Tories were Anglican Puritans, and the Anglican Church became the established church of Virginia, Maryland, New York, North Carolina, South Carolina, and Georgia during the Colonial Period.

Episcopalians

In 1789, just a decade after the American Revolution, the Anglican Church reorganized itself into autonomous churches each with their own bishops and self-governing structure. With this restructuring, the Anglican Church became known as the Episcopal Church. In the nineteenth and early twentieth centuries, it was the predominant religion of the ruling class. More than a quarter of all presidents of the United States have been Episcopalians.[169]

Episcopalians define themselves as the "middle way between Roman Catholic and Protestant traditions." Like the Catholic Church, the Episcopal Church upholds the sacraments as essential to salvation and like Protestant churches, it denies the supremacy of the Pope as the Vicar of Christ on earth. Today the Anglican Communion has eighty million members worldwide in thirty-eight different church organizations, including the Episcopal Church.[170]

Puritans

Puritans in England were followers of Calvinism. They became an active movement in 1558, shortly after Elizabeth came to power. They were the protestant extremists who wanted the Anglican Church to make a total break with its Catholic heritage and adapt the principles of Calvinism. They found themselves, however, blocked from changing the established church from within, and were severely restricted in England by laws controlling the practice of religion.

In their opposition to the Anglican Church and its Episcopal system, they criticized clerical dress and developed their own style of dressing. Facing persecution after the *Restoration of 1660*,[171] in which Charles II seized control of the governments of England, Ireland and Scotland, almost all Puritan clergy left the Church of England and many of them went to America. As Calvinists, the Puritans supported the merchant class. They advocated greater purity of worship and doctrine as well as group piety. They brought these values and their support for the capitalists to American shores.[172] Samuel Adams, the father of the American Revolution was a Puritan. His fight against the Tories was based on over a century of religious conflict as well as on a personal vendetta.[173] It can be said without question that the English Puritan's vision of a Christian state has been instrumental in forming the ideology of contemporary conservatism ever since the beginning of the American Revolution.

Presbyterians

A "presbyter" is a member of the governing body of an early Calvinist Reformed Church. He could be a bishop, priest, deacon, or even a layperson. Presbyterians owe their ideology to Calvinism and also followed his lead in making their organizational structure more democratic in comparison to the Church of England that was governed by bishops.

John Knox (1505–1572), a Scot who had spent time studying under Calvin in Geneva, returned to Scotland and urged his countrymen to reform the Church in line with Calvinist doctrines. In 1733, a group of ministers seceded from the Church of Scotland to form the Associate Presbytery. Another group seceded in 1761 to form the Relief Church. This turmoil led to the *Disruption of 1843*, which was a part of the schism within the established Church of Scotland. The Disruption saw four hundred and fifty evangelical ministers of the Church break away, over the issue of the Church's relationship with the State. The result was the formation of the Free Church of Scotland. The Disruption had huge effects not only within the Church, but also upon Scottish civic life.

In England, Presbyterianism was established in secret as early as 1592. By the eighteenth century, many English Presbyterian congregations had become Unitarian in doctrine.

Presbyterianism officially arrived in Colonial America in 1703 with the establishment of the first Presbytery in Philadelphia. In 1717, the presbytery would be joined by two more to form a synod that would eventually evolve into the Presbyterian Church in the United States of America in 1789. Most Presbyterian churches today trace their heritage back to this church.

In the United States, Presbyterian influence helped give root to modern Evangelicalism:

> Evangelicalism itself . . . is quintessentially a North American phenomenon, deriving as it did from the confluence of Pietism, Presbyterianism, and the vestiges of Puritanism. Evangelicalism picked up the peculiar characteristics from each strain—warmhearted spirituality from the Pietists, doctrinal precisionism from the Presbyterians, and individualistic introspection from the Puritans—even as the North American context itself has profoundly shaped the various manifestations of evangelicalism: fundamentalism, neo-evangelicalism, the holiness movement, Pentecostalism, the charismatic movement, and various forms of African-American and Hispanic evangelicalism.[174]

Congregationalists

The Congregationalists were another nonconformist movement within the Church of England. The early Congregationalists were called separatists or independents to distinguish them from the Calvinist-Presbyterians. The Congregationalists rejected all form of church hierarchy and made each congregation or church independent and autonomous in running its own affairs.

Their most well-known leader was John Cotton, who began writing and organizing in 1633. Cotton's writings persuaded John Owen, the academic administrator at the University of Oxford, to separate from the Presbyterian Church. Once in America, however, church leaders became distressed by the colony-wide decline of religious piety and church discipline. In 1700, they called a meeting that resulted in the *Saybrook Platform*, which was in essence a new constitution for the church. The constitution rejected the local control that had been inherited from England and replaced it with a system similar to what the Presbyterians had. This amounted to a counter-revolution against the nonconformist tide and resulted in a centralized authority.

Congregationalist churches were widely established in the Plymouth Colony in Massachusetts and spread to Connecticut and then into New England. From there they spread to New York and then into Illinois, Indiana, Michigan, Ohio, and Wisconsin, whose territory was won from the British during the American Revolution.

Congregationalists are credited with having formed some of the first colleges and universities in America including Harvard, Yale, Dartmouth, and Amherst.[175]

Pietists

While the dominant strain of Protestantism in the United States derived from Calvinism, the secondary strain derived from Lutheranism. Reforms within the Lutheran movement gave rise to Pietists, Methodists, Baptists, and also supported Evangelicals. The earliest of these reforms was that of Pietism.

Pietism was a movement within Lutheranism that began in the late seventeenth century, reached its zenith in the mid-eighteenth century, declined through the nineteenth century, and had almost vanished in America by the end of the twentieth century. While it declined as an identified Lutheran group, it inspired Anglican priest John Wesley to begin the Methodist movement and Alexander Mack to begin the Brethren movement. The Pietist movement put its emphasis on individual piety and living an active Christian life. Though pietism shares an emphasis on personal behavior with the Puritan movement, and the two are often confused, there are important differences, particularly in the concept of the role of religion in government.

The direct originator of the Pietist movement was Philipp Jakob Spener. Born in Alsace, a part of German territory at the time, but French by 1635, Spener was convinced of the necessity of a moral and religious reformation within German Lutheranism. Pietism, as a distinct movement in the German Church, began with religious meetings at Spener's house where he preached his sermons, expounding on passages of the New Testament, and induced those present to join in conversation on religious questions. In 1675, Spener published his *Earnest Desire for a Reform of the True Evangelical Church* (Pia desideria), the title giving rise to the term "Pietists." In this treatise, Spener made six proposals as the best means for restoring the life of the German Lutheran Church:

1. The earnest and thorough study of the Bible in private meetings;
2. The laity should share in the spiritual government of the Church;
3. Academic knowledge of Christ was not enough, one had to be a practicing Christian;
4. Instead of attacking the unbelievers, extend sympathetic and kindly treatment to them;
5. Reorganize theological training of the universities, giving more prominence to devotion; and
6. Instead of intellectual sermons, a different style of preaching was needed to impact the soul of man.

His work split the Lutheran Church. The main difference between the new Pietistic Lutheran school and the orthodox Lutherans arose from the Pietists' conception of Christianity as chiefly consisting in a change of heart and consequent holiness of life. Orthodox Lutherans rejected this viewpoint as a gross simplification and a vague form of mysticism. They renewed their call for a strong church administration with sound theological underpinnings. Spener stressed the necessity of a new birth (born again) and separation of Christians from the world. His emphasis on home study also tended to weaken the power of church administration.

Authorities within the state-endorsed religions were suspicious of Pietist doctrine which they viewed as a social danger because it generated an excess of evangelical fervor and disturbed the public tranquility and because it promoted a mysticism so nebulous as to obscure the imperatives of morality.

Pietism, with its emphasis on personal faith, rather than church doctrine, is considered the major influence that led to the creation of the "Evangelical Church of the Union" in Prussia in 1817. The King of Prussia ordered the Lutheran and Reformed churches in Prussia to unite; they took the name "Evangelical" as a name both groups had previously identified with. Those Lutherans who rebelled against the king's decree, became known as the Old Lutherans who formed their own free churches. Many, of whom, immigrated to the United States to avoid persecution where they formed what later became the Lutheran Church—Missouri Synod. Many immigrants to America, who agreed with the union movement, formed the German Evangelical Lutheran and Reformed congregations, that later combined into the Evangelical Synod of North America, which is now a part of the United Church of Christ.

Pietism also had a major influence on John Wesley and others who began the Methodist movement in eighteenth century Great Britain. The fruit of Pietist influence can be seen in the modern American Methodists and members of the Holiness movement.

Along with Presbyterianism and Puritism, Pietism gave Evangelicalism an emotional fervor in its church services.[176]

Women under Protestantism

Very few things changed for women under Protestantism. In marriage, a wife still remained subordinate to her husband and was expected to be silent, obedient, and to perform her domestic chores without complaint. These chores included raising the children, caring for the home, making clothing for her family, and tending the garden and livestock. The identification of these chores as "women's work" harkens back to the role of women among the barbarian tribes of Europe before they became Christian. Women, under Protestantism, however, were taught to read so that they could read the Bible and teach it to the children.[177]

Women were still not allowed to teach or preach in public, however, because of Paul's admonition (Timothy 2: 11-15):

> "Let the woman learn in silence with all subjection. But I suffer not a woman to teach, nor to usurp authority over the man, but to be in silence. For Adam was first formed, then Eve. And Adam was not deceived, but the woman being deceived was in the transgression. Notwithstanding she shall be saved in childbirth, if they continue in faith and charity and holiness with sobriety."

The only exception to Protestant sexism, was the Anabaptist religion, where women could preach in church. The only evidence of works or writings that are written by women were from their letters or through the confessions of the woman who were being questioned by the Inquisition, but these were often written by the Inquisitors themselves.[178]

From a spiritual perspective, Protestantism provided even less options to women than Catholicism. Catholicism provided an alternative to marriage for women by joining a convent, but under Protestantism even this was no longer an option. Thus, the only option of a full-time religious role for women was eliminated. Both Luther and Calvin agreed that a woman's place was in the home.[179] [180]

Protestant clergy, unlike priests, were allowed to marry. This limited the sexual aberrations that long plagued the Catholic Church due to its rule of celibacy.

It does not seem to matter which Protestant denomination we discuss; they all suppressed women's spiritual expression in public. The Baptist theologian Dr John Gill stated:

> In Gen_3:16, "thy desire shall be to thy husband, and he shall rule over thee". By this the apostle would signify, that the reason why women are not to speak in the church, or to preach and teach publicly, or be concerned in the ministerial function, is, because this is an act of power, and authority; of rule and government, and so contrary to that subjection which God in his law requires of women unto men....[181]

Methodist founder John Wesley (1703–1791) and Methodist theologian Adam Clarke (1762–1832) both upheld male supremacy, but allowed that spiritual Christian women could publicly speak in church meetings if they "are under an extraordinary impulse of the Spirit."[182]

The Puritan theologian Matthew Poole (1624–1679) concurred with Wesley, adding, "But setting aside that extraordinary case of a special afflatus [strong Divine influence], it was, doubtless, unlawful for a woman to speak in the church."[183]

Matthew Henry (1662–1714), a Puritan theologian, granted that "praying, and uttering hymns inspired" by women, as such "were not teaching."[184]

Congregationalist A. Hastings Boss, D.D. wrote in 1870 that he found no sanctioned "instance in the Bible of a woman's speaking in public." In his attempt to dismiss the Jewish judges Miriam, Deborah, Huldah, and Anna, he states:

> If these prophetesses had each been called to public speaking, they would have been exceptions to the general rule, in striking contrast with the conduct of all other women under the law. Certainly no rule could have been or can now be founded upon these exceptional cases. Joel predicts [Joel 2:28-32] and Peter quotes [Acts 2:17-21] that "in the last days" God's Spirit should lead "daughters" and hand-maidens," as well as men, to "prophesy"; but neither prophet nor apostle specifies any particular place, as the church, in which it should be done. Now Paul nowhere forbids women to prophesy, except "in the churches." They could have exercised their gift in private, or in a congregation of women, as did the four virgin daughters of Philip . . . A prophetess would have had enough to do among her own sex, without speaking in the assemblies.[185]

Dr. John Gill also believed that: "The extraordinary instances of Deborah, Huldah, and Anna must not be drawn into a rule or example in such cases [of women preaching in public]." [186]

The Presbyterian quarterly, April, 1889, expressed concern about the dangers of revival meetings and stated:

> "Meetings of pious women by themselves for conversation and prayer, whenever they can conveniently be held, we entirely approve. But let not the inspired prohibitions of the great apostle of the Gentiles, as found in his Epistles to the Corinthians and to Timothy, be violated. To teach and exhort, or to lead in prayer in public and promiscuous assemblies, is clearly forbidden to women in the holy oracles."[187]

While Protestant preachers, to this day, continue mechanically to reference Paul as the originator of this admonition (certainly it was not Jesus Christ), they forget that Paul was raised as a Jewish Pharisee and that this belief originated with the patriarchal scribes of Judaism.[188] Unfortunately, some Protestant preachers continue this patriarchal cultural disrespect for women even today.

Yet, despite men's attempt to keep women in a subservient position, women did begin to make strides based on their own initiative. Women joined the Protestant movements only in the company of their husbands or fathers. Those who did convert were mostly middle class like their husbands. Because literacy was now extended to women to read the Bible, many women began to preach as well, but this alarmed the men. They were not allowed to receive formal theological training, so they could hardly preach. The women, for their part claimed direct illumination from God for their ideas, as had the Catholic female mystics. Silenced at the pulpit, they nonetheless began to write sermons, hymns, and poems that were used during Church services.

Because Protestants valued marriage above celibacy as the ideal, Protestant clergy, many who were former priests, began to marry and many married former nuns. Martin Luther married the former nun, Katherine Bora, and fathered six children. Calvin also married. With the closing of convents, the number of marriage-age women increased, and so did their struggle to survive. In England, statistics show nearly thirty percent of nuns married and twenty-five percent of monks did.

But many, who did not marry, had to resort to domestic servitude, day labor, or even prostitution.

To the Protestants, marriage was not a sacrament to be administered by the Church. Philosophically, they looked at marriage as a cooperative relationship based on mutual responsibility. Women were praised for their biblical vocation as mothers and housewives and no longer relegated to the stereotypes of a virgin mother or the temptress Eve. Even so, Protestant sermons on the subject of marriage continued to instruct husbands to keep their wives in their place.

For the Catholic Church, sexual intercourse was for procreation only. Both Luther and Calvin rejected this teaching and also rejected the legal double standard for fornication and adultery. In reality, however, the double standard did prevail for Protestants until the twentieth century. Women were persecuted for adultery while men were not. Even so, the divorce rate remained low, around two percent, and did not change until the twentieth century.

The Protestants condemned the worship of saints, both male and female, and dethroned the Virgin Mary as the mother of God and protector of women in childbirth. This was especially hard on Protestant women because it eliminated the only female deity to whom they could pray. Luther, himself, said that he had trouble breaking his wife of saying her "Hail Marys."

After all was said and done, women were equal to men in the presence of God according to the Bible, but remained inferior to men on Earth. They were to remain obedient to their husbands and to keep silent in public. Calvin rudely enjoined: "Let the woman be satisfied with her state of subjection and not take it ill that she is made inferior to the more distinguished sex." He incessantly chastised women for their fashionable dress, adornments, and immodest behavior. Consistent with the Catholic tradition, he also blamed them for the sins of men: "There have been too many examples of how men, otherwise inclined to behave virtuously have been debauched and turned from the right way by women."

As the Reformation and then the Counter-Reformation took hold in Europe, the horrendous laws against witchcraft and infanticide ignited, creating the most cataclysmic time for women in all of human history.

In summary, the Protestant Reformation was a European revolution against the beliefs and practices of the Roman Catholic Church in the sixteenth century. It focused on certain beliefs and rituals and was exacerbated by ambitious political rulers who wanted to extend their power and control at the expense of the Church. The Reformation ended the unity imposed by the hegemony of the Catholic Church and signaled the ascension of the modern era. The movement quickly gained adherents in the German states, the Netherlands, Scandinavia, Scotland, and portions of France due in large part to sincere reformers, but quickly turned into chaos and universal warfare throughout the entirety of Europe as opportunists fought for control of church property. In this process, Christians forfeited their sense of humanity in their descent into moral anarchy.

As the hope of reforming the Catholic Church faded, the reformers separated from Roman Catholicism, resulting in the formation of Lutheran churches in Germany, Scandinavia and some eastern European countries, the Reformed churches in Switzerland and the Netherlands, Presbyterian churches in Scotland, the Anglican church in England, and other diverse elements, all of which have evolved into the Protestant denominations of today.[189]

The positive aspect of the Protestant Reformation was that it led to a more sober and dignified life, as a hundred years of anger, hatred, brutality, and immorality played themselves out. This led to a rejection of religious blind faith and supported the rise of rationality. The Protestant Reformation also set the stage for the Enlightenment period that followed, during which, after so many years of war, the rebirth of philosophy and science, that had begun with the Renaissance, began to flourish anew. Because Protestants valued rational thought and a more "get down to business" view of life, the need to understand material reality in order to succeed in life helped to support and ultimately lead to the rise of capitalism and the beginning of the modern era.[190]

Chapter Three: The Enlightenment

THE POLITICAL REVOLUTION THAT occurred during the Protestant Reformation continued during the Age of Enlightenment, thereby increasing the challenge to Church hegemony in Europe and the New World.

While the Protestant Reformation attacked Church corruption, it also challenged some of its fundamental dogmas. During the Enlightenment, on the other hand, intellectuals began to question the validity of Christianity itself. Many were sick and tired of religion and the chaos that it had brought to European life. Such people rejected Divine revelation and replaced it with respect for human reason. They replaced Faith with Science. And they sought to replace the power of the Papacy with local authority, which, by consequence, set the rise of independent nation states.

The Church after the Thirty Years War

During the late seventeenth century, the Church faced a barrage of new "heresies." In France, ideas such as *Gallicanism, Councilarism,* and *Jansenism* sought to diminish papal authority. Gallicanism held that civil authority should lie in the hands of local authorities such as the monarch, state authority, or even local bishops but not in the hands of the pope.[191]

Councilarism held that the supreme authority in the Church should reside with an Ecumenical council and not with the pope. The movement emerged in response to the Western Schism in which popes in Rome and Avignon vied for authority.[192]

There was also Jansenism, which was a movement within the Church that supported the ideas of Calvinism, by focusing on original sin, human depravity, the necessity of divine grace and predestination. [193]

Such heresies were only the start of the Church's troubles. The Enlightenment also brought ideas such as *Secularism*, the belief that religion should not play any role in government, education, or other public parts of society, and *Relativism*, which held that there is no such thing as absolute truth, only relative, subjective values based upon differences in perception and consideration.

Later, as the merchant/capitalist class rose to ascendency throughout the Western world, the Church also faced the heresies of *Modernism, Materialism, Consumerism, and Hedonism.*[194] But by now, they no longer had the authority to declare such ideas illegal or persecute those who ascribed to them.

Toward the latter part of the seventeenth century, Pope Innocent XI focused on the increasing attacks by the Ottoman Turks as the greatest threat to Catholicism. He built a Polish-Austrian coalition and was able to defeat the Turks in Vienna in 1683. Scholars have called him a saintly pope because he reformed abuses by the Church, including simony, nepotism, the large drain of capital resulting from the Thirty Years War, and lavish papal spending.

In 1685, the Gallicanist King Louis XIV of France issued the *Edict of Fontainebleau* that made it illegal, after a century of religious toleration, to be a Protestant in France. He ordered the destruction of Huguenot churches, as well as the closure of Protestant schools. He also made the Huguenots quarter dragoons (French cavalry) within their homes and assume the burden of this expense. It is estimated that from two hundred and ten thousand to nine hundred thousand Calvinists left France during this time. Louis XIV also forced local bishops to support conciliarism and deny Papal infallibility. The king threatened the pope with a general council and a military take-over of the Papal state.[195] This absolutist policy of the French State allowed it to control virtually all major Church appointments in France as well as many of the Church's properties. Gallicanism spread to Belgium and Germany as well. A hundred years later, the Emperor Joseph II of Austria would also apply the principles of Gallicanism to regulate Church services, appointments, and the confiscation of Church properties.[196]

The Church in North America

During this period, the Church, in conjunction with the Spanish crown, also sent missionaries to the Americas. Junípero Serra, the Franciscan priest in charge of this effort, founded a series of missions and fortresses (presidios) in California that became important economic, political, and religious institutions. Coastal and overland routes were established from Mexico City and mission outposts in Texas and New Mexico had led to thirteen major California missions by 1781. The impact on the native population was devastating as the Europeans brought new diseases that killed off a third of the population. The impact was similar to the Black Plague that had previously ravaged Europe.

The Church in South America

To their credit, in South America, the Catholic Jesuits attempted to protect the native people from being enslaved by the Portuguese and Spanish colonialists by establishing semi-independent settlements for them. After some time, in 1839, Pope Gregory XVI, challenging Spanish and Portuguese sovereignty altogether, appointed his own candidates as bishops in the colonies, and outright condemned the slave trade in 1839. He also approved the ordination of native clergy in spite of government racism.[197]

The Absolute Monarchies of France, England, and Russia

When the Thirty Years War came to an end, England and France were in the best position to develop their mercantile economies. The Dutch economy had already peaked and was on a decline due to wars with the English and French who were jealous of its success during the sixteenth century. The Holy Roman Empire, run by the Hapsburgs, who controlled Spain and Austria, were preoccupied with stopping the Ottoman Empire from coming into Western Europe. Germany was still divided into small warring states and Italy remained divided.

France

France, like Germany, was in a state of anarchy during the days of the religious wars. After the wars, the French people still found themselves subject to internal violence as armed bands under aristocratic leaders terrorized them. The people looked to a strong king to stop the violence. At the time, however, Louis XIII had died and the government was in the hands of his widow, Anne of Austria, who served as the Regent, and Cardinal Mazarin, who served as the Chief Minister. Anne's son, the legendary Louis XIV, was only five years old at the time. Mazarin, who was the protégé of the famous or infamous Cardinal Richelieu, followed his policy of creating a strong monarchy by controlling the power of the nobility.

Richelieu had imposed heavy taxes on the nobility in order to pay the debt incurred in the Thirty Years War. Because the nobility held many positions in the French bureaucracy, he began to replace them with an organization of officials (*intendants*) loyal only to the king.[198] The intendants spread throughout the kingdom, ensured that taxes were paid and reported any instances of corruption or rebelliousness against the king. The intendants soon began to replace the bureaucratic role of the nobility and set up a parallel structure to the feudal system. When Richelieu died in 1642, Cardinal Mazarin filled his position.[199] Just as the nobility hated Richelieu, they hated Mazarin and schemed to overthrow the monarchy. They started a series of rebellions from 1648 to 1653, known as the *Fronde*.[200] Mazarin faced the combined opposition of the princes, the nobility, the law courts (parliaments), and most of the French people, and yet won out in the end. Nonetheless, during the revolt, Anne was forced to escape from Paris with the young Louis.

Mazarin ruled France until his death in 1661. During this time, the young Louis concentrated his energy on internal reforms to strengthen his power.

The Fronde, which was a series of civil wars initiated by the French nobility against the king, had alarmed him and Louis sought a way to build a better army loyal only to him. He standardized uniforms and equipment, established good supply lines, and insisted on strict discipline and training.

Louis also embraced economic reforms. France had already established colonies in North America and mercantile capitalism was on the rise. Gold and silver was becoming the new measure of wealth, while land and title were on the wane. Louis supported this development by building new roads, creating a merchant marine, and developing the colonies. He also set up new domestic industries to cut imports and strengthened the French colonies to increase access to raw materials. While the merchants appreciated these developments, they also bristled under Louis' tight control. Everything became the property of the state, thereby limiting the initiative of the new merchant class.

By the late 1660s, Louis began to follow more aggressive policies. He moved his throne from Paris, which he hated, and created the Palace of Versailles. There a court of ten thousand people lived a lavish existence. Louis also drove the Calvinist Huguenots out of France and anyone who preached or attended a Protestant assembly faced life terms as a galley slave if a man, and imprisonment if a woman. In addition, all of their property was confiscated. Louis' attack on the Protestants caused tens of thousands to leave France and move to England and Prussia (in Germany).[201] This damaged his economy because of the loss of so many skilled workers.

Louis' improvement of the French army, along with his increased wealth and his antagonistic policy toward non-Catholics, caused much of Europe to ally against him to maintain a balance of power. In the subsequent wars, flintlocks were improved and pre-measured powder loads made firing quicker. Bayonets replaced pikemen. This new weaponry made warfare more deadly and caused the monarchies of other nations to maintain tighter control of their armies. Louis's long and bloody wars and his lavish lifestyle at Versailles eventually ruined the economy and led to the French Revolution.[202]

When Louis died in 1715, Louis XV (1715-1774) and Louis XVI (1774-1792) proved to be weak kings and drove France deeper into debt.

Conditions were exacerbated by a serious crop failure due to outdated technology and the rise, once again, of the nobility under the weak monarchies. At the same time, the kings were unable to curtail Enlightenment ideas that called for liberty, democracy, and a new vision of the role of government. The people became angrier about the injustices they witnessed in French society and the government. The bourgeoisie spent their money on noble titles and land rather than investing in technology and businesses. Louis XVI called a general assembly (*Estates General*) of the clergy, nobles, and merchants in 1789 to raise taxes to cover the debt incurred by the monarchy.[203]

The assembly failed when the merchants (the Third Estate),[204] supported by the French people, withdrew from the Estate General and declared itself the National Assembly. A Paris mob stormed the Bastille, a fortified prison, as Louis posted troops around the city. Panic and riots (the *Great Fear*)[205] swept across the people, inflamed by rumors of an "aristocratic conspiracy," led by the king and the privileged, to overthrow the Third Estate. The merchant class created a national guard to compete with the king's army. Aristocrats were captured and tortured for their long years of oppressing the people. They were forced to give up their feudal rights and many left France creating fears of revolution across Europe.

Many members of the nobility were put under the guillotine. In 1789, the people, under the leadership of women who were close to rioting over the high price and scarcity of bread, marched on Versailles, seized Louis from his Palace and brought him back to Paris. The middle class merchants created a constitutional monarchy in 1791 that called for jury trials and an end to torture. Louis was executed in 1793. Is spite of these developments, the new government was faced with continuing economic and political turmoil.

People's armies "liberated" Holland and Switzerland and the revolution spread. In 1793, fearing an attack by foreign powers, the French government massacred fifteen hundred political prisoners in what became known as the *September Massacres.*[206] At this time, England, Holland, Austria, Prussia, and Spain formed a coalition to stop the revolution. In the chaos, revolts spread through the French countryside. The Jacobins,[207] the most radical and ruthless of the political groups, seized power in Paris and, in association with Robespierre, they instituted the *Reign of Terror* [208] that brought tens of thousands of "enemies of the revolution" to their deaths, most under the blade of the guillotine. It is noteworthy that Robespierre highly valued the enlightenment ideas of a new form of government and was always honored as an outspoken defender of the poor.[209]

The revolution, its reforms, and its bloodshed, came to an end when Napoleon Bonaparte seized power in 1799 and established a military dictatorship.

England

During the last six years of the Thirty Years War, England was going through a civil war. The conflict between the Protestants and Catholics continued to heighten during the absolutist reigns of James I and Charles I (1625 to 1649). The Catholic monarchs clashed with the rising Puritan merchant class who controlled Parliament. The result of the Civil War was that the Parliament, under Oliver Cromwell,[210] won the fight against Charles. Cromwell had Charles beheaded in 1649 and set up a military dictatorship. He also set up a professional army along the lines of Louis XIV.

Cromwell conquered Protestant Scotland and ruled it with moderation. When he took over Ireland, however, because it was Catholic, he ruled it with brutality. He also started wars with Spain and the Dutch.

At home, Cromwell heavily taxed the people to pay for his army. He closed racetracks, theatres, pubs, and other means of entertainment. In the Calvinist tradition, he also discouraged fashionable clothing.

Due to these actions, Cromwell became very unpopular among the people. After his death in 1658, the monarchy, as mentioned above, was restored in 1660 and Charles II came to power.[211] Charles II was a frivolous ruler who reopened sources of entertainment for the people. He lived lavishly because more money was coming in from his North American colonies. At the same time, he was secretly receiving money from Louis XIV to restore the power of the Catholic Church in England. During this time, the Calvinist Parliament split into two parties, the

Whigs and the Tories. The Whigs supported the Presbyterian Church and the Tories supported the king and the Anglican Church.

When Charles II died in 1685, the monarchy seemed strong, but the accession of James II (1685-1688) to the throne resulted in the rule of a stubborn and autocratic leader who openly favored Catholicism and worked to create an absolute monarchy.[212] This caused the Whigs and Tories to join together. Their contest with the king led to the *Glorious Revolution* in 1688 and the creation of a constitutional monarchy that placed English law above the divine right of kings. The constitutional monarchy introduced freedom of speech and religion and the right to due process under the law to all English citizens. This new faith in the government led to investment in a new Bank of England,[213] which was privately owned. The freedom gained from government restrictions led to the Industrial Revolution and put England decades ahead of its competition in the development of a capitalist infrastructure.

Eastern Europe

During this period in Eastern Europe, the Hapsburg Austrian Empire was concentrating on fighting the Ottoman empire. In 1683, the Turks invaded Austria and laid siege to Vienna, the capital. A polish army, under King Jan Sobieski defeated the Turks.[214] A coalition of papal forces, Austria, Venice, Poland, and Russia soundly defeated the Ottomans in 1697. In the Treaty of Karlowitz in 1699, Austria gained control of Slavonia, Transylvania, and the rest of Hungary making it once again a great power.[215] Even so, long-term problems within Austria continued to fester. Nobles continued to oppress the serfs and threaten Hapsburg rule. The Hapsburgs allowed the nobles to continue to oppress the serfs so long as they did not bother the Hapsburgs. Austria was also the common ground of many different ethnic groups and cultures that divided the empire. While the Hapsburgs tried to unify them by imposing the German language and Catholic religion, this only gave rise to resentment and calls for freedom.

The German ruling class established itself in the cities but unsanitary conditions continually killed off the population due to cholera and other diseases. There was a gradual influx of Slavs into Austria to replace the German population that was lost. The Slavs were drawn to the cities where the industrial revolution had produced a need for a large factory workforce. The Germans became xenophobic and created a backlash against the Slavs. As resistance grew, Austria slowly declined and continued to do so until World War I. The Hapsburg Empire collapsed for good at the end of the war. [216]

In Russia, the people had long been subject to the harsh rule of the Mongols that included a slave trade that had existed for centuries. The Grand Duchy of Moscow, which was a late medieval Rus' (Viking) principality centered around Moscow and the predecessor state of the early modern Tsarist Russia, paid tribute to the Mongols until Ivan IV, better known as "Ivan the Terrible," led a revolt against them.[217] Using European weapons and technology, Ivan destroyed the Tatar khanates and opened Siberia to the Russians.

Peter I (1682-1725) became Tsar after the death of Ivan's son, Ivan V. When Peter came to power, Russia was not connected to the rest of Europe because it was geographically isolated and practiced a different religion. Nonetheless, Peter, commonly known as Peter the Great, wanted Russia to become stronger and to compete with western countries. He achieved this by increased trade, the study of technology, taking over the church of Russia, and building a powerful army.[218] Through a number of successful wars, he built a large empire and turned Russia into a major European power. Peter fostered the ideas of the Enlightenment in Russia, creating a cultural revolution that replaced traditionalist and medieval social and political systems with ones that were modern, scientific, and westernized. Many of the institutions created by Peter are still in existence today. He died as he had lived, a hero to the people. After diving into freezing water in an attempt to rescue several drowning sailors, he died of pneumonia in 1725.[219]

After Peter's death, his reform movement was sidelined by a conservative backlash that caused Russia to fall behind the West in economic development. In the late 1700s, Catherine the Great (1729-1796), the longest-ruling female leader of Russia, came to power following a *coup d'état* in which her husband, Peter III, was assassinated. Russia grew stronger under her reign and again became one of the great powers of Europe.[220]

In the south, after it defeated the Ottoman Empire during the Russo-Turkish wars, Russia annexed the Crimean Khanate, a vassal state of the Ottoman Empire and an important center in the slave trade.[221] Russia at the time also colonized the vast territories of Novorossiya (New Russia) along the coasts of the Black and Azov Seas.

Map 4-1: Map of New Russia (Novorossiya)

In the west, Stanislaw August Poniatowski (1732-1798) now ruled the Polish-Lithuanian Commonwealth. He had been romantically involved with Catherine when they were young and Catherine had helped Stanislaw become elected king of the Commonwealth. Against the expectations of neighboring countries, Stanislaw began to strengthen the ailing Commonwealth. This alarmed Catherine, as well as the powers of Prussia and Austria, who desired to keep the commonwealth weak. The king also faced opposition from the conservative nobility who viewed his reform effort as a threat to their traditional privilege. This situation led to a series of wars in which Poland was gradually partitioned. The king was stripped of all power and abdicated in 1795. Russia gained the largest share of Poland in a territorial takeover.

In the east, Russia also started to colonize Alaska. From 1733 to 1867, its holdings spanned parts of Alaska, California, and Hawaii. Many of its possessions were eventually abandoned and, in 1867, Russia sold its last remaining possessions to the United States for $7.2 million about $130 million in 2018 dollars.

Catherine also instituted administrative reforms and many new cities and towns were founded on her orders. While she attempted to modernize Russia using the West as a model, military conscription and the Russian economy continued to depend on the serfs. As greater demands were continually being placed on the serfs by the state and private landlords, the situation created a series of revolts, including the large-scale Pugachev's Rebellion (1773-1775), the largest peasant revolt in Russian history.[222]

Catherine is considered by historians to be an "enlightened despot." While she built the Russian empire and created a Golden Age for the nobility, she abused and punished the common people. At the same time, she was a patron of the arts and established the first state-financed higher education institution for women in Europe.[223]

The next important leader in Russia was Alexander II (1818-1881). He was the Tsar (Emperor) of Russia from 1855 until his assassination in 1881. He was also the King of Poland and the Grand Duke of Finland.

In 1854, Alexander became embroiled in the Crimean War in which Russia was defeated by an alliance of France, England, the Ottoman Empire, and Sardinia. Ostensibly, the war was started over the rights of Christian minorities in the Holy Land, controlled by the Ottomans. France wanted protection for the Catholics, while Russia wanted protection for the Eastern Orthodox Christians. In reality, the war was fought because the alliance did not want Russia to gain territory and power at the Ottoman's expense.[224] The war was known for its "notoriously incompetent international butchery."[225]

Emancipation of the Serfs in Russia

The emancipation of serfs in 1861 by Alexander is considered to be his greatest accomplishment. But it is worth taking a look beneath the surface of this political action because it provides an object lesson in how the propensities for self-aggrandizement on the part of a ruling class, regardless of nation, is hidden by its apparent support of good works.

At the time, the feudal system in Russia tied the peasants irrevocably to their landlords. It was technically not slavery because, unlike in the United States, the serfs were not "owned" outright by the landlords, but the reality was the same because a serf could not leave the land without the landlord's permission. The purpose of this development was to make the nobles dependent upon and loyal to the tsar. As in Europe, the nobles had to express their loyalty by serving as military officers or public officials. By this device, the tsars built up their empire using nobles who now had a vested interest in maintaining the state. In this way, the ruling class was established in feudal Russia. The serfs made up just over a third of the population.

In the West, serfdom was abandoned as it moved into the industrial age, but Russia found itself trapped in the old system and remained economically and socially backward. Many Russians had come to believe that reform was unavoidable if their nation was to progress.

Serfdom became the easy target for the intellectuals to explain all Russia's weaknesses: its military incompetence (it had just lost the Crimean War), food shortages, over population, civil disorder, and industrial backwardness.

The Tsar used the humiliating defeat of the Crimean War to call for the emancipation of the serfs. Perhaps it was a noble act on his part.[226] The army had always been the great symbol of Russia's worth. So long as the army remained strong, Russia could ignore its backwardness as a nation. But now it had failed to provide the caliber of soldier Russia needed.

But freeing the serfs presented its own dangers, particularly from the nobility that depended upon them for their rich lifestyle. In order to get the support of the landlord nobility for the emancipation, Czar Alexander put the ball in their court by announcing that "the existing condition of owning souls cannot remain unchanged. It is better to begin to destroy serfdom from above than to wait until that time when it begins to destroy itself from below. I ask you, gentlemen, to figure out how all this can be carried out to completion."[227] Over the next five years, thousands of officials sat down in committees and drafted plans for the abolition of serfdom. When they presented their work to Alexander, he issued a formal Imperial Proclamation. The year was 1861.

While their new "freedoms" sounded great, in actuality, the serfs found themselves in a worse condition. The landlord nobility had actually created a document that served only their own self-interest. The serfs now had to compensate the landlords for the land they worked at a price far above its market value. The landlords also decided which part of their holdings they would give up so they kept the best land for themselves and the serfs got the left-overs. The records show that the landlords retained two-thirds of the land, while the serfs received only one-third. So limited was the amount of land now available to the serfs that they could farm only small strips of the worst land and could not afford to stay alive by farming anymore.

Because the serfs had to buy this land from the landlords and because they had no savings to do so, they were advanced mortgages but the payments and interest became a lifelong burden that they had to hand down to their children.

To prevent emancipation from creating too much disruption, the government urged the peasants to remain in their localities. This was easy to achieve because the great majority of the ex-serfs bought their allotments of land from the estates where they were already living. The government then reorganized local governments into village communes (*mirs*) that became the administrative system for the collection of taxes to which the freed serfs were now liable, and the means to keep control in the countryside. The "freed" Russian peasant was now more restricted than he had been as a serf. Instead of being tied to the lord, the peasant was now tied to the state.[228]

As the Industrial Revolution progressed in Russia, the serfs faced the same conditions as did the displaced serfs in Europe. This led to a mass migration to the cities in search of work. People faced overcrowding in poorly built tenements, low wages, and no job security. They died from diseases caused by polluted air and water and from spoiled food.

In 1903, Japan defeated Russia in a war over control of Manchuria. Both empires sought control of Port Arthur on the Pacific Ocean in Manchuria. Vladivostok, a Russian port town on the east coast, was operational only during the summer, whereas Port Arthur was operational all year. The cost of the war and the rising influence of Marxism led to a revolution in 1905. The Duma, the parliament controlled by the nobility, got stripped of power and land reform allowed many peasants to get their own land.

The ruling class of the tsarist system proved unable to adapt to the capitalist mode of production as a way to develop its agriculture and industry to the point where it could sustain its growing population and compete with its European and Asian neighbors. It needed the support of the people to do so, but it used its power instead to continue to suppress the people. In such a way, all ruling classes eventually lose power and are swept away by historical forces.

The Society of Middle Class Merchants

One of the distinct elements of the bourgeois Enlightenment culture was the introduction of the *public sphere* into the fabric of social life. The public sphere was an opportunity within social life for individuals to come together to freely and openly discuss and debate any topic in order to influence political action. The vehicle for the public sphere became salons, coffee houses, theatres, and other means for public expression.

The public sphere arose at the time in which the middle class required a vehicle for communication among themselves in order to discuss and debate, not only business issues, but all social issues as well. As the middle class merchants became a more prominent political force, the public sphere became a means by which they could connect the world of ideas, science, art, philosophy, etc., to the needs of business, society, and ultimately to the decisions made by the state. The distinction between the state, economic markets, and public associations became essential to the formation of democratic theory. The public sphere, therefore, rested on the values of participatory democracy and the value of public opinion.[229]

Ideally, the theory behind the public sphere was that public discussion and debate should steer government's laws and policies. In fact, the very legitimacy of any government rested on its ability to listen to the public sphere. "Democratic governance rests on the capacity of and opportunity for citizens to engage in enlightened debate".[230]

The idea of a *public sphere* did not previously exist in European society. Under Church rule there was no opportunity to discuss any matters in an open forum. There was no such idea as a "common concern." Social knowledge and political ideas were excluded from public discussion, but now they were open to critical examination by the public. In this examination, it was human reason, not an imposed religious faith, which guided discussion. Secrecy of all sorts was opposed.[231]

The manifestation of the *public sphere* was a concomitant development with the rise of the modern nation-state and the rise of the merchant/capitalist class. It signaled a progressive step in the evolution of human society. It increased the need for self-awareness and the need for an exchange of information. It was the development of the public sphere that gave rise to the ideas of the Enlightenment.

It should also be noted that, just as it happened in the Renaissance, the explosion of science, art, and philosophy at this time rested on the new wealth introduced by the merchant class as a result of the Industrial Revolution. Economic expansion, increased urbanization, and the new means of communication obliterated the stagnation of the century given to the religious wars.[232]

We must keep in mind, however, that the *public sphere* did not really constitute the public at large, but generally only the nobility, merchants, and intellectuals. Enlightenment thinkers contrasted their conception of the "public" with that of the "people." Condorcet contrasted "opinion" with "populace," Marmontel "the opinion of men of letters" with "the opinion of the multitude," and d'Alembert the "truly enlightened public" with "the blind and noisy multitude."[233] Also there were many men who excluded women from the conversation, although, it was rich women who came to dominate the salons as hostesses and referees among the gatherings of the elite. Within the coffeehouses and Masonic lodges, people of different social classes were able to meet.[234]

Salons

Wealthy members of the aristocracy had always drawn poets, writers, and artists to their drawing rooms, usually with the lure of patronage, but the salons rejected the idea of the aristocracy and social hierarchy. They were, after all, a product of the middle class or the *nouveau riche*. The most daring salons encouraged socializing between sexes, as well as between classes. In this way, they provided a strong impetus for the development of Enlightenment ideas.

The salons were an Italian invention of the sixteenth century city-states, but also flourished in France throughout the seventeenth and eighteenth centuries. During the Renaissance period in Italy, the salons were galvanized by the presence of a beautiful and educated patroness, such as Isabella d'Este or Elisabetta Gonzaga.[235]

Because the salons took place within private homes, and because it was a normal function of "woman's work" to throw parties and host private events, it was quite natural that intelligent and gracious women came to assume the role of hostesses of salons. The women selected their guests and decide the topics to be discussed at the meetings. The topics were generally about social, literary, or political issues. The women also served as mediators and moderators if discussion became too heated. Their sense of propriety and graciousness permitted discussion and debate to occur within the bounds of civility.

The salon actually became an informal university for women through which they were also able to exchange ideas, give and receive criticism, read their own works, and hear the works and ideas of other intellectuals.[236]

Two of the most famous seventeenth century literary salons in Paris were the Hôtel de Rambouillet, established in 1607 by the Marquise de Rambouillet, and the Le Marais, established by Madeleine de Scudéry in 1652.

The Hôtel de Rambouillet was the Paris residence of Catherine de Vivonne, Marquise de Rambouillet. Members of her salon included some of the leading ladies of the day, as well as social luminaries such as Balzac and Richelieu. The group strove to overcome the crass, ostentatious, and corrupt nature that defined the French court and replace it with civility, restraint, and decorum. Conversation was a sacred art through which the group developed its refined taste.[237]

Madeleine de Scudéry was part of a movement in the late Renaissance in England and France where women used classical rhetorical theory as their own. She helped revise the medium of discourse and modeled it on conversation rather than public speaking. The speaker in the salon built on the ideas of the speaker before them, seeking consensus rather than argument.

Madeleine was also a novelist and her works became the delight of Europe. Her novel, *Artamène*, which contains over two million words, was the longest novel ever published. It derived its length from endless conversations and successive abductions of the heroines, conceived and told with great propriety. Her readers also enjoyed her novels because they gave a glimpse into the life of important contemporary figures that were often disguised as Persian, Greek, or Roman warriors and maidens.

Her work, *Les Femmes Illustres,* published in 1642, addressed itself to women and defended education, rather than beauty or other superficial qualities, as the means of social mobility.[238]

From Italy, and then France, the salon movement spread throughout Europe, led by great women that included Mariquita Sánchez of Argentina, Elizabeth Montagu, and others of England, Constance Trotti of Belgium, and Henriette Herz and Rahel Varnhagen of Germany. In Spain, the salon movement was led by Maria Cayetana de Silva and in Greece by Alexandra Mavrokordatou.

In Poland, the Duchess Sieniawska held a salon at the end of the seventeenth century and they became very popular during the eighteenth century, the most notable were those held by Zofia Lubomirska and Izabela Czartoryska. Salons were introduced in Sweden by Sophia Elisabet Brenner and in Denmark by Christine Sophie Holstein and Charlotte Schimmelman.

In America, "society hostesses" such as Perle Mesta performed a function similar to that of the hostesses of the European salon. During the Harlem Renaissance, Ruth Logan Roberts hosted a salon that brought together leading figures in the culture and politics of Harlem at the time.

Jewish women also established salons in Germany to bring Jews and Gentiles together and to overcome the enculturated stigmas of being women and also Jews.[239]

The fact that women were able to establish salons, and not men, speaks to the strong skills that women have in the realm of interpersonal communication. They have stronger verbal skills and are exceptional at facilitating discussion and in moderating emotional tensions. Women can be serious but they can also be light hearted, when required. This same reality exists today. Women are better communicators and better facilitators, particularly in interpersonal relations and one-on-one exchanges. These skills were developed quite early in human evolution because women were responsible for raising the young collectively. This situation required a greater need for cooperation and sharing. Men, on the other hand, in order to hunt or anticipate attack, developed stronger skills in being silent for long periods of time and also being able to focus intently on a single object. While men's brains tend to be superior in focusing on a single problem and blocking out other stimuli, it nonetheless inhibits their verbal skills and their ability to socialize. We are in a crisis today that requires a balance between the skills of men and the skills of women. While it is good to be able to focus on a single problem, without the socializing and nurturing skills of women, peaceful solutions to a problem are less likely to be actualized. The Plan A of our male leaders, is the same as it was for male leaders in the past. Fight, compete, establish dominance, and seize the resources. In a globally interdependent world like we have today, this solution has become bankrupt and is leading us closer to the edge of societal breakdown and environmental collapse. Today, we require the strong pervasive leadership of women at every tier of social organization if we are to back away from the edge and create the future for our children that we all want to see.

Coffeehouses

In England, it was not so much the salons, but the coffee houses that brought people together. In the late 1600s and early 1700s, over three thousand coffee houses hosted a more free-wheeling clientele. Instead of the polite discussion of Parisian salons, the coffee houses were venues for caffeine-fuelled raucous debates, deal making, and male gossip-mongering.

Britain's first coffee shop opened in Oxford in 1650 and two years later a shop opened in London and became an immediate success. Previously men had gathered in taverns but due to drunkenness and fights they proved unable to provide a pleasant enough environment to exchange ideas and talk business. Coffee, on the other hand, *"will prevent drowsiness and make one fit for business."*[240]

Soon, intellectuals, professionals and merchants were heading to the coffee houses to debate, distribute pamphlets, make deals, smoke pipes, and, of course, consume a drink said to resemble *"syrup of soot and essence of old shoes."*[241] Newsletters and gazettes (the precursors of newspapers) were distributed in coffee houses as well as notice boards announcing social events and business opportunities.

Soon coffeehouses began to draw distinct clientele. In 1688, Edward Lloyd's coffee house on Tower Street earned a reputation as the place to go for marine insurance. It later evolved into the world-famous insurance market, Lloyd's of London. In 1698, the owner of Jonathan's coffee house in Exchange Alley began to issue a list of stock and commodity prices called "The Course of the Exchange and other things," starting the London Stock Exchange. Auction houses like Sotheby's and Christie's also had their origins in coffee houses.

Physicians used Batson's coffee house in Cornhill as a consulting room. Chapter in Paul's Alley was the chosen rendezvous for publishers and booksellers. Scientists like Sir Isaac Newton and Professor Halley preferred the Grecian on the Strand. While the wits of the day, including the playwright Dryden, gathered at Will's on Russell Street, Covent Garden.

Not everyone was in favor of these 'penny universities.' Women, in particular, objected to the amount of time their husbands spent in such establishments. In 1674, the Women's Petition Against Coffee was launched. King Charles II tried to ban the coffee shops as "places where the disaffected met and spread scandalous reports concerning the conduct of his Majesty and his Ministers."[242] But a public outcry forced him to withdraw his proclamation almost before the ink was dry. Coffee houses were vindicated as "the sanctuary of health, the nursery of temperance, the delight of frugality, an academy of civility, and a free-school of ingenuity."[243]

By the mid-eighteenth century, coffee shops began to wane in popularity as the nation's tastes turned to tea drinking. First made fashionable by Charles II's wife, Queen Catherine, the hugely powerful East India Company flooded the domestic market with tea to boost its trade interests. The coffee shops that remained began to serve a more aristocratic clientele by charging membership fees. This was the birth of The Gentleman's Club.[244]

Republic of Letters

Another means of expanding the *public sphere* was the Republic of Letters.[245] Letters were the only means to transmit ideas across long distances and national boundaries. The Republic of Letters consisted of an intellectual community in the late seventeenth and eighteenth centuries in Europe and America. It was a self-proclaimed community of scholars and literary figures that transcended national boundaries.

The circulation of handwritten letters enabled intellectuals to exchange published papers and pamphlets. They considered it their duty to bring others into the Republic through the expansion of correspondence.

The Republic eventually established permanent literary and scientific academies in Paris and London under royal patronage. The foundation of the Royal Society in 1662 was particularly important in legitimizing the movement in England and provided a European center of gravity for the movement. The Royal Society primarily promoted science, which was undertaken by "gentlemen of means" acting independently. The Royal Society created its charters and established a system of governance. Its most famous leader was Sir Isaac Newton, president from 1703 until his death in 1727.[246]

Women in the Enlightenment

Although women played an important role in providing venues for the exchange of ideas in bourgeois society, especially in France, the enlightenment movement did little to support women's rights. In fact, rights were being stripped away from them in favor of men. For example, women in London owned and managed businesses but following Enlightenment reforms they lost that right. Their education was also lowered in quality. Women were offered training in music, drawing, singing, painting, and other fine arts because men believed that these things would make for a better wife. However, an education in the sciences, or any knowledge that might allow women to compete in the economy, was not made available to them. Women's rights were few and far between and this sparked people to advocate for the rights of women.

Men's views of women during the Enlightenment are reflected in the writings of Rousseau who stated that women should be "passive and weak," "put up little resistance," and are "made specially to please man."[247] In his novel *Emile* he says: "Always justify the burdens you impose upon girls but impose them anyway.... They must be thwarted from an early age.... They must be exercised to constraint, so that it costs them nothing to stifle all their fantasies to submit them to the will of others."[248]

He portrayed the ideal woman as someone who takes care of the home and children, but has no role in social matters. Rousseau even raised eyebrows among men because of his insistence that male children should have greater independence and autonomy, but that female children did not need serious intellectual preparation for life and therefore did not require a formal education.

Just why Rousseau was such a misogynist is difficult to say but certainly his direct experience with women must have had something to do with it. Mary Wollstonecraft, a contemporary of Rousseau's, who wrote *A Vindication of the Rights of Women,* largely in response to Rousseau's position on women's education, speculated that Jean-Jacques Rousseau wrote such harsh things about women because his wife was so ignorant and passive. She writes, "And why was he thus anxious? Truly to justify to himself the affection which weakness and virtue had made him cherish for that fool Theresa. He could not raise her to the common level of her sex; and therefore he labored to bring woman down to hers."[249]

Other women also spoke out against Rousseau and the misogynist ideas that other enlightenment writers were proselytizing. Among those speaking out were Denis Diderot, Lady Mary Wortley Montagu, Mary Astell, Madame du Chatelet, Mary Wollstonecraft, the Marquis de Condorcet, and Madame Condorcet. All of these people were champions of women's rights and made their voices heard on the issue of women's education

As the salons gained popularity in bourgeois society, these women and others championed the idea that the values of life, liberty, freedom, democracy, individual expression, etc., should also apply to women. Such ideas inspired women to participate in the French Revolution where they actually fought in the streets for women's rights. This is an interesting story and bears telling.

Women in the French Revolution

Male liberals during the Enlightenment did not consider women to be an oppressed minority and therefore not worthy of attention as a social issue. At the time, most of the female population worked as peasants, shopkeepers, laundresses, nannies, but unlike men they were not identified by their occupations but rather by their gender and their relationship to men by marriage.

This so-called "enlightened" thought regarding women would not have changed if it were not for the French Revolution. When Louis XVI convened the meeting of Estates General and brought the clergy, nobility, and the merchant class together to address the problems of France with the intention of raising taxes, he unleashed a torrent of discussion. The merchant class was anticipating that he intended government reform when he asked for a list of their grievances.

Because the King had not invited women to meet as women to draft their grievances or name delegates to the general assembly, a few took matters into their own hands and sent him petitions with their concerns. They wanted better education and protection of their property rights. None yet dared to raise the issue of civil or political rights.

After the Bastille fell on July 14, 1789, and the people arrested the deputies and closed the Estates General, they knew that the plans of the aristocracy were dead in the water. A few months later, in October, the revolutionaries were confronted by a shortage of bread, and in the fear of the moment, rumors circulated that the royal guards at Versailles, the palace where the King and his family resided, had trampled on the revolutionary flag (red, white, and blue) and were plotting to invade Paris. In response, a crowd of women gathered to march to Versailles to demand an accounting from the King. They trudged twelve miles from Paris in the rain, soaked and tired. By the next morning, the women were joined by thousands of men who had left from Paris to join them. The next day the crowd grew more belligerent and broke into the royal apartments, killing two of the King's bodyguards. To prevent further bloodshed, the King agreed to move back to Paris.

After this, women began to attend meetings of political clubs, and soon both men and women were agitating for the guarantee of women's rights. In July 1790, a leading male intellectual and aristocrat, Marie-Jean Caritat, the Marquis de Condorcet, published a newspaper article in support of full political rights for women. Women were now in the spotlight. A small band of proponents soon gathered around Condorcet and launched a campaign for women's rights in 1790–91 that included liberal divorce laws and reforms in inheritance laws

The boldest statement for women's political rights came from the pen of Marie Gouze (1748–93). She published the *Declaration of the Rights of Woman*, modeled on the *Declaration of the Rights of Man and Citizen* that was passed by France's National Constituent Assembly (the first people's assembly after the fall of the monarchy) in August 1789. The Declaration of the Rights of Man and Citizen was the first document of the French Revolution, influenced by Thomas Jefferson and General Lafayette. Unfortunately, it did not address the rights of women. Thus, Marie Gouze, following the structure and language of this declaration, showed how women had been excluded from its promise. Like many of the other leading female activists, she eventually suffered persecution at the hands of the government; however, while most others had to endure imprisonment, Gouze was sent to the guillotine in 1793. She had given her life in support of the rights of women.

While most deputies thought the idea of women's rights was outlandish, it did not stop women from participating in the events that unfolded. Women demonstrated and even rioted over the food prices; some joined women's clubs; others took part in movements against the Revolution. The most dramatic individual act of resistance to the Revolution was the assassination of the deputy Jean-Paul Marat by Charlotte Corday in 1793. Marat published a newspaper, *The Friend of the People*, that called for violence against anyone who opposed the leadership of the Revolution. He even attacked moderates like Condorcet who supported the revolution, but spoke out against its use of violence and intimidation. Corday gained entrance to Marat's dwelling and stabbed him while he was taking a bath.

Most women acted in a more collective fashion. Their biggest concern was providing food for their families. The high price of food led to riots in February 1792 and again in February 1793. In these disturbances, which often began at the doors of shops, women usually played a prominent role, egging on the men to demand lower prices. They also confiscated high priced goods and sold them at a "just" price.

A small but vocal minority of women activists set up their own political clubs. The best known of these was the Society of Revolutionary Republican Women established in Paris in May 1793. The members advocated for stringent measures against hoarders and counterrevolutionaries and proposed ways for women to participate in the war effort.

The women in the revolution succeeded in getting the revolutionary government to establish liberal divorce laws and granting women the right to inherit family property. While the men continued to reject every call for equal rights for women, they now had to explain themselves. Rejection of women's rights was no longer automatic.[250]

As the political situation grew more turbulent and dangerous in the fall of 1793, the revolutionary government became suspicious of the Society of Revolutionary Republican Women. Despite attempts to respond to the charges of its critics, the club was outlawed as were all women's clubs on October 30, 1793. The Queen was executed in the same month. In November, Gouze was put to death, then Marie-Jeanne Roland. Roland was one of the leading political figures and was the wife of a minister and hostess of one of Paris's most influential salons. A city official declared that women should no longer involve themselves in politics.

After the suppression of women's clubs, the Terror did not spare even ordinary women. Many went to prison for complaining about food shortages, or for making disrespectful remarks about the authorities, or for challenging local officials.

The police gathered information every day about the state of discontent and despite their fear, the women, in order to feed their families, continued to prod the men to attack the local and national authorities. When bread rations dropped from $1\frac{1}{2}$ pounds per person in March to $\frac{1}{8}$ of a pound in April, rioting broke out. In May, a large crowd of women and men, armed with guns, pikes, and swords, rushed into the meeting place of the National Convention and chased the deputies from their benches. They killed one and cut off his head. As soon as the government gained control of the situation, it arrested as many rioters as it could find. From thenceforth, women were prohibited from observing its meetings or from attending any kind of political assembly, or even gathering in groups of more than five in the street.

Although women had not gained the right to vote or hold office and would not do so in France until 1944, they became more aware of their status in society.

Despite the fact that women were silenced once again by the men, they nonetheless became symbols of the revolution. In paintings and sculpture, abstract values like "liberty," "equality," and "freedom" were given female bodies. Women made good symbols because they could not hold office or officially participate in politics. The French were extremely worried that one man might take power and establish a dictatorship. They preferred symbols that could not be identified with any specific male political leader. Instead, "liberty" became the dominant political figure.[251]

While it was the bravery of the women in the French Revolution that inspired the men to action, while it was the women who marched on Versailles to confront the king, while it was the women who fought for the food that the men ate to keep themselves alive during the turbulent years of the revolution, while the women fought shoulder to shoulder with the men during the revolution, the men remained complacent and asleep to their contribution. In the days ahead, we will not be able to afford such complacency.

Women in England

While the women in France were going through a political revolution in the mid to late 1800's, the women of England were going through an economic revolution.

The Industrial Revolution developed in England almost one hundred years before it developed in the rest of Europe, giving the country a big start in the competition for capital, technology, colonies, and markets.

The Industrial Revolution produced an upheaval in peoples' lives as they were driven off the land and were forced to move to the towns and cities for jobs. Women played a significant role in this transformation.

As technology developed, the need for men's physical strength diminished and women were able to compete with men for jobs. The men reacted and pushed women out of "male" occupations. They could not participate in guilds or have access to educational institutions. Nonetheless, the rise of the merchant middle class provided more leisure for some women. Now literate, at home, and aware of social issues, they began to get involved in charitable causes. They set up relief operations for the poor. At the same time, they began to fight for women's rights as a whole. Just as the men had defined "male occupations" the women sought to define "female occupations," which included teachers, secretaries, etc., areas where they fought to create more jobs for women. They also fought for more social mobility and less confining fashions. They wanted access to universities and the right to vote.

Therefore, we can say that the Industrial Revolution, in good measure, was quickened by the economic need of many women, both single and married, to find money through work outside their home. Women mostly found jobs in domestic service, textile factories, and piece-work shops. They also worked in the coal mines. For some women, the Industrial Revolution provided independent wages for the first time in history. It also allowed social mobility and a better standard of living. For the majority, however, factory work and laboring in the mines in the early years of the nineteenth century meant only a life of grueling hardship.

In England and Wales, Parliamentary commissions in the early 1840s, began to collect testimonies from women and children regarding their jobs. Inspectors visited the women in the mills, mines, and shops to see how they were affected by the Industrial Revolution. Information received indicated that the jobs performed by women and children were dangerous and the working conditions were often unsanitary. However, there was opposition to proposals that sought to abolish child and female labor in dangerous jobs.[252] The demands of work prohibited the pursuit of education. Home life suffered as women had to spend long hours at work. On the job, men assumed supervisory roles over women and received higher wages. Young women away from home generated fears about their safety and fate within society. Nonetheless, families needed their wages to exit in a cash economy.

The strategy developed by factory and mine owners to control and discipline their workforce was to demand long working hours, issue fines for disregarding rules or quotas, and pay low wages.

A normal shift ran twelve to fourteen hours a day, with extra time required during busy periods. Workers were often required to clean their machines during their mealtimes. Children were often forced to crawl inside machines and clean them while they were moving. Up to forty per cent of accident cases at Manchester Infirmary in 1833 were factory accidents.

A typical wage for male workers was about fifteen shillings a week, but women and children were paid much less, with women earning seven shillings and children three shillings. For this reason, employers preferred to employ women and children. Many boys were fired when they reached adulthood and then had to be supported by their wives and children.

A good example of conditions in textile mills can be seen from information derived from the silk mill that was built by Samuel Courtauld in 1825 in Halstead in southeast England. Before the Industrial Revolution, Halstead was an agricultural community in which most people worked the land as serfs. There was, however, a small cottage industry producing woolen cloth. In Halstead, as elsewhere, unemployment, due to being ousted from the land, depressed farming households, resulting in women, as well as men, having to find other work in order to survive. Because their labor was cheap, women, more than men, were recruited into the textile factories that sprang up all over Britain in the nineteenth century. A look at Halstead's wage chart shows that it had a labor force of 1013 people, of which 899 were women. Their jobs consisted of gauze examiners, assistant overseers, warpers, twisters, wasters, weavers, and winders. Their weekly salary ranged from two to ten shillings. On the other hand, the one hundred and fourteen men worked in jobs like managers, overseers, clerks, mechanics, carpenters, blacksmiths, machine attendants, packers, messengers, sweepers, coachmen, and watchmen. Their salaries ranged from ten to twenty shillings per week. Only the thirty-eight men who served as winders made the same as their female counterparts, two to four shillings per week.[253]

Workers were often subjected to cruel punishment. The children suffered the most. Orphans from workhouses in southern England were "apprenticed" to factory owners, supposedly to learn the textiles trade. They worked twelve-hour shifts, and slept in barracks attached to the factory, in beds just vacated by children about to start the next shift. Children were punished by being beaten with leather straps. They were also punished by hanging iron weights around their necks, hanging them from the roof in baskets, nailing their ears to the table, and dowsing them in buckets of water to keep them awake.

Fines were imposed for talking or whistling, leaving the room without permission, or having a little dirt on a machine. Employers were known to alter clocks to make their workers late so that they could fine them. Some employers demanded that their overseers raise a minimum amount each week from fines.

The air pollution in textile factories was legendary. The air inside the factories was a constant cloud of tiny textile fibers, which led to chest and lung diseases. The loud noises of the machines also damaged workers' hearing.

Conditions in the coal mines were even worse.[254] Men, women, and children worked inside the mines. The jobs in the coal mine consisted of hewers, putters, hurriers, and trappers. Hewers were usually men who cut the coal with pickaxes. Putters were normally children who pushed the tubs for the hewers. Women and children hurriers pulled the full tubs with a chain that went around their middles and between their legs to the horse-ways, passages where horses were used for hauling. Trappers as young as four years old sat all day in the dark, opening the doors for the horse drawn coal trucks to pass through.

Fig. 4-21: Woman Lowering Children Down Into Coal Mine (from Esther M. Zimmer Lederberg at the Esther M. Zimmer Lederberg Memorial Website)

While women and children were used to haul the tubs of coal, women were also hired to crank a windlass to raise and lower coal and workers from a deep shaft mine.

Fig. 4-22: Woman Pulling Coal Tub

Miners were paid by the tub and if their tub was underweight, they were not paid. There were severe fines for any violation of rules and it was not unheard of that some miners ended a week's work owing money to the mine owner.

Accidents such as falling roofs, explosions, shaft accidents, and drowning were frequent.

If a man joined a trade union, he was not only fired but also blacklisted by all the mine owners in the area so he became unemployable. Many employees were required to sign "the Document" promising they would not join a union. In some mines, especially in Scotland, a miner had to sign "the Bond" before he was given a job, in which he promised not to leave for another job. These conditions continued to enslave the working people.[255]

Before 1842, there were no-protection laws, nor limits for the age of child labor. The initial laws, once passed were weak and not enforced. Testimonies of women and children from South Wales Mines reveal the lives they led:

Six year old girl:
"I have been down six weeks and make 10 to 14 rakes a day; I carry a full 56 lbs. of coal in a wooden bucket. I work with sister Jesse and mother. It is dark the time we go."

Jane Peacock Watson.
"I have wrought in the bowels of the earth 33 years. I have been married 23 years and had nine children, six are alive and three died of typhus a few years since. Have had two dead born. Horse-work ruins the women; it crushes their haunches, bends their ankles and makes them old women at 40."

Maria Gooder
"I hurry for a man with my sister Anne who is going 18. He is good to us. I don't like being in the pit. I am tired and afraid. I go at 4:30 after having porridge for breakfast. I start hurrying at 5. We have dinner at noon. We have dry bread and nothing else. There is water in the pit but we don't sup it."

Mary and Rachell Enock, ages 11 and 12 years.
"We are door-keepers in the four foot level. We leave the house before six each morning and are in the level until seven o'clock and sometimes later. We get 2p a day and our light costs us 2 1/2 p. a week. Rachel was in a day school and she can read a little. She was run over by a tram a while ago and was home ill a long time, but she has got over it."

Isabel Wilson, 38 years old.
"I have been married 19 years and have had 10 bairns [children]:... My last child was born on Saturday morning, and I was at work on the Friday night...None of the children read, as the work is no regular. When I go below my lassie 10 years of age keeps house...."[256]

When reformers called attention to the living conditions of the workers, demanding better wages and improved working conditions, opposition from the capitalists and their paid lawyers and economists was immediate. We hear the same arguments against higher wages and human concerns today. Economists argued that increased costs would ruin the industry, which made a major contribution to the wealth of the country. This was later proved wrong because better-fed, less tired workers produced more, not less.

The capitalists argued that the workers would only spend the extra time and money in drunkenness and crime. This later proved false because better conditions led to less crime.

Others argued that the severe working conditions were necessary to discipline the workers. They claimed that peasants and domestic workers were not used to the needs of the factory and had to be trained.

Titus Salt, a manufacturer and politician from Manchester, argued that it was better for children to work in a factory or a mine and earn a wage that provided food and clothes, than to be forced to stay outside and starve or freeze to death. Who could argue with this paragon of human virtue.

Some argued against labor reforms on philosophical grounds claiming that it was wrong for the government to interfere in the free working of the economy.

Even the famous economist Adam Smith, the darling of the capitalists, argued that children had always been employed, and that poor conditions in the factories were exaggerated.

In addition to becoming wage slaves, the working people also had to survive in an urban environment. They faced pollution from the burning of coal to heat houses, overcrowding, low wages and high rents, and disease including typhus, typhoid, tuberculosis and cholera. Poorly constructed tenements, inadequate waste disposal, and lack of fresh water also added to human misery.[257]

In time, labor reforms were made. While still exploitive, they allowed a family to meet their basic needs. The capitalists, surprisingly, did not go bankrupt and society survived. In due course, as the consumer society evolved, and the middle class expanded, women became targeted by the capitalists as consumers. They bought more than the men because they bought not just for themselves but for their families and households. This situation gradually allowed women to gain some measure of leverage and social empowerment.

In 1918, British women received the right to vote. In 1919, American women gained the right to vote, and in 1944, women's suffrage was finally passed in France.[258]

Liberalism

Theological Liberalism

What then does it mean to follow Jesus? It means to hope and pray for a world structured on principles that would turn present society upside down. It means to live now as far as possible from those principles, and that means to relate to others in ways that create countercultural communities. It means to do what we can to influence the larger society to change in the direction called for by these principles. It means to do all this nonviolently and without antagonism to those who oppose our efforts. It means to keep on keeping on even at personal risk. It means to know God's love and forgiveness in the midst of this life. It means to trust God's working in us and amongst us. It means to do all this while remaining open to ideas and ways of being of quite different sorts. And it means to share this way of being and thinking with others as good news, the best there is. John B. Cobb Jr.[259]

Modern philosophy began in an attempt to blend faith in God with human reason. This effort was called *Theological Liberalism*. It was also called *Liberal Theology*, *Religious Liberalism*, or *Liberal Christianity* and represented an approach to the concept of God that is based on rational thought and humanism. Theological liberalism focuses on one's personal religious experience. It is not a secular criticism of religion, nor is it a criticism of other religions. At the same time, it differs from Christian fundamentalist or conservative approaches that are based on an unquestioned faith in the concept of God as defined by the church as well as on a literal interpretation of scripture.[260]

Religious liberalism attempted to reconcile the long Christian tradition with modern society. Today, the major Christian denominations in the Western World and also the reform movement in Judaism have incorporated liberal tenets within their religions. Islam, because it did not have to contend with the Reformation or the Enlightenment that affected Christian and Jewish religions, was not largely affected by the development of liberal thought.[261]

Liberal Christianity, unlike fundamentalist Christianity, did not originate as a belief structure, and as such it was not dependent upon any Church dogma or statements of faith. Instead, "liberalism" from the start embraced the methodologies of Enlightenment rational thought as the basis for understanding God, the Bible, life, faith, and theology.

The liberal theologians/philosophers desired to develop an objective point of view, without preconceived notions of the authority of scripture or the correctness of Church dogma. Importance was laid upon "scientific" interpretations of scriptural texts and the reason for human morality.

Behind the evolution of liberal theology was the desire to be liberated from the coercion of church and state and to explore the inner spiritual impulse. It emerged during the Reformation, blossomed in the Enlightenment period, and was characterized by the rejection of the myths, stories, and dogmas that had been perpetrated by traditional Catholic authority.

Liberal theology can be traced to the seventeenth century French philosopher Rene Descartes whose ideas also laid the ground for the tenets of secular liberalism that lasted through the nineteenth century. Descartes's worldview is based upon the ideas of the immanence of God, the importance of human reason, the progress of human nature, and the primacy of the individual. The many persons that influenced religious thought in this period included Spinoza, Leibniz, Lessing, John Locke, and Samuel Clarke. The ideas of liberal theology were also disseminated through the English writers and philosophers known as the Cambridge Platonists and the Deists.[262]

Liberal theology, in the late eighteenth century, also gave rise to Romanticism. The Romantics included some of the greatest poets in Western history, including Wordsworth, Coleridge, Keats, Shelley, Byron, and Goethe. The Romantics believed in the uniqueness of the individual and the significance of individual experience as a source of divine inspiration. Their emphasis upon personal experience, human emotion, individual creativity, and the sacredness of nature exceeded every other value. The American and French revolutions provided the symbol of their spirit of independence and dramatically exemplified it in political action.

The value of individual experience took root in the claim by Protestant liberals that each believer could have direct access to the Bible and to the God who is revealed therein. Some leaders of the Reformation then built upon this claim of individual freedom and taught that the same God who had inspired the scriptures now directly inspired individual believers. This began to move the West in the direction of mystical thought again. However, as usual, the major church reformers were again frightened by this development. Personal spiritual experience minimized the authority of the new churches, but the liberal theologians, like the well-intentioned priests of the Catholic hierarchy, did have a practical concern. Without the guidance of a spiritual ideology and practice, they believed that it was too easy to mistake the various impulses and ideas that arise in one's mind with the guidance of God. The diversity of such impulses and ideas could lead to fragmentation and very questionable behavior. Hence, Luther and the major Reformers emphasized *sola scriptura,* that is, only the Bible could be the source of authority. In this way, the words in the Bible took absolute precedence over any church authority or private religious experience.

This emphasis on the Bible has been prominent in Protestantism ever since, but the appeal of personal experience could not be so easily squashed and came to play an important role in the history of Protestantism. The Quakers are heirs of this spiritual impulse, as were the early Pietists.

The contradiction between faith in the authority of the Bible versus a desire for a personal experience of God split Protestant theology between the Fundamentalists and the Liberals. While the liberals believed in a merciful God who forgave one's sins and granted a person freedom of discovery, the Fundamentalists succumbed to an unquestioned faith that the scriptures were completely true and without human error.

We can say that Liberal theology grew out of the Pietist movement. Unlike later secular philosophy, however, it did not engage in critical biblical study or directly challenge the literalism of the official teaching. Rather, it simply shifted the emphasis from the supernatural claims of the Bible to an emphasis on the personal experience of God. It also served to share the gospel message with others. The missionary work of the protestant churches and its service to the poor stem largely from the Pietist movement.

The father of liberal theology was Friedrich Schleiermacher.[263] As a Pietist, he developed the first Christian theology based on spiritual experience and provided Christians with a context for understanding such experience. The emphasis on "experience," rather than "faith" or "reason," is still a strong characteristic of liberal theology to this day.

While the Pietist movement had some influence on the Lutheran and Calvinist churches, it directly affected the Methodists, whose founder John Wesley was at the heart of the Pietist movement. Wesley was an evangelist and he believed that individual Christians should demonstrate their faith by serving the needy. This contradicted the belief of Luther and Calvin who believed that such service was of no value or even of negative value.

Through the eighteenth century, most intellectuals believed that the laws of nature and basic moral tenets pointed to a God who was a lawgiver, but they debated whether these laws applied simply to the creation or to human history as well. It was a simplistic intellectual pursuit based upon an erroneous assumption that human history somehow existed outside the creation.

But in England, David Hume provided a much greater challenge to theological liberalism. Hume argued that knowledge that arose from sense experience could provide no basis for the existence of God. In Germany, Immanuel Kant agreed and argued that it is the human mind that presents us with an ordered world and not God. Kant's philosophy changed the context for intellectual debate in Europe. The assumptions that provided the Christian affirmation of God or that claimed authority of the Bible were now nonstarters.

Hegel provided a third strand. He accepted Kant's view that the ordered world is created by the human mind and then pointed out that the way the mind orders the world varies from culture to culture and evolves within individual cultures. Nonetheless, despite these differences, the human mind (Geist) moves toward some final and perfected state that for Hegel was the Divine. This introduced the idea that everything is moving toward God as a natural projection of cosmic motion. We now have an idea of natural evolution as a return to God.

Such thinking reveals the intention of the Enlightenment thinkers to collaborate in creating the best possible logic and to display the truth of

Christianity in that context. While such radical thought flourished among the philosophers, the Orthodox and conservative forms of Protestantism continued to affirm the authority of scripture against any new forms of thought. These fundamentalists insulated themselves against the dominant intellectual changes of their day and continue to do so today.

A contemporary liberal Protestant minister has this to say about liberal theology:

> To be a liberal Protestant . . . means that one never rejects an idea simply because it is not biblical or not compatible with the Bible. One may, however, find insights in the Bible that provide public arguments against the idea and show that thinking more continuous with Christian teaching is better. One is open to all evidence, but one may believe that dominant secular and atheistic interpretations of that evidence are inadequate.
>
> Despite their diversity, all forms of liberal Protestantism affirm that the Bible is rightly studied with critical historical methods. There is nothing sacred about its texts. The truth about the historical Jesus can only be recovered through these methods. There is nothing sacred about Jesus. The history of the church, likewise, should be studied critically, and the negative aspects of Christian history should be fully acknowledged. Similarly, other religious traditions should be studied critically, but with no prejudice against them because of unfamiliar features of their thought or practice. If one remains a Christian, it must be because the best knowledge one can gain about all these matters provides sufficient reason for doing so.[264]

Given the damage done to the dictatorship of the Catholic Church during the Renaissance and Reformation periods and by the rise of capitalism, the Enlightenment, more than any other period in history, represented the flowering of secular ideas in the western world. The development of these ideas and new worldviews, independent of the shackles of blind faith in Church dogma, followed an identifiable pattern. In the beginning, as we might expect, the philosophers continued to struggle with the concept of Divinity. But now faith played little part in their conclusions. God was now subject to rational and critical analysis. If God existed, He had to be substantiated by reason. The Bible, as well as other scriptures, was also submitted to the test of critical scrutiny. As rational thought transitioned from faith-based beliefs to attention on this relative world, the philosophers began to wrestle with definitions of nature, the state, society, the economy, and the rights of the individual. The chart below demonstrates the time period in which this transition occurred and who were the major contributors to the rise of theological liberalism and secular thought.

Contributer	Dates	Affiliation	Secular or Religious	Country
John Wycliffe	1320-1384	Translated Bible	Religious	England
Balthasar Hubmaier	1480-1528	Anabaptism	Religious	Germany
Martin Luther	1483-1546	Lutheranism	Religious	Germany
Ulrich Zwingli	1484-1531	Dutch Reformed Church	Religious	Germany
Henry VIII	1491-1547	Anglicanism	Religious, State	England
William Tyndale	1494-1536	Translated Bible	Religious	England
John Knox	1505-1572	Presbyterianism	Religious	Scotland
John Calvin	1509-1564	Dutch Reformed Church	Religious, State	Switzerland
Sir Francis Bacon	1561-1626	Empiricism	Philosophy, science	England
John Smyth	1570-1612	Baptist	Religious	England

John Cotton	1585-1652	Congregationalism	Religious	England
John Hobbes	1588-1679	Empiricism	Political Philosophy	England
Rene Descartes	1596-1650	Rationalism	Philosophy/Math	Holland
George Fox	1624-1691	Puritan/Quaker	Religious	England
Baruch Spinoza	1632-1677	Rationalism	Philosophy	Holland
John Locke	1632-1704	Liberalism/Empiricism	Philosophy	English
Philipp Spener	1635-1705	Pietism	Religious	Germany
Gottfried Liebniz	1646-1716	Rationalism	Philosophy/Math	Germany
Charles Montesquieu	1689-1755	Liberalism	Political Philosophy	France
John Wesley	1703-1791	Methodism	Religious	England/US
David Hume	1711-1776	Empiricism	Philosophy	Scotland
Jean-Jacque Rousseau	1712-1778	Romanticism	Political Philosophy	France
Adam Smith	1723-1790	Empirist	Political Economy	English
Immanuel Kant	1724-1804	Kantianism	Politics, ethics, etc	Germany
Friedrich Schleiermacher	1768-1834	Protestantism	Liberal Theology	Germany
Georg Hegel	1770-1831	Idealism	Logic, dialectics	Germany
Arther Schopenhauer	1788-1860	Post-Kantianism	Will, Reason,	Germany

| John Stewart Mill | 1806-1873 | Liberalism | Political Economy | England |
| Karl Marx | 1818-1883 | Marxism | Political Economy | Germany |

As we can see, during the fifteenth and early sixteenth centuries religious thought still dominated. In the second half of the sixteenth century, however, the secular philosophers came on the scene. During the seventeenth century, religion and secular thought co-existed. By the eighteenth century, however, the big thinkers were all secular philosophers. Even Schleiermacher was engaged in synthesizing Protestant thought with the secular ideas of the Enlightenment. This was the time of the French and American revolutions and the attention of the intellectuals was devoted to questions about the role and structure of the state, social values, the role of the individual, and economics. It was also the time when philosophers were wrestling with the nature of reality to determine if it was primarily a mental or physical phenomenon.

The philosophers split into two camps. The first camp argued that only by reason could one come to know the nature of reality. They became known as the *rationalists*. The second camp argued, just as convincingly, that only by a rigorous analysis of sensory data could one determine the nature of reality. They became known as the *empiricists*. The empiricists were the first scientists.

In this struggle, both camps made cogent arguments in defense of their worldview, but the dualism inherent in the thought process of western civilization prohibited a synthesis from being made. This dualism is still deeply ingrained in current thought. Consequently, a synthesis concerning the nature of this psycho-physical reality has remained elusive. We shall examine this situation in the second book of this trilogy, which contains an exposition of universal ideology in which a synthesis is made possible.

Let us now take a look at how philosophy and science evolved during the Enlightenment period. This is an important concern because we must be able to understand and overcome the contradictions inherent in these worldviews if we are to solve our current social and environmental problems. If not, we will be doomed to repeat our past thinking, a way of thinking that has brought us to the brink of the social and environmental collapse, which we now are facing.

Secular Liberalism and the Birth of Modern Philosophy and Science

As previously stated, secular thought came to dominate modern thought in the mid-eigheenth century. The American and French revolutions were right around the corner and intellectuals were less concerned about challenging traditional doctrines and dogmas than they were in defining a civil society based on reason, natural law, and science. In Paris, this philosophic movement was led by Voltaire, Jean-Jacques Rousseau, and Montesquieu.

In England, Bacon, Hobbes, Locke, Hume, Smith, Wollstonecraft, and Mills dominated secular thought. In Holland, Descartes and Spinoza made their voices heard and in Germany, Liebniz, Kant, Hegel, Schopenhauer, and Marx helped to shape the modern mindset. In America, Franklin, Jefferson, Paine, and Samuel Adams contributed to the definition of governance, human rights, and civil society. Among these European and American thinkers, some sought accommodation with the powers of church and state and some were true revolutionaries who sought a clean break with the past. The revolutionaries advocated democracy, individual liberty, freedom of expression, and eradication of any imposed religious authority. Both the liberal reformers and the revolutionaries were opposed by the conservative Counter-Enlightenment.

After having undergone fifteen hundred years of Church law, and subjection to the rule of warlord kings and nobles, after being continuously threatened by a god who could damn you to eternal hell fire on the least provocation, after being burned to death as a heretic or witch for having an original thought, the intellectuals, whether rationalist or empiricist, whether reformer or revolutionary, were finally free to think for themselves. This was the dawn of the Enlightenment period and the beginning of modern western philosophy and science.

In his famous essay *"What is Enlightenment?"* (1784), Immanuel Kant described enlightenment simply as freedom to use one's own intelligence. Basically, the Enlightenment period is marked by an increasing development of rationalism, empiricism, scientific rigor, and the rejection of blind faith based on religious dogma.

While Descartes is considered the first great philosopher of the Enlightenment period, it is worth exploring the life of Sir Francis Bacon who was born just as the life of John Calvin was coming to an end, but which overlapped for three decades with the life of Descartes. A product of religious ferment, he was arguably the most secular thinker of his day and set the course for empirical thinking in England and then on the continent. It is also instructive to look at the ideas of Thomas Hobbes who lived from 1588 to 1679 because it was Hobbes, more than any other philosopher that contributed to modern ideas of politics, governance, and democracy.

Sir Francis Bacon (1561-1626)

When Francis Bacon was born, the Protestant revolution was in full swing. Lutherans, Calvinists (Dutch Reformed), Anglicans, Puritans, and Presbyterians were already in existence and the Baptists and Congregationalists would come into being in his lifetime. War raged between countries, localities, communities, and within families. It raged between brothers and husbands and wives.

By virtue of his clear thinking, Bacon served as a Member of Parliament, Attorney General, and Lord Chancellor of England during his life. He sympathized with the Puritans who were seeking reform within the Anglican Church and stood strongly against the Catholic Church and, in 1586, openly called for the execution of Mary, Queen of Scots.[265] This, however, was probably more for political reasons than religious ones because Bacon had only a mild interest in religion.

His interests lay mainly with secular matters. He is considered the father of empiricism and the man who created the *scientific method*.[266] Bacon believed that knowledge did not come from God, intuition, revelation, or *a priori* reasoning (i.e., without sensory experience). Rather, he postulated, that knowledge came only from evidence of the senses. This belief called empiricism gave rise to Western science and the scientific method. The scientific method holds that when one makes a statement (hypothesis) about natural or social reality it can only be verified by being tested by observation and experiment.[267] The hypothesis gains credibility as others come to the same conclusion by their own observation and experiment.

Sir Francis Bacon set the stage for John Locke, Thomas Hobbes, George Berkeley, and David Hume who were the primary proponents of empiricism in the eighteenth century Enlightenment. Because of Locke's in-depth analysis of sensory perception and rational thought, he is also called the founder of empiricism. Empiricism differs from *rationalism,* which states that knowledge may be derived from reason independent of the senses.

Bacon played a leading role in establishing the British colonies in North America, especially in Virginia, the Carolinas, and Newfoundland in northeastern Canada. His government report on "The Virginia Colony" was submitted in 1609. In 1610, Bacon and his associates received a charter from the king to form *the Tresurer and the Companye of Adventurers and planter of the Cittye of London and Bristoll for the Collonye or plantacon in Newfoundland*[268] and sent John Guy to found a colony there. Newfoundland is the oldest British colony and became the model for English colonialism under Queen Elizabeth and subsequent rulers.[269]

Thomas Jefferson, the third President of the United States and author of the Declaration of Independence, wrote: "Bacon, Locke, and Newton. I consider them as the three greatest men that have ever lived, without any exception, and as having laid the foundation of those superstructures which have been raised in the Physical and Moral sciences." [270]

The Rosicrucian organization, AMORC, believes that Bacon's work, *The New Atlantis,* inspired a colony of Rosicrucian mystics led by Johannes Kelpius to sail to North America in the late seventeenth century. Kelpius and his followers settled on the shores of Wissahickon Creek, in the colony of Pennsylvania, where they became known as "Hermits of Mystics of the Wissahickon" or simply "Monks of the Wissahickon." According to AMORC, this and other Rosicrucian communities "... made valuable contributions to the newly emerging American culture in the fields of printing, philosophy, the sciences, and arts."[271]

Thomas Hobbes (1588-1679)

Thomas Hobbes was an English philosopher, who was one of the first to focus on political philosophy. His book *Leviathan* was the first text to articulate the relationship between the *ruler* and the *ruled* as one that was determined by a *social contract*.[272] The Leviathan addressed the questions of the origin of society and the legitimacy of the authority of the state over the individual. Hobbes was a monarchist, who believed that absolute authority should be focused without question in the hands of a single individual. The surrender of the people to the authority of the monarch was justified by the fact that they now came under the protection of the monarch and therein could enjoy certain rights and live their lives free from chaos.

This idea of social contract between the ruler and the ruled continued to be developed by Enlightenment philosophers. Those who espoused free will held that the contract required the individuals' consent, either explicitly or tacitly, to surrender some of their freedoms and submit to the authority of the ruler, or decision of a majority, in the case of democracy, in exchange for protection of their rights. The relation between natural and civil rights, therefore, was often an aspect of social contract theory.[273] The idea of social contract became a central tenet of democracy and was debated and expanded upon by philosophers who followed Hobbes, namely Locke, Rousseau, and Kant.

Hobbes's philosophy progressed from first developing a doctrine of physical bodies in terms of motion. He then singled out man from the realm of nature and plants. In another treatise, he showed what specific bodily motions were involved in the production of the peculiar phenomena of sensation, knowledge, affections, and passions whereby man came into relation with man. Finally, he considered, in his crowning treatise, how men were moved to enter into society and argued how this must be regulated if men were not to fall back into "brutishness and misery." Thus he proposed, in *Leviathan*, to unite the separate phenomena of body, man, and the state.[274]

At the time that Hobbes was working on his theory of bodies in motion, The English Civil War broke out in 1642. It was a result of continuous ferment between King Charles 1, who was an Anglican, and a Parliament composed of Puritans. Due to these religious differences and the Puritans' rejection of the king's authority, a series of civil wars broke out in England.

These armed conflicts between the king and his supporters (Cavaliers) and the Parliamentarians (Roundheads) was principally over the question of governance. The wars ended with the Parliamentarian victory at the Battle of Worcester on September 3, 1651.

The overall outcome of the war was the trial and execution of Charles I; the exile of his son, Charles II; and the replacement of the monarchy with the Commonwealth of England (1649–53). This was followed by the Protectorate (1653–59) under Oliver Cromwell. Constitutionally, the wars established the precedent that an English monarch cannot govern without Parliament's consent. The monopoly of the Church of England on Christian worship in England also ended with the victors consolidating the established Protestant Ascendancy in Ireland.[275]

In 1640, just prior to the advent of the civil wars, Hobbes wrote and circulated a treatise called *The Elements of Law, Natural and Politic* in which he defended the legitimacy of the monarchy. Fearing for his life after the Parliamentarians gained ascendency, Hobbes fled to Paris.

As the Royalist cause continued to decline many of the king's supporters left England and went to Paris. This revitalized Hobbes's political interests and he published *De Cive* (The Citizen) in 1655. *De Cive* is the first of a trilogy of works written by Hobbes dealing with human knowledge, the other two works in the trilogy being *De Corpore* ("On the body") published in 1655, and *De Homine* ("On man"), published in 1658. *De Cive* is comprised of three parts: Libertas (liberty), Imperium (dominion), and Religio (religion). In the first part, Hobbes describes man's natural condition, dealing with the natural laws; in the second, the necessity of establishing a stable government. Finally, in the third part, he writes about religion.[276]

Hobbes' master work *Leviathan or The Matter, Forme and Power of a Common Wealth Ecclesiasticall and Civil* was published in 1668. While it is a discussion of state governance, its name derives from the biblical Leviathan, which signifies a monster or Satan. *Leviathan* argues for a social contract and rule by an absolute sovereign. Hobbes wrote that the civil war and the brute situation of a state of nature ("the war of all against all") could only be avoided by a strong undivided government.

Though a champion of royal sovereignty, Hobbes also developed some of the fundamentals of European liberal thought: the right of the individual; the natural equality of all men; the artificial character of the political order (which led to the later distinction between civil society and the state); the view that all legitimate political power must be "representative" and based on the consent of the people; and a liberal interpretation of law which leaves people free to do whatever the law does not explicitly forbid.

Leviathan has three parts: (1) Of Man, (2) Of Commonwealth, and (3) Of a Christian Commonwealth. In the section on man, Hobbes presents an image of man as matter in motion, attempting to show through example how everything about humanity can be explained materialistically, without recourse to God or any authority outside the human mind. The "good" denotes our desires and our tendency to move toward those objects we desire. Bad is its obverse. Hope is nothing more than a desire for a thing combined with opinion that it can be had.

Hobbes refutes the idea of the greatest good (*summum bonum*) as superfluous. Given the variability of human desires, he reasoned, there could be no such thing. Consequently, any political community that sought to provide the greatest good to its members would find itself driven by competing conceptions of that good with no way to decide among them. The result would be civil war. Having no concept of the greatest good to guide and unify society, Hobbes concludes that the natural state of man is not to be found in a political community. Yet, to be outside of a political community is to be in a state of anarchy. Given human nature, the variability of human desires, and the need for scarce resources to fulfill those desires, the state of anarchy (nature), must be a war of all against all. Even when two men are not fighting, there is no guarantee that the other will not try to kill him for his property or just out of an aggrieved sense of honor, and so they must constantly be on guard against one another. It is even reasonable to preemptively attack one's neighbor. Here is Hobbes' famous quote about what life would be like without the state:

> In such condition there is no place for industry, because
> the fruit thereof is uncertain, and consequently, not

culture of the earth, no navigation, nor the use of commodities that may be imported by sea, no commodious building, no instruments of moving and removing such things as require much force, no knowledge of the face of the earth, no account of time, no arts, no letters, no society, and which is worst of all, continual fear and danger of violent death, and the life of man, solitary, poor, nasty, brutish, and short.[277]

While there is no greatest good to motivate society, according to Hobbes, there is the greatest evil (a *summum malum*). This is the fear of violent death. A political community can be oriented around this fear.

In the second part of Leviathan, Hobbes explains the purpose of the commonwealth, which is a political community for the common good.

> The final cause, end, or design of men (who naturally love liberty, and dominion over others) in the introduction of that restraint upon themselves, in which we see them live in Commonwealths, is the foresight of their own preservation, and of a more contented life thereby; that is to say, of getting themselves out from that miserable condition of war which is necessarily consequent, as hath been shown, to the natural passions of men when there is no visible power to keep them in awe, and tie them by fear of punishment to the performance of their covenants...[278]

The commonwealth is instituted when all agree in the following manner: *I authorise and give up my right of governing myself to this man, or to this assembly of men, on this condition; that thou give up, thy right to him, and authorise all his actions in like manner.*

According to Hobbes, the monarch or "sovereign" had twelve principal rights:

1. because a successive covenant cannot override a prior one, the subjects cannot (lawfully) change the form of government.

2. because the covenant forming the commonwealth results from subjects giving to the sovereign the right to act for them, the sovereign cannot possibly breach the covenant; and therefore the subjects can never argue to be freed from the covenant because of the actions of the sovereign.
3. the sovereign exists because the majority has consented to his rule; the minority have agreed to abide by this arrangement and must then assent to the sovereign's actions.
4. every subject is author of the acts of the sovereign: hence the sovereign cannot injure any of his subjects and cannot be accused of injustice.
5. following this, the sovereign cannot justly be put to death by the subjects.
6. because the purpose of the commonwealth is peace, and the sovereign has the right to do whatever he thinks necessary for the preserving of peace and security and prevention of discord. Therefore, the sovereign may judge what opinions and doctrines are averse, who shall be allowed to speak to multitudes, and who shall examine the doctrines of all books before they are published.
7. to prescribe the rules of civil law and property.
8. to be judge in all cases.
9. to make war and peace as he sees fit and to command the army.
10. to choose counsellors, ministers, magistrates and officers.
11. to reward with riches and honour or to punish with corporal or pecuniary punishment or ignominy.
12. to establish laws about honour and a scale of worth.

Hobbes explicitly rejected the idea of Separation of Powers (separation of church and state). He favored censorship of the press and restrictions on the rights of free speech should they be considered desirable by the sovereign to promote order.

Hobbes said there were three kinds of commonwealth, monarchy, aristocracy and democracy. Of these, he favored monarchy.

In part three, Hobbes looked at the question of a Christian Commonwealth. This immediately raised the question of which scriptures we should trust, and why. If any person may claim supernatural revelation superior to the civil law, then there would be chaos, and Hobbes's fervent desire was to avoid this. Hobbes thus began by establishing that we cannot infallibly know another's personal word to be divine revelation:

> When God speaketh to man, it must be either immediately or by mediation of another man, to whom He had formerly spoken by Himself immediately. How God speaketh to a man immediately may be understood by those well enough to whom He hath so spoken; but how the same should be understood by another is hard, if not impossible, to know. For if a man pretend to me that God hath spoken to him supernaturally, and immediately, and I make doubt of it, I cannot easily perceive what argument he can produce to oblige me to believe it.[279]

Having said this, Hobbes was concerned that this would lead to the entire Bible being rejected. So, he said, we need a test, and the true test was established by examining the books of scripture:

> So that it is manifest that the teaching of the religion which God hath established, and the showing of a present miracle, joined together, were the only marks whereby the Scripture would have a true prophet, that is to say, immediate revelation, to be acknowledged; of them being singly sufficient to oblige any other man to regard what he saith.

> Seeing therefore miracles now cease, we have no sign left whereby to acknowledge the pretended revelations or inspirations of any private man; nor obligation to give ear to any doctrine, farther than it is conformable to the Holy Scriptures, which since the time of our Saviour supply the place and sufficiently recompense the want of all other prophecy.[280]

"Seeing therefore miracles now cease" means that without the proof of a miracle, only the books of the Bible can be trusted. Hobbes then discussed the various books which were accepted by various denominations and the "question much disputed between the diverse sects of Christian religion, from whence the Scriptures derive their authority." To Hobbes, "it is manifest that none can know they are God's word (though all true Christians believe it), but those to whom God Himself hath revealed it supernaturally." And therefore, "The question truly stated is: by what authority they are made law?"

Unsurprisingly, Hobbes concluded that ultimately there is no way to determine this other than the civil power:

> He therefore to whom God hath not supernaturally revealed that they are His, nor that those that published them were sent by Him, is not obliged to obey them by any authority but his whose commands have already the force of laws; that is to say, by any other authority than that of the Commonwealth, residing in the sovereign, who only has the legislative power.[281]

In part four, which Hobbes entitled *Of the Kingdom of Darkness*, he attacks those religionists who deceive their fellow men. Falsehood is created by: (1) those who claim that the Kingdom of God can be found in the church, (2) heathen poets and the worship of saints, and images, and relics, practiced in the Catholic Church; (3) those who punish scientists for speaking truth about the natural world, and 4) those who comingle Greco-Roman and Catholic traditions based on a feigned or uncertain history.[282]

While Hobbes is to be commended for attempting to sort out the questions of human nature, governance, and religion, his philosophical conjecture that dependence upon a government by man, as opposed to a government by the word of God, suffers from the exact same problems. By depending upon the "rule of man," societies suffer through the same injustices that they had under the Church, only now such injustices are committed by monarchs, fascists, communists, republicans, and democrats, instead of a priest class, and these new leaders' penchant to secure their rule by self-interest, gross injustices, terror, or death, is equal in proportion to any government set up on religious beliefs. While all religious beliefs are dangerous because they are dogmatic, divisive, and willing to destroy the *unbeliever*, this is no reason to determine, as Hobbes has done, that there is no such thing as *the greatest good*. His rejection of this idea, based upon the different desires of individuals and groups, does not discount that there is a greatest good for humanity as a whole and that this good ultimately is the attainment of Absolute Divinity, not as a limited god by religious definition, but one who is the loving creator and witness to creation and a well-wisher of the progress of the entire universe.

The ideas in Leviathan had an immediate impact on its times. Hobbes found himself more praised and damned than any other thinker of his day. Because of his rejection of religious governance, the first effect of its publication was to sever his link with the exiled royalists. The secular spirit of his book greatly angered both Anglicans and French Catholics, forcing him to appeal to the protestant English government for protection. Ironically, Hobbes was forced to flee back to England, arriving in London in the winter of 1651. Following his submission to the Council of State he was allowed to live a private life.[283]

Rene Descartes (1596-1650)

Descartes was a French philosopher and scientist, who spent most of his life in the Dutch Republic.

On the night of November 1, 1619, at 23 years old, while in the army stationed in Neuburg an der Donau, Germany, Descartes climbed into an "oven" to escape the cold. While inside, he had a vision and believed that a divine spirit revealed to him a new philosophy. Upon exiting he had formulated *analytical geometry* and the idea of applying the mathematical method to philosophy. He concluded from his vision that the pursuit of science meant the pursuit of true wisdom, which became the central part of his life's work. Descartes saw that all truths were linked with one another, so that finding a fundamental truth and proceeding with logic would open the way to all science. [284]

Descartes's contribution to mathematics helped turn it into a science. Believing that physics and mathematics should be linked, he applied the principles of physics to geometry. He created behaviors that still are used by modern mathematicians. For example, he introduced the practice of using x, y, and z to describe unknowns in problems and a, b, and c to describe knowns. He also used superscripts to indicate the power of numbers, such as 2^3. Descartes established the place for algebra in our current system of knowledge. He also established the base for calculus, which Sir Isaac Newton and Leibnitz would later develop. In the field of optics, he discovered the law of reflection.

Not only was Descartes a mathematician, he was also considered the father of modern Western philosophy. Unlike Bacon, who believed that only sensory data could be trusted to reveal the truth, Descartes, believed it was the mind that determined what was real. As opposed to empiricism, he pioneered the philosophy of *rationalism.*

While Descartes claimed to be a Catholic, he was not concerned with religious doctrine, nor with the Protestant revolution that swirled around him like a tornado. Rather than being concerned about arguments of faith, he was more concerned about the rational use of the mind and material science. It was Descartes who said "I think therefore I am." His rationale was such:

1. Thoughts exist
2. Thoughts cannot be separated from me
3. Therefore I exist
4. If I doubt this, there must be a doubter
5. Thus I exist, whether I believe or doubt.

Descartes rejected empiricism because he believed that sensory information was unreliable. To prove this he used his Wax Argument.

> Let us take, for example, this piece of wax: it has been taken quite freshly from the hive, and it has not yet lost the sweetness of the honey which it contains; it still retains somewhat of the odour of the flowers from which it has been culled; its colour, its figure, its size are apparent; it is hard, cold, easily handled, and if you strike it with the finger, it will emit a sound. Finally all the things which are requisite to cause us distinctly to recognise a body, are met with in it. But notice that while I speak and approach the fire what remained of the taste is exhaled, the smell evaporates, the colour alters, the figure is destroyed, the size increases, it becomes liquid, it heats, scarcely can one handle it, and when one strikes it, no sound is emitted. Does the same wax remain after this change? We must confess that it remains; none would judge otherwise. What then did I know so distinctly in this piece of wax? It could certainly be nothing of all that the senses brought to my notice, since all these things which fall under taste, smell, sight, touch, and hearing, are found to be changed, and yet the same wax remains.
>
> We must then grant that I could not even understand through the imagination what this piece of wax is, and that it is my mind alone which perceives it.[285]

Descartes ultimately concluded that the only thing that he could be sure of was that he was a thinking being. And thinking was every activity of which a person is immediately conscious. Philosophy was a thinking system that he described as such:

> Thus, all Philosophy is like a tree, of which Metaphysics is the root, Physics the trunk, and all the other sciences the branches that grow out of this trunk, which are reduced to three principals, namely, Medicine, Mechanics, and Ethics. By the science of Morals, I understand the highest and most perfect which, presupposing an entire knowledge of the other sciences, is the last degree of wisdom.[286]

In Descartes's philosophy, he offered a proof of the existence of God; he actually offered two, but they are generally the same. This is a reconstruction of his "trademark argument":

1. I have an idea of God.
2. Everything which exists has a cause.
3. Therefore, there is a cause of my idea of God.
4. The cause of an effect must contain at least as much reality as the effect.
5. Therefore, the cause of my idea of God must contain at least as much reality as my idea of God.
6. The idea of God contains perfection.
7. Therefore, the cause of my idea of God must contain perfection.
8. No being which is not God contains perfection.
9. God is the cause of my idea.
10. If something is the cause of something else, that something exists.
11. Therefore, God exists.

Descartes's "proof" was criticized by others, including David Hume an empiricist, who argued that the idea of God could be arrived at by considering qualities within oneself (wisdom, strength, goodness) and magnifying them. Another argument against this approach was that if I have an idea of a perfect island, that does not imply that it really exists.[287]

While the religious thinking of the protestant reformation freed man from the religious dogma and ritual of the Catholic Church, Descartes and the secular philosophers who followed were more concerned with the nature of being (ontology), the nature of knowledge (epistemology), and how these ideas of being and knowing interacted with the mental and physical world. The study of thought became known as *philosophy* and the study of the material world became known as *science*. The split between the protestant faith on one hand and philosophy/science on the other set the contradiction between conservatives and liberals that still exists today. While the conservatives form their opinions based on religious dogma, the liberals form their opinions based on the dogmas of philosophy and science. This helps to explain why the liberals shy away from questions of faith in God and why conservatives are so adamantly averse to the findings of science.

Perhaps the most significant contribution that Descartes made to liberal thought and to the ideas of personal freedom (liberty and individualism) was to change the focus from "What is true?" to a focus on "Of what can I be certain?" *Truth* implies an external authority while *certainty* relies on the judgments of individuals. This change shifted the nucleus of authority from God to human beings. By emancipating human beings from Christian revelation and church doctrine, Descartes helped set the base for individual liberty. The idea of free will for secular thinkers eventually came to trump church authorities and church dogmas such as God's predetermination of whether we would be eternally damned or not.

Baruch Spinoza (1632-1677)

Spinoza was a contemporary of Rene Descartes. They were born in the same year and both lived in the Dutch Republic.

Spinoza was a lens grinder by trade and had no higher education, although he knew radical students and became interested in their ideas. Like Descartes, Spinoza was a rationalist. He did not believe that evidence or observations gained from the senses could account for the nature of reality. Having said this, neither did Spinoza trust religion. He was one of the first to engage in biblical criticism, a field of study that was later picked up by Thomas Hobbes and Richard Simons.

Biblical criticism views biblical texts as having human rather than supernatural origins. It asks when and where a particular text originated; how, why, by whom, for whom, and in what circumstances it was produced; what influences were at work in its production; what sources were used in its composition; and what message was it intended to convey. It also addresses the physical text, including the meaning of the words and the way in which they are used, its preservation, history, and integrity. Biblical criticism draws upon a wide range of scholarly disciplines including archaeology, anthropology, folklore, linguistics, Oral Tradition studies, and historical and religious studies.[288]

Spinoza examined the first five books of the Old Testament (the Jewish Torah) and concluded that these books (Genesis, Exodus, Leviticus, Numbers, and Deuteronomy) traditionally believed to be authored by Moses, contained major inconsistencies that made such a belief improbable.[289] His efforts got him ostracized by the Portuguese Jewish community of which he was a member.

In his greatest work, *Ethics,* Spinoza rejected the idea of a providential God, one who intervenes in the world. As such, he rejected the God of Abraham and the line of Jewish prophets. God did not give out any Laws like the Ten Commandments and therefore they were not binding on Jews.

God did exist for Spinoza, but it was an impersonal God. God was One because two infinities could not exist as equals. God was the substance of Nature/Universe and was expressed through Nature/Universe. Everything in Nature has a cause and an effect and is driven by this necessity. Therefore, Spinoza was a determinist and did not believe in free will. Neither did good and evil have any absolute meaning, they were only relative to circumstances and belief. Prayer was also meaningless because everything was determined by cause and effect.

Spinoza saw the Universe as an extension of God's thought. Knowledge of God required reason. There were three types of knowledge—opinion, reason, and intuition. Of these, intuition provided the greatest satisfaction of mind. The more conscious we are of ourselves and Nature/Universe, the more perfect and blessed we are. Only intuitive knowledge is eternal. Opinion and reason are relative.

Spinoza rejected the body-mind duality introduced by Descartes and held that physical and mental realities are intertwined, each causing and being effected by the other.

He did not believe that reason could defeat emotion, only a stronger emotion could do that. To master emotion, one had to detach from external causes.

Through his writings, Spinoza became known as one of the greatest philosophers to ever live. His thinking laid the groundwork for the eighteenth century Enlightenment. His reasoning ability and independence of faith in a providential god provided secular thinkers powerful arguments in their fight against church authority as well as the godlessness of empirical science. In his day, he was valued for having provided an alternative to materialism, atheism, and deism.

His philosophical accomplishments and moral character prompted twentieth century philosopher Gilles Deleuze to name him "the prince of philosophers."[290]

John Locke (1632-1704)

John Locke was an English philosopher and physician. He is known as the "Father of Classical Liberalism." From a contemporary point of view, Locke is full of contradictions. For example, he considered himself an empiricist but at the same time he believed that the Bible was consistent with human reason. Locke was a primary author of the justification of slavery in the United States, while arguing for personal liberty in his writings. Locke argued that people are created equal yet believed the state should allow individuals to amass as much wealth as possible regardless of the impact on others. In this way, he mirrored Calvinist thought.

Regarding religion, Locke began as a Calvinist Trinitarian believing in God the Father, the Son, and the Holy Spirit. Both his parents were Puritans. In time, his ideas regarding Christ and the Holy Spirit changed, but he remained an ardent defender of the Bible until his death.

Locke was convinced that the entire content of the Bible was in agreement with human reason. Although he advocated tolerance, he urged the authorities not to tolerate atheism, because he thought the denial of God's existence would undermine the social order and lead to chaos.[291] This included the secular philosophers who questioned the existence of God. In Locke's opinion the cosmological argument[292] was valid and proved God's existence. The cosmological argument is an argument in which the existence of God is inferred from alleged facts concerning causation, explanation, change, motion, contingency, dependency, or finitude with respect to the universe or some totality of objects.

Locke's concept of man started with the belief in creation. We have been "sent into the World by [God's] order, and about his business, [we] are his Property, whose Workmanship [we] are, made to last during his, not one another's Pleasure." [293]

Locke was at times not sure about the subject of original sin, so he was accused of Socinianism, Arianism, or Deism. But he did not deny the reality of evil.

Locke derived the fundamental concepts of his political theory from biblical texts, in particular from Genesis 1 and 2 (creation), the Decalogue (Exod 20), the Golden Rule (Matt 7:12), Jesus' doctrine of charity (Matt 19:19), and the letters of Paul. The Decalogue (Ten Commandments) puts a person's life, his or her honorable reputation (i.e. honor and dignity), and property under God's protection.[294]

Freedom is another major theme in the Old Testament that Locke defended. God's actions in liberating the Israelites from Egyptian slavery created the Ten Commandments (Exod 20:2). Moreover, Locke derived basic human equality, including the equality of the sexes ("Adam and Eve") from Genesis 1:26–28. To Locke, one of the consequences of the principle of equality was that all humans were created equally free and therefore governments needed the consent of the governed. Only when Locke had derived the fundamental aspects of his concept of man and ethics from the biblical texts—life, equality, private property, etc.,—did he examine as a philosopher what the consequences were. Following Locke, the American Declaration of Independence founded human rights on the biblical belief in creation: "All men are *created* equal ... they are endowed by their *Creator* with certain unalienable rights ... life, liberty, and the pursuit of happiness." Locke's doctrine, which was built on Hobbes, that governments needed the consent of the governed, is also central to the Declaration of Independence.[295]

Regardless of the fact that Locke depended upon the Bible for his political thought, it nevertheless became the basis of Classical Liberalism. Thus, classical liberalism had its birth in religious as well as political thought.

The emphasis of classical liberalism is to secure the liberty of individuals from the power of government. As such, it advocates for personal guaranteed freedoms that the government cannot abridge, either by law or by judicial interpretation. Though the scope of the term differs amongst various countries, examples of civil liberties include the right to life, the right to liberty and security, freedom of conscience, freedom of press, freedom of religion, freedom of expression, freedom of assembly, freedom of speech, the right to privacy, the right to equal treatment and due process, and the right to a fair trial. Other civil liberties include the right to own property, the right to defend oneself, the right to bodily integrity, and freedom from torture and death.[296]

Classical liberalists also argued for limited government, rule of law, private property and laissez faire economics, individual liberty, natural law, utilitarianism, and the idea of progress.

Of these values, Locke inspired the liberal tradition in its idea of individualism, the consent of the governed, rule of law, the government as the trustee of the governed, the significance of property, and religious toleration. These ideas laid the base for democracy and a republic, replacing the argument of divine right of kings. As a trustee of the people, government must serve the interest of the people and not the rulers. The rulers were subject to the law as are everyone else. Locke's idea, that authority is derived from the consent of the governed and not the state, was a revolutionary idea and as such influenced revolutionary thought across Europe and the United States.

His arguments influenced the written works of Alexander Hamilton, James Madison, Thomas Jefferson, and other Founding Fathers of the United States. In fact, one passage from Locke's *Second Treatise* is reproduced verbatim in the Declaration of Independence, the reference to a "long train of abuses." Such was Locke's influence that Thomas Jefferson considered him to be one of the greatest men that has ever lived.[297]

Locke assumed that people established a civil society to resolve conflicts in a civil way with help from the government. Locke also advocated governmental separation of the executive, legislative and judicial branches of government to assure a check and balance on political power and believed that revolution is not only a right, but an obligation in some circumstances. These ideas would come to have profound influence on the Declaration of Independence and the Constitution of the United States.

Most scholars trace the phrase "life, liberty, and the pursuit of happiness," in the American Declaration of Independence, to Locke's theory of rights.

While Locke is often tied to liberalism in general, and also to the founding of the United States, he has serious detractors. In 1671, Locke was a major investor in the English slave-trade through the Royal African

Company. In addition, he participated in drafting the *Fundamental Constitutions of Carolina* while working for the 1st Earl of Shaftesbury, the Lord Chancellor. This document established a feudal aristocracy and gave a master absolute power over his slaves. At the time, Locke was appointed as a secretary to the Council of Trade and Plantations (1673-4) and a member of the Board of Trade (1696-1700), and was in fact, "one of just half a dozen men who created and supervised both the colonies and their iniquitous systems of servitude."[298] Some see his statements on unenclosed property as having been intended to justify the displacement of the Native Americans. Because of his opposition to aristocracy and slavery in his major writings, he is accused of hypocrisy and racism, or of caring only for the liberty of English capitalists.[299]

Gottfried Liebniz (1646-1716)

Liebniz began life in Leipzig, Saxony toward the end of the Thirty Years War. He became an academic whose father was a professor of Moral Philosophy at the University of Leipzig. Gottfried inherited his father's library and, in this way, was introduced to the ancient philosophers as well as important Church theologians.

In philosophy, Leibniz is considered one of the three top rationalists of the century along with Descartes and Spinoza. Leibniz was an idealist and developed arguments against materialism. He did not believe that perception and consciousness could be derived at through sensory data. As such, perception and consciousness could not be physical processes. Leibniz's argument has the reader imagining himself or herself entering a large machine. The visitor, upon entering it, would observe nothing but the properties of the parts, and the relations they bear to one another. But no explanation of perception or consciousness can possibly be deduced from this conglomerate. No matter how complex the inner workings of this machine, nothing about them reveals that what is being observed are the inner workings of a conscious being. Hence, materialism must be false, for there is no possible way that the purely mechanical principles of materialism can account for the phenomena of consciousness.[300]

To account for consciousness, Leibniz identifies the "I feeling" or the soul in us. In his *New System of Nature* (1695), he writes:

> Furthermore, by means of the soul or form, there is a true unity which corresponds to what is called the *I* in us; such a thing could not occur in artificial machines, nor in the simple mass of matter, however organized it may be. [301]

Regarding the question of Nature, Leibniz argued that our world is the best among possible worlds because it was created by an all powerful and all knowing God, who would not choose to create an imperfect world if a better world could be known to him or possible to exist.

Leibniz attempted to bridge the contradiction between religion and rational thought by asserting that the truths of religion and philosophy cannot contradict each other, because reason and faith are both "gifts of God" so that their conflict would imply God contending against himself. Because reason and faith must be entirely reconciled, any tenet of faith, which could not be defended by reason must be rejected. Leibniz then approached one of the central criticisms of Christian belief: if God is all good, all wise and all-powerful, how did evil come into the world? Leibniz answered that, while God is indeed unlimited in wisdom and power, his human creations are limited both in their wisdom and in their will (power to act). This predisposes humans to false beliefs, wrong decisions, and ineffective actions in the exercise of their free will. God does not arbitrarily inflict pain and suffering on humans; rather he permits both *moral evil* (sin) and *physical evil* (pain and suffering) as the necessary consequences of *metaphysical evil* (imperfection), as a means by which humans can identify and correct their erroneous decisions.

Further, although human actions flow from prior causes that ultimately arise in God, there is in creation the existence of "wonderful spontaneity" that provides individuals an escape from predestined damnation.

Perhaps Liebniz's greatest contribution to humanity is in the field of mathematics. He is believed to have developed *calculus,* either independently or in consort with Isaac Newton, and his mathematical notation has been widely used ever since it was published. He became one of the most prolific inventors in the field of mechanical calculators and created the internal workings for the first mass-produced mechanical calculator. Liebniz also refined the binary number system, which is the foundation of virtually all digital computers.

Leibniz made major contributions to physics and technology and anticipated notions that surfaced much later in philosophy, probability theory, biology, medicine, geology, psychology, linguistics, and computer science.

He also wrote on the topics of politics, law, ethics, theology, history, and philology. Leibniz's contributions to this vast array of subjects were scattered in various learned journals, in tens of thousands of letters, and in unpublished manuscripts. He wrote in several languages, but primarily in Latin, French, and German. There is no complete gathering of the writings of Leibniz.

Liebniz proposed that the earth has a molten core, anticipating modern geology. In embryology, he proposed that organisms are the outcome of a combination of an infinite number of possible microstructures and of their powers. In the life sciences and paleontology, one of his principal works on this subject, *Protogaea*, unpublished in his lifetime, has recently been published in English for the first time. In medicine, he exhorted the physicians of his time—with some results—to ground their theories in detailed comparative observations and verified experiments, and to firmly distinguish between scientific and metaphysical points of view.

Much of Leibniz's work went on to have a great impact on the field of psychology. His theory regarding consciousness in relation to the principle of continuity can be seen as an early theory regarding the stages of sleep. Psychologists embraced his ideas of psycho-physical parallelism. This idea refers to the mind–body problem, stating that the mind and brain do not act upon each other, but act alongside one another separately but in harmony.

Leibniz believed that the mind had a very active role in perception, and plays a larger role than sensory input. He focused heavily on perception, distinguishing between the type of perception where we are conscious of a stimulus, and the other where we are aware of a distinct perception. He believed that there are many small perceptions of which we are unaware. For example, when a bag of rice is spilled, we see the rice but are not necessarily aware of how many grains are in the pile. Under this principle, there are an infinite number of perceptions within us at any given time that we are unaware of. For this to be true there must also be a portion of the mind that we are unaware of at any given time. In this respect, Leibniz's theory of perception can be viewed as one of many theories leading up to the idea of the *unconscious*. Additionally, the idea of subliminal stimuli can be traced back to this theory. Leibniz was a direct influence on Ernst Platner, who is credited with originally coining the term "unconscious."

Charles Montesquieu (1689-1755)

Charles Louis de Secondat, Baron de Montesquieu was born on January 18, 1689, at the castle of La Brède near Bordeaux.[302]

Montesquieu was a French lawyer who is famous for his political philosophy. More than any other philosopher during the Enlightenment period, he dedicated himself to an examination of laws and the types of governments they engendered.

Montesquieu published his great work, *The Spirit of the Laws,* in 1748. It reveals his premise that laws are based upon different environmental and social relationships that change according to different societies. Combining the traditions of customary law with those of the modern theories of natural law, Montesquieu redefined law as "the necessary relationships that derive from the nature of things" and concluded that laws "must be adapted to each peoples."[303]

The Spirit of the Laws helped to lay the basis of the eighteenth-century movement for constitutionalism (government run by established law) instead of monarchy or dictatorship. His work helped engender the French Revolution of 1789 that empowered the middle class bourgeoisie against the failures of King Louis XVI and his royals, many of whom were killed by the guillotine. *The Spirit of the Laws* was immediately celebrated as one of the great works of French literature.

Montesquieu constructed an account of the various forms of government and of the causes that made them what they were and what advanced or constrained their development. He used this account to explain how governments might be preserved from corruption. He saw despotism, in particular, as a standing danger for any government not already despotic and argued that it could best be prevented by a system in which different bodies exercised legislative, executive, and judicial power and in which all those bodies were bound by the rule of law. This theory of the separation of powers had an enormous impact on liberal political theory and on the framers of the constitution of the United States of America.

While most of Montesquieu's peers were ignorant of the potential corruption within a democracy, focused as they were on the corruption of the Church and Monarchy, he began to envision how this corruption might take form.

Montesquieu held that there are three types of governments: republican governments, (which can take either democratic or aristocratic forms), monarchies, and despotisms. Each form of government has a principle, a set of "human passions which set it in motion" (SL 3.1); and each can be corrupted if its principle is undermined or destroyed.

In a democracy, the people are sovereign. They may govern through ministers, or be advised by a senate, but they must have the power of choosing their ministers and senators for themselves. The principle of democracy is political virtue, by which Montesquieu means "the love of the laws and of our country" (SL 4.5), including its democratic constitution. The form of a democratic government makes the laws governing suffrage and voting fundamental. The need to protect its principle, however, imposes far more extensive requirements. In Montesquieu's view, the virtue required by a functioning democracy is not natural. It requires "a constant preference of public to private interest" (SL 4.5); it "limits ambition to the sole desire, to the sole happiness, of doing greater services to our country than the rest of our fellow citizens" (SL 5.3); and it "is a self-renunciation, which is ever arduous and painful" (SL 4.5). Montesquieu compares it to monks' love for their order: "their rule debars them from all those things by which the ordinary passions are fed; there remains therefore only this passion for the very rule that torments them. . . . the more it curbs their inclinations, the more force it gives to the only passion left them" (SL 5.2). To produce this unnatural self-renunciation, "the whole power of education is required" (SL 4.5). A democracy must educate its citizens to identify their interests with the interests of their country, and should have censors to preserve its mores. It should seek to establish frugality by law, so as to prevent its citizens from being tempted to advance their own private interests at the expense of the public good; for the same reason, the laws by which property is transferred should aim to preserve an equal distribution of property among citizens. Its territory should be small, so that it is easy for citizens to identify with it, and more difficult for extensive private interests to emerge.

According to Montesquieu, democracies can be corrupted in two ways: by "the spirit of inequality" and by "the spirit of extreme equality" (SL 8.2). The spirit of inequality arises when citizens no longer identify their interests with the interests of their country, and therefore seek both to advance their own private interests at the expense of their fellow citizens, and to acquire political power over them. The spirit of extreme equality arises when the people are no longer content to be equal as citizens, but want to be equal in every respect. In a functioning democracy, the people choose magistrates to exercise executive power and they respect and obey the magistrates they have chosen. If those magistrates forfeit their respect, they replace them. When the spirit of extreme equality takes root, however, the citizens neither respect nor obey any magistrate. They "want to manage everything themselves, to debate for the senate, to execute for the magistrate, and to decide for the judges" (SL 8.2). Eventually, the government will cease to function, the last remnants of virtue will disappear, and democracy will be replaced by despotism.

In the United States today, we can witness both these types of corruptions. The capitalists are guilty of perpetrating the "spirit of inequality," while the federal government leans toward the "spirit of extreme equality." The capitalists move our society to abject selfishness and exploitation of others, while the federal government moves our government evermore toward capitalist despotism.

Producing a despotic government is relatively straightforward. A despotism requires no powers to be carefully balanced against one another, no institutions to be created and maintained in existence, no complicated motivations to be fostered, and no restraints on power to be kept in place. One need only terrify one's fellow citizens enough to allow one to impose one's will on them; and this, Montesquieu claims, "is what every capacity may reach" (SL 5.14). For these reasons despotism necessarily stands in a different relation to corruption than other forms of government: while they are liable to corruption, despotism is its embodiment.

According to Montesquieu, political liberty is "a tranquility of mind arising from the opinion each person has of his safety" (SL 11.6). Liberty is not the freedom to do whatever we want: if we have the freedom to harm others, for instance, others will also have the freedom to harm us, and we will have no confidence in our own safety. Liberty involves living under laws that protect us from harm while leaving us free to do as much as possible and that enable us to feel the greatest possible confidence that if we obey those laws, the power of the state will not be directed against us.

If it is to provide its citizens with the greatest possible liberty, a government must have certain features. First, since "constant experience shows us that every man invested with power is apt to abuse it . . . it is necessary from the very nature of things that power should be a check to power" (SL 11.4). This is achieved through the separation of the executive, legislative, and judicial powers of government. If different persons or bodies exercise these powers, then they can check the others if they try to abuse their powers. But if one person or body holds several or all of these powers, then nothing prevents that person or body from acting tyrannically; and the people will have no confidence in their own security.

Liberty also requires that the laws of government be limited only to threats to public order and security, since such laws will protect us from harm while leaving us free to do as many other things as possible. Thus, for instance, the laws should not concern offenses against God, since He does not require their protection. They should not prohibit what they do not need to prohibit: "all punishment which is not derived from necessity is tyrannical. The law is not a mere act of power; things in their own nature indifferent are not within its province" (SL 19.14). The laws should be constructed to make it as easy as possible for citizens to protect themselves from punishment by not committing crimes. They should not be vague, since if they were, we might never be sure whether or not some particular action was a crime. Nor should they prohibit things we might do inadvertently, like bumping into a statue of the emperor, or involuntarily, like doubting the wisdom of one of his decrees. If such actions were crimes, no amount of effort to abide by the laws of our country would justify confidence that we would succeed, and therefore we could never feel safe from criminal prosecution.

Finally, the laws should make it as easy as possible for an innocent person to prove his or her innocence. They should concern outward conduct, not (for instance) our thoughts and dreams, since while we can try to prove that we did not perform some action, we cannot prove that we never had some thought. The laws should not criminalize conduct that is inherently hard to prove, like witchcraft; and lawmakers should be cautious when dealing with crimes like sodomy, which are typically not carried out in the presence of several witnesses, lest they "open a very wide door to calumny" (SL 12.6).

Here Montesquieu's limiting the arena of law to public order and security ignores the necessity of creating laws against economic injustice. His thinking also allows for the creation of a police state, in which so-called protection from "terrorists" leads to laws that in an emergency will take away all of our citizens' natural and civil rights. Such laws now exist on the books in the United States.

According to Montesquieu, commerce was the best of all ways for a country to enrich itself. It was preferable to conquering and plundering other nations or setting up colonies to mine gold. Commerce, he believed, has no such disadvantages. It does not require vast armies or the continued subjugation of other peoples. It does not undermine itself, as the extraction of gold from colonial mines does, and it rewards domestic industry. It therefore sustains itself, and nations, which engage in it, over time. While it does not produce all the virtues, it is naturally attended with that of frugality, economy, moderation, labor, prudence, tranquility, order, and rule" (SL 5.6). In addition, it "is a cure for the most destructive prejudices" (SL 20.1), improves manners, and leads to peace among nations.

Montesquieu did not realize that the English slave trade had already begun in America and that the fruits of his beloved commerce became exactly what he had denounced—vast armies and the continued subjugation of other people's.

Religion did not play a major role in Montesquieu's thinking. God created nature and its laws. Having done so, God plays no further explanatory role. Montesquieu does not explain the laws of any country by appeal to divine enlightenment, providence, or guidance. In the *Spirit of the Laws*, Montesquieu considers religions "in relation only to the good they produce in civil society" (SL 24.1), and not to their truth or falsity. Nonetheless, it is interesting to note his identification of Protestantism with capitalist government. For example, he regarded different religions as appropriate to different forms of government. Protestantism, he believed, is most suitable to republics, Catholicism to monarchies, and Islam to despotisms.

Montesquieu's view was that it is generally a mistake to base civil laws on religious principles. Religion aims at the perfection of the individual; civil laws aim at the welfare of society. Given these different aims, what these two sets of laws should require will often differ; for this reason religion "ought not always to serve as a first principle to the civil laws" (SL 26.9). The civil laws are not an appropriate tool for enforcing religious norms of conduct: God has His own laws, and He is quite capable of enforcing them without our assistance. When we attempt to enforce God's laws for Him, or to cast ourselves as His protectors, we make our religion an instrument of fanaticism and oppression; this is a service neither to God nor to our country.

If several religions have gained adherents in a country, those religions should all be tolerated, not only by the state but by its citizens. The laws should "require from the several religions, not only that they shall not embroil the state, but that they shall not raise disturbances among themselves" (SL 25.9). While one can try to persuade people to change religions by offering them positive inducements to do so, attempts to force others to convert are ineffective and inhumane.[304] This observation has proven quite prescient and stands in contradiction to the current Protestant Dominion Theology which seeks to make a white Christian nation of the United States.

David Hume (1711-1776)

David Hume is considered one of the great empiricists of modern history. He was a product of the Scottish Enlightenment. Jonathan Israel, a prominent scholar on Dutch history and the Enlightenment, argued that the Enlightenment had its roots in Scotland and from there spread to the mainland and across to America. By 1750, Scotland's major cities had already created an intellectual infrastructure of mutually supporting institutions, including universities, reading societies, libraries, periodicals, museums, and masonic lodges. The Scottish network was "predominantly liberal Calvinist, Newtonian, and 'design' oriented in character, which played a major role in the further development of Enlightenment ideas in America. In France, Voltaire said "we look to Scotland for all our ideas of civilization."[305] Historian Bruce Lenman says their "central achievement was a new capacity to recognize and interpret social patterns."[306]

The first major philosopher of the Scottish Enlightenment was Francis Hutcheson, who held the Chair of Philosophy at the University of Glasgow from 1729 to 1746. A moral philosopher who produced alternatives to the ideas of Thomas Hobbes, he argued that virtue is that which provides the greatest happiness for the greatest numbers.

Much of what is incorporated in the *scientific method* (the nature of knowledge, evidence, experience, and causation) and some modern attitudes towards the relationship between science and religion were developed by Hutcheson's protégés David Hume, and Adam Smith.

Hume was a skeptic. Knowledge could only be derived and truth could only be established from sense experience. It was on such a hardline that the empirical sciences evolved in Western thought.

Along with other Scottish thinkers, Hume developed a "science of man" that investigated how humans behaved in ancient and primitive cultures and, in so doing, provided the roots for modern *sociology*.

Hume rejected the rationalist approach of Rene Descartes, arguing that inductive reasoning, and thus causality, could not be justified.

He also argued that it was *desire* not reason that governed human behavior. He did not believe in innate ideas, which were ideas present in the mind from birth. For example, while Descartes believed that the existence of the self (I think, therefore I am), the existence of God, and some logical propositions like, *from nothing comes nothing*, where innate ideas,[307] Hume believed that humans had no actual conception of the self and what we call "self" was only a bundle of sensations. Such ideas placed Hume as the forerunner of *utilitarianism*, *logical positivism*, the *philosophy of science*, and *analytic philosophy*.

Hume's position on religion is unclear and his contemporaries considered him to be an atheist. That is understandable because in his *A Treatise of Human Nature* he declared:

> Tis evident that all the sciences have a relation, more or less, to human nature . . . Even Mathematics, Natural Philosophy, and Natural Religion, are in some measure dependent on the science of Man.[308]

Later, he wrote that the science of man is the only solid foundation for the other sciences and that the method for this science requires both experience and observation as the foundations of a logical argument. As for religion, he dismissed it by saying that all religions derive simply from fear of the unknown. He said it was impossible to deduce the existence of a Deity from the existence of the world.

Hume helped establish science as an expression of materialism that was to propel modern industrial society in its understanding of the material conditions in which we live, as well as its understanding of the relation of matter and energy. Unfortunately, Hume's limited view of *Man* ruled out any understanding of the mind or spirit of mankind, the consequences of which, just as assuredly as the religious concept of predetermination, have brought humanity to the brink of disaster. Take away the human mind and the soul and we have little more left to us than a colony of ants. By rejecting the I-feeling, Hume also rejected the idea of unit consciousness and in so doing left humanity without a moral compass or means of achieving human unity.

On the subject of morality, Hume argued that it was not reason but emotions that produced or prevented actions. In this regard, Hume consigned moral behavior to the realm of sentiments rather than reason and thus helped propagate the continual drift within capitalist society toward the moral ambiguity and ambivalence that we experience today. Hume was unable to envision that it was only by acting in a moral way that we could balance the turbulence between the individual and the environment. Nor could he understand that morality was the foundation of spiritual progress, that it had a specific role to play in human evolution and was not just a matter of circumstance.

As for Hume's writing on politics, he is more conservative than liberal. This most likely stems from the social conditions that characterized his environment. Civil war and religious wars had destabilized society and left it deeply divided politically and religiously. While he advocated that society should be governed by an impartial system of laws, he was not concerned about what kind of government was in power. Hume was suspicious of attempts to reform society that broke from long established custom. He counseled people not to resist the government except in cases of the most egregious tyranny. However, Hume also supported freedom of the press and was sympathetic to democracy. Basically, he supported government by consent, separation of powers (executive, legislative and judicial), decentralization, giving people with property the right to vote and limiting the power of the clergy. In this position he had a major impact on James Madison's writings.

In the study of economics, Hume wrestled with the ideas of private property, inflation, and foreign trade. Unlike Locke, he argued that private property is not a natural right. It is justified only because it is in limited supply. If property were unlimited it would be ludicrous to privatize it. He did not believe in the equal distribution of wealth because this would destroy the impetus for thrift and industry. Perfect equality would therefore lead to impoverishment. Here we see the Calvinist argument reappear as a justification for bourgeois freedom at the expense of society.

Jean-Jacque Rousseau (1712-1778)

There is probably no philosopher that is more confusing than Rousseau. He is considered, as we have seen, to be one of the greatest misogynists among philosophers. At the same time, he wrestled with ideas that no one in his time had a handle on. As such, he made enemies of Catholics as well as Calvinists, philosophers as well as scientists. He is the greatest example of the limits of philosophy. His writings are full of conjectures, flights of fantasy, undeveloped ideas, and unanswered questions. At the same time, to his credit, he introduced the topics of the arts, music, literature, education, popular sovereignty, and the beauty of the natural world to the realm of philosophy.

Rousseau is most famous for his political philosophy because it had a major impact on the French Revolution. He is also considered a pre-Romantic for his love of nature and his use of literature to describe its beauty.

Rousseau had a fascinating although dysfunctional life. He was always on the run because his ideas challenged popular dogmas and beliefs. He was at different times at odds with the governments of Geneva, France, and England.

Rousseau was born in Geneva, the center of Calvinism and the birthplace of the Protestant Christian state. His family had property and therefore voting rights in the city. At the time of his birth, Calvinism was approaching two hundred years of dominance. Geneva, in theory, was governed democratically by its male voting citizens. They were a small minority compared to the people who were not allowed to vote. In reality, the city was ruled by a small number of wealthy families that made up the "Council of Two Hundred." They delegated their power to an executive group of twenty-five members that was called the "Little Council." There was much talk about the sovereignty of the people, an idea of which the bourgeoisie ruling class made a great mockery. In 1707, a democratic reformer, Pierre Fatio protested the rule of the elite saying "A sovereign that never performs an act of sovereignty is an imaginary being."[309] He was shot by order of the Little Council. Rousseau's grandfather was a supporter of Fatio and was punished.

In 1695, as a young woman, Suzanne Rousseau, who was Jean-Jacque's mother, and who was raised as a Calvinist, had to face charges that she had attended a street theatre disguised as a peasant woman so she could gaze upon an actor whom she fancied, despite his being married. She was chastised and henceforth forbidden to even look at the man. She died after giving birth to Rousseau seventeen years later.

While being deeply moved by religious services, Rousseau renounced his Calvinist faith and became a Catholic because he could not tolerate Calvinism's insistence on the dogma of the total depravity of man. The liturgy at the time still required people attending church services to declare "We are miserable sinners, born in corruption, inclined to evil, incapable by ourselves of doing good."[310] Rousseau preferred the Catholic doctrine of forgiveness of sins and, in moving to France, became a Catholic.

Rousseau found himself involved in a *ménage a trois* with a woman mentor whose circle included educated members of the French Catholic clergy. Here he was introduced to the world of letters and ideas. Later, he had a child with a seamstress whom he supported, along with her mother, but convinced his lover to give up the newborn to a foundling hospital.

When in Paris, Rousseau became a close friend to the French philosopher Diderot who led a group of intellectuals called the *Encyclopedistes*, who compiled writings from many French thinkers, especially scientific works. During this time he had a revelation that the arts and sciences were responsible for moral degeneration of mankind, which was basically good by nature. His argument was that people go to plays and, watching the actors, identify with them as good people, then return to their normal life and their evil ways, while believing they remain good people. An interesting notion and one that could equally be attributed to the impact of church services on people.

In 1754, Rousseau returned to Geneva and reconverted to Calvinism to regain his citizenship. In Geneva, he wrote his three greatest works, the novel *Julie*, which was sentimental and pre-Romantic, his political philosophy in *Of the Social Contract, Principles of Political Right*, and his novel *Emile* or *On Education*.

Emile was intended to be a defense of religious belief, but his writing was interpreted as a defense of Unitarianism, which espoused One God instead of Three Gods in One. Rousseau also questioned the idea of original sin and predestination.[311] Because he rejected original sin and Divine revelation, both the Catholics and the Calvinists were enraged. Rousseau also believed that all religions were good because they led people to virtue. This was interpreted as "religious indifference" and resulted in his book being banned from France and Geneva. The authorities burned his books and issued warrants for his arrest.

Rousseau took refuge in England where he stayed with David Hume who remarked: "Rousseau had not had the precaution to throw any veil over his sentiments, and, as he scorns to dissemble his contempt for established opinions, he could not wonder that all the zealots were in arms against him.[312]

While living with Hume, Rousseau, never emotionally stable, and not being able to speak English, was plagued by paranoid fantasies about plots against him involving Hume and others. Hume wrote to a friend, "He is plainly mad, after having long been maddish."

In 1770, Rousseau was allowed to return to Paris with the condition that he was not allowed to publish any more books.[313]

Just as Rousseau contradicted the religious dogma of his day, he also had a quarrel with the philosophers whom he saw as rationalizers of self-interest, apologists for tyranny and forces that helped to alienate people from their natural impulse for compassion. As a man driven by his emotions and sentiments, Rousseau, it seems, was feeling the weight of capitalism and its ruling institutions even during this formative period. His greatest concern was how to preserve human freedom in a world where people are increasingly dependent upon each other to meet their basic needs. Rousseau believed that in modern society, people come to derive their sense of self from the opinion of others, destroying freedom and individual authenticity.

The Social Contract is considered Rousseau's most important work. In it, he tries to lay the groundwork for constructing political institutions that allow for the co-existence of free and equal citizens, in which they make their own laws. In *Emile*, he proposes that education should also be a way to train people away from the destructive aspects of self-interest. While Rousseau believed intellectually that equality and freedom are possible, he was constantly overwhelmed by pessimism that people would ever escape their alienation, oppression, and slavery.[314]

Rousseau introduced sentiments and other matters of the heart to the field of philosophy. He "felt" for humanity, and in this respect, superseded his contemporaries who remained lost in the labyrinths of dry logic. Nonetheless, in being subject to sentiment rather than rationality, he suffered lack of clarity and inner strength. As a musician and novelist, he introduced aesthetics while at the same time arguing against them. Rousseau was confused in logic and emotions, but he remained true to his convictions and a champion of humanity against tyranny for his entire life.

Adam Smith (1723-1790)

Adam Smith was the son of a Scottish judge and comptroller. His father died two months after he was born leaving his wife a widow. Smith grew up close to his mother Margaret, and it was she who encouraged his studies. He attended the University of Glasgow at age fourteen and studied moral philosophy under Francis Hutcheson.[315] Here, Smith developed his passion for liberty, reason, and free speech.

Upon graduation, he toured France where he made a living as a tutor. In France, he saw firsthand how the wealth of the country was virtually destroyed by Louis XIV and Louis XV in ruinous wars, and by aiding the American insurgents against the British. He also observed that the excessive consumption of goods, services, and luxuries on the part of the monarchy contributed to the declining wealth of the country. Given that the English economy of the day stood in marked contrast to that which existed in France, Smith attributed this difference to the fact that labor was used productively in England, while being used unproductively in France. The distinction between productive versus unproductive labor became a predominant issue in the development of what would become classical economic theory.

As a person, Smith was a bit quirky. He was described by several of his contemporaries as having peculiar habits of speech and gait, and a smile of "inexpressible benignity."[316] During his childhood he had conversations with imaginary companions and this led to him talking to himself as an adult. His absent mindedness was also a source of amusement to those that knew him. According to one story, Smith took Charles Townshend on a tour of a tanning factory, and while discussing free trade, Smith walked into a huge tanning pit from which he needed help to escape. He is also said to have put bread and butter into a teapot, drunk the concoction, and declared it to be the worst cup of tea he ever had. According to another account, Smith distractedly went out walking in his nightgown and ended up fifteen miles outside of town, before nearby church bells brought him back to reality.[317] In Boswell's *Life of Johnson*, we find the story that Smith believed that speaking about his ideas in conversation might reduce the sale of his books, so he "made it a rule when in company never to talk of what he understood."[318]

Nonetheless, for all his quirkiness, Adam Smith became a legend within capitalist society. As a philosopher, he was interested in morality and political economy. Today, he is held to be the father of modern economics and is still one of the most influential thinkers in the field of capitalist economics today. His two classic works are *The Theory of Moral Sentiments* (1759) and *The Wealth of Nations* (1776). The latter work, published in the same year as the United States gained its independence from the British, provided a philosophical rationale for the inherent cosmic goodness of capitalism. Smith theorized that self-interest and competition inevitably lead to economic prosperity. This argument provided the foundations for the notion of "free markets," i.e., economic exchange unregulated by any government oversight.[319]

Smith argued that an "invisible hand" guided individual economic transactions so that despite the fact that such actions are taken for personal gain, nonetheless, collectively they contribute to the greater social good. This argument was fuzzy at best, for it did not take into account the exploitation of labor or resources in the accumulation of capital. It did not account for the use of slaves to create wealth, nor the wage slavery of serfs, nor the loss of the fingers and hands of little children forced to work in factories for twelve hours a day. Nonetheless, like Calvin, Smith helped provide a rationale for the merchant class to gain greater freedom from government control. Smith's argument of the "invisible hand" is still proffered by apologists for capitalism today even as this economic system, under the control of a few multinational corporations, continues to impoverish the human population and the life-support systems of the planet.

Interestingly, Smith came to realize that the cause of the increase in national wealth was human labor and not the amount of gold or silver held in the national treasury, which was the premise of mercantilist theory that was still the dominant economic theory at the time.

Smith's work on morality argued that one acts morally, not based on a "moral sense" nor because it is useful, but because one has empathy with another. Unfortunately, Smith never bridged the contradiction in capitalism that prevented the capitalists from acting in a moral way toward their workers. The same contradiction remains today. Capitalists could not afford to "empathize" with the workers and at the same time amass wealth at their expense. Thus, Smith's contribution to humanity is at best ill-conceived, even though he remains a hero to the capitalist class and their apologists. The disconnect in Smith's theorizing can be seen as the capitalists evolved their rationale for exploitation of others by applying Darwin's "survival of the fittest" theory of evolution to the capitalist class structure. Called *Social Darwinism*, this theory held that the capitalists have the right to rule over and exploit other men and species because they are the strongest and therefore, they can take whatever they want in any manner that they want. We will discuss this idea in the next chapter on the History of Capitalism.

Immanuel Kant (1724-1804)

Immanuel Kant was born 207 years after Martin Luther challenged the Catholic Church with his revolutionary treatise *95 Theses* and one hundred and nineteen years after Sir Francis Bacon published *Of Proficience and Advancement of Learning Divine and Human*, which set the base for empirical thought in the new Europe. The religious wars had mostly been fought and the Protestant movement had gained ascendency throughout Europe. Thus, Kant was born at a time when religious thought had already gone through a revolution and when secular thought in the form of philosophy and science were being taught in the universities.

Kant was born in Königsberg, near the Baltic Sea. Today Königsberg has been renamed Kaliningrad and is part of Russia. But during Kant's lifetime, Königsberg was the capital of East Prussia, and its dominant language was German. Though geographically remote from the rest of Prussia and other German cities, Königsberg was then a major commercial center, an important military port, and a relatively cosmopolitan university town.[320]

Kant's father was a master harness maker and although his family was never destitute, his father's trade was in decline during Kant's youth and his parents at times had to rely on their extended family for financial support.

His parents were Pietists. Pietism was the evangelical offspring of Lutheranism that emphasized personal conversion, reliance on divine grace, and the experience of religious emotions. It involved regular

Bible study, prayer, and introspection. Kant reacted strongly against the forced soul-searching to which he was subjected at his Pietist high school. He sought refuge in the Latin classics, which were central to the school's curriculum. Afterward, Kant attended college at the University of Königsberg, where his early interest in classics was quickly superseded by philosophy, which all first year students studied, including mathematics, physics, logic, metaphysics, ethics, and natural law. At the University, Kant was exposed to Leibniz (rationalist) and Newton (empiricist). After college, he spent six years as a private tutor to young children outside Königsberg.

Kant wrote several papers in Latin, which resulted in an invitation to be an unsalaried lecturer at his alma mater. He was paid directly by the students who attended his lectures, so he needed to teach many hours and to attract many students in order to earn a living. Kant held this position from 1755 to 1770, during which period he would lecture an average of twenty hours per week on logic, metaphysics, and ethics, as well as mathematics, physics, and physical geography. His ideas at the time were strongly influenced by the works of David Hume, the Scottish empiricist and skeptic. Kant credited David Hume with awakening him from "dogmatic slumber." Hume, the first great empiricist, had stated that experience consists only of sequences of feelings, images, or sounds. Ideas such as "cause" or "goodness" were not evident in experience, so why do we believe in the reality of these? Kant felt that reason could remove this skepticism and he set himself to solving these problems. It would take him eleven years before he published *Critique of Pure Reason* in an attempt to address the main philosophical contradictions of his day, those between feelings and thoughts and between reason and sensory data.

In 1770, at the age of forty-six, Kant was appointed to the chair in logic and metaphysics at the University, after teaching for fifteen years as an unsalaried lecturer. When Kant was finally promoted, he gradually extended the scope of his lectures to include anthropology, rational theology, pedagogy, natural right, and even mineralogy and military fortifications. In order to inaugurate his new position, Kant also wrote one more Latin dissertation: *Concerning the Form and Principles of the Sensible and Intelligible World* (1770), which is known as the Inaugural Dissertation.

In this work, Kant was the first to reject the rationalist view that sensibility (emotion) is only a confused sense of intellectual cognition, and he replaced this with his own view that sensibility is distinct from understanding and brings to perception its own subjective forms of space. Sensibility gives us access to the sensible world, while understanding enables us to grasp a distinct intelligible world. In this paper, Kant rejects the view of Hume that moral judgments are based on feelings of pleasure or pain. He contends that moral judgments are based on pure understanding alone.

After 1770, Kant always held that emotions and thoughts are distinct ways of knowing, that space and time are subjective forms of human sensibility, and that moral judgments are based on reason alone.

Kant is considered the first of the Germany Idealists, a long tradition that ends with Hegel. Kant was considered a *transcendental idealist*, whereas Hegel was considered an *absolute idealist*. Idealism, itself is a belief that only mental entities are real, so that physical things exist only in the sense that they are perceived. Berkeley defended his "immaterialism" on purely empiricist grounds, while Kant and Fichte arrived at theirs by transcendental arguments. German, English, and (to a lesser degree) American philosophy during the nineteenth century was dominated by the absolute idealism of Hegel, and later Bradley and Royce.[321]

In 1781, after a decade of work, Kant published his masterpiece *Critique of Pure Reason*. Among the major books that rapidly followed were the *Groundwork of the Metaphysics of Morals* (1785), Kant's main work on the fundamental principle of morality; the *Metaphysical Foundations of Natural Science* (1786), his main work on natural philosophy in what scholars call his critical period (1781–1798); the second and substantially revised edition of the *Critique of Pure Reason* (1787); the *Critique of Practical Reason* (1788), a fuller discussion of topics in moral philosophy that builds on (and in some ways revises) the *Groundwork*; and the *Critique of the Power of Judgment* (1790), which deals with aesthetics and teleology. Kant also published a number of important essays in this period.

With these works Kant secured international fame and came to dominate German philosophy in the late 1780s. It was only a few years after the United States gained its freedom from England.

Kant retired from teaching in 1796. For nearly two decades, he had lived a highly disciplined life focused primarily on completing his philosophical system, which began to take definite shape in his mind only in middle age. After retiring, he came to believe that there was a gap in this system separating the metaphysical foundations of natural science from physics itself, and he set out to close this gap in a series of notes that postulate the existence of an *ether* or "caloric matter." These notes, known as the *Opus Postumum*, remained unfinished and unpublished in Kant's lifetime. Interestingly, scholars disagree on their significance and relation to his earlier work. They postulate that these notes show unmistakable signs of Kant's mental decline, which became tragically precipitous around 1800. Kant died February 12, 1804, just short of his eightieth birthday. From Prabhat Rainjan Sarkar's presentation of a universal ideology, which is the subject of Book II of this trilogy, ether is the first and most subtle material factor to condense within the field of macrocosmic conscious vibration. As such, it appears that Kant was on the verge of linking universal mental and physical reality but was not yet able to do so. His critics still do not understand what he was attempting to do, or why he was concerned with ether (space).

Kant remains a central figure in the evolution of modern Western philosophy. His life's work was to synthesize early modern rationalism and empiricism which, as we have seen, constituted the great divide between western philosophers ever since intellectuals broke completely from religious constraints and established a secular discourse. Kant set the basis for much of nineteenth and twentieth century philosophy, especially in the fields of metaphysics, epistemology, ethics, political philosophy, and aesthetics.

More than any other philosopher leading up to his time, Kant did the most to elucidate the tenets of a universal ideology. His attempt to synthesize rational thought and sensory data led him to develop a worldview that, as mentioned above, closely corresponds to Sarkar's universal ideology. Let us take a look now at what Kant discovered.

At the age of forty-six, Kant was engaged in the fundamental problem of the connection between sensory perception and rational conception, which are related but very different processes. This problem concerns itself with how human knowledge is derived.

In his attempt to resolve this contradiction, Kant argued that sense data is purely subjective without first being processed by pure reason. On the other hand, reason without testing it by experience only leads to theoretical illusions. Kant hoped to move beyond what he took to be failures of traditional philosophy and metaphysics. He attempted to put an end to what he considered an era of futile and speculative theories of human experience.

Kant believed that the concepts of *space* and *time* are integral to all human experience, as are our concepts of *cause* and *effect*. One important consequence of this view is that one never has *direct* experience of things, the so-called *noumenal* world (a thing as it is, independent of the mind). Rather we only experience the *phenomenal* world, which is what is conveyed by our senses.

By the time of Kant, the development of the natural sciences had led to an understanding of how data reaches the brain. Sunlight falls upon a distant object, whereupon light is reflected from various parts of the object in a way that maps the surface features (color, texture, etc.) of the object. The light reaches the eye of a human observer, passes through the cornea, is focused by the lens upon the retina where it forms an image similar to that formed by light passing through a pinhole into a camera obscura. The retinal cells next send impulses through the optic nerve and thereafter they form a mapping in the brain of the visual features of the distant object. The interior mapping is not the exterior thing being mapped. But yet, to Kant's contemporaries their belief that there is a meaningful relationship between the exterior object and the mapping in the brain depends on a chain of reasoning that was not fully grounded.

Kant saw that the mind could not function as an empty container that simply receives data from the outside. Something must be giving order to the incoming data. Images of external objects must be kept in the same sequence in which they were received. This ordering occurs through the mind's perception of *time*. The same considerations apply to the mind's function of constituting *space* for ordering mappings of visual and tactile signals arriving via the already described chains of physical causation.

Kant asserted that *experience* is based both upon the perception of external objects and *a priori* (previous) knowledge. The external world provides those things that we *perceive* through our senses. It is our mind, though, that processes this information about the world and gives it order, allowing us to *conceive* or comprehend it. Our mind supplies the conditions of space and time in order for us to experience objects. According to the "transcendental unity of apperception," the concepts of the mind (understanding) and the perceptions that garner information from phenomena (sensibility) are synthesized by comprehension. Without the concepts, perceptions are nondescript; without perceptions, concepts are meaningless—thus the famous statement, "Thoughts without content are empty, perceptions without concepts are blind."[322]

Kant also makes the claim that an external environment is necessary for the establishment of the *self*. Although Kant wanted to argue that there is no empirical way of observing the self, we can see the logical necessity of the self when we observe that we can have different perceptions of the external environment over time. By uniting all of these general representations into one global representation, we can see how the idea of a transcendental self emerges. "I am therefore conscious of the identical self in regard to the manifold of the representations that are given to me in an intuition because I call them all together my representations."[323] Thus an individual will believe they are the same being at three years old, twenty years old or sixty years old.

Kant asserted that, because of the limits of argumentation in the absence of irrefutable evidence, no one could really know whether there is a God and an afterlife or not. Nonetheless, for the sake of morality and as a ground for reason, Kant asserted, people are justified in believing in God, even though they could never know God's presence empirically. He explained:

> All the preparations of reason, therefore, in what may be called pure philosophy, are in reality directed to those three problems only [God, the soul, and freedom]. However, these three elements in themselves still hold independent, proportional, objective weight individually. Moreover, in a collective relational context; namely, to know *what ought to be done*: if the will is free, if there is a God, and if there is a future world. As

> this concerns our actions with reference to the highest aims of life, we see that the ultimate intention of nature in her wise provision was really, in the constitution of our reason, directed to moral interests only.[324]

Kant's teachings placed the active, rational human subject, i.e., the "I-feeling," at the center of the cognitive and moral worlds. He argued that the rational order of the world as known by science was not just the fortuitous accumulation of sense perceptions.

Conceptual integration is carried out by the mind through "categories of the understanding" (concepts) operating on the perceptual world, within space and time, which are not concepts, but are forms of sensory knowledge that are *a priori* necessary conditions for any possible experience. Thus, the objective order of nature and the causal necessity that operates within it are dependent upon the mind's processes that Kant called, "synthesis" rather than analysis.

The notion of the "thing in itself," i.e., a thing independent of the mind's interpretation of it, was much discussed by those who came after Kant. The German Idealists argued that since the "thing in itself" was unknowable, its existence could not simply be assumed. Another group arose to ask how our presumably reliable accounts of a coherent and rule-abiding universe were actually grounded. This new kind of philosophy became known as Phenomenology, and its founder was Edmund Husserl.

According to the modern philosopher, P. R. Sarkar, as we shall see in Book 2, *Universal Ideology*, the "thing in itself" exists in the mind of the Macrocosmic consciousness, whereas an individual's interpretation of it exists within the mind of the unit consciousness. This duality between the internal and external realities exists until the unit I-feeling transcends its limited definition of itself and merges with the Cosmic I. Ultimately there is no inside, nor outside. It is all consciousness. Everything that is, exists in the macrocosmic mind of God.

Kant believed that morality does not exist outside of the mind, but rather is a product of the good will of the individual. He believed that a good will is one that acts in accordance with a universal moral law that the individual chooses to live by. This law obliges one to treat humanity as an *end in itself* rather than as *means to other ends* that the individual might hold. To act morally depends upon practical self-reflection in which we universalize our reasons. This analysis is close to Sarkar's in that it assumes a universal moral law. If people act according to it, they reflect morality, if not, they lack morality. However, for Sarkar, morality is the foundation of spiritual practice while Kant had no concept of spirituality. Sarkar would agree with Kant that morality entails appreciating people and things for what they are, without calculating how to manipulate them. According to Kant it requires "self-reflection" to develop this sense of morality. For Sarkar, it also requires spiritual practice. While it can be argued that these two requirements are the same, spiritual practice leads to an expanded definition of the self, whereas this is not apparent in Kant's thinking.

Kant believed that if an action is not done with the motive of duty, then it is without moral value. He thought that every action should have pure intention behind it; otherwise it was meaningless. He did not necessarily believe that the final result was the most important aspect of an action, but that how the person felt while carrying out the action determined the value of the result. This is also true for Sarkar. It is the intention of an act, either good or bad, that creates one's karma.

For Kant, everything has either a *price* or a *dignity*. Whatever has a price can be replaced by something else as its equivalent; on the other hand, whatever is above all price, and therefore admits of no equivalent, has a dignity. That which constitutes the condition of being an end in itself has more than mere relative worth, i.e., price. It also has an intrinsic worth, i.e., a dignity. This same observation caused Sarkar to write that all life has a utilitarian value as well as an existential value. One can put a price on the use of something, but its existence reflects its inherent dignity, that is above price.

Kant did not give a lot of time or thought to political philosophy. If he had his druthers, he wanted to see a world of constitutional republics based upon a law that sought eternal peace. There is nothing new here. He was, however, clearly opposed to democracy, believing that majority rule posed a threat to individual liberty. He stated, " . . . democracy is, properly speaking, necessarily a despotism, because it establishes an executive power in which 'all' decide for or even against one who does not agree; that is, 'all,' who are not quite all, decide, and this is a contradiction of the general will with itself and with freedom."[325] As with most writers at the time, he distinguished three forms of government i.e., democracy, aristocracy, and monarchy with mixed government as the most ideal form of it. He did not discuss, however, how individual liberty could be realized within a social system.

Kant's influence on Western thought has been profound. Over and above his influence on specific thinkers, Kant changed the framework within which philosophical inquiry had been carried out. He accomplished a paradigm shift that consisted in several closely related innovations that have become axiomatic in philosophy as well as in the social sciences and humanities. These are:

- He bridged the contradiction between the rationalists and the empiricists by postulating that objective experience is actively constituted or constructed by the functioning of the human mind;
- He placed the role of the human subject or knower at the center of inquiry into our knowledge, such that it is impossible to philosophize about things as they are independently of us or of how they are for us;
- His invention of critical philosophy that allowed philosophers to discover and systematically explore possible inherent limits to our ability to know through philosophical reasoning;
- His creation of the concept of "conditions of possibility", that things, knowledge, and forms of consciousness rest on prior conditions that make them possible, so that, to understand them, we must first understand these conditions. This is similar to the concept of karma;
- His notion that moral autonomy is central to humanity; and

- His assertion that human beings should be treated as ends rather than as means[326]

Kant's philosophy became known as Transcendental Idealism because he reasoned that knowing requires a subject-based component (the I-feeling) rather than just an activity that directly comprehends the things as they are in themselves.[327] In other words, the will or the doer requires an I-feeling to validate its actions. This I-feeling for philosophers, prior to Kant, did not exist and was thus considered "transcendental" to the actual experience of knowledge.

The reason that we made several comparisons between Kant's thinking and that of P. R. Sarkar is that we want to demonstrate that Kant synthesized the philosophical ideas of the West in his day in an attempt to create an all-encompassing vision of reality. In like manner, P. R. Sarkar, a contemporary philosopher, has attempted to synthesis the ideas of his day, which not only include the ideas of Western philosophy, but also Eastern philosophy, thereby addressing the relationships of the body, mind, and soul, as well as the relation of the individual to society, economically, politically, and culturally. His philosophy also includes ideas related to the individual's and society's relation to the Divine and the natural world. The value in having such a perspective is more than being able to have an interesting discussion on the evolution of ideas, rather the value in having a universal philosophy is that it provides us, as human beings, with a means by which we can overcome our divisive points of view and begin to act as a human society to solve our common problems of individual alienation, social disintegration, and environmental decline. Please consider the ideas of the philosophers that we will continue to discuss from this perspective. Do their ideas move us closer to enlightenment and human unity or do they only add to our general confusion.

Friedrich Schleiermacher (1768-1834)

Friedrich Daniel Ernst Schleiermacher was a German theologian, philosopher, and biblical scholar who attempted to synthesize the philosophies of the Enlightenment with Protestant Christianity. He became influential in the evolution of Higher Criticism or hermeneutics, which is the scientific method for analyzing historical texts, particularly the Bible and other scriptures. He is often called the "Father of Modern Liberal Theology."

As a theology student, Schleiermacher was a skeptic. He pursued an independent course of study that omitted the Old Testament. During his years as a student, he completely lost his faith in Christ and Christianity. Writing to his father, he said: "Alas! dearest father, if you believe that without this faith no one can attain to salvation in the next world, nor to tranquility in this—and such, I know, is your belief—oh! then pray to God to grant it to me, for to me it is now lost. I cannot believe that he who called himself the Son of Man was the true, eternal God; I cannot believe that his death was a vicarious atonement."[328]

Yet, while he confessed his lack of faith in private, he continued his education and graduated from the University of Halle. He now had the credentials to serve in the role of chaplain, pastor, or professor. After graduation, Schleiermacher became a tutor to a wealthy aristocratic family and immersed himself in the arts, sciences, and philosophy. Over the course of his life, he developed his philosophy of liberal theology.

While serving as a professor of theology at the University of Halle, he gained much attention for his ideas, despite being charged as an atheist or pietist. Schleiermacher took a prominent role in the foundation of the University of Berlin in 1810 and was given a theological chairmanship. He also became the secretary of the Prussian Academy of Sciences.

He played a prominent role in the reorganization of the Prussian church and advocated for the union of the Lutheran and Reformed (Calvinist) divisions of German Protestantism. This activism paved the way for the Prussian Union of Churches[329] that emerged in 1817 from a series of decrees by Frederick William III of Prussia. It became the biggest independent religious organization in the German Empire and later Weimar Germany with about eighteen million parishioners.[330]

In his Sunday sermons and class lectures, Schleiermacher addressed every branch of theology and philosophy, including the introduction to and interpretation of the New Testament, ethics, dogmatic and practical theology, church history, history of philosophy, psychology, dialectics, logic, metaphysics, politics, pedagogy, translation, and aesthetics.

In politics, Schleiermacher supported liberty and progress.

Schleiermacher's chief theological work is *Der christliche Glaube nach den Grundsätzen der evangelischen Kirche*, translated as the *Doctrine of Faith*. His fundamental idea is that it is one's feeling of absolute dependence on God, as described by Jesus, through the church, which is the source of theology and not creeds, scripture, or rationalistic understanding. His work describes this religious feeling as emanating from the soul in its relations to God. The aim of the work was to reform Protestant theology by putting an end to blind faith in miracles, as well as the superficiality of rationalism, and to deliver religion from dependence on temporal philosophy. Here, we see Schleiermacher striving to create a universal ideology free from the limits of religious rational thought.

Though the Doctrine of Faith added to the reputation of its author, it increased the rancor of the theological schools whose work he had just declared irrelevant. At the same time Schleiermacher's defense of the right of the church to frame its own liturgy in opposition to the arbitrary dictation of the monarch or his ministers added to his troubles. He felt isolated, although his church and his lecture-room continued to be crowded.

Schleiermacher spent the remainder of his life defending his theological position and died in 1834 from a bout of pneumonia.

Georg Hegel (1770-1831)

"We may affirm absolutely that nothing great in this world has been accomplished without passion."—*Lectures on the Philosophy of World History*

Georg Wilhelm Friedrich Hegel was a major figure in German Idealism. His holistic approach to philosophy revolutionized European thought and was an important precursor to Marxism.

Hegel developed a method to understand the relationship between opposing forces in a dynamic manner, rather than seeing them as fixed polar opposites. He saw that opposites, by continual contact, interpenetrate each other and in doing so change into each other, bringing each to a higher synthesis. This process became known as *dialectics*. With such a methodology, he examined the relation of mind and nature, the subject and object of knowledge, and the contradictions in psychology, the state, history, art, religion, and philosophy. He believed all things develop in a dialectical fashion until they achieve their final synthesis, which is mergence with the Oneness. It was God, the Spirit, or Oneness that manifested itself in a set of contradictions (waves) that are ultimately integrated and reunited, without eliminating either pole or reducing one to the other. By applying his dialectical method to all aspects of thought and nature, Hegel was able to develop a comprehensive system where the Absolute's creative process is explained through its own internal dynamics. In this work, Hegel provided a precursor to Sarkar's creation theory by grasping the general outline of the movement of the universe from *subtle to crude* (consciousness into matter) and *crude to subtle* (the evolution of matter to reflect greater consciousness). Hegel failed however to describe the relationship between brain and mind, mind and unit consciousness, or the relation of absolute consciousness to any of these manifestations. Thereby his genius did not receive the credit it deserved, but rather it was rejected by both the left and the right in his day.

Hegel was born in Stuttgart Germany and baptized Georg Wilhelm Friedrich. His close family knew him as Wilhelm. His father, Georg Ludwig, was secretary to the revenue office at the court of Karl Eugen, Duke of Württemberg. Hegel's mother, Maria Magdalena Louisa, was the daughter of a lawyer at the High Court of Justice at the Württemberg court. She died of a "bilious fever" when Hegel was thirteen. Hegel and his father also caught the disease but narrowly survived. Hegel had a sister, Christiane Luise (1773–1832), and a brother, Georg Ludwig (1776–1812), who died as an officer in Napoleon's Russian campaign of 1812.

Hegel studied Latin from the time he was five years old. He attended Stuttgart's Gymnasium Illustre (high school) in 1776, the same year as the founding of the United States. During his adolescence, Hegel was a voracious reader. His high school graduation speech was entitled, "The abortive state of art and scholarship in Turkey."

At the age of eighteen, Hegel entered a Protestant seminary attached to the University of Tübingen, where he met two fellow students, the future poet Friedrich Hölderlin and philosopher Friedrich Wilhelm Joseph Schelling. Sharing a dislike for the restrictive religious environment of the seminary, the three became close friends and mutually influenced each other's ideas. All greatly admired Hellenic civilization and, additionally, Hegel steeped himself in Rousseau and Lessing during this time.

Having received his theological certificate from the Tübingen Seminary, Hegel became a tutor to an aristocratic family in Bern and then to a wine merchant's family in Frankfurt. Afterward, he took a job as an unsalaried professor at the University of Jena. Money was scarce.

Hegel was working on his book, the *Phenomenology of Spirit*, when Napoleon engaged the Prussian troops on October 14, 1806, in the Battle of Jena in which Hegel was now living. On the day before the battle, Napoleon entered the city of Jena. Hegel recounted his impressions in a letter to a friend:

> I saw the Emperor – this world-soul – riding out of the city on reconnaissance. It is indeed a wonderful sensation to see such an individual, who, concentrated here at a single point, astride a horse, reaches out over the world and masters it . . . this extraordinary man, whom it is impossible not to admire.[331]

Although Napoleon chose not to close down the University of Jena as he had other universities, the city was devastated and students deserted the university in droves, making Hegel's financial prospects even worse.

Following some teaching jobs and the publication of his *Phenomenology of Spirit* in 1808 and his *Science of Logic* in 1812, Hegel received offers of a post from the Universities of Erlangen, Berlin, and Heidelberg. Hegel chose Heidelberg, where he moved in 1816. He published *The Encyclopedia of the Philosophical Sciences in Outline* (1817) as a summary of his philosophy for students attending his lectures at Heidelberg.

In 1818, Hegel accepted the renewed offer of the chair of philosophy at the University of Berlin, which had remained vacant since Johann Gottlieb Fichte's death in 1814. Here he published his *Philosophy of Right* (1821). Hegel devoted himself primarily to delivering his lecture courses on aesthetics, the philosophy of religion, the philosophy of history, and the history of philosophy. His fame spread and his lectures attracted students from all over Germany and beyond.

Hegel was appointed Rector of the University in 1830, when he was sixty. In August 1831, a cholera epidemic reached Berlin and by November 14 of that year Hegel was dead.[332]

Hegel's contribution to universal ideology is that he created a holistic philosophy taking life as a process and not as a static entity. He took Kant's dualism regarding nature vs freedom (thesis vs antithesis) and synthesized them within "Spirit".

Although Hegel had many publications, his most significant thinking is expressed in four books: the *Phenomenology of Spirit* (or *Phenomenology of Mind*), his account of the evolution of consciousness from sense-perception to absolute knowledge, published in 1807; the *Science of Logic*, the logical and metaphysical core of his philosophy, in three volumes, published in 1812, 1813, and 1816; *Encyclopedia of the Philosophical Sciences*, a summary of his entire philosophical system, which was originally published in 1816 and revised in 1827 and 1830; and the *Elements of the Philosophy of Right*, his political philosophy, published in 1822. He also published some articles early in his career and during his Berlin period. A number of other works on the philosophy of history, religion, aesthetics, and the history of philosophy were compiled from the lecture notes of his students and published posthumously.[333]

Hegel forwarded the work of previous philosophers of Idealism (the world is a mental creation) and synthesized their positions. His thinking, which became known as Absolute Idealism is a philosophy that deals with the subject of being and existence (ontology),[334] while positing a single source for everything (monism).[335] That source is God.

Absolute idealism is the attempt to demonstrate the unity between human consciousness (the subjective I-feeling) and the world (objective reality) using a new method which required new concepts and rules of logic. According to Hegel, the absolute ground of being is essentially a dynamic, historical process that unfolds by itself in the form of increasingly complex forms of being and of consciousness, ultimately giving rise to all the diversity in the world and in the concepts with which we think and make sense of the world. This belief essentially undergirds the science of evolution.

Hegel's science of logic follows the same dialectical method found in all of his other writings because, for Hegel, it is the structure of all being. Thus, what Hegel means by logic is very different from the conventional meaning of the term that expresses static formal laws of thinking because his intention was to elucidate the unfolding of reality as conscious thought. In Chapter 3 of Book 2, we will see this concept echoed in the philosophy of P. R. Sarkar.

For Hegel, we understand the world not as something static, but rather dynamic. Thus, there was a need to create a method to understand motion, i.e., dialectics. Thoughts, things, and history all follow the law of dialectics. In the *Phenomenology of Spirit*, Hegel presents a history of human consciousness as a journey through stages of explanations of the world. Each successive explanation creates problems and oppositions within itself, leading to tensions, which can only be overcome by adopting a view that could accommodate these oppositions in a higher unity. Thus, at the base of social consciousness lies rational development. This means that the absolute itself (God) is exactly that rational development. The assertion that "All reality is spirit" means that all of reality rationally orders itself and while doing so creates the oppositions we find in it.

Hegel created dialectics as a means to describe motion. In this method, the *thesis* is a thing in-itself, the second stage is the direct opposite, the annihilation, or at least the subsuming, of the first. It is the *antithesis* or the thing out of itself. The third stage, the *synthesis*, is the first stage returned to itself in a higher, truer, richer, and fuller form. The three stages are, therefore, styled:

- in itself (*An-sich*) (thesis)
- out of itself (*Anderssein*) (antithesis)
- in and for itself (*An-und-für-sich*) (synthesis)

These three stages describe the process of motion that characterizes all thought and being.[336]

The aim of Hegel was to show that the world is not other than us. Rather, both the mind and the world are ordered according to the same rational principles. In this way, Hegel created security in the fact that we can know God, which had been lost to philosophers since Kant's position that the Oneness was ultimately inaccessible.[337]

In essence, what Hegel was saying is that all things are forms of consciousness that dissolve again into consciousness. In a similar way, the waves of an ocean dissolve back into the ocean. Finite and particular forms dissolve into absolute consciousness. And the means by which they do this is through the dialectical method, or laws of motion.
Hegel went further than any previous philosopher in the development of a universal ideology. He developed a system that incorporated spirit, logic, nature, history, political thought, morality, and religion.

Like Sarkar, he views relative reality as an active process rather than as a static entity. Yet, where Sarkar is concerned with the relation of the individual to the Absolute, Hegel ignores the singularity of each person, place, or thing that complements and/or conflicts with others, and sees the achievement of unity only within the historical process. Whereas, he shares the macro analysis of Sarkar, he does not understand the dynamics between the absolute and the individual. Hegel's vision is also an idealistic and rationalistic approach that does not incorporate sense data or the material condition into his analysis, as does Sarkar's ideology.

In his thinking, Hegel was influenced by the writings of Jakob Böhme, a German Lutheran mystic, who lived from 1575 to 1624 about one hundred years after Luther. Bohme had mystical visions that he believed revealed to him the spiritual structure of the world, as well as the relationship between God and man and good and evil. At the time of his visions, fearing reprisal, he chose not to speak of his experience openly. Yet, Böhme wrote about his experiences. He believed that the Fall of Man was a necessary stage in the evolution of the universe,[338] while the process of evolution was the result of God's desire for complete self-awareness that was now fragmented in psycho-physical forms. When Bohme's writings became known, they were considered scandalous and Böhme was forced to leave town.

"Mind" and "Spirit" are the common English translations of Hegel's use of the German "Geist." Geist combines the meaning of spirit—as in god, ghost or mind—with an intentional force. In Hegel's early philosophy of nature (draft manuscripts written during his time at the University of Jena), Hegel's notion of "Geist" was tightly bound to the notion of "Aether" from which he also derived the concepts of space and time; however, in his later works (after Jena), Hegel did not explicitly use his old notion of "Aether" any more.[339] Here we see that Hegel did not make a clear distinction between mind and unit consciousness (spirit) that is required by Sarkar. It is interesting, however, that, like Kant, Hegel felt it necessary to explore the idea of ether, in order to determine a transition stage between the mental and physical stratum. But like Kant, he also gave up on determining the role of ether in the creation of the manifest universe.

Hegel also shares Sarkar's idea of the relationship of mind and external objects. Central to Hegel's conception of mind (and therefore also of reality) was that the mind externalizes itself in various forms and objects that stand outside of it or opposed to it, and that, through recognizing itself in them, is "with itself" in these external manifestations. Consequently "external" objects are simultaneously mind and other-than-mind. This notion of identity in difference, which is intimately bound up with his conception of contradiction, is a principal feature differentiating Hegel's thought from other philosophers. Hegel, however, did not have a concept of karma. According to Sarkar, objects perceived by the mind are defined by one's karma. We are predisposed to see an object in a certain way because of our past experiences. Sarkar would agree with Hegel that objects, so long as a mind is governed by karma, will be both mind and other-than-mind. Only in overcoming karma will this duality between subject and object, between internal and external reality, be resolved.

Many philosophers challenged Hegel's focus on God. He is seen as offering a metaphysico-religious view of God *qua* "Absolute Spirit," as the ultimate reality that we can come to know through pure thought processes alone. In short, Hegel's philosophy is treated as exemplifying the type of pre-critical or "dogmatic" metaphysics against which Kant had reacted in his *Critique of Pure Reason*, and as a return to a more religiously driven conception of philosophy to which Kant had been opposed.

Insofar as Hegel's contribution to political philosophy is concerned, in his *Elements of the Philosophy of Right*, he made a valuable distinction between civil society and state. In this work, the dialectic between civil society and the state centered on the relationship of the state and the family. Political order has its origins in family life, in which the basic needs of all individuals are served by mutual feeling, without any formal principle of organization. The antithesis to this is civil life, in which the incorporation of many more individual units often leads to a system of purely formal regulation of conduct, demanded by law without any emotional bond. The synthesis of the two, then, is the State, whose purpose, Hegel believed, was to unite society into a sort of civil family, organized in legal fashion, but bound together by a profound emotional sense of devotion.

According to Hegel, then, the modern nation must serve as an actualization of the self-conscious ethical will of a people (*Völk*). Although this sounds something like *Rousseau's* general will, Hegel's version puts all of the emphasis on the collective expression of what is best for the people rather than on each individual's capacity to discover it for herself or himself. This view of the state fit well with the rise of modern nationalism in Europe during the nineteenth century, where the national spirit (*Völkergeist*) of each group emerged distinctively from every other.[340]

While most people ridiculed Hegel for his interpretation of the state, they found his concept of "civil society" to be more useful. As such, it became defined from a left-wing and right-wing perspective. To the left, Karl Marx's used the term to define society's economic base; to the right, it became a description for all non-state aspects of society, including culture, society, and politics.

Today the term "civil society" is used by the left to define people's organizations and movements as opposed to the functions of government agencies. This wide range of interpretations was due to the fact that Hegel's distinction, as to what he meant by civil society, was largely unclear.

The weakest part of Hegel's system is his writings on society. According to Hegel, it is through the *state* that the Spirit returns into itself at the level of institutions. Ethics and right culminate in the state as the concrete manifestation of the Spirit through human interaction. But first, on the level of law, Hegel deals with the notion of crime and punishment. Punishment is seen as the negation of the crime and Hegel even states that the criminal implicitly calls for his punishment as the logical outcome of his crime. This law is then internalized in conscience on the level of morality. This morality then is manifested at the successive levels of family, society, and state.

Hegel's emphasis on the state has the connotation of oppression. He looked at national wars as necessary and inevitable in the process by which one state negates another to drive history forward. He also considered the German people to be the first to achieve the full awareness of the freedom of the human spirit.[341] By placing human institutions above human beings, Hegel showed his ignorance of how the individual achieves liberation. Freedom of the human spirit can never be achieved at a state level, or any group level. It is a personal, and thus a subjective experience.

Despite Hegel's detractors, his influence was immense both within philosophy and in the other sciences. Throughout the nineteenth century many chairs of philosophy around Europe were held by Hegelians. Søren Kierkegaard, Ludwig Feuerbach, Karl Marx, and Friedrich Engels, among many others, were all deeply influenced by, but also strongly opposed to, many of the central themes of Hegel's philosophy. After less than a generation, Hegel's philosophy was suppressed and even banned by the Prussian right-wing and was firmly rejected by the left-wing in multiple official writings.

Hegel's influence did not make itself felt again until the philosophy of British Idealism and the twentieth century Hegelian Western Marxism that began with György Lukács. The more recent movement of communitarianism also has a strong Hegelian influence.

In conclusion, Hegel made a large leap in Western philosophy toward the description of a universal ideology. He declared that the inner movement of reality is the process of God's imagination manifested in the evolution of the universe. Hegel argued that when fully and properly understood, "reality" is something that is continually being thought by God and understood by individuals in their comprehension of this process. Since human thought is the image and fulfillment of God's thought, God is not ineffable (so incomprehensible as to be unutterable), but can be understood by an analysis of thought and reality. As humans continually correct their concepts of reality through a dialectical process, so God himself becomes more fully manifested through the dialectical process of becoming. This principle underlies the author's presentation of history insofar as humans can be seen evolving as our definition of the Divine expands and becomes more subjective. We will return to this discussion of evolution and the divine in Chapter 3 of Book 2.

The uniqueness of Hegel in the history of Western thought is that, while he remained an Idealist, he changed his conception of reality from a static (metaphysical) view to a dynamic (dialectical) view. This is to say that instead of seeing reality as a system of fixed eternal principles, he began to see it as a process. To Hegel, Reality was the self-unfolding of the Absolute Idea from God to his creation and the return into Himself again.

Hegel, we may say, was the culmination of what some have called "The Great Tradition" or the doctrine of the establishment. Throughout the entire Middle Ages, and reaching into the nineteenth century of the modern era, the orthodox segments of European society, i.e., the Church, the King, and the nobility, insisted on the unquestioned acceptance of a Christian heritage which, when applied to the political realm, meant two things: (1) a divinely sanctioned monarchy, and (2) a "natural law" based on "reason" that, in a word, kept the class domination of the priest class and the aristocracy intact. In Hegel's day, this tradition was alive in the formation of the nation-state and in a system based on reason. The theologians and philosophers who amplified this Great Tradition had not yet realized, however, that the old ruling class was being rapidly replaced by the emergence of the new class of wealthy merchants. This observation, and the consequences thereof would not be fully appreciated until the coming of Karl Marx who was thirteen years old when Hegel died.

Arthur Schopenhauer (1788-1860)

Arthur Schopenhauer was a German philosopher best known for his book, *The World as Will and Representation* in which he claimed that our world is driven by a dissatisfied will, continually seeking satisfaction. Influenced by Eastern philosophy, he maintained that the "truth was recognized by the sages of India";[342] consequently, his solutions to suffering were similar to those of Vedantic and Buddhist thinkers (e.g., asceticism). The influence of Kant's "transcendental idealism" led him to choose atheism.[343]

Arthur Schopenhauer was born on February 22, 1788, in the city of Danzig (currently Gdańsk), the son of Heinrich Floris Schopenhauer and Johanna Schopenhauer, both descendants of wealthy German patrician families. When he was five years old, Danzig became part of Prussia and Heinrich removed his family to Hamburg.

Schopenhauer became a student at the University of Göttingen in 1809. There he studied metaphysics and psychology and concentrated on Plato and Immanuel Kant. In Berlin, from 1811 to 1812, he attended lectures by the prominent post-Kantian philosopher Johann Gottlieb Fichte and the theologian Friedrich Schleiermacher. Fichte was the father of German Idealism. He introduced new thinking about the "I-feeling" and the nature of self-consciousness.[344] Freidrich Schleiermacher, as we have seen above, introduced liberal theology.

In 1814, at the age of twenty-six, Schopenhauer began his seminal work, *The World as Will and Representation* (*Die Welt als Wille und Vorstellung*). At the time, his professor, Johann Fichte was wrestling with the problem of the feeling of "I am" or self-consciousness. He had dedicated his studies to the topic of "I do," which is the feeling of the will or ego; i.e., individual motivation was his principle topic of study.

Before Schopenhauer, Hegel had popularized the concept of *Zeitgeist*, the idea that society consisted of a collective consciousness, which moved in a distinct direction, dictating the actions of its members. Schopenhauer, a reader of both Kant and Hegel, criticized their logic and the belief that individual morality could be determined by society and reason. Schopenhauer believed that humans were motivated by only their own basic desires, or *Wille zum Leben* ("Will to Live"), which directed all of mankind.[345]

For Schopenhauer, human desire was futile, illogical, directionless, and, by extension, so was all human action in the world. The Will was a malignant, metaphysical existence which controlled not only the actions of individuals, but also, ultimately, all observable phenomena; an evil to be terminated via mankind's duties: asceticism and chastity.[346] He is credited with one of the most famous opening lines of philosophy: "The world is my representation".

According to Schopenhauer, whenever we make a choice, "we assume as necessary that decision was preceded by something from which it ensued, and which we call the ground or reason, or more accurately the motive, of the resultant action."[347] Therefore, choices are not made freely. Our actions are necessary and determined because "every human being, even every animal, after the motive has appeared, must carry out the action which alone is in accordance with his inborn and immutable character."[348] Here we see Schopenhauer touching on the topic of karma, although he was not influenced directly by this teaching. Nor, according to the law of karma is character immutable.

Schopenhauer believed that willful criminal acts should be punished by the state, so that the state must be able to exercise a specific punishment for every kind of criminal act. He believed in capital punishment, asserting: "For safeguarding the lives of citizens, capital punishment is therefore absolutely necessary." The murderer, his life, his person, must be the *means* of fulfilling the law, and thus of re-establishing public security."[349]

His strong support of the state as a punishing entity stemmed from his belief that people cannot be improved. They can only be influenced by strong motives that overpower criminal motives. Schopenhauer declared that, "real moral reform is not at all possible, but only determined from the deed. . . ."[350] Here we see Schopenhauer reflecting the Calvinist perspective of man's inherent depravity.

Schopenhauer's moral theory proposed that only compassion can drive moral acts. Compassion alone is the good of the object of the acts, that is, acts cannot be inspired by either the prospect of personal utility or the feeling of duty. Mankind can also be guided by egoism and malice. Egotistic acts are those guided by self-interest, desire for pleasure or happiness. Acts of malice are different from egotistic acts in that their aim is to cause damage to others, independent of personal gains.

Schopenhauer's understanding of the Will was incompatible with belief in God. He rejected the dogmas of Christianity and hypothesized that if God existed, he would be evil. The "Last Judgment" is no longer preceded by anything—"the world is itself the Last Judgment on it." Whereas God, if he existed, would have no other purpose in creating life than for his own evil amusement.

Schopenhauer finished his chief work in 1818 and published it the following year. In 1820, he became a lecturer at the University of Berlin. He scheduled his lectures to coincide with those of Hegel's whom Schopenhauer described as a "clumsy charlatan."[351] However, only five students turned up to Schopenhauer's lectures, and he dropped out of academia.

In 1831, a cholera epidemic broke out in Berlin and Schopenhauer left the city. He settled permanently in Frankfurt in 1833, where he remained for the next twenty-seven years, living alone. The numerous notes that he made during these years, amongst others on aging, were published posthumously under the title *Senilia*.

Schopenhauer had a robust constitution, but in 1860 his health began to deteriorate. He died of heart failure on September 21, 1860 while sitting at home on his couch with his cat. He was seventy-two.

Schopenhauer believed that apart from the ancient Hindus and Egyptians, the highest civilizations and cultures are found exclusively among the white races. All this is due to the fact that necessity is the mother of invention because those tribes that emigrated early to the north, and there gradually became white, had to develop all their intellectual powers and invent and perfect all the arts in their struggle with need, want, and misery, which in their many forms were brought about by the climate. This they had to do in order to make up for the parsimony of nature and out of it all came their high civilization.[352]

While some called Schopenhauer a racist for this analysis, he was not devoid of brotherly love. In fact, he was adamantly against differing treatment of races, was fervently anti-slavery, and supported the abolitionist movement in the United States. He describes the treatment of "[our] innocent black brothers whom force and injustice have delivered into [the slave-master's] devilish clutches" as "belonging to the blackest pages of mankind's criminal record."[353]

Schopenhauer was very concerned about the welfare of animals.[354] For him, all individual animals, including humans, are essentially the same, being phenomenal manifestations of the one underlying Will. The word "will" designated, for him, force, power, impulse, energy, and desire; it is the closest word we have that can signify both the real essence of all external things and also our own direct, inner experience. Since everything is basically Will, then humans and animals are fundamentally the same and can recognize themselves in each other. For this reason, he claimed that a good person would have sympathy for animals, who are our fellow sufferers.

Compassion for animals is intimately associated with goodness of character, and it may be confidently asserted that he who is cruel to living creatures cannot be a good man.[355]

Schopenhauer read the Latin translation of the Upanishads. He was so impressed by their philosophy that he called them "the production of the highest human wisdom," and considered them to contain superhuman conceptions. The Upanishads were a great source of inspiration to Schopenhauer and in writing about them he said:

> It is the most satisfying and elevating reading (with the exception of the original text) which is possible in the world; it has been the solace of my life and will be the solace of my death.[356]

The Upanishads are a collection of texts in the Vedic Sanskrit language, which provide a synthesis of Aryan Vedas and Shiva Tantra. As such they contain some of the earliest revelation of the central concepts of yoga. These include rebirth, karma, liberation, ascetic techniques, and renunciation. These topics have entered into the religions of the East, particularly Hinduism, Buddhism, and Jainism. The Upanishads are sometimes referred to as *Vedanta* ("Last part of Veda"), but while the Vedas are concerned with the religious rituals of the Aryans, the Upanishads are an inquiry into the nature of Absolute Consciousness (Brahma).[357]

Schopenhauer also became familiar with Buddhism in later life and noted a similarity between his doctrines of the Will and the Four Noble Truths of Buddhism. In his first discourse after attaining enlightenment, the Buddha addressed four "noble" truths. These are:

1. Life is suffering (*dukkha*);
2. The cause of suffering is a desire for things outside ourselves (*samudaya*);
3. The extinction of desire leads to liberation (*nirhodha*); and
4. Desire is extinguished by spiritual practice (the eightfold path) (*magga*).[358]

Schopenhauer's thought corresponded to the first three truths of Buddha that life involves suffering, that suffering is caused by desire, and that the extinction of desire leads to liberation. Unfortunately, Schopenhauer did not take the important last step of being diligent in a spiritual practice. Thus, he remained only a philosopher and not a practitioner of the spiritual science.

Among ninteenth century philosophers, Arthur Schopenhauer was considered to be a thorough going pessimist. Yet, he did advocate that through artistic, moral, and ascetic forms of awareness, one could overcome a frustration-filled and fundamentally painful human condition. Since his death in 1860, his philosophy has had a special attraction for those who wonder about life's meaning, along with those engaged in music, literature, and the visual arts.[359]

Schopenhauer had a strong influence on the Russian novelist Leo Tolstoy, the German composer Richard Wagner, the German philosopher Friedrich Nietzsche, and the Argentine writer Jorge Luis Borges.[360]

As regard to Schopenhauer's understanding of a universal ideology, he shared certain ideas with P. R. Sarkar. These include the fact that suffering is caused by a thirst for limitlessness that tries to find fulfillment in psychological or material objects. Secondly, that people are controlled by a Will over which they have no control. Sarkar clarifies this contention, however, by demonstrating that the Will of Schopenhauer is not the same as one's karma, which governs one's actions despite one's rational intent. Karma is programming. The third truth that Schopenhauer touched upon, but misinterpreted, was that the Will does not derive from a good or evil God, but rather from one's own self-identified actions, which became the cause for consequent actions. This reality, however, is not incompatible with the existence of God, but rather constitutes a law inherent in the process of evolution. Ultimately God is not an evil entity, but a benevolent entity that uses cause and effect to goad individuals out of their complacency and seek a more subtle understanding of reality.

John Stewart Mill (1806-1873)

John Stuart Mill was a British philosopher and political economist. His fields of study were social theory, political theory, and political economy.

He has been called "the most influential English-speaking philosopher of the nineteenth century."[361] Mill became the champion of secular liberal ideology when he defined personal freedom in opposition to unlimited state control. He held that an individual's efforts for self-development and pursuit of greatness constituted true freedom. This attitude toward freedom and accomplishment through self-improvement inspired many people and became the bedrock of secular liberal thought. The virtues that one admired could be attained by efforts to improve oneself.[362]

Mills was the main proponent of *utilitarianism*, an ethical theory holding that the proper course of action is the one that maximizes utility, usually defined as maximizing total benefit and reducing suffering or the negatives. This theory led to an economic analysis that had a moral foundation and was human-centered rather than capital-centered. In utilitarianism, the moral worth of an action is determined only by its resulting consequences. According to Jeremy Bentham, who founded utilitarianism, "it is the greatest happiness of the greatest number that is the measure of right and wrong."

In *A System of Logic*, Mill's most comprehensive and systematic philosophical work, he presents his thoughts on inductive logic and the shortcomings of the use of syllogisms to advance deductive logic.[363] Syllogisms are arguments derived from general principles, in which two premises are used to deduce a conclusion. His insights helped refine the scientific method of inquiry, which remains the basis of empirical thought. To be termed scientific, the method of inquiry must be based on measurable evidence subject to specific principles of reasoning.[364] Simply stated, the steps of the scientific method are to:

1. Pose a Question;
2. Do Background Research;
3. Construct a Hypothesis;
4. Test Your Hypothesis by Doing an Experiment;
5. Analyze Your Data and Draw a Conclusion; and
6. Communicate Your Results.[365]

John Stuart Mill was born in London, the eldest son of the Scottish philosopher, historian, and economist James Mill, and Harriet Burrow.

John was educated by his father, with the advice and assistance of Jeremy Bentham. He was given an extremely rigorous upbringing and was deliberately shielded from association with children his own age other than his siblings. His father, a follower of Bentham, had as his explicit aim to create a genius intellect that would carry on the cause of utilitarianism and its implementation after he and Bentham had died.[366]

At the age of eight, Mill began studying Latin, the works of Euclid, and algebra and was appointed schoolmaster to the younger children of the family. His main reading was still history, but he went through all the commonly taught Latin and Greek authors and by the age of ten could read Plato and Demosthenes with ease. His father also thought that it was important for Mill to study and compose poetry. One of Mill's earliest poetry compositions was a continuation of the Iliad. In his spare time, he also enjoyed reading about natural sciences and popular novels, such as *Don Quixote* and *Robinson Crusoe*.[367]

By twelve, Mill was reading Aristotle and studying the economic writings of Adam Smith and David Ricardo. Ricardo, who was a close friend of his father, used to invite the young Mill to his house for a walk in order to talk about political economy.[368]

At the age of fourteen, he stayed in Paris for a few days in the house of the renowned economist Jean-Baptiste Say, another friend of Mill's father. There he met many leaders of the Liberal party, as well as other notable Parisians, including Henri Saint-Simon.

This intensive study, however, had injurious effects on Mill's mental health and state of mind. At the age of twenty he suffered a nervous breakdown. His depression eventually began to dissipate, as he began to find solace in the *Mémoires* of Jean-François Marmontel, a French civil servant who wrote about society under King Louis XV.[369] He also treasured the poetry of William Wordsworth, arguably the greatest of the English Romantic poets.[370]

As a nonconformist who refused to subscribe to the Thirty-Nine Articles of the Church of England, Mill was not eligible to study at the University of Oxford or the University of Cambridge. Instead, he followed his father to work for the East India Company until 1858 and attended University College in London. He was elected a Foreign Honorary Member of the American Academy of Arts and Sciences in 1856.

From 1865 to 1868, he was a Member of Parliament for City and Westminster and was associated with the Liberal Party. During his time as an MP, Mill advocated easing the burdens on Ireland. In 1866, he became the first person in the history of Parliament to call for women to be given the right to vote, vigorously defending this position in subsequent debates. Mill became a strong advocate of such social reforms as labor unions and farm cooperatives. In *Considerations on Representative Government*, Mill called for various reforms of Parliament and voting, especially proportional representation, the single transferable vote,[371] and the extension of suffrage.

In his views on religion, Mill was an atheist, having grown up without religious training.[372] Mill died in 1873 in Avignon, France. He was godfather to the philosopher Bertrand Russell.

In his most famous work, *On Liberty*, Mills addressed the nature and limits of power that can be legitimately exercised by society over the individual. His definition of liberty does not extend to all individuals and all societies. He states that, "Despotism is a legitimate mode of government in dealing with barbarians."[373] Therefore, Mills approved of colonialism, but was against slavery. Regarding colonialism, Mills thought that the best form of government for a colony was "benevolent despotism." This sort of pseudo-charitable outlook masked racist and nationalist sentiments (geo- and socio-sentiments) as well as feelings of superiority over other peoples. This pseudo-humanism has proven to be as contagious among the white liberal left as it has among the Christian right. It is a sort of thinking that overlooks the spiritual nature of most native peoples, that has, in many instances, proven more humanistic and reflective of universally morality than the so-called civilized societies in the West. It is a bankrupt view that provided the justification for the repressive economic policies of neo-liberalism.

Here we see the same limits of morality that has characterized many so-called liberal thinkers. For religious or secular intellectuals, morality only extends to one's group. Everyone or anything else is fair game for exploitation.

For Mill, the only legitimate reason that institutional power can be rightfully exercised over any member of a *civilized community*, against his will, is to prevent his harm to others. Over himself, over his own body and mind, the individual is sovereign. As we have seen, this principle did not apply to third world or conquered peoples or, for that matter, does it apply today to women or minorities in the United States.

Mill believed that it is acceptable to harm oneself as long as the person doing so is not harming others. However, because no one exists in isolation, harm done to oneself may also harm others, and destroying property deprives the community as well as oneself. Mill excuses young children and those living in "backward states of society" from this principle. Harm could be an act of omission or commission. For example, it was harmful to not help someone in need.

Mill was a strong proponent of free speech. He defended allowing people to air false opinions because he believed that people are more likely to abandon false opinions if ideas are exchanged in an open forum; and secondly, giving people the opportunity to re-examine and re-affirm their ideas kept ideas from declining into dogma. It is not enough for Mill that one simply has an unexamined belief that happens to be true; one must understand why the belief in question is the true one. Mill also eloquently argued that freedom of expression allows for personal growth and self-realization. He said that freedom of speech was a vital way to develop talents and realize a person's potential and creativity. He repeatedly said that eccentricity was preferable to uniformity and stagnation. Mill also held that vituperation on the side of prevailing opinion deterred people from expressing contrary beliefs and from listening to those who expressed them.

Mill believed that the struggle between Liberty and Authority is the most conspicuous feature of history. He defined "social liberty" as protection from "the tyranny of political rulers." He introduced different forms that tyranny can take and referred to them as social tyranny and tyranny of the majority, respectively.

Social liberty for Mill had to do with the power, which can be legitimately exercised by society over the individual. It could be realized through granting political liberties or rights and, secondly, by establishing a system of "constitutional checks."

Social liberty also implies putting limits on the ruler's power so that he would not be able to use his power based on his own wishes and make decisions which could harm society; in other words, people should have the right to have a say in the government's decisions. However, in Mill's view, limiting the power of government was not enough. He stated:

> "Society can and does execute its own mandates: and if it issues wrong mandates instead of right, or any mandates at all in things with which it ought not to meddle, it practices a social tyranny more formidable than many kinds of political oppression, since, though not usually upheld by such extreme penalties, it leaves fewer means of escape, penetrating much more deeply into the details of life, and enslaving the soul itself."[374]

Unfortunately, we do not know what Mr. Mill would have said about the corrosive propaganda of mainstream media.

Mill did prove to be a champion of women, so long as they were from a civilized society. He is considered among the earliest women's rights advocates. In *The Subjection of Women,* Mill attempted to prove that the legal subjugation of women is wrong and that it should give way to perfect equality. He talks about the role of women in marriage and how he felt it needed to be changed. Mill comments on three major facets of women's lives that he felt are hindering them: society and gender construction, education, and marriage. He felt that the oppression of women was one of the few remaining relics from ancient times, a set of prejudices that severely impeded the progress of humanity.

Regarding economic philosophy, Mills supported free markets and a flat tax because he believed that a progressive tax penalized those who worked harder and saved more and was therefore "a mild form of robbery."

Given an equal tax rate regardless of income, Mill agreed that inheritance should be taxed. A utilitarian society would agree that everyone should be equal one way or another. Therefore, receiving inheritance would put one ahead of society unless one was taxed on the inheritance.

Later, he altered his views toward a more socialist bent, adding chapters to his *Principles of Political Economy* in defense of a socialist outlook.[375] For example, he proposed that the whole wage system be abolished in favor of a co-operative wage system. This led Mill to promote economic democracy instead of capitalism. See Book IV, Chapter 5 in which he speaks of workers' cooperatives, peoples banks, etc. He says:

> The form of association, however, which if mankind continue to improve, must be expected in the end to predominate, is not that which can exist between a capitalist as chief, and work-people without a voice in the management, but the association of the laborers themselves on terms of equality, collectively owning the capital with which they carry on their operations, and working under managers elected and removable by themselves.[376]

Mill's *Principles*, first published in 1848, was one of the most widely read of all books on economics in the period. As Adam Smith's *Wealth of Nations* had during an earlier period, Mill's *Principles* dominated economics teaching. In the case of Oxford University, it was the standard text until 1919, when it was replaced by Marshall's *Principles of Economics*.

In regard to political democracy, his writings in *Considerations on Representative Government* defend two fundamental principles, extensive participation by citizens and enlightened competence of rulers. His arguments were not clearly thought out, however. At one point he proposed that educated people have more than one vote, and at a later point argued that universal suffrage would educate the masses.

To his credit, Mill was an avid proponent of the natural environment. In Book IV, Chapter VI of *Principles of Political Economy*, he argues that the logical conclusion of unlimited growth was destruction of the environment and a reduced quality of life. He concluded that a stationary state could be preferable to unending economic growth:

> I cannot, therefore, regard the stationary states of capital and wealth with the unaffected aversion so generally manifested towards it by political economists of the old school.
>
> If the earth must lose that great portion of its pleasantness which it owes to things that the unlimited increase of wealth and population would extirpate from it, for the mere purpose of enabling it to support a larger, but not a better or a happier population, I sin-

cerely hope, for the sake of posterity, that they will be content to be stationary, long before necessity compel them to it.[377]

Mill supported the Malthusian theory of population. By population he meant the number of the working class only. He was therefore concerned about the growth in number of laborers who worked for hire. He believed that population control was essential for improving the condition of the working class so that they might enjoy the fruits of the technological progress and capital accumulation. Mill advocated birth control. In 1823, Mill and a friend were arrested while distributing pamphlets on birth control to women in working class areas.[378]

Mill's economic analysis has not survived with any great impact. He followed in his father's footsteps, who was credited with creating "classical economics," which is widely regarded as the first modern school of economic thought. Aside from his father, its major developers were David Ricardo, Adam Smith, Jean-Baptiste Say, and Thomas Malthus.

The publication of Adam Smith's *The Wealth of Nations* in 1776 is usually considered the beginning of classical economics. The school was active into the mid nineteenth century and was followed by neoclassical economics in Britain beginning around 1870. The term "classical economics" was coined by Karl Marx.

Classical economists claimed that free markets regulate themselves, when free of any intervention. Adam Smith referred to a metaphorical "invisible hand," which will move markets towards their natural equilibrium, without requiring any outside intervention.[379]

In summary, John Stewart Mills made the following contributions to Western secular thought. He:

- Advanced the modern development of the scientific method;
- Demonstrated how cherished values could be attained by self-development;
- Defined freedom as the opportunity for self-development;
- Defined the greatest virtue as creating the greatest benefit and the least harm (after Bentham);

- Defined the only legitimate power of the state as the duty to protect people from harm by others;
- Distinguished harm that was caused by authority from harm caused by social sentiment;
- Was one of the earliest champions of women's rights, abolition, free speech, animal rights, and the environment;
- Spoke in defense of economic democracy as opposed to capitalism and sought the development of farmer and worker cooperatives; and
- Was the first to consider a healthy natural environment in the study of economics.

Having said this, we can see how Mill became the champion of liberal thought. Even so, his understanding of reality was insufficient to enable him to craft a universal ideology. For example, in lacking a spiritual perspective, he was unable to develop a concept of human progress that existed outside the confines of western civilization. While not a racist per se, he did consider the white race superior to "backward cultures" and permitted "civilized society" the right of dictatorship over colonized people. He held this view despite the fact that most native peoples share a greater spiritual outlook and identity with the natural world than does the materialistic white culture.

Even so, Mill's racist view was quite tempered when one considers his relationship with his authoritarian father who was a blatant racist. According to Thomas Trautman's account, "James Mill's highly influential *History of British India* (1817)—most particularly the long essay 'Of the Hindus'—is the single most important source of British Indophobia and hostility to Orientalism." In the chapter titled General Reflections in 'Of the Hindus,' Mill wrote "under the glossing exterior of the Hindu, lies a general disposition to deceit and perfidy." According to James Mill, 'the same insincerity, mendacity, and perfidy; the same indifference to the feelings of others; the same prostitution and venality' were the conspicuous characteristics of both the Hindoos and the Muslims. The Muslims, however, were perfuse, when possessed of wealth, and devoted to pleasure; the Hindoos almost always penurious and ascetic; and 'in truth, the Hindoo like the eunuch, excels in the qualities of a slave.'

Furthermore, similar to the Chinese, the Hindoos were 'dissembling, treacherous, mendacious, to an excess which surpasses even the usual measure of uncultivated society.' Both the Chinese and the Hindoos were 'disposed to excessive exaggeration with regard to everything relating to themselves.' Both were 'cowardly and unfeeling.' Both were 'in the highest degree conceited of themselves, and full of affected contempt for others.' And, above all, both were 'in physical sense, disgustingly unclean in their persons and houses.'[380]

James Mill's work became an instant success, made him rich, and totally transformed the way India was governed by the British.

It is interesting to note that while James Mill worked for the East India Company, he never visited India. His racist vituperations, as is often the case, appear to be just a projection of his own small-mindedness. It may be relevant that James Mill started his career as a minister of the Church of Scotland.[381]

It is not surprising that John Stewart Mill was an atheist with a penchant for racism. By lacking a spiritual perspective, he also lacked a universal morality. While he advanced morality to include women, slaves, animals, and nature, he lacked a full understanding of the inter-relationship of all things and the full nature of human beings.

When Mill had his breakdown as a young man, he came to realize that the forced education of his intellect by his father left him emotionally immature and devoid of spiritual insight. While he broke from the indoctrination of his father, he never managed to develop these suppressed qualities of his human nature.

Before we leave this section on the Enlightenment philosophers, we must acknowledge that the philosopher who had the greatest single impact on the future development of the world was Karl Marx. A German philosopher and revolutionary who lived from 1818 to 1883, Marx was the first philosopher to break with the Idealist tradition and attempt to apply scientific principles to the development of society and the capitalist economic system. His writings inspired revolutionaries around the world and led to the communist revolutions in Russia, China, and other countries. Rather than discuss Marx at this time, however, we will discuss his work as part of the chapter on the History of Capitalism because without an understanding of the development of capitalism, it would be difficult to understand why Marx has such an impact on human society. There would be no context for his theory.

When people think about the Enlightenment, they think about a cultural revolution that occurred in the seventeenth and eighteenth centuries, when secular thought, based upon human reason, flourished completely unhindered by religion. In actuality, however, the Enlightenment, while it diminished the value of faith in religious dogma, continued to address the riddle of an Absolute Divinity. Whether religious or secular thought, the same thirst for knowledge concerning fundamental questions continued into the Enlightenment. Is there a God? How did this world come about? What is the nature of reality? Who am I? Such questions continued to pose a challenge to human beings and the philosophers of the Enlightenment were no exception. In many respects, the Enlightenment was a continuation of the Renaissance that occurred after the religious wars of the sixteenth and early seventeenth centuries. Art and science emerged again and new ideas, regarding the nature of Divinity, the world, the state, and the individual began to surface again. It was a time of revolutionary developments in art, science, philosophy, and politics. The Enlightenment flourished at the time of political and social upheaval, in which the Church fought kings and kings fought nobles and each other. It was a time when the merchant class rose to power and overthrew the monarchies in a series of political revolutions. In this upheaval the values of the Enlightenment arose and continue to resonate in American and European culture today. These are the values of free will, democratic process, equality, the separation of church and state, and trust in God. Philosophically, the intellectuals at the time were guided by a concept of rational humanism in which the goals of an ideal society were knowledge, freedom, and pursuit of happiness.

Chapter Four: The Making of the United States

THE UNITED STATES BEGAN to emerge at the same time that England was transitioning out of its phase of laissez faire capitalism and was entering the phase of monopoly capitalism. Monopolies were granted to organizations, like the East India Company, which were chartered companies formed by investors (shareholders) for the purpose of trade, exploration, and colonization.

Fig. 4-23: The British East India Company

In the United States, the British Crown granted monopolies to the following chartered companies: Virginia Company (1606), Plymouth

Company (1606), Massachusetts Bay Company (1629) and the Hudson's Bay Company (1670). The Crown also granted charters to colonizers in the Caribbean Islands, Central America, Africa, India, etc.[382]

When these companies came to North America, they immediately began to establish fortifications, harvest resources, and trade with the Native Americans. They also brought labor with them from England, including those who sought a better opportunity and an escape from religious persecution. Capitalism at the time of European colonization was non-existent in the Americas. Neither was feudalism. Rather, the Natives lived a tribal lifestyle similar to that of the European tribes prior to the rise of Christianity and the centralization of political and military power across Europe. Let us look at what was happening in North America at the time.

Native Americans

The map below indicates the main language groups of the native tribes of North America prior to the coming of the European colonists. There is no strict relationship between language groups and ethnic groups, just as there was no relationship in Europe between those who spoke an Indo-European language and the ethnic cultures that diverged from the core group over time. What we do know, however, is that at one time in the past, all the tribes spoke a common language.

Archaeologists previously believed that the Native Americans arrived approximately twelve thousand years ago from northeast Asia by crossing a land ridge between Siberia and Alaska during the last ice age.[383] They brought the *Clovis culture* with them that is known for its unique spear points that are associated with various sites in North America. Recent discoveries, however, together with genetic research, make the case for an earlier wave of immigrants.[384]

Genetic testing has revealed ties between Native Americans and the Altaian people who are a Turkic people who still live in the Siberian Altai Republic.[385] The last common genetic ancestor between the Altaians and the Native Americans goes back to twenty to twenty-five thousand years ago. Archeologists now believe that the New World's earliest settlers left their homeland at this time and arrived in what is now Alaska between fifteen thousand to twenty thousand years ago.

While nobody knows why the Altaian people moved east, scientists know that their land in Siberia was pretty densely settled by thirty thousand to thirty-five thousand years ago and that this region was never able to support huge numbers of people. Inclement weather, similar to that which drove the Aryans out of central Russia, might also have encouraged the people to migrate. Scientists now believe that the Altaian people who left their homeland in Siberia twenty-five thousand years, but did not arrive in North America until twelve thousand years ago may have spent that interim in the land of Beringia which was the connecting land mass between Siberia and Alaska.[386] See the map below.

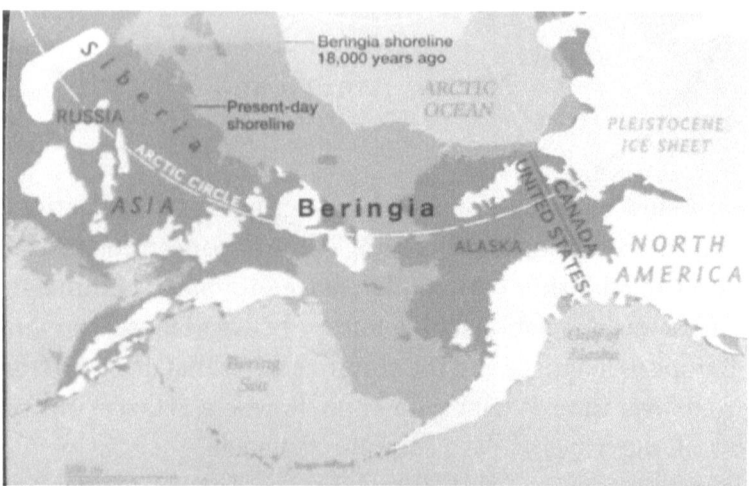

Map 4-2: Land of Beringia

This means that the people were moving toward the Americas during the last glacial period when the ice sheets were at their greatest extension.

In any case, the earliest settlers to North America spoke Algic. From this point, as they dispersed across the continent, different languages developed to express different experiences.

When the European colonists arrived on the eastern seaboard of North America, the natives they encountered spoke Algic, the largest language group, and the language of the Algonquian and Iroquois tribes.

These tribes shared much in common in terms of lifestyle and social structure, but they were continually at war with one another. The Native

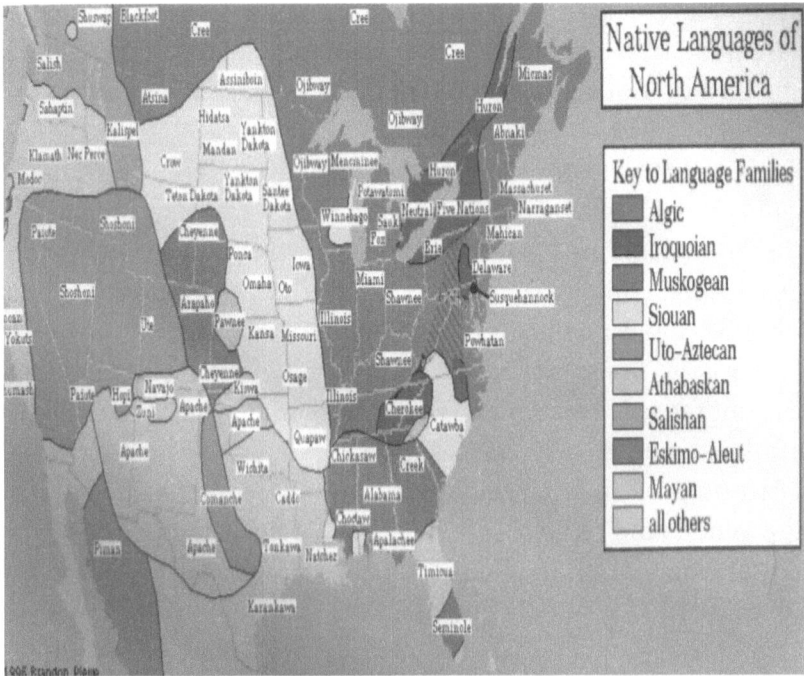

Map 4-3: Native Languages of North America

Americans were warrior tribes and much like the native tribes of Europe, before their conquest by Rome, they were engaged in the summer months with raiding their neighbors for blood revenge, booty, and prestige. Like the Europeans, they could also be quite cruel in their torture of prisoners and their blood thirstiness in battle. When prisoners were brought back to their settlements, the women elders would decide who lived and who died and what the torture would be used. Insofar as the Native American tribes were still governed by the rules of blood revenge, torture was usually weighed against the nature of the crime they were avenging. While the Native American tribes could be cruel, the cruelty was not random. It was based on the tradition of blood revenge, which, in turn, was based on the higher principle of natural balance. If someone took a life, the debt had to be repaid, either by the perpetrator or by a relative or someone in his clan.

The Algonquian Tribes

It appears that the *Algonquian* speaking tribes first settled the large area (coded green in the above map) and that at some time later the *Iroquois* tribes invaded this territory (coded blue in the map). Historians do not know where they came from or when this move occurred.

Because the *Cherokee* tribes who settled in Georgia, Tennessee, Virginia, North Carolina, and South Carolina were linked linguistically to the Iroquois tribes who settled in the northern states of New York, Pennsylvania, Ohio, and up into Canada, historians debate whether some tribes moved north or some tribes moved south.

In any case, when the Dutch, English, and French colonists landed on the shores of North America, they were met by tribes belonging to either the Algonquin or Iroquois language group. The animosity between the Algonquians and the Iroquois was to some extent exploited by the English and French who sought allies among the native peoples in their quest for dominance of colonial North America. In this process, the Algonquin tribes generally fought on the side of the French, while the Iroquois tribes fought on the side of the British. When we look closer at these people, we find that they were very similar to the early European tribes, before the introduction of iron, Rome, Christianity, and modern warfare. Like the Europeans, they belonged to matriarchal clans and tribes and their lives were similarly organized.

As for the Algonquian, there is no Algonquian tribe per se. The Algonquians are a widespread North American native language group with tribes originally numbering in the hundreds of thousands. Even today, thousands of individuals identify with various Algonquian peoples. Historically, the peoples were prominent along the Atlantic Coast and in the interior along the St. Lawrence River and around the Great Lakes.

In Canada, the French encountered Maliseet, Abenaki, Mi'kmaq, Betsiamites, Atikamekw, Anishinaabe, and Montagnais/Naskapi (Innu). In northern New England, the colonists first met the Wampanoag, Massachusett, Nipmuck, Pennacook, Passamaquoddy, and Quinnipiac. The Mohegan, Pequot, Pocumtuc, Tunxis, and Narragansett lived in southern New England. All these tribes practiced agriculture, hunting, and fishing.

In the mid and south Atlantic areas, the Delaware lived in what is now known as eastern Pennsylvania, Delaware, New Jersey, the lower Hudson Valley, and western Long Island in New York. They met Giovanni da Verrazzano in New York Harbor in 1524. Branches of the Pequot occupied eastern Long Island.

Further south were the Powhatans, a loose group of tribes numbering in the tens of thousands. They first encountered Europeans in the area of the Chesapeake Bay. Other tribes also included the Nanticoke, Wicocomico, and Chickahominy peoples.

In the Midwest, as they explored the Mississippi and Ohio rivers, the French encountered the Shawnee, Illini, Kickapoo, Menominee, Miami, Sauk, and Fox.

In the upper Midwest the Ojibwe/Chippewa, Ottawa, Potawatomi, and the Cree lived in Upper Michigan, Western Ontario, Wisconsin, Minnesota, and the Canadian Prairies. The Arapaho, Blackfoot, and Cheyenne lived in the Great Plains area.

Farther west, the ancestors to the Cheyenne and Arapaho tribes lived in the present states of Wyoming, Colorado, southwestern Nebraska, and northwestern Kansas.

All of the tribes mentioned above spoke a common language, or their language was rooted in a common Algonquian language.[387]

Before Europeans came in contact with these tribes, their basic social structure was the village. It was composed of a few hundred people that were related by the clan structure. The clans were united into tribes, each having a separate chief.

In the earliest oral history, the Algonquins came from the Atlantic coast. Because there is no known history of people traveling to the Atlantic coast before Leif Erikson in the tenth century, it is probable that the Algonquin peoples had traveled across the continent from the Pacific to the Atlantic through northern Canada and then came south to Montreal. From there they continued to journey up the Saint Lawrence River and settled along the Ottawa River, which was an important route for trade and cultural exchange. Some of the tribes continued to move further west and settled around present day Detroit about two thousand years ago.[388]

About one thousand years ago, they were manufacturing copper tools and weapons. Local pottery artifacts from this period show widespread similarities that indicate the continuing use of the river for cultural exchange throughout northern Canada.

As the change of seasons affected the food supply, clan villages tended to be temporary and mobile as people moved to locations where the food supply was greater. As they did so, they often broke into smaller units or recombined as circumstances required.

In warm weather, the tribes constructed light wigwams, wickiups, or teepees for portability. In the winter, they erected the more substantial long houses in which more than one clan could reside. In the winter, they also stored their food supplies in more permanent, underground structures like root cellars.

In the spring, when the fish were spawning, they left the winter camps to build villages at coastal locations and waterfalls. They caught smelt, alewife, sturgeon, trout, smelt, striped bass, salmon, and flounder in the estuaries and streams. They also fished the ocean for cod, whales, porpoises, walruses, and seals. On the shores, the women and children gathered scallops, mussels, clams, and crabs, items, which are still on the menus in New England today.

During the summer months, the people hunted migratory birds like Canadian geese, mourning doves, and others. They also enjoyed the eggs of these birds. The people also foraged for strawberries, raspberries, blueberries, and nuts. In September, they split into smaller groups and moved to the edge of the forests where the men hunted beaver, caribou, moose, and white-tailed deer.

The hard months were in the winter. As the snows began, the people built long houses and lived from their root cellars. In February and March they would fast for several days at a time.

The Algonquian tribes that lived further south in New England relied predominantly on slash-and-burn agriculture. They cleared fields by burning for one or two years of cultivation, after which the village moved to another location. By planting corn (maize), beans, and squash, these southerners were able to improve their diet. This led to a larger population than their northern cousins, who were mainly foragers and hunters.

Farming tended to create fixed villages and a division of labor between men and women.[389] The women farmed and the men fished and hunted.

This ancient division added to the dominant male and female psychology in which the women grow life to live and the men kill life to live.

The Algonquian tribes of the eastern Canada, New England, and the Great Lakes regions in North America practiced a religion called *Mide*, which was based on the worldview of the Ojibwa peoples. They believed that the "Great Spirit" was the creator of the world. It was a spiritual force that was inherent in all things, both living and non-living. There were also many lesser spirits, both good and evil.

Dreams were of great spiritual significance, and their interpretations was an important responsibility of the shamans who were believed to be able to communicate with the spirit world. People sought the counsel of the shamans (priests) for guidance for a successful hunt, for healing the sick, and for guidance on important matters of life. They believed that after death the spirits of hunters went on to pursue the spirits of animals. They also had a great fear of witchcraft, fearing to use their real names in case of misuse by enemies with spiritual power and evil intent.[390]

Contact with the Colonists

When the European colonists arrived on the shores of North America, they were met by Algonquian tribes, who controlled vast tracks of land in eastern Canada and the eastern and midwestern United States. The tribes, however, were mostly concentrated in the New England region. Here, the Algonquian tribes were in frequent battles with the Iroquois tribes, especially with those who were concentrated in central New York.

From the seventeenth to the nineteenth century, the Algonquians tribes also fought with the European settlers. They signed hundreds of peace treaties with them, but ultimately were driven off their lands. They first met the French, with whom they became trading partners. However, this partnership led to battles with the Iroquois who were allied with the Dutch and the English and who ultimately defeated them. The partnership was also troubled by the fact that the French were always trying to convert them to Catholicism, which led to internal problems among the Algonquian tribes.

At the time of their first meeting with the French in the early seventeenth century, the various Algonquin bands probably had a combined population somewhere in the neighborhood of six thousand.

Upon their arrival in North America, the French had claimed a huge part of North America as their own. They called it *New France*. It extended from Newfoundland in eastern Canada to the Rocky Mountains and from Hudson Bay to the Gulf of Mexico.[391] Unfortunately for the French, they could not support their greed with the necessary manpower to defend such a large tract of land.

In 1632, an English adventurer and colonist, Sir David Kirke, occupied a large part of eastern Canada and set up his own trading company.[392] Seeing themselves thus outmanned, the French colonials started to trade guns to the Algonquians as allies against the British. This is when the British began to trade guns to the Iroquois to also act as their surrogates.

Algonquian warriors fought in alliance with France until the British conquered Quebec in 1760 as part of the Seven Years War. As a consequence, the British oppressed the natives after the war. Infuriated by the way the British treated them, warriors from numerous tribes, most of them Algonquian, joined an uprising that became known as Pontiac's War, in an effort to drive British soldiers and settlers out of the region. The war is named after the Odawa leader Pontiac, the most prominent of many native leaders in the war.

The war began in May 1763 when Native Americans attacked a number of British forts and settlements. Eight forts were destroyed, and hundreds of colonists were killed or captured, with many more fleeing the region. Hostilities came to an end after British Army expeditions in 1764 led to peace negotiations over the next two years. While the Native Americans were unable to completely drive away the British, the uprising prompted the British government to modify its policies that had provoked the conflict.[393]

Later the Algonquian tribes would fight against the American revolutionaries on behalf of the British Crown during the contest over territory in Canada.

Their support of the British was not reciprocated. Tory settlers (white settlers loyal to England) began encroaching on Algonquin lands in New England and Canada shortly after the American Revolution. Later, in the nineteenth century, the lumber industry began to move up the Ottawa valley, and the Algonquians were forced into a few small reservations.[394]

In New England, the Wampanoags fought with Puritan farmers over the encroachment of their land. All along the coast, the colonists organized militia to fight the natives, except for the Quakers who refused to form a militia.

In the south, centered in Virginia, the Algonquians were organized into the Powhatan confederacy, which took its name from Powhatan who became the chief of many Algonquian tribes.[395] His real name was Chief Wahunsonacock, but the English called him Chief Powhatan. He ruled the tribes whose lands were being invaded by the French from the west and the English from the east coast. It was Powhatan's daughter, Pocahontas who talked her father into sparing the life of John Smith, the president of the Jamestown colony, when he was captured by the natives.[396] The Powhatan also fed the English settlers through the first winter. Without this help they certainly would have died. Later, Pocahontas would marry John Rolfe who grew the first successful tobacco crop and introduced this industry to Virginia and the south. Pocahontas and John would have a son, Thomas Rolfe, who became the ancestor of many Virginians. Even today many of the First Families of Virginia[397] have both English and Virginia Indian ancestry.[398]

Other marriages between the colonists and the Powhatan took place, but these attempts at peace were not enough to prevent war because the colonists' main intent was to settle the Native Americans' land and would do anything to gain control of it. The whites were also outraged because black slaves, who escaped from the whites, were welcomed by the Powhatan and became members of their tribes.

Iroquois Confederation

Unlike the Algonquian, who included thousands of tribes and were primarily associated by language, the Iroquois were an actual confederation of six tribes. It appears that they settled in New England after the Algonquian tribes had already settled the region. Where they came from originally is unknown, although they are connected linguistically to the Cherokee who settled in the states of Alabama, Georgia, North Carolina, South Carolina, Virginia, West Virginia, Kentucky, and Tennessee.

As a small confederation living within a small area, there is more information about the Iroquois social structure, lifestyle, and politics then we have concerning the diverse Algonquian tribes. At the time the Europeans met them, they were already a sophisticated society with about six thousand people.

The "Five Tribes" that formed the Iroquois Confederacy were the Mohawk, Oneida, Onondaga, Cayuga, and Seneca. They lived in central New York State. It is unknown where the word "Iroquois" came from, but it is probably a bastardization from the French language. The native people called themselves Haudenosaunee (pronounced "hoo-dee-noh-shaw-nee"), or "people surpassing all others." In 1723, the Tuscaroras joined them, and they became known as "The Six Nations Confederacy."[399]

The Iroquois tribes, although they shared a common culture and language, were nearly in constant warfare with each other until sometime between 1350 and 1600 when relations among the Five Tribes deteriorated to a state of near-constant warfare. The infighting, in turn, made them vulnerable to attacks from the surrounding Algonquian tribes.

On the banks of Onondaga Lake, sometime between 1350 and 1600, Deganawidah established the Iroquois Confederacy, a league of nations that shared a positive code of values and lived in mutual harmony. Out of respect, the Iroquois refer to him as the Peacemaker. His name means "Two River Currents Flowing Together."[400] He is a man surrounded by myth and legend. Some hold that he was born a Huron from a virgin mother.[401] Others say he was born an Onondaga and was later adopted by the Mohawk.

In any event, it appears that he was a mystic who counseled peace among the warring tribes. According to some legends, his first ally was Jigonhasasee who is now called the Mother of Nations.[402] Jigonhasasee means "she who lives on the road to war." It is said that in the many wars between the Iroquois tribes, combatants from any tribe were welcomed in her home for food or counsel. In this way, she came to know warriors from all the tribes and was considered a friend to all. It was Jigonhasasee, who, along with Deganawidah, Hiawatha, and Tadadaho, formed the

Iroquois confederation, the tenets of which became a basis for the U.S. Constitution when the founding fathers sought a model to define and implement a democracy in the modern world.[403]

The Political Structure of the Iroquois Confederation

The Great Peace forged by Deganawidah produced a clearly defined framework for the Iroquois Confederacy. The league foundation was based upon three principles, which addressed both personal and social well being. The *Good Word* signified righteousness in thought, word, and deed and also signified justice through balancing rights and responsibilities. The principle of *Health* referred to maintaining a sound body and mind and peace among individuals and between groups. Thirdly, *Power* meant physical strength, military, or civil authority; it also denoted spiritual power. The founders envisioned the resulting peace spreading beyond the original five tribes, so that eventually all people would live in cooperation. In time, a sixth tribe belonging to the Cherokee people in the southeast came north to join the confederation.

Under the structure of the Confederacy, the fifty clan chiefs within the tribes came together to confer about questions of common concern. A chief chosen as chairman would oversee the discussion, which continued until a unanimous decision was reached. If no consensus could be achieved, each tribe was free to follow an independent course on that matter.

The League fostered peace among the Six Nations. If the tribes failed to agree regarding an external dispute, such as one between the French and the Dutch, they would find a way to fight their respective enemies without confronting another League tribe. However, they were unable to do this during the American Revolution. The Confederacy nearly collapsed in the wake of that war, and traditionalists are still trying to rebuild it.

It is held by historians that the Iroquois Confederacy served as a model for the U.S. Constitution. Benjamin Franklin and Thomas Paine were well acquainted with the League and John Rutledge, chairman of the committee that wrote the first draft of the Constitution, began the process by quoting some passages from the Haudenosaunee Great Law.

The Iroquois form of government was based on democracy and personal freedom and included elements equivalent to the modern political tools of initiative, referendum, and recall. In 1987, Senator Daniel Inouye sponsored a resolution that would commemorate the Iroquois' contributions to the formation of the federal government.[404]

Social Structure

The Iroquois tribes were organized into eight clans, which were grouped in two confederations (moieties): Wolf, Bear, Beaver, and Turtle; and Deer, Snipe, Heron, and Hawk.[405] In ancient times, intermarriage was not allowed within each four-clan group, but eventually intermarriage was only forbidden within each clan. All Wolf clan members were considered to be blood relatives, regardless of whether they were members of the Mohawk, Seneca, or other Iroquois tribes. At birth, each person became a member of the clan of his or her mother.

Within a tribe, each clan was led by the clan mother, who was usually the oldest woman in the group. In consultation with the other women, the clan mother chose one or more men to serve as clan chiefs. Each chief was appointed for life, but the clan mother and her advisors could remove him from office for poor behavior or dereliction of duty.

The Iroquois were not big on laws and rules. Life was relatively simple and based upon common sense and regard for community. For example, regarding marriage, if a man and woman wished to marry, they would tell their parents, who would arrange a joint meeting of relatives to discuss the suitability of the two people for marriage to each other. If no objections arose during the discussion, a day was chosen for the marriage feast. On the appointed day, the woman's relatives would bring her to the groom's home for the festivities. Following the meal, elders from the groom's family spoke to the bride about wifely duties, and elders from the bride's family told the groom about husbandly responsibilities. Then the two began their new life together.

Adultery was rare. If a couple decided to separate, both of their families would be called to a council. The parties would state their reasons for wanting a divorce, and the elders would try to work out a reconciliation. If those efforts failed, the marriage ended. In ancient times, fathers kept their sons and mothers kept their daughters when a divorce occurred; by the early eighteenth century, however, mothers typically kept all of the children.[406]

Children were valued among the Iroquois. Because of the matrilineal society, daughters were somewhat more prized than sons. The birth of a couple's first child was welcomed with a feast at the mother's family home. The couple stayed there a few days, and then returned to their own home to prepare another feast.

Birthing took place in a hut located outside the village. A woman with support from other women would remain there a few days after the birth. When she returned to her work, the baby was secured to a cradleboard[407] that the mother would hang from a tree so that the baby could watch as the mother worked.

Fig. 4-24: Iroquois Cradleboard

Babies were named at birth but given an adult name at puberty. Names referred to natural phenomena (such as the moon or thunder), landscape features, occupations, and social roles. Such names might be Center of the Sky, Hanging Flower, He Carries News, or Mighty Speaker. A person was never addressed by his name during conversation.

Mothers had primary responsibility for raising their children and children learned informally from their family and clan elders. Children were not spanked, but they might be punished by splashing water in their faces. Difficult children might be frightened into better behavior by a visit from someone masked as Longnose, the cannibal clown.

Puberty marked the time of acceptance into adulthood. It was a time of physical and mental trials. At the time of her first period, a girl would retire to an isolated hut. She had to perform difficult tasks, such as chopping wood with a dull axe, and was prohibited from eating certain foods. When her period was over, she would return to her mother's house. The period of initiation for a young man was lengthier. When his voice began to change, he went to live in a secluded cabin in the forest for up to a year. An old man or woman took responsibility for overseeing his well-being. He ate sparsely, and his time was spent in physically demanding activities such as running, swimming, bathing in icy water, and scraping his shins with a stone. His quest was completed when he was visited by his spirit, which would remain with him during his adult life.[408]

Religion

From ancient times, the Iroquois (Haudenosaunee) believed that a powerful spirit called Orenda permeated the universe. He created everything that is good and useful. The Evil Spirit made things that are poisonous, but the Great Spirit gained control of the world. This view was identical to the view of Zoroaster, the Jewish priests, and the Christians.

In 1666, trying to make inroads into Iroquois territory, the French attacked the Mohawk tribe in New York. After driving the people from their homes, the French burned three of their villages on the south side of the Mohawk river, destroying the longhouses, wigwams, and the women's corn and squash fields.[409] Among those who escaped with their lives was a ten-year old girl named Tekakwitha who fled with her family into a cold October forest.[410]

After their defeat by the French forces, the Mohawk were forced into a peace treaty that required them to accept Jesuit missionaries in their villages. The Jesuits established a mission that later grew into the town of Auriesville, New York.

Tekakwitha, the little girl, who escaped from the French when her village was destroyed, converted to Roman Catholicism at the age nineteen.

She was baptized and renamed Kateri, in honor of the mystic Saint Catherine of Siena. Because her face was scarred from small pox, she had refused to marry and moved to a Jesuit mission. There she took a vow of perpetual virginity.

Leading the life of isolation and prayer, Tekakwitha was said to have put thorns on her sleeping mat and to have lain on them while praying for the conversion and forgiveness of her kinsmen. Piercing the body to draw blood was a traditional practice of the Mohawk and other Iroquois nations.

When she died at the age of twenty-four, the Catholics said that her scars had vanished and that her face was radiant and beautiful. Known for her chastity and mortification of the flesh, she was admired by the Catholics, while many of her people shunned her for converting to Catholicism. In any case, she became the first Native American to be canonized by the Catholic Church in 2012 by Pope Benedict XVI at Saint Peter's Basilica. The Mohawk people who did not convert to Catholicism remember her as the first virgin of the Mohawk people.[411]

In time, Quakers, Baptists, Methodists, and an interdenominational Protestant group called the New York Missionary Society joined the effort to proselytize to the Iroquois.

In 1799, as a result of the white colonialists continued attempts to force their religion on the Iroquois, a revival of the traditional religion developed.

A Seneca chief known as Handsome Lake, who squandered much of his life in drink and promiscuous sex, experienced a profound dream at sixty-five years old and began to spread the Good Word among his fellow Iroquois. The Good Word by now was basically the old religion with a little Quaker ethics thrown in. Major tenets of Handsome Lake's religion included shunning of alcoholic beverages, abandonment of beliefs in witchcraft and love potions, and denunciation of abortion. It included prayers to the Great Spirit. The fact that Handsome Lake's message had come in a dream made a profound impact among the Haudenosaunee.

Handsome Lake would later meet Thomas Jefferson after he had become president of the United States and explain his religious beliefs to him. His combination of old beliefs with Christian ethics provided the Iroquois with a faith that revitalized their civilization at a time when it was threatened with extinction by the white man's culture.[412] The religion served to show the Iroquois people how to retain their own culture while adapting to a world increasingly dominated by the white colonists.

The old religion has continued to be a major spiritual force among the Iroquois people. Some adhere solely to its practice, while others maintain a parallel membership in a Christian church.

Settlements

The Iroquois were an agricultural society in which the women farmed and the men hunted.

The people's name for themselves referred to the construction of their homes, in which extended families of up to fifty people lived together in bark-covered, wooden-framed houses that were fifty to one hundred and fifty feet long. They shared a vision that their extended community occupied a symbolic longhouse some three hundred miles long, with the Mohawk guarding the eastern door and the Seneca the western.[413]

The longhouses in which they lived were constructed with a large common room at each end that all residents could use. Within the length of the house, a central corridor eight feet wide separated two banks of apartments. Each apartment, measuring about thirteen feet by six feet, was occupied by a nuclear family. A wooden platform about a foot above the ground served as a bed by night and chair by day; some apartments included small bunks for children. An overhead shelf held personal belongings. Every twenty feet along the central corridor, a fire pit served the two families living on its opposite sides. Bark or hide doors at the ends of the buildings were attached at the top; these openings and the smoke holes in the roof fifteen to twenty feet above each hearth provided the only ventilation.

The villages of three hundred to six hundred people were composed of six to twelve longhouses and were protected by a triple-walled stockade of wooden stakes fifteen to twenty feet tall. Every two years or so, the men would find and clear an alternate site for the village, which would then be completely rebuilt. This was done in order not to overhunt or deplete the soil and firewood within an area.

The primary food crops were corn, beans, and squash and were called the "Three Sisters." Corn provided stalks for climbing bean vines, while squash plants controlled weeds by covering the soil. These crops also possessed complimentary nutrient needs and soil-replenishing characteristics that extended the useful life of the fields. In addition to providing food, the corn plants were used to make a variety of other goods. From the stalks were made medicine-storing tubes, corn syrup, toy war clubs and spears, and straws for teaching children to count. Cornhusks were fashioned into lamps, kindling, mattresses, clotheslines, baskets, shoes, and dolls. Animal skins were smoked over corncob fires.[414]

Hunting weapons consisted of bows and arrows tipped with flint or bone. Blowguns were used for smaller prey.

Elm bark served many useful purposes, including constructing houses, building canoes, and fashioning containers. Baskets were woven of various materials and pottery vessels were decorated with angular combinations of parallel lines.

Wampum (cylindrical beads) were made from large clam shells. White and purple beads were made from the different sections of the shells. The beads were used as ornamentation on clothing but were also used for other purposes. For example, strings of the beads were used in mourning rituals or to identify a messenger as an official representative of his nation. Wampum belts served as symbols of authority or of contract. Patterns or figures woven into wampum belts recorded the terms of treaties. Because of its important uses, wampum became a valuable commodity and was sometimes used as a form of currency in trading.

Traditional Iroquois games ranged from lively field contests like lacrosse to more sedentary activities involving dice. A favorite winter game called "snow-snake" involved throwing a long wooden rod and seeing how far it would slide down an icy track smoothed out on a snowy field.

The Iroquois had no stringed musical instruments. Single-tone rhythm instruments provided the only musical accompaniment for ceremonial dancing and singing. Rattles were made by placing dried corn kernels inside various materials including turtle shells, gourds, bison horns, or folded, dried bark. The traditional drum was about six inches in diameter, made like a wooden pail, and covered with stretched animal skin;

just the right amount of water was sealed inside to produce the desired tone when the drum was tapped with a stick.

Festivals

The annual cycle consists of six regular festivals that are still observed among the Iroquois. There are additional ceremonies for wakes, memorial feasts, burials, adoptions, or sealing of friendships.

The new year began with the Mid-Winter Festival held in late January or early February. It lasted five days, followed by another two or three days of game playing. This was a time of spiritual cleansing and renewal, and included a ritual cleaning of homes. Thanks were offered to the Creator for protection during the past year. Particular attention was devoted to dream guessing during the Mid-Winter Festival. Names were conferred on babies, young adults, and adoptees so they could participate in the upcoming ceremonies.

In the spring, when the sap rose, it was time for the Thanks-to-the-Maple Festival. This one-day celebration included social dances and the ceremonial burning of tobacco as a peace offering to the maple tree.

In May or June, corn seeds saved from the previous year were blessed at the Corn Planting Ceremony. This was a half-day observance in which the Creator was thanked and spirit forces were implored for sufficient rain and moderate sun.

In June, ripening strawberries signaled time for the Strawberry Festival. Dancers mimicked the motions of berry pickers. This one-day celebration was a time for giving thanks.

In August or early September, the corn was ready to eat. This event was marked by the Green Corn Festival, which involved ceremonies on four successive mornings. The first day included general thanksgiving, a Feather Dance honoring those who worked to put on the festival, and the naming of children. The second day saw more dances and the bestowing of names on young adults and adoptees. The third day was dedicated to personal commitment and sacrifice, and included a communal burning of tobacco. Speeches and dancing were followed by a feast. On the fourth day, the ceremonial dice game was played as it was at the Mid-Winter Festival. Finally, the women who worked the fields sang thanksgiving for the crops.

When all the crops had been harvested and stored away, and before the men left for the fall hunt, the Harvest Festival was held. This one-day celebration took place in October.[415]

Households

The provision of food, shelter, clothing, and health care were primary concerns for the Iroquois, as they are for all people. Regarding food, it has been said that the Iroquois were hunters, gatherers, and farmers. Corn was the traditional staple of their diet. It was baked or boiled and eaten on or off the cob; the kernels were mashed and either fried, baked in a kettle, or spread on corn leaves that were folded and boiled as tamales. Some varieties of corn were processed into hominy by boiling the kernels in a weak lye solution of hardwood ashes and water. Bread, pudding, dumplings, and cooked cereal were made from cornmeal. Parched corn coffee was brewed by mixing roasted corn with boiling water.

Besides corn, beans, and squash, the Iroquois people ate a wide variety of other plant foods. Wild fruits, nuts, and roots were gathered to supplement the cultivated crops. Berries were dried for year-round use. Maple sap was used for sweetening, but salt was not commonly used.

The traditional diet featured over thirty types of meat, including deer, bear, beaver, rabbit, and squirrel. Fresh meat was enjoyed during the hunting season, and some was smoked or dried and used to embellish corn dishes during the rest of the year. The Iroquois used the region's waterways extensively for transportation, but fish were relatively unimportant as food.

Clothing for men consisted mainly of a breechcloth made of a strip of deerskin or fabric. Passing between the legs, it was secured by a waist belt, and decorated flaps of the breechcloth hung in the front and back. The belt, or sash, was a favorite article; sometimes worn only around the waist, and sometimes also over the left shoulder, it was woven on a loom or on the fingers and might be decorated with beadwork.

Items that were worn by both sexes included a fringed, sleeveless tunic, leggings, moccasins, and a robe or blanket. Clothing was adorned with moose-hair embroidery featuring curved line figures with coiled ends. Decorated pouches for carrying personal items completed the costumes.

Women used burden straps, worn across the forehead, to support litters carried on their backs.

By the end of the eighteenth century, cotton or wool, traded by colonists, replaced deerskin as the basic clothing material. Imported glass beads became decorative elements.

Regarding healthcare, medicine women or men (witch doctors) used herbs and natural ointments to treat maladies including fevers, coughs, and snake bites. Wounds were cleaned, broken bones were set, and in the case of poisoning or upset stomach, medicinal emetics were given.

Figs. 4-25 & 4-26: Traditional Iroquois Dress

Another type of healer, known as a conjurer, sang incantations to combat maladies caused by bad spirits through witchcraft. They might remove an affliction from the patient's body by blowing or sucking. Twice each year they would visit each house in the village to combat disorders caused by evil spirits.

In the realm of mental health, the Iroquois practiced dream guessing. If a person was mentally troubled, he or she would tell everyone what they were dreaming. In response, everyone in the community had a responsibility to resolve conflicts and unmet needs made evident through any person's dreams.

Iroquois Women

Much like the German tribes, before the introduction of large-scale warfare and Christianity, the Iroquois treated their women with great respect. They were the "mothers" who gave them birth, cared for the land and its creatures, and introduced them to the Great Spirit. They created a model society that still remains an example for how men and women can work together. This is something that is critical for us to learn as we move into an uncertain future.

Iroquois women had many more rights than colonial women. As such, they served as an example that inspired the first suffragettes like Susan B. Anthony, Elizabeth Cady Stanton, Lucretia Mott, and Matilda Joslyn Gage, who worked for women's rights and the right for women to vote. The first women's convention was in Seneca Falls, which takes its name from one of the confederacies and is located in the middle of Iroquois territory.[416]

The Iroquois women succeeded in creating a democratic government, a spiritual religion, a code of honor, and laws of hospitality, which excelled those of all other nations at the time, including the Europeans. They were never the "savages" that the colonials made them out to be.

"Savage" was a Euro-American word that the whites used to denigrate the Native Americans. It implied that the natives lived in a cruder civilization. The Spanish used the same word to describe the Aztec, the Mayan, the Zapotec, and the Mixtecs of Mexico. Despite this put-down, the Native Americans at the time had a more advanced culture than did the Europeans. Tenochtitlan, the city-state that was the Aztec capital when Cortez met them in what is now Mexico City, had large zoos, great gardens, and magnificent causeways. It produced architectural wonders that the Europeans had never seen before and observatories to chart the movement of the heavens.

Aside from the derogatory use of the word "savage", the whites also used the word "squaw" that was the word for female genitalia. To the whites, every native woman was no more than a squaw.[417] As part of the ancient patriarchal tradition that snaked its way from the Jewish and early Christian priests, through the ancient societies of the Greeks and Romans, up through the nations of Europe and across the Atlantic to the shores of America, white men still felt a keen disrespect for women.

While they called other people savages and whores, they themselves behaved as savages and harassed the women.

It is ironic that it was the work of "squaws" that provided our Founding Fathers with the inspiration for creating the Constitution of the United States of America.

Influenced by the patriarchy of the dominant, white man's culture, the Iroquois Mohawks officially discarded their traditional clan-based structure in 1802. In 1848, a faction of Seneca instituted a similar change. Voting rights were denied to Seneca women, who had historically chosen the tribal leaders. Women's suffrage was not reinstated until 1964. Other tribes eventually followed suit, either abandoning their ancestral governments or modifying them to discount women's leadership. Not everyone subscribed to the destruction of the clan system and the inherent disrespect for women, however. Today two competing sets of governments exist on several reservations.[418]

Fortunately, for the Native American women in North America, the Catholic Church no longer had the power to conduct witch hunts here, although the women in South America were still subject to witch hunts and violence under the rule of the Spanish Catholics.[419]

Relations with the Colonists

The French in Canada were trading with the Algonquian for over fifty years before they met the Iroquois. During this time, the Iroquois began to acquire European trade goods through raids on Algonquian villages. They found the metal axes, knives, hoes, and kettles far superior to their implements of stone, bone, shell, and wood. They were also fond of woven cloth and began to use it in place of animal skins for their clothing.

The raids by the Iroquois prompted the French to help their Indian allies attack the Iroquois in 1609. This fight introduced the Iroquois to weaponry they had never seen before. French body armor was made of metal, whereas that of the Iroquois was made of wood. The French fought with firearms, while the Iroquois used bows and arrows, stone tomahawks, and wooden war clubs.

This led the Iroquois to change their military tactics to include stealth, surprise, and ambush. They became guerilla fighters. Their motive for fighting also changed. In the past, they had fought for prestige or revenge, or to obtain captives or goods. Now they fought for economic gain. They fought for control over the beaver hunting grounds or stole beaver skins to trade for European goods.[420] In short, they were becoming "civilized."

Although it provided the Indians with better tools and shiny new stuff, the European invasion, we know, was disastrous for the indigenous people. In the 1690s alone, the Iroquois lost between sixteen hundred and two thousand people in fighting with the Algonquians. They lost many more people to smallpox, measles, influenza, lung infections, and even the common cold because their bodies had developed no immunity to these diseases and they knew no cures for them.

The Iroquois people adopted outsiders into their tribes to replace members who had died. While some captives were tortured to death, others were adopted into Iroquois families. Who would lived or died was determined by the elder clanswomen. If one lived through this trial and was adopted into the tribe, they were treated with the same affection, given the same rights, and expected to fulfill the same duties as his or her predecessor, even if they were of a different gender or age.

Iroquois society, it appears, was still more humane than that of the whites. Natives who were educated by the English would always return to their native cultures at the first opportunity. Conversely, many colonists chose to become tribal members. They would do this by joining voluntarily, by not trying to escape from captivity, or by staying with their captors in the wake of peace treaties that gave them the freedom to return home.

Early in the eighteenth century, the Tuscarora, another Iroquoian-speaking tribe that lived in North Carolina, moved into the territory occupied by the Iroquois Confederacy. They were exhausted by the continual encroachment of colonial settlers, by their fraudulent treatment by white traders, and by repeated raids that captured their people for slaves. In a war with the British, Dutch, and German settlers in 1711, they suffered a terrible defeat, losing hundreds of their people who were either killed or enslaved.[421] Those who escaped such fates made their way north and became the sixth nation of the Iroquois League.

During the first half of the eighteenth century, the Iroquois made peace with the French and assumed a position of neutrality between the

French and the English. Even when the French and Indian War broke out, the Confederacy remained neutral. Nonetheless, the Mohawk tribe sided with the English, and the Seneca with the French.

Before long, the colonists were again fighting among themselves and the Iroquois were faced with the American Revolutionary War. For years, they had looked at the English and the English colonists as one and the same. But now, the Iroquois Confederacy had to deal with two governments. This made it impossible to maintain a neutral stance, because the governments would get jealous and belligerent if the Confederacy was interacting or trading more with one of the governments over the other, or even if there was a perception of that. Because of this challenging situation, the Six Nations had to choose sides. The Oneida and Tuscarora decided to support the Colonists, while the rest of the Iroquois League (the Cayuga, Mohawk, Onondaga, and Seneca) sided with the British and Loyalists.[422]

The Iroquois Confederation, as a political entity, was all but destroyed by the Revolutionary War and its tribal members suffered death and devastation. After the war, American retaliatory raids, destroyed many Iroquois villages and crops, and drove the people from their homelands.[423]

During the nineteenth century, the Iroquois sold large amounts of land in exchange for European goods. Chiefs were sometimes induced to support such sales by the offer of lifetime pensions.[424] Shrinking land holdings made hunting difficult and left the men with little to do. In this condition, the Quakers' helped the Iroquois transition to agricultural work. Families were encouraged to leave the longhouses and live separately on small farms so the men could work in their fields without being embarrassed by being seen doing women's work. Today, longhouses are used only for religious and ceremonial purposes.

The Cherokee

The Cherokee are a people native to North America who, at the time of contact with European settlers in the seventeenth century, inhabited the mountain and inland regions of the southeastern United States in present-day Tennessee, Virginia, North Carolina, South Carolina, and Georgia.[425]

There are two prevailing views about Cherokee origins. Some historians believe that the Cherokees came to Appalachia as late as the thirteenth century. Others hold that they've been there for thousands of years.

Unlike other Indians in the American southeast at the time, the Cherokee spoke an Iroquoian language. Some historians believe that some of the Iroquois in New England moved south to form the Cherokee, while others believed that Cherokees moved north to create the Iroquois. In either case, the split occurred long ago, perhaps as early as 1,500 BC, because a linguistic analysis shows a large difference between Cherokee and the northern Iroquoian languages.[426]

Social Structure

John Howard Payne (1791 to 1852), an American actor and playwright who spent time with Cherokee elders learning their traditions, described a social structure in which a "white" organization of elders represented the seven clans. This group was responsible for religious activities such as healing, purification, and prayer. A second group of younger men, the "red" organization, was responsible for warfare. Warfare was considered a polluting activity, which required the purification of the priest class before participants could reintegrate into normal village life.

The white government consisted of the tribal chief, a counselor from each clan, a council of elders composed of men and women, and a Council of Grandfathers. They made decisions during the times of peace. The red government consisted of a war chief, his second, a counselor from each clan, ceremonial officers, messengers, and scouts. The seven war counselors were in charge of declaring war when they felt the circumstances made it necessary. The Council of Grandmothers would declare the fate of captives and prisoners that were taken in times of war.[427] The elders said that the Cherokee revolted against the abuses of the "white" government.[428] This may have referred to a transition from matriarchy to fratriarchy or the onset of patriarchy among the tribe. Or it may have signaled the rise of the warrior administration due to increased conflict.

The Cherokee were still matrilineal when they encountered the Europeans and descent was traced through the mother's side of the family. As is true of all matriarchal societies, the most important man in the life of any Cherokee child was their mother's brother. Discipline and instruction in hunting and warfare rested not with the child's father, but with his maternal uncle. The mother's brother was also responsible for the protection of the household.

The Cherokee adhered to the ancient custom of blood revenge. This was usually carried out by the mother's oldest brother or uncle to preserve the balance of forces between the spirit world and the physical world. Blood revenge was exacted on the perpetrator to free the soul of the victim and let it pass from this world to the next. In 1808 the Cherokee National Government abolished the Ancient Law of Blood Revenge. The Ancient Cherokee (Ah-ni-yv-wi-ya) tribe was traditionally grouped around seven clans. These were the:

- *Blue Clan* (*a-ni-sa-ho-ni*) made a medicine called the Cherokee black drink from a bluish colored plant for purification ceremonies.
- *Long Hair Clan* (*ah-ni-gi-lo-hi*) wore their hair in elaborate styles and walked in a proud manner. The Peace Chief was usually from this clan.
- *Bird Clan* (*a-ni-tsi-s-qua*) kept the birds and were skilled in using blowguns and snares for bird hunting.
- *Paint Clan* (*a-ni-wo-di*) made red paint and gathered the sacred colors used in the ceremonies.
- *Deer Clan* (*a-ni-a-wi*) kept the deer and were known as fast runers and deer hunters.
- *Wild Potato Clan* (*a-ni-ga-do-ge-wi*) gathered the wild potato in swamps along streams for food.
- *Wolf Clan* (*a-ni-wa-ya*) was the largest and most prominent clan providing most of the tribe's war chiefs. They were keepers of the wolf and the only clan who could kill a wolf.[429]

While, the clan provided care for orphans and the destitute, punished offenses by its members, and took revenge on those who violated its rules, they also provided hospitality for visiting clan members from other villages. They were like a large extended family.

Cherokee Women

As we have said, the Cherokee were matrilineal. All children and property was under the control of the women who were the heads of their households. Women were sought for their advice regarding spiritual, political, and economic decisions, as well as matters of war. Some women also went to war.[430]

Europeans were also astonished that women were the heads of Cherokee households. Several generations (grandmother, mother, grandchildren) lived together as one family. Such a large family needed a number of different buildings including a summer and a winter house. The large summer house was built of bark, while the tiny winter house had thick clay walls and a roof, which kept in the heat from a central hearth. The household also had corn cribs and storage sheds. All these buildings belonged to the women in the family, and daughters inherited them from their mothers. A husband lived in the household of his wife (and her mother and sisters). If a husband and wife decided to separate, the husband went home to his mother while any children remained with the wife in her home.[431]

The family had a small garden near their houses and also cultivated a section of large communal fields, which lay outside the village. Women did most of the farming. They used stone hoes or pointed sticks to cultivate corn, beans, squash, pumpkins, and sunflowers. Old women sat on platforms in the fields and chased away any crows or raccoons that tried to raid the fields.

In the winter when men traveled hundreds of miles to hunt bears, deer, turkeys, and other game, women stayed at home, kept the fires burning in the winter houses, made baskets, pottery, clothing, and other things the family needed, cared for the children, and performed the chores for the household.

The Cherokees made decisions only after they discussed an issue for a long time and agreed on what they should do. The council meetings at which decisions were made were open to everyone including women. Sometimes they urged the men to go to war to avenge an earlier enemy attack. At other times they advised peace. Women occasionally even fought in battles beside the men. They were called the "War Women," and all the people respected and honored them for their bravery.

By the 1800's, the Cherokees had lost their independence and had become dominated by the white colonists, who did not allow women to vote, speak in public, work outside the home, or even control their own children. The Cherokee men began to imitate whites and Cherokee women lost much of their power and prestige. In the twentieth century, all women have had to struggle to acquire many of those rights that Cherokee women once freely enjoyed.[432]

Religious Beliefs

The Cherokee creation myth envisions earth as a great floating island surrounded by seawater that hangs from the sky by cords attached at the four cardinal points. The story tells that the first earth came to be when Beaver's Grandchild (Dâyuni'sï), a little water beetle, came from the sky realm (Gälûñ'lätï) to see what was below the water. He scurried over the surface of the water, but found no solid place to rest. Consequently, he dove to the bottom of the water and brought up some soft mud. This mud expanded in every direction and became the earth.

The other animals in the sky realm were now eager to come down to the new earth and first birds were sent to see if the mud was dry. Buzzard was sent ahead to make preparations for the others, but the earth was still soft. When he grew tired, his wings dipped very low and brushed the soft mud, gouging mountains and valleys in the smooth surface, and the animals were forced to wait again. When it was finally dry they all came down. It was dark, so they took the sun and set it in a track to run east to west; at first setting it too low and the red crawfish was scorched. They elevated the sun several times in order to reduce its heat.

The animals were told to stay awake for seven nights, but only a few animals, such as owl and panther, succeeded and they were given the power to see and prey upon the others at night. Only a few trees succeeded as well, cedar, pine, spruce, and laurel, so the rest were forced to shed their leaves in the winter.

The first people were a brother and sister. Once the brother hit his sister with a fish and told her to multiply. Following this, she gave birth to a child every seven days and soon there were too many people, so women were then forced to have just one child every year.[433]

The Cherokee had a concept of a universal supreme being they revered as the Great Spirit or the Great Mystery[434] who created the world and presided over all things. She made the earth to care for her children. The Cherokee believe that signs, visions, dreams, and powers were all gifts of the spirits, and that the material world is intertwined with and presided over by the spirit world.

Traditionally, there is no universal evil spirit corresponding to Satan in Cherokee theology. There are spirits, however, who are malevolent. These spirits portray the people's existential angst. There is Uya, for example, who opposes the forces of right and light;[435] or Nun'Yunu'Wi or Kalona Ayeliski, evil spirit monsters who torment their victims and prey on their souls. Medicine men were required to drive away such evil spirits.

There were also Great Thunder and his sons, the two Thunder Boys. The lightning and the rainbow were their clothing. The thunders were good in that they brought rains for the people. They could also cause harm to people.

The thunder beings are viewed as the most powerful of the servants of the Great Spirit and are revered in the first dance of the Green Corn Ceremony held each year, as they are directly believed to have brought the rains for a successful corn crop.

The Cherokee also believed that all human disease and suffering originated from animal spirits, ghosts, or witchcraft and that the plants, feeling bad about the suffering in the world, made a medicine to cure each sickness that entered the world.[436] As such it must have been incomprehensible to face the diseases that the white man brought with him that wiped out thousands of Native Americans.

Settlements

The Cherokee were not nomadic. They did not travel to follow the game they hunted. They never lived in tepees, but in settled villages. Since they lived in the high hills and mountains, the winters were cold, and they built houses of log and clay. The villages, which contained as many as one thousand villagers, were surrounded by a stockade wall and used for protection from intruders and wild animals. To enter the village, one had to pass through a long, narrow opening, large enough for only one person. The long passage made it possible for the guard on duty to capture would-be intruders.[437]

The villages were built near water and the people were accomplished at creating irrigation systems that ran through the village so all would have easy access to water. The Cherokee villagers also devised some of the world's first fish traps. Houses varied in size and were built by placing poles in the ground vertically, then weaving cane or branches, basket style, between the poles until the walls were complete. Mud was plastered on both sides to form a fairly solid house for that time. Summer homes had bark roofs.

Some homes were "whitewashed" on the inside with a material made from crushed seashells, which they traded with other Indians. They were decorated with colorful rugs, baskets, and wall hangings. Each home had a fire burning in the center and a smoke hole at the top to let out the smoke. Beds were made of branches or woven cane, placed alongside the walls, and covered with skins.

Fig. 4-27: Traditional Cherokee House

Aside from the regular houses, the village also contained the Council House, which was a large seven-sided structure that provided seven sections of seats within, giving each clan a section for its representatives within the governmental structure. The seven sections of seats surrounded a sacred fire.

Households

Following the ancient taboo, it was forbidden to marry within one's clan or to someone in the clan of one's father. Such marriage was considered incest and punishable by death at the hands of the offender's own clan and by no other.[438]

When a Cherokee boy married a girl, which took place around seventeen years of age, he would move to the girl's clan. The women were considered the heads of households among the Cherokee, with the home and children belonging to her should she separate from a husband. Maternal uncles were still considered more important than fathers.[439]

Property was inherited and bequeathed through the clan and held in common by it. Cherokee, or any outsiders who were taken into the tribe in ancient times, had to be adopted into a clan by a clan mother. If the person was a woman who had borne a Cherokee child and was married to a Cherokee man, she could be taken into a new clan. Her husband was required to leave his clan and live with her in her new clan. Men who were not Cherokee and married into a Cherokee household had to be adopted into a clan by a clan mother; he could not take his wife's clan.[440]

The Cherokee people were farmers, hunters, and foragers and their meals included plants, fish, and animals. Their most important crops were corn, beans, pumpkin, squash, tomatoes, and sunflowers. They were also accomplished hunters.

Whenever the Cherokee needed food, they would take only what they needed because they did not believe in wasting food. For example, they did not hunt for sport. The men only hunted for what they needed to feed their families and every part of the animal was used. The most important animal for their needs was the deer. They hunted turkey, fox, rabbit, elk, and bear.[441] They also hunted turtles for food and used turtle shells for rattles. Wasting anything was considered bad luck that would bring sickness to the village.

Cherokee men wore deerskin breechcloths in the summer and added leggings, shirts, and robes in the winter. Cherokee women wore wraparound skirts made out of deerskin, or later, woven cloth. They all wore moccasins on their feet. Men decorated their faces and bodies extensively with tribal tattoo art and also painted themselves bright colors in times of war. Women also made jewelry of shells and silver and painted clay beads.[442]

Festivals

There were six main festivals or religious observances before the Cherokee were removed by the whites. The festivals were observed at the capital and the Chief, the seven principle counselors, and the seven clans all participated. The festivals were based on the annual cycle of life and were opportunities for prayer, spiritual cleansing, giving thanks to the Great Spirit, socializing, and celebrating.

The first festival was the *First New Moon of Spring*. This festival was held in March. The seven Principal Counselors determined when the moon would appear and a messenger would announce the upcoming festival to all the Cherokee people. Men were designated to hunt deer, dress it, and prepare it.

On the first evening, selected women performed the friendship dance. The next day, everyone went to the water for ritual purification. The third day, the people fasted. On the fourth day everyone participated in friendship dances and ended the ceremony. Afterwards the Seven Counselors scheduled the sacred night dance. They would have a religious dance, a new sacred fire was built, and all old fires in the Cherokee homes were put out. Medicine prepared by the Medicine Men was taken and white deerskins were presented to the Festival Priests.

The *Green Corn Ceremony* was celebrated during late June or early July for four days. The dates scheduled for the celebration depended upon the time the first corn ripened. Included in the rituals were the stomp dance, feather dance, and buffalo dances.

At certain points of the ceremonies, the people prayed, fasted, performed ritual bathing, played stickball, made corn sacrifices, and took medicine. Then after the ceremonial fasting, they would feast.

The Cherokee believed that when you perform a ritual bath, it washes away bad deeds and starts a new life. A priest performed the cleansing ceremony. Bathing was followed with fasting and praying and other sacred practices.

The third Cherokee festival was called the *Mature Green Corn Ceremony*, which was held about forty-five days after the New Green Corn Ceremony. Before the festival, women performed a religious dance and decided when the festival would be held. Hunters were sent out to bring back game and there was a committee appointed for the festival.

An arch was built with green branches, making an arbor in the ceremonial grounds. The evening before the Green Corn Ceremony, all the clans took a branch that they used the next day during a noon ritual. People drank a special tea called the "Black Drink" that they used for cleansing and purifying. Afterwards the people would dance for four days while feasting on game and corn.

The *Great New Moon Festival* was held around October. This marked the beginning of the Cherokee New Year. It was believed that the world was created in autumn.

The seven counselors determined when the new moon would appear. As in previous festivals, hunters were sent out to catch game seven nights before the festival. Seven men were selected to take charge of all the planning and seven women were chosen to prepare the food. The evening before the main gathering, the women performed a religious dance and again the people went to the river for purification, making offerings to the sacred fire and praying. When the people gathered for the feast the next day, they ate deer meat, corn, pumpkin, and beans among other foods. Each family also offered food to the priest.

The fifth festival was held about ten days after the Great New Moon Festival. It was called the *Friends Made Ceremony*. The purpose of this festival was to renew friendships, make new friends, and cleanse oneself. A new sacred Fire was built by the Fire Keeper and his assistants. The Fire keeper and his assistants fasted for seven days before the festival. Others fasted during special designated days. This festival renewed the Fire and the people. It also brought friendship by ceremonially forgiving conflicts from the previous year. This was seen as a brand new start. There was also a cleansing ritual that was performed at the river in running water. This festival lasted four days.

The sixth festival was the *Winter Festival.* It was a celebration of sacred offerings, dancing, and feasting. Tobacco was gathered from the people who participated in the feast. The dance consisted of alternating pairs of males and females. During the dance, women, wearing their turtle shells, formed a circle with the men moving counter-clockwise in a circle. Each dancer took two twigs of spruce and waved them up and down like pigeon wings. The fourth night, they made offerings to the sacred fire.

Today, many Cherokee traditionalists still observe these festivals. Many ceremonial grounds observe some, and a few observe all of the occasions.[443]

When the Europeans came, they met people who were honest, decent, hard-working, loving, and spiritually humble. If the Christian settlers had been more spiritual themselves, they would have discovered people with a very kindred spirit.

It is a small testament to the consciousness of the white settlers that they considered the Cherokee to be one of the "Five Civilized Tribes" whom they encountered.[444] The Cherokee were the first of the Native peoples to develop a written language.

Relations with the Colonists

The Cherokee first made contact with Europeans in 1540, when a Spanish expedition led by Hernando de Soto passed through Cherokee country in what is today Tennessee.[445] Diseases brought by the Spaniards and their animals decimated the Cherokee and other Eastern tribes.[446]

A second Spanish expedition came through Cherokee country in 1567 led by Juan Pardo. The troops built six forts in the interior southeast and tried to dominate the Cherokee but were unsuccessful and retreated to the coast.

A little over a hundred years later, in 1673, a fur-trader from Fort Henry (Petersburg, Virginia) hoped to forge a direct trading connection with the Cherokee. The trader called them *Rickohockens* in his book on the expedition. The map accompanying the book, showed the Rickohockens occupying all of present day southwestern Virginia, southeastern Kentucky, northwestern North Carolina, and the northeastern tip of Tennessee.

By the late seventeenth century, colonial traders from both Virginia and South Carolina were making regular journeys to Cherokee lands. The trade was mainly deerskins, which were used by the booming European leather industry. In exchange, the British offered iron and steel tools (kettles, knives, etc.), firearms, gunpowder, ammunition, rum, and whiskey. In 1705, traders complained that their business with the Cherokee was lost because the Governor of South Carolina, James Moore, had set up a Cherokee slave trade.[447] He commissioned whites to "set upon, assault, kill, destroy, and take captive as many Indians as possible." When the captives were sold, in order to ameliorate the traders, the Governor spilt the profits of the slave trade with them.[448]

In the early eighteenth century (1715 to 1717), the main colony of white settlers lived in Charles Town (Charleston), South Carolina.[449] The town was named after King Charles II of England, when he was restored to the throne after Oliver Cromwell's Protectorate was defeated. At the time, Charleston was the hub of the African slave trade. An estimated forty percent of the total four hundred thousand Africans transported and sold as slaves into North America are estimated to have landed at Sullivan's Island, off the port of Charles Town. It is described as the "hellish Ellis Island." The main ethnic groups of Africans sold as slaves came from the Bakongo, Mbundu, Wolof, Mende, and Malinke.[450]

By this time, the Native American tribes in the southeast had their fill of the white men. Many tribes, including the Cherokee, Yamasee, Muscogee, Chickasaw, Catawba, Apalachee, Apalachicola, Yuchi, Savannah River Shawnee, Congaree, Waxhaw, Pee Dee, Cape Fear, Cheraw, and others launched attacks throughout South Carolina in an attempt to destroy the Charles Town colony.

This resulted in what became known as the Yamasee War. In this war, Native Americans killed hundreds of colonists and destroyed many settlements. Traders were killed throughout the entire southeastern United States. Abandoning their settled frontiers, the European settlers fled to the protection of Charles Town. Here starvation set in as supplies ran low. The people barely survived in 1715, but the tide turned in 1716 when the Cherokee sided with the colonists against the Creek, their traditional enemy. This internal conflict caused the last of the Native tribes to withdraw from the conflict in 1717 bringing a fragile peace to the colony.

The Yamasee War was one of the Native Americans most serious challenges to European dominance. For over a year the colony faced the possibility of annihilation.[451]

Hostility and sporadic raids between the Cherokee and Creek (Muscogee) over claims to shared territory continued for decades until things came to a head at the Battle of Taliwa in 1755 in present day Georgia.[452] The story is told of a heroic young widow, Nan'yehi, who at eighteen years old, took up her slain husband's gun, and singing a war song, led the Cherokees to victory. This gained her the title of "Beloved Woman" and lasting respect from the Cherokee people.[453]

After the battle, political power among Cherokees again decentralized with towns acting autonomously. In 1735, the Cherokee were estimated to have sixty-four towns and villages and six thousand fighting men.

About this time, the Cherokee accepted a German radical named Gottlieb Priber into their tribe who advocated for a region-wide confederation among all the tribes to oppose European colonization. Before the people could give this much thought, however, a small pox epidemic in 1738 wiped out nearly half the Cherokee nation. Hundreds more committed suicide due to disfigurement from the disease.

In 1756, the Cherokees fought alongside the British in the French and Indian War; however, mutual suspicion and misunderstandings between the two allies arose quickly, resulting in the 1760 Anglo-Cherokee War.[454] The Royal Proclamation of 1763 resolved the conflict, as the French and Indian War drew to an end.[455] The proclamation was issued by King George III and forbade British settlements west of the Appalachian crest. It was an attempt on the part of the Crown to give temporary protection from colonial encroachment to the Cherokee, but it proved difficult to enforce. England needed time to breathe and it could not afford another war with the Native Americans. It was at this time that the Algonquian tribes to the north had just fought the British in the Pontiac War. The King's decision, nonetheless, was a burr in the britches of the colonists, especially the Tories, who viewed the king as favoring the savages instead of them. The entire reason for their settling in America was to seize greater areas of territory.

In 1776, allied with the Shawnee and led by Cornstalk, Cherokees attacked settlers in South Carolina, Georgia, Virginia, Washington DC, and North Carolina in the Second Cherokee War. Nanyehi, the Warrior Woman who led the Cherokee against the Creek in the Battle of Taliwa, and who sat in council with the chiefs believed in peaceful coexistence with the European settlers and served as a negotiator and ambassador with them. She had warned settlers of the impending aggression. This resulted in American militia destroying over fifty Cherokee towns. In 1777, most of the surviving Cherokee leaders signed treaties with the new government of the United States of America.

In 1817, the US government established a Cherokee Reservation in Arkansas.[456] The Cherokees who settled there became known as "Old Settlers."

The Cherokees were being displaced from their ancestral lands in northern Georgia and the Carolinas in a period of a rapidly expanding white population. Some of the rapid expansion was due to a gold rush in Georgia in the 1830s. In June of that year, a delegation of Cherokees led by Chief Ross brought a case to the US Supreme Court that challenged the ability of state governments to override their tribal sovereignty. In the case *Worcester v. Georgia*, the Supreme Court held that Cherokee Native Americans were entitled to federal protection from the actions of state governments.

It was an act of deception, however, because Congress, under President Andrew Jackson had already passed the *Indian Removal Act* a couple months earlier. This law authorized the president to remove southern Indian tribes to federal territory west of the Mississippi River in Oklahoma. Jackson was not alone in his racist attitude. He merely sanctioned a racism that had persisted for many years among most white colonialists. Even Thomas Jefferson, who often cited the Great Law of Peace of the Iroquois Confederacy as the model for the U.S. Constitution, supported Indian Removal as early as 1802.[457]

Thus, despite the Supreme Court ruling, the majority of Cherokees were forcibly relocated westward to Oklahoma in 1838 and 1839. This forced exile became known as the "Trail of Tears."

The Trail of Tears was a series of forced relocations of Native American nations in the United States following the Indian Removal Act of 1830.

The relocated people suffered from exposure, disease, and starvation while en route, and more than ten thousand died before reaching their various destinations. The removal included members of the Cherokee, Creek, Seminole, Chickasaw, and Choctaw nations. Among the native tribes were some European Americans, African American freedmen, and African American slaves owned by the Cherokee. The exiles were forced to march to their destinations by state and local militias.[458]

Something should be said at this point about the Cherokee owning black slaves. Slavery did not exist among the Cherokee before the coming of the Europeans. Both the Spanish and the French histories refer to taking natives as "slaves," but because the word was also interchanged with the word "prisoner," historians demur over the distinction between the two. Nonetheless, the reality is that prisoners who were used in forced labor were the same as slaves.

Native Americans who were captured by the whites were usually sold into slavery, but were not so easily sold as blacks because they could afford to be more belligerent and resistant as they were in their own environment. This was a critical advantage that blacks did not have.

Soon after the colonization of their territory by the whites, the Cherokee, Creeks, Seminoles, Cherokees, Choctaws, and others came into possession of runaway slaves. The Indians were quick to perceive their value as servants and soon were buying and selling black slaves.[459]

Once introduced to the white man's ways, the Cherokee copied the ways of the white slavers. This triggered the 1842 Slave Revolt against the Cherokee once they arrived in the "Indian Territory" of Oklahoma. The revolt started when a group of twenty African-American slaves owned by the Cherokee escaped in an attempt to reach Mexico, where slavery had been abolished in 1829.[460] Along their way south, they were joined by fifteen slaves escaping from the Creek in Indian Territory.

Later, they ran into two slave catchers taking a family of eight slave captives back to Choctaw territory. The black fugitives killed the hunters and allowed the family to join their party. The Cherokee and Choctaw raised an armed group of more than one hundred warriors to pursue and capture the fugitives which they did. In the aftermath of this escape, the Cherokee passed stricter slave codes, expelled freedmen from the territory, and established a 'rescue' (slave-catching) company to try to prevent additional losses.[461]

The Native tribes that met the white colonialists were warrior tribes. They were not easily imposed upon and it took hundreds of years of constant immigration by the whites, who finally succeeded in outnumbering and outgunning the native peoples to destroy their societies and banish the survivors to the stark environments of the western states where they have since lived in poverty. Such was the fate of a strong, proud, and decent people.

The Coming of the Colonialists

Now that we have seen the impact of the European settlers on the Natives of the east coast, let us backtrack and look at the coming of these colonists and what drove them to act in America as they did. The Dutch, Spanish, French, and English had all explored North America and laid claim to its territories. They each set up colonies and claimed for themselves vast tracts of land that overlapped, setting the stage for war among themselves and with the Native Americans who occupied the lands they claimed.

The Dutch

In 1602, the government of the Republic of the Seven United Netherlands chartered the Dutch East India Company to explore North America for a passage to the Indies and to claim any uncharted areas for the Netherlands. This led to several expeditions and the creation of the province of *New Netherland*.[462]

New Netherland extended from Cape Cod in present day Massachusetts to include territory in New York, New Jersey, Delaware, and Connecticut, with small outposts in Pennsylvania and Rhode Island.[463]

The colony was set up to exploit the North American fur trade. During its first decades, New Netherland was settled rather slowly, partially as a result of mismanagement and partially as a result of conflicts with Native Americans. During the 1650's, however, the colony grew dramatically and Manhattan became a major port for trade in the North Atlantic. Wall Street actually was the northern wall of the settlement intended to keep out Native American tribes who lived in the north. A long trail from the north end of the island to the southern tip, which had been established by the natives became Broadway Ave.

The Dutch had gotten a prosperous colony off the ground, but in 1664, an English naval expedition, ordered by Prince James, Duke of York and brother to the king, sailed into the harbor and facing its cannons at the island of Manhattan, threatened to attack the settlement. Being greatly outnumbered and outgunned, the Director-General, Peter Stuyvesant, surrendered the settlement to the English. It was renamed New York (from James's English title). The region between the lower Hudson and the Delaware was deeded to proprietors and called New Jersey.

The loss of the colony led to a couple of Wars between the Dutch and the English, but eventually the Dutch gave up their claims to the land.

The inhabitants of Manhattan at the time were Native Americans, Europeans, and African slaves. Descendants of these original settlers played a prominent role in colonial America. For two centuries, New Netherland Dutch culture characterized the region around Albany, the Hudson Valley, western Long Island, northeastern New Jersey, and New York City.

The Spanish

The presence of the Spanish empire was mainly felt in South and Central America, as well as the Caribbean Islands. In North America, it had conquered Mexico and set up a colony in Florida. Spanish Catholic priests also set up missions in California. In their conquest, the Spanish utterly destroyed the Aztec, Mayan, and Inca civilizations.

The Aztecs in Mexico greatly resisted being colonized and it took almost a century and a half to dominate them. This strong resistance occurred even though the Aztec warriors lacked a functional wheel, horses, iron, steel, or gunpowder and were extremely susceptible to European diseases.[464] Eventually, the natives under the leadership of a Spanish priest, Miguel Hidalgo, who was inspired by the ideas of the Enlightenment, fought a revolutionary war and the people gained their independence from Spain in 1821.[465] The Mexican territory at the time included Texas and southern California. Fearing that the Catholic missions in California would provide Spain with a foothold to attack Mexico in the future, the Mexican republic passed *An Act for the Secularization of the Missions of California*, and took away much of the California Mission land and sold or gave it away in large grants.[466] This act brought an end to Spanish influence in the American west.

In the east, however, the Spanish still held Florida, which was a thorn in the side of the English and the French, who were fighting among themselves for supreme dominance of North America. Florida, named by Ponce de Leon, means "The Flowery." It was the site of the Seminole Wars fought between the US Army against Native Americans and African Americans. It was also a stronghold slave state during the American Civil War.[467]

The Spanish had established the town of St. Augustine in 1565 and retained a tenuous control over the native tribes by converting them to Christianity. Their influence diminished, however, as the English established colonies to the north and the French set up colonies to the west. The English attacked St. Augustine several times, burning the city and its cathedral to the ground until Spain built the Castillo de San Marcos (in 1672) and Fort Matanzas (in 1742) to defend it.

The Spanish attempted to destabilize the English colonies by offering asylum to slaves of the British colonies. In 1693, the Spanish Crown declared that runaway slaves would find freedom in Florida if they converted to Catholicism and serve four years in the Spanish army. The Spanish also created a settlement for blacks called Gracia Real de Santa Teresa de Mosé just north of St Augustine. This action served two purposes. It helped destabilize the British plantations and also provided a buffer between the British and the Spanish in the case of attack. Gracia Real de Santa Teresa de Mose was the first free black settlement of its kind in what became the United States.[468] Today Fort Mose Historic State Park commemorates this settlement.[469]

Spain was a mild annoyance to the French and the British in North America, who stood toe to toe with each other for dominance of the North American continent.

The French and the English

France founded colonies in Canada, throughout the east coast of North America, and along the Mississippi River. The purpose of these colonies was to export fish, sugar, and furs back to France. As the French established their forts and settlements, they grew into towns and cities, some of which still exist today, including, Quebec and Montreal in Canada, Detroit MI, Green Bay WI, New Orleans LA, Baton Rouge LA, St Louis MO, Cape Girardeau MO, Mobile AL, and Biloxi MI.[470]

As for the English, they populated the east coast of North America with settlers who formed thirteen distinct colonies. These colonies today form the states of Connecticut, Rhode Island, Massachusetts, New Hampshire, Delaware Pennsylvania, New Jersey, New York, Virginia, Maryland, North Carolina, South Carolina, and Georgia.[471]

During the fifteenth to the seventeenth century, the French and the English had fought several wars on American soil, but neither country was able to win a clear victory. The contest in North America was largely settled, however, by the Seven Years War that convulsed Europe between 1755 and 1764. Historians have called this war the "first world war" because it included all the major powers of the day with the exception of the Ottoman Empire.

The war bore different names depending upon the location and the combatants. In French-speaking Canada, it is known as the War of the Conquest, while it is called the Seven Years' War in English-speaking Canada. It is called the Pomeranian War (between Sweden and Prussia, 1757–1762), the Third Carnatic War (on the Indian subcontinent, 1757–1763), and the Third Silesian War (between Prussia and Austria, 1756–1763). In the thirteen colonies of America, it was called the French and Indian War.

Aiming to curtail Britain and Prussia's ever-growing might, France formed a coalition with Austria to stop them. Realizing that war was imminent, Prussia preemptively struck Saxony, a state in the Holy Roman Empire, and quickly conquered it. The result caused an uproar across Europe. Austria formed an alliance with France and most of the states of the Holy Roman Empire split between the contesting coalitions. Sweden, fearing Prussia's expansionist tendencies, went to war in 1757 to protect its Baltic dominions (Swedish Pomerania, parts of Livonia, and Prussia). Spain intervened on behalf of France and together they launched a disastrous invasion of Portugal in 1762 where they were beaten by an Anglo-Portuguese alliance. The Russian Empire, which was originally aligned with Austria, fearing Prussia's ambition on the Polish-Lithuanian Commonwealth, switched sides upon the succession of Tsar Peter III in 1762.

Some of the smaller powers in Europe, for example, the Dutch Republic and Denmark-Norway, tried to steer clear of the escalating conflict. The war ended with the Treaty of Paris between France, Spain, and Great Britain and the Treaty of Hubertusburg between Saxony, Austria, and Prussia, in 1763.[472]

In North America, the conflict between Great Britain and France had to do with the fact that both France and England laid claim to a large tract of land called the "Ohio Country."

Things came to a head when the French sent soldiers to the Ohio Country to woo the native inhabitants to their side and select sites for fortifications. British officials saw that if the French won control of the Ohio Country, the English would be hemmed in between the Atlantic and the Appalachians, caught between new France to the North and West, and Spanish Florida to the south. Western land speculators would lose a fortune, English colonists would be denied the promise of land and the dream of a mighty British Empire would die.[473]

Robert Dinwiddie, the English governor of Virginia and one who was personally invested in the Ohio Country, immediately alerted London to the danger. He was advised to send a messenger to the French army in the Ohio Country informing them that the region belonged to Virginia. Dinwiddie selected young George Washington for the mission. George was twenty-one years old, with no military experience but he had wanted to be a soldier and his half-brother Lawrence, who had married into the wealthy and powerful Fairfax family, proposed that Dinwiddie hire him for the job. In November 1753, Washington departed for the Ohio country with a party of six men. As they slogged up and down the Appalachian hills and valleys in freezing weather, the group explored the forks of the Ohio River as possible sites for fortifications.

Nearly one hundred miles north of the forks of the Ohio, just south of Lake Erie, the men came upon their destination. It was Fort Le Boeuf, a well-armed compound with about one hundred soldiers. The French received the young soldier with hospitality and after an enjoyable dinner complete with French wine, George delivered Dinwiddie's message. The

French response was that the Country belonged to them by virtue of discovery and exploration. While the men remained cordial throughout, they all knew that war was now on the horizon.[474]

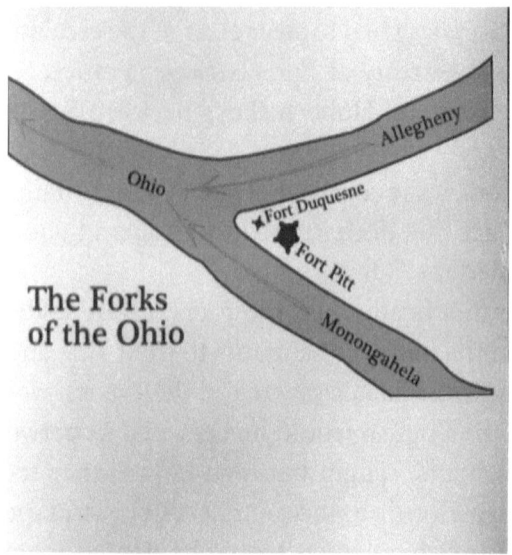

Map 4-4: Forks of the Ohio River

When Washington made his report to Dinwiddie, the governor immediately created the Virginia Regiment and named Washington as its commander. His mission was to proceed to the forks of the Ohio and build a fort. If the French had already arrived there, he was to drive them out.

Late in May 1754, Washington, now twenty-two years old, marched his ill-trained, rag tag group of one hundred and fifty men to the forks of the Ohio. About forty miles from his destination, he received a scouting report that a party of French soldiers had been spotted. Washington immediately moved with forty men to intercept the French and came upon them. Having a comparable number of men, Washington decided on a surprise attack. Once they surrounded the French, Washington gave the order to fire. Caught off guard, and without adequate cover, the French surrendered.

For whatever reason, be it inexperience or blood lust, Washington then stood by while his Indian allies massacred the French. Washington did not know that at that time, the French were on a peace mission not unlike the one Washington had previously taken to Fort Le Boeuf.[475] While war clouds had been on the horizon for months, there is little doubt that this massacre led to a series of battles and an official declaration of war by the British in 1756, which ignited the Seven Years War in America.[476]

During 1754 and 1755, the French retaliated for the massacre of their peace mission and defeated George Washington, Genera; Edward Braddock, and Braddock's successor, Governor William Shirley of Massachusetts. Throughout this period, the British military effort was hampered by several factors: lack of interest at home, rivalries among the American colonies, and France's greater success in winning the support of the Indians.

The tide turned in 1757 in favor of the British because William Pitt, who would become Prime Minister of Britain, saw America as the key to building a vast British empire. Borrowing heavily to finance the war, he paid Prussia to fight in Europe while offering to reimburse the colonies for raising troops in North America.

In July 1758, the British won their first great victory at Louisburg, (named after Louis XIV) near the mouth of the St. Lawrence River in Nova Scotia when a twelve thousand man army laid siege to an encampment of three thousand French soldiers.[477] By the end of August, the British also took Fort Frontenac where Lake Ontario drains into the St. Lawrence River. Here the British confiscated a large cache of supplies destined for French forts in the Ohio Country. This included more than sixty cannons, hundreds of barrels of provisions and bales of furs.[478]

Then the British closed in on Quebec. The Battle of Quebec, also known as the Battle of the Plains of Abraham, was a pivotal battle in the French and Indian War. The battle, which began in September 1759, was fought by the British Army and Navy against the French Army on a plateau just outside the walls of Quebec City, on land that was originally owned by a farmer named Abraham Martin, hence the name of the battle. After a three-month siege by the British, a French column attacked the British, employing new tactics that had proved extremely effective against standard military formations in the European conflicts, but proved unsuccessful now. Both generals were mortally wounded during the battle and the French were forced to evacuate the city.[479]

With the fall of Montreal in September 1760, the French lost their last foothold in Canada. Spain had also tried unsuccessfully to support the French from the south. At the peace conference in 1763, the British took Canada from France and Florida from Spain, but permitted France to keep its West Indian sugar islands and gave Louisiana to Spain. The treaty strengthened the British American colonies significantly by removing their European rivals to the north and south and opening the Mississippi Valley to westward expansion.[480]

Yet to the dismay of British land speculators and many colonists, the Royal Proclamation by King George III, in 1763, curtailed westward expansion by drawing a boundary line between white and native lands and declared that the land west of the Appalachian Mountains was reserved for Native Americans. While apparently altruistic, this proclamation served the Crown in several ways. First, it calmed the Native Americans who had a close relationship with the French and were angry now to find themselves under British rule. Secondly, the British did not have the necessary troops on American soil to continue a war with the Native Americans. Thirdly, because the proclamation outlawed private purchase of Native American land, it was required that any future purchase of land be made through Crown officials. Colonists were forbidden to move west of the line and colonial officials were forbidden to grant lands without royal approval. Thus, the proclamation gave the King a monopoly on all future land purchases from the Native Americans. Finally, the proclamation served to keep the British colonists on the east coast participating more directly in the British economy.

In any case, the line drawn by the English was not meant to create a permanent divide between the Natives and the colonists. Rather it was a "temporary boundary" that would allow for expansion west in a more "orderly and lawful manner".

Immediately, however, prominent American colonists joined with land speculators in Britain to lobby the government to move the line further west. As a result, the boundary line was adjusted in a series of treaties with Native Americans. The Treaty of Fort Stanwix,[481] and the Treaty of Hard Labor,[482] were both signed in 1768, and the Treaty of Lochaber,[483] in 1770, opened much of what is now West Virginia and Kentucky to British settlement.

The American Revolution

The Seven Years' War was tremendously costly for both France and England. For France, the military defeat and the financial burden of the war weakened the monarchy and led to the French Revolution. For the British, the war nearly doubled its national debt. In order to pay off the debt, it attempted to impose new taxes on the American colonies. These attempts were met with increasingly stiff resistance, until troops had to be called in to ensure that representatives of the Crown could safely perform their duties. These acts ultimately led to the start of the American Revolutionary War.

Sam Adams

"I pity Mr. Sam Adams for he was born a Rebel." John Adams

When Americans think of the Founding Fathers of the American Revolution, they think of George Washington, Thomas Jefferson, Benjamin Franklin, Alexander Hamilton, John Adams, Thomas Paine, etc. They rarely think of Samuel Adams, who, in fact, at the time was considered by everyone, including those mentioned above, to be the "Father of the American Revolution."[484]

Sam Adams was the political strategist behind every protest against English rule leading up to the American Revolution. Years before any of his countrymen considered breaking with England, Sam Adams saw the handwriting on the wall and realized that Americans would eventually have to choose between freedom or submission. As a consequence of his vision, once the British began to impose increased tax burdens on the colonists to pay for the French and Indian War, Adams was prepared. He meticulously charted a course to achieve self-rule for his countrymen who followed his lead step by step to that end. Sam Adams cherished his countrymen and provided leadership for them not with emotional diatribes like a demagogue, but by appeals to reason and spiritual inspiration.[485] The story of the American Revolution is the story of Sam Adams, for one cannot be told without the other.

Adams was an organizer, journalist, and political strategist without equal. He was, arguably, the greatest revolutionary that ever lived. We would indeed be blessed today to have his calm, resolute, clear-thinking leadership as we struggle to achieve freedom for humanity against the one percent, and their national governments, who continue to push us toward the brink of social and environmental disaster.

How did Sam Adams do it? How could one insignificant, local organizer take a group of totally diverse people, scattered along the eastern seaboard, who had never even considered themselves to have common interests and mold them into a fighting force with a shared vision of freedom, self-governance, and natural human rights? How did he give them the will to fight against the greatest empire in the world and defeat it? How was he able to create an independent nation called the United States of America? Let us take a look.

Sam Adams was born in 1722 in a house that overlooked the Boston Harbor. At the time, Boston was the largest city in North America. Sam's father, also named Sam, was a deacon in the Puritan Church. He also ran a successful brewery and was a leading figure in local politics. Sam Jr. had great respect for his father and learned his basic political skills by watching his actions as a labor organizer.

Deacon Adams had watched his working-class parishioners suffer for years because they could not get access to credit. The dockworkers, carpenters, ship builders, craftsmen, farmers, etc., were shut out by the local British aristocracy. The rich only loaned to each other and thereby grew richer as they were able to take advantage of economic circumstances, while the workers were stifled in their efforts to make any progress economically. The policy of the Governor and other Crown appointed officials was that the colonies were to provide raw materials to England and serve as a market for English goods. At the time, Boston was involved in what was known as the Triangular Trade. New England provided timber, fish, and manufactured goods to the Caribbean Islands and received molasses in return from which the colonists made rum. The rum was then traded in Africa for slaves who then ended up back in the colonies.

In support of his parishioners and the townspeople of Boston, Deacon Adams helped form the Boston Caucus, which was an informal political organization made up of working-class people. In time, it was powerful enough to help shape the agenda of the Boston Town Meeting, i.e., the city government. The Town Meeting was not simply a gathering of citizens but a formal meeting of elected officials. Deacon Adams was an elected official who also became a member of the Massachusetts House of Representatives. These bodies, controlled by Massachusetts residents, resisted any encroachment by the royal officials on the rights of the people as described in the Massachusetts Charter of 1691.

The Government of William and Mary, the co-rulers of the Kingdom of England, had issued the charter. It defined the government of the Massachusetts colony and while it supplanted local officials with royally appointed governors, it also established freedom of worship and eliminated any religious restrictions on voting. Economically, it reserved fishing rights to British citizens only. Towns across the colony grew in status as a result of the charter.[486] Deacon Adams worked with Elisha Cooke Jr., who founded the Boston Caucus, to form a political party, "the popular party," that later became known as the Whigs or Patriots.

The younger Samuel Adams entered Harvard College in 1736. His father had hoped that his schooling would prepare him for the ministry, but Sam was more interested in politics. He earned a Master's Degree in 1743 and in his thesis he argued that it was "lawful to resist the Supreme Magistrate, if the Commonwealth cannot otherwise be preserved." Like his father, Sam was oriented towards colonial rights.

Quite often, when Sam was young, his father would invite members of the Boston Caucus and other tradesmen to his house for meetings and conversations. In this way, Sam got an early education concerning the oppression of British rule. What completely changed Sam into a rebel, however, was a situation that happened to his father while Sam was at Harvard.

In 1739, Massachusetts was faced with a serious currency shortage and in response, Deacon Adams and the Boston Caucus created a "land bank," which issued paper money to borrowers among the workers who could mortgage their land as security. The land bank was supported by the citizenry and the "popular party," which dominated the House of Representatives and the lower branch of the General Court.

Nonetheless, the "court party" of aristocrats who were supported by the royal governor, the Governor's Council, and the upper chamber of the General Court opposed the land bank because it destroyed their monopoly on credit. The aristocrats used their power to have the British Parliament dissolve the land bank. In addition, the Directors of the land bank, including Deacon Adams, became personally liable for the currency still in circulation, payable in silver and gold. The government sued Deacon Adams multiple times, liquidated his property and destroyed his health. Lawsuits over the bank persisted for years, even after Deacon Adams' death in 1748, the younger Samuel Adams would often have to defend the family estate from seizure by the government. Thus, Sam came to see firsthand the vindictiveness of the British ruling class and to realize early on how they could exercise their authority over the colonies in arbitrary and destructive ways. Sam Adams had had enough.[487]

Events Leading to the American Revolution

1764	Sugar Act	1775	Lexington and Concord
1765	Stamp Act	1776	Washington Crosses the Delaware River
1765	Stamp Act Congress	1776	Common Sense
1765	Quartering Act	1776	Declaration of Independence
1765	Sons and Daughters of Liberty	1777	Battle of Saratoga
1766	Declaratory Act	1778	France enters the war
1767	Townshend Act and Writs of Assistance	1781	Articles of Confederation ratified
1768	Adam's Circular Letter	1781	Siege of Yorktown
1770	Boston Massacre	1783	Treaty of Paris
1772	Committee of Correspondence	1785	The Land Ordinance of 1785
1773	Tea Act and Boston Tea Party	1786	Shay's Rebellion

1774	Coercive Acts	1787	Constitutional Convention
1774	Boston Port Bill	1787	The Northwest Ordinance
1774	First Continental Congress	1788	Constitution ratified
1775	Olive Branch Petition	1789	Washington Elected President
1775	Capture of Fort Ticonderoga		

The Sugar Act

In April, 1764, one year after the French and Indian War ended, the British imposed the Sugar Act on the colonies. The act revived duties on wool, hats, and iron, and increased taxes on textiles, coffee, indigo, wines, and sugar. In addition, it authorized a court to be set up in Nova Scotia to try smuggling cases. The preamble to the act stated: "it is expedient that new provisions and regulations should be established for improving the revenue of this Kingdom . . . and . . . it is just and necessary that a revenue should be raised . . . for defraying the expenses of defending, protecting, and securing the same."[488] Boston was the first town to receive this news when a cargo ship arrived from London.

Sam immediately saw this Act as in infringement on colonial rights, but was shocked to find out that the Bostonians he talked to were not concerned about the tax. Most were either unaware of the tax or remained unconcerned because they could pass the tax on to their customers in the price of their goods. Even the people's elected officials remained indifferent to the tax. But Adams knew that the tax would lead to more taxes, more royal officials and eventually the end of self-governance for the people. Sam met with members of the Town Hall Assembly, but no one had voiced any opinion on the matter; worse, the colony's representative in London had not been given any instruction on how to respond to Parliament regarding the tax. Most people, even if they agreed with Adams, that there was a risk in accepting the tax, felt that it was futile to oppose it.[489] The colonists had little influence in London and they felt that complaints about taxes would undoubtedly raise little more than a yawn from Parliament. Convincing

Parliament, a government body, three thousand miles away, to reverse its course on taxes was virtually impossible.

Nonetheless, Adams was determined to take a stand. And herein, is reflected the first sign of his political genius and his character as a man. Sam had been honing his skills as a political organizer since the death of his father. He had become an accomplished journalist and was also a member of the Boston Town Meeting. Even so, he was little more than a background figure on the outer reaches of the empire. He had no channels to the power in London, no material wealth to launch a lobbying campaign, and no political connections outside Boston. He was, in short, only a local activist. But he did have the experience of his father's battle with the land bank and he knew that the English merchants who used the wharfs of the Boston Harbor had the ear of the king and Parliament.

Sam Adams immediately began to develop a strategy to turn the English merchants into lobbyists on behalf of the colony by creating a boycott of English goods. It was a novel tactic of his own invention and was not easily achieved because it would require the support of the other twelve colonies. This was a tall order for someone who did not even hold a post in his own colonial assembly.[490]

Not to be dismayed, Sam used his position in the Boston Town Meeting to impress his point on the citizens of the Massachusetts colony. Speaking in a serious tone that stirred his listeners, he explained that the Sugar Act was not like a tax levied by the Massachusetts assembly in which local people voted for representatives. The freedom of the colonists rested on their power of self-governance and self-taxation. If an outside body like Parliament were allowed to tax them, their liberty was gone.

In May, when the Boston Town Meeting elected its representatives to the Massachusetts House, it was customary that the Town Meeting provide its representatives with a set of written instructions as to what actions to take in the House of Representatives. Adams was selected to write these instructions and he addressed the dangers he perceived in what he called "taxation without representation":

> "For if our Trade may be taxed, why not our Lands? Why not the Produce of our Lands & everything we

possess or make use of? This we apprehend annihilates our Charter Right to govern & tax ourselves. It strikes at our British privileges, which as we have never forfeited them, we hold in common with our Fellow Subjects who are Natives of Britain. If Taxes are laid upon us in any shape without our having a legal Representation where they are laid, are we not reduced from the Character of free Subjects to the miserable State of tributary Slaves?"[491]

When the Boston Town Meeting approved Adam's instructions, it became the first political body in America to go on record stating Parliament could not constitutionally tax the colonists. Adam's directives also contained the first official recommendation that the colonies present a unified defense of their rights."[492]

In his instructions, Sam chastised the Massachusetts assembly for responding so slowly to the tax that their agent in London had no instruction to voice the colonists' opposition to it. He then instructed the representatives to demand that the taxes be repealed on the grounds that the taxes would "prove detrimental to Great Britain itself; upon which account we have reason to hope that an application, even for a repeal of the act, should it be already passed, will be successful."

Adams then stated his economic argument. He held that trade helped both economies to expand. Taxes only slowed this growth and could actually hinder it. Americans spent millions on British goods, which outweighed any tax in terms of providing revenue for England. This argument that taxes could reduce government revenues in the long term was unknown to European intellectuals. Adams wrote this thirteen years before Adam Smith's "Wealth of Nations," who would then use Adam's argument that trade restrictions, duties, and counter-duties were bad for the economy.

Adams then turned his attention to his fellow citizens and appealed to their sense of independence and freedom.

In roughly fifteen hundred words, Adams had presented the first public document to question Parliament's right to tax the colonies, issue a call for the colonies to unite in protest in a congress, and the first to denounce non-American juries to try Americans. It also contained the first threat of a boycott.

The instructions were published in newspapers and pamphlets and widely read in the other colonies as well as in London. Sam's instructions became a manifesto on colonial rights that lit a "smoldering fire in the hearts of many readers across the continent," including Patrick Henry who ran for a seat in the House of Burgesses in Virginia with the intention to fight British taxes.[493]

While the Boston assembly accepted Sam's instructions, many of his peers became extremely nervous that Sam's position was moving them toward the conclusion that Parliament did not have sovereignty over the colonies. This was unthinkable to his associates but for Sam, this was indeed his intention, but he had to be ever mindful not to state this intention openly.

When the Boston representatives carried Adams' instructions to the Massachusetts assembly, the governor, Francis Bernard, who was appointed by the Crown, shut down the assembly preventing the measure from being heard. Nonetheless, the die had been cast.

Sam had framed the debate over the Sugar Act as a civil rights issue. As a result, many of his countrymen agreed and began to see British taxes in this light. As far as the British were concerned, they were completely flummoxed by Adams. For them, taxes were a simple manner of recouping their losses in America for the French and Indian War. The war had cost the British about sixty million pounds and they were only hoping to recoup around one hundred thousand pounds through the Sugar Act to pay for administrative costs in America.

Adams began to develop innovative strategies of civil disobedience. His maxim was to "put and keep the enemy in the wrong." Once the word of his Instructions spread, he began to promote his idea of a "boycott" of English goods. This tactic was so new that there was not even a word for it at the time. He used the term "non-importation agreement" in meetings that he set up with professional clubs, trades, and associations. He argued that if British taxes went unopposed, more taxes would follow and their hard-earned profits would be sent overseas. If, however, they stopped buying British goods and cancelled orders, the British merchants would complain to their government and call for a repeal of the Sugar

Act. Some Boston shop owners began to cancel orders for luxury goods and soon the non-importation policy began to spread to surrounding colonies in New England.

Even so, it was not enough. Sam Adams knew that he had failed to defeat the Sugar Act. Governor Bernard had shut down the legislature the previous summer to prevent his call for a congress of the other colonies to discuss the Sugar Act. He also felt that Jasper Mauduit, Massachusetts's agent in London was too cozy with British officials. In fact, Jasper was praised in London for his submissive cooperation, and other colonial agents were equally obliging.

The Stamp Act

To make matters worse, several agents of the colonists, including Pennsylvania's Benjamin Franklin, in a meeting with the First Lord of the Treasury, George Grenville, in February 1765, not only dismissed protests over the Sugar Act, but also consented to a more extensive tax plan, a Stamp Act. The Stamp Act required government-issued seals be placed on all printed materials sold within the colonies, except books. The act included all legal documents, newspapers, almanacs, broadsides, pamphlets, insurance policies, ship's papers, and many other articles. The act meant that a British stamp of approval was required for colonial governments to operate, court proceedings to convene, and marriages to be officially sanctioned. The stamps would also be required to validate deeds and wills. This act represented total control of all social communication and potential censorship of any public opinion.

Proceeds from the tax were earmarked to pay a third of the cost of putting ten thousand British troops in America. Franklin believed protesting the Stamp Act would be senseless. "We might as well have hindered the sun's setting," he remarked.

The only concerns in London over the proposed Stamp Act came from British merchants, who worried about additional boycotts. They held millions of pounds of orders to American importers that stood to be cancelled if the tax plan was approved. Thanks to Sam Adam's initial groundwork with the Sugar Act, the news of the latest tax measure created a firestorm in Boston. Ministers spoke against it from their pulpits, citizens complained in town meetings, and legislators drafted resolutions against the tax. Stamp agents were also threatened.

When he got word of the Stamp Act, Adams worked nonstop on a strategy to stop the measure. Unlike Franklin's complicit response, Adams called together a meeting of local merchants and tradesmen and explained that Britain would be able to control the American economy if the tax measures were successful. He told them that London viewed the colonies not as trading partners but as trade rivals and wanted to check their growth. He urged them to continue and expand the boycott and they agreed. At the Boston town meeting, he warned the crowd that complicity regarding the Stamp Act was equal to servitude. He told his audience that the colonies were not responsible for England's debt, that the colonies had their own debt from the French and Indian War to repay.

He also told the people that if England were allowed to station ten thousand troops on American soil, it would mean the end of self-government. The military, he argued would not be under the rules of the local voters but answerable only to the Crown.

He concluded by asking them to keep up the boycott, to produce their own goods and to resist any attempts by the stamp agents to implement the tax.

Adams did not stop there. He wanted to renew his call for a congress of the colonies to discuss the issue of British taxes. If the Massachusetts house renewed the call for a congress, he knew that each colonial assembly would be forced to take up the debate over the tax even if they turned down the invitation to attend the congress. The question of Parliament's authority to levy taxes on the colonists would be discussed at hundreds of town meetings, in taverns, working guilds, and in daily conversations on street corners. Countless publishers and pamphleteers would write editorials. His instructions from the previous year spelled out the position of the Massachusetts House on Parliament's authority to tax. Other legislatures would have to form their own position and decide whether to attend the congress.

Adams knew that to call for a congress would likely cause the Governor to shut down the state assembly again, but the House would have to approve the measure before the Governor could react.

Governor Bernard opened the general assembly of the House in May. He urged compliance with the Stamp Act and stated that Parliament had the right to legislate for the colonies. "Submission to the decrees of the supreme legislature, to which all other powers in the British Empire were subordinate, was the duty and the interest of the colonies."[494]

In June, James Otis, a representative of the Boston Town Assembly and collaborator of Sam Adams, called for the colonies to participate in a Stamp Act congress. He proposed that the Massachusetts' House send out invitations to the other colonists. The measure passed and letters were immediately sent to speakers of each colonial legislature.

Governor Bernard then, as suspected, shut down the assembly again. But this time he was too late to stop the call for a colonial congress. Bernard informed London, telling them not to worry, but it would be good to increase the number of royal appointments in Massachusetts to strengthen his hand and offset the power of Adams and the popular leaders. The Lieutenant Governor Thomas Hutchinson scorned the idea of a congress: "No two colonies think alike; there is no uniformity of measures; the bundle of sticks thus separated will be easily broken."[495]

The initial reactions to the invitations to the Stamp Act congress were not encouraging for Adams, but the tide turned when the South Carolina legislature agreed to send representatives. Within weeks, eight other states accepted the invitation: Connecticut, Delaware, Maryland, Massachusetts, New Jersey, New York, Pennsylvania, and Rhode Island. All through the summer months, the debate in churches, in meeting halls, and at dinner tables continued despite the predictions of Bernard and Hutchinson.

It was at this time that Adams began to consider the idea of complete independence from England. Yet, in 1765, most colonists could not imagine life without Britain. Even Adams wondered if his imagination was deluding him. The hope of prodding the colonies into a break with England seemed absurd. Could he split an empire?

In writing Boston's instructions to the Stamp Act Congress, Adams needed to consider his neighbors, his fellow citizens of Massachusetts, members of each of the thirteen colonies, as well as officials in London.

His instructions directed James Otis, the Boston representative to the Stamp Act congress, to get approval of a statement of colonial rights and a petition to King George III to address their grievances.

Meanwhile, in Boston, the Sons of Liberty was secretly organized to pressure stamp masters to resign. They organized an event to hang the colony's appointed stamp master in effigy. On August 14, they gathered at an elm tree near the Boston Common, which soon after became known as the Liberty Tree. Adams was not a part of the protest. A stuffed effigy of the stamp master, Andrew Oliver, was tied to a rope, slung over a branch of the tree, hoisted in the air, and swung in a mock public hanging, to jeering laughter from the crowd. A sign was posted: "A goodlier sight whoe'er did see? A Stamp man hanging on a tree."[496] In the evening, the figure was cut down and carried through town on a plank. As they moved in procession, the Sons of Liberty were joined by a crowd of more than two thousand. They marched up King Street, where they came upon the unfinished frame of a building that was to be the stamp master's future office. The crowd demolished the structure. Not yet satisfied, the crowd moved to Fort Hill and built a bonfire and the effigy was beheaded and burned at the stake.

Many in the crowd headed for their homes, but a small group visited the home of the stamp master and torched his coach, trampled his garden, destroyed the outdoor furniture, smashed windows, and got drunk on wine from his cellar. Andrew Oliver resigned as stamp master the next day.

Things quieted down, but twelve days later, the Lieutenant Governor Hutchinson heard rumors that a crowd planned to attack the customs house and the admiralty office later that night. As night descended, a mob formed at the office of the admiralty, setting fire to its records. It proceeded to ravage the customs office, then turned toward the Hutchinson mansion.

This mob was not led by the Sons of Liberty, who were satisfied with Oliver's resignation. This mob was composed of criminals, debtors, rowdy seafarers, and dockworkers who felt powerless and wanted to unleash their anger on the authorities. Smallpox had recently decimated the population and a weak economy left many without work. To make matters worse, the British were enslaving men by conscripting them into the royal navy.

When the angry mob descended on the Lieutenant Governor's house, they stripped it of its possessions and destroyed it. Hutchinson and his family fled in fear for their life. This was very bad news for Adams. Whatever moral high ground he was trying to maintain in the protests over the Stamp Act suddenly vanished. His claims of the "natural rights" of life, liberty, and property for Americans rang hollow after a mob destroyed property and threatened the lives of others. Adams believed in the rule of law, that freedom entailed an obligation of moral and rational behavior. He sought not to overturn colonial society but to preserve it from British intrusion. The destruction of Hutchinson's home vindicated British claims that American resistance was not born of high ideals but of base motives. It confirmed the notion that the colonies could not govern themselves without lawlessness breaking out. It also fed suspicions that a lack of respect for royal authority would unleash latent passions resulting in upheaval.

This event proved a valuable lesson for Adams. In order to keep public opinion on his side, he realized that all future protests must be carefully orchestrated and that nonviolent passive resistance was preferable. Demonstrations must be kept within the law and they must portray British interference as unconstitutional. Adams decided that petitions, boycotts, and well-designed campaigns would be the chief components of popular protests in Boston.

The acts of destruction were condemned and resolutions were drawn up asking for town officials to prevent future vandalism. Townspeople pledged their assistance in keeping the peace and Samuel Adams denounced the misguided demonstration as "high-handed outrages."

By September 5, Governor Bernard openly acknowledged that the Stamp Act was unenforceable in Massachusetts. The seals were expected to arrive by ship any day. With Oliver's resignation, the governor himself became the de facto stamp master. An unwilling target, Bernard told the council that, "he had no warrant whatsoever to unpack a bale of them or to order anyone else to do so; and it could not be conceived that he should be so imprudent as to undertake the business."[497]

The ship carrying the stamps from London entered Boston Harbor four days later, bringing news that the Grenville ministry had been dismissed by the king and replaced by the Marquis of Rockingham, who was sympathetic with the colonists. The stamps were unloaded at the barracks on Castle William Island and a guard was placed around them.

The Massachusetts House was scheduled to reconvene in mid-September after three months of inactivity. One of Boston's four representatives in the assembly had died during the summer and Adams decided to run for the vacant seat. He won the election.

Governor Bernard addressed the opening session of the legislature by arguing that Parliament would not repeal the Stamp act so long as colonists denied its authority over America. He warned that lawless chaos would result if the courts and customhouses were closed because of a refusal to use stamped paper. Bernard was furious to discover the next day that the assembly had introduced a bill expressing the need to carry on business without the stamps. He retaliated by closing the assembly once again.

During the same week, the Stamp Act congress wrapped up its efforts in New York. Nine states participated: Connecticut, Delaware, Maryland, Massachusetts, New Jersey, New York, Pennsylvania, Rhode Island, and South Carolina. New Hampshire was absent but sent word that it would abide by the group's actions. Georgia sent representatives to transcribe the proceedings. The Stamp Act congress had hammered out a series of resolutions and the first-ever united petition to the King of England and Parliament. The Congress stated that taxation without representation violated basic civil rights of all British subjects and they maintained that only colonial legislatures could levy taxes in America. The jurisdiction of the vice-admiralty courts over the enforcement of the Stamp Act was protested as unconstitutional.

Sam Adams was extremely pleased with the results. He wrote to a friend:

> "What a blessing to us has the Stamp Act eventually or, to use a trifling word, virtually proved, which was calculated to enslave and ruin us. When the colonies saw the common danger, they at the same time saw their mutual dependence, and mutually called in the assistance of each other; and I dare say such friendships and connections are established between them as shall for the future deter the most virulent enemy from making another open attack upon their rights as men and subjects."[498]

Sam's work in preparation for the Stamp Act congress forced him to change his legal strategy against England. A problem had developed, a significant problem. Sam had always argued that the Massachusetts charter had granted the citizens of that colony the same rights as the citizens of England. Now, however, he found that he could not make the same argument for the colonies in general. Only three of the colonies held charters and each had its own framework. Some were unchartered and had been granted to individuals like Lord Baltimore (MD) or William Penn (PA). Others were under the direct control of the king. Therefore, he could no longer talk about legal rights in regards to the colonies as a whole. Instead, while drafting Massachusetts' opposition to the Stamp Act, Adams changed his argument from legal rights to "unalienable rights." These rights were natural rights common to all men that no law or society could take away from them without violating the law of God and of nature. For the first time, in preparing his instructions for the Stamp Act congress, he expressly denied Parliament's authority over Massachusetts based on these unalienable rights. He wrote:

> All acts made by any power whatever, other than the general assembly of this province, imposing taxes on the inhabitants, are infringements of our inherent and unalienable rights as men and British subjects, and render void the most valuable declarations of our charter.[499]

When Adams wrote these words, the colonists still thought of Parliament as their government, despite complaints about taxation. When, the congress voted, however, to approve Adam's statement that had become known as the *Massachusetts Resolves,* it was widely distributed. When the Lieutenant Governor Hutchinson read them, he called them a colonial Magna Carta. London dismissed it as "ravings of a parcel of wild enthusiasts."[500]

The Stamp Act was scheduled to become law the first day of November. The people of Boston held a demonstration but were careful to avoid violence and destruction. Nonetheless, their message was clearly demonstrated. They gathered around the Liberty Tree and hung effigies of George Grenville, the head of the British treasury, and other officials. By mid-afternoon, they took the effigies in a solemn procession to Boston Neck and hung them again. Then they tore them to pieces and threw them in the wind. Governor Bernard had no idea how to handle the situation. The Massachusetts stamps were still under guard on Castle William Island in the middle of Boston Harbor.

Adams went to work at the Boston Town meeting. He came up with ways to allow businesses to continue without the stamps, and he protested the cost of the troops guarding the stamps. As chair of yet another committee, he was responsible for forming a legal team to appeal to Governor Bernard to open the judicial courts. He hired his cousin John Adams to appear before the governor to make the plea. He argued that the courts must reconvene, regardless of the absence of stamps. Bernard denied their request.

While attending to local matters, Sam also had the assembly hire Dennys DeBerdt, a successful English merchant, to represent the colony in England. Adams instructed him to warn British merchants of America's vow to continue the boycott. He told DeBerdt:

> There will be a necessity of stopping in a great measure the importation of English goods. And indeed the people of the colonies seem more and more determined to do without them as far as possible.[501]

He reiterated his argument that Americans already paid extra fees to boost the English economy, that this was the entire purpose of regulating colonial trade. He argued that if Americans were overburdened with taxes, their economy would collapse.

English merchants held cancelled orders from American customers and many worried about going bankrupt. Adam Smith, observing the situation wrote:

> The expectation of a rupture with the colonies . . . has struck the people of Great Britain with more terror than they ever felt for a Spanish armada or a French invasion. It was this terror, whether well-or ill-grounded, which rendered the repeal of the Stamp Act, among the merchants at least, a popular measure."[502]

The merchants called on the British ministry to repeal the Stamp Act. Parliament was forced to consider it in early 1766. Grenville, the Lord of the Treasury, was replaced by the Whig prime minister Charles Watson-Wentworth. In February, at a secret meeting of Parliament, Benjamin Franklin, who was considered a moderate, was summoned as an agent for the colonists and questioned:

> Parliament: Can the colonists afford to pay the tax?
>
> Franklin: In my opinion there is not gold and silver enough in the colonies to pay the stamp duty for one year.
>
> Parliament: Did America not have an obligation to pay for the cost of protection?
>
> Franklin: That is not the case. The colonies raised, clothed and paid, during the last war, near twenty-five thousand men, and spent many millions.
>
> Parliament: Would America pay a modified stamp tax?
>
> Franklin: No, never, unless compelled by force of arms.[503]

The House of Commons voted to rescind the tax. But when the issue went to the House of Lords, they reaffirmed the doctrine of "virtual representation." Lord Mansfield argued that there were twelve million people in England and Ireland who were not represented and the idea that every subject must be represented was preposterous. Nonetheless, Sam Adam's vision about the merchants becoming lobbyists for the colonists held true. On March 17, the leading British merchants who exported goods to America met to draft a petition to the king asking that he rescind the tax. Once written, they boarded fifty coaches and rode in a procession to the House of Lords to meet with his majesty. The following day when King George III, resplendent in his royal robes, traveled to Parliament to give his assent to the repeal of the Stamp Act, the streets were lined with people clapping and cheering. Church bells in London rang out. Ships were immediately sent to America with the news.[504]

When news of their victory reached Boston Harbor on May 16, spring was in full bloom and the townspeople rushed into the streets to celebrate.

Even Governor Bernard was caught up in the excitement and voiced his approval. The celebration continued into the night. Crowds again gathered at the Liberty Tree but now they hung lanterns instead of effigies. People opened their houses to each other and John Hancock gave out wine from his house across from the Commons. Adams publicly expressed gratitude toward the British merchants who helped win a repeal of the Stamp Act in a statement that was printed in newspapers in America and London.

When Sam Adams first decided to protest the Sugar Act two years earlier, the idea that he could make the slightest impression on the policies of the king and the British government was ridiculous. He was just a local organizer on the lowest rung of civil officials, and few people, if any, questioned the tax. Yet Samuel Adams was a political genius and his accomplishments so far were stunning. In two years time, he had galvanized Americans across the continent, engineered the first boycotts, helped unite the colonies, implanted a reverence for liberty based on individual rights, and gave his fellow citizens not only the reasons to fight for their rights but with the political weapons to do battle.[505] This is in part why he became known as the Father of the American Revolution by this contemporaries.

We have taken the time to go into great detail concerning the actions of Sam Adams in stirring his country toward revolution against British imperialism. But this was just the beginning of the battle for Sam and for the American people. We will not be able to touch on future struggles in such depth due to the limited scope of this book. Nonetheless, as Americans, it will serve us to remember the passion and struggle that our forefathers exerted to guarantee the freedoms which we have always enjoyed, but which are being systematically eroded today, accomplished in secrecy, and covered over with fabrications and demagoguery. We will address the erosion of our freedoms in Book 1, Volume 5 on Contemporary History, but for now let us continue with the story of the American Revolution.

The good news of the repeal of the Stamp Act came with a fly in the ointment. In repealing the Stamp Act, Parliament had created the Declaratory Act, which mandated that the colonies were completely under the authority of the King and Parliament. They were not free men as they might fantasize, but remained subjects of the Crown. While the English government had been forced to make another embarrassing concession to the colonists, they were not persuaded in the least by arguments about colonial rights. In fact, things had just become very serious.

The Townshend Acts

King George looked at the repeal of the Stamp Act as a "fatal compliance" and he found a champion in Charles Townshend, his newly appointed Chancellor of the Exchequer. Townshend proclaimed to the House of Commons, "So long as I am in office, the authority of the laws shall not be trampled upon."[506]

In true imperialist fashion, he told Parliament that the American charters should be taken away from the Americans and that all governors, judges, and attorneys should be appointed by the Crown and furthermore, the colonists should have no say over legal matters.

In June of 1767, Townshend issued, through what became known as the Townshend Acts, a tax against glass, paint, paper, and tea. Townshend intended to raise forty thousand pounds a year from the tax to pay for agents of the King positioned in America, as well as military troops who would be beyond the authority of local elected legislatures. The acts also freed custom officials, judges, and governors from any control by local assemblies. They also permitted searches of colonist properties if they were suspected of smuggling (i.e., trading without paying British taxes).

Adams saw that a puppet government was being installed to rule over Americans. He recruited his cousin John Adams and John Hancock to work beside him. While some of their constituents now advocated armed resistance, Sam continued his policy of economic warfare. Because Boston remained quiet while Sam worked with his companions on expanding the boycott and other non-consumption agreements, the Governor and the Tories, who were the American aristocrats loyal to the King, began to believe that the radicals were too discouraged to protest.

News reached the colonies in October that Townshend had died and was replaced by Lord Frederick North, a favorite of the King, and just as determined as Townshend to bring the colonies under control. Three more custom officials arrived in Boston. In addition to five already stationed there, this team was mandated to collect taxes and ensure that no smuggling took place.

The Townshend Acts destroyed the democratic institutions of the colonies and rendered home rule meaningless. The American experiment of freedom and liberty was officially over. The New York assembly had already been dissolved by Parliament for refusing to comply with the Quartering Act. The Massachusetts charter was in danger of being revoked and the chief justice was now on the king's payroll. Servitude was no longer hypothetical. It had become starkly real.

Sam had to make his countrymen realize that the American dream was being destroyed by the Townshend Acts. His strategy was to write a petition to the King that would express the true sentiments of Americans and become a policy statement for all the colonies. In a measured tone, he set out a rational argument in which he rejected any vision of society without property rights and where everything was controlled by government. He linked property rights to self-governance and warned how England's actions were going to ruin the liberties of America. Sam did not believe his words would favorably impact the King or Parliament, rather they were written to organize a united front of resistance among his fellow Americans. He published his petition to the King as a "circular letter" that was sent to each provincial legislature with letters that detailed Adam's case against the Townshend Acts. The letters invited other colonists to discuss the tax and coordinate efforts between assemblies.[507]

Sam took pains in his letter to ensure the other colonists that Massachusetts was not trying to break from England or that it wanted to lead an independent America. He was careful not to provoke provincial jealousies or raise fears of Massachusetts. As a result of his hard work, the circular letter was well received in the other colonies.

In London, the circular letter was viewed as the most defiant act yet toward the British government and a cry went up to send an army to America to reduce them to reason.

Lord Hillsborough, the American Secretary of State for Britain, refused to forward the petition to the king and instead sent his own letter to the governors of the colonies telling them to suppress the petition even if it meant suspending the assemblies.

In Massachusetts the Governor and his team were in a panic. In a secret letter to London, he requested a fleet and regiments to protect them. Boston was now seen as a breeding ground for revolutionaries. Hillsborough told Governor Bernard to force the assembly to rescind the circular letter and if they refused, he was to dissolve the assembly for good. He also ordered General Gage, stationed in New York, to "maintain the public tranquility."

But again, things did not go according to the British plan. By the end of April, 1768 the legislatures of Connecticut, New Hampshire, New Jersey, and Virginia passed resolutions in support of the circular letter.

Sam had provided Americans with a treatise of their rights that became known in the press as *The True Sentiments of America*. The English, in turn, expressed their true sentiments by sending a battleship with fifty guns to Boston Harbor.

The Boston Massacre

The intent of the British was to strike fear into the hearts of Bostonians and to cow the other colonists. The British began to quarter troops in the homes of the people, although, for the most part they used vacant buildings. They also began to round up men to serve in their navy and to seize American merchant ships suspected of smuggling. One of those ships, the *Liberty*, belonged to John Hancock.

The citizens of Boston held a public meeting and decided to send Sam Adams and James Otis to see Governor Bernard to address their grievances. The Governor politely told them that he sympathized with their complaints but unfortunately there was nothing he could do about it. A week later, he ordered the state assembly to rescind the circular letter and delete it from public record. If they refused to do so, he was ordered to dissolve them. The order had come directly from the King. To defy the king now would mean more battle ships and more troops.

Adams told the assembly to stand firm. He said it would be fruitless to rescind the letter because it had already been sent out and gotten responses. What was illegal, anyway, about being able to communicate with other colonies?

As the assembly put off the governor by extending their deliberation about the circular letter, a committee drafted a petition to the king requesting that he remove the governor from office. The petition claimed that the breakdown of self-government meant that Bernard had lost credibility with the citizens.[508]

The stand taken by the Massachusetts assembly inspired the other colonies, as Adams hoped it would, but it further inflamed London. Bernard dissolved the assembly on June 31, 1768. He also sent a secret letter to the King claiming that open rebellion was at hand. Anxiety among the British merchants caused the London stock market to fall sharply. There was only one solution now. Force was needed to subdue the rebel town.

The British also turned their attention to Sam Adams as the lead instigator. Bernard labeled him "one of the principal and most desperate of the chiefs of the faction." Hutchinson, the Lieutenant Governor, called him "the all in all" who needed to be "taken off." Plans were made to charge Adams with treason and the government began to seek out witnesses to testify against him.

England sent two ships to Boston with one thousand troops. The Boston Town meeting selected Sam to form a committee to determine how to deal with the troops. They decided that they needed to gain the support of the other towns in Massachusetts and called for a convention.

Adams also wanted to demonstrate the resolve of the Bostonians by having a show of arms. He had people bring their guns to the next town meeting under the pretense that they believed that war with France was imminent and they intended to support the mother country. Over four hundred muskets were stacked on the floor of the meeting hall and emotions were ready to explode.

When the British troops arrived they took over the State House and made it into a barracks. Adams knew, at this point, that he had always been right in his belief to seek complete independence from England.

His strategy was to continue the boycott, demonstrate that the military occupation was unjustifiable, and refuse to pay the taxes. He encouraged his fellow citizens to behave lawfully and to follow the British constitution and the colonial charter. His most powerful weapon continued to be his pen. He challenged every British action and, using reason, kept them in the wrong. He knew that the Achilles heel of the empire was its fear of being embarrassed and so he did just that. Again and again, he dismantled British reasoning and made them look ridiculous. His articles were read throughout the colonies and he gave the colonists retorts to every British argument to justify their rule and occupation.

Fig. 4-28: 1772 Portrait of Sam Adams Pointing to the Massachusetts Charter

The British were outflanked by Adams. The strategy to send troops to frighten the people was a failure and only led to greater resistance. It did not take long before the lid to blow. The British soldiers were young, homesick, bored, and were often unruly. The residents insulted them. They became resentful and anxious. The residents told the troops that everyone carried a pistol and a knife and were waiting for the signal for an all-out attack.

By the end of 1769, protests against the occupation began to grow violent. Townspeople tarred and feathered a man who had collaborated with the customs officials. In November, a British captain told his troops to bayonet anyone who touched them. In March 1770, some soldiers asked if they could earn some extra money working in a rope factory. When they came to work, they were insulted and made to clean the outhouse. A fight broke out and the soldiers were beaten. Upon hearing of this, the other soldiers were humiliated and vowed to get even. They began to move around the city in small bands yelling at and cursing the townspeople. A boy insulted a soldier and the soldier struck him. This got the attention of other angry residents who began to insult the soldier. Children threw snowballs at him. He yelled for help and the British captain Thomas Preston called his men into the streets. About fifty residents confronted the line of soldiers who now protected the soldier who struck the boy. Some in the crowd taunted the British to shoot knowing that they could not do so without the Governor's orders. Yet in the middle of the confusion, the soldiers fired into the crowd, killing five people.

Adams called for the immediate withdrawal of the troops saying that the citizens and the soldiers could no longer live together in safety. He led a group of fifteen local officials to a meeting with the Lieutenant Governor Hutchinson and the highest officers of the British army and navy stationed in Boston. While they were assembled in their white wigs and full military regalia to impress the locals, it was Sam Adams who made their knees quiver.

Otis described Adams as a man who was "too firm to be intimidated, too haughty for condescension, his mind was replete with resources that dissipated fear, and extricated in the greatest emergency."[509]

Adams demanded the complete removal of the troops. Hutchinson said it was not in his power to do so. Adams told him that it would be perilous for him if he did not. He motioned to the crowd of three thousand residents who stood in the streets outside the meeting. Messengers had already been sent to nearby towns to come to Boston's aid.

As the energy pulsated inside Adams and his eyes bore into Hutchinson's brain, the Lieutenant Governor caved. He dreaded the thought of facing the residents without the troops and he was forced to concede. Adams had alluded to ten thousand citizens of Massachusetts who would see to the removal of the troops if necessary. The troops were gone within two weeks and Sam Adams had once again forced the British to retreat and to change its policy towards America.[510]

Sam Adams convinced his cousin John Adams to serve as the lawyer for the British captain Thomas Preston who had called out the soldiers who were involved in the shooting. John Adams gave a brilliant summation that resulted in the jury dropping charges against him. At a second trial of eight soldiers, all but two were acquitted and two were convicted of manslaughter and had their thumbs branded.

Sam did not like the verdict because he believed that evidence had been suppressed but, in a series of articles, he defended the townspeople who were the victims of this "massacre." He argued that the soldiers were not in mortal danger from snowballs and that the soldiers were looking for trouble as a result of the fight at the rope factory. He placed the blame on British policy toward the town. "Let me observe," he wrote, "how fatal are the effects, the danger of which I long ago mentioned, of posting a standing army among a free people!"[511]

The Committee of Correspondence

Once the British had removed their troops from the streets of Boston, things quieted down. The residents felt that they had gotten everything they wanted from the British and went about their daily business. Understandably, they wanted peace and a chance to relax. Some began to break the boycott on British goods.

This was a dark period for Sam Adams, because he still understood England's intentions and while he tried to keep his countrymen alert, few people were willing to listen to him now. Nonetheless he persevered.

In November 1772, in a Boston Town Meeting, Adams proposed to create a "Committee of Correspondence." The committee would have twenty-one members and their intention would be "to state the rights of the Colonists and of this Province in particular, as men and Christians and as subjects; to communicate and publish the same to the several towns in this province and to the world as the sense of this town, with the infringements and violations thereof that have been, or from time to time may be made." He also requested of each town a free communication of their sentiment on this subject. Happily the motion passed unanimously.[512]

While there were skeptics concerning the idea and some high-profile patriots like John Hancock and Thomas Cushing declined to serve on the Committee, Adams was undeterred. He stocked the committee with men who he had brought into the cause. The first publication of the committee was entitled "Rights of the Colonists." It was approved by the Boston Town Meeting and immediately caused a sensation across the colonies. Ben Franklin reprinted it in England. The publication provided a framework for the Declaration of Independence and the First Amendment of the American Constitution that followed.[513]

Within a few months, "committees of correspondence" were springing up in other towns and colonies. Cambridge was the first to respond, then Roxbury. Then other colonies joined in; first Rhode Island then Virginia who appointed Thomas Jefferson, Patrick Henry, and Richard Henry Lee to the committee. By July, Connecticut, New Hampshire, and South Carolina had joined the movement. Sam was elated and followed up with a barrage of articles extolling civil and religious liberties. He had rekindled the fire of revolution in the hearts of his countrymen once again. Thomas Hutchinson, who had since been appointed Governor of Massachusetts, was forced to respond. He delivered a speech at an emergency session of the State Assembly in which he warned of the dangerous direction in which Adams was leading the country. He concluded: "Is there anything which we have more reason to dread than independence?"[514]

Adam's response to Hutchinson was classic. He wrote: "the great design of our ancestors in leaving the kingdom of England, was to be freed from a subjection to its spiritual laws and courts and to worship God according to the dictates of their consciences."[515]

And now something happened that allowed Sam Adams to make the next great leap in the movement toward revolution—a call for a Continental Congress made up of representatives of the thirteen English colonies. Sam had his smoking gun.

The Hutchinson Scandal

Benjamin Franklin was stationed in London to represent the colonies of Pennsylvania and Massachusetts in their relations with Parliament. He loved the sophistication of England, its arts, music and theatre, but he sympathized with the struggles of his countrymen and insofar as the residents of Boston were concerned, he sensed among the English "a certain malice against us."[516]

In the days leading up to Christmas, Thomas Whatley, a sympathetic British Treasury official, presented Franklin with a packet of six letters that had been written by Governor Hutchinson, Lieutenant Governon Andrew Oliver, and custom officials stationed in Boston. The letters excoriated Sam Adams and the radical faction in Boston and pleaded for troops to subdue the populace. Governor Hutchinson had written, "There must be an abridgment of what are called English liberties."[517] The letter from the Lieutenant Governor Oliver went even further in its specifics. He recommended the arrest of Adams and the other "incendiaries" and proposed the creation of a colonial aristocracy that would take over the city council and the state assembly. The letters had been secretly sent to leaders of Parliament and obviously meant for the King's eyes.

Franklin was astonished by what he read and realized now why the King and Parliament believed that Boston was on the verge of revolution. Adams had previously warned Franklin that the timing of British repressive measures coincided with the colonists' political battles with the Governor.[518] Franklin sent the letters to Sam Adams asking that they remain confidential. They could be shared with the assembly but were not to be published in the press.

When Adams received the letters, he finally had proof of Governor Hutchinson's desire to end the liberties of the citizens of Massachusetts and reintroduce military occupation. It seemed insane not to publish the letters, but not knowing Franklin's political position back in London, he honored his request.

In the meantime, the Governor wanted, once and for all, to confront Adams's "The Rights of Colonists," which he called a "declaration against the authority of Parliament."[519] He wrote an essay for publication, which, he believed, "would make apparent the reasonableness of coercion and justify it to the world."[520]

His leading argument was that settlers for generations had accepted the authority of Parliament and that the Massachusetts Charter did not exempt the colonists from Parliament's authority; it simply laid out the rights common to all English subjects. Every English citizen in the entire world came under the authority of Parliament whether they were directly represented in Parliament or not. He argued that the Charter had been granted to the Massachusetts Bay Colony for financial reasons and was never intended to be a constitution for a colony. He maintained that the colonists who left England had surrendered their democratic rights to direct representation in Parliament when they chose to leave England by their own free will. If they had remained in England they would have had the same rights of representation as those living in the mother country. Nothing had been taken from the colonists that they had not forfeited by themselves. Adams and the rebels were in the wrong to claim otherwise. Hutchinson concluded that the supremacy of Parliament could not be denied and that the grievances of the colonists should be ignored and forgotten.

Confident in his iron-clad reasoning, Hutchinson invited Adams to respond. Sam solicited the help of his cousin to write a response on behalf of the Massachusetts assembly. They prepared two lengthy papers that were approved unanimously.

Adams argued that it was virtually impossible to determine the difference between a universal and absolute rule of Parliament from no authority at all. This was common sense and therefore the reason that the Massachusetts Charter was required and why it gave the settlers the right of self-governance. The charter stated that the settlers could pass their own laws as long as they were "not repugnant to the laws of England." Adams took this to mean that English and colonial laws were separate and that the laws derived from local assemblies stood outside the laws of Parliament.

He quoted King James I who said, "America was not annexed to the realm, and it was not fitting that Parliament should make laws for those countries." If this were so, Adams argued, the American colonies were not a part of the kingdom, and consequently not subject to the legislative authority of the kingdom. Only the realm of England was subject to the laws of England.

Adams rejected the argument that the settlers gave up their rights of self-governance when they left England. He said that they were persecuted and enslaved in England and they left for America to enjoy their own self-governance.

In the second paper, Adams scoffed at Hutchinson's referral to an "antiquated form of government" that he referred to as the feudal system. He argued that beginning with the Magna Carta, liberties had consistently been enlarged and Hutchinson's arguments, based on past precedents, was meaningless.[521]

Adam's response forced those colonists who remained loyal to England to question their allegiance. Once again Adam's ideas were distributed throughout the country and debated in committees of correspondence and legislatures, workplaces, and homes.

Having discredited Governor Hutchinson, it was now time to strike at the heart of the problem. Adams had sat on the letters received from Franklin for two months. Now in May of 1773, he decided to read them to the assembly.

When the letters were read to the assembly, they, of course, created outrage. Some immediately called for a petition to remove Hutchinson from office. He was reduced to the status of a repugnant traitor. Adams called for a statement that the purpose of the letters was to "subvert the constitution and introduce arbitrary power into the province."[522]

Hutchinson sent a message to a friend in England to burn his letters. Adams told the House that since copies of the letters had been distributed to crown officials and had been leaked in Boston, there was no sense in not publishing them. They had already become part of the public discourse. The assembly agreed. They also approved a petition to be sent to London to remove Hutchinson from his post.

The table had completely been overturned. Now Hutchinson was the "odious" politician and Adams was free to blame the persecution of Americans on "a plan for the ruin of American liberty" created by a few men governed by avarice and a lust for power.[523]

The time had finally arrived for Adams to issue a call for a united America. He sent out a letter to the committees of correspondence in each colony advocating the creation of a "Congress of American States." For the first time he wrote that he believed that the only security for American freedom resided in the creation of a new nation.

In a letter in the Boston Gazette, he made his plan known to the public:

> As I have long contemplated the subject with fixed attention, I beg leave to offer a proposal to my countrymen,

namely, that a Congress of American States be assembled as soon as possible; draw up a Bill of Rights, and publish it to the world; choose an ambassador to reside at the British Court to act for the united colonies; appoint where the congress shall annually meet, and how it may be summoned upon any extraordinary occasion, what farther steps are necessary to be taken.[524]

At the time of Sam's proposal, the idea of a Congress of American States was a pipe dream. Few took it seriously. The English, who had envisioned Adams as being an eminent lawyer or wealthy business man, were stunned to discover he was a penniless nobody. They offered him a bribe of a royal post. Hutchinson said that Sam would not accept it and that, if he would, he would be even more dangerous. While people talked about a Congress, it remained just that—talk. What was needed was a crisis to bring Americans together. Fortunately for the Americans, the English obliged.

Boston Tea Party

In October, news reached Boston of the new Tea Act. The East India Company was near bankruptcy because of the American boycott on English tea. The plan was to ship tea to America without charging taxes to the Company so that they could undercut the price of tea and sell it for a price that even smugglers could not compete with. It was a cagey idea because they could establish a tax in America, which even while slight, would establish their power to tax and thereby break the leadership of Adams. The plan would work if the colonists bought the tea to save money.

Adams alerted the committees of correspondence about the English plan and soon newspapers across the land were condemning the Tea Act. In Boston, Adams secretly met with the Sons of Liberty and they began to harass the custom agents. He also called a meeting of leaders of nearby towns to see if they would stand with Boston to reject the tea and they agreed. When three ships carrying three hundred and forty-two chests of tea arrived in the Harbor, the Bostonians demanded that the tea remain aboard the ships and sent back to London. Hutchinson called in the British navy. Warships were dispatched and upon arriving trained their cannons on the docks to ensure that the tea was unloaded. They had orders to fire on any colonists who tried to interfere with the unloading.

An immense mob of thousands of people had gathered for a meeting, most of which were standing in the streets for lack of space inside. While the town leaders had managed to put off the unloading of the tea for several days, they now had run out of options and the tea was expected to be unloaded the next morning. All eyes were now on Adams. Should he raise a finger, he knew the mob would run out and destroy the three ships. Yet to do so would mean another occupation by the army and martial law. England would want to make an example of Boston. The leaders of the town would be rounded up and punished as traitors and the real traitors would be hailed as patriots. If he defied the king, he was as good as dead. His wife would be a widow and his children fatherless. The struggle had now come down to two options; either destroy the tea and become lawless or give up the fight. The fate of America and the British Empire would be determined in his next few words.

Adams composed himself and said, "This meeting can do nothing more to save the country." He adjourned the meeting.[525]

Upon this signal forty men standing in the doorway of the meeting hall yelled out, "Boston Harbor a tea-pot tonight."[526] The group of men with painted faces carried blankets and hatchets. They immediately formed a line and headed to the wharf. Soon their numbers swelled to eighty men. Upon arriving at the wharf, they divided into three groups, one for each ship. They boarded the ships, split each chest of tea with their hatchets and threw them overboard. In three hours, all three hundred and forty-two chests had sunk to the bottom of the sea.

The British admiral stood on his warship unable to act. If he fired, he would destroy the ships and kill many innocent spectators who stood on the wharf watching the spectacle. It would be a political disaster. Nonetheless, everyone knew that war was now inevitable.

Three months later, the British retaliated by passing the Boston Port Bill, which forbid all commercial shipping in Boston Harbor. Three thousand five hundred workers lost their jobs. The British provided an ultimatum that the law would stay in place until restitution for the tea was made.

In addition, the British passed other laws that became known as the Coercive Acts. These included the Massachusetts Government Act, which disbanded the Massachusetts assembly and put power in the hands of a Governor's Council with members appointed by the king. It also restricted Town Hall meetings to once a year. The Impartial Administration of Justice Act allowed the governor to send government officials to London to stand trial instead of having to face local juries. Finally, the Quartering Act allowed troops to use local buildings as barracks.

Adams kept up a brave face and scoffed at the British attempts at control. He wrote that they were so absorbed in luxury and dissipation, that to support themselves in their vanity and extravagance they had to seize the honest earnings of the industrious colonists. When the army of occupation arrived, the Bostonians threw a big party to welcome them with all civility. The Coercive Acts, like all the acts that preceded it, failed to intimidate the people of Boston.

The colonists outside Massachusetts stood to make windfall profits with the closing of Boston Harbor, but Adams sent out letters to the committees of correspondence saying that the Bostonians had made a big sacrifice on behalf of American liberty and asked that the other colonists stand firmly with them. He argued that the British were using their old ploy of divide and conquer and that the other colonists should not fall for it.

In the meantime, the state assembly, reconvening in June and employing great secrecy, for every move of the Whig leaders was being watched by the British, planned a charade that totally caught the Tory appointees off guard. While locking the doors so that the Tories could not leave to notify the British military authorities, they voted on sending delegates to a continental congress to be held in Philadelphia in September. When the meeting was adjourned, the leaders unbarred the doors and the army moved in to shut down the assembly.

The call for a Continental Congress was received with great excitement throughout the colonies, and local assemblies voted to send representatives. Closer to home, Adams met with Dr. Joseph Warren to plan a convention in Suffolk county to also be held in September in a town about ten miles outside of Boston. Since Adams would be attending the Continental Congress at the same time as the proposed convention, he and Warren drafted a series of proposals that they wanted the nearby towns to agree upon and then send the convention's resolutions to the Continental Congress.

They proposed that the Coercive Acts should be rejected as an attempt to enslave America and that Massachusetts's residents deny the authority of judges, sheriffs, and any other officers appointed by the king as being unconstitutional. They demanded that any appointed members of the Massachusetts council should resign and that the residents should arm themselves and form local militias as quickly as possible to acquaint themselves with the art of war, but fight only if attacked. They proposed that taxes be withheld until a constitutional government could be reconvened. Finally, they encouraged the people not to engage in riots or attacks on private property.

Adams also reached out to the nearby native tribes telling them that the British would be returning to fight a war in New England and asking them to fight alongside the colonists to protect their lives and liberties. The Mohawk did not respond, but the St. John's tribe and the Penobscot tribe from Maine agreed to fight alongside the colonists against the "People of Old England."[527]

As Adams made preparations to go to Philadelphia, the local people came to help repair his house and build a barn for his family. They chipped in for new clothes and promised their support, thanking him for his efforts on their behalf. He said good bye to his wife Betsy, whom he loved dearly, and to his son Samuel who was now twenty-three and studying medicine at Harvard, and to his daughter, Hannah, who was eighteen and becoming a young woman.

He left town in a coach with the other delegates on a three hundred-mile journey. When they reached Philadelphia a long line of carriages eager to introduce themselves came to meet him. For the first time, the delegates could put faces to the names they had read on communications from the various committees of correspondence.

Now the politics began. Some men were jealous and suspicious of Adams and felt they needed to distance themselves from him. Others were Tories that were bitter at his presence. But Adams had a core of people whom he could count upon including Richard Henry Lee of Virginia, Thomas Lynch of South Carolina and Colonel George Washington. Sam knew that he had to play a subdued role at the Congress so as not to divide the delegates.

Religion was also an issue. The delegates were divided into five religious denominations, Anglicans in the south, Quakers in Pennsylvania, Anabaptists, Presbyterians, and Congregationalists spread throughout the colonies. Many were mistrustful of the Massachusetts Puritans who had a reputation for intolerance. To ease religious tensions, Sam Adams declared before the delegates that he would gladly bow his head in prayer with any pious and virtuous man who loved his country. Unknown to most, he had already made arrangements for a well-respected rector of the United Parishes of Christ's Church to lead the delegates in a prayer each morning to start the proceedings. Adams was sincere in his universal religious beliefs and his statement to the delegates did much to relieve tensions among the group.[528]

As the deliberations began, it became evident that the body was split into two main groups—moderates, who wanted to repair relations with England, and radicals, who wanted independence. Despite the moderates reasoned arguments, the leaders of the committees of correspondence across the country were forming local militias and Sam, through his network of contacts, was able to monitor events better than any delegate at the Congress. While John Adams became a champion of the radicals through his public addresses, Sam organized in the background. They were an unbeatable team. Patrick Henry remarked that, "the good that was to come from these congresses was owing to the work of Samuel Adams."[529]

While ideas were exchanged and politics rumbled thickly in the air, in September the Suffolk Resolves reached the Continental Congress, carried by Paul Revere, who covered the three hundred miles from Boston in six days. They were read, endorsed, and orders were given to publish them with the Congress' endorsement. The Congress followed the Resolves by also halting trade with Great Britain and approved an association to enforce the boycott and embargo.

The moderates were outflanked once again by Adam's strategy and the royal government began to drift. Without tax receipts there were no funds to run their royal offices. News also arrived that General Gage, the military commander who occupied Boston, seized gunpowder from local citizens and town armories in Charleston and Boston. This changed the mood of the Congress. The armchair philosophers were now forced to become committed revolutionaries.

When Adams returned to Boston in November, after three months of deliberations in Pennsylvania, he was pleased to discover that efforts to train militia units were in full swing. Experienced fighters from the French and Indian War stepped up to train the tradesmen and farmers. Massachusetts hoped to raise a fighting force of twelve thousand men by January. They also put out a call to other colonies to send another twenty thousand men to Boston.

Emboldened by military fervor, colonists in other states began to attack British forts and seize cannons and gunpowder. They also sent a steady stream of provisions under cover of darkness to the citizens of Boston who had lost their jobs when the British closed the Harbor. Defiance was no longer limited to Massachusetts. In Virginia, Patrick Henry, aroused his fellow assemblymen with his clear resolve —"Give me liberty, or give me death."

Revolution

Now anarchy broke out in Boston. Soldiers broke into Hancock's house and trashed it. They made an assassination attempt on Adam's life as the people attended a commemoration of the fifth anniversary of the Boston Massacre. Gage ordered the arrest of Adams and Hancock, whom he knew was in charge of training militia. He also gave orders to make a preemptive strike against any citizens or surrounding towns who were stockpiling munitions. For his part, Adams was being counseled to seize Fort Ticonderoga and Crown Point from which the British were making plans to invade the colonies from Canada. Benedict Arnold and Ethan Allen agreed to lead the attack on the fort.

These developments put Adams and Hancock on the run. They stayed with Reverend Jonas Clarke in Lexington about twelve miles north of Boston and planned their assault on the forts to the north and also their strategy for the next Continental Congress, which was scheduled to meet in May. Meanwhile, the Sons of Liberty were monitoring the movements of the British troops stationed in Boston and saw that a contingent of troops were preparing to sail up the Cambridge River to Lexington to arrest Adams and Hancock or go to Concord to destroy the munitions stored there by the colonists. They dispatched Paul Revere to warn Adams and Hamilton and he arrived at 2:00 am to tell the men that the British were coming. A local militia was activated with loaded guns, but were told not to fire the first shot. When the British arrived beating drums they were met by seventy-five militiamen. A shot was fired and the British let loose a volley that killed seven men and wounded nine. They cheered at this easy victory.

The war for American independence began in this early morning of April 19, 1775 in Lexington, Massachusetts with these shots that became known as the "shots heard round the world."

The townspeople had smuggled Adams and Hancock out of town just as the British arrived. They were headed for the second Continental Congress. Along the way, they stopped for strategy sessions and in New York City thousands lined the roads to escort Adams and Hancock into town. Many carried guns and vowed to stand with the Bostonians in battle.

Upon arrival in Pennsylvania, an urgent need was to appoint a commander of the American army. Hancock wanted this role, but Adams knew that he had a divisive personality and so he quietly lobbied to have George Washington appointed commander. At about the same time, the Congress received word that Arnold and Allen had been successful in capturing Ticonderoga along with a great arsenal of weapons and munitions.

Adams met often with the representatives from Virginia with whom he had strong allies. His intention was to make Virginia the leaders of the American cause so that people would see the struggle as a national struggle and not a regional struggle by New England states. There were still many in the Congress who, while favoring armed struggle with England, still did not want to break with her.

Among the Virginians at this second Congress, Adams met Thomas Jefferson. He was, at the time, thirty-two years old while Adams was fifty-three. He considered Adams an elder statesman whom he greatly respected but, because of the difference in age, did not feel intimate.

Meanwhile Boston was in chaos. The British troops were not well disciplined and lootings and beatings were common. People who were Sam's friends and acquaintances were leaving the city and he was worried about his family whom he knew would be prime targets for revenge. In August, the Congress recessed and Adams returned to Boston laden with several thousand pounds sterling from Americans for the citizens of Boston. Upon arrival in Massachusetts he was pleased to see the caliber of the colonists' military leadership. It contained officers and engineers and men with skills beyond the firing of a gun.

In Boston, his stay with his family was brief. Betsy had moved the family to an American army encampment in Cambridge and told him not to worry that, if the British attacked, she had her escape route planned. He confided in Betsy that he was continually searching his conscience to make sure that he was not fooling himself by encouraging a break with England, but in his self-examination he felt that he was not acting from a selfish motive but was guided by a pure motive to save his countrymen from the tyranny of British control.

Upon returning to Philadelphia to resume the Congress, he wrote to his wife:

> The Affairs of our country are at this moment in the most critical situation. Every wheel seems now to be in motion. I am so fully satisfied in the justice of our cause that I can confidently as well as devoutly pray that the righteous disposer of all things would succeed our enterprises. If he suffers us to be defeated in any or all of them I shall believe it to be for the most wise and gracious purpose and shall heartily acquiesce in the divine disposal.[530]

Now back in Philadelphia, Adams was embroiled in the battle between the delegates over the question of independence. While many, like Franklin and Jefferson, still supported armed struggle, they remained firmly against a break with England. The Tories were now better organized and argued vehemently against armed struggle and independence.

It was a mark of Adam's genius that he was able to move the delegates to a position of independence. This session of the Congress created the Declaration of Independence, which was primarily penned by Thomas Jefferson. When the Declaration was approved by the Congress, John Hancock was the first to sign. He did so in large letters exclaiming that His Majesty King George III would then be able to read his name without the aid of eyeglasses. Adams wrote his name in "unadorned, small letters."[531]

George Washington

As Adams was preoccupied with building a consensus on the question of independence among the delegates of the Continental Congress and shepherding them through the development of legal documents, including the Constitution and the Bill of Rights, George Washington was on the front lines poised to fight the largest, best trained, and best equipped army in the world.

In fact, one of the reasons that consensus on the Declaration of Independence was reached was because the British army had increased in Canada and was about to descend on New York City. This battle, most believed, would determine the fate of America and it was imperative that Congress resolve its differences and stand united as a country.

When Arnold and Allen conquered Fort Ticonderoga and seized its weaponry they came into possession of fifty-nine cannons that weighed sixty thousand tons. Washington had sent Henry Knox, a twenty-five year old Bostonian, with instructions to bring the cannons to the outskirts of Boston. After seventy-five days of intense labor and the use of eighty-two sleds, one hundred and sixty oxen, and one hundred and twenty-five horses, Knox had succeeded in moving the cannons and munitions down to Albany, across the Hudson River, through the Berkshire Mountains to the outskirts of Boston.[532]

Under the cover of darkness on March 5, 1776, Washington positioned his artillery atop Dorchester Heights above Boston. From here, the cannons could decimate the British ships in the Harbor and sever General Howe's supply line to England. When Howe was informed of Washington's cannons, he proposed to Washington that if he were to spare his ships, he, in turn, would not destroy Boston. Washington agreed and the occupation of Boston finally came to an end.

Washington knew that the next target for the British troops would be New York City. It was a crucial part of the British plan to isolate and, if necessary, to destroy the city and thereby crush the uprising in New England. From New York, the English would move to capture the Hudson River, and thereby cut New England off from the other colonists to the south and thereby strangle the rebellion.

Washington had five months to build his fortification in New York before British and Hessian troops landed on Long Island, just east of Manhattan. Washington was confident that they would give the British a whipping but things turned out differently than expected.

Ten thousand British and Hessian troops landed on Staten Island in June 1776. All during July and August more reinforcements came until General Howe had a combined force of thirty-two thousand men, the largest army England had ever sent overseas.

As the insert map below shows, Washington had built fortifications on the western shore of Long Island today known as Brooklyn Heights. Underestimating the number of British troops, he only had an army of six thousand men in Brooklyn.

At the end of August, Howe attacked Washington's fortifications and crushed his army, forcing him to withdraw his troops to Manhattan. Here he stationed half his troops on lower Manhattan and sent the other half up north a few miles to Harlem Heights. Again, Washington's inexperience was on display. When the British discovered that he had split his troops, they landed a large force on Manhattan's east side in Kips Bay, which is considered midtown today. This force now stood between Washington's divided troops. Another cataclysmic loss seemed inevitable with half his army now trapped in lower Manhattan surrounded by the East River, the Hudson River, and the New York Harbor. It was only by the grace of Providence that he was able to escape with this troops.

The Congress, hearing of Washington's defeat, became demoralized. Those who advocated peace with England once again vehemently raised their voices. Others criticized the inexperienced troops who ran in panic in the face of the Red Coats. Washington himself came under criticism for his blunders. He was, after all, not a professional soldier but a private citizen who had been in a couple of battles. He was greatly outmatched in experience, strategy, troops, and weaponry by the British. Frozen by indecision and the need to overly process the advice of his senior officers, Washington allowed the British in mid-November to overrun Fort

Washington in Harlem Heights and also seize supplies of the American army from Fort Lee across the Hudson River in New Jersey.

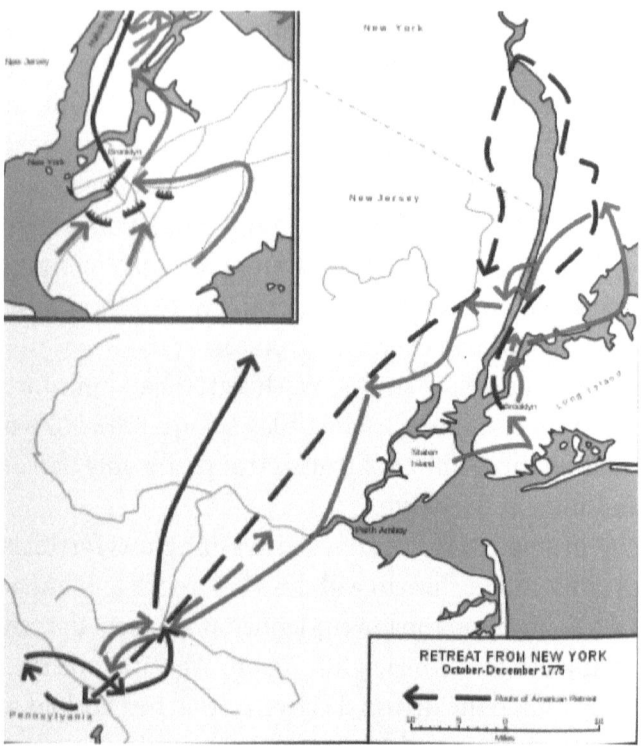

Map 4-5: Battle of Long Island

In the battle for Fort Washington, the Americans had lost about three thousand troops, who were either killed, wounded, or captured. The losses of Fort Washington and Fort Lee were inexcusable. Washington almost lost his entire army as the British moved to cut off all exits out of Harlem. Only because the British had poor maps and were unfamiliar with the terrain was Washington able to get his rag tag troops out of New York City and into the wilderness of New Jersey.[533]

Washington ran for his life down the entire coast of New Jersey with General Cornwallis in hot pursuit. Often, as the Americans were exiting a small town from the south, the British were entering it from the north. Washington escaped New Jersey, crossed the Delaware River, and encamped his troops in Pennsylvania. It was the dead of winter and his troops were hungry and ill-clothed. The British set up their encampment on the New Jersey side of the river near Trenton and waited things out. They knew the winter would destroy Washington's army and they had nothing to do but wait and conduct a mop up operation when the weather got warmer.

Congress was now in a black mood. John Adams acknowledged that Washington's troops were "much disgusted" with his leadership and his fatal indecisiveness.[534]

Washington was faced with the reality that the enlistment period of his troops was about to expire and that no one would join an army on the run and that faced consistent defeat. Yet, in this darkest hour, in an act of complete desperation, Washington risked it all. Only "dire necessity," he later admitted, moved him to action.

He had gathered good intelligence from German-Americans in Trenton who had told him that the Hessians, who were German mercenaries, were full of confidence and distracted with celebrating Christmas. Washington decided that they were vulnerable to a surprise attack. His plan worked perfectly. Crossing the Delaware River in the dark of night, he caught his enemy unaware in a cold dawn assault. More than one thousand Hessian troops were killed, wounded, or captured and many supplies and weapons were confiscated.[535] After the battle, Washington moved the majority of his troops back to Pennsylvania, leaving some to control Trenton. The victory fired up his troops and recharged the imagination of the American colonists. Now Washington went on the offensive.

General Cornwallis had sent an army to Trenton where he hoped to engage Washington again. He recaptured Trenton as Washington's troops moved south of the town and set up fortifications along Assunpink Creek. From their defenses, the Americans fired volley after volley into the advancing Red Coats causing heavy casualties. On the same night, Washington moved his troops in Pennsylvania back across the Delaware and made a surprise attack on Princeton NJ, a few miles north of Trenton. Cornwallis was caught off guard because Washington had left decoy troops in Pennsylvania who built campfires, repaired fortifications and made enough noise to suggest that the entire army had remained in the camp.

Washington's victory in Trenton had galvanized militia in New Jersey, Pennsylvania, Delaware, New York, and Connecticut and they now came to join the fight. The Americans set up cannons and blasted Nassau Hall of Princeton University where the British were headquartered. This forced them to surrender. Cornwallis immediately moved to engage Washington's army but the Americans had sabotaged a bridge, which prevented his troops from crossing.[536] The British were soon forced into an enclave around New Brunswick, giving up the rest of New Jersey.

The British strategy was to overwhelm the Americans, cut them off from each other, and crush any military opposition that could be mustered. After their defeats in New Jersey, they realized that they had failed and it was going to be a long war.

Washington's military victories caused even the most cynical hearts to swell with pride. The Continental Congress became more cooperative with each other and put aside their egos and petty differences. The American people picked up Thomas Paine's *Common Sense* and began to see themselves as an independent people just as the Declaration of Independence said they were. The year 1776 proved to be very big for what would become the United States of America.

In 1778, the French would send their fleet to America to aid the revolution. The English were compelled to sue for peace and grant the colonies their independence. George Washington was elected the first president of the new government. The definition of this new republic and the shape of its political economy would be debated and hammered out with great difficulty. In this struggle, two names stand out as driving forces in establishing the United States of America. These men were Washington's Secretary of the Treasury, Alexander Hamilton and his Secretary of State, Thomas Jefferson.

Hamilton vs Jefferson

The quarrel between Hamilton and Jefferson is the best known and historically the most important in American political history. Hamilton's and Jefferson's incompatibility was heightened by the wish of each to be Washington's principal and most trusted advisor.[537]

Alexander Hamilton (1755-1804) began his political career as the *aide-de-camp*[538] to General George Washington during the Revolutionary War. After the war, he became Washington's Secretary of the Treasury, and, as such, was the author of the administration's economic policies. In this role, he founded the nation's financial system, and can be considered the father of American capitalism. He built a centralized economy through the design and lobbying for a series of actions. These included advocating that the paying of the states' debts that were acquired during the Revolutionary War be assumed by the Federal government. To pay the debts of the national and state governments, he created a system of taxes and established a national bank. He also strongly advocated for friendly trade relations with England. To help realize his goals, he created the Federalist Party to create legislation and also the New York Post to popularize support for his economic vision.

Hamilton's plan was soon opposed by those who realized that it would unfairly benefit the northern capitalists at the expense of local, rural people and certainly the south. Thomas Jefferson and James Madison of Virginia led the opposition and formed the Democratic-Republican Party to protect the interests of the average person. Jefferson feared that Hamilton, and the Tories who supported him, longed to play Britain's game of empire building and once again place the country in England's financial debt. Jefferson and Madison were patriots in the mold of Sam Adams. Like Adams, they despised British imperialism and knew that if Hamilton's polices were put into law, they would weaken state's rights and destroy the democratic republic that Americans had fought so hard to establish. They saw a conspiracy developing among the wealthy to take over the national economy by merging their interests with the English capitalists. As things turned out, Hamilton had his way and the fears of Jefferson and Madison were realized.

Hamilton's Plan

Hamilton was an Enlightenment thinker who understood how capitalism worked. He believed that those nations that adapted a capitalist economy would become, in his words, "prosperous at home and respectable abroad." At the Constitutional Convention, he told the delegates that, "Safety from external danger is the most powerful director of national conduct."[539] He argued that if nations were insecure, they tended to be less free as they were compelled to adopt institutions that destroyed civil and political rights. Conversely, nations that were powerful achieved security and maintained their freedoms. What made nations powerful? Hamilton's answer was "commerce." Commerce generated wealth and wealth generated power. In turn, power resulted in national security. In order to be a "commercial people" American's must be able to defend their commercial ventures against other nations. This circular argument still forms the basis of US political policy today. Unfortunately, being circular, it allows no room for expansion of thought or necessary change.

To build its commercial empire, Hamilton knew that the United States needed to industrialize and to do this, it required credit from financiers not only in America but also in Europe where most of the money was. To establish credit with European capitalists, his task was to first resolve the problem of the national debt that Americans had accrued due to the Revolutionary War.[540]

With the formation of the new government in 1789, the first House of Representatives directed Alexander Hamilton to draw up a plan for the support of public credit. In January of 1790, Hamilton submitted his First Report on the Public Credit, which became the foundation for subsequent action taken by Congress to fund and pay the public debt.

The report analyzed the financial standing of the United States of America and made recommendations to reorganize the national debt and to establish the public credit.[541] The report called for full federal payment at face value to holders of government securities. It also called for the national government to assume funding of all state debt.[542]

From a capitalist perspective the plan was brilliant. In the proposed refinancing of the debt, new securities were to be exchanged for the old, but instead of liquidating the debt immediately, it was funded through regular interest payments. Regarding the states wartime debts, Hamilton recommended that the creditors would exchange their state securities (IOUs) for new federal securities. Creditors of national or state debt could opt to hold their old IOUs, but incentives were built into Hamilton's plan to exchange them for new IOUs.

The new public debt was to be funded at four percent interest and be backed by the pledge that the government would guarantee payment throughout the life of the loan.

To raise revenues to pay the new loans, Hamilton proposed a tariff on certain items being sold from other nations to Americans. Because ninety percent of this tax would be paid by British merchants, who were at the time the American's greatest trading partners, it was important for Hamilton that the US maintain good working relations with them.

Hamilton knew that the bulk of the new securities would be held by the northern capitalists—merchants, professionals, and men of old wealth. There would also be investors and speculators from Europe, the Dutch banks, and the wealthy of England and France. Foreign investment was crucial for Hamilton because, at the time, the US economy was not large enough to finance his strategy. Other options for generating local capital were ruled out by Hamilton. These included agriculture in the south and expansion westward.

Hamilton appealed directly to the capitalists, especially the northern American capitalists because he knew this would put them in a position to fully support a federal government. If the government failed, their new securities would be worthless.[543]

Hamilton's vision, which came to be known as "Hamiltonianism,"[544] was based upon the model of the English capitalists. As such, he sought to turn the US economy into a "cash" economy with a constantly expanding money supply. He also sought to minimize the power of the states (colonies) in relation to the federal government by reducing their power to collect taxes. In this way, Hamilton, wanted to control the colonies just as the English had previously controlled them. Only now it would be a federal government, funded by northern capitalists, who would sit on the throne.

According to Gordon Wood, the highly acclaimed author of *Radicalism of the American Revolution*, Hamilton was clearing the way for the day when the "whole society should be taken over by moneymaking and the pursuit of individual interest."[545]

The Opposition of Madison and Jefferson

When Hamilton presented his plan to Congress, it went generally unopposed except for James Madison from Virginia, who opposed Hamilton's proposal to fund the domestic debt at face value and to assume the state debts. Madison, who was a seasoned, back room political infighter sensed something was wrong with Hamilton's proposal, but he did not have the vision or scope to completely wrap his mind around it. Instead, he argued that Hamilton's plan ignored the small farmers, soldiers, and townspeople who had supported the war but who, finding themselves in debt, sold their original securities to monied speculators who bought them for pennies on the dollar. He proposed instead that six percent interest be paid on the entire debt with the current security holders only being paid at face value while the interest would be returned to the original holders. Madison also opposed the national government assuming state debt. Virginians believed that they had paid most of their debt and they did not feel that it was their responsibility to pay federal taxes to bail out other states. Madison knew that his argument would not hold water but it prevented an immediate approval of Hamilton's plan.

As the battle waged on, Madison was joined by his friend, Thomas Jefferson, who had become Washington's Secretary of State in the spring of 1790. Hamilton joined the administration in September 11, 1789, giving him a six-month lead in forming and implementing his strategy.[546]

Fig. 4-29: Alexander Hamilton

Fig. 4-30: James Madison

Fig 4-31: Thomas Jefferson

At the time, Jefferson had not been in the country for long, having traveled to France and England. Jefferson supported the French Revolution, but was appalled by the living conditions of the common man in England. He was struck by the "utter powerlessness of the people of Europe. They seemed uninspired and hopeless compared to the American revolutionaries.

The Compromise of 1790

When he returned to the states and entered the fray, Jefferson was a newbie unfamiliar with the subtleties of the national politics in play. At the time, much of the debate over Hamiltonianism took place over dinner conversations during which the state representatives shared their opinions and positions. Hamilton encouraged Jefferson and Madison to come to dinner at his house to try to resolve their impasse. He had secretly hoped to persuade Jefferson to abandon his support of Madison and see things his way. Jefferson agreed to host the private dinner at his own home on 57 Maiden Lane in New York City. At the dinner, Hamilton got what he wanted.

What some call the "dinner table bargain"[547] and others call the Compromise of 1790, produced an agreement between the contestants and set the course for Congress to pass the Funding Act of 1790. Jefferson later described the encounter between the men accordingly:

> They came. I opened the subject to them, [acknowledged] that my situation had not permitted me to understand it sufficiently but encouraged them to consider the thing together. They did so. It ended in Mr. Madison's acquiescence in a proposition that the question [i.e., assumption of state debts] should be again brought before the house by way of amendment from the Senate, that he would not vote for it, nor entirely withdraw his opposition, yet he would not be strenuous, but leave it to its fate. It was observed, I forget by which of them, that as the pill would be a bitter one to the Southern states, something should be done to soothe them; and the removal of the seat of government to the [Potomac] was a just measure, and would probably be a popular one with them, and would be a proper one to follow the assumption.[548]

Later Jefferson would rue his decision to support Hamilton's scheme as the worst mistake of his political career. He said he felt that he had been used by Hamilton, or, in his own words, he had been "made a tool for forwarding the schemes of others."[549]

When they realized that they had been duped, Jefferson and Madison formed the Democratic-Republican party to challenge Hamilton's Federalist party. This set the stage for a political struggle that lasted for several decades. From a greater perspective, it also defined the main contradiction within America society to this day—between democracy for the common man vs the power of the capitalists and their money.

The compromise cleared the way for Congress to approve Hamilton's plan. They passed the Funding Act of 1790.[550] Without going into the particulars of the bill, it allowed for the creation of new federal debt and the federal assumption of state debts. By relinquishing their debt payments, the states were able to reduce the need for state taxes. This resulted in the lowering of taxes in many states. However, the savings were an illusion because there was a subsequent imposition of federal taxes. Essentially the status quo was maintained. The advantage to the states, however, was that the Funding Act immediately provided substantial revenue through the federal securities, which they now held in place of their old debt. This new income made up nearly one-fifth of total state revenue and thereby enabled states to directly invest in industry and economic enterprises.[551]

With the unqualified support of President Washington and Congress and with the Federalist Party in the driver's seat, Hamilton pushed through laws that provided several more building blocks for the realization of his vision. He immediately pushed through the Bank Bill of 1791. This bill created a national bank "in order to manage the national finance, to obtain loans for the federal government, and to promote trade and industry." The bank was granted the right of corporate personhood and given a monopoly over any business with the federal government. The bank would not be owned by the government but by its shareholders who were private subscribers who bought the shares.[552] Only the wealthy could afford to buy shares in the bank. Washington signed the Bank Bill into law in 1791.

Jefferson Sees the Writing on the Wall

Jefferson now grasped the big picture. The federal government was now to be controlled by the private capitalists who controlled the government's purse strings. Democracy for all intents and purposes would no longer have meaning. Independence would be lost and once again the people would become subservient to the designs of the capitalists' ambition. The Bank Bill, to Jefferson, meant that once again Americans would be subservient to British wealth, which would continue to concentrate in the hands of the rich. He was utterly dismayed, after making his case to President Washington that he was completely ignored. Washington supported Hamilton in everything.

Jefferson began to seriously reassess his thinking. He now believed that the ideals of the revolution were under serious assault. He studied the behavior of those around him. He hosted dinner parties to learn what people were thinking. He was stunned to realize that there was strong support for creating an American aristocracy and even turning the presidency into a monarchy. Jefferson became sensitive to warnings in some newspapers that a movement was growing among rich and powerful Americans to expand the powers of the national government under their control. The papers noted with dismay President Washington's regal formality and the social style of those around him.

John Adams, the Vice President, had actually advocated calling the president "His Highness," an idea that appalled his cousin Sam Adams, who was back in Massachusetts and no longer a part of the national political scene. As for Alexander Hamilton, he had previously proposed at the Constitutional Convention that the President and the Senate should be elected for life. Hamilton argued, "And let me observe that an executive is less dangerous to the liberties of the people when in office during life than for seven years."[553] Hamilton wanted someone like the King of England who could never be impeached.

Jefferson and Madison knew that they could no longer depend upon the President for support. In the ten months since he had joined Washington's cabinet, Hamilton had won every battle on funding, assumption of state debt, taxes, and the Bank.[554] He had also led the Federalist campaign against decentralization. What was worse, Jefferson realized that Hamilton's power was growing among the wealthy and the politicians who stood to personally profit by Hamilton's position on bonds and securities. At the same time, Jefferson knew that most Americans neither supported Hamiltonianism, nor the higher taxes and big government that went with his proposals. They could feel their power at the local level slipping from their grasp.

The Jefferson Strategy

Jefferson knew that he had to stop Hamilton if the South and, for that matter, small town people everywhere were to escape the capitalist strategy of Hamilton and the Federalist Party. He knew he had to mobilize the opposition. This involved a strategy that was not so much based on organizing as it was activating. He knew the enemies of Hamiltonianism were the southern states as well as the progressive decentralists in the north who fought for local and state rights. For his part, Jefferson's first step was to create a newspaper that would publicize the viewpoint of the resistance. The Federalists already had created the *Gazette of the United States* that promoted their vision. Hamilton had also created the *New York Evening Post* that still exists today as the *New York Post*. To counter the offensive of these publications, Jefferson secretly negotiated with Philip Freneau, a journalist who mirrored the ideas of Thomas Paine, to create an opposition newspaper. Freneau agreed and the *National Gazette* was born.[555] It published its first issue on October, 1791.

Next, Jefferson sent out letters to local organizers in several states to determine their response to the Bank Bill and Hamilton's vision. He was encouraged to find that there was significant dismay with Hamilton's initiatives as well as the sudden expansion of congressional powers as reflected in their authority to influence state economies and create a national bank.[556]

Madison, who had been a strong proponent of a central government, now realized that Jefferson was right. He began to warn people that the Federalists were an "anti-republican party" who believed that the American people were incapable of self-governance. He criticized their strategy to keep the American people quiet and docile through "pageantry of rank, the influence of money and emoluments, and the terror of military force."[557]

While Jefferson and Madison led the insurrection against the capitalist assault on self-governance and democracy, there were many local organizers who saw things their way. They had already set up committees of correspondence in the example of Sam Adams and held true to the beliefs of Thomas Paine who stood for an independent democracy. These people remembered how Tom had inspired the entire country during the period of hopelessness as George Washington's army was being ruthlessly pursued by the English and the Hessians down the coast of New Jersey during the cold winter months of 1776. It was Thomas Paine who encouraged them with the words: "These are the times that try men's souls: The summer soldier and the sunshine patriot will, in this crisis, shrink from the service of his country; but he that stands for it NOW, deserves the love and thanks of man and woman."[558] Washington was so inspired by these words that he had them read to his troops on Christmas night immediately before they crossed the Delaware and won their first victory at the Battle of Trenton.

Paine championed the dignity of the common man. He consistently fought against the idea of the Federalists who believed that ordinary people were not fit to govern themselves. He said that every age and generation must be free to act for itself because it is the living and not the dead who should be accommodated. He said that every individual is born equal in terms of the rights of his contemporaries.[559]

Paine's pamphlets were read throughout the colonies, in churches, and in public squares so that even illiterate people could hear his words of independence. Paine was a relentless critic of the British monarchy and Parliament and a staunch defender of republicanism. Paine won the hearts of the people because he was always optimistic about the course of history, about the perfectibility of human beings, and the vision of political and social equality. It was Thomas Paine, more than any other American, even Sam Adams, who convinced the American people to stop thinking of themselves as British subjects and embrace the cause of American liberty.[560]

It was to Thomas Paine, therefore, and not Thomas Jefferson, that the local people and local organizers turned for inspiration. And it was they who began to build a political party to opposed Alexander Hamilton and the Federalists.

Back in Pennsylvania, Madison was also working on the idea of creating a political party to uphold the vision that mankind is capable of governing itself. He pointed out that political organizations were not new. There were the Whigs and the Tories, the Federalists and Anti-Federalists who had emerged during the struggle to create a Constitution, and now a new party was needed to resist the "opulent" who had seized the government for its own purposes. He proposed the name *Republican Party* because it would support the republic and preserve the dream of the American Revolution that hereditary power would not control a free people.[561] Madison made the same argument that Karl Marx would later make, and after Marx, many of our own contemporaries who contrast the interests of the one percent against the common interests of the American people. These people all understand the problem inherent in centralized capitalism and the inevitability of class conflict under the capitalist system.

By early 1793, Jefferson thought that the threat posed by Hamilton and the Federalist was on the wane. An opposition press had been established and there were now Republicans in Congress to fight the Federalists. There were certainly grounds for optimism, but the class struggle of which Madison spoke has persisted until this day.

When George Washington retired in 1797, his Vice President, John Adams, a Federalist, won the next election for President. Even so, the Republicans were strong enough to have Thomas Jefferson elected as his Vice-President. After four years in office, Thomas Jefferson defeated Adams and became the President for the next eight years, 1801 to 1809. When Thomas Jefferson was elected to the presidency, Sam Adams, whose sentiments lay more with the new president than with his cousin, wrote Jefferson to express his delight in his election.[562]

After Jefferson's term, Republicans James Madison and James Monroe served for two terms until John Quincy Adams, a Federalist, was elected. The political landscape would shift again with the election of Andrew Jackson in 1829.

Thomas Jefferson made a lasting impression on American history and his name has become synonymous with democracy. He held a deep optimism about human reason and believed that the will of the people, expressed through elections, should direct the course of the republic.

He also felt that the federal government should be frugal and simple. As president, he reduced the size and scope of the federal government, the size of the army and navy and paid off the government's debt. He believed this was consistent with the intention of the Constitution.

Jefferson also struggled to support human rights, especially the protection of civil liberties and minority rights. As he explained in his inaugural address in 1801, "though the will of the majority is in all cases to prevail, that will, to be rightful, must be reasonable; that the minority possess their equal rights, which equal laws must protect, and to violate would be oppression."[563]

Jefferson did have his faults, however. He lacked a credible economic policy to rival the well-organized financial strategy of Alexander Hamilton. Because most of the people in the country at the time were farmers, he identified farming with democracy. He believed that "Those who labor in the earth are the chosen people of God."

While he believed in international trade and modern technology, he was wary of urban industrialization and financial speculation. He believed that they robbed men of their independence. Debt was the main enemy of liberty.

Ever since the dawn of capitalism, the well wishers of humanity have wrestled with the problem of how liberty and democratic equality could be reconciled with social and economic changes that continually increase inequality? Jefferson believed that if every farmer owned his own land and could meet his basic needs, then democracy and liberty could be achieved. But there were flaws in this simplistic approach. He did not see how poverty pushed women and children into forced labor. Nor did he consider a place for the Native Americans or African slaves. Jefferson saw these people as inferior races and not deserving of full and equal citizenship. While declaring that, "all men are created equal," he owned slaves all his life and, unlike Washington, never set them free.[564] Our final assessment of Jeffersonian Democracy, therefore, rests upon a profound contradiction. While Jefferson was the single most powerful defender of democracy as expressed in his Declaration of Independence "that all men are created equal, his definition of "all men" was severely limited to only white men and did not include women, children, or racial minorities.

Many of the economic problems that early Americans faced continue to exist today. The class struggle persists and government has become beholding to the capitalist class wealth and power. This condition could not be mitigated by Jefferson's inadequate presentation of an alternative economic model nor by his sexist and racist attitudes. This situation will be discussed more fully in *Revolution*, the third book of this trilogy on *History, Ideology and Revolution*.

Women of the Revolution

When John Adams became President, he tried to move the government closer to England just as his mentor, Alexander Hamilton, had desired. His leanings were explicitly conservative, and while he might have spoken out against the rich who totally disrespected democracy, in reality, he was extremely anxious about the common man raising himself out of oppressive circumstances to challenge authority. Adams complained that "our struggle has loosened the bands of government everywhere. That children and apprentices were disobedient—that schools and colleges were growing turbulent—that Indians slighted their guardians and Negroes grew insolent to their masters."[565]

He wrote this in a letter to his wife, Abigail, but if he expected to gain comfort from her in his anxiety, he was much mistaken. Abigail, like many women who had suffered through the revolution, had made the connection between government of the society and government within the household. She told her husband, that in the course of making laws, he should remember the women and be more generous than his ancestors were. She warned him, "Do not put such unlimited power into the hand of the husbands. Remember all men would be tyrants if they could. If particular care and attention is not paid to the ladies, we are determined to foment a rebellion, and will not hold ourselves bound by any laws in which we have no voice or representation."[566]

The language that she used expressed the same sentiments that Sam Adams had expressed when he spoke about the injustice faced by the American colonists in being bound by the laws of Parliament when they had no representation in its deliberations. To be bound as such was to be a slave, to be a subject to another. The revolution made women more aware of the inequality that existed in their marriages that allowed their husbands to treat them cruelly and exercise arbitrary power over them. The British rule of thumb on how to treat wives, which was still held by colonial men, was that it was permissible for husbands to beat their wives so long as the stick or club did not exceed the thickness of a male thumb.[567] John dismissed his wife's warning with a laugh. He wrote to Abigail that men knew better than to repeal their "masculine systems." Men, he scoffed, would never be subject to the "despotism of the petticoat."[568]

Abigail simmered over her husband's callous response. She knew that laws could be revised to gain legal protection for women against abusive husbands. There was also need to change the British laws that held that women, once married, ceased to have any independent legal, political, or economic existence. Under the legal doctrine of *coverture*, a wife became a *feme covert* and her identity was absorbed into that of her husband, symbolized by her taking of his name. A wife could not bring suit in court, sign a legally binding contract, vote, or acquire property or income in her own name.[569] Once married, a woman was forced to surrender her property and wages to their husband. According to Abigail, such flagrant sexism violated the principles of God, nature, and human morality.

If her husband was going to be unyielding on such a fundamental principle, Abigail resolved to have her friends petition Congress. While John worried that to concede power to women would be to concede power to anyone with a social grievance and thereby destroy class privilege, Abigail's vision embodied a universal human sentiment: "I will never consent to have our sex considered in an inferior point of light. Let each planet shine in their own orbit. God and nature designed it so—if man is Lord, woman is Lordess—that is what I contend for." Her goal was to "restore liberty, equality, and fraternity between the sexes."[570]

The question of women's rights had been a subject of public debate before John Adams became President. James Otis, a compatriot of the Adams cousins in Boston, as early as 1764, had raised the question in his *The Rights of the British Colonies Asserted and Proved*, "Are not women born as free as men?" At Yale, senior students had debated "Whether women ought to be admitted into the Magistracy and Government of Empires and Republics." But the row between the aristocratic John Adams and his activist wife Abigail sent out ripples that created changes beyond their family dynamics.[571]

Early Social Reform Movements

The truth is that the American Revolution failed to bring significant changes to women's rights as citizens. The marriage laws remained intact. The control of women by men continued. The purpose of women was to nurture their husbands and to raise virtuous children so that the United States republic would flourish. This concept later become known as *Republican Motherhood*.[572]

While only a small number of people believed that the ideals of *life, liberty, and the pursuit of happiness* should also apply to women, nonetheless, women began to gain power through reform movements like the temperance movement and the abolition movement of the 1820s to 1840s. These early social movements, and the meetings and conventions that they required, offered women their first public platform by which to express themselves collectively. Over time, women abolitionists began to realize that they should be fighting for their own rights as well.[573]

One of these women was Elizabeth Cady Stanton, who used the Declaration of Independence as a model to create the *Declaration of Sentiments*, which she presented at the first Women's Rights Convention in Seneca Falls, New York in July 1848.

The Declaration of Sentiments began:

> We hold these truths to be self-evident; that all men and women are created equal; that they are endowed by their Creator with certain inalienable rights; that among these are life, liberty, and the pursuit of happiness.

While the Declaration met with scathing criticism by the male press and husbands everywhere, causing some of the original signees to withdraw their signatures, the women's movement finally had a list of the rights that women were seeking and this fact alone inspired many other women to stand up for their rights.

Suffrage Movement

A second women's rights movement emerged after the Civil War. Convinced that women would never enjoy equality until they won the right to vote, Elizabeth Cady Stanton and Susan B. Anthony formed the *National Woman Suffrage Association* in 1869.[574]

The same year, Lucy Stone, Henry Blackwell, and Julia Ward Howe started the American Woman Suffrage Association, which concentrated on gaining voting rights through individual state constitutions. The two organizations merged in 1890 to form the National American Woman Suffrage Association. It was not until the decade of 1910 that states stopped preventing women from voting and it was not until 1920 that voting rights for women was ratified as an amendment to the U.S. Constitution.[575] In their relentless march to equality, Susan B Anthony, Matilda Joslyn Gage, and Elizabeth Cady Stanton, on behalf of the National Woman Suffrage Association, wrote a four page *Declaration of Rights of the Women of the United States* in 1876 which made the following statement:

> The history of our country the past hundred years, has been a series of assumptions and usurpations of power over woman, in direct opposition to the principles of just government, acknowledged by the United States at its foundation, which are:
>
> *First*. The natural rights of each individual.
>
> *Second*. The exact equality of these rights.
>
> *Third*. That these rights, when not delegated by the individual, are retained by the individual.
>
> *Fourth*. That no person can exercise the rights of others without delegated authority.

The document concluded with the simple statement: We ask of our rulers, at this hour, no special favors, no special privileges, no special legislation. We ask justice, we ask equality, we ask that all the civil and political rights that belong to citizens of the United States, be guaranteed to us and our daughters forever.[576]

It took almost a century and a half from the signing of the Declaration of Independence in 1776 to 1920 for women to gain the right to vote in the United States. It was a long and arduous journey in which every step taken was condemned by the male establishment. For all the greatness of this accomplishment in achieving their political rights, women in this country have yet to achieve their economic rights that will give them equality with the ruling capitalist class. This battle, which includes both women and men in the ranks of its patriots, is still being fought and the victory of the average citizen in this struggle is much more critical to universal human justice than any battle that has ever proceeded it.

Andrew Jackson (1767–1845)

Andrew Jackson was the seventh President of the United States (1829-1837). He was born in the backwoods, somewhere near the border between North and South Carolina of a newly immigrant Scots-Irish farming family from Ulster.[577] The family settled in an area that still belonged to Native Americans who didn not share the whites' idea of property rights, so there was often conflict, and life on the farm was an anxious one. Just before Andrew was born, his father injured himself while working, fell ill, and died leaving his wife Elizabeth with two children and Andrew on the way. She moved into her sister's house and tried to ensure that her son who never knew a father would get an education and become a god-fearing man in the Presbyterian tradition.

Andrew was a wild child, however, with a strong will and nasty temper. A school mate of his recalled that in a fight he would always be thrown to the ground three or four times, but "he would never stay throwed."

During the Revolutionary War, the British navy delivered an army to the Carolinas in 1780 in an attempt to divide the colonists north and south. They outfitted local Tories under a Lieutenant Colonel Banastre Tarleton to fight the rebels. Tarleton turned out to be a particularly cruel man and his men massacred any rebels they came across, raped local women, and recognized no established rules of combat. Andrew Jackson was thirteen years old at the time and his mother was an ardent rebel. While she tried to protect him from the British, he joined a local militia. The men would not let him engage in combat but they used him as a messenger. It was not too long before the British destroyed his family's house and farm and took him prisoner. As a prisoner, he was interrogated and refused to speak. To humiliate him, a British officer demanded that Andrew clean the mud off his boots. Andrew, filled with rage, refused. The officer, incensed by the boy's resistance, drew his sword and aimed a blow at the boy's head. Andrew raised his arm and received a severe gash on his hand and another on his head. With blood pouring from his head and hand he stood his ground and defied the officer again.[578]

The officer overcame his urge to kill Andrew on the spot and forced him to lead his dragoons to a local rebel named Thompson. There were too paths to Thompson's house and Andrew took the dragoons on the longer route giving Thompson a chance to escape. Such was the early experience of Andrew Jackson and a demonstration of his mettle as a young warrior.

While it is unknown what qualities Andrew inherited from his father, it is clear what he inherited from his mother. When she found out that her son was taken to a prison in Camden, New Jersey, she braved the cold, Tories, Natives, and outlaws to rescue her son. Hiding her rebel sentiments, she persuaded the British to exchange her son for some British prisoners that her militia could no longer afford to keep.

Her parting words to her son, as she later left for Charleston to care for the patriot soldiers were:

> Andrew, if I should not see you again I wish you to remember and treasure up some things I have already said to you: In this world you will have to make your own way. To do that you must have friends. You can make friends by being honest, and you can keep them by being steadfast. You must keep in mind that friends worth having will in the long run expect as much from you as they give to you. To forget an obligation or be ungrateful for a kindness is a base crime – not merely a fault or a sin, but an actual crime. Men guilty of it sooner or later must suffer the penalty. In personal conduct be polite, but never obsequious. No one will respect you more than you esteem yourself. Avoid quarrels as long as you can without yielding to imposition. But sustain your manhood always. Never bring a suit at law for assault and battery or for defamation. The law affords no

> remedy for such outrages that can satisfy the feelings of a true man. Never wound the feelings of others. Never brook wanton outrage upon your own feelings. If you ever have to vindicate your feelings or defend your honor, do it calmly. If angry at first, wait till your wrath cools before you proceed.[579]

This counsel from his mother inspired Andrew for his entire life. He went on to become a lawyer and was elected to the U.S. House of Representatives in 1796, and then to the U.S. Senate in 1797. In 1801, the President appointed him brigadier general of the Tennessee militia. It was in this role that he accomplished his decisive victory over the British army in the Battle of New Orleans as part of the War of 1812 and as a consequence gained national recognition for his victory.

The War of 1812 (1812–1815), was fought by the United States of America against Great Britain and its Native American allies. Even after the Revolutionary War, England kept its troops in America and was supported in this effort by colonial Tories, northern industrialists, and the Federalist Party.

The United States, during the presidency of James Madison, declared war again on the British for several reasons. These included the impressment of approximately ten thousand American merchant sailors into the Royal Navy[580] and the insult to national honor in the Chesapeake-Leopard Affair when an English ship fired upon and boarded an American ship off the coast of Virginia.[581] The Americans also were angry with the British for supporting Native American tribes against the desire of the colonists to expand into Native territory.[582] It was not that the British supported the Natives out of good will, but they did so only to divide and conquer.

The war was fought on the US-Canadian frontier, down along the Atlantic coast, and into the Gulf of Mexico. It was in the Gulf of Mexico that the Battle of New Orleans was fought in which Andrew Jackson prevented the British Army, Royal Marines, and a large Royal Navy fleet, commanded by Admiral Alexander Cochrane and General Edward Pakenham, from seizing the town of New Orleans and establishing a base by which to control the Mississippi River and split the power of the colonies.[583]

It was during the presidency of Thomas Jefferson that Napoleon had sold the Louisiana territory to the Americans for hard cash. The Americans acquired 827,000 square miles of territory west of the Mississippi River for fifteen million dollars or three cents an acre. By this act, the French relinquished their claim to lands in the United States.

The British never accepted the transfer of the Louisiana Territory to the Americans. By seizing New Orleans, they hoped to seize this territory and keep the Americans bottled up east of the Mississippi River.[584]

Map 4-6: Louisiana Purchase

Jackson was given responsibility for protecting the city. He still remembered what the British had done to his friends and family during the Revolutionary War and he still bore the scars on his wrist and forehead from the attack by the British officer. The odds were heavily stacked against him. The British had the advantage of mobility and control of the Gulf waters. They also had a professional army that was much larger than Jackson's reluctant militia, which was composed of Americans, Frenchmen, Spaniards, whites, blacks, persons of mixed race, rich, and poor, all speaking different languages. Some willingly responded to the call to arms, but most were reluctant. Some hoped for success, others for failure.[585]

Upon a late arrival, Jackson immediately declared martial law. Every individual entering the city had to report to the military. A curfew was set and all street lights were extinguished by nine o'clock.

Jackson had to inspire the men of New Orleans to fight. He took a different tact with each group. He reminded the Americans of the Revolutionary War fought by their fathers. He reminded the Frenchmen that the English were their eternal enemies and the Spaniards that the English had plotted with the Creek Indians to lay Siege to Pensacola, then one of two major settlements in Spanish Florida.[586] He also made an appeal to the black militia, after convincing the plantation owners that their lives depended upon arming free men of color. He addressed the blacks by saying:

> "Soldiers! From the shores of the Mobile I called you to arms. I invited you to share in the perils and to divide the glory of your white countrymen … I knew that you could endure hunger and thirst, and all the hardships of war. I knew that you loved the land of your nativity and that, like ourselves, you had to defend all that is most dear to man. But you surpassed my hopes. I have found in you, united to those qualities, that noble enthusiasm which impels to great deeds."[587]

While Jackson struggled to inspire his militia, the English landed thousands of regular troops on an island in Lake Borgne, which, due to coastal erosion, is no longer a lake but a lagoon extension of Gulf waters.[588] The English rowed sixty miles across the lake and reached hard ground where they began to capture outlaying homes and arrest their inhabitants. One man escaped and reported the English location to Jackson. They were only two miles from New Orleans before he got the message. As the townspeople learned of their situation many panicked. Many, listening to rumors, believed that the English would rape the women and kill the men so many families began to pour out of the city.

Jackson's implacable response was to order his aide-de-camp, "Say to them not to be alarmed. The enemy shall never reach the city." It was the truth.

He immediately loaded a number of his militia on a sailing vessel and moved to confront the British. Hungry and cold, the British had set up fires for cooking and warmth. They saw a ship approach at dusk but thought it was British until a voice called out: "Give them this for the honor of America!" Immediately cannons began to roar and grapeshot from anti-personal shells splintered the ranks of men gathered around the camp fires. The British responded with musket shots but to no avail. Now Jackson began an assault at several points in the enemy lines. In the dark, it became impossible for them to tell how many Americans there were or where they were coming from. The battle lasted most of the night with men fighting hand to hand, bayonet to bayonet and saber to saber."[589] It was the night before Christmas.

When the fighting stopped neither side knew who won. Both claimed victory, but in war ties go to the defender, and the strong showing of the American militia greatly increased the morale of the city inhabitants. Jackson had said they would not reach the city and he had stopped them cold.

While the battle was being fought, English and American diplomats were meeting in Ghent, Belgium and had concluded a peace treaty, which concluded the war.[590] The news however did not reach American shores until weeks later. By that time, Jackson had fought another seven days with the English army and had defeated them. The Battle of New Orleans was the most decisive victory of the Americans during the war and its final major battle.[591]

President Andrew Jackson

After Jackson's victory at the Battle of New Orleans, his name became a household word. He was now one of the most famous men in America and definitely the most popular. His supporters, mostly poor and middle-class white people, rallied to make him the next president. The Democratic-Republican Party of Jefferson and Madison was now simply called the Democratic Party.[592] In opposition to them, those with Federalist tendencies regrouped under the banner of the Whig Party. While, as we have seen, the Whigs during the Revolutionary War, were a progressive force in their fight against the English aristocrats (Tories), after the war the Whigs became a conservative force, who supported the English economic system against the people's expectations of a democratic nation.

Both parties built grassroots organizations to maximize the turnout of voters, which often reached eighty to ninety percent. Both parties created big city political machines and national networks of newspapers. The Democratic Party that ran Jackson for president, was a proponent for farmers, urban workers, and new immigrants. The Whig party, on the other hand, fought for businessmen, plantation owners, and later, social reformers who sought to abolish slavery. It was at this time that the small slave owners of the south joined the Democratic Party that supported their efforts as plantation owners and farmers.

The Democratic Party advocated westward expansion (Manifest Destiny)[593], greater equality among all white men, and opposition to the national banks.

Jackson agreed to run for President out of a sense of duty to his countrymen but, in accepting his election, he lost his beloved wife Rachel, who suffered a heart attack as the Jacksons prepared to leave their home, the *Hermitage*, in Tennessee and move to Washington. She was extremely anxious about the ill treatment that she and her husband had been subject to in the Washington press. In going to Washington DC, the Jacksons would be totally out of their element and she knew they would be the victims of the suave city gentry and the political insiders who were repelled by this rustic "military chieftain." Rachel's fears were not unfounded.

The regal tendencies of the Washingtonians that first manifested among the Hamiltonian Federalists were now firmly ingrained in Washington society. Jackson's predecessor was John Quincy Adams, the son of John and Abigail Adams. He was a Federalist who promoted big business and international trade deals. During his administration, goods, money, and people traveled more rapidly and efficiently than ever before.[594] At least this was true for the northern industrial states, if not the country.

Like his father, John Quincy was an aristocrat who reveled in the court society of Washington DC. As one member of the gentry explained, "Every look, word, and gesture in this aspiring city is regulated by the most fastidious etiquette. It is as much as your reputation is worth to transgress the rules provided for the defense of fashionable life."[595]

Another commented, "Woe to the simple, unsophisticated visitor to Washington, who, in obedience to the promptings of nature and observance of the uncourtly manners that he had practiced in his native village or woods, ventures to speak, dress, look, eat, or perform any ordinary office of life without deference to fashion!" The elite and powerful in Washington had almost forgotten the idea of democracy and held tightly to the aristocratic vision of turning Washington into a European court.

The elite were appalled, therefore, when a vast army of unsophisticated Americans descended on Washington to witness Andrew Jackson's inauguration. As one resident declared," . . . it seemed as if half the nation had rushed at once into the capital. It was like the inundation of the northern barbarians into Rome. . . . "

What made matters worse was that the people were defiant. They were sick of the power politics and economic exploitation of Washington, with its creeping control over their lives and freedoms. They had come to reinstate democracy.

When Jackson stepped out between the columns of the portico of the Capitol building to be officially inaugurated, a crowd of fifteen thousand supporters emitted a roar that shook the city. They had also brought their own cannons and fired them without reprieve until Chief Justice Marshall stepped forward to administer Jackson's oath. While, in many ways, the day was a mob scene "with a rabble, a mob of boys, negroes, women, children, scrambling, fighting, romping," the gentry of Washington had to admit, as one socialite confessed, that, "It was the People's day, and the People's President, and the People would rule."[596]

The Spoils System

Jackson began his administration by attempting to repair the damage done to democracy. He began by firing nearly ten percent of all government employees, (nine hundred and nineteen people) and replacing them by his own supporters. He argued that this would help to ensure the new administration's commitment to democracy. It would also create a more efficient government in which the new employees would be more committed to follow the lead of the President and his cabinet. His critics, however, referred to this process as a "spoils system" comparable to a situation where a victorious army loots the territory of its adversary after his loss. There was an element of truth in their complaint, for the wholesale firing of people by the Jackson administration introduced the *spoils system* into American politics.[597] The spoils system eliminated the merit system, in which employees kept their jobs by virtue of their performance and led to the spread of corrupt patronage jobs.

The post office, for example, was the largest department in the federal government at the time and hired even more personnel than the war department. In one year four hundred and forty-three postmasters were deprived of their positions, most with extensive records of good service.[598]

Federal Rights vs States Rights

One of the most immediate crises that Jackson faced was to clean up a mess created by his predecessor, John Quincy Adams. During the former President's rule, the Congress had passed a tariff designed to protect industry in the northern states that was suffering from cheap goods being imported from England. It was a protectionist measure to promote American manufacturing after the War of 1812. By adding a tax to British goods, the northern merchants could compete with British prices on goods. The tariff, however, hurt the southern states that now had to pay higher prices for goods not produced in their region. Furthermore, the reduction of the import of English goods made it more difficult for the British to pay for the cotton that they imported from the South to supply their textile industry. The South called the tax, the Tariff of Abominations.[599]

This situation led to what became known as the *Nullification Crisis*[600] as South Carolina declared that the federal tariffs were unconstitutional and therefore null and void within the sovereign boundaries of the state. It was the first example of the contest between federal and state rights that would later ignite into the Civil War between the Union and the Confederacy.

By 1828, South Carolina state politics increasingly organized around the tariff issue. Its opponents expected that Jackson as President would significantly reduce the tariff, but when he failed to take any actions to address their concerns, local organizers advocated that the state itself declare the tariff null and void within South Carolina.

By 1832, a state convention in South Carolina adopted the Ordinance of Nullification, which declared that the Tariffs of 1828 and 1832 were unconstitutional and unenforceable in the state. They began to mobilize an army to resist anticipated federal enforcement. On March 1, 1833, Congress passed the Force Bill authorizing the President to use military forces against South Carolina. However, it also negotiated a new tariff, the Compromise Tariff of 1833, which was satisfactory to South Carolina. The tariff rates were reduced and remained low to the satisfaction of the South, but the states' rights doctrine of nullification remained unresolved. By the 1850s, the argument of states' rights to expand slavery into the western territories and the threat of their growing power in the federal government became the central issue for the nation.[601]

Taking on the Bank of the United States

In keeping with his platform of economic decentralization, Jackson vetoed the renewal of the charter for the Second Bank of the United States, which pitted the proponents of democracy against the aristocrats largely composed of northern industrialists and the American business elite. The battle between the people and the one percent reached a feverish pitch under Jackson and exposed the main contradiction that, while often masked over, nonetheless, had always controlled the direction of American capitalism.

It was Hamilton, as we recall, who established the First Bank of the United States. After Hamilton left office in 1795, the new Secretary of the Treasury, Oliver Wolcott, Jr., informed Congress that the federal government needed more money. He suggested that this could be achieved either by selling the government's shares in the bank or by raising taxes. Congress agreed to sell the government's shares in the bank. In 1811, the Senate voted not to renew the bank's charter.[602]

In 1816, however, President James Madison was faced with a wicked currency inflation due to the cost of fighting the War of 1812. The government was printing up money to pay its debts and, in doing so, flooded the local economy with money so that its value was continually falling. At wits end, in an effort to stabilize the dollar, he supported the creation of the Second Bank of the United States.

Similar to the First Bank, it was set up as a private corporation that assumed some public duties. The bank handled all fiscal transactions for the U.S. Government, and was accountable to Congress and the U.S. Treasury. The federal government owned twenty percent of its capital, making it the bank's single largest stockholder. Four thousand private investors held eighty percent of the bank's capital, including one thousand Europeans.[603] The bulk of the stocks was held by a few hundred wealthy American capitalists. At the time, the bank was the largest financial corporation in the world.[604]

Trouble broke out during the Jackson administration when the Democrats fought the renewal of the bank's charter because of its fraud and corruption. Many called it a monstrous threat to American liberties. The Democrat's effort to kill the bank, was met by strong resistance led by Henry Clay who, in 1832, was running for President against Jackson as a member of the Whig Party and Nicholas Biddle who was the president of the bank.

Both sides made their case to the public. While Jackson's Democrats held more power in the south and among those who worshipped him as a leader in the fight for democracy, the Whigs fared well among all classes of people in urban communities engaged in commerce. They also had strong support among evangelical Protestants, abolitionists, and persons unhappy with the brutal treatment of blacks and Native Americans.[605] Like the Republican party of today, whom the Whig party would eventually become, the Whig leaders often acted like religious zealots rather than party leaders. Yet for all their religious posturing, the Whigs were as realistic and efficiently organized as their Democratic opponents.

After the War of 1812, the American economy boomed, in large part because American agricultural products, including cotton, were in demand in Europe due to the devastation caused by the Napoleonic Wars. The Bank aided this boom by providing loans to business. It also provided loans for land speculation. Similar to the housing bubble that peaked in 2006, land speculation, in 1819 alone, three years after the bank was chartered, led to the sale of over fifty-five million acres. The turnover of this land resulted in the doubling and tripling of money for the speculators. With land fever at this scale, not a lot of people were concerned about the widespread fraud occurring at the Bank.

Nonetheless, in the summer of 1818, the national bank managers realized that they were massively over-extended in their lending and began to call in their loans. This led to the Panic of 1819.

The Panic of 1819 was the first major peacetime financial crisis in the United States. It led to the general collapse of the American economy that persisted through 1821.[606] The Panic essentially revealed the flaws in American laissez faire capitalism with its continual boom and bust cycles, which the banks have long ago learned how to manipulate to milk the American people of their savings. The banks create bubbles by promoting investment in certain sectors of the economy and then when the Ponzi scheme peaks, they are the first to withdraw their investments, leading to a panic and collapse, to be followed by recessions, Depressions, or Great Recessions.

During the Panic of 1819, the central bank refused to cash in its own paper for hard currency (gold or silver) when the smaller state banks requested them to do so. This caused the state-chartered banks to foreclose on the heavily mortgaged farms and business properties they had financed.[607] This led to widespread bankruptcies and mass unemployment. Because most Americans do not know their history, they allow the same thing to happen again and again and are still letting it happen.

The financial disaster and the following depression, as could be expected, provoked popular resentment against the banks and a general mistrust of government economic policy. The people, many for the first time, became politically engaged so as to defend their local economic interests.[608]

This widespread discontent was channeled by Jackson's Democrats who advocated a return to Jeffersonian agrarian precepts. The *Era of Good Feelings* was over. It was followed by the Bank War and the rise of Jacksonian democracy that advocated for the common white man.[609]

The Bank War was the name for the political struggle that developed over the issue of renewing the charter of the Second Bank of the United States (BUS) during Jackson's administration.[610] Jacksonian Democrats mobilized in opposition to the national bank's re-authorization on the grounds that the bank conferred economic privileges on financial elites and violated the U.S. constitutional principles of social equality. They argued that it was an illegitimate corporation whose charter violated state sovereignty and therefore posed a threat to the agriculture-based economies, particularly of the U.S. southern states.

When Congress voted to reauthorize the Bank, Jackson promptly vetoed the bill. His veto message spoke for "farmers, mechanics, and laborers" against the "monied interest" and argued against the Bank's constitutionality. Pro-Bank Whigs (National Republicans) warned the public that Jackson would abolish the Bank altogether if granted a second term.[611]

Nonetheless, Jackson overwhelming beat Senator Henry Clay of the National Republicans and was reelected to his second term. Knowing that reprisals would come swiftly, Jackson addressed his cabinet with these words:

> The divine right of kings and the prerogative authority of rulers have fallen before the intelligence of the age. Standing armies and military chieftains can no longer uphold tyranny against the resistance of public opinion. The mass of the people have more to fear from combinations of the wealthy and professional classes – from an aristocracy which through the influence of riches and talents, insidiously employed, sometimes succeeds in preventing political institutions, however well adjusted, from securing the freedom of the citizen."[612]

He related to them how the bankers had gained complete control over the currency and consequently could levy taxes on the people without representation just as England had done to Americans before the Revolutionary War. These secret taxes, he said, took the form of premiums and interest that were limited only by the quantity of paper currency the Bank was able to print.

He immediately moved to remove federal deposits from the Bank and distributed the funds to several dozen private banks throughout the country.

Biddle, the president of the Central Bank, had his own plan. He knew he could buy off politicians within Jackson's administration as well as members of Congress. He boasted to an intimate acquaintance:

"I can remove all the constitutional scruples in the District of Columbia. Half a dozen presidencies [of bank branches], a dozen cashierships, fifty clerkships, a hundred directorships, to worthy friends who have no character and no money."[613]

In response to Jackson's actions, Biddle, launched a counter-attack. He offered lucrative positions to Jackson loyalists if they would abandon him. At the same time, he called in loans and tightened credit. While he stated publicly that the reason for this was to strengthen the bank against the uncertainty caused by Jackson's hasty actions, his real intent was to prove that people could not live without the Bank. To convince them this was so, he intentionally, and single-handedly, threw the economy into a depression. A panic spread from New York across the entire country. The greater the financial pain of the people, the greater was Biddle's resolve to crush Jackson and force Americans into subservience to his will.

He told any who pleaded with him to expand credit, to take their case to Jackson and the Congress, for it was they who were destroying the economy. Jackson was bombarded with petitions to return the federal deposits to the Bank, but he was as equally determined as Biddle not to give in. He knew what was at stake. If he could hold out long enough for the state banks to relieve the liquidity crisis by making loans and issuing credit, the economy would begin to correct itself. And so, it happened.

The Bank War broke the power of Biddle and the big capitalists. There was further good news. By 1835, the US government was no longer in debt. Jackson, since the first day he took office, began to repay the national debt. He had always seen national debt as a plot to fatten bankers and subvert the public. And so, it remains today. Jackson had provided the American people with a great service. He had forever proven that the bankers' claim that a democracy could never control its appetite for money, and thus needed the bankers, was a complete and utter falsehood and simply another argument in their arsenal of weapons to confuse the people.

Unfortunately, because things are never simple, especially when a nation's money supply is concerned, while Jackson was victorious in the Bank War against the Second Bank of the United States, he did not anticipate what would happen next. In short, the state banks, being free of Biddle's control, began to issue state bank notes to stimulate local economies without regard for the well-being of the economy as a whole. This led to another land speculation bubble. While he could not stop the state banks because he had no control over their charters, Jackson still hoped to quell inflation and speculation by giving an Executive Order, called the *Specie Circular*, which required that payment for government land be made in gold and silver.[614] This act caused the greater economy to sputter and led to the Panic of 1837 and another depression.[615]

Such a development must be understood if the American people desire to create a financial system that is free of corruption at the national level and parochialism at the local level. Despite the depression which lasted for seven years, the American people owe Andrew Jackson a great debt by clarifying our thinking about the need for a Federal Reserve Bank and teaching us how to confront the corruption to which such an institution gives rise.

Jackson and Slavery

Jackson lived in Tennessee which was a slave state. Despite his political principles, as a member of the southern elite, he owned and traded slaves and grew cotton. He built a mansion for himself, or rather, his slaves built a mansion for him called The Hermitage that sat on a one thousand acre plantation. The African American slaves, men, women, and children, sustained Jackson's family and the plantation through their labor. Most were employed producing cotton as the cash crop. As more ground was put under cotton production, the more slaves Jackson bought.

He purchased his first slaves in 1794. By the time he bought The Hermitage land in 1804, he owned nine slaves. After twenty-five years, thanks to slave labor, Jackson owned over one hundred slaves through purchase and reproduction. Over the course of his life, Jackson would own over three hundred men, women, and children. The maximum he ever owned at any one time was about one hundred and fifty. At the time of his death in 1845, he owned approximately one hundred and fifty people who lived and worked on his property.[616]

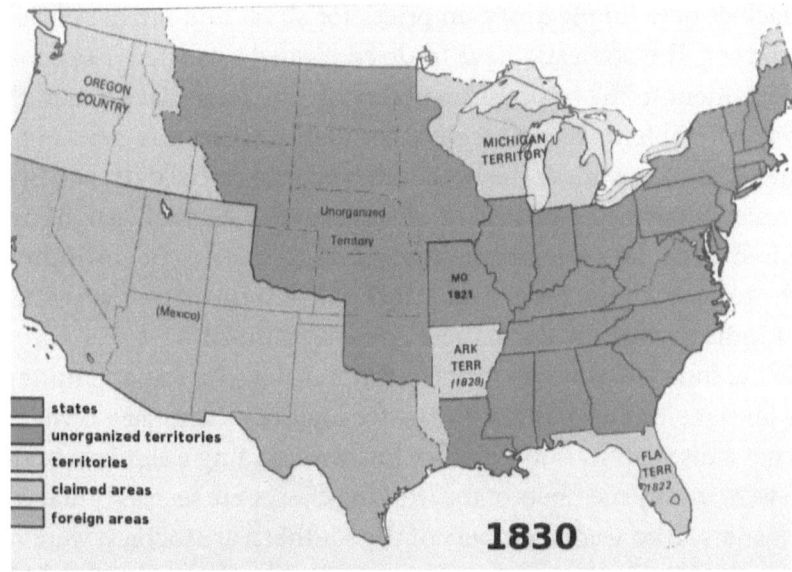

Map 4-7: United States in 1830

As was typical at the time, slavers liked to portray slavery as just another kind of labor system. Slaves were called servants, boys, girls, or my men.[617] They were seen as members of an "extended family," which was an idyllic myth that covered over the cruelty and moral depravity of slavery. Many people in the south still hold to this myth.

As a slaver, Jackson encouraged his slaves to form family units. Although the slaves could not be legally married, the coupling of African American men and women in plantation "marriages" increased the slave population and also discouraged slaves from trying to escape as it was more difficult for an entire family to safely flee their captivity.

As long as the slaves did as they were told, Jackson treated them with a modicum of humanity, but if they crossed him, it was another story. When one slave escaped, Jackson offered a reward of fifty dollars and expenses for his return and another ten dollars for every hundred lashes any person would give the slave, up to thirty dollars for three hundred lashes. It is difficult to believe that any human being could endure such torture. More likely Jackson just wanted to punish the man out of spite and also set an example for any other slave who might entertain the idea of escape.

In 1808, Congress had outlawed the importation of slaves, but slavers were allowed to keep those they had for as long as they wanted. In fact, the lack of new supply drove up prices for slaves and further enriched the slavers. The domestic slave trade continued unabated. I suppose it is a testament to the business mentality of American slavers, that their slaves were able to reproduce fast enough to meet the needs of the domestic market while in the West Indies (Caribbean islands) and Brazil, the exceedingly cruel treatment of slaves and their high rate of death required a regular replenishment of slaves to sustain the institution.[618] At the time, both the French and the English were active slavers in the West Indies, while the Portuguese controlled Brazil.

By the time Jackson was running for president, he was attempting to hide his slave-trading past. In the twisted logic of racism, slave ownership was not a disqualification for office but slave trading was. Slave traders, who were mostly members of the working class, were seen as brutal while the owners, who were members of the southern aristocracy, were not.

Nonetheless, both the ownership and the trading of human beings in the history of the United States is a mark of moral degeneracy that to this day prevents the efforts of the American people to realize life, liberty, and the pursuit of happiness, and hinders all attempts at political democracy and spiritual unity. It serves as the basis of American bigotry that still churns in our conscious and subconscious mind.

By the time of Jackson's presidency, the inhumanity of slavery was beginning to assault the consciousness of the American people. As opposition grew, tensions between the northern and southern states grew more extreme. The issue of slavery entered every aspect of American society—politics, economics, religion, and culture. Within a few decades, it led to a Civil War.

Native Americans

The Cherokee had a nickname for Andrew Jackson. They called him "Sharp Knife." Jackson waged his first war against the Creeks after President Jefferson had appointed him to appropriate Creek and Cherokee lands. In his military campaign against the native tribes, Jackson recommended that troops systematically kill Indian women and children after massacres in order to complete the extermination.[619] The Creeks lost twenty-one million acres of land in southern Georgia and central Alabama, paving the way for cotton plantation slavery.[620]

Before the turn of the century, most of the Native American tribes in the northeast had been systematically removed, but it was in the early 1800's, that the United States government began a systematic effort to remove Native American tribes from the southeast.[621] The Cherokee nation, as well as the Chickasaw, Choctaw, Creek, and Seminole, referred to as the "Five Civilized Tribes" by white settlers, in reference to the tribes' adoption of aspects of colonial culture, had been established as autonomous nations in the southeastern United States as early as the presidency of George Washington.

These Native tribes did everything they could to accommodate the white settlers, expecting that, by doing so, they could live peaceably among them. The acculturation of these Native American tribes was well under way, especially among the Cherokee and Choctaw by the beginning of the 1800's. Native peoples had converted to Christianity, learned to speak and read English, and adopted European-style economic practices such as the individual ownership of land and property (including the ownership of African slaves).[622] Once the tribes were removed from Georgia and Alabama, Thomas Jefferson allowed the Five Tribes to remain east of the Mississippi, provided they adopt the ways of the white man. But as the Europeans continually pressed westward in their bid for new wealth and land, Andrew Jackson decided to move the Native tribes even further west. The method in which he chose to do so was consistent with his history of political and military action. In his 1829 State of the Union address, Jackson called for removal of the Native tribes.[623]

Congress passed the *Indian Removal Act* in the following year having gained widespread support in the South from men eager to seize the tribes' land and expand their plantations.

Jackson agreed to divide the United States territory west of the Mississippi into districts for tribes in order to replace the land from which they were being removed. He falsely promised that the land west of the Mississippi would be owned by the Indians forever even though a Supreme Court case in 1823[624] had previously made a decision that Native Americans could occupy lands within the United States, but could not hold title to those lands.

While Native American removal, according to the law, was voluntary, everyone knew that the law meant the inevitable removal of most Indians from the states. The Removal Act paved the way for the forced expulsion of tens of thousands of American Indians from their traditional homelands to the West, and led to a death march widely known as the "Trail of Tears."

In his effort toward nation building, Jackson remained blind even to the most rudimentary principles of human justice. He could not support the native tribes' sovereignty over land in the colonized United States. He believed that for their own survival, tribes who were being attacked by and removed by white settlements must either assimilate as individuals or be removed to the west where there were still no states to contend with. He was not willing to defend the Natives against infringement on their land by white men.

The Chickasaws and Choctaws, under pressure and outright threats, submitted readily, while the Creeks did so under duress. Only the Cherokees resisted to the bitter end. Tired of their legal battles with the United States government, Jackson ordered that they be systematically rounded up and sent on a death march of over twenty-two hundred miles under armed guard. It was a march in which ten thousand men, women, and children died en route, the biggest massacre of Native Americans in the history of the United States. This ranks along with the most egregious acts of genocide in human history.

The treaties between the US government and the Natives regarding their removal, was full of promises for fair payment for their land and goods, safe transportation to the West and, sustenance upon arrival, including protection for their personal property, but proved to be no more than empty lies as corrupt contractors, unscrupulous traders, and white trespassers, backed by state authority, preyed on the Natives. In the systematic genocide of the Native Americans, Jackson must bear full responsibility for the *Trail of Tears* death march because while he politically spoke out against the abuses, he did not lift a finger to stop them.[625]

President Jackson, who did so much for the American nation in his victory over the English imperialists, and who taught us the lesson of how to confront the international banker aristocracy, unfortunately could not see one inch beyond the notion of white privilege, thus dwarfing his status as a human being and fortifying the racist sentiment of white Americans throughout our history.

The Ladies Take Jackson Down a Peg

Jackson had come to Washington knowing full well that the Washington aristocracy would be lying in wait to ambush him at every turn. He was especially angry at the women who controlled the cultural climate of Washington, just as the French women had controlled Paris during the years of the French Revolution.

In Washington, the ladies who were mustered against Jackson, were the white elite and the middle-class women who were related to government officials. While each state and national elections brought new people to Washington, the wives of prominent men with long careers were capital fixtures.

Ruling-class women, as we have seen, had played an important, albeit behind the scenes, role in every major political contest, but the Washington women enjoyed particular powers and freedoms. The wives and daughters of the Founding Fathers had helped to instill the courtly culture of salons in Washington in which they "dispensed patronage, made political deals, and entertained a good deal of legislative business."

In Washington, the ladies not only hosted politics, they played it.[626] While men feared corruption charges for dispensing government jobs, their wives could sponsor candidates without reprisal. Any man who wanted a government post knew the best route lay in petitioning a powerful woman.

During the presidential campaign, the supporters of Jackson's opponent, President John Quincy Adams, painted Andrew Jackson as a violent and crude rustic. They also painted Rachel Jackson as a "loose woman."

Believing that Rachel's heart attack and death was triggered by her anxiety over moving to Washington because of vicious rumors about her character, Jackson was determined to sweep his administration free of the back biting aristocracy. The battleground between Jackson and the women of the Washington aristocracy was Jackson's choice of his cabinet members. While the women had hoped that establishment politicians would be chosen in order to curb his temper, they were disappointed when Jackson brought his own people into power. In response, the women focused their attack on Margaret Eaton, the wife of Jackson's old friend, John Eaton, whom he had recent appointment as the Secretary of War.

The Washington women, led by Floride Calhoun, wife of Vice President John C. Calhoun, painted Margaret as a local boardinghouse keeper's daughter with a dubious sexual reputation.[627] Because Jackson was a widower, as was his Secretary of State, Martin Van Buren, they held that Margaret would be the de facto First Lady. The women, however, loudly complained that they would now be forced to interact with this woman of ill repute at official events. Their swipe at Margaret had little to do with her personally, but was targeted against the rustic, lower class President.

Jackson saw the attacks on Margaret on par with the attacks on his beloved Rachel and he was not willing to listen to counsel that he make peace with the women. The contest between Jackson and the ladies nearly cost him his administration. The first shot, in what became known as the "Petticoat War" was fired at the Inaugural Ball.

At the ball, the ladies of the administration refused to be introduced to or to speak with Margaret. From that night on Floride Calhoun and her allies, including some Cabinet wives, persuaded even the President's own daughter-in-law and hostess, Emily Donelson, to join with them against Margaret. By their use of invitations and their behaviors at social events, the ladies of Washington turned every party and ball into a demonstration of whether one supported Jackson or not. Social events had always been somewhat partisan but now they made bi-partisanship impossible. [628]

Under the circumstances, the men continually jockeyed to gain political advantage.

At first it seemed that Jackson's stubbornness would win, as he gave parties and dinners with Margaret Eaton on his arm. But when Emily Donelson, his own daughter-in-law continued to side with his opponents, he sent her home, signaling that he could not even control the women in his own family. Cabinet meetings descended into battles over the sexual propriety of Margaret with the President roaring at his Cabinet to visit and socialize with Margaret.

By the spring of 1831, as the affair dragged on, Washington society became paralyzed with fear of offending someone important. The parlors of the city closed and political business stalled from the Cabinet on down. "The mighty Andrew Jackson, who fought like a lion in battle, could not prevail against a battalion of Washington ladies."[629]

Martin Van Buren and John Eaton withdrew from their positions in order to break the stalemate. When other Cabinet members with wives who were against Margaret Eaton refused to follow suit, Jackson fired them. Now suddenly the Eaton Affair became a national story. The press had a field day fueled by former cabinet members who had returned to their own states.

In the end, everyone lost. Andrew Jackson only knew the white man's world and was unaware of the role of women in politics and nation-building. Such limited vision destroyed his presidency and made his life miserable. For their part, the elite women of Washington had overstepped their influence and had to learn the hard lesson that in the capitol, society was always subservient to politics.

Slavery

"If you are a white authority, you're constantly trying to figure how tightly you want to impose the lid with respect to people running away. How fierce should the punishments be? Should it be a whipping? Should it be the loss of a finger or a hand or a foot? Should it be wearing shackles perpetually?"- Peter Wood, historian

We have seen that every major race, culture, nationality, and religion from ancient times to the present day has enslaved their fellow human beings. Slavery began with the institution of marriage and then expanded when bands of men raided the settlements of others and enslaved captive women and children. Later, when men learned how to enslave other men, captives were used for hard labor or to fill the ranks of armies. Throughout history, however, the position of slaves was vastly different in different times and places.[630]

Slavery can be traced back to the earliest civilizations of Mesopotamia and Egypt. The earliest written legal records, such as Code of Hammurabi (c. 1760 BC), refer to slavery as an established institution. In the wars between the inhabitants of the Middle East and Europe, Christians took Muslim slaves and Muslims took Christian slaves. During the Middle Ages, slavery was common in the British Isles. In modern history, during the rise of mercantile capitalism, the Portuguese, Spanish, Dutch, French, and English all used slaves to forward their colonial expansion. Slavery was a legal institution in each of the thirteen American colonies and England played a dominant role in financing the Atlantic slave trade. At the beginning of the 1800s, it is estimated that three quarters of all people on the planet were trapped in bondage against their will, either as serfs or slaves.[631]

Although slavery is no longer legal anywhere in the world, except in territories controlled by certain terrorist groups like ISIS, human trafficking remains an international reality and an estimated 24.9 million people are living in illegal slavery today.[632]

Slavery became a major industry with the dawn of capitalism. Because capitalism is an economic system based on the appropriation of another's labor, it could not have developed without the cheap labor that slavery provides. Cheap labor means more profits and more profits means larger projects and economies of scale, which leads to even more profits. If one is to understand the origins of capitalism, which is the driving force of the modern world, it is necessary to understand the role of slavery in its development. Insofar as the United States is the greatest capitalist country in the world, we will concentrate here on the role that slavery played in the development of the American economy.

After the Revolutionary War, the thirteen English colonies formed the United States of America. At the time, its economy was principally agricultural. More than half of the nation's exports from 1800 to 1860 were raw cotton, almost all of it grown by slaves. Just as English capitalists were entirely dependent upon the cheap labor of displaced serfs to kick start their economy, so also slaves were required to kick start the early American economy. In this effort, it was the South that was the economic dynamo of the economy. It produced cotton more cheaply than did the serfs of Europe so that the English textile industry, the largest in the world, was largely dependent upon the American South for its supply of cotton as its raw material.

In the late 1700's, the southern states had largely grown tobacco, but they had exhausted their land in this effort and the South faced an economic crisis. The demand for slaves plummeted. However, it was at this same time that England was mechanizing its textile industry and there was a huge demand for cotton. Unfortunately, it was difficult to harvest cotton because of the difficulty in removing the seeds that were embedded in the cotton fiber, so production was minimal despite the demand. This was true until Eli Whitney, a young schoolteacher, invented the cotton gin that efficiently removed the seeds. The year was 1793. Whitney's invention revolutionized cotton production in the south and led to large-scale plantations that depended upon slave labor.[633] Thus, the slave trade also boomed.

We should not forget, however, that slavery was just as necessary for the Northern capitalists as it was for the southern plantation owners. Slaves worked in the offices of accountants and lawyers in Lower Manhattan, in the spinning mills of New England, and in the factories of Massachusetts and Rhode Island. It was not only that Northerners owned slaves to work in their industries, however, but it is also more important to understand that many of the big financial institutions on Wall Street today got their start by capitalizing the slave trade.[634]

For example, the Brown brothers turned their mercantile linen business into a bank in 1825. Later, they merged with the Harriman Brothers to form Brown Brothers, Harriman and Company still one of the largest banks on Wall Street. During the 1840s, James, one of the brothers, sat in his office in Lower Manhattan hiring overseers for the slave plantations that his defaulting creditors had left to him. Because plantation owners needed ever more funds to invest in land and slaves, they needed capital from the banks of New York and London. Without this capital, the expansion of slave agriculture in the American South would have been impossible. Thus, slavery fueled the northern banking industry as surely as it fueled the cotton industry in the South.

Citibank, Lehman Brothers, Aetna, J.P. Morgan, Wachovia, and Berkshire Hathaway all made their fortunes on slavery.[635] Established European banks, like Barings and Rothschild, also profited greatly from the American slave trade. The investment in slavery led to financial innovations in tabulating the cost and productivity of human labor. This was made possible because the slave owners had complete control over their workers and could experiment upon them in any way they chose in order to increase their production. Insurance companies worked out new actuary tables to indemnify slaveholders from loss or damage to the men and women they owned. Slaves were depreciated as they grew older.[636]

As new methods of "labor management" developed, torture became more widespread. As John Brown, a fugitive slave, observed in 1854: "When the price [of cotton] rises in the English market, the poor slaves immediately feel the effects, for they are harder driven, and the whip is kept more constantly going."[637]

It was not only the Northern banks that benefitted from slavery, but also Northern manufacturers who provided the plantations with clothing, brooms, plows, furniture, and hundreds of other commodities. Thus, slavery, from the very beginning was embedded in the very core of the American economy.[638]

The Cabots, one of the original blue-blood families of Boston, made their fortune by shipping slaves, opium, and rum.[639] Many other Boston Brahmin families[640] like the Lowells[641] and Slaters[642] all profited greatly from cheap, slave-grown cotton.

As profits accumulated in the cotton trade, many Northern congregations, hospitals, and universities were also built on the backs of African American slaves. Craig Steven Wilder's book *Ebony & Ivy: Race, Slavery, and the Troubled History of America's Universities* links the growth of Ivy League colleges and universities to slavery. Brown, Harvard, Princeton, Columbia, Yale, Dartmouth, Pennsylvania, and William and Mary are named in his book.[643] The universities played a central role in creating the ideological justifications for slavery.

Recently, the Harvard Law School, one of the most elite universities in the United States and the world, voted to remove its shield that it had used for eighty years, after a group of students challenged its use because it is based on the family crest of a wealthy slave-owning family. Isaac Royall Jr. endowed Harvard's first law professorship with a bequest in his will and in the 1930s, the image with three sheaves of wheat was adopted by the institution.

As the university wrote to the student body, "We cannot choose our history but we can choose that for which we stand. Above all, we rededicate ourselves to the hard work of eradicating not just symbols of injustice but injustice itself."[644] While apologies are always healing to some extent, one would have greater respect and appreciation for such words if they were to reciprocate with tangible projects to help the descendants of the slaves whose forced labor and suffering was responsible for the wealth and prestige that made Harvard such a great university.

Capitalism is not that difficult to figure out. It is simply a case of the strongest and most immoral pushing themselves to the front of the line and gorging themselves on the bounty of the planet. As they have taken way too much to feed themselves, they parcel some of the bounty out to others who come after them at a dear price so as to force them to do the capitalists' bidding.

The following generations of American capitalists rarely started from scratch, but instead drew on wealth generated earlier in the initial economy built by slave labor. Fathers who made their fortunes loaning money to slaveholders and outfitting slave ships for distant voyages bore sons who used their fathers' money to build factories, charter banks, invest in railroads, speculate in new financial instruments, and protect their capital by investing in government bonds.

Slavery and American Politics

As for the impact of slavery on politics, we need only recall that George Washington, Thomas Jefferson, James Madison, James Monroe, and Andrew Jackson, in fact, all but four of the first twelve presidents of the United States were from the South.[645] The Democratic Party[646] was also formed among southerners intent on protecting the interest of the Southern plantation owners against the northern establishment whose interests in industrialization clashed with their own.

This contest would continue in American history from the clash of Jefferson and Hamilton, through to the clash between John Quincy Adams and Jackson, and would continue to smolder until it ignited the American Civil War. Culturally, the divide between the North and the South continues to exist in American society.

The differences between John Quincy Adams, who inherited the vision of Hamiltonianism from the northern industrialists, and Andrew Jackson, who favored the agriculturalism of the South, gave rise to the Democratic Party. The supporters of Adams called themselves the National Republicans. Jackson, whose strength lay in the South and West, referred to his followers simply as Democrats.[647]

It was the issue of slavery that divided the nation and gave rise to the two-party political system that we have today in the United States. From 1828 to 1856, the Democrats won all but two presidential elections (1840 and 1848). It was during the 1840s and 1850s, that the Democratic Party fought among themselves over the issue of extending slavery to the Western territories. Southern Democrats, led by Jefferson Davis, wanted to allow slavery in all the territories, while Northern Democrats, led by Stephen A. Douglas, who was feeling the heat from northern industrialists and abolitionists, proposed that each territory should decide the question for itself through referendum. The issue split the Democrats. During the 1860 elections, each side proposed its own candidate, Breckinridge for the Southern Democrats and Douglas for the Northern Democrats. The split severely weakened the Democratic Party and allowed Abraham Lincoln, the candidate for the newly established antislavery Republican Party to win the election. Lincoln was elected president with only forty percent of the vote, while his opponents took eighteen percent and twenty-nine percent respectively.

The election of 1860 changed party loyalties and gave rise to the Democrat and Republican two-party system. In federal elections from the 1870s to the 1890s, the parties were roughly balanced in terms of voters nationally, but in the South, the Democrats continued to dominate because the whites there blamed the Republican Party for the American Civil War (1861–65) and the Reconstruction (1865–77) that followed. While slavery was no longer legal, the southern states under the Democrats created repressive legislation. They used physical intimidation to prevent African Americans from voting, despite the passage of the Fifteenth Amendment in 1870, which gave them the right to vote. This inbred racist mentality ensured that the South would remain staunchly Democratic for nearly a century.

The Slave Trade

The Atlantic Slave Trade and the institution of slavery constitute the darkest era in American history. The slave trade remains a crime against humanity and a potent negative force that denigrates all who perpetrated it and those who continue to share its racist ideology. It remains one of the greatest affronts to our human nature and to human society.

The Atlantic Slave Trade originated with the Europeans, but was quickly adapted by American colonists to create the labor force for its systems of agricultural mass production. These included sugar, tobacco, and rice, but mainly cotton. Between the sixteenth and ninetheenth centuries, approximately ten to fifteen million people from Africa were enslaved by European and American slave traders. The impact of losing so many people left Africa a tortured and destitute continent, the effects of which continue to plague the continent to this day. With the loss of so many people, Africa also lost its rich heritage of traditions, know-how, and ideals.[648] When we think of Africa and the struggle of Afro-Americans, it remains our duty to persistently remember this underlying reality and to acknowledge the painful contribution that black people have made to the current welfare of human society. More than this, we must take action to assist black people who have suffered so much and have remained oppressed and impoverished to this day in the United States.

Like the Native Americans, the tribes of Africa were victims of a totalitarian system of economic, political, social, and sexual exploitation that was based on force, violence, torture, and the ideology of institutional racism, much of which continues to exist despite the Emancipation Proclamation.

The country of Portugal, which as we have seen, was the first European country to seek a new route to the riches of the Far East, was the first country to start selling African slaves. The first slave purchase is said to have taken place in 1441 when the Portuguese adventurers caught two African males when they docked at a site in what is today Ghana along the western coast of Africa. The Africans in the nearby village paid them in gold for their return.[649] For over four hundred years, the Europeans built countless castles and forts along the coastline of Ghana.[650] Back then, Ghana became known as the Gold Coast due to its vast quantities of gold and the European strongholds which served to protect the slavers from attacks by Africans and other Europeans. Placed strategically as links in the slave trade routes, these forts, many of which still exist today, were attacked, seized, exchanged, sold, and abandoned during the struggle between European powers for domination over the Gold Coast. The growing demand for human labor in the New World (Americas and the Caribbean) triggered the African slave trade. The forts became prisons of misery and despair for slaves awaiting transport from their homeland. From Ghana alone, six million people were enslaved. Of these ten to fifteen percent, or nine hundred thousand people, died in the rat-infested squalor of the holds of slave ships, never reaching their final destination. Look closely at the illustration below to see how people were packed into the ship's hold. Now consider living like that on a rocking ship for two months in the dark without showers, toilets, or medicine to keep disease from spreading. Among you are men, women and children.

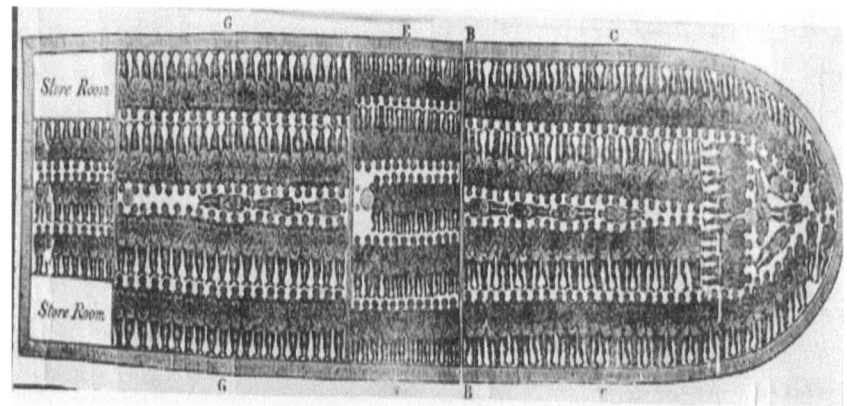

Fig. 4-32: Interior Hold of a Slave Ship

In 1807, England passed a bill prohibiting the slave trade, and the next year the United States outlawed the importation of slaves. To enforce these laws the British and Americans patrolled the sea around Africa to stop suspected slavers and free the slaves.

The Reverend Robert Walsh served aboard one of the ships assigned to intercept the slavers off the African coast. On the morning of May 22, 1829, a suspected slaver was sighted and the naval vessel gave chase and boarded the ship. Below are comments from his account of what he saw.[651]

> She was called the *Feloz*, commanded by Captain Jose' Barbosa, bound to Bahia.
>
> She had taken in, on the coast of Africa, 336 males and 226 females, making in all five hundred and sixty-two, and had been out seventeen days, during which she had thrown overboard 55. The slaves were all enclosed under grated hatchways between decks. The space was so low that they sat between each other's legs and [were] stowed so close together that there was no possibility of their lying down or at all changing their position by night or day.

Walsh reported that, because they were bought by different owners, they were branded with a red hot-iron "under their breasts or on their arms."

> Over the hatchway stood a ferocious-looking fellow with a scourge of many twisted thongs in his hand, who was the slave driver of the ship, and whenever he heard the slightest noise below, he shook it over them and seemed eager to exercise it. I was quite pleased to take this hateful badge out of his hand, and I have kept it ever since as a horrid memorial of reality, should I ever be disposed to forget the scene I witnessed.

Reverend Walsh reported how the slaves responded when the rescuing sailors opened the hatches to let in some light. Some tried to get up on their knees to kiss their hands, while others were hopelessly dejected and emaciated. The children "seemed dying."

What struck Walsh and the sailors most forcefully was how it was possible to pack people so tightly. He described three feet high cells, shut out from light or air with temperatures in the nineties and a stench that prevented them from entering.

> The space between decks was divided into two compartments 3 feet 3 inches high; the size of one was 16 by 18 and of the other 40 by 21; into the first were crammed the women and girls, into the second the men and boys:

> 226 fellow creatures were thus thrust into one space 288 feet square and 336 into another space 800 feet square, giving to the whole an average of 23 inches and to each of the women not more than 13 inches.

When the officers of the patrol boat wanted to let the slaves on board to get air and water, the slaver insisted that if they did so, he would kill them all. As the people came up from their three-foot high dungeon, Reverend Walsh reported:

> It is impossible to conceive the effect of this eruption—517 fellow creatures of all ages and sexes, some children, some adults, some old men and women, all in a state of total nudity, scrambling out together to taste the luxury of a little fresh air and water. They came swarming up like bees from the aperture of a hive till the whole deck was crowded to suffocation front stem to stern, so that it was impossible to imagine where they could all have come from or how they could have been stowed away. On looking into the places where they had been crammed, there were found some children next to the sides of the ship, in the places most remote from light and air; they were lying nearly in a torpid state after the rest had turned out. The little creatures seemed indifferent as to life or death, and when they were carried on deck, many of them could not stand.

Walsh explained how the fifty-five slaves who were thrown overboard had died of dysentery even though only seventeen days before they had boarded in good health. He witnessed slaves with dysentery lying on the deck in the last stages of emaciation in a "state of filth and misery not to be looked at."

While expressing his horror to an officer of his ship, Walsh was told that the conditions on this slave ship were not the worst that the officer had seen. The officer said that on other slave ships that he had seen, the cells were only eighteen inches high "so that the unfortunate beings could not turn round or even on their sides, the elevation being less than the breadth of their shoulders; and here they are usually chained to the decks by the neck and legs."

The officer also described boarding a slave ship in which people were chained in twos and threes. Due to being suffocated many were foaming at the mouth in agony while many were also dead. A living man was sometimes dragged up, and his companion was a dead body. Many people became crazed in their torture and killed each other in the hope of having more air to breathe. Upon being freed, "Many unfortunate creatures took the first opportunity of leaping overboard and getting rid, in this way, of an intolerable life."[652]

Despite such conditions, the people persisted and resisted. There are accounts of the people who made it through the voyage alive; then to face a life of hard-labor, humiliation, terror, torture, and rape. They lived a life of prisoners, far from home and family, with little chance of escape.

Resistance

The African people did not surrender easily to slavery. There is a great deal of evidence of resistance when people were first kidnapped and of resistance on the shore, in the prison forts, and on ships. In some cases, "resistance" involved attacks from the shore on slave ships. Without weapons or the means to resist, other captives also fought their enslavements by taking their own lives, by jumping from slave ships, or refusing to eat.

Over fifty major mutinies occurred on slave ships in the Middle Passage between 1699 and 1865.[653] David Richardson, Director of the Wilberforce Institute for the Study of Slavery and Emancipation, has provided evidence of four hundred and eighty-five acts of violent resistance by Africans against slave ships and their crews. These include ninety-three cases of attacks from the shore against ships or longboats and three hundred and ninety-two cases of revolt on shipboard that involved more than three hundred and sixty ships. They also include twenty-two instances of planned rather than actual rebellion. Perhaps as many as ten percent of slave ships experienced an insurrection.[654]

On the plantations, many enslaved Africans slowed down the pace of work by pretending to be ill, causing fires or "accidentally" breaking tools. This earned them the reputation for being a lazy, good for nothing people deserving of punishment. Whenever possible, enslaved Africans ran away. Some escaped to South America, England, or North America. All of these acts made slavery less profitable for the slaveholders. Some enslaved Africans came back to fight the slavers after escaping. Others set up free communities in the dense forests and adapted guerrilla tactics to attack the plantations.

Resistance was extremely difficult in the Americas and the Caribbean considering that the African people had few resources in this foreign land. Enslaved Africans who escaped were easily recognized as runaways and returned to be punished by their owners. Unarmed, African people had to be brave to fight their overseers who possessed guns and relied on bounty hunters, hunting dogs, and a trained army to recapture the runaway slave and return him for punishment. Yet despite overwhelming odds, there were hundreds of slave revolts.

As the oppression increased, the revolts got bigger. The people made it known that if they were not set free, they would free themselves. In their struggle, the people from Africa had their own legendary heroes, both men and women, who included Nzinga Mbemba of the Congo,[655] Nanny[656] and Cudjoe[657] in Jamaica, Cuffy,[658] Quamina Gladstone[659] in Guyana, and Bussa[660] in Barbados. In the United States black heroes in the struggle against slavery include Richard Allen[661], Mary Ann Shadd Carey,[662] Maria Weston Chapman,[663] Joseph Cinque,[664] Samuel Cornish,[665] Frederick Douglas,[666] Sojourner Truth,[667] and Harriet Tubman.[668]

In addition, there were many whites who were active in the anti-slavery movement who have gained respect from people across the planet for their humanity and bravery.

How the Haitian Slave Revolt Changed History

The African people's resistance to slavery in the Americas took the form of insurrections that were ultimately so damaging to the European slavers that slavery no longer proved economically viable. At the same time, the blacks were fighting against the slavers, the Enlightenment ideas and the revolutions by white colonists against the French and English aristocracies and Church gave rise to a new definition of human freedom that caused many whites to support freedom for all human beings, not just whites. In the US, such people formed the anti-slavery abolitionist movement in the North inspired by the spiritual revival of the Second Great Awakening.

The insurrection that had the greatest impact on the abolitionists was the Haitian Revolution that took place in the French colony of Saint Domingue between 1791 and 1804 on the island of Haiti in the Caribbean Sea. The revolution sent chills down the spines of the slavers in the United States who feared the contagion of a domestic rebellion.[669]

In 1791, at the same time as the first term of President George Washington, a general insurrection began that set the stage for the abolition of slavery and the War of Independence on the island.[670] The revolution on Haiti was inspired by Enlightenment ideas and the beginning of the French Revolution.

In Haiti, when the slaves liberated themselves from the slavers, they also established their own government, which became the sovereign state of Haiti. It was the greatest slave rebellion in the Western world since Spartacus fought the Roman Empire nineteen hundred years earlier.[671] In fact, Toussaint L'Ouverture, who let the revolution, was nicknamed "Black Spartacus."

The Haitian Revolution was the only slave uprising that led to the founding of a state free from slavery and ruled by non-whites and former captives. It challenged head-on the racist ideology and cherished myths of European governments, capitalists, and Christian ministers that blacks were an inferior race. The black rebels' organizational capacity and their bravery and tenacity under pressure became the stuff of rumors that shocked and frightened American slave owners.[672]

Once established as an independent nation, the Haitians also helped blacks throughout the Caribbean and the US in their own insurrections. The Haitian Revolution provided aid to Simon Bolivar, a military and political leader who played the leading role in establishing Venezuela, Ecuador, Bolivia, Peru, and Colombia as sovereign states independent of Spanish rule.[673] The Haitian Government also provided weapons and ammunition to the Mexicans led by General Mina who started a resistance war with Spain that led to the Mexican War of Independence.

The Haitians also gave aid or inspired rebellions in Columbia, Cuba, Guadeloupe, Martinique, British Guyana, Jamaica, and Puerto Rico. Haitians even came to the United States and inspired rebellions in Louisiana, Virginia, and South Carolina, led by such heroes as Gabriel Prosser,[674] Denmark Vesey,[675] and Nat Turner.[676]

Of greater significance for all Americans is the fact that the Haitian Revolution was directly responsible for Napoleon selling the Louisiana Purchase to the United States under Thomas Jefferson. If this sale had not occurred Americans today living west of the Mississippi would not even be citizens of the United States. Napoleon did not envision Louisiana as a valuable strategic territory on its own. Rather, he saw it as a massive granary that could feed supplies to the profitable sugar plantations on Saint-Domingue. So, when the French forces could not regain control of Saint-Domingue, Napoleon decided to give up on Louisiana as well. He did not want to sell it to the British, so he instructed his ministers to sell it to the United States. The Louisiana Purchase Treaty was signed on April 30, 1803.

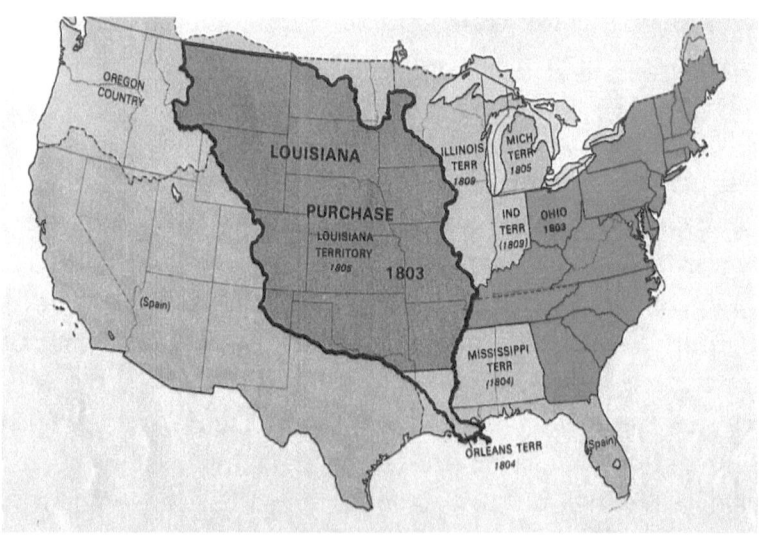

Map 4-8: Louisiana Purchase

The United States nearly doubled its size, in no small part due to the slave revolt on Saint-Domingue.[677]

The Haitian Revolution set off an irresistible process of liberation throughout the Western Hemisphere. Like the American Revolution, it was based on the ideas of freedom, equality, and independence and was supported by the almost unimaginable bravery of its people.[678] Just as the Americans had overthrown the mighty English Empire in North America, the black slaves of the little island of Haiti overthrew the mighty French Empire in South America and in the Caribbean islands. In this gigantic accomplishment, it should be remembered that the people of Haiti accomplished this feat without ships, or army, or resources, at a time when their people were bound in chains across many islands and lands.

This revolution ate away at the foundations of the slave trade in the New World. Well before Britain launched its crusade against the Atlantic slave trade, Haiti was alone in its struggle to overcome slavery.

When the Spanish colonists began using American Indians as a labor force, they employed the *encomienda*[679] system that started in Spain during the days of the Roman Empire. It was essentially a "protection racket" in which the conqueror preyed on the weak in exchange for a service. The Spanish monarch would assign a Spaniard (conquistador) with the task of "protecting" a specific group of Native Americans.

In this system, the leader of the native tribe would then be held responsible for mobilizing labor and tribute (metals, corn, wheat, pork, etc.) to give the Spanish. In exchange for their goods and labor, the Native tribes earned the right to learn Christianity and the Spanish language. And, of course, they would be protected from other tribes in the vicinity and from other European pirates. In the first decade of Spanish presence in the Caribbean, Spaniards divided up the natives and worked them relentlessly. The men who rebelled were killed and the women were burned as witches at the stake.

By the beginning of the seventeenth century, the *encomienda* system was considered to be too abusive because too many Native Americans were being killed to make it economical. It was replaced by the *repartimiento* system.[680] Under this new system, the natives were forced to do low-paid or unpaid labor for a certain number of weeks or months each year on Spanish-owned farms, mines, workshops (*obrajes*), and public projects. The *repartimiento* was not considered to be slavery because the worker was not owned outright. He or she was free to live their life so long as they met their labor requirement. This worked better on the plantations because work was intermittent, but it still mirrored slavery in the mines, where workers were driven to exhaustion, illness, and death.

Even under these "improved" conditions, the Native Americans rebelled and the Spanish responded by killing a sizable number of them. This caused the Spanish to import a huge supply of African slaves. As you can see on the map below, the great majority of slaves from Africa went to the Caribbean and South America.

More than half of the black slaves were employed on the sugar cane plantations in the Caribbean and in Brazil. For the people of Africa, the slave trade was a holocaust. For every slave that reached his or her destination, five others died during the various phases of raiding, conflict, and capture in the African villages, during the forced march towards the prisons on the Atlantic, shore and during the journey across the ocean. For those who arrived alive, their life expectancy was only five or six years.[681]

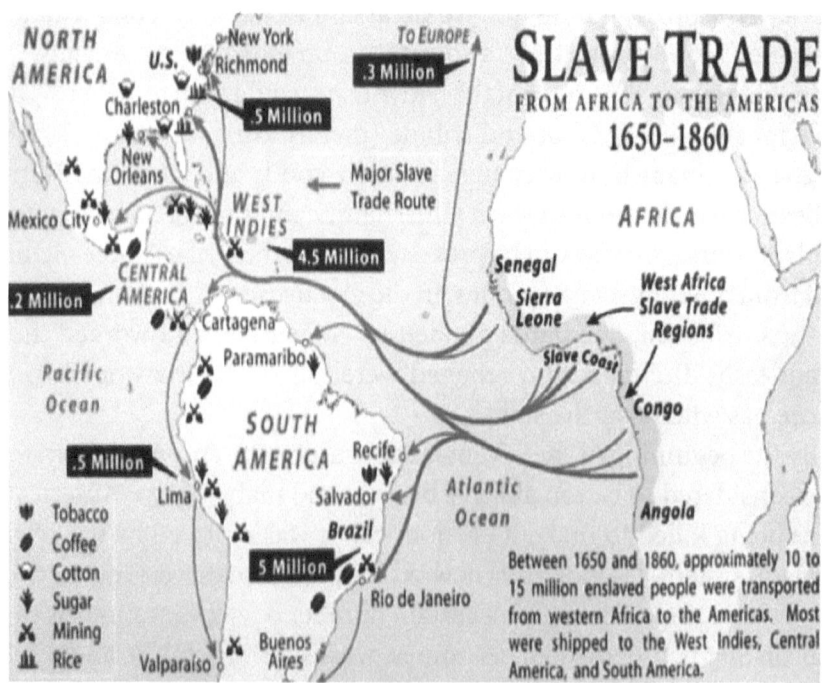

Map 4-9: Slave Trade Routes from Africa to the Americas

From Indentured Servitude to Racial Slavery

When the US colonies began, blacks, as well as whites who were drawn from the serfs and urban poor of England, were equal in stature as indentured servants. After the term of their contract, they were freed and usually given a piece of land, some supplies, and a gun. This was true of black and white laborers.[682]

The Catholic Church had established a general rule that while it was fine to own slaves, they could not be Christian slaves. Europeans, as we have seen, had slaves prior to the establishment of the colonies. In these cases, slavery was not usually life long and a slave could gain his or her freedom by becoming a Christian. The early colonialists did not therefore define themselves as "whites." They were Christians or Englishmen or members of a particular class.

The development of racial slavery developed over time as we can see from a few historical records from Virginia. They give an account of an African-American known as "Antonio the negro" as he was named in the 1625 Virginia census.[683] Antonio was brought to the colony in 1621. At this time, English law did not define racial slavery and Antonio was considered to be a "servant" but not a slave. Later, Antonio changed his name to Anthony Johnson, married an African American servant named Mary, and they had four children. The family became free after the termination of their contract and soon owned land and cattle and had indentured servants of their own. By 1650, Anthony was one of four hundred Africans in the colony of nineteen thousand settlers. In Johnson's own county, at least twenty African men and women were free and thirteen owned their own homes.[684]

The situation began to change in 1640, the same year that Anthony and Mary bought their first property. Three servants fled a Virginia plantation and were caught and returned to their owner. Two had their servitude extended four years. However, the third, a black man named John Punch, was sentenced to "serve his said master or his assigns for the time of his natural life." John Punch became the first black slave in Virginia and in the English colonies in America. In 1661, the first reference to slavery appears in Virginia law. It was directed at white servants who ran away with a black servant. The following year, Virginia went one step further by stating that children born would be bonded or free according to the status of the mother.

The transformation into black slavery had begun and it would be codified into law in the Slave Codes of 1705 that sealed the fate of Africans in Virginia and soon within the Southern states. The Codes stated:

> "All servants imported and brought into the Country... who were not Christians in their native Country... shall be accounted and be slaves. All Negro, mulatto and Indian slaves within this dominion ... shall be held to be real estate. If any slave resist his master... and shall happen to be killed in such correction... the master shall be free of all punishment... as if such accident never happened."[685]

The code imposed harsh physical punishments. For robbery and other "major offenses" the slave would receive sixty lashes and be placed in stocks, where his ears would be cut off. For minor offenses, such as associating with whites, slaves would be whipped, branded, or maimed. A slave owner who sought to break a rebellious slave now had permission to inflict any torture he wanted to, including death, without legal reprisal. It was obviously not true that slavery was "just like an extended family."

While Europeans could communicate with each other across the ocean, the African people who were now enslaved were completely cut off from their roots and thus could be exploited without mercy. There would be no reinforcements coming to save the day. Slavery started out as a religious issue, but by the second half of the seventeenth century the sole determinate of slavery in North America was based on race.

Once the racial hierarchy was established in the South, the whites felt it necessary to keep blacks in their place. They did this through intimidation and violence. The goal was to break these people mentally and spiritually. Any black people who succeeded in any respect became a big threat to the Southern way of life. Even if the whites were not of the aristocratic class, they still benefitted from black slavery, in that they had someone below them to hate and to blame for their own miserable existence. This hatred gets transmitted from generation to generation and keeps racism alive even today.

The rhetoric of white supremacy was seen as sanctioned by God and was repeated in churches across the South. The Confederate States of America made sure to invoke the power of the Divine in their own constitution.

Slavery and Christianity

Racial slavery arose in relation to specific economic conditions within the evolution of American society. It is not a God given nor God sanctioned phenomenon. It is not a part of "human nature" to hate people of other races. Neither is it a component of our spiritual nature. From a spiritual perspective, human beings have the same status and no race is superior to another. According to Jesus Christ, God-realization can only be experienced through love of God and love of neighbor. The true Christian loves all things and all people as a manifestation of the Divine.

Yet, like so many other perversions of true Christianity, institutions that supported racial slavery used the cloak of Christian righteousness to justify themselves. White Christians created the largest slave trade in the history of the world and, in doing so, used the Bible to justify their oppressive exploitation of other human beings. The Bible, as we have seen, was written during an era of primitive human development when slavery was endemic to societies in the Middle East.

Consequently, those who revere the Bible as the "word of God" are able to justify any behavior they desire, no matter how perverse. The majority of southern Christians prior to the Civil War were convinced that their personal relationship with Jesus Christ justified, and even authorized, their ownership of slaves.

The Bible, aside from Christ's teachings, is full of passages that justify slavery. For example, in the Tanakh (Old Testament) of the Jews we find:

> If you buy a Hebrew slave, he is to serve for only six years. Set him free in the seventh year, and he will owe

> you nothing for his freedom. If he was single when he became your slave and then married afterward, only he will go free in the seventh year. But if he was married before he became a slave, then his wife will be freed with him. . . . But the slave may plainly declare, 'I love my master, my wife, and my children. I would rather not go free.' If he does this, his master must present him before God. Then his master must take him to the door and publicly pierce his ear with an awl. After that, the slave will belong to his master forever. (Exod. 21:2-6)
>
> When a slave owner strikes a male or female slave with a rod and the slave dies immediately, the owner shall be punished. But if the slave survives a day or two, there is no punishment; for the slave is the owner's property (Exod. 21:20-21).

In the New Testament, we have the words of Paul and Peter corrupting the teachings of Jesus in order to gain influence with wealthy slave owners:

> Let all who are under the yoke of slavery regard their masters as worthy of all honor, so that the name of God and the teaching may not be blasphemed. Those who have believing masters must not be disrespectful to them on the ground that they are members of the church; rather they must serve them all the more, since those who benefit by their service are believers and beloved. (1 Tim. 6:1-5)
>
> Slaves, obey your earthly masters with fear and trembling, in singleness of heart, as you obey Christ; not only while being watched, and in order to please them, but as slaves of Christ, doing the will of God from the heart. (Eph. 6:5-60)
>
> Slaves, accept the authority of your masters with all deference, not only those who are kind and gentle but also those who are harsh. For it is a credit to you if, being aware of God, you endure pain while suffering unjustly. If you endure when you are beaten for doing wrong,

what credit is that? But if you endure when you do right and suffer for it, you have God's approval. (1 Pet. 2:18-29)

This distortion of the words of Jesus Christ were carried on by the Church Fathers who created the Catholic Church. St Augustine believed that slavery was part of the mechanism to preserve the natural order of things.[686] John Chrysostom, regarded as a saint by Eastern Orthodoxy and Roman Catholicism, argued that slaves should be resigned to their fate, as by "obeying his master he is obeying God."[687] Thomas Aquinas opined "Slavery among men is natural, for some are naturally slaves.[688]

In the Americas, the Anglican Church's Society for the Propagation of the Gospel in Foreign Parts owned the vast Codrington Plantation, in Barbados, that contained several hundred slaves. The slaves were branded on their chests with the word *Society*.[689] The fact that funds from slavery were used to further propagate Christianity among the slaves indicates why the churches were hesitant to condemn slavery among its Christian parishioners.[690]

The racist ideology of the South gained a major impetus from George Whitefield who sparked the first *Great Awakening*, a religious movement particularly strong in the South, which gave rise to the Methodist and Baptist religions and the rise of evangelicalism in general. Whitefield was an Anglican cleric and arguably the most famous religious figure of the eighteenth century, both in England and America. It is said that he preached at least eighteen thousand times to perhaps ten million listeners.[691] Whitefield fought to preserve slavery in the Americas and went on to own several hundred slaves himself.[692]

As racial slavery became more ingrained in the American society over time, white people no longer needed religious justifications. A typical secular justification for black slavery can be found in *The Right of American Slavery* by T. W. Hoit published in 1815.[693] Hoit's justification includes the following arguments:

> Africans have always been slaves.
> Africans are barbarians and as such should be subservi-

ent to civilized men. Civilized men have a nature right to control barbarians.

Even if a Black becomes civilized, he is still not legally entitled to freedom because as a barbarian he became the property of a civilized man who now has a vested right to him. Because the slave's transition from barbarity to civilization was at the expense of his owner, the black owes his slavery to his master as an equivalent for teaching him to be civilized.

The slave labor of blacks is not degrading because labor is good and slave labor is better than no labor. Coercion does not degrade a man but ennobles him because it helps to civilize him. It is preposterous to talk about the degradation caused by slave labor.

It is wrong to claim that what brought the blacks to America was the goal of profit and therefore his coming was not justifiable. "Commerce is the handmaid of civilization, and if his coming was only incidentally right, yet that incident belongs to civilization, which is amenable to the moral code, and is also to be commended."

The intimate commercial relations between America and Europe require that we continue to make progress. And since our progress is based on the agricultural production of slaves, to attempt to end slavery would be to imperil civilization and destroy the principles of right and justice, which demand that barbarism shall always be subservient to civilization.[694]

In our attempt to create a universal human society, this brand of racism, as a group sentiment, remains a pernicious adversary and requires sufficient energy to stamp it out. Every possible means at our disposal should be dedicated to cure this social cancer.

Abolition

Fortunately, not all white people are racists, nor are all Christian churches racist. In the colonies, the Quakers, who were mostly Dutch and German settlers in Pennsylvania, were early leaders in the abolitionist movement. Some members of the church had already begun to speak out against slavery as far back as 1688.[695]

In 1787, following the American Revolutionary War, the British had evacuated thousands of freed African-American slaves and resettled them in Canadian and the Caribbean colonies, Some also were sent to London,[696] even though it was all but impossible for black people to survive in London and a charitable organization called the Committee for the Relief of the Black Poor[697] was formed to assist them. They pressured the British Crown to repatriate them back to Africa. The Crown obliged and the settlement of Sierra Leone was formed, which would later become an independent country in Africa.

During the same year, the Society for Effecting the Abolition of the Slave Trade[698] was also formed in London. The majority of the founders were Quakers. By 1807, with the help of William Wilberforce, who was a Member of Parliament and an Evangelical Christian, the Society was able to push through the 1807 Slave Trade Act.[699] It was a stupendous effort that banished the slave trade within the British Empire and set the stage for the complete abolition of slavery with the enactment of the Slavery Abolition Act of 1833.[700]

In North America, many Methodist and Presbyterians evangelicals also spoke out against slavery, including John Wesley, the founder of Methodism. The Methodist church made the rejection of slavery a requirement for membership in their church.

Gaining inspiration from developments in England, in 1816, the American Colonization Society[701] was founded as a coalition made up mostly of evangelicals and Quakers who advocated for the repatriation of American blacks to Africa. To accomplish their goal, they created the colony of Liberia in West Africa. Liberia was founded, established, colonized, and controlled by citizens of the United States and ex-Caribbean slaves as a colony for former African American slaves and their free black descendants. From 1821, thousands of free black Americans moved to Liberia from the United States. Over twenty years, the colony continued to grow and establish economic stability. In 1847, the legislature of Liberia declared the nation an independent state.

It is interesting to note that some American slaveholders also supported the repatriation of free blacks back to Africa because they posed a continual threat and incitement to black slaves seeking to rebel. The Society closely controlled the development of Liberia until its declaration of independence. By 1867, the ACS had assisted in the movement of more than thirteen thousand Americans to Liberia.[702]

The South struck back against what they believed was an infringement on their God-given right to own slaves. They burned anti-slavery literature and even refused to allow it to be sent through the post office.[703]

After the Civil War, slavery was constitutionally banned in the United States. This however, did not stop the Southern Baptist plantation owners from continuing their defense of slavery on religious grounds, nor their continual oppression of black people. Christian movements like Christian Identity arose that were based on white supremacist theology. Christian Identity preached that all non-whites (people not of wholly European descent) on the planet will either be exterminated or enslaved in order to serve the White race in the new Heavenly Kingdom on Earth under the reign of Jesus Christ. In this new kingdom, only whites can achieve salvation and paradise.[704] This racist belief system is still held by many poor whites and white gangs like the Aryan Brotherhood.

The Ku Klux Klan, another white racist group, also arose after the Civil War to terrorize blacks and keep them from running for political office.[705] Today, it still serves as a catalyst for white racism and uses the Bible as a means to justify its belief in white supremacy.[706]

Slaves in the United States, who escaped slavery, tried to make their way to Canada via the "Underground Railroad,"[707] which was a network of secret routes and safe houses set up by black and white abolitionists. One estimate suggests that by 1850, one hundred thousand slaves had escaped via the "Railroad".[708] The more famous of the African American abolitionists included former slaves Harriet Tubman, Sojourner Truth, and Frederick Douglass. Many more people who opposed slavery and worked for abolition were northern whites, such as William Lloyd Garrison and John Brown.

American Religions

The American colonies were settled by people who brought their religions with them. Many came to escape religious persecution back in Europe and to be able to worship freely in America. Religion meant something to them. Yet, despite the religious leanings of the European settlers, when the United States government was established, it was not based on theological principles, but rather on the principles of the secular Enlightenment. In fact, the US Constitution was the first document written by political leaders with the express purpose of maintaining a separation of Church and State. Why was this so?

Religion of the Founding Fathers

If the colonies were based on explicit religious aspirations, how did the United States come to be the first modern nation-state that was unquestionably committed to the separation of church and state? Obviously, not everyone was on the same page. Frank Lambert who wrote *The Founding Fathers and the Place of Religion in America* explains what happened.

Lambert tells us there were two sets of founding fathers who defined the place of religion in early America. The first he calls the "Planting Fathers," who brought the Old World Calvinist ideas with them and dreamed of building a "City upon a Hill." This phrase was taken from a sermon by Puritan John Winthrop in 1630, when the Massachusetts colonists were still aboard the ship *Arbella*. Winthrop told the future Massachusetts Bay colonists that their new community in Boston would be "as a city upon a hill," watched by the world. The Puritans' community in New England, Winthrop said, would set an example of communal charity, affection, and unity to the world. Winthrop's sermon gave rise to the widespread belief in American folklore that the United States of America is "God's country." It arguably could be called the first case of American exceptionalism,[709] even if its intent was simple pride in his co-religionists and thankfulness to God.

The second group were the "Founding Fathers," those who actually determined the constitutional arrangement of religion in the new republic. While the former proselytized the "one true faith," the latter emphasized religious freedom over religious purity.[710] The Founding Fathers saw the wisdom of certain secular ideas of the Enlightenment thinkers.

In the mid-eighteenth century, during the years leading up to the American Revolution, the colonies contained a wide diversity of religious denominations. These religions were both challenged by and revitalized by a domestic religious revival known as the *Great Awakening*, which was an evangelical movement that swept Protestant Europe and British America during the 1730s and 1740s and left a permanent impact on American Protestantism.

The movement originated with revivalist evangelical preachers, who started preaching in people's homes and later spread their teaching throughout the country by creating tent-revivalist fairs. Evangelical preachers appealed to the emotions of their audience, giving them a deeper sense of their connection to God through Jesus Christ. The new evangelists taught that the trappings of churches, with their rituals, ceremony, dogma, and hierarchy were unnecessary for one to achieve a personal relationship with God. The movement inspired the average person to develop a deeper sense of spiritual conviction by encouraging self-introspection and a commitment to a higher standard of personal morality.[711]

In the New England states, the movement pitted the revivalists against the Anglicans, Lutherans, and others who strongly believed in the importance of church authority and the continuance of ritual, dogma, and tradition. The movement had a major impact in reshaping the Congregational Church, the Presbyterian Church, the Dutch Reformed Church, and the German Reformed Church. It also greatly influenced the emerging, but still small, Baptist and Methodist denominations. These new religions were strong in the South where the revivalist movement also affected the African slaves and free blacks who were exposed to it and subsequently converted to Christianity in the form of the Black Baptist churches.

At the same time, new immigrants were continually arriving in the British colonies and fed the growth of the religious denominations. These growing denominations of Christian Protestants competed with each other for members and also to have the last word on the one true religion. This, of course, led to the same kind of religious rancor that had occurred back in Europe. Having to contend with strong contradictory religious views, and while still remembering the religious wars that rocked Europe for over a hundred years, the American Founding Fathers sought not to duplicate this situation. In order to avoid increasing religious self-righteousness, the Founding Fathers chose to minimize the influence of religious theologies upon the founding principles of the new republic. Their solution was ingenious. They granted freedom of religion to all groups, while simultaneously refusing to incorporate contentious theological positions within the new government's laws or structure. They supported religious pluralism and praised it for giving Americans a wider religious choice in which to believe.

In the daunting task of uniting thirteen disparate colonies, the Founding Fathers felt that the separation of Church and State was required to avoid discord. While they resisted the input of religious dogma into the American legal documents, they also kept religions free of government intervention, except for the guarantee that all people were free to worship as they chose.[712]

The Founding Fathers did not deny religious organizations from trying to seek political influence so long as they understood that all voices would be heard in government deliberations.

Where the founding fathers atheists or secularists? They were a mixed group actually and their decision to separate Church and State was encouraged by the fact that they had the chore to develop a common constitution upon which all could agree. Of the fifty-five delegates to the 1787 Constitutional Convention, for example, forty-nine were Protestants, and two were Roman Catholics. [713] Among the Protestant, the majority (thirty-one) were members of the Church of England (Anglican/Episcopalians), sixteen were Presbyterians, eight were Congregationalists, three were Quakers, two were Lutherans, two were Dutch Reformed (Calvinist), and two were Methodists. Others, including Thomas Paine, were Deists. John Adams, Jefferson, Franklin, Wilson, Morris, Madison, Hamilton, and Washington were neither Christians nor Deists, but rather supporters of a hybrid "theistic rationalism." Sam Adams, the Father of the American Revolution, who did not participate in the Constitutional

Convention because he did not support expanding the powers of a centralized government,[714] was a practicing Puritan.[715]

When the Founding Fathers wrote The Treaty of Tripoli, in 1797, in cooperation with the Islamic government of Tripoli, in order to serve their mutual interest in fighting pirates, they stated: "

> As the Government of the United States of America is not, in any sense, founded on the Christian religion" and "has no enmity against the laws, religion, or tranquility of the Musselman [Muslims]; and, as the same States never entered into any war, or act of hostility against any Mohametan nation, it is declared by the parties, that no pretext, arising from religious opinions, shall ever produce an interruption of the harmony existing between the two countries." The treaty was passed unanimously by the Senate and signed by President John Adams. [716]

Thus, there can be no doubt that while Christians created the foundation of the United States of America, it was not their intention to create a Christian national government. Religion would not determine US laws nor would it affect US relationships with other countries.

While most religions of the Founding Fathers can be traced back to their European roots, there were new Protestant movements that took root and flourished on American soil. Of these, the Methodist and Baptist religions stand out.

Methodists

The Methodist religion derives its inspiration from the life and teachings of John Wesley, Charles Wesley, and George Whitefield, who led the movement. Methodism began as a spiritual revival within the eighteenth century Church of England (Anglican) and became a separate Church following Wesley's death. In 1784, John Wesley ordained preachers from Scotland, England, and America with the power to administer the sacraments. This was the major reason for the Methodists' final split from the Anglican Church.

Because Methodism derived from the Anglican Church rather than the Calvinist Reform movement, it is not averse to offering charity to the poor or average person. Its legacy has been the establishment of hospitals, universities, orphanages, soup kitchens, and schools. In its service, the church seeks to follow Jesus's exhortation to spread the good news and serve all people.

Methodists believe that building loving relationships with others through social service is a means of working towards the inclusiveness of God's love. As opposed to the Calvinist tradition, most Methodists teach that Christ died for all of humanity, (not just the elect) and that everyone is entitled to God's grace. Theologically, this view is known as Arminianism. It supports the notion of free will and denies the Calvinist doctrine that God pre-ordained an elect number of people to eternal bliss while others were destined to perish for eternity. However, Whitefield and several other early Methodists had Calvinist leanings and were considered Calvinistic Methodists.[717] This dichotomy gives the Methodists a wide variety of biblical interpretations as well as forms of worship. Like all Christians, however, Methodists believe that one must be a Christian in order to be saved.

Early Methodists were drawn from all levels of society, but the Methodist preachers took their message to laborers and criminals who tended to be ignored by the organized religions at that time. In England, the Methodist Church had a major impact on the making of the working class (1760–1820). In the United States, it became the religion of many slaves who later formed "black churches" in the Methodist tradition.[718]

Like their Pietistic ancestors, Methodist preachers in America were evangelists known for their enthusiastic sermons that often led them to be accused of being fanatics by their critics within the staid traditional religions. Their doctrines of being born again in Christ and of salvation achieved through free will (as opposed to a predetermined elect) were not appreciated by the Reformed movement. But the Methodist movement thrived among the working class. During its periods of spiritual revitalization, it spread a message of true mysticism within the Christian religion.

The growth of the Methodist church in America began with *The First Great Awakening* in the 1730s and 1740s. The movement began in New

Jersey in private homes, then spread to New England, and eventually south into Virginia and North Carolina. The English Methodist preacher George Whitefield played a major role, traveling across the colonies and preaching in a dramatic and emotional style, accepting everyone as his audience.

The new style of sermons and the personal manner in which people practiced their faith breathed new life into religion in America. People became passionately and emotionally involved in their religion, rather than passively listening to intellectual sermons given in a detached manner. People began to study the Bible at home. The effect was akin to the renewal of the individual that was present in Europe during the reform of the Lutheran Church.

The *Second Great Awakening* was a nationwide wave of revivals, from 1790 to 1840, following the American Revolution. In New England, the renewed interest in religion inspired a wave of social activism among the Yankees. Methodism grew rapidly in the Second Great Awakening, becoming the nation's largest denomination by 1820. From 58,000 members in 1790, it reached 258,000 in 1820 and 1,661,000 in 1860, growing by a factor of 28.6 in seventy years, while the total American population grew by a factor of eight.[719] Northern Methodists were active in the Underground Railroad, but this caused a split with the southern Methodists who were slave owners or dependent upon slavery for their livelihood.

The *Third Great Awakening* from 1858 to 1908 saw another enormous growth in Methodist church membership.

Today, there are seven World Methodist Council denominations in the United States: the African Methodist Episcopal Church; the African Methodist Episcopal Zion Church; the Christian Methodist Episcopal Church, the Church of the Nazarene; the Free Methodist Church; The Wesleyan Church; and the United Methodist Church.

Baptists

Baptists comprise a group of denominations and churches that subscribe to a doctrine that baptism should be performed only for professing believers as opposed to infant baptism, and that it must be done by complete immersion.[720] Other tenets of Baptist churches include: (1) *soul competency* (each person is responsible before God for their own actions), (2) salvation through faith alone, (3) Scripture alone as the rule of faith and practice, and (4) the autonomy of the local congregation. Baptists recognize two ministerial offices, pastors and deacons.

Diverse from their beginning, those who identify as being Baptists today differ widely from one another in what they believe, how they worship, their attitudes toward other Christians, and their understanding of what is important in Christian discipleship.

Historians trace the earliest church labeled "Baptist" back to 1609 in Amsterdam, with English Separatist John Smyth as its pastor. In accordance with his reading of the New Testament, Smyth rejected the practice of baptism of infants and instituted baptism only of believing adults. Baptist practice spread to England, where the *General Baptists* considered Christ's atonement to extend to all people, while the *Particular Baptists* believed that it extended only to the elect. At this time of religious turmoil and innovation, individuals and entire congregations were willing to give up their theological dogmas if they became convinced that a more biblical "truth" had been discovered.[721]

When the Church of England (Anglicans) separated from the Roman Catholic Church, some Christians were disappointed that the Church of England had not gone far enough to correct the errors and abuses of the Catholic Church. Of those most critical of the Anglican Church's direction, some chose to stay within the Church and try to reform it. These became known as "Puritans". Others decided they must leave the Church because of their dissatisfaction. They became known as the "Separatists." Modern Baptist churches trace their history to the Separatist movement in the century following the rise of the original Protestant denominations.

Another milestone in the early development of Baptist doctrine occurred in 1638 with John Spilsbury, a Calvinistic minister, who reestablished the practice of a believer's baptism by immersion.

At the same time in the United States, Roger Williams established the first Baptist congregation in the North American colonies. In the mid-eighteenth century, the *First Great Awakening* increased Baptist growth in both New England and the South. At this time the evangelists spoke out against slavery. Fifty years later, with The *Second Great Awakening* in the South, the Baptist church grew rapidly due to the fact that, for the most part, the Baptist preachers spoke less about abolition and the need for slave owners to free their slaves.[722] Finding a sympathetic religion many slave owners became Baptists in the South. Often slave owners also became Baptist ministers. Southern Baptists, therefore, became the main proponents for slavery and used their religion to justify it.

This duplicity was allowed to exist because there is no hierarchical authority within the Baptist religion. Each church is autonomous and there is no official set of Baptist theological beliefs. Differences exist between churches and associations of churches. Today, the largest association of Baptist churches is the Southern Baptist Convention.

The Southern Baptist Convention was formed by nine state conventions in 1845, founded in part on the premise that the Bible sanctions slavery and that it is acceptable for Christians to own slaves. They believed slavery was a human institution that Baptist teaching could make less harsh. Not only were there many planters in the Southern Baptist churches, in some denominations, prominent preachers like Rev. Basil Manly Sr. were slave owners. Manly was also the president of the University of Alabama.[723]

At the time of the rise of Baptist churches in the South, white southerners tried to keep their black slaves from worshipping in their churches. Furthermore, church services typically emphasized the responsibility of the slave to be obedient and provided biblical justification for black bondage. Slaves had no voice in church affairs and were relegated to the rear of the church or the gallery. In other words, they were allowed to be spectators but not members of the congregation.

Black Baptists

Despite their ill treatment in southern white churches, blacks came to practice their own form of Christianity. This began in earnest during the Second Great Awakening following the American Revolution when Baptist and Methodist itinerant ministers began to appeal directly to the black population. Inspired by the ideals of individual freedom and direct communication with God, the ministers preached to the blacks using a simple language that conveyed a message of hope and redemption. These preachers, infused with spiritual energy, also accepted the blacks' manners of worship, which they carried with them from Africa. These included spirit possession, call-and-response singing, shouting, and dancing.[724] Called a shout or ring shout, the slaves would perform an ecstatic, transcendent religious ritual in which worshipers move in a circle while shuffling and stomping their feet and clapping their hands.[725]

Slave Christianity became an extraordinarily creative patchwork of African and Christian religious tradition.[726] Beside a wide array of tribal traditions that originated across the African continent, the blacks also brought with them the religious traditions of tribal shamanism and Islam.

The blacks, like the European tribes who had encountered Christianity centuries before, blended Christian influences with their traditional rites and beliefs. Symbols and objects, such as crosses, were combined with charms carried to ward off evil spirits. Christ was interpreted as a healer similar to the priests of Africa. In the New World, fusions of African spirituality and Christianity led to distinct new practices among slave populations, including voodoo or vodun in Haiti and Spanish Louisiana. Although African religious influences were also important among Northern blacks, exposure to Old World religions was more intense in the South, where the density of the black population was greater.[727]

Despite ritual difference among the tribes, they all shared a common spiritual heritage. Much like the Native Americans, they did not distinguish between the spiritual and the material. All life was sacred and the supernatural was present in every facet and focus of life. Most tribal traditions accessed the spiritual through rituals that encouraged the ecstatic experiences of the supernatural. This was the reason for the ritual song and dance, which the early Christian ministers referred to as idolatrous dancing. The traditional Christians could not understand that the experience of being "possessed by the spirit" meant to be taken over by an intuition of the Divine. Having an intuitive realization like this is how one actually communes with the Divine.[728] Being possesses by the spirit means being in a state of ecstatic love.

During the decades of slavery in America, any association of black people was a constant source of concern to slave owners. As such, black religious meetings were considered to be the ultimate threat to white existence. The slave owners would gladly have prohibited them from occurring but this would have punctured their justification for slavery as being a civilizing endeavor. How could the Baptist slaveholders forbid the slaves from worshipping Jesus Christ without destroying their entire rationalization for slavery. Faced with this dilemma, the most that the slavers could do was to intimidate the worshippers and watch their religious gatherings to detect plans for escape or insurrection. After all, insurrections, such as that led by Nat Turner in Virginia, were born out of the religious inspiration of slaves.

Black religious services were often broken up by the whites. Slaves risked flogging to worship God.[729] Despite their oppression, black people continued to establish their churches in order to seek refuge from slavery as well as replenish their faith in God.

While we can speak of Black Baptists, the idea of a "Black Church" is a misnomer.[730] It implies that all Black churches share or have shared the same beliefs aspirations and strategies for creating cohesive African-American communities. This is not true, and there were numerous differences found among Black communities, which were reflected within their community churches. Black communities differ from region to region. They have always been divided along social lines, composed of persons from different economic levels, and have maintained varying political philosophies. Black communities in the inner cities of the United States have traditionally differed from those in rural areas, etc.

Nonetheless, for many African-American Christians, regardless of their denominational differences, black churches have always represented their religion, community, and home.

One of the first known black churches in America was created before the American Revolution, around 1758. Called the African Baptist or "Bluestone" Church, this house of worship was founded on the William Byrd plantation near the Bluestone River, in Mecklenburg, Virginia. Following the example of white southern Baptists, Africans at the time believed that only adult baptism by total immersion was doctrinally correct.

The First African Baptist Church of Savannah, Georgia was begun in 1777. This is said to be the oldest Black church in North America. It was originally called the First Colored Church and was founded by George Liele who was its first preacher. Liele was born into slavery in Virginia in 1752, but was taken to Georgia where he was converted to Christianity around 1774 by Rev. Matthew Moore, who was the minister of a Baptist church in which Lisle's owner was a deacon.

Liele was freed by his owner Henry Sharp before the American Revolution began. He then went to Savannah, Georgia, where he helped organize the First African Baptist Church.[731]

In 1787, blacks in Philadelphia organized the Free African Society, the first organized African American society. Absalom Jones and Richard Allen were elected as overseers and they established contacts and created relationships with similar black groups in other cities.

The end of the Confederacy signaled freedom for millions of southern black people and prompted the emancipation of black churches, which became separate institutions.

After emancipation, black churches became virtually the only place for African-Americans to find refuge. During this time, a black church had to submit a petition for separation from its white church sponsor. For example, in 1867, thirty-eight black members of the predominantly white Fairfield Baptist Church in Northumberland County, Virginia, filed a church separation petition. Referring to the new political and social status of African Americans, the petitioners said they wanted to "place ourselves where we could best promote our mutual good" and suggested "a separate church organization" as the best possible way. A month later, the white members of the church unanimously acceded to the petitioners' request, setting the stage for the creation of the all-black Shiloh Baptist Church.[732] During the Civil War many parishioners were assisted in a move to Washington DC by Union troops where they soon formed the Shiloh Baptist Church of Washington DC. The Church is still active and, as president, Barack Obama worshipped there.

Just as blacks sought their own religious communities, so the white racists also began to shun blacks from their church services, especially in the South.[733]

Once established, black churches spread rapidly throughout the South. In 1808, the Abyssinian Baptist Church in New York City was founded.[734] Other new churches also emerged because of the missionary activities of black ministers. The Reverend Alexander Bettis, a former South Carolina slave, single-handedly organized more than forty Baptist churches between 1865 and his death in 1895.[735]

Working-class Baptist and Methodist churches carried on the fusion of African and European forms of worship.[736] Church buildings also doubled as community centers and schools until permanent structures could be built. During the Reconstruction period after the Civil War, they also served as political halls. The black church provided shelter for visitors as well as temporary community theaters and concert halls where religious and secular plays and programs were presented. Church members also provided care for the sick or incapacitated and gave financial aid to students bound for college. They also sponsored virtually all of the many fraternal lodges that emerged in the nineteenth-century South. As racially motivated violence and terrorism ran rampant across the country, Black churches were staunch in their resistance.[737]

In 1886, blacks organized the National Baptist Convention and in 1895, a meeting was held in Atlanta, Georgia in which two thousand black clergymen attended. The three largest conventions of the day: the Baptist Foreign Missionary Convention, the American National Baptist Convention and the National Baptist Educational Convention merged to form the National Baptist Convention of the United States of America. This brought both northern and southern black Baptist churches together. Among the delegates was Rev. A. D. Williams, pastor of the Ebenezer Baptist Church and grandfather of Rev. Martin Luther King, Jr.

However, the more involved black churches became in fighting the racial intolerance and violence targeted against them, the more the white churches ostracized them and their members. The Presbyterian and Episcopalian churches also saw the division of their memberships into white and black denominations.

The Church of God in Christ

In his attempt to describe the spiritual experience, John Wesley, the founder of the Methodist movement, taught that there were two distinct phases in the Christian experience, salvation and sanctification. During salvation, the believer received forgiveness and became a Christian. During the phase of sanctification, the believer was purified and became holy. Wesley taught that sanctification could be an instantaneous experience, or a gradual process.[738] Within the Methodist church, sanctification became the goal of a Christian life.

The idea of sanctification gave rise to the concept of a *second work of grace* in which the life of a Christian is significantly transformed for the better in his or her relation with God. Sanctification could actually lead to *Christian perfection*. Christian perfection has been defined in different ways, including the attainment of perfect love; heart purity; the baptism of the Holy Spirit; the fullness of the blessing; Christian holiness; the second blessing; the baptism of fire; and entire sanctification.[739] The idea of Christian perfection is consistent with the belief of mysticism and the teachings of Jesus Christ when he speaks of becoming one with the Father. This idea is refuted, however, by the Lutheran and Reformed churches who say that this believe contradicts their doctrine of salvation by faith alone.

The concept of Christian perfection reemerged in the *Holiness movement* in the 1860s at the time of the Second Great Awakening when the teachings of Methodism were being reinvigorated. Holiness preachers taught that sanctification was an instantaneous experience. One could be "saved" or "reborn" in an instant, if one's heart was pure and he or she believed in Jesus Christ.

In the early nineteenth century, the Pentecostal Movement emerged from the Holiness Movement largely through the efforts of Charles Fox Parham[740] and William Seymour.[741] It emphasized that one could have a direct personal experience of God through the baptism of the Holy Spirit.

Today Pentecostal churches are distinguished by their belief in the empowerment of individuals by the Holy Spirit. Gifts of empowerment are reflected in the ability to "speak in tongues" and heal others through divine power. Pentecostals believe that we are living in the end days when the Second Coming of Christ will spiritually renew the Christian Church and restore spiritual gifts to the world.[742]

The Church Of God in Christ emerged from the Pentecostal-Holiness denomination with a predominantly African-American membership.

According to the Yearbook of American and Canadian Churches, The Church of God in Christ is the third largest church in the United States with 5.5 million members. It follows the Southern Baptist Convention with 16.2 million members and the United Methodist Church with 7.8 million members.[743]

During the mid-ninteenth century, other Protestant religions formed, among them the Jehovah's Witnesses,[744] the Mormons,[745] and the Seventh Day Adventists.[746]

Summary

In the chapter on the Protestant Reformation we saw how Calvinism played the dominant role in moving Christianity to support capitalism as a God-endowed political economy. We have also seen how Calvinism gave rise to the model protestant nation-state and how it encouraged protestant Christians to engage in political activity. In this activity, the capitalist is viewed as the ideal man whose ethical qualities (thrift, prudence, sobriety, etc.), that are required to make money, are the same qualities necessary to enter the kingdom of heaven. The capitalists were made the chosen of God (the *elect*), according to Calvin. The capitalists are never held accountable for their negative qualities, however, the qualities of greed, cruelty, waste, oppression of others, etc., that destroy the natural environment and shred the social fabric. The capitalists are exonerated from having any responsibility to the poor or the slaves. Social service is not required to get to heaven; in fact, charity actually became a sin in that it robbed the poor of self-discipline. Now we can understand the link between Protestantism, particularly the Reformed churches, and capitalism. Insofar as the ideas of Calvinism permeated most subsequent protestant churches, these ideas were transported to America with the coming of the European colonists.

Nonetheless, as the traditional European religions continued to alienate the average person by their tired sermons, staunch dogmatic style, dry rituals, and physical punishments, a wave of spiritual rejuvenation called the Great Awakening spread throughout the colonies. In this spiritual awakening, newer religions like the Methodists and Baptists adopted the ideas of personal salvation and mystical connection with God. These ideas resonated with the working class and black slaves who were directly approached by spiritually inspired preachers. Because the blacks had brought with them a rich mystical heritage from Africa, it was easy for them to synthesize their traditions with this new expression of American Christianity. Nonetheless, a strong contradiction immediately developed between those who were inspired by the mystical expression of Christianity and those who clung to the established conventions of the old religions, many in order to maintain their economic advantage or in the case of poor whites, their position of white privilege.

This fundamental contradiction existed throughout the nineteenth and twentieth centuries and continues to exist today. It manifests in the continuing racism of white society and the arch-conservative strain of Christian fundamentalists, whose voices have been so prevalent in the Republican Party. It continues in the language and demonstrations of white racists, neo-Nazis, and white nationalists.

Chapter Five: A Global Capitalist Empire in the Making

BEFORE THE UNITED STATES could become a capitalist empire, it had to resolve the contradiction between the Southern/Northern divide. The South's economy was based on plantations, slavery, and mercantile values and had no need to industrialize, while the North, based on manufacturing, banking, and big cities, dreamed of expanding into a world empire. This divide existed from the very founding of the nation and festered for almost a century, before it was finally resolved by the American Civil War.

This chapter will take us through the events leading up to this war, the military conflict, and its aftermath. Once freed from the political and economic resistance from southern politicians, the North was free to unleash industrial capitalism. This resulted in the rise of the Robber Barons who monopolized the finance, steel, transportation, and oil industries, which are the essential infrastructure needed to build a capitalist industrial economy. This chapter will explore the dynamics that gave rise to these super rich captains of industry and the consequences for the general public. It will look at how the state became an integral player in the advance of monopoly capitalism and the development of the Federal Reserve Bank. As the US Empire rose to a position of power among the industrialized western world, we will also examine its involvement in World War I and how finance capitalism crashed the US economy and pushed the country into the Great Depression.

Events Leading to the Civil War

From the time the United States was formed, a conflict existed between slave owning states in the South and free states in the North. This conflict simmered and grew for over a hundred years as differences over economic policy, frontier expansion, and slavery continually bubbled to the surface. As the conflicts grew, so did the enmity between the North and South. The conflict was fueled by the on-going process of admitting new territories and states to the country. As new states petitioned for admission, politicians at the national level fought over whether slavery should be abolished in that state or allowed. From the time of the thirteen original colonies, the country had grown to include thirty-nine states by the time of the Civil War. As a result of this escalating conflict, eleven southern, slave-owning states eventually seceded from the United States to form their own country, called the Confederate States of America or the Confederacy or "the South".[747]

In the political struggle leading to the Civil War, individual states in the north were passing state legislation based upon abolitionist principles, while in the South, the states were passing legislation to strengthen slavery.[748]

Even though the United States Declaration of Independence declared, "that all men are created equal, that they are endowed by their Creator with certain unalienable Rights, that among these are Life, Liberty and the pursuit of Happiness," slavery remained legal in the colonies even after the Revolutionary War. George Washington, a southerner, condemned slavery and freed his slaves, while Thomas Jefferson spoke out against slavery but kept slaves his entire life. Benjamin Franklin, an abolitionist, organized against it. Sam Adams could not have created a revolution by speaking out against slavery because he needed the Southern colonies to stand united with the north against England. He nonetheless was adamant that no slave live in his house. When he married his second wife Elizabeth who owned an enslaved woman named Surry, Adams insisted that "A slave can not live in my house; if she comes she must be free."[749] John Adams and Alexander Hamilton never owned slaves.

In 1777, just after the Revolution, Vermont prohibited slavery in its state constitution. A year later, Thomas Jefferson convinced the Virginia legislature to ban the importation of slaves in that state. It was the first state to ban the slave trade. Slavery, however, still remained legal.

In the next ten years, Pennsylvania, New Hampshire, Rhode Island, and Connecticut adopted laws that provided for the gradual emancipation of slaves within their states. During this time, Virginia relaxed its laws regarding the freeing of slaves by allowing a man to free his slaves by deed or will.

In 1781, the Continental Congress ratified the Articles of Confederation that united the thirteen colonies into a single nation that could be recognized by other countries. By 1781, the Articles were used to legally justify the Northwest Ordinance[750] by which the nation was expanded to include the Northwest Territory, which is the land occupied by the midwest states.[751]

Map 4-10: Northwest Territory in 1787

The territory, as the above map indicates, later became the states of Illinois, Indiana, Michigan, Ohio, Wisconsin, and Minnesota. In the ordinance, Congress prohibited slavery and involuntary servitude in the Northwest Territory, but required that fugitive slaves found in the territory be returned to their owners. The federal law no longer applied, however, once the states came into existence. Nonetheless, anti-slavery Northerners would cite the ordinance through the years as precedent for the limitation, if not the abolition, of slavery in their states. Despite the terms of the ordinance, Southern-born settlers tried and failed to pass laws to allow slavery in Indiana and Illinois.[752]

The Northwest Ordinance was considered a key legislative act because it set the precedent whereby the federal government now held sovereignty over all lands explored in the westward expansion of white settlers. No longer would individual states have the sovereignty to expand their territorial boundaries without federal approval.[753]

The prohibition of slavery in the Northwest Territory essentially established the Ohio River as the boundary between free and slave territory between the Appalachian Mountains and the Mississippi River. This division drew a line in the sand between slave and free states in the 1800s and established the "North" and the "South" in the Civil War, which began in 1861.

In 1803, President Jefferson purchased a huge tract of land west of the Mississippi from Napoleon that became known as the *Louisiana Purchase*.[754] This purchase proved a boon to the South because slavery already exists in the territory and the federal government did not have the resources to restrict it. Consequently, the new land allowed for a great expansion of slave plantations.[755]

In 1807, Congress, with the urging of President Jefferson, outlawed the Atlantic slave trade in order to damper the expansion of slavery in the West. At the time, slavers were bringing about fourteen thousand black slaves to the United States and its territories each year. After the slave trade was outlawed, smugglers continued to bring in about one thousand per year.

Southern slavers led by John Randolph, a Congressman from Roanoke Virginia, who although a member of Jefferson's Democratic-Republican Party, argued vehemently against Jefferson's anti-slavery legislation, char-

Map 4-11: Louisiana Purchase

ging that it was a pretext for universal emancipation and that if this occurred it would "blow up the constitution." There is no question that the outlawing of the slave trade deepened the divide between the states that supported slavery and those that did not.

Randolph became the leader of the right-wing faction of the Democratic-Republican Party that argued for "states' rights" as a means to stop the federal government from intervening in the rights of Southern states to own and trade slaves. Randolph's faction would later help to form the Democratic Party that ran Andrew Jackson, who was a slave owner, for President. Soon after the formation of the Democratic Party, the abolitionists would form the Republican Party that got Abraham Lincoln elected. Randolph's party gained support for their promotion of the principle that individual states could judge the constitutionality of central government laws and decrees and could refuse to enforce those laws they deemed unconstitutional.[756] This actually was one of the original principles of Jefferson and Madison's Democratic-Republican Party.

During the turn of the ninteenth century, Kentucky, Tennessee, Louisiana, Mississippi, and Alabama were admitted to the union as slave states. Illinois was admitted as a free state.

Tensions continued to mount as Texas, Florida, and Arkansas entered the union as slave states, while Massachusetts and eight other states passed personal liberty laws under which state officials were forbidden to assist in the capture of fugitive slaves.[757]

In 1820, Speaker of the House, Henry Clay proposed the *Missouri Compromise*[758] as a means to break the deadlock between the slave states and free states concerning westward expansion. The Missouri Compromise asserted that land west of the Mississippi River acquired from the Louisiana Purchase should be divided among slave states and free states according to a boundary established at 36°30' latitude.[759] The line ran roughly along the southern boundary of Missouri. The Compromise stated that, except for Missouri, no state north of the 36°30' latitude could be a slave state.

Many Southerners bristled at the exclusion of slavery from such a large area of the country. About twenty-five years later, the *Kansas-Nebraska Act* of 1854[760] would repeal the Compromise. This Act created the states of Kansas and Nebraska with the goal of opening up thousands of new farms and plantations and also set the stage for the creation of a Transcontinental Railroad.

The law contained a "popular sovereignty clause" that allowed residents of the territory to vote on whether they wanted to be admitted to the Union as a free or slave state. This led slavers and abolitionists to pour into Kansas with the goal of voting slavery up or down. The popular sovereignty clause proved to be a formula for violent confrontation between slavers and abolitionists that earned Kansas the epitaph *Bleeding Kansas.*[761]

The violence between the opposing sides resulted in two hundred deaths and two million dollars worth of property damage. Later findings showed that over ninety-five percent of the pro-slavery votes in the election of a Kansas territorial legislature in 1855 were determined to be fraudulent.[762]

In 1855, anti-slavery Kansans drafted the Topeka Constitution[763] and elected a new legislature, which actually represented the majority of legal voters. In reaction to being stymied in their illegal activity, pro-slavery men sacked and burned the anti-slavery town of Lawrence, Kansas. This led John Brown, an abolitionist, and his five sons to kill five pro-slavery men in retaliation. John Brown believed that the only way to defeat the oppressive system of slavery was through violent insurrection.[764]

During the presidential election of 1856, the tempers of politicians were rising and Congressional meetings were filled with rancor. The anti-slavery, Republican candidate, John C. Frémont's campaign slogan was "Free speech, free press, free soil, free men, Frémont and victory!" The Southern Democrats threaten that Fremont's election could lead to civil war. They were successful in their campaign. The Democratic Party candidate, James Buchanan carried five northern and western states and all the southern states except Maryland to win the election.

As President, Buchanan was often called a "doughface";[765] that is, a Northerner who could easily be molded by Southerners. Buchanan's efforts to maintain peace between the North and the South actually alienated both sides and led the Southern states to declare their secession from the Union. This ended any further discussion between the North and the South regarding slavery and set the stage for the American Civil War. Ever on the fence, Buchanan held that secession was illegal, but going to war to stop it was also illegal.[766]

Historians have ranked Buchanan as one of the worst presidents in American history because of his inability to identify a means of peace between the pro-slavery and anti-slavery forces, but this is a harsh criticism considering the history leading up to the war, that we have just observed. The handwriting was already on the wall when Buchanan took office and both sides disdained any attempt at compromise.

The Civil War

In 1860, Abraham Lincoln won the presidential election on a platform that included the prohibition of slavery in new states and territories. On November 7, South Carolina authorities in Charleston arrested a Federal officer. The officer was attempting to move supplies from the Charleston Arsenal to the federal Fort Moultrie. Two days later, South Carolina raised its flag over the Charleston harbor batteries. One month later, South Carolina officially seceded from the United States of America. The pot, long simmering, now began to boil. There was no going back.

On January 3, 1861, South Carolina commissioners proposed a meeting with other slave states to form a provisional government. In the same month Mississippi, Florida, Alabama, Georgia, and Louisiana seceded from the United States. Texas seceded in early February.

In February, the secessionists convened in Alabama to create a Provisional Congress of the Confederate States of America. The convention drafted a provisional constitution[767] that was signed by seven secessionist states.[768] The states were South Carolina, Georgia, Florida, Louisiana, Alabama, Mississippi and Texas.[769] It also chose Jefferson Davis to be the provisional president.[770] The United States government did not recognize the Confederacy, nor did any foreign nations.

Events moved very quickly now as both sides prepared for war. Southern states began to seize federal arsenals within their boundaries, while politicians developed legal documents to officially declare their secession from the Union. Individual states held meetings to allow their citizens to vote for or against secession. Skirmishes, battles, and riots began.

On March 4, Abraham Lincoln was inaugurated as sixteenth President of the United States. He stated his intention was not to interfere with slavery where it existed and to preserve the Union. The Union began to garrison soldiers in their forts and sent two hundred and fifty extra men to Fort Sumter in North Carolina to secure it from attack. Fort Sumter has thick, high walls and was one of many federal forts built after the War of 1812.

On April 12, 1861, Confederate artillery fired on the Union garrison stationed there. These were the first shots of the Civil War. The bombardment lasted all day and the fort, cut off from its supply line in the fight, surrendered the next day.[771] The Confederates allowed the Union to evacuate its garrison on Navy vessels.

The next day, President Lincoln called on the states to provide seventy-five thousand militiamen to recapture the fort and suppress the rebellion.

In response, Virginia, Arkansas, North Carolina, and Tennessee declared their secession from the Union and joined the Confederacy. Missouri and Kentucky, two border states, were admitted to the Confederacy, although they continued to support the Union.

President Lincoln then declared a naval blockade of the Confederate States, focusing on ports in Virginia and North Carolina.[772]

By the end of the year, seven hundred thousand troops were being trained in Union camps.[773] In the following year, 1862, major battles were fought at Shiloh, Richmond, Bull Run, Antietam, and Fredericksburg. As a result of the Union's blockade of the southern seacoast, its control of the waterways into the South, and its successful military campaigns, the South steadily lost control of its land.

On January 1, 1863, Lincoln delivered the Emancipation Proclamation.[774] This executive order changed the federal legal status of more than threemillion people from "slave" to "freedman." As a war measure, it allowed escaped slaves who reached Union territory to become legally free. Eventually, as the Union army took control of all Southern states, the Proclamation reached and liberated all of the designated slaves.

However, slaves in states that had not seceded from the Union were still considered slaves. Therefore, the proclamation applied only to three million of the four million slaves at the time. The Proclamation also provided for freedmen to enroll in the Union army. The Proclamation did not compensate the slavers, but it did not outlaw slavery or grant citizenship to the ex-slaves.[775]

As the Union armies moved southward, large numbers of plantation slaves were freed. Many joined the Union as soldiers and laborers. The most notable Union military campaign was Sherman's "March to the Sea" in late 1864.[776] The campaign began with General Sherman's troops leaving the captured city of Atlanta, Georgia, on November 15 and ended with the capture of the port of Savannah five weeks later. In this march, Sherman's army destroyed everything in its path. Not only military targets, but industries, infrastructure, and civilian property were destroyed. These included telegraph operations, railroads, and bridges. Sherman's *scorched earth* warfare, or total war, was revolutionary in the annals of military history. The campaign severely disrupted the Confederacy's economy and its transportation networks,⁷⁷⁷ making internal movement increasingly difficult and limiting its army's mobility.

The losses of men, supplies, and finance so disadvantaged the Southern army that public support for the Confederate administration eroded dramatically. After four years of fighting, Union forces captured Richmond, Virginia in April 1865. Shortly afterward, Confederate General Robert E. Lee surrendered to Union General Ulysses S. Grant, effectively destroying the Confederacy and ending the Civil War.⁷⁷⁸

While the politics of the war were extremely complex and took center stage in government deliberations, other political business continued at a normal pace. The transcontinental telegraph was completed in 1861 and as states and territories were formed during the westward expansion, government offices were being filled. The Homestead Act of 1862 opened vacant land to settlers.⁷⁷⁹ This Act encouraged Western migration by providing small farmers and settlers with one hundred and sixty acres of public land. In exchange, the homesteaders paid a small filing fee and were required to complete five years of continuous residence before receiving ownership of the land. After six months of residency, homesteaders also had the option of purchasing the land from the government for $1.25 per acre. The Homestead Act led to the distribution of eighty million acres of public land by 1900. Another important piece of legislation at the time was the Morrill Act that transferred over seventeen million acres of federal land to the states to raise funds for the creation of agricultural and mechanical universities.⁷⁸⁰

During the war, the United States also managed to maintain diplomatic and trade relations with foreign powers. While the Union blockade of Confederate ports created trade frictions and political intrigues, successful negotiations kept nations like Britain and France neutral.⁷⁸¹

An Economic Lesson

In 1805, there were just over one million human beings forced into slavery in the United States. Their labor value was calculated at three hundred million dollars. By the time the Civil War began in 1860, there were four million people enslaved whose labor value was calculated at three billion dollars. In the Confederate states, four out of ten people were enslaved and they accounted for more than half the agricultural labor in those states. In the cotton regions, the economic impact of slave labor was even greater. The value placed on enslaved people roughly equaled the total value of all farmland and farm buildings in the South. Each year the labor value of enslaved people in the United States increased.

Slave labor, the vilest form of capitalist exploitation of human labor was an increasingly prosperous business in the South. Almost a third of the wealth of white southerners in the cotton states was due to the expropriation of slave labor.[782] It is no wonder that Southerners, even those who did not own slaves, viewed any attempt to free black slaves as a catastrophic threat to their entire economic system. They were willing to do anything, even risk war, to keep blacks enslaved.

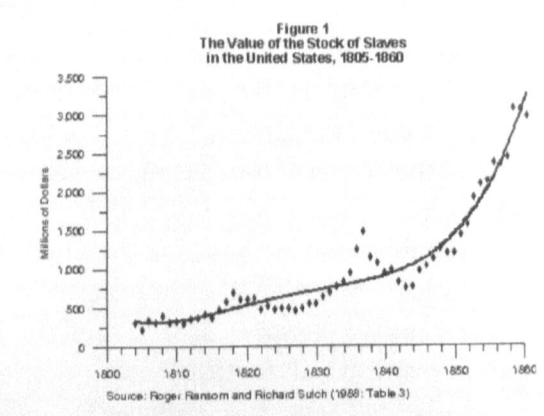

Fig. 4-33: Value of the Stock of Slaves in the US, 1805-1860
(Source: The Economics of the Civil War Roger L. Ransom, University of California, Riverside)

The Northern states also had a huge economic stake in slavery. By the mid 1830s, cotton shipments accounted for more than half the value of all exports from the United States. As cotton exports increased, so did the number of slaves. Slave labor allowed the price of raw cotton produced in the American South to remain low and this enabled textile manufacturers in the United States and in Britain to expand production and thus their profits. In turn, this reduced the cost of textiles to white consumers and added to their increased quality of life. As manufacturing of all kinds expanded in the United States and abroad, markets expanded and at the root of all this economic stimulus was the labor exploited from slaves. When James Hammond exclaimed in 1859 that "Cotton is King!" no one rose to dispute the point.[783]

In 1860, the year the Civil War began, 6.1 million people, or twenty percent of the population of the United States, lived in an urban county. By contrast, less than seven percent of people in the eleven Southern states lived in urban counties. Cotton cultivation with slave labor did not require local financial services or nearby manufacturing activities that might generate urban activities.

Settlement of western lands was a major bone of contention between the North and the South. How the federal government distributed land to people would have a major impact on the nature of farming in a region. Northerners wanted to encourage the settlement of farms, which would depend primarily on family labor by offering cheap land in small parcels. The plantation aristocrats feared that such a policy would inhibit the establishment of large plantations. This all came to a head with the passage of the "Homestead Act" of 1860. Northern and western congressmen strongly favored the bill in the House of Representatives, but the measure received only a single vote from slave states' representatives.

Federal government support for railroads was another contentious issue. The railroads needed government assistance to be viable, but Southerners had no need for the railroads. When the Pacific Railway Bill of 1860 was proposed to create a transcontinental railway between the East and West coasts, the South kept the bill from passing.[784]

The South also strongly objected to the imposition of taxes on imported goods (tariffs), which made consumer goods more expensive for them. The North, on the other hand, desired import taxes to give their industries a competitive advantage against goods from Europe that could be produced more cheaply than domestic goods. These tariffs were also the main source of federal government revenues at the time, thus the issue resulted in continual infighting between the industrial North and the agricultural South.

Another volatile economic issue between the North and the South was banking. The Northern states wanted central control over the banking industry, while the South wanted local control. When Andrew Jackson, a southerner, vetoed the recharter of the Second Bank of the United States, bank charters and regulations were largely put in the hands of private banks at the state level. In 1860, a Republican proposal to create a National Banking System was killed by Southern opposition.

The rancorous debate around each of these economic issues created ample support for those Southerners who clamored to leave the Union in 1861.

Historians have questioned the motivation of the North in getting involved in the Civil War. Why did not the Union just let the South secede? The strongest argument made by historians is that the North wanted to control the expansion of slavery in new territory and thus its mode of economic production and that the only way that they could do this was to keep the South in the Union. Abraham Lincoln, in his second inaugural address, simply answered: "Both parties deprecated war, but one of them would *make* war rather than let the nation survive, and the other would *accept* war rather than let it perish, and the war came." What did the war cost? The most comprehensive attempt to answer this question is the work of Claudia Goldin and Frank Lewis.[785]

Table 3 The Costs of the Civil War (Millions of 1860 Dollars)			
	South	North	Total
Direct Costs:			
Government Expenditures	1,032	2,302	3,334
Physical Destruction	1,487		1,487
Loss of Human Capital	767	1,064	1,831
Total Direct Costs of the War	3,286	3,366	6,652
Per capita	376	148	212
Indirect Costs:			
Total Decline in Consumption	6,190	1,149	7,339
Less:			

Effect of Emancipation	1,960		
Effect of Cotton Prices	1,670		
Total Indirect Costs of The War	2,560	1,149	3,709
Per capita	293	51	118
Total Costs of the War	5,846	4,515	10,361
Per capita	670	199	330
Population in 1860 (Million)	8.73	27.71	31.43
Source: Ransom, (1998: 51, Table 3-1); Goldin and Lewis.			

While these figures are at best a rough estimate, they provide an educated guess as to the cost of the war. The direct cost of the war as calculated by Goldin and Lewis was 1.5 times the total gross national product of the United States for 1860, an enormous sum in comparison to any military effort by the United States before or after. What stands out in addition to the enormity of the bill is the disparity in the burden these costs represented to the people in the North and the South. On a *per capita* basis, the cost to a Northerner was about on hundred and fifty dollars—or roughly equal to one year's income. The Southern burden was two and a half times that amount—three hundred and seventy-six dollars per each man, woman and child.

No war in American history strained the economic resources of the US as did the Civil War. Governments on both sides were forced to resort to borrowing on an unprecedented scale to meet the financial obligations of the war. The North, with its developed markets and industrial base was better prepared to meet the cost. The South, on the other hand, had always relied on either Northern or foreign capital markets for their financial needs, and they had virtually no manufacturing establishments to produce military supplies. Thus, the Confederate states had to rely heavily on funds from Europe to finance their costs.

In 1862 and 1863 the Union covered less than fifteen percent of its total expenditures through taxes. To increase tax revenues, they imposed higher tariffs on imported goods and introduced the first income tax in American history. Even so, by the end of the war, only twenty-five percent of the cost of the war was collected as taxes. Of the remaining seventy-five percent, some was met by printing money without the backing of gold. This amounted to two hundred and fifty million dollars worth of "Greenbacks." But this only met another eighteen percent of the cost of the war. This still left a huge shortfall in revenue that was not covered by either taxes or the printing of money.

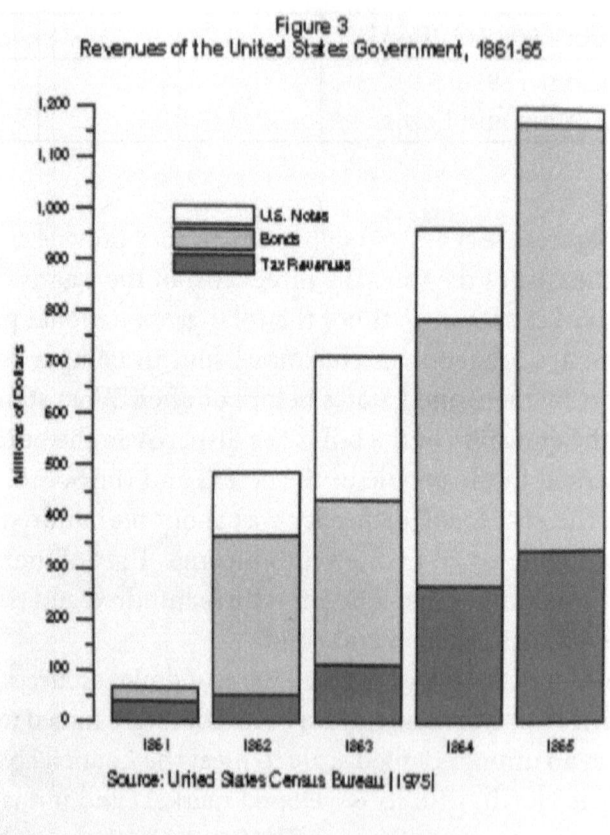

Fig. 4-34: Revenues of the US Government, 1861-1865
(The Economics of the Civil War Roger L. Ransom, University of California, Riverside)

The remaining revenues were obtained by borrowing funds from the public. Between 1861 and 1865, the debt obligation of the Federal government increased from $65 million to $2.7 billion. Even the robust financial institutions of the North were strained by these demands, but they managed to come up with the money. In all, Northerners bought almost two billion dollars worth of treasury notes and absorbed seven hundred million dollars of new currency. Consequently, the Northern economy was able to finance the war without a significant reduction in private consumption. Several economic historians have claimed that the creation and subsequent retirement of the Civil War debt ultimately provided a significant impetus to post-war growth.[786] [787]

Wartime financing put the spotlight on the bankers again and prompted a significant change in the banking system of the United States. Andrew Jackson's legacy in which he destroyed the central bank to clean out the capitalist "vipers" who were controlling the national government, now came to an end. State banks that had replaced the federal bank now lost their power. In 1862, Congress, under the determined leadership of President Lincoln, passed legislation to create a privately-owned national bank again. It was now called the National Banking System.

As far back as 1839, two years after Nicholas Biddle intentionally threw the country into a depression in revenge for Jackson's resistance to renewing the privately-owned national bank, a move that ultimately led to the Panic of 1837, Lincoln addressed the issue of Jackson's *Independent Treasury System*[788] in a speech. His speech compared the centralized Second Bank of the United States to the decentralized hard money-only "sub-treasury" system with which Jackson's followers had replaced it. Lincoln claimed that a decentralized banking system produced vastly inferior results. His speech gained Lincoln the support of the big banks and cast him into the political spotlight.[789] Lincoln had a point. By creating a central banking system, money flowed more easily and its use was optimized:

> "The [National] Bank was permitted to, and did actually loan [public revenues] out to individuals, and hence the large amount of money annually collected for revenue purposes, which by any other plan would have been idle a great portion of time, was kept almost constantly in circulation. Any person . . . will reflect, that money

> is only valuable while in circulation, [and] any device which will keep the government revenues, in constant circulation, instead of being locked up in idleness, is no inconsiderable advantage.
>
> "By [contrast, under] the Sub-Treasury [Jackson' Independent Treasury System], the revenue is to be collected, and kept in iron boxes until the government wants it for disbursement, thus robbing the people of the use of it, while the government does not itself need it, and while the money is performing no nobler office than that of rusting in iron boxes. The natural effect of this change of policy, everyone will see, is to reduce the quantity of money in circulation ... [resulting in] distress, ruin, bankruptcy, and beggary.[790]

Consequently, when Lincoln won the presidency, he spared no effort to get Congress to pass the National Bank Act,[791] prepared by his Treasury Secretary Salmon P. Chase. The Act created the national banking system and the Office of the Comptroller of the Currency as its supervisor. Although promoted partly as a wartime measure, Lincoln conceded that he wanted to create a central banking system that would exist into the future:

> The national banking system is proving to be acceptable to capitalists and to the people.... That the government and the people will derive great benefit from this change in the banking systems of the country can hardly be questioned. The national system will create a reliable and permanent influence in support of the national credit, and protect the people against losses in the use of paper money.[792]

While Lincoln supported a national banking system, he did not necessarily support a national banking system in the hands of private bankers. In fact, by his second term, he was already considering revising the National Bank Act to put the finance of the country into the hands of the federal government. His experience with the private bankers had left a bad taste in his mouth.

When President Jackson had killed off the Central Bank that was privately controlled, the power over the money supply devolved to the state banks. The big banks were furious that they had lost control and were determined to get it back. Most of the money invested in the US banking system up to this time had come from private European banks like the Rothschilds who were quite outspoken about their intentions. We can see this from a quote from Otto von Bismark the Chancellor of Germany, shortly after the Civil War:

> The division of the United States into federations of equal force [North and South] was decided long before the Civil War by the high financial powers of Europe. These bankers were afraid that the US, if they remained as one block, and as one nation, would attain economic and financial independence, which would upset their financial domination over the world.[793]

When the Civil War began in April of 1861, Lincoln needed money to finance the war effort and he went with his secretary of the treasury, Salmon Chase, to New York to apply for the necessary loans. The bankers offered loans at twenty-four percent to thirty-six percent interest. Lincoln essentially told them to stick it. He then put an old acquaintance, Colonel Dick Taylor, who was a friend and confidante of General Grant during the war, in charge of solving the problem of how to finance the war. His response to Lincoln was: "Just get Congress to pass a bill authorizing the printing of full legal tender treasury notes ... and pay your soldiers with them and go ahead and win your war with them also."

When Lincoln asked if the people of America would accept the notes Taylor said: "The people or anyone else will not have any choice in the matter, if you make them full legal tender. They will have the full sanction of the government and be just as good as any money; as Congress is given that express right by the Constitution."[794]

Lincoln was later to reply to his old friend:

> My dear Colonel Dick:
> I have long determined to make public the origin of the

greenback and tell the world that it was Dick Taylor's creation. You had always been friendly to me and when troublous times fell on us, and my shoulders, though broad and willing, were weak, and myself surrounded by such circumstances and such people that I knew not whom to trust, then I said in my extremity, 'I will send for Colonel Taylor — he will know what to do.' I think it was in January 1862, on or about the 16th, that I did so. Said you: 'Why, issue treasury notes bearing no interest, printed on the best banking paper. Issue enough to pay off the army expenses and declare it legal tender.' Chase thought it a hazardous thing, but we finally accomplished it, and gave the people of this Republic the greatest blessing they ever had — their own paper to pay their debts. It is due to you, the father of the present greenback, that the people should know it and I take great pleasure in making it known. How many times have I laughed at you telling me, plainly, that I was too lazy to be anything but a lawyer.

Yours Truly.
A. Lincoln[795]

On Taylor's advice, Lincoln printed four hundred and fifty million dollars worth of the new bills using green ink on the back to distinguish them from other notes. Speaking before the Senate in 1865, he said:

The government should create, issue and circulate all the currency and credit needed to satisfy the spending power of the government and the buying power of consumers. . . . The privilege of creating and issuing money is not only the supreme prerogative of Government, but it is the Government's greatest creative opportunity. By the adoption of these principles, the long-felt want for a uniform medium will be satisfied. The taxpayers will be saved immense sums of interest, discounts and exchanges. The financing of all public enterprises, the maintenance of stable government and ordered progress, and the conduct of the Treasury will become matters of practical administration. The people can and will be furnished with a currency as safe as their own government. Money will cease to be the master and become the servant of humanity. Democracy will rise superior to the money power."[796]

Having the money supply under the hands of the government instead of private bankers was working so well that Lincoln considered making it a permanent policy. He would have done so in his second term, if he had not been assassinated. Lincoln's plan benefitted everyone except the big bankers. Realizing how dangerous his intentions were to their ability to exploit the American people, they wasted no time in expressing their view in their *Hazard Circular*, which was the big bankers' trade publication. One of their comments came to be published in the London Times:

> If this mischievous financial policy, which has its origin in North America, shall become endurated down to a fixture, then that Government will furnish its own money without cost. It will pay off debts and be without debt. It will have all the money necessary to carry on its commerce. It will become prosperous without precedent in the history of the world. The brains, and wealth of all countries will go to North America. That country must be destroyed or it will destroy every monarchy on the globe."[797]

The *Hazard Circular* was also discovered and circulated throughout the country by community organizers. It gave additional information as to the thinking of the bankers:

> The great debt that capitalists will see is made out of the war and must be used to control the valve of money. To accomplish this government bonds must be used as a banking basis. We are now awaiting Secretary of Treasury Salmon Chase to make that recommendation. It will not allow Greenbacks to circulate as money as we cannot control that. We control bonds and through them banking issues.[798]

If Lincoln supported the idea of a national currency in public hands, why did he create the National Bank Act of 1863, which put the private bankers back in charge of the U.S. economy? In 1863, Lincoln was unable to get congressional authority to issue more greenbacks. Salmon Chase convinced Lincoln that the only way to raise money was from the passage of the National Bank Act. The Act was approved by Congress. From this point on the entire US money supply was created out of the public debt owed to bankers who bought government bonds and monetized them at a great cost to the public. This insidious development, something that our enlightened leaders had fought against since the American Revolution, led to the situation that even though the federal government ran a surplus in many years, it still could not pay off the public debt because to do so would mean there would not be any bonds to back the national bank notes (currency). In other words, to pay off the debt was to destroy the money supply. This same situation exists today, although the government no longer runs surpluses. But remember, despite the Republicans call to end the federal debt, it is an impossible task to accomplish because of the way that the bankers set up the national bank. Through their arrangements, the American people can never get out of debt to the bankers, and can only go deeper into debt to them.

Lincoln discovered this truth during his first term in office and was intent on ending the monopoly of the public finances by the bankers but he had to first end the war and get nominated for a second term. Like Jackson, he would certainly have killed off the bankers' monopoly had he not been killed himself only forty-one days after being re-elected.

After Lincoln's death, the bankers had their way. On April 12th, 1866, the American Congress passed the Contraction Act, that had the Treasury call in and retire most of the federally issued greenbacks, To strengthen their position, the bankers began to call in existing loans and refused to issue new loans. They spread the word through the newspapers that unless the National Bank was recertified, additional hardships would ensue. After destroying the federally issued greenbacks, the bankers then developed their plan to demonetize silver so that people could not use it as money in daily transactions. By demonetizing silver, the bankers knew that the only money available to people would be the federal reserve notes that they themselves created.

Due to the restricted money supply in 1877, riots broke out all over the country. The bank's response was to do nothing except to campaign against the idea that greenbacks should be reissued. The American Bankers Association secretary James Buel expressed the bankers' position in a letter to fellow members of the association:

> It is advisable to do all in your power to sustain such prominent daily and weekly newspapers, especially the Agricultural and Religious Press, as will oppose the greenback issue of paper money and that you will also withhold patronage from all applicants who are not willing to oppose the government issue of money. To repeal the Act creating bank notes, or to restore to circulation the government issue of money will be to provide the people with money and will therefore seriously affect our individual profits as bankers and lenders. See your congressman at once and engage him to support our interest that we may control legislation."[799]

In 1881, James Garfield became President. He also grasped the underlying problem with the economy:

> Whosoever controls the volume of money in any country is absolute master of all industry and commerce ... And when you realise that the entire system is very easily controlled, one way or another, by a few powerful men at the top, you will not have to be told how periods of inflation and depression originate.[800]

Within a week of releasing this statement President Garfield was also assassinated.

In 1891, a major fleece of the people was being planned. The secretary of the Associated Bankers of New York sent out this message to bankers across the country, "On September 1, 1894, we will not renew our loans under any consideration. On September 1, we will demand our money. We will foreclose and become mortgagees in possession. We can take two-thirds of the farms west of the Mississippi, and thousands of them east of the Mississippi as well, at our own price . . . Then the farmers will become tenants as in England. . . ."[801]

It may be, as Lincoln claimed, that a centrally controlled bank serves to maintain the optimum circulation of currency better than local banks, but history has taught us that when the national bank is in the hands of private capitalists and they are above the law, the capitalists simply confiscate other peoples wealth and destroy the purchasing power of the average person. The impact of such a system, now called the Federal Reserve System, has led today to a situation in which the "richest one percent in the United States now own more than the bottom ninety percent".[802] If the American people are to ever regain control of their banking system, we must not forget the lesson learned from Union financing of the Civil War, both its positive and negative aspects.

The efforts of the Confederate government to pay for their war effort were far more chaotic than in the North. In most cases, reliable expenditure and revenue data are not available. Over the course of the war, tax revenues accounted for only eleven percent of all revenues, as opposed to the Union's twenty-five percent. The South also printed money at a greater quantity than did the North. Over a third of the Confederate government's revenue came from the printing press. In addition, the majority of funds were raised by issuing bonds (IOUs), many of which were sold abroad in either London or Amsterdam. By mid-1864 the costs of paying interest on outstanding government bonds absorbed more than half all government expenditures. In the last year of the war, collecting taxes and issuing new bonds became so difficult that the total revenues collected by the Confederate Government actually declined.[803]

The exorbitant printing of money in the South created hyperinflation while excessive borrowing created crushing debt. By the beginning of 1862, the prices of consumer goods had already doubled; by the middle of 1863 they had increased by a factor of thirteen. By the end of the war, inflation had reached a point where the Confederate currency was virtually worthless. People took to barter or using Union dollars (if they could be found) to conduct their transactions. Simply put, the collapse of the Confederate monetary system demonstrated that the economy was not strong enough to sustain the war effort.[804]

Insofar as inflation, which is a sudden rise in prices, affects wage earners and the poor the hardest, the average person in the South saw the real value of their wages practically disappear by the end of the war. This resulted in wide spread poverty and destitution. At the same time, many freed blacks also entered the labor market reducing the number of jobs available to poor whites. This stoked white hatred and resentment for blacks even more.

The end of slavery meant that the entire Southern economy had to be rebuilt. This task was far greater than anyone at the time imagined and the burden persisted long after the war had ended.

During the war, white farmers had abandoned their land in order to fight in the war. As a result, their property was neglected and its worth depreciated. Further, slaveholders lost their investment in the slaves due to emancipation. Planters were consequently strapped for capital in the years immediately after the war, forcing them to borrow money to survive. Because the slaves were now free, the farmers and plantation owners had to negotiate with them to procure their labor. The freedmen and their families understandably were not so eager to work for slavers and a third of their previous labor value now was completely eliminated from white control. This created an apparent labor "shortage" for the plantation owners and convinced white landlords that a free labor system could never work with the ex-slaves. While they were able, for the most part, to cling to their landholdings, the ex-slavers were forced to break up their large plantations and rent small parcels of land to the freedmen using a new form of rental contract called "sharecropping." Now the South suddenly became an agricultural economy characterized by tenant farms, much like England during the feudal era, the small exception being that the tenant farmers did not belong to the land if it was sold.

The Southern economy remained heavily committed not only to agriculture, but to the staple crop of cotton, although production in the South fell dramatically at the end of the war, and still did not recover fifteen years later. Per capita income of whites in 1857 had been one hundred and twenty-five dollars; in 1879 it was just over eighty dollars.[805] By the end of the nineteenth century, Southern per capita income had fallen to roughly two-thirds of the national level, and the South was locked in a cycle of poverty that lasted well into the twentieth century.[806]

Neither the dreams of those who fought for an independent South, nor those who believed that Reconstruction would create a New South after the war were realized. Even so, the South, at the end of the war, went through a twelve-year period, in which the federal government and forces from the North attempted to reconstruct the economy on the South independent of slave labor.

Reconstruction

The process of southern "Reconstruction" lasted from 1865 to 1877 under the administration of four presidents, Abraham Lincoln, Andrew Johnson, Ulysses S. Grant, and Rutherford B Hayes.

This period saw the ratification of the 13th, 14th, and 15th Amendments to the Constitution. The 13th amendment formally abolished slavery in the United States. The 14th amendment granted citizenship to "all persons born or naturalized in the United States," which included former slaves. It also forbade states from denying any person "life, liberty, or property, without due process of law" or to "deny to any person within its jurisdiction the equal protection of the laws." By directly mentioning the role of the states, the 14th Amendment greatly expanded the protection of civil rights to all Americans and is cited in more litigation than any other amendment.[807]

The 15th amendment granted African American men the right to vote by declaring that the "right of citizens of the United States to vote shall not be denied or abridged by the United States or by any state on account of race, color, or previous condition of servitude." Although ratified in 1870, the promise of the 15th Amendment would not be realized until a century later. Southern states were able to effectively keep blacks from voting through such devices as poll taxes, literacy tests, terrorism, murder, and other means. It would take the Civil Rights movement, led by Martin Luther King, to secure the passage of the Voting Rights Act of 1965 before the majority of African Americans in the South were registered and allowed to vote.[808] Even today, politicians continue to disenfranchise black voters in the South.

The purpose of Reconstruction was to help the eleven states that seceded from the Union to become part of the Union again, to regain their Congressional seats and self-government. Presidents Lincoln and Johnson were moderates in their approach to Reconstruction.

Motivated by a desire to build a strong Republican party in the South and to end the bitterness between the North and the South, Lincoln issued a *Proclamation of Amnesty and Reconstruction* in an attempt to reunite the once United States. This proclamation was made in 1863 even before the war had ended, but he intended it to apply immediately in those areas of the Confederacy occupied by Union armies.[809] The Proclamation offered a pardon to any Confederate who would swear to support the Constitution and the Union. Once a group in any conquered state reached the size of one tenth of that state's total vote in the presidential election of 1860 and took the prescribed oath and organized a government to abolish slavery, he would grant that government executive recognition.

Lincoln's plan was sharply opposed by the progressives in Congress who believed that his plan would simply restore to power the old planter aristocracy, which it did. After the war, the political aristocracy of the South immediately passed laws to restrict black freedom and compel them to work in a labor economy based on low wages and debt. These laws, known as *Black Codes*, were part of the larger pattern of Southern whites to suppress the emancipated African Americans and return them to conditions of slavery.[810]

The Black Codes allowed no voting rights and no citizenship to blacks. Blacks could not own firearms, serve on a jury in a lawsuit involving whites, or move about without employment. The Black Codes outraged northern opinion and led to the Civil Rights Act of 1866, which granted full legal equality with whites except for the right to vote.

As the South had little desire to forsake black slavery, nor their previous way of life, the progressives were correct in demanding an immediate and strong intervention against the Black Codes and the persistent terrorism, brutality, and murder of blacks.

Northern officials reported on conditions of the freedmen in the South. One assessment came from Carl Schurz, who was a Union Army General during the war and later became the Secretary of the Interior under Rutherford B. Hayes.[811] His report documented dozens of killings of blacks without trial by local governments. He also claimed that hundreds or thousands more African Americans were killed:

> The number of murders and assaults perpetrated upon Negroes is very great; we can form only an approximate estimate of what is going on in those parts of the South which are not closely garrisoned, and from which no regular reports are received, by what occurs under the very eyes of our military authorities. As to my personal experience, I will only mention that during my two days sojourn at Atlanta, one Negro was stabbed with fatal effect on the street, and three were poisoned, one of whom died. While I was at Montgomery, one Negro was cut across the throat evidently with intent to kill, and another was shot, but both escaped with their lives. Several papers attached to this report give an account of the number of capital cases that occurred at certain places during a certain period of time. It is a sad fact that the perpetration of those acts is not confined to that class of people which might be called the rabble.[812]

The report included sworn testimony from soldiers and officials of the Freedmen's Bureau. In Selma, Alabama, for example, Major J. P. Houston noted that whites, who killed twelve African Americans in his district, never came to trial. Many more killings never became official cases. Captain Poillon described white patrols in southwestern Alabama:

> . . . who board some of the boats; after the boats leave they hang, shoot, or drown the victims they may find on them, and all those found on the roads or coming down the rivers are almost invariably murdered. The bewildered and terrified freedmen know not what to do—to leave is death; to remain is to suffer the increased burden imposed upon them by the cruel taskmaster, whose only interest is their labor, wrung from them by every device an inhuman ingenuity can devise; hence the lash and murder is resorted to to intimidate those whom fear of an awful death alone cause to remain, while patrols, Negro dogs and spies, disguised as Yankees, keep constant guard over these unfortunate people.[813]

Much of the violence that was perpetrated against African Americans was shaped by sexist prejudices. Because whites portrayed black women as sexually greedy, it was virtually impossible to convict a white man of rape during this time. In fact, because black women had so little virtue, white society held they could not legally be raped. Sexual assaults on African-American women were so pervasive, particularly on the part of their white employers, that black men sought to reduce the contact between white males and black females by having the women in their family avoid doing work that was closely overseen by whites.[814] Black men were also stereotyped as being extremely sexually aggressive and their supposed threat to white women was often used as a pretext for lynching and castration.

To counter such virulent racism, rape, and murder, the progressives passed the Wade-Davis Bill,[815] which required that fifty percent of a state's male voters take an "ironclad" oath that they had never voluntarily supported the Confederacy. Lincoln vetoed the bill, thinking it too radical. His plan, outlined in his *Proclamation of Amnesty and Reconstruction*, however, never worked and, in fact, acted to reinstate the slaver elite to power. Congress, in opposition, refused to seat the Senators and Representatives elected from the Southern states. By the time Lincoln was assassinated, the President and Congress were at a stalemate.

President Andrew Johnson, who came to power after Lincoln's assassination, ensured that Lincoln's policies prevailed until the elections of 1866 when the progressives came to power. Frustrated by Johnson's opposition to Congressional Reconstruction, they filed impeachment charges against him, but the action failed by one vote in the Senate. They immediately passed the Freedmen's Bureau and Civil Rights Bills and sent them to Johnson. The first bill extended the life of the Freedmen's Bureau, which was originally established by Lincoln as a temporary organization charged with assisting refugees and freed slaves. The second defined all persons born in the United States as national citizens who were to enjoy equality before the law. Johnson vetoed the bills and this caused a permanent rupture in his relationship with Congress, one that eventually resulted in his impeachment in 1868. The Civil Rights Act of 1866 became the first major bill to become law over a presidential veto.[816]

Once in power, the progressives removed former Confederates from power and enfranchised the freedmen. A Republican coalition emerged in nearly all the southern states to accomplish this work. Their goal was to transform the South by setting up an economy independent of slave labor by using the U.S. Army and the Freedmen's Bureau to get the job done.[817] In this process, thousands of Northerners went south as missionaries, teachers, businessmen and politicians. Most of these people truly wanted to create a new South that did not depend upon slavery. They were the predecessors of the Civil Rights activists that went to the South to register black voters in the 1960s. Of course, some opportunists also moved into the south motivated by self-interest. Southerners derisively referred to such people as *Carpetbaggers* because of their cheap luggage. Southerners, who supported the Republican civil rights campaign, were derisively called *Scalawags* by the supporters of slavery. Due to the Republican civil rights campaign, sixty Republicans from the South were elected to Congress.[818]

Among those elected were freedmen. Between 1865 and 1877, many African Americans served in state and local politics. Fourteen black men served in the House of Representatives between 1869 and 1877, six served as lieutenant governors, and more than six hudred served in southern state legislatures. When the Reconstruction ended in 1877, however, African Americans were driven out of government by the Ku Klux Klan.[819]

What caused the end of the Reconstruction period? The process began with the presidential election of 1876. To this day, it is considered to be the most contentious and controversial presidential election in history.[820] The contest was between Rutherford B. Hayes (Republican) and Samuel J. Tilden (Democrat). While Tilden beat Hayes with the popular vote, the distribution of electoral votes threatened to cause a political crisis. After a first count of electoral votes, Tilden had won one hundred and eighty-four votes to Hayes's one hundred and sixty-five, but twenty votes were unresolved. These twenty electoral votes were in dispute in four states: Florida, Louisiana, South Carolina, and Oregon. In the first three states, each party reported its candidate had won the state, while in Oregon one elector was declared illegal and replaced. The question of who should have been awarded these electoral votes continues to be a source of controversy. As Republicans and Democrats fought over the disputed votes, the nation was again threatened with ruin. To prevent a crisis of democracy and keep the nation from splitting, a backroom deal was struck to resolve the dispute. This deal was called the *Compromise of 1877*.[821] It awarded all twenty electoral votes to Rutherford B Hayes, the Republican candidate, thus giving him the presidency. In return for their acquiescence, the Southern Democrats received a promise from the Republicans to withdraw federal troops from the South and end Reconstruction. The Compromise effectively ceded power in the Southern states to the Democratic *Redeemers*,[822] and cast the black population in the South into a lower region of hell than even slavery had inhabited.

The Redeemers were a Southern white political coalition that sought to oust the Radical Republican coalition of freedmen, "carpetbaggers," and "scalawags" and return Southern politics to the days of slavery. The Redeemers were generally led by the rich plantation owners, businessmen, and professionals, who came to dominate Southern politics in most areas from the 1870s to 1910.

The Redeemers were not willing to accept the constitutional amendments that granted rights to blacks and they prevented black political activity by any means at their disposal. The Redeemers, as the leaders of the Democratic Party, were supported by paramilitary organizations that conducted insurgencies and assassinations. The most well known of these groups were the White League,[823] the Red Shirts,[824] and the KKK.[825]

The White League and the Red Shirts operated openly with the expressed goal to violently overthrow Republican rule and suppress black voting. The Ku Klux Klan, on the other hand, was a clandestine terrorist organization.

The White League, or the "White Man's League," was primarily composed of Civil War veterans who knew how to use weaponry and were trained in the art of war. They developed chapters throughout the rural south and received financing and weapons from the wealthy. Their activities included the Coushatta Massacre[826] and the Battle of Liberty Place. In 1874, the White Man's League assassinated six white Republican officeholders and many black witnesses outside Coushatta, Louisiana, which was then a predominately black town. Later in the same year, the League, in an attempt to overthrow the Republican governor of Louisiana, brought five thousand men to New Orleans where they overwhelmed the police and state militia and ransacked the state house and city hall. They retreated only when President Grant dispatched federal troops to the city.[827]

Similarly, the Red Shirts, another paramilitary group, arose in 1875 in Mississippi and the Carolinas. Like the White League they operated as a "military arm of the Democratic Party," to restore white supremacy. They broke up Republican meetings, disrupted their organizing, and intimidated black voters at the polls. Many blacks stopped voting from fear, and others voted for Democrats under threats of violence. The Red Shirts drove voting blacks from their homes and whipped them. Black leaders and activists were murdered without reprisal. During the 1876 presidential election, the Red Shirts ensured that the white Democrats voted multiple times at the polls while blacks were barred from voting.[828]

Armed and mounted Red Shirts also accompanied the Democratic candidate for governor of South Carolina, Wade Hampton[829] on his tour of the state, in order to intimidate Republicans and the black population. By such maneuvers, the Democrat slavers and racists regained their power throughout the South.

As for the Republicans, a split developed between the Southerners and the Northerners within the party. The Southerners, who took a more conservative position in decisions influencing reconstruction, were often sidelined by the Northerners and many, in frustration, joined the Southern Democrats. In 1868, for example, Georgia Democrats, with support from some conservative Republicans, expelled all twenty-eight black Republican members from the state house, arguing since blacks were ineligible to vote they could not hold office.[830]

The blacks during this period of time had begun to demand a bigger share of the offices and patronage. In their quest for justice, they often contested elections of their carpetbagger allies arguing that the hard realities of Southern political life required that blacks be represented by black officials. Ironically, some of the more prosperous freedmen joined the Democrats because they were angry with the Republicans for failing to address land reform. The South was "sparsely settled," and in states like Louisiana and Mississippi only ten percent of the arable land was being cultivated. Because blacks did not have the financial stake to buy land, they hoped that the government would help them acquire land, which they could work. W. E. B. Du Bois, a black activist and historian,[831] promoted coalitions of poor whites and blacks, but they never got off the ground. Neither side looked with favor upon cooperation. The blacks did not trust the whites and the whites resented the job competition from the freedmen.

As the struggle for civil rights continued in the South and as white Democrats and their paramilitary arms continued to fight against any attempt at cooperation on civil rights, (their military activities often required US army intervention), the people of the North grew tired of the struggle. They drifted into belief in the mythology that Confederate nationalism and slavery were dead and the goals of the Civil War were achieved. Even the Republican leadership adapted a "let it be" attitude claiming that any further military intervention would be undemocratic and a violation of Republican values. This attitude permeated the presidential election of 1876 in which Hayes and the Republican party abandoned the unarmed and vulnerable southern blacks to the vile white racists of the South, who were now even more driven by hate and the desire to torture and terrorize than they were during the days of slavery.

In summary, the Civil War destroyed the economy of the South and threw many people into poverty and destitution. Prior to the Civil War, the Southern economy was one of mercantile capitalism. Industrialization, the mark of laissez-faire capitalism, was curtailed by the plantation system. This conflict of interest prevented Northern legislators from passing legislation regarding monetary and banking reform, a transcontinental railroad, and incentives for settling the West. After the war, when efforts were made to rebuild the southern economy based on an industrial model, such efforts were met with opportunism on the part of some Northerners and hostility and uncooperativeness on the part of the majority of southern whites. The social stratification based upon institutional racism became even more virulent and the southern elite made every effort to restore the conditions of slavery that had preceded the war. Consequently, the South remained mired in rural poverty similar to the conditions of feudal Europe before the birth of capitalism.

Because the Civil War and the destruction of the South's economy occurred so recently, it is little wonder that the social memory of the war and its impact on people's lives still vibrates in the minds of Southern people today. In this respect, we can certainly sympathize with their suffering. Unfortunately, many southern conservatives still maintain their racist hatred of black people and persist in blaming them for their suffering that they only created by themselves. Such people continue to justify their racist hatred and their crimes against humanity by using the Christian religion. Consequently, the South, despite the persistent efforts of many good people, continues to remain at the heart of American racism until this day. And this racist mentality continues to create social divisiveness and to greatly hinder further human progress in the country. Today, our current President has done everything in this power to fan the flames of this racist fire and, in doing so, has divided the nation once again.

Robber Barons: Laissez Faire Capitalism Reaches the United States

Even as the Civil War was being fought, telegraph lines and railroad lines continued to be built. These inventions allowed people to communicate over great distances almost instantaneously and to transport people and goods from different regions of the country with increased speed. Such inventions allowed for the large-scale advancement of the industrialized economy of the United States that followed immediately after the Civil War.

With the North's victory in the war, it was no longer shackled by opposition from Southern politicians. Industrial capitalism in the United States could fully advance into the next stage of capitalist expansion, that of Laissez Faire capitalism. This is the time when monopoly capitalists like Morgan, Rockefeller, Carnegie, and Vanderbilt gained control over the key industries of the economy. Their business practices included buying off politicians, seizing control of national resources, paying extremely low wages, and once having established their monopolies, raising prices that kept the American people in a general state of fear that they would be unable to meet their basic needs.

The robber barons were also known for their manipulation of the stock market and the crashes and depressions that followed their acts of defrauding the public. They invented the "boom and bust" cycle by selling the stock of worthless companies at inflated prices to unsuspecting investors. When they had suckered in enough money, they would dump their own stock on the market, destroy the company in the process and impoverish the investors.⁸³² This description of the capitalist method for milking the economy holds true today. The boom and bust cycle caused by stock manipulation is now called creating "bubbles" and "recessions."

Fig. 4-35: "The Robber Barons"

A couple of quotes from these robber barons enlighten us as to their mentality:

> "What do I care about the law? Ain't I got the power?" Cornelius Vanderbilt⁸³³
>
> "I can hire one half of the working class to kill the other half." Jay Gould⁸³⁴
>
> "The way to make money is to buy when blood is running in the streets." John D. Rockefeller⁸³⁵

Such men, who were either deified as Captains of Industry or vilified as Robber Barons, created the first large scale corporations in the United States. Their corporations reshaped the American economy and in doing so, profoundly influenced every aspect of American society from its politics, culture, religion, and education systems.

A list of nineteenth and early twentieth century monopoly capitalists is listed in Josephson's, Robber Barons as well as other books written on this subject.⁸³⁶ How many names do you recognize:

- John Jacob Astor (real estate, fur) – New York
- Andrew Carnegie (steel) – Pittsburgh and New York
- William A. Clark (copper) – Butte, Montana
- Jay Cooke (finance) – Philadelphia
- Charles Crocker (railroads) – California
- Daniel Drew (finance) – New York
- James Buchanan Duke (tobacco) – Durham, North Carolina
- Marshall Field (retail) – Chicago
- James Fisk (finance) – New York
- Henry Morrison Flagler (railroads, oil) – New York and Florida
- Henry Clay Frick (steel) – Pittsburgh and New York
- John Warne Gates (barbed wire, oil) – Texas
- Jay Gould (railroads) – New York
- Edward Henry Harriman (railroads) – New York
- Charles T. Hinde (railroads, water transport, shipping, hotels) - Illinois, Missouri, Kentucky, California
- Mark Hopkins (railroads) – California
- Collis Potter Huntington (railroads) - California
- Andrew W. Mellon (finance, oil) - Pittsburgh
- J. P. Morgan (finance, industrial consolidation) – New York
- John Cleveland Osgood (coal mining, iron) - Colorado
- Henry B. Plant (railroads) – Florida
- John D. Rockefeller (oil) – Cleveland, New York
- Charles M. Schwab (steel) – Pittsburgh and New York
- Joseph Seligman (banking) – New York
- John D. Spreckels (water transport, railroads, sugar) – California
- Leland Stanford (railroads) - California
- Cornelius Vanderbilt (water transport, railroads) – New York
- Charles Tyson Yerkes (street railroads) – Chicago

It is interesting to note that the industries in which the robber barons concentrated their attention are the same industries, by and large, that kicked off the industrial revolution in England a hundred years earlier—land, coal, iron, steel, railroads, water transport, and finance. Understanding this, it is easy to see how an economy the size of the United States can still be controlled by a small handful of people. In short, they hold a monopoly on the building blocks necessary to establish and maintain an industrial economy. The Occupy Wall Street movement in 2011, which spread to eighty-two countries, chanted slogans against the one percent versus the people who constitute ninety-nine percent of the population. The protestors were angry that less than one percent of the population, the monopoly capitalists, controlled over fifty percent of the country's wealth. They understood our economy to be a *monopoly*, controlled by an oligopoly that stood in direct opposition to *democracy*.

This process of the concentration of wealth into a few hands was set in motion by the robber barons, the first monopoly capitalists of the United States. From the very beginning, they came to monopolize the infrastructure upon which all the remaining sectors of the economy depended. Among the robber barons, four men stood out, Cornelius Vanderbilt (transportation), John. D. Rockefeller (energy), Andrew Carnegie (steel) and J.P Morgan (finance). These were the poster boys of the age. Each of these titans of industry were driven by a common vision, to amass as much personal wealth and power as was humanly possible. In each instance, the fortunes they amassed were extracted from the labor of others and from the natural resources of the planet.

Let us now take a look at these four men to see how they amassed their fortunes and how their actions affected the lives of people in the United States during the initial stage of industrial capitalism.

Cornelius Vanderbilt (1794 – 1877)

Cornelius Vanderbilt was descended from Dutch settlers who came to America in the mid-1600s. He was born on a farm on Staten Island in 1794, during the presidency of George Washington. His father supplemented the farm income by ferrying produce and merchandise between Staten Island and Manhattan in his two-masted sailboat. As a boy, Cornelius worked with his father on the water and attended school. As a teenager, he transported cargo around the New York harbor in his own boat. Eventually, he acquired a fleet of small boats and learned about ship design.

In 1813, Vanderbilt married his cousin Sophia Johnson, and the couple had thirteen children. After a long marriage, his wife died in 1868. A year later, Vanderbilt married another cousin who was oddly named Frank Armstrong Crawford. She was more than forty years younger than he was.

It can be said with little exaggeration that Vanderbilt was the first and greatest capitalist of the transportation industry, first in sea transport and then with railroads. Having lived a long and prosperous life, he made deals with Rockefeller, Carnegie, and Morgan who stood in his shadow and were jealous of his vast fortune.

Recognizing his skill in sea going transport, a wealthy man named Thomas Gibbons[837] hired him to captain his steamboat in 1817. Steamboats had recently been invented and so Vanderbilt entered the transport industry just as it was beginning to be revolutionized.[838]

At the time, a few wealthy land-owning aristocrats controlled American politics and business. New York's constitution, which went into effect in 1777, established a three-tiered class structure, with escalating property requirements for voting. Only those in the top bracket could cast ballots for governor and the state senate.[839] Consequently, Hamilton's revolution resulted in no more than exchanging English capitalists for American capitalists despite the promise of democracy.

Regarding the steamship business, New York State had already granted a monopoly on steamboat transport to Robert R. Livingston, the head of a prestigious Tory family. Livingston who shared the monopoly with its inventor Robert Fulton passed it to his heirs as a hereditary right. Later, the state of New Jersey granted a monopoly to Aaron Ogden,[840] a former governor and president of Princeton University, who took Thomas Gibbons on as a partner. The two eventually split as a result of internal discord, competed with each other, and were rivals in several court cases concerning which legal entity had the authority to control steamboat transportation in New York. As the trials wound on, Gibbons hired Cornelius Vanderbilt, who, because of his expertise, was able to cut the going rate for transport in half. When Ogden lowered his rate to meet that of Gibbons, Gibbons retaliated by agreeing to transport goods for free. This competitive strategy was unheard of among the Tory elite who saw Gibbons as a destructive force to the established order of things.

Nonetheless, Gibbons won the court battle, *Gibbons v. Ogden*, in 1824 when Chief Justice John Marshall ruled that states could not erect barriers to interstate commerce.[841] Soon after the ruling, Ogden went to debtor's prison, and Gibbons died in 1826. This left the field wide open for Vanderbilt who emerged thereafter as a steamboat proprietor in his own right. He concentrated on trade as it shifted across the east coast, always with one end in New York City. When the Erie Canal opened, he competed for control of the route between New York and Albany. When textile mills began to operate in New England during the industrial revolution, he switched to Long Island Sound, on the route to Boston. Everywhere he went, he was feared as the most effective competitor, one who either destroyed his enemies or extracted a ransom in return for leaving a market. As one businessman wrote "I confess if we are to be opposed I'd sooner have *him* with us, than against us."

When the California Gold Rush[842] whipped the country into a frenzy, Vanderbilt abruptly left the regional transportation market around New York and competed in the trans-continental steamship business. He built steamships to run on both the Atlantic and Pacific coasts, and connected them via a transit route he established in 1851 that ran across Nicaragua, farther north than the established crossing in Panama. By doing so, he was able to offer lower fares and faster passage to the gold prospectors eager to strike it rich in California. This route made Vanderbilt a fortune.

The competition between the California steamship lines set the course of American big business. The lines stretched thousands of miles, with stations in distant countries. When they fought each other, the repercussions were felt by hundreds of thousands of travelers, residents, and businesses. The demands of these enterprises also fed the shipbuilding and steam-engine works in New York, in which Vanderbilt also invested. By 1850, Vanderbilt was a household name in the United States.

The steam ships commanded the transportation sector until the coming of the railroads. The Union Pacific and Central Pacific completed the first transcontinental railway link in 1869.[843] The railroads would far surpass the steamship lines and in doing so set the course for large-scale monopoly capitalism in America.

Vanderbilt saw the inevitability of this transition. While still running his steamship business, he began, in the 1860s, to invest heavily in railroads just as growth was exploding. Everywhere tracks for new lines were being built. By virtue of his investments, he gained control of a number of railway lines operating between Chicago and New York and set up a coordinated network between them. At this time, travel between the cities, depended upon local railway lines, each with its own procedures and timetables. This made shipping and transport extremely difficult and time consuming. When Vanderbilt established his network, he created a coherent system that traversed several states, sped up travel time, increased efficiencies and lowered transportation costs for passengers and the shipment of goods. Vanderbilt also instigated the construction of Manhattan's Grand Central Depot, which opened in 1871. The station eventually was torn down and replaced by the present-day Grand Central Station, which opened in 1913.[844]

To raise money to purchase railway stock, Vanderbilt sold off this steamship interests. While he did so, he was mocked by Wall Street brokers and the press who questioned his expertise in railroads. The fact was that he knew more about the practical aspects of running a profitable railroad than Wall Street brokers or even his competitors. His steamboats had connected with New England's early railways, and in 1847 he had seized the presidency of the Stonington Railroad, a strategic line in Rhode Island and Connecticut that connected New York City, Providence, and Boston.[845] During the 1850s, he helped to save the endangered Erie Railway and New York & Harlem Railroad, by lending them money and helping to restructure their debt. When he took the presidency of the Harlem Railroad in 1863, he already had deep experience with the workings of the stock exchange, corporate finance, and the railroad industry.

Vanderbilt had simply wanted to show that he could turn a bankrupt railroad into a profitable enterprise, but to do so proved to be a daunting task. For one thing, the "railroad system" was completely fragmented and consisted of an incomplete network of small lines each built to serve its local community rather than a national network. This situation led to continual rivalry between the owners of these companies who competed with each other to expand. Vanderbilt's technique was to pursue diplomacy with his competitors and seek an amicable agreement. When his attempt failed, a conflict would ensue leading to lawsuits, backstabbing, and stock manipulations. In the end, Vanderbilt would triumph because he had more money to wage war and would usually end up buying out his competitors.

After he assumed the presidency of the Harlem line in 1863, Vanderbilt ran into trouble with the neighboring Hudson River Railroad. He took control of it in 1864, which gave him a monopoly on the railways that entered Manhattan. In January 1867, he engaged in a struggle with the New York Central railroad. Vanderbilt refused to allow any transfers from their line to his lines, thus eliminating their ability to transport their passengers to New York City. The Board of the New York Central was forced to accede to the sale of their railroad to Vanderbilt.[846]

Around 1877, Vanderbilt, through a manipulation of the stock exchange, gained a majority of stock of the Lake Shore and Michigan Southern Railway. The line extended the New York Central main line from Buffalo west to Chicago, along with another route across southern Ontario (Canada Southern Railway and Michigan Central Railroad). On December 22, 1914, the New York Central and Hudson River Railroad merged with the Lake Shore and Michigan Southern Railway to form the New York Central Railroad.[847]

One particular conflict between Vanderbilt and his rivals gained a lot of attention from the press and crystallized the idea of "robber baron" in the minds of the people. It was the only struggle that resulted in a loss of fortune for Vanderbilt. The conflict occurred when Vanderbilt tried to corner the stock on the Erie Railroad in 1868. The Erie Railroad Company began in the 1830s and by 1851 had established a track between Buffalo and New York City. At the time, the Erie was the longest line in the world.

During the Civil War years, the line prospered. Daniel Drew and two other unscrupulous board members, James Fisk[848] and Jay Gould,[849] emerged as the Erie's controlling directors. Once in power, they proceeded to drain the line, divert funds into their own pockets, and allow the railroad to deteriorate.

Vanderbilt, who previously had bad dealings with Drew, launched a hostile bid to take control of the Erie. But as Vanderbilt continued to buy Erie stock, Drew, and his partners in crime, began to issue thousands of new, illegal shares that inflated the value of the railroad's outstanding stock to more than three times their true worth. The unsuspecting Vanderbilt was eventually thwarted in his attempt to buy controlling stock in the railroad and lost heavily in the process.

After discovering that he had been duped, Vanderbilt alerted public officials (whom he had bribed over the years) to issue arrest warrants for Drew, Fisk, and Gould. Before the police could apprehend them, however, the three escaped to New Jersey. Unbeknownst to Vanderbilt, however, the three soon returned to New York where they proceeded to buy the votes of the state's legislators in Albany who reciprocated by passing new laws that prevented the New York Central and Erie railroads from merging and legitimized the trio's earlier stock-watering exploits. As it turned out, the man whom Vanderbilt previously had turned to for assistance was Boss Tweed,[850] who controlled politics and finance in New York City. Tweed stabbed Vanderbilt in the back when he was offered cash, stock, and a seat on the Erie board for deserting Vanderbilt.[851] While Vanderbilt fumed, Gould, Fisk, and Drew went on their merry way. The Erie, crippled by enormous debt due to the exploits of Drew, Fisk, and Gould, would not become profitable for the next seventy years of operation.[852]

The *Erie War* came to symbolize the rampant corruption of the enormous new railroad corporations as they purchased legislators to do their bidding. By the same token, politicians also extorted the railroads by threatening to pass harmful laws unless corporations paid them off.

Despite being beaten in the Erie War, Vanderbilt remained one of the most successful businessmen attaining enormous wealth and influence. The "Railroad King," as he was referred to in the newspapers was indeed a "robber baron," who made a great fortune by manipulating politicians and undermining democracy. His manipulation of the stock market also undermined and destroyed the investments and savings of average families. On the other hand, Vanderbilt can also be credited with being a "captain of industry," who improved the organization of railroads, lowered costs, and made possible the building of the infrastructure that created the greatest national economy the world has ever seen. Monopoly allowed for more efficient central control of an industry, but the money value of such a development accrued only to the great capitalists and not to the American people who had performed the labor to make it possible.

John D. Rockefeller (1839 – 1937)

John Davison Rockefeller was born on July 8, 1839, in Richford, New York, the son of a traveling salesman. As an enterprising boy, he earned money by raising turkeys, selling candy, and doing jobs for neighbors. In 1853, his family moved to Cleveland, Ohio where John attended high school.

In 1855, at age sixteen, he got a job as an office clerk in a firm that bought, sold, and shipped grain, coal, and other commodities. Four years later, in 1859, Rockefeller and a partner established their own firm. During the same year, America's first oil well was drilled in Pennsylvania. In 1863, as the Civil War was at its height, Rockefeller and several partners entered the new oil industry by investing in a Cleveland refinery.

In 1864, Rockefeller married Laura "Cettie" Spelman (1839-1915), the daughter of a prosperous merchant, politician, and abolitionist who was active in the Underground Railroad. Spelman College was named after Laura. It is located in Atlanta Georgia and is one of the oldest black women's colleges in the country.[853] The Rockefellers had four daughters and one son.

John D. Rockefeller established Standard Oil in 1870 along with his brother William and several other men. John was its president and largest shareholder. By the early 1880s, Standard Oil controlled an astonishing ninety percent of US refineries and pipelines! While the company did everything from building its own oil barrels to employing scientists to determine new uses for petroleum by-products, such actions alone could not have led to such a rapid monopolization of a vast American industry, on which everyone was dependent.

Standard Oil provided fuel oil for the lamps that lit the nation's streets, offices, and houses before the invention of electric lights. It also provided lubricants for machinery. The sale of these essential products must surely have created handsome profits for the company, but this still does not explain how a start up company came to control over ninety percent of the booming energy industry in such a short time. The answer lies in the illegal methods used by John D. Rockefeller to destroy competition.

Rockefeller engaged in predatory pricing schemes that crushed his competitors and then he bought their assets for a song. He colluded with Vanderbilt's railroads to eliminate his competitors. The collusion took the form of rebates and kickbacks. As the biggest client of the railroads, Standard Oil got extremely favorable terms for shipping their oil. But the relationship was much more devious. The rebates worked like this. For each destination, a public rate for the transport of oil was published. But the rate was artificially set high. Standard Oil would receive a substantial rebate that amounted to thirty to fifty percent off the declared price, but the other oil companies that were not party or knowledgeable of this secret arrangement had to pay the full, declared price. Let's say it was $2.56 a barrel while Rockefeller paid only $1.56 per barrel. Now, here's where things get subversive. The railroad would actually pay Rockefeller the one dollar difference for each barrel that its competitors paid. Because the cost of shipping oil was such a major expense to producers and refiners, this backroom deal allowed Rockefeller to charge a significantly cheaper price for oil and thereby strangle his competitors who could not meet his price.[854] Smaller competitors across the country were forced to sell their refineries one after the other for a song to Rockefeller. For its part, the railroad received $1.56 per barrel from all competitors and this was a profitable rate that was large enough to create a fortune for them.

Even when this system of preferential treatment became known to the public, the government did not challenge it until many years later. It did not, however, escape public condemnation from people like Dr. Washington Gladden that was reported in the New York Times in April 1905. Gladden was a nationally known Congregationalist minister who waged a ceaseless war against economic injustice. When he discovered that his own Church had accepted one hundred thousand dollars of Rockefeller's blood money, he gave a sermon that was reported in the Times:

> In a sermon delivered at Columbus, last Sunday, he [Gladden] discussed Rockefeller's gift, and said: "The money proffered to our Hoard of Missions comes out

of a colossal estate, whose foundations were laid in the most relentless rapacity known to modern commercial history. The success of this business from the beginning until now has been largely due to unlawful manipulations of railway rates. The United States Government is now engaged in a strenuous attempt to ferret out and punish this injustice. And the people of the Tainted States have a tremendous battle on their hands with the corporate greed, which has entrenched itself in this stronghold and has learned to use the railways for the oppression and spoliation of the people."[855]

Rockefeller also bribed men to spy on competing companies and coerced rivals to join the Standard Oil Company under threat of being forced out of business. He used any means he could to gain a monopoly over the oil industry. By virtue of such business practices, he was able to build an enormous fortune on the ruins of other men and their families.

In 1890, the U.S. Congress passed the Sherman Antitrust Act, the first federal legislation prohibiting monopolies like Rockefeller's from restraining trade. Two years later, the Ohio Supreme Court dissolved the Standard Oil Trust. Through crafty lawyers, however, the businesses within the trust became part of Standard Oil of New Jersey, which functioned as a holding company. In 1911, after years of litigation, the US Supreme Court ruled Standard Oil of New Jersey was in violation of anti-trust laws and forced it to be broken up into more than thirty individual companies. Many of these, however, were still owned by the Rockefellers, including Amoco, Mobil, Exxon, and Chevron. Later ExxonMobil joined together once again. Originally these companies had been Standard Oil of New Jersey and Standard Oil of New York.[856] Today ExxonMobil is a greater threat to climate catastrophe than any other corporation on the planet.

Rockefeller retired from the day-to-day business operations of Standard Oil in the mid-1890s. Inspired in part by fellow tycoon Andrew Carnegie (1835-1919), who made a vast fortune in the steel industry and then became a philanthropist to give away the bulk of his money, Rockefeller donated more than half a billion dollars to various educational, religious, and scientific causes, among these, the University of Chicago and the Rockefeller Institute for Medical Research, now Rockefeller University.[857] As was demonstrated above, much of Rockefeller's donations were instrumental in winning over people and organizations to his side as he plundered the oil industry. Yet, apparently Rockefeller also gave away money out of the goodness of his heart. He had always considered himself a devout Christian.

When Standard Oil was at its peak, Rockefeller's fortune (in today's figures) was around six hundred and sixty-three billion dollars. Compare this to Bill Gates' fortune at sixty billion dollars or Mark Zuckerberg's at thrity-four billion dollars. [858] Given this mind-boggling wealth, his donation to charity amounted to less than one percent of his fortune.

Andrew Carnegie

Andrew Carnegie was another robber baron/captain of industry and a contemporary of Vanderbilt, Rockefeller, and J. P. Morgan. Carnegie made his fortune in steel and although ruthless with competitors and employees, he had an altruistic streak that caused him to give most of his fortune away after he retired.

Carnegie was born in Scotland in 1835 in the heart of the linen industry. His father was a weaver, but the industrial revolution in the English textile industry destroyed his craft. The steam engine, introduced in 1847, laid off hundreds of weavers, including Andrew's father.

"I began to learn what poverty meant," Andrew would later write. "It was burnt into my heart then that my father had to beg for work. And then and there came the resolve that I would cure that when I got to be a man."[859]

Andrew's mother, Margaret, fearing for the survival of her family, pushed the family to leave Scotland for America. In 1848, the family joined two of Margaret's sisters in Pittsburgh, then the center of iron manufacturing in the country.

Carnegie worked as a messenger boy in the city's telegraph office. One of the men he met there was Thomas A. Scott, who was just beginning a career at the Pennsylvania Railroad. Scott liked the boy, his hard work, quick mind, and eagerness to learn and hired him as his private secretary and personal telegrapher at thirty-five dollars a month. Carnegie later said, that, at the time, he could not imagine what to do with so much money.

The railroads were the first big businesses in America, and the Pennsylvania Railroad was one of the largest of them all. By working with the company, Carnegie learned about management and cost control and the other systems required for big business. More importantly, Carnegie learned how to manipulate the capitalist system from his mentor Thomas Scott.

Scott helped Carnegie with his first investments. Many of these were part of the corrupt insider trading deals in which Scott and the Pennsylvania president, John Edgar Thomson, indulged. Though excellent managers, they also indulged in unethical and often illegal schemes to skim money out of the Pennsylvania's transactions. For example, they would often demand stock in companies that contracted with the railroad, and would even rout business through shell companies that they personally controlled.

They also took kick backs as part of the secret quid pro quo agreements that we saw in the Vanderbilt—Rockefeller relationship. Through such corrupt methods, Carnegie was able to invest five hundred dollars in the Adams Express Company[860] that delivered personal packages throughout the east coast and the south. The company, at the time, had contracted with the Pennsylvania Railroad to carry its messengers. A few years later, Carnegie received a few shares in Theodore Tuttle Woodruff's sleeping car company,[861] as a reward for holding shares that Woodruff had given to Scott and Thomson as a payoff. By reinvesting his returns from inside deals in railroad-related industries like iron, bridges, and rails, Carnegie slowly accumulated capital that he would use to later form his own companies.

By working his way up the ladder in the Pennsylvania Railroad, Carnegie succeeded Scott as superintendent of the Pittsburgh Division. When the Civil War broke out, Scott was hired to supervise military transportation for the Union forces and Carnegie worked as his right hand man.

The Civil War caused a boom in the iron industry, and by the time the war was over, Carnegie saw the potential in the field and resigned from Pennsylvania Railroad. He founded the Keystone Bridge Company in 1865. At that time, wooden bridges were being replaced by iron and steel. The company held a patent for wrought iron bridges and advertised its services as building steel, wrought iron, wooden railway, and road bridges. The company also supplied wrought iron columns for buildings.[862] In three years Carnegie had an annual income of fifty thousand dollars.

One would think that Carnegie would be happy to have such success in business, but he wrote in a letter at the age of thirty-three, "To continue much longer overwhelmed by business cares and with most of my thoughts wholly upon the way to make more money in the shortest time, must degrade me beyond hope of permanent recovery." He was determined to retire at thirty-five while spending the next two years educating himself.[863]

But this would not prove to be the case. Carnegie continued to build his fortune for the next thirty years. At thirty-five, he became enamored by the possibility of a new steel refining process developed by Henry Bessemer that could convert huge batches of iron into steel. Steel was much more flexible than iron and could be used in the production of more products than iron. Carnegie used his own money and raised additional capital to build a new steel plant near Pittsburgh. Carnegie's motto was "watch costs and the profits take care of themselves." At the macro-level, however, he could read economic trends and if he saw the possibility of something that had the potential to rapidly expand, he was willing to take great risks in order to profit from its expansion. Throughout his career, he maintained close relationships with Scott and Thomson. As he set up his businesses to supply rails and bridges, he was granted contracts from the two in exchange for a stake in his enterprises.

Raised as a poor boy, Carnegie was unusual among the capitalists of his day because he preached for the rights of laborers to unionize and to protect their jobs and, in fact, allowed his workers to join a union. However, driven by a conflicting desire to keep costs down, Carnegie still paid the steel workers low wages and pushed them to long hours.

Eventually, the workers revolted from the oppressive conditions and called a strike. Carnegie's plant manager, Henry Frick, retaliated by locking the workers out and hiring Pinkerton Agents (a private army used to break strikes).[864] The event, which came to be known as the Homestead Strike, was one of the most serious confrontations in US labor history, standing with the Ludlow Massacre[865] and the Battle of Blair Mountain.[866] The strike, which began on June 30, 1892, culminated in a violent battle between strikers and Pinkerton agents a week later. Many men were killed in the conflict. The event ended with the state militia being called in. Rather than support the workers, the state busted the strike and the workers' pay was reduced.[867] It was a major setback in the effort of workers to organize for fair pay and basic rights in this country. The episode, it is said, hurt Carnegie's reputation and haunted him for the rest of his life.

Even so, Carnegie Steel proved unstoppable. The country needed steel and by 1900, the company produced more steel than all the steel mills of England combined. It was in this year, that J. P. Morgan, ever vigilant for new industries to monopolize, determined to take over Carnegie Steel. Carnegie believed he could beat Morgan in a battle of attrition, but it would last five, ten, or fifteen years. It was a fight that did not appeal to him because he was now sixty-four years old and wanted to spend time with his wife Louise and their daughter Margaret.

Carnegie wrote the asking price for his steel business on a piece of paper and had the offer delivered to Morgan. Morgan immediately accepted, buying the company for $480 million. When the deal was finalized, Morgan said, "Congratulations, Mr. Carnegie, you are now the richest man in the world."[868] With the Carnegie Steel Corporation as its centerpiece, Morgan proceeded to buy up other steel companies to create the monopoly called the US Steel Corporation.[869]

One year before he sold his steel company, Carnegie wrote his famous article, "Wealth," which appeared in the June 1889 issue of the *North American Review*. "Wealth," more commonly known as "The Gospel of Wealth," held that philanthropy was a responsibility of the new class of self-made men.[870] In the article, Carnegie proposed that the best way to deal with the issue of wealth inequality was for the wealthy to redistribute their surplus wealth in a responsible and thoughtful manner. He contrasted this approach with the traditional model of patrimony where wealth is handed down to heirs or is willed to the state for public purposes. Carnegie argued that surplus wealth produces the greatest net benefit to society when it is administered carefully by the wealthy. He argued against the wasteful use of capital in the form of extravagance, irresponsible spending, or self-indulgence and promoted the prudent distribution of capital over the course of one's lifetime toward the cause of reducing the wealth imbalance between the rich and poor. Surplus wealth should be distributed, however, in a manner that does not encourage "the slothful, the drunken, the unworthy." He concluded by saying that a "man who dies rich dies disgraced."[871] Not surprisingly, his ideas were not pursued by the monopoly capitalists. Nor did his ideas encourage the government to enforce distribution of this wealth even though it was gained by the work of the people. Political democracy without economic democracy has led to one percent of the population controlling fifty percent of the national wealth in today's economy.

To his credit, Carnegie, within one year after making his moral code known, turned his attention to giving away his fortune. As a self-made man, he abhorred charity and instead he put his money into helping people help themselves. He used much of his fortune to establish over twenty-five hundred public libraries as well as support institutions of higher learning.

Carnegie was also one of the first to call for a "League of Nations" and to further the cooperation between nations, he built the *Peace Palace,* an international law administrative building in The Hague, in the Netherlands. Today, this building serves as the seat of international law. It houses the *Permanent Court of Arbitration* that helps states resolve legal issues involving territorial boundaries, human rights, and international trade and investment.[872] It also houses the *International Court of Justice,* which serves as the principal judicial body of the United Nations.[873] The Court settles legal disputes submitted to it by states and provides advisory opinions on legal questions submitted to it by duly authorized international branches, agencies, and the UN General Assembly. The Peace Palace also includes the Hague Academy of International Law and the Peace Palace Library.[874]

According to his wife, Louise, his "heart was broken" by the events leading up to World War I. The last entry in his autobiography was the day World War I began.[875] He had watched helplessly as his hopes for creating a civilized world were dashed beneath the juggernaut of war.

J. P. Morgan (1837-1913)

John Pierpont Morgan was an American banker and industrialist. His life took him through the Civil War and the Progressive Era. He is by all accounts the father of monopoly capitalism in this country, having built cartels that monopolized the railroad, electricity, farming, and steel industries. When he died, he was also working on a plan to monopolize the finance industry as well. This task, however, was left to his son John who unbeknownst to the public, helped create and legalize the Federal Reserve Bank in 1913.

Morgan's strategy for creating monopolies was derisively called "morganization" by the peoples' movements of the day. During the time of his rule (late nineteenth century), the United States was coming out of the Civil War and the businesses created during the American Industrial Revolution were ripe for consolidation. In 1869, the nation's first transcontinental rail line was completed and the U.S. railroad industry was experiencing rapid overexpansion and heated competition.[876] This competition was viewed as too unruly by J. P. Morgan and some might say with good reason. Often men from competing railroads were encouraged by their bosses to form small armies and fight it out with the employees of their competitors to save the owners from having to file suits and obtain injunctions.[877]

Because of his links with his father's banking firm in London, J. P. Morgan had intimate and highly useful connections with the London financial world, and during the 1870s, he was able to provide the growing industrial corporations of the United States with much-needed capital from British bankers. In 1885, his attention turned to the railway industry when he arranged an agreement between two of the largest railroads in the country, the New York Central Railroad and the Pennsylvania Railroad. This act, we are told, minimized a potentially destructive rate war and rail-line competition between them. In 1886, he reorganized two more major railroads with the aim of stabilizing their financial base. In the course of these corporate restructurings, Morgan demanded that he become a member of the board of directors of these railroads. In such a way he was able to amass great influence over them. Between 1885 and 1888, he concentrated his influence on rail lines based in Pennsylvania and Ohio, and after the financial panic of 1893 he was called upon to rehabilitate a large number of the leading rail lines in the country, including the Southern Railroad, the Erie Railroad, and the Northern Pacific. By doing so, he was able to reorganized or "morganize" the railroad industry into a giant monopoly that discouraged competition and secured high prices from shippers and passengers across the country. By gaining control of much of the stock of the railroads, he became the world's most powerful railroad magnate, controlling about five thousand miles (eight thousand kilometers) of American railroads by 1902.[878] He eventually controlled an estimated one-sixth of America's rail lines. To give you a sense of the size of the monopoly J. P. Morgan created, railroad stock comprised sixty percent of the New York Stock Exchange issues at the time.[879]

The story of Morgan's involvement with the *Northern Pacific* railroad is worth telling because it combined many aspects of the process that he used to monopolize not only the railroad industry but several other industries as well. It began with a colossal manipulation of the stock market, and ended by J. P. Morgan getting into bed with the federal government as a means to further his strategy to monopolize the country. His dealings with the Northern Pacific also reveal how American monopoly finance capital came into being.

To tell this story we need to back up a little bit. In 1871, J. P. Morgan was thirty-four years old and his father Junius Morgan, who ran the J. S. Morgan Bank in London, was concerned about his son's fiery temper and spontaneous business decisions. He recommended that he take as a partner Tony Drexel[880] who was forty-five and professionally refined. As a result of their meeting, J. P. became a partner in Drexel and Company in Philadelphia, and he would also manage their partnership in New York City called Drexel, Morgan, and Company. This new company was the forerunner of J. P. Morgan and Company.[881] J. P. Morgan is now ranked as the top investment bank in the world.[882]

The partnership between Morgan and Drexel added a high society image to the Morgan bank and established Morgan's foothold in New York, Philadelphia, London, and Paris. Soon after the partnership was formed, the federal government decided to refund, at a lower interest rate, three hundred million dollars in bond debt remaining from the Civil War.

Until then Jay Cooke,[883] Drexel's chief rival in Philadelphia had a virtual stranglehold over government bonds in the United States. While government bonds were historically the exclusive province of the super rich and European banks like the Rothschilds, Cooke gained attention of the Union government by marketing Civil War bonds to the average man. During the war, he employed twenty-five hundred agents to peddle government bonds across America, winning President Lincoln's undying gratitude. In the early 1870s, the phrase "rich as Jay Cooke" had the same resonance as "rich as Rockefeller" had in the twentieth century. Cooke was invincible as an investment banker until he financed the Northern Pacific Railroad in 1869. His promotion of the railroad bonds, it turned out, was built upon lies, fraud, and political bribery. To lure European funding, he created what author Ron Chernow called "brazenly surreal lies."[884] His advertising made small wood-shack railroad towns look like full-blown metropolises.

Congress had chartered the Northern Pacific Railway Company in 1864 with the goal of connecting the Great Lakes with Puget Sound on the Pacific, opening vast new lands for farming, ranching, lumbering, and mining, and linking Washington and Oregon to the rest of the country. Congress granted the railroad forty million acres of land in exchange for building rail transportation to an undeveloped territory.

For the first six years, the railroad struggled to find financing. In 1870, Jay Cooke began to finance and promote the railroad and the first tracks were laid. The crews had to transverse swamps, bogs, and tamarack forests and were subject to attacks by Sioux, Cheyenne, Arapaho, and Kiowa warriors in North Dakota and Minnesota, which resulted in the US Army providing protection.

Nonetheless, the railroad made progress due to the fact that the land was perfect for growing grains and attracted settlers to the Red River Valley along the Minnesota-North Dakota border.[885] This led to the Northern Pacific opening offices in Germany and Scandinavia through which they offered US farmers cheap transportation for their grain and purchase deals in Europe.

However, after the Franco-Prussian War, grain prices in Europe collapsed and with them the fortunes of the Northern Pacific Railroad. This was a major blow to Cooke who had much of his fortune tied up in the railroad. When the federal government wanted to refinance three hundred million dollars of Civil War debt, in 1873, he formed a partnership with the Seligman bank and the Rothschilds' bank to obtain the three hundred million dollars to refund the government issue. This time, however, he was met by a challenge by Morgan and Drexel and a syndicate that they had put together. Financing of such magnitude was too big for a single bank to shoulder and thus syndicates were required to raise the money.

The Morgan team put intense pressure on the government to refuse the bid of Cooke's cartel. They also spread damaging rumors about Cooke's other business ventures. Bowing to the pressure, the Secretary of the Treasury decided to grant half the issue to each syndicate. The year 1873 was also one in which the stock market was panicky because of the Credit Mobilier [886] scandal. The company that was building the Union Pacific Railroad was exposed as a pit of fraud and corruption. The scandal took down several congressmen in the process. By August, European investors refused to touch any American bonds. Debilitated by the Northern Pacific loss and unable to secure additional capital, the mighty house of Jay Cooke declared bankruptcy on Black Thursday, September 18, 1873.[887]

The failure caused a Wall Street panic. The New York Stock Exchange closed its doors for ten days and before things settle down, five thousand businesses and fifty-seven stock exchange firms had gone belly up. In addition, European investors lost six hundred million dollars in American railroad stock. To the people of that generation, this catastrophe was as significant as the Wall Street panic of 1929, and the Great Recession of 2007.

The crash of the Cooke empire and the Panic of 1873 that it generated stands as an early example of the destructive social consequences when a monopoly capitalist falls. Jay Cooke was an entrepreneur. He sold government debt at the retail level across America, by employing twenty-five hudred workers and supported the efforts of the North to preserve the United States. For his services, he deserved a reward that he received in cash. He also received the primary role as the purveyor of US government bonds going forward. This proved to cost great harm to the American people. Through the sale of government bonds, he was allowed to amass a great fortune that put the welfare of the country as a whole at risk. Cooke inappropriately used this fortune to fund the Northern Pacific Railroad and in doing so, found it necessary to lie to the public, defraud fellow businessmen, and bribe government officials. By these actions, he destroyed his fortune and the fortunes and livelihoods of thousands, perhaps hundreds of thousands of people in the deflation and depression that followed the Wall Street Panic resulting from his bankruptcy. This was the cost of one man's greed to the society at large. Although his wealth was generated collectively, by allowing such a vast accumulation of wealth to a single individual and making it subject to personal greed and selfishness, the capitalist system created a tragedy for average families across the country. This event, and those like it, continue to unfold in the capitalist system revealing a fundamental flaw within the system that the government has never addressed.

For Drexel Morgan bank, however, the fall of Cooke, was a boon. The catastrophe provided these shrewd capitalists the ability to concentrate even more wealth into their hands. With Jay Cooke out of the picture, the Morgan bank now found itself in the position of principle provider of American government finance. Even so, the extended deflation and depression that followed the fall of the Cooke empire created a gloom over Wall Street and the entire country. Even Morgan was shaken by the event and vowed to only deal with the strongest companies and avoid speculative ventures.

Working for his father's bank in London, before coming to America, J. P. followed the banking "ethics" of the established moneyed families of Europe. They submitted to what was called the Gentleman Bankers' Code. Bankers felt responsible for the bonds that they sold and felt obliged to intervene on behalf of their customers (investors) when things went awry. Everyone knew that the American railroad industry was going awry. As Morgan continued his work with the railroad industry, his ethics, however, became less about protecting his customers and more about adapting the tactics of robber baron Jay Gould who came to own the Erie Railroad after engaging in fraud and stock manipulation.[888]

When investors boycotted an Erie Railroad bond issue in 1871, Gould proposed to run the railroad by bringing in outside coal, railway, and banking interests to run the railroad as "voting trustees." To please the Wall Street crowd, Gould proposed that Junius Morgan become a trustee. The idea never flew, but it taught J. P. Morgan a valuable lesson. Gould had introduced a strategy by which investors could take control of a company from management and run it according to their own designs. When the Erie railroad went bankrupt, the irate bondholders, now under the leadership of the Morgans, created a "voting trust" to run operations. This was *the* pivotal moment in which the bankers gained the upper hand over the industrialists. The bankers from here on were able to control the railroad men instead of standing by powerless when bad management lost their investments. Morgan would use this simple device to bring the country's rail system under his personal control. Through such trusts, he would convert bankers from being servants of industry to being masters of it. This single strategy set the stage for the development of monopoly capitalism in the United States.

J. P. Morgan went on to use the *voting trust*, syndicates, and corporate mergers to dominate key industries in the country and bring the economy under the rule of the bankers. In 1892; he arranged the merger of Edison General Electric and Thomson-Houston Electric Company to form General Electric. This created a monopoly within the electrical-equipment manufacturing industry.

After financing the creation of the Federal Steel Company, in 1901, he merged it with the Carnegie Steel Company, the Consolidated Steel, and Wire Company, and several other steel and iron businesses to form the United States Steel Corporation as a monopoly.[889]

In 1902, Morgan brought together the leading agricultural equipment manufacturers to form the International Harvester Company.

Morgan's involvement in government finances was also leading to a monopoly over finance capital. During the depression that followed the panic of 1893, Morgan had formed a syndicate that resupplied the US government's depleted gold reserve with sixty-two million dollars worth of gold in order to relieve a Treasury crisis.[890]

In the process of becoming the most powerful banker in the United States and the controller of its major industries, Morgan became more despotic. He expected everyone to bow at his feet. The captains of industry, other bankers, and even the federal government were in his debt. As the reigning god of greed, Morgan ruled over those possessed by greed.

When John Calvin sanctified the emerging capitalists at the dawn of the Protestant Age by calling them the "elect" of God, he could not have envisioned how the capitalist psychology would manifest itself over time, nor could he have understand the consequences of the nations of the world being ruled by such men who embodied his definition of virtue.

If the capitalists were the elect of God, then Morgan would certainly now be sitting at the left hand of God (we suppose Jesus would still be sitting on the right). Morgan was the very archetype of an unbridled capitalist. In him, we witness the core of the capitalist psychology that still exists today although it is now hidden beneath smooth manners, elegant parties, encouraging words, clever commercials, and the never-ending public relations campaigns to justifying corporate agendas or create scapegoats to blame for the destruction they cause in the lives of billions. How easy it has become to point to blacks, Latinos, women, whistleblowers, Muslim terrorists, etc., as responsible for the problems of American society.

Morgan was an anti-Semite his entire life. Although he took great caution to hide it, he refused to partner with any Jewish banks, unless it was forced upon him by circumstance. The reality is that he was probably a racist, but because he had no relations with Blacks, Latinos, or Native Americans in his line of work, it is impossible to verify. This is not to say that his bank and his banking partners, like Aetna Insurance Company, were not involved in the slave trade by providing insurance to slave owners on their slaves.[891]

Morgan was also a sexist. He did not allow women to work in his bank and when George Perkins was hired and wanted to bring his female secretary with him from Aetna Insurance, Morgan roared, "I will not have a damned woman in the place."[892] She was kept in another building. Later, Morgan relented and let Perkins bring her to his office at the Morgan bank building, but she could not be seen on the main floor. Regarding marriage, Morgan believed that it should be based on discretion rather than fidelity. He was a womanizer and an adulterer.[893]

Morgan never gave a dime to charity for social welfare. He was not interested in the problems of poverty. When he did part with crumbs from his fortune, he gave to art and education and other pursuits of the ruling class.[894] There is no doubt that Morgan was a classist. As a member of the ruling class, he believed that God gave him the privilege to do whatever he wanted, regardless of the consequences. It did not matter in the least to him what the public thought, or whether his actions caused mass poverty. This is the mark of a sociopath. The definition of a sociopath is a person whose behavior is antisocial, often criminal, and who lacks a sense of moral responsibility or social conscience.

It might be argued that by monopolizing the key industries, Morgan benefitted the US economy by giving it order and structure. Some historians point to the time when Morgan single-handedly bailed out the federal government, after the Panic of 1893 had plunged the country into another depression. But upon examination, the Panic of 1893 occurred because the bankers had over-invested in the railroads and created an unsustainable bubble. Morgan was involved in the very machinations that caused the Panic in the first place. Now, in order to save the federal government from being drained of its gold and potentially going bankrupt as a result of the social chaos caused by the Panic, Morgan put together an international cartel to buy gold for the Treasury. While this kept the government solvent, it was now firmly in Morgan's debt. His gesture of "good will" strengthened his bank and increased the profits he made from the federal government. There was no patriotism in Morgan, except when it profited him. Nor is there any patriotism in the J. P. Morgan bank that continues to control the US economy today.

If it is argued that Morgan brought order and structure to the American economy, then we must ask if this could not have been done in a way in which the people of America were not victimized in the process and large sections of the population impoverished.

Morgan's despotism clearly revealed itself in 1901 in his manipulation of the stock market in order to achieve the majority of shares in the Northern Pacific railroad. In this instance, more than in others, we can see the greed and reckless abandon that drives the capitalists, despite their endearing commercials and foundation grants that lead one to believe they actually care about people.

As we have said, Morgan had always been anti-Jewish and although it was prudent to conceal his prejudice, he took deliberate steps to avoid partnering with Jewish banks if at all possible.[895] The rivalry for control of the great Northern Pacific pitted Edward H. Harriman, William Rockefeller, the National City Bank, and Kuhn Loeb[896] on one side against J. P. Morgan and Co. on the other. This was a battle of titans that shook the foundation of the US economy and by their dirty tactics threw the country into a deep depression. The conflict between these two cartels had been brewing since 1895 when Morgan autocratically declared that he would not reorganize the Union Pacific railroad, which he described as "two streaks of iron rust across the plains."[897] His willingness to write off the major rail system in the southwestern states provided an opening for outsiders. Edward Harriman took control of the Union Pacific in 1897 and became its president. He merged it with the Southern Pacific in which he also served as the president. By this move, he and his Jewish bankers, Kuhn and Loeb, came to dominate the southwestern railroads as invincibly as Morgan did those in the East and the Northwest.

The rivalry over the Northern Pacific began when James J. Hill, who was the CEO of the Great Northern and the Northern Pacific, sought to buy the Chicago, Burlington, and Quincy railroad (CB&Q).[898] This move was part of his plan to build a transcontinental transportation system across the United States. He already controlled transportation between Seattle and Minneapolis, but the CB&Q would allow him to directly connect to Chicago and then, with links to Morgan-controlled railroads, he could access the east coast. Hill already had a working relationship with Morgan who had helped him consolidate the Great Northern and the Northern Pacific into a rail system that controlled the northwestern United States. As such, they both had the same interest in building the first transcontinental railroad between New York and Seattle.[899]

Meanwhile, Harriman's goal was also to create a transcontinental transportation system. He knew that that if Hill was able to purchase the CB&Q, it would provide Hill with the opportunity to create a rival transcontinental transportation system. Harriman and his banker Schiff[900] went to Hill and Morgan and pleaded with them for a stake in the Northern Pacific, but were rebuffed. It is suspected that Morgan's anti-Jewish prejudice played a role in his decision. Schiff responded that Morgan and Hill were engaged in a hostile act for which there would be consequences. In the following days, Harriman and Schiff plotted to swallow up the Northern Pacific by secretly buying the companies stock.

In August 1901, the raiders entered the stock market and bought seventy-eight million dollars worth of Northern Pacific shares, the largest stock purchase in history. While doing so, they created the rumor that the rise in the stock price was a result of the railroads recent purchase of the CB&Q. For his part, Morgan thought the rise in the stock price was due to the bullish market that resulted from the launch of US Steel. As the stock price rose, Morgan's man Bacon sold railroad stock, as did several members of the railroad's board. The Harriman con job was also camouflaged by the recent reelection of McKinley and a bullish market in general.

Then in May the stock shot way up. At this point, the Harriman-Schiff forces were only forty thousand shares short of majority control of the Northern Pacific railroad. On a Saturday morning, Harriman ordered Kuhn Loeb to buy the needed stock, but Schiff was attending services in the temple and did not place the order. The lapse was fateful because now Morgan sensed trouble and ordered his man Bacon to purchase one hundred and fifty thousand shares at any price. That Monday morning, Morgan's brokers fanned out across the Exchange floor and began an insane bidding for the stock. The pitched battle between Morgan and Harriman caused the stock price to skyrocket. On Tuesday, May 7, the stock closed at over one hundred and forty-three, up seventy points in three days. The next day, it shot up to two hundred. This spectacle usually signals a scam called cornering the market. It is a trap set for speculators who kept "shorting" the stock, i.e., selling borrowed shares in the belief that the bubble would pop and enable them to buy back the shares at a cheaper price. Instead the stock kept rising due to the battle between Morgan and Harriman that went on behind the scenes. As the stock price kept rising, the speculators were forced to liquidate shares of other companies that they owned to pay for their borrowed Northern Pacific shares. Thus, the entire stock market became endangered by the feud between the titans.

By Wednesday, the price of almost every stock on the Exchange was crashing with money sucked from them to feed the Northern Pacific frenzy. On Thursday, people fell victim to the biggest crash in a century. Northern Pacific zoomed up as much as two hundred to three hundred per trade, finally hitting one thousand. Then it dropped four hundred points on a single trade. The scene of the Exchange was mayhem with men pushing and shoving each other, screaming, wide-eyed with panic, awash in fear and greed.

The event came to be known as the Panic of 1901. It was the first stock market crash on the New York Stock Exchange and it resulted in thousands of lives being ruined. At the end of the day, Morgan had control over the railroad, but the cost was that thousands of people lost their money and their nest eggs. Half the firms on Wall Street were now bordering on bankruptcy. When asked by reporters as to his response to the chaos he helped create, Morgan shot back, "I owe the public nothing."[901] Morgan and his ilk were like wild drunks in a china shop without the least concern for the collateral damage that they caused. A depression enveloped the country.

On the streets, the public was seething. The stock market crash reinforced the socialist view that the welfare of the American people was held hostage to the stock manipulations of a few Wall Street moguls. What made things worse, the people were soon to learn that the capitalists involved in the stock market manipulation got away unscathed. In fact, soon after the crash, Harriman and Schiff, Hill and Morgan joined forces to form a holding company, the Northern Securities Company, to control the Northern Pacific, the Great Northern, and the Burlington.[902]

The so-called Progressive Era arose at this time in response to the public outrage over the lost jobs and savings of thousands of people across the country. The people felt that the capitalists had finally gone too far and that it was now the responsibility of the federal government to step in and create justice for the people. The people needed protection and this was, after all, a democracy in which the majority decision should determine the course of events.

J. P. Morgan Meets Theodore Roosevelt: the Rise of State Monopoly Capitalism

We have demonstrated above how J. P. Morgan almost single-handedly created monopoly capitalism in the United States. Now let us look at how he also became the spearhead for the development of *state monopoly capitalism*, the stage just preceding the final stage of capitalist expansion that would be realized in our lifetime, *Globalism*.

Our story begins with his partnership with that legendary "trust-buster" Teddy Roosevelt. American myth tells us that Morgan and Roosevelt were enemies and that Roosevelt used the federal government to bring Morgan's empire under control on behalf of the American people. Apart from this leftist dogma, however, American history tells a different story.

President McKinley, a staunch supporter of monopoly capitalism, had nothing to say about the Northern Pacific cornering of the market even though it bankrupted thousands of people. Robert Bacon, Morgan's man in the fight, however, lost his health and his nerve because of serving as Morgan's chief lieutenant in this Wall Street stock market crisis. To recuperate, he went on vacation and when he came back he became employed by the McKinley administration as Assistant Secretary of State, then Secretary of State, and finally ambassador to France.[903] In this instance, we see how the government rewards those who defraud the American people by giving them high positions in government and even promoting them over time. Sometimes the people will take matters into their own hands rather than continue to be offered up as lambs to the slaughter. McKinley was assassinated on August 6, 1901 and his Vice-President, Theodore Roosevelt, came to power.

Roosevelt was considered a progressive in much the same way as the late president Obama was considered a progressive. Progressives historically believe that human progress can be achieved by advancements in science, technology, economic development, and social organization. Its proponents, historically, consisted of a wide variety of people including British Prime Minister Benjamin Disraeli, Chancellor Otto von Bismark, Pope Leo XIII, Woodrow Wilson, and John Stewart Mills who strongly influenced the liberal movement in this country. They all considered themselves to be progressives. Theodore Roosevelt considered himself to be a progressive.

In Roosevelt's day, this meant that he, and others, believed that societal problems like poverty, violence, corporate greed, and racism could best be mitigated by having government develop and impose solutions to them. This view was opposed by the conservatives and even moderate liberals who believed that social problems would solve themselves, if left to the crooked meanderings of the free market and the choices of individual corporations. The progressives, however, pointed to the crises created by big business when there was no legal oversight. They countered that continuing to take a hands-off approach would only create more economic inequality, more monopolistic corporations, and thus more oppression of the working people of America.

As far as Teddy Roosevelt was concerned, he did not mind monopoly capitalism, he just wanted the federal government, his government, to benefit more directly from it. In addition to being a progressive, Roosevelt was also a showman. He correctly read the people's anger over the Northern Pacific stock manipulation that sent a wave of depression and pain across the land. He knew that he had to confront Morgan and the Wall Street crowd. In doing so, he also saw an opportunity to accrue more power to himself and the federal government that was now almost exclusively in the hands of the monopolists.

Morgan, of course, had no intention of sharing his power with the government or with labor. He knew he had to keep an eye on Roosevelt. He began by sending his lieutenants to see Roosevelt who had just been sworn into office, to laud him and to warn him to not act too hastily to make changes. Roosevelt told them that he wanted reform. Knowing that the public was appalled by the Northern Pacific debacle, he filed an antitrust suit against the Northern Securities Company, which was formed between Harriman and Morgan as a truce. Morgan was appalled by the actions of this *class traitor*. But after being calmed by his lieutenants, he whined to Roosevelt that he had not been given advance notice about the suit. Speaking down from his heavenly throne, he told Roosevelt that in the future he should just "send your man to my man and we can fix it up."[904]

As a showman, Roosevelt knew just how to attack the image of Morgan in public. He frequently lambasted Morgan and Wall Street in his speeches. Behind the scenes, however, it was a different matter as the two "secret blood brothers"[905] collaborated to expand their wealth and power. While criticizing Morgan to the domestic press, Roosevelt partnered with Morgan on international exploits, or should we say exploitation. The Panama Canal affair is a good case in point. Roosevelt lobbied Congress for funds to build a canal for shipping that would link the Atlantic and Pacific oceans. In 1902, Congress authorized Roosevelt to pay forty million dollars to

France for its assets in the Isthmus of Panama and the right to continue the canal they had started. Roosevelt chose Morgan to finance the deal. Morgan organized an "exchange syndicate" to raise the money that was comprised of eight banks, five in Paris and three in New York. The firm's Paris affiliate, Morgan, Harjes & Co., managed the business in France, and J. P. Morgan & Co. headed the New York account.[906] We do not know Morgan's commission on this deal, but we do know that it was the largest real estate deal in American history at the time.

Interestingly, J. P. Morgan & Co. was also appointed in 1903 as the fiscal agent for the newly independent Republic of Panama after Roosevelt had strong-armed Columbia into giving up its isthmus. Panama had been a part of the sovereign state of Columbia at the time.

Within six months after the Congress gave Roosevelt permission to raise funds for a canal, Secretary of State John Hay signed a treaty with Colombian Foreign Minister Tomás Herrán to build the new canal. Not surprisingly, the financial terms were unacceptable to Colombia's congress, and it rejected the offer.

President Roosevelt responded by fomenting revolution in Panama[907] and dispatching US warships to Panama City (on the Pacific) and Colón (on the Atlantic) in support of "Panamanian independence." Unable to move ships by sea due to the blockade, the Colombian troops could only defend the isthmus by land, but this proved futile because they were unable to cross the dense jungles of the Darien Strait, which separated the isthmus from the mainland. The Columbians in Panama were forced to declared independence on November 3, 1903 with the US guaranteeing full support for the "revolutionary junta." At the time, many of the people of the new country of Panama thought the US control of the canal was a good deal. Later they would realize that they had been exploited. [908]

It was Teddy Roosevelt who gave Morgan the power to capitalize the debt of the US as well as collect fees from the junta in Panama for brokering the Panama Canal deal.

J. Pierpont Morgan took this in stride as an offering from an underling. He remained distrustful of government and labor, seeing them as competitors for his wealth. His lieutenants had more foresight, however, and could see the profitable advantage of partnering with government. Cooperating on foreign policy in such exploits as the Panama Canal obviously meant more money for the bank. And partnership with the federal government would also allow them to strengthen their control over domestic labor.

Morgan's brightest lieutenant was a man named George W. Perkins. It was he who brought Roosevelt and Morgan together in what would become an on-going collaboration. In his career at Morgan Bank, Perkins became employed by both Roosevelt and Morgan and was thereby able to cement a relationship between the two of them.

Perkins was a handsome, imaginative man with a silver tongue. It was Perkins who put together the International Harvester deal that resulted in a monopoly that controlled eighty-five percent of the farm-equipment market.[909] While J. P. Morgan gave no attention to theory and strategy, serving instead as a blunt instrument in financial warfare, Perkins was more sophisticated. He gave many speeches and published many papers. He preached a gospel of industrial cooperation, contending that it was small businesses that depressed wages[910] and retarded technological advancement. In a time when capitalism and communism were battling for the mind of the working class, Perkins begged the question as to what would be the difference "between the US Steel Corporation as it was organized by Mr. Morgan, and a Department of Steel as it might be organized by the Government?"[911] He offered up a social philosophy he called "private socialism." Perkins realized that the monopolies created by Morgan were too big and, as such, exposed to public criticism. The welfare of millions of people's lives was in the balance. To accomplish his private socialism, Perkins proposed government licensing. This included licensing of interstate companies and workers benefits. It could also extend to include profit sharing, social insurance, and old-age pensions. This, he boasted would be "socialism of the highest, best and most ideal sort."[912]

Morgan grudgingly bought the package because the giant monopolies required stability and predictability and were constantly being threatened by "upstart" companies. In the 1904 presidential campaign, the Morgan bank gave one hundred and fifty thousand dollars toward Roosevelt's reelection. Roosevelt responded by chastising Morgan at a dinner at the Gridiron Club at which he thundered about business reform. All was right in the world of monopoly capitalism.

Both Morgan and Roosevelt supported monopoly capitalism and their cooperation set the stage for state monopoly capitalism in which the monopolists were able to use the government to forward their quest for wealth and power while the federal government was able to have access to ready cash to realize their own plans for expansion and conquest.[913]

> Roosevelt saw trusts as natural, organic outgrowths of economic development. Stopping them, he said, was like trying to dam the Mississippi river. Both TR and Morgan disliked the rugged, individualistic economy of the ninteenth century and favored big business; they wanted to promote US entry into world markets. But whereas Roosevelt thought economic giantism warranted an equivalent growth in government regulation, Morgan saw no need for countervailing powers. A Victorian gentleman banker at bottom, Pierpont saw trust, honor, and self-regulation among businessmen as providing the needed checks and balances.[914]

Well it all sounds so neat and tidy when its put this way, but we all have witnessed, as have preceding generations, how well the capitalists have been able to "self-regulate" their greed. We also have seen what a joke government regulation of capitalism has become. Under state monopoly capitalism, the state's role is not to regulate the capitalist corporations, rather it is to regulate the middle class, working class and the poor to accept the interest of capital, period. The capitalists remain above the law.

We have taken the time to explore in some detail the workings of J. Pierpont Morgan because he provides the role model and archetype for capitalist bankers even to this day. Not only did he create the monopolies that continue to dominate the American economy, he also helped build the banking establishment that today controls the US dollar and US debt. Although it was left to his son John Pierpont Morgan Jr. to bring the international bankers together to set up the Federal Reserve Bank in 1913, it was Pierpont Sr. who made the plans. While most people still do not realize it, the Federal Reserve Bank is not a public institution. It is a private bank whose shares belong to private banks that are administered by private bankers and it is they who reap the profits. Despite the fluff about the Fed being set up by orders of Congress and being at the service of Congress and the American people, there is *absolutely* no office in Washington DC, whether it be that of a representative, senator, or judge, or the Congress, Supreme Court or even the Presidency that has any control over the Federal Reserve Bank. It should then come as no surprise to the American people that the bankers control the political economy of the United States. They would not have bothered to set up the Federal Reserve Bank in the first place if they were not to profit on the lives of others. The monopoly bank, called the Federal Reserve Bank, is owned by international capitalists, who, through it, own our government because they hold its debt and issue its credit. Our government is simply in their employ.

Today, after a hundred years of liberal and progressive "reforms" in which our relatives and families slogged through WWI and WWII, and the Great Depression, as well as numerous local imperialist wars, we continue to face the same economic threats to our children and ourselves, because the government does nothing to stop the behavior of the capitalists. The in-house liberals, progressives, and democratic socialists continue to perpetrate a lie, a myth, a left-wing dogma that capitalism can be reformed to serve the majority of the people. If we understand history, we must reject this myth outright. If we are to survive and prosper, it is on us to free ourselves from our slavery.

Is it moral to support capitalism, no. Is it moral to support conservatism, no. Is it to our advantage to support liberalism, progressivism or democratic socialism, no. None of these systems serve us now. None of these worldviews and organizations can save the human race nor prevent the destruction of the planet's life support systems. We need a new ideology and a new army to fight for our survival. It is a do or die situation we are now confronting. If humanity survives, how will our generation be remembered? How will we be remembered by our grandchildren if we leave them a barren wasteland?

As it turned out, it was not the Roosevelts or the socialists that fought a battle against the monopolists, it was small businesses and common people fighting at the local level. This is the same situation that exists today.

How Does State Monopoly Capitalism Work?

Today we are living through the downscaling of the middle class in America and the further impoverishment of the lower class. People are joining the ranks of the poor and half of the US population is marginally able to pay their bills. Forty-six percent of Americans, (people of all colors), do not have four hundred dollars in savings to meet an emergency.[915] It does not take much to erroneously convince white people that it is the blacks and colored people's fault for taking their jobs. Other capitalist PR campaigns blame "the economy," a nebulous entity, in which people have no control. Still others blame politicians who make false promises but are unable to provide jobs or change any aspect of the economy. While we labor in our pre-constructed work environment going through our daily lives, we remain eternally fearful that we may not have enough money to meet our basic needs, yet hopefully we will find a way out, if we keep doing what we are doing.

In order to change the system, we first need to understand how it works, and how we are exploited. In his short book, entitled *Austrian And Marxist Theories Of Monopoly-Capital*,[916] Kevin A Carson begins by referring to the US depression of the 1890s, which resulted from the Cooke panic on Wall Street.

While capitalist economists view such panics and depressions as a "natural or inevitable outgrowth of a market society," Carson tells us that such events are neither natural nor inevitable. Rather, as we have seen, they result from the manipulation of the financial system by powerful capitalists, and from their ability to make deals with the federal government to support their monopolistic stranglehold over the different sectors of the economy in exchange for increasing the power of the government to control the public. They do this by "legally" setting limits on striking workers, running prisons to contain the surplus labor populations, and by providing minimal social services. Such government services are not meant to put people back on their feet or allow them a decent standard of living, rather they are meant to regulate the poor and the desperate at the minimum outlay necessary to prevent rebellion against the system.

Of course, such an interpretation of events flies in the face of the in-house leftist intellectuals who hold sacred the belief that during the late nineteenth century's rise of monopoly capitalism, the federal government rose up to break the control the corporations had over the people. Carson makes the argument that the Roosevelt government's new regulations on monopoly capitalists did not curtail their power, but actually increased it by giving them the cover they required to mute the growing revolutionary fervor of the American people at the time. He argues that the effect of the government's subsidies and regulations were to: (1) encourage production on a large scale that, in some cases, led to overproduction and thus depressions; (2) promote monopoly prices above market levels; and (3) set up market entry barriers that put new or smaller companies at a competitive disadvantage.

Of equal, if not greater significance, the back room deals that created government regulations at the beginning of the twentieth century led to a process of increasing cooperation between the federal government and monopoly capitalists to cover up economic crises.[917] We saw how Morgan's man George Perkins created the ideology of "private socialism" that linked the monopoly capitalists to big government and how Theodore Roosevelt sanctioned the monopolies as part of his deal to impose some federal regulation over them as a sop to the public. We must also remember that it was J. P. Morgan's son, John, who created the ultimate monopoly—the monopoly on money supply that was granted to the capitalist banks through the creation of the Federal Reserve Bank in 1913. The Federal Reserve still maintains its control of the country's money supply and thus continues its stranglehold over wages, interest rates, credit, debt, and the global economy. Every nation on earth, every person on earth, remains in the Fed's debt and thus in the debt of those banks that own the shares of the Fed. Does the housing crisis and the Fed's bail-out of the big banks *too large to fail* ring a bell? Was the Fed and J. P. Morgan's bank directly involved in the biggest destruction of American jobs since the Great Depression? We all know the answer to this.

Instead of controlling the monopolists, the progressive government got into bed with them and created the next phase of capitalism—State Monopoly Capitalism.

This idea was echoed in the rise of socialism and communism in the world during the twentieth century and specifically by the student movement in the 1960s and 1970s. The students understood how the monopoly corporations had merged with the federal government in a system they simply called *The Establishment.* The "Establishment" to this generation (baby-boomers) did not simply mean the people of the older generation. Rather it meant the existing power structure controlled by the elite in society including their groups, political and economic institutions, and their authority.[918]

Samuel Huntington who was a leading intellectual within the Trilateral Commission, which was initiated by David Rockefeller to create a world government under corporate control, made this revealing comment about whom the president of the United States was beholding to, and it was not to the people:

> " . . . the President act[s] . . . with the support and cooperation of key individuals and groups in the executive office, the federal bureaucracy, Congress, and the more important businesses, banks, law firms, foundations, and media, which constitute the private sector's "Establishment." . . . The day after [the President's] . . . election, the size of his majority is almost—if not entirely—irrelevant to his ability to govern the country. What counts then is his ability to mobilize support from the leaders of key institutions in a society and government. . . . . This coalition must include key people in Congress, the executive branch, and the private-sector 'Establishment.'"[919]

The student movement did not subscribe to the argument put out by the liberals and organized labor that the government was a "progressive" force dedicated to restraining big business.

The marriage between big business and the government, as we have seen, had its roots in the actions of the "secret blood brothers," Morgan and Roosevelt. It began in 1901 immediately after McKinley was assassinated and Roosevelt, his vice-president, came to power. At this time Morgan had already created monopolies in the railroad, electric utilities, steel, and farming industries. He was also the primary purveyor of government bonds. While President McKinley, as a conservative, publicly supported the creation of US monopolies, so did the progressive Theodore Roosevelt, although he was obliged to hide his support from public view, choosing to lambast Morgan and Wall Street in public while cutting deals with them in the back room. The roots of state monopoly capitalism, begun by the collaboration of Morgan and Roosevelt, sprouted with the creation of the Federal Reserve Bank and flowered with the advent of World War I. This cozy relationship of the state with monopoly capital became the prototype for twentieth century American capitalism that has only strengthened to this present day.

Murray Rothbard, a disciple of Ludwig von Mises, the founder of the Austrian school of economics characterizes state monopoly capitalism as:

> "a new order marked by strong government, and extensive and pervasive government intervention and planning, for the purpose of providing a network of subsidies and monopolistic privileges to business, and especially to large business interests. In particular, the economy could be cartelized under the aegis of government, with prices raised and production fixed and restricted, in the classic pattern of monopoly; and military and other government contracts could be channeled into the hands of favored corporate producers. Labor, which had been becoming increasingly rambunctious, could be tamed and bridled into the service of this new, state monopoly-capitalist order through the device of promoting a suitably cooperative trade unionism, and by bringing the willing union leaders into the planning system as junior partners.[920]

Even today most liberals and progressives believe the myth that the growth of the welfare and regulatory state is a restraint on the power of big business. According to their perception, the Progressive programs and New Deal programs were forced on corporate interests by the federal government against their will. In this cock-eyed view of the world, big government is a protector of the people against the exploitation of the corporate elite. This view is still shared by the Rand Corporation and the Chicago school on the right and by the populist leaning leftists as well. It is, in fact, the official ideology of the public school system, whose history texts recount heroic legends of the "trust buster" Theodore Roosevelt combating the "malefactors of great wealth." It is expressed in almost identical terms in right-wing, homeschool texts by Clarence Carson and the like, who bemoan the defeat of business at the hands of the collectivist state.[921]

The problem with these conventional assessments is that they are an almost exact reverse of the truth. The student movement, which became known as the New Left,[922] produced massive amounts of evidence that virtually demolished the revisionist official version of American history. The problem is that the consensus myth still lingers on propped up daily by TV news programs, newspaper articles, commercials, movies and the debates and commentary by corporate owned talking-head news reports. By such means the Big Lie continues to befuddle what people's own experience tells them to be true. Scholars like Noam Chomsky,[923] Paul Sweezy,[924] James Weinstein,[925] Gabriel Kolko,[926] and William Appleman Williams,[927] in their historical analyses of "corporate liberalism," have demonstrated that the main forces behind both Progressive and New Deal "reforms" were powerful corporate interests. To the extent that big business protested the New Deal, it was a simple case of Brer Rabbit's plea not to fling him in the briar patch.[928]

At the time of the Morgan and Roosevelt partnership, the International Socialist Review (1912) warned American workers not to be fooled into identifying social insurance or the nationalization of industry with true "socialism." They warned that the state programs such as workers' compensation and insurance for health and old age, were simply measures to strengthen and stabilize capitalism. Nationalization of certain corporate functions simply reflected the capitalist's realization "that he can carry on certain portions of the production process more efficiently through the government than through their private corporations." [929]

The liberal/progressive support of capitalism and their justification for state monopoly capitalism initially gained support from the emerging middle-class intellectuals, who populated the government bureaucracy. Such people, who were good at planning and defining "professionalism" saw the American people as human raw material to be managed for their own good. Such people were the inspiration for the English Socialist Party (Ingsoc) that created the political ideology of the totalitarian government of Oceania in George Orwell's dystopian novel *Nineteen Eighty-Four*.[930] Orwell described them in this way:

> The new aristocracy was made up for the most part of bureaucrats, scientists, technicians, trade-union organizers, publicity experts, sociologists, teachers, journalists, and professional politicians. These people, whose origins lay in the salaried middle class and the upper grades of the working class, had been shaped and brought together by the barren world of monopoly industry and centralized government.[931]

The key to efficiency, for this new class of federal bureaucrats, was to remove as much of people's lives as possible from the domain of "politics" (i.e., the democratic process) and to place it under the control of "competent" authorities. "Democracy" was shrunken into an occasional voting ritual, with the people going home after casting their vote to their proper role of sitting down and shutting up. In virtually every area of life, the average citizen was to be transformed from a self-sufficient and resourceful member of the community into a client of some bureaucracy or other.

The educational system was also designed to render us into passive and easily managed recipients of the "services" of one institution after another.[932] As it became incumbent upon the corporate elite to have a docile workforce, they began to invest money into a public education system. The intention for such a system was made perfectly clear. In 1901, Edward A. Ross, a progressive American sociologist, eugenicist, and major figure of early criminology, wrote in his book, *Social Control*, "Plans are underway to replace community, family, and church with propaganda, education and mass media." [933]

In 1906, the first report of the Education Board (Rockefeller's Occasional letter No. 1) set up by John D. Rockefeller expressed their goal this way:

"In our dream . . . people yield themselves with perfect docility to our molding hands. The present educational conventions [intellectual and character education] fade from our minds, and unhampered by tradition we work our own good will upon a grateful and responsive folk. We shall not try to make these people or any of their children into philosophers or men of learning or men of science. We have not to raise up from among them authors, educators, poets or men of letters. We shall not search for embryo great artists, painters, musicians nor lawyers, doctors, preachers, politicians, statesmen, of whom we have ample supply. The task we set before ourselves is very simple . . . we will organize children . . . and teach them to do in a perfect way the things their fathers and mothers were doing in an imperfect way."[934]

President Woodrow Wilson defined the goal of public education in this way:

"We want one class to have a liberal education. We want another class, a very much larger class of necessity, to forego the privilege of a liberal education and fit themselves to perform specific difficult manual tasks."[935]

By the second quarter of the twentieth century, the goal of public education was firmly established. Ellwood Cubberley, the Dean of the Stanford Graduate School of Education and a pioneer in the field of educational administration, wrote in his book, *Public School Administration*:

"Our schools are, in a sense, factories in which the raw products (children) are to be shaped and fashioned into products to meet the various demands of life . . . It is the business of the school to build its pupils according to the specifications laid down. Every manufacturing establishment that turns out a standard product or series of products of any kind maintains a force of efficiency experts to study methods of proce-

dure and to measure and test the output of its works
. . . [Building pupils demands] continuous measurement of production to see if it is according to specifications [and] the elimination of waste in manufacture."[936]

In this process of government education, individual creativity was crushed. It should not come as any surprise now why the student movement of the 1960s, as well as radicals up to the present, consider the education system of the United States to be "irrelevant" to their needs as human beings. The public school system was established, based on the agreement between the monopoly capitalists and the federal elite, specifically to train the American people as cogs to function in the industrial system of the corporations.

Health, learning, dignity, independence, and *creative endeavor*—these human qualities became little more that bureaucratic platitudes that enhanced the lobbying efforts of government institutions to procure corporation grants and tax allocations for more resources to manage their hospitals, schools, and other agencies in question.

As a corollary of this principle, the public was taught to view healing oneself, or teaching one's children, as irresponsible. These were unreliable actions. In the same way, community organizing, when not paid for by those in authority, was viewed as a form of aggression or subversion.[937]

While the liberal/progressive ideology is as much associated with this bureaucratic worldview, as is the conservative ideology, they also intersect with the "enlightened" capitalists who see paternalism as a way of getting more out of workers. As far as the monopoly capitalists and the Washington elite were concerned, both the companies and the bureaucrats were to be dominated and coordinated from the central office. Given this total control, the ruling elite was willing to extend such things as housing projects, old age pensions, death payments, wage and job schedules, and bureaus charged with responsibility for welfare, safety, and sanitation.[938]

The new mania for planning was also reflected in the Taylorist cult of "scientific management" in which the workman was deskilled, work became piecemeal, and control of the production process was shifted upward into the white-collar hierarchy of managers and engineers.[939]

In summary, state monopoly capitalism arose because the liberal and progressive intellectual bureaucrats believed they could be quite comfortable in this reformed version of capitalism. In turn, the capitalists came to believe in the value of creating welfare and regulatory agencies to maintain social stability and control of the people. This all contributed to the profitable bottom line, which could now be accomplished in the name of the people. This devil's pact led Hilaire Belloc to write of the "Progressive" intellectual:

> Let laws exist which make the proper housing, feeding, clothing, and recreation of the proletarian mass be incumbent on the possessing class, and the observance of such rules be imposed, by inspection and punishment, upon those whom he pretends to benefit, and all that he really cares for will be achieved.[940]

The desire to mold people to their will by using a public education system was a goal of the corporate elite and the government under the system of State Monopoly Capitalism. The elite wanted a docile and unimaginative workforce who would not question the legitimacy of the status quo. This led them to explore the concept of eugenics. Eugenics was a set of beliefs and practices that aimed at "improving" the genetic quality of the human population by either promoting higher rates of sexual reproduction for people with desired traits (i.e., the ruling elite) and reducing the rate of sexual reproduction and sterilization of people with less-desired or undesired traits.[941]

In 1904, German Alfred Ploetz founded the *Archive for Racial and Social Biology*, which became the chief journal of the German eugenics or "race hygiene movement." Ernst Haeckel popularized eugenics in Germany.

This philosophy influenced John D. Rockefeller's "Occasional Letter No.1," mentioned above in his attempt to "perfect human nature."

In the same year, the Eugenics laboratory was established at Cold Springs Harbor on Long Island. This was the location of the estates of both Dulles brothers. The laboratory facility was funded in excess of eleven million dollars by the Harrimans and the Rockefellers.

In 1909, the Rockefeller Foundation was established with the aim of supporting the Eugenics movement. This included support for the Kaiser Wilhelm Institute in Germany. The Rockefeller Foundation made major contributions to the fields of brain research and psychiatry as well as the construction of different scientific institutes working on research concerning the control of human consciousness. The institutes that were beneficiaries of Rockefeller's largesse eventually played the leading role in the development, implementation and exploitation of the racial programs of Hitler's Third Reich as Kaiser-Wilhelm scientists joined with the Nazi state in order to "improve the people's health" (*Volksgesundheit*). There major emphasis was on eugenic and racial purification. The collaboration between science and the Nazi state legitimized the policies and programs of the Hitler regime that resulted in the exploitation, mutilation, and murder of untold millions of innocent victims by physicians and scientists associated with some of the world's leading universities and research institutes.[942]

Today the Kaiser Wilhelm Society is called the Max Planck Society and serves as an umbrella organization for many institutes, testing stations, and research units spawned under its authority.[943]

The Federal Reserve Bank

The unbridled and unregulated cutthroat competition and stock manipulations on the part of the robber barons caused the "Panics" of 1873, 1884, 1890, 1893, 1896, 1901, and 1903, each of which decimated the lives of millions of average Americans. In 1907, another panic occurred. This time a Wall Street banker named Charles W. Morris, who had previously cornered the ice market in New York City, teamed up with magnates F. Augustus and Otto Heinze who owned United Cooper, to corner the copper market using a stock manipulation scheme.

Believing that a significant number of the Heinze's shares had been borrowed and sold short by speculators who were betting that the stock price would drop, these robber barons devised a scheme to aggressively purchase as many remaining shares as possible on the belief that this would force the short sellers to pay for their borrowed shares. The strategy was that by aggressively purchasing outstanding shares, the price would be driven up and the short speculators would be unable to find shares elsewhere, and have no other recourse than to buy the shares from Morris/Heinz at a higher price. The scheme, which was put in operation by Otto Heinz, went terribly awry.

Otto had misread the market and did not have the money necessary to corner the cooper market. As he began to purchase stock in United Copper, the shares rose in one day from thirty-nine dollars to fifty-two dollars. The next day he issued the call for short sellers to return the borrowed stock. The share price rose to nearly sixty dollars, but the short sellers were able to find plenty of United Copper shares from sources other than the Heinzes. As a result, the share price of United Copper began to collapse. The stock closed at thirty dollars on Tuesday and fell to ten dollars by Wednesday. Otto Heinze was ruined. [944] His brokerage house, Gross & Kleeburg declared bankruptcy. The collapse of the stock prices also sunk many other banks that had either held stock in United Cooper or were associated with the Heinzes and Morse. Runs occurred on six national banks, and ten state banks on whose boards Heinz and Morse held directorships. A week later, many regional stock exchanges throughout the nation had closed or were limiting trading. Then, the big banks of Wall Street began to tumble. The Knickerbocker, the Trust Company of America, and the Lincoln Trust Company all suffered panicky runs on their banks. Other banks across the country also began to collapse. It was at this point that George F. Baker, President of the First National Bank, and James Stillman, President of the National City Bank, met with J. P. Morgan to examine the assets of the troubled banks. They agreed to offer loans to any of the banks that remained solvent. The Secretary of the Treasury, George B. Cortelyou, offered the New York bankers use of government funds to help prevent a meltdown of the system. At the time of the Panic, President Theodore Roosevelt was on a hunting trip in Louisiana. By the fall of 1907, the country was again in a depression.

The bank panic of 1907 with its falling stock market caused industrial production to fall more than any other time in American history. Production fell by eleven percent and imports by twenty-six percent. Unemployment rose to eight percent from under three percent. Immigration dropped to 750,000 people in 1909, from 1.2 million two years earlier.

The monopoly of the banking system by a handful of capitalists had proven once again that the system was susceptible to contagion because the capitalists sat on each other's boards and were so interconnected in their business dealings, that a problem in one bank could quickly spread to the others. What made matters worse was that the federal government had no authority over the bankers who were able to mercilessly exploit the people at will.

Once again, the public clamored for banking reform and the option again was promoted that the government should control the national banking system as had occurred under Jefferson, Jackson, and Lincoln. Fearful that the forces of democracy might gain the upper hand, the bankers fought back. Yes, a central bank was required, but it should remain in their hands, not the hands of the public. The result was the founding of the Federal Reserve Bank in 1913. Here is how it occurred.

Soon after the 1907 panic, Congress formed the National Monetary Commission to review banking policies in the United States. The committee was chaired by Senator Nelson W. Aldrich of Rhode Island, a man firmly under the control of the international banking cartel. Aldrich went to Europe where he was schooled by the bankers on how to set up the Federal Reserve Bank. When he returned, he called a meeting on Jekyll Island, with the permission of J. P. Morgan, far from the eyes of the people or the press, to which he invited several bankers and economic scholars. While meeting under the ruse of a duck-shooting excursion, the purpose of the meeting was to restructure the banking system in such a manner that the banking elite would remain in power but be able to control future economic panics, a goal, not surprisingly, they never accomplished. They did manage, however, to tighten their grip on the nation's finances.[945]

The 1910 "duck hunt" on Jekyll Island included Senator Nelson Aldrich, his secretary Arthur Shelton, a former Harvard University professor of economics; Dr. A. Piatt Andrew; Henry P. Davidson, a partner in J. P. Morgan & Co; Frank A. Vanderlip, president of National City Bank; and Paul W. Warburg, a partner in Kuhn, Loeb, and Co.

Knowing that any exposure of their collusion would result in a public outcry, the group proceeded with the greatest caution, refusing to even use each other's last names. On Jekyll Island the group developed the plan that eventually became the Federal Reserve Banking System.[946] In 1913, the Congress approved the Federal Reserve Act and the monopoly capitalists have since then controlled the banking system of America against the interests of the American public, who remain unaware that the Fed is really a private bank that acts in its own interest.

For years afterward, the members of the Jekyll Island Club would recount the story of the secret meeting and by the 1930s the recounting of the narrative was considered a tradition. Although Congress did not pass the exact reform bill submitted by Senator Aldrich, it did approve a similar proposal in 1913 called the Federal Reserve Act. The Federal Reserve System of today mirrors in essence the plan developed on Jekyll Island in 1910. We shall look more closely at how the Federal Reserve Bank works in Volume 5 of this book.

World War I

World War I began in 1914, one year after the Federal Reserve Bank was set up in the United States. The "Great War," however, was not primarily an American war. It was initiated by the empires of Europe who vied for dominance among themselves, while they also sought to colonize countries abroad. Their governments were driven by the values of nationalism, militarism, and imperialism, while the capitalists steered their economies. Religion was no longer the primary cause of the war. The idea of the nation and the sense of belonging associated with a fixed land base created pride and arrogance within the people. Many minority ethnic groups, such as the Poles, Czechs, and Slovaks craved to have their own independent nations.

The empires of Europe were continually expanding their armies. Great Britain, which relied on its navy for the vast majority of military protection, felt threatened by Germany as the size of its navy began to swell. Having "peace time" armies grow at alarming rates created palpable tension and grave mistrust among the nations of Europe. This occasioned the formation of alliances whose treatise stipulated that if a country was attacked, its allies were bound to defend them.

The long history of internal wars that had ravaged Europe for centuries had now reached a stage where two great Alliances contended for power. The Central Powers (Triple Alliance) consisted of Austro-Hungary, Germany, and Italy,[947] while the Allied Powers (Triple Entente) consisted of France, Great Britain, and Russia. Later the Allied Powers would be joined by the United States when it declared war on Germany in April 1917.[948]

While a restless balance of power existed between the "Powers" their member nation-states competed aggressively with each other to build colonies in different lands. Germany, France, and Great Britain still had colonial empires abroad, while Austria-Hungary controlled the states in the Balkans. The lands of the Middle East and Africa were also hotly contested between the Allies and Central Powers.[949]

The powder keg of tensions, fueled as they were by the competitive sentiments of nationalism, militarism, and imperialism, set the stage for a human holocaust. On June 28, 1914, a teenage boy assassinated the Archduke Franz Ferdinand and in doing so, lit the fuse to the worse nightmare Europe had ever experienced in its long history of nightmares.

The explosion, known as the Great War (World War I), killed seventeen million people and transfigured the map of Europe.

As with most wars, the Great War started almost by accident. A teenage boy named Gabriel Princip killed the Archduke Franz Ferdinand and his wife Sophie because their driver, while traveling in a motorcade, unintentionally turned down a side street. As he stopped immediately to back onto the main boulevard, a teenager, standing just a few feet from the car, pulled out a gun and fired a bullet into the duke and then into his wife, killing them instantly. While the boy had been sent to kill the duke a few months earlier, the circumstances in which he did so were impossible to stage. The duke's death was a freak accident. At the time, Franz Ferdinand was the heir to the Hapsburg Empire and the archduke of Austria-Hungary one of the most powerful empires on the planet.

Events Leading to World War I

When the Archduke was assassinated, the Austro-Hungarian Empire was a multinational state composed of the Austrian Empire and the Kingdom of Hungary that resulted from the Austro-Hungarian Compromise of 1867. The compromise stated that the Austrian and Hungarian states were co-equal. While foreign affairs and the military came under joint oversight, all other governmental affairs were divided between the respective states.[950]

In 1914, the Austria-Hungary Empire was geographically the second-largest country in Europe after the Russian Empire, at 239,977 square miles.[951] It was the third-most populous country after Russia and the German Empire.[952] It also had the fourth largest industrial base in the world, after the United States, Germany, and Great Britain.[953]

The Austria-Hungary Empire had controlled Bosnia and Herzegovina from 1878 when it took control of the territory from the Ottoman Empire (Turkey).[954] In 1908, the Austro-Hungary Empire fully annexed the two provinces. This led to what became known as the *Bosnian Crisis*.[955]

Pan-Slavism and the Bosnia Crisis

At the time of the annexation, the largely Slavic population of the two provinces yearned to create their own nations, while their fellow Slavs, in next-door Serbia, schemed to annex them to further their own pan-Slavic ambitions.

Pan-Slavism, a movement that crystallized in the mid-nineteenth century, was based on a political ideology that promoted the advancement and unity of the Slavic peoples. While there were many Northern Slavs who supported Pan-Slavism, the idea was considerably stronger in the south where the Slavic peoples had been controlled by non-Slavic empires for hundreds of years. These included the Byzantine Empire, the Austro-Hungary Empire, and the Ottoman Empire.[956]

Austria feared that the Pan-Slavic movement threatened its empire. It especially was concerned about the great number of Slavs within its own territory. In Austria-Hungary, Southern Slavs were distributed across the land. There were Slovenes and Croats in Austria and Croats and Serbs in Hungary. There were also Slavs in the autonomous Kingdom of Croatia-Slavonia and in the autonomous Kingdom of Dalmatia. There were also many Slavs in Bosnia and Herzegovina.

The Austrians were particularly alarmed by Pan-Slavism because certain Serbian intellectuals sought to unite all of the Southern Slavs, whether Catholic (Croats, Slovenes), Muslim (Bosnians), or Orthodox (Montenegrins, Serbs) as a "Southern-Slavic nation of three faiths".

Among the Southern Slavs the most powerful were the Serbs because they were dispersed among several regions, and they also controlled their own independent nation, the Kingdom of Serbia. The Serbs were the strongest advocates for the independence of Southern Slavs in Austria-Hungary. Their vision was to unite all Southern Slavs into a common state under a Serbian monarchy.

This situation is why Austro-Hungary's annexation of Bosnia and Herzegovina greatly disturbed Serbia and, for that matter, most Southern Slavs, especially those in Bosnia and Herzegovina. Serbia, at the time, was also allied with Russia that wanted to maintain a presence in the Balkans. This added poignancy to the unfolding drama. Even so, Russia, at the time, was militarily weakened by its war with Japan over their imperial ambitions in Manchuria and Korea,[957] It was, therefore, forced to submit to the annexation, but it still did everything it could to encourage pro-Russian, anti-Austrian sentiment among the Slavs in the Balkan provinces. This, of course, added to Austrian fears of Slavic expansionism in the region and increased its desire to subdue Serbia.

At the height of these tensions, Austro-Hungary cut a backroom deal with Germany that if Austria were to invade Serbia and if Russia was to intervene on Serbia's behalf, Germany would go to war on the side of Austro-Hungary. In addition, Germany eager for a fight, would also declare war on France who was Russia's ally to the west.

In the summer of 1914, when the struggle for power in the tumultuous Balkans morphed into the war, Germany would keep its promise and the stage was set for World War I.[958]

The Balkan League and the Balkan Wars

The Pan-Slavic movement in the south often turned to Russia for support. Russia also required their allies in the Balkans to contribute to the balance of power against Germany, Austria-Hungary, and the Ottoman Empire.

Map 4-12: WWI Military Alliances in 1914

With the encouragement of Russian agents, a series of agreements were concluded between Serbia and Bulgaria in March 1912 related to retaking Slavic lands presently controlled by the Ottoman Empire. Even so, a military victory against the Ottoman Empire was not possible so long as the empire could reinforce its troops from its vast population in Asia by way of the Aegean Sea. Because Greece was the only Balkan country with a navy powerful enough to stop the Ottoman Empire in the Aegean, Bulgaria signed a treaty with Greece in May 1912. At around the same time, Montenegro concluded agreements between Serbia and Bulgaria while Bulgaria also signed treaties with Serbia to divide the territory of northern Macedonia, presently under Ottoman control.

The alliances between Greece, Serbia, Bulgaria, and Montenegro gave rise to what became known as the Balkan League.[959] Even though, the League was loose at best, Montenegro declared war on the Ottoman Empire in the summer of 1912. The remaining members entered the conflict in October.

The Balkan League bested the Ottoman Empire in the Slavic territories and the war ended officially with the Treaty of London on May 1913.[960]

Though the Balkan allies had fought together against the common enemy and won, it was not enough to overcome internal rivalries that led almost immediately to a Second Balkan War.[961]

Map 4-13: Treaty of Bucharest, 1913

Bulgaria was dissatisfied with its share of the spoils of the First Balkan War and within a month after the Treaty of London was signed, it attacked its former allies, Serbia and Greece. The Serbian and Greek armies repulsed the Bulgarian offensive and counter-attacked, entering Bulgaria. Because Bulgaria was also involved in territorial disputes with Romania, Romanian took advantage of the war to also attack Bulgaria. As Romanian troops approached its capital, Sofia, Bulgaria asked for an armistice. This resulted in the Treaty of Bucharest,[962] in which Bulgaria was forced to cede portions of its First Balkan War gains to Serbia, Greece, and Romania.

The Second Balkan war proved to be a catastrophic blow to Russian policies in the Balkans. First, it ended the Balkan League, which was a strategic component in Russia's system of defense against Austria-Hungary.

Second, Bulgaria's uncompromising position forced Russia to adopt a strong pro-Serbian position. In the process, Bulgaria adapted the Central Powers policy concerning an anti-Serbian front. This isolated Serbia militarily against Austria-Hungary. Because Russia could not afford to lose its last ally in the Balkans, when the crisis between Serbia and Austria broke out in 1914, Russia was forced to support Serbia. This position inevitably drew her into World War I with devastating results. Russia was less prepared (both militarily and socially) for the war than any other Great Power.

The Black Hand

In the summer of 1911, a group of officers in the Serbian army created a secret military society, led by Colonel Dragutin Dimitrijević "Apis," whose purpose was to unite all of the territories that had a South Slavic majority not ruled by either Serbia or Montenegro.

By 1914, the organization had hundreds of members who were being trained as guerilla fighters and saboteurs. The Black Hand was organized at the grassroots level in three to five-member cells and supervised by district committees and then by a ten-member Central committee in Belgrade led by Colonel Dragutin Dimitrijević "Apis." To ensure secrecy, members rarely knew much more than the members of their own cell and one superior above them. New members swore an oath by the Sun, the Earth, God, the blood of his forefathers, his honor, and his life, to serve and be prepared to die for the organization. In addition, recruits were further required to . . . "swear by my God, by my honor, and by my life, that I shall keep within myself all the secrets of this organization and carry them with me into my grave. May God and my brothers in this organization be my judges if at any time I should wittingly fail or break this oath."[963]

It was in 1914 that Apis allegedly decided to have Archduke Franz Ferdinand assassinated. He recruited three young Bosnian Serbs who were trained in bomb throwing and marksmanship by members of the Serbian military. Those involved probably realized that their plot would result in war between Austria and Serbia, but they had every reason to expect that Russia would side with Serbia. They likely did not, however, anticipate that the assassination would start a chain of events leading to world war.[964]

After Gabriel assassinated the Archduke on June 28, 1914, the long-existing tensions between Serbia and Austria-Hungary eventually drew the other European powers into the conflict and this escalated into World War I.

Austria-Hungary Invades Serbia

Austria-Hungary immediately suspected Serbia of being responsible for the assassination of the Archduke and demanded that they be able to conduct an investigation into the matter on Serbian soil. Serbia refused and Austria-Hungary immediately recalled its ambassador from Serbia. In July, the empire, with the understanding that Germany would come to their assistance, declared war against Serbia. Unbeknownst to them, however, France and Russia had also made a secret alliance in 1892 similar to that made between Austria-Hungary and Germany.[965] England, fearing the power of the Triple Alliance, reluctantly joined sides with France and Russia, and soon all the Great Powers of Europe were at war. Only Italy demurred, citing a clause in the Triple Alliance treaty that it was only bound to defend an ally if it was attacked, not if it attacked another country. Because Serbia had not declared war on Austria-Hungary, Italy chose to remain neutral. The invasion of Serbia by Austria-Hungary was the first act of aggression in World War I.

Meanwhile Russia began to mobilize its own military against Austria. Russia's allies, Britain and France, feared that the Balkans conflict, if entered into by Russia, would explode into a general European war. As an attempt to keep this from happening, Britain proposed an international convention to moderate the conflict, but Germany was not interested.

On August 1, Germany demanded that Russia halt mobilization immediately. When Russia failed to respond within twenty-four hours, both Germany and France ordered the mobilization of their troops. The stock exchanges of Europe panicked and many were closed. Germany formally declared war against Russia and on the next day, it delivered an ultimatum to Belgium requiring that she remain neutral while German troops occupied the country while en route to fight France. The following day the British Parliament stated that Britain would fight to defend Belgium if necessary.

The Belgian King, Albert I, rejected Germany's ultimatum and on August 4, German troops invaded Belgium. This led to Britain announcing a state of war with Germany.

In a fever of nationalistic and militaristic sentiment, the people of Europe responded with overwhelmingly enthusiasm. They looked at the war as little more than a bar fight and believed that the war would be over by Christmas.[966] Thus, in the summer of 1914, the major powers in the Western world, with the exception of the United States and Italy, flung themselves headlong into what became the First World War.[967]

The Russian Revolution

By the time World War I began, the capitalists were in control of the national economies of Europe, but the socialist movement was gaining international strength. The liberals of the nineteenth century, whose philosophy provided the rationale that freed the capitalists from the control of monarchs, had by now come to believe that liberty could only be accomplished by economic independence and security. The writings of Alexander Hamilton clearly show this development in capitalist thought. When put into practice, this came to mean powerful national governments having strong militaries. The blind faith in religious dogma that had characterized the Middle Ages was long gone. It had been replaced by the celebration of greed, a Protestant virtue that drove the economy and provided prosperity for all. In this new paradigm, poverty was considered a character flaw and the poor were punished by harsh laws designed to drive them to work. On the other hand, any efforts on the part of the workers to organize to improve their conditions were met with fierce resistance.

In the first half of the nineteenth century, the working classes suffered under many forms of exploitation. Feudalism at least had provided security regarding a home and food (except in cases of natural disaster or plagues), but capitalism denied workers even this fundamental security. Men and women were hired or fired at will and their pay rate kept at a level that barely offered survival. At the same time, people who were unemployed, (surplus labor) created a competition between all workers that led to a survival of the fittest mentality. The factories ran twenty-four hours a day, in two twelve-hour shifts, seven days a week. Many industries severely polluted their environments while machinery maimed and killed workers. Food was of poor quality in the towns and the living standards and educational levels declined among the workers as women and children were brought into the work force because they worked for a lower wage than men.[968]

The workers also had to deal with an existential angst created by the bust and boom cycle, which appeared to have no rhyme or reason and thus was believed to be out of control of human intervention. Even the middle class, as we have seen, were not exempt from losing their homes and savings. It was the insightful work of Karl Marx and Frederick Engels, however, that solved the riddle of the boom and bust cycle and demonstrated for the workers, the manner in which the capitalist bankers created this pattern. Marx also explained how the exploitation of labor by the capitalists was the key element in their ability to control workers and amass profits from their work. Marx took the "people first" idea of socialism (as opposed to the "money first" idea of capitalism) to a scientific level well beyond the earlier utopian visions promoted by European intellectuals.

Socialists, at the time of the Great War, advocated a democratically controlled economy run for the benefit of all. The unfettered competition of capitalists was to be replaced by cooperation; the bust and boom cycle by economic planning. Like the early Christians, many socialists believed that private ownership of industry and land should be abolished and ownership of property shared in common.

Communism as an ideology grew out of socialism and was a specific form of it. Communism came to mean people living in groups and sharing labor and property collectively under the central control of the state. Communists did not believe capitalism could be reformed; rather it was to be overthrown by a new revolutionary movement. Marx's ideas strongly resonated among the working class across Europe. There were strong workers movements in England, France, German, Italy and Spain. The workers had begun to organize labor unions to fight for their rights. As they did so, the capitalists fought back, breaking their strikes and hiring private armies to kill them if necessary. They also created laws against promoting socialist ideas.[969]

The capitalists saw any form of unionizing, no matter how mild, as a threat. Marxists saw this obsessive effort to suppress the workers as living proof that the capitalists exploited the worker and that the only way to overcome this situation was to create a revolution.[970]

It was in Russia, while the country was engaged in WWI, that the first communist revolution occurred. Russia was the nation in which capitalism was the weakest and the institutions required for capitalist rule almost non-existent. The empire was a monarchy ruled by a tsar and the economy was still largely feudal. Agriculture prevailed and capitalist dominated industry was just beginning. As such, the Tsarist government paid little attention to Marx's writings whose theory introduced the *proletariat* as urban workers fighting for justice in industrialized factories. Marx's writings were allowed to be distributed in Russia even though they were banned in many other countries. "The Communist Manifesto" and "Das Kapital" became influential for many of the early Russian socialists and communists.

Marx's writings had a profound impact on Vladimir Lenin and Leon Trotsky, who would, in turn, promote communist ideas in Russia through the publication of a Marxist periodical called *Iskra* ("The Spark").[971] Lenin became the most influential political figure during the years of turmoil between the Revolution of 1905 and the Revolution of 1917. He also led the Revolution of 1917. Lenin's *Bolshevik* branch of communism,[972] advocated revolution rather than reform and when he came to power, he quickly deposed other socialist groups that would not support the revolution. Marx believed that the communist revolution would take place on an international scale. Lenin, however, realized that the Russian working class was in the vanguard of socialism in Europe and that it was operating under the gravest conditions. He therefore turned his attention from the idea of international revolution and dedicated himself to establishing communism within Russia.

Upon seizing power, Lenin created his "New Economic Policy (NEP)" or what he called "state capitalism," (not to be confused with the state monopoly capitalism created by Morgan and Roosevelt). Lenin's plan, rather, was to nationalize all industries of the economy and set up farming collectives in the countryside. The experiment was a colossal flop in large measure because immediately after the 1917 revolution, a civil war erupted in Russia that lasted until 1922.

Realizing that he could not fight a war internally, while the country was also engaged in World War I, Lenin signed a peace treaty with Germany on March 3, 1918, giving them huge tracts of land that had been the Ukraine and Poland in exchange for peace on his eastern front. This was a benefit to Russian and Germany, but the peace allowed the German command to shift soldiers to the Western Front, where the French, British, and Americans bore the brunt of a larger, revitalized German army.[973]

The Russian Civil War was unavoidable.[974] In the power vacuum created by the Revolution of 1917[975] and the abdication of the Tsar, many political factions vied to determine Russia's future. The two largest combatant groups were Lenin's Red Army, fighting for the Bolshevik form of socialism, and the loosely allied forces known as the White Army, which included the monarchists (old ruling class), the capitalists, and the other socialist groups that were still smarting from Lenin's rejection of their reformist approach.

During the civil war, no less than eight foreign nations intervened against the Red Army, including the Allied Forces and pro-German armies.[976] In the end, the Red Army triumphed over its adversaries, although minor battles continued as late as 1934 in different parts of Russia. The civil war was long and brutal and fought under the worst conditions imaginable. The casualties of the Russian Civil War numbered between seven million to twelve million people, mostly civilians.

Outside of Russia proper, many pro-independence movements emerged to free themselves from what was once the tsarist empire. Armenia, Azerbaijan, Georgia, Finland, Estonia, Latvia, Lithuania, Poland, and Ukraine were established as sovereign states having fought their own civil wars and wars of independence. Many, however, were later consolidated into the formation of the Soviet Union.[977]

After years of war, the NEP economic plan created by the Bolsheviks under Lenin was modified. A mixed economy was put into place that allowed private individuals to own small businesses and farms, while the state still controlled the banks, foreign trade, and large industries.[978] In addition, the revised economic plan abolished forced grain requisition and introduced a tax on farmers, payable in the form of raw agricultural products.

After Lenin died in 1924, there was a brief power struggle between two of his chief lieutenants, Leon Trotsky and Josef Stalin. Trotsky, ever the internationalist, believed that the world needed to be in a state of constant revolution for communism to survive. Stalin, like Lenin, believed that communism could succeed in a single nation and that it could coexist with other forms of government until the working class in other countries staged their own revolutions. In the end, Stalin came to power and his view of Marxist-Leninism prevailed in Soviet Russia. Stalin created a small but powerful ruling party that enforced his policies in the name of the Communist Party by any means necessary. While Trotsky was an intellectual, Stalin was a warrior, and a ruthless one at that. Under his rule, any suspected challenge to the Communist Party's leadership was dealt with severely. A secret police force spied on everyone and political opponents were routinely assassinated. Any form of protest was brutally repressed. Stalin controlled almost every aspect of the Soviet people's lives. The leaders who followed him, from his successor Nikita Khruschev to Mikhail Gorbachev each made changes relaxing some of the harsher controls on the Russian people. They admitted that Stalin had not exemplified the best ideals of Marxism, which held that the dictatorship of the proletariat would give way to a society in which government was unnecessary, not a totalitarian dictatorship.[979]

Lessons Learned from the Russian Communist Experiment

The Russian revolutionaries and the Russian people are to be praised for their valiant, life and death struggle to create an alternative to monopoly capitalism in the world. Russia provided an antithesis to the rapacious U.S. and European capitalism, provided the working class of the world with an inspiration to fight for a fair wage, and opposed the capitalists' unchallenged assault on third world countries and their resources.

Yet, Russian communism was beset with its own limitations and it is important that we see them for what they are. Because its theoretical foundation, like capitalism, was based on materialism, people were still seen as little more than cogs in the state apparatus.

While capitalism stressed individual freedom to the exclusion of collective welfare, communism stressed collective welfare at the expense of individual freedom. Each system, therefore, presents us with an extremist interpretation of human good in which there is no possible balance to be achieved between the social and personal aspects of human nature. We have seen the effects of this imbalance under capitalism in which the collective welfare suffers at the expense of a hyper individualism that has given rise to an elite one percent who control the lives of ninety-nine percent of the people living under the capitalist system. On the other hand, communist extremism has meant for many years the suppression of individual expression. This has taken the form of religious (spiritual) suppression, artistic expression (aside from political propaganda), and freedom of thought. This lack of individual creativity has resulted in static forms of social production, including the design of buildings and structures, the lock step control of a party bureaucracy and a lack of speed in all modes of production. Furthermore, the enforced collectivist mentality only led to a new ruling class, now composed of the Communist Party elites who prospered at the expense of the people. Because the materialist communist ideology is too limited in scope, any attempt that is made to grant more freedom to individuals has simply resulted in a return to capitalism.

The overriding question for humanity moving forward is how do we ensure that everyone receives their basic needs (food, shelter, clothing, health care, and education) and has incentives to grow personally as well as contribute to the social welfare, within a socio-economy that balances individual and collective needs. As human beings, we require individual freedom as well as social security to prosper. Any advance in socio-economic theory, therefore, must take this into account. And because human beings are simultaneously physical, mental, and spiritual beings, we must also move beyond political economic theories that only account for the physical and mental components of our being. Neither materialism nor idealism, in themselves, are adequate to that task.

The War Rages On

In the spring of 1917, just as the Russian revolution was beginning, the Americans entered the world war on the side of England and France.

By this time, the war had been going on for almost three years and there had already been great damage to the combatants and the countryside of Europe.

When the Germans had first entered the war in August 1914, they immediately invaded Belgium. A year later, they suffocated two French divisions at Ypres by firing more than one hundred and fifty tons of lethal chlorine gas into their lines.[980] This was the first time a large amount of poison gas was used in a battle. Nonetheless, the Germans were unable to capitalize on their assault and break through the French line. A month later, in May 1915, a German U-boat sunk the passenger liner *Lusitania* as it was crossing the Atlantic. At the time it was carrying 1,198 people. There were 128 Americans on board. The Germans had been warning the Allied Powers that they would blow up any ship entering the waters around England and specifically told passengers that if they traveled on Allied ships to England that they were doing so "at their own risk." The German government even took out ads in the New York Tribune and the Washington Times to make their case. Newspaper articles were written about the German ads in papers across the country and the Lusitania was specifically mentioned in the discussions.[981] Nonetheless, the ship set sail and the Germans torpedoed it. They suspected that the US had smuggled weapons and supplies to England on the ship. The world reacted in outrage. This led Kaiser Wilhelm to restrict submarine warfare. He knew if he did not, the United States would enter the war, but by restricting his submarines, his effort to keep the Americans from sending war munitions and supplies to France and England was hampered.

In September 1916, the British army employed the first tanks ever used in battle at Delville Wood. This battle was part of the larger *Somme Offensive* fought by the armies of the British and French empires against the German Empire on both sides of the upper River Somme in France.[982] It was the largest battle of World War I on the Western Front. In this single battle, more than three million men participated and one million men were wounded or killed. As for the tanks, while they were useful at breaking through barbed wire and clearing a path for the infantry, they were still primitive and failed to be the decisive weapon that their designers thought they would be.

By early February 1917, The Germans resumed unrestricted submarine warfare in the waters around England and France. As Kaiser Wilhelm had initially feared, this drew the United States into the war, and led to the eventual defeat of Germany.

In the same month, British intelligence intercepted a telegram from the German foreign secretary, Arthur Zimmerman, addressed to the Mexican government. It proposed that Mexico side with Germany in the event that the United States entered into the war. In return, Germany promised to return Texas to Mexico including a large portion of the Southwest. While Mexico declined the offer, the news of the "Zimmerman Telegram" pushed US public opinion to support entering the war.[983]

In April, President Wilson made his case for going to war and Congress authorized a declaration of war against Germany. Congress also passed the Selective Service Act authorizing the draft. The draft was completely undemocratic and people criticized Wilson for destroying democracy at home while fighting for it abroad. President Wilson claimed he had no other option and signed the bill into law.

In March 1918, when Lenin made peace with Germany, the German army sent fifty additional divisions to the Western Front, hoping to defeat the Allies before U.S. forces could be fully deployed. It failed to do so.

In May 1918, at the Battle of Cantigny, the American army fought its first battle taking the town of Cantigny from the Germans.[984] This victory by the Americans, under the command of General Pershing, although small, inspired the French and English troops. This battle was a part of the German army's third major offensive.

This offensive brought the German army to the north bank of the Marne River at Château-Thierry, about sixty miles from Paris. On May 31, the American 3rd Division stopped the German advance at Château-Thierry amid retreating French troops earning for itself the nickname "Rock of the Marne."[985]

On June 3, the Americans counterattacked. The battle changed into a larger battle at Belleau Wood in which the U.S. Marine Corps and the German army attacked each other across an open field of wheat. The area changed hands six times during the three week battle. Each side suffered significant casualties. The Americans lost ten thousand men.

The number of dead Germans was not reported. The battle marked the farthest advance of the German army on Paris.[986]

In September, three hundred thousand American forces accompanied by one hundred and ten thousand French troops, under the command of General Pershing, attacked the town of St. Mihiel as part of Pershing's plan to break through the German lines and capture the fortified city of Metz in northeastern France. This was the first major offensive launched solely by the United States and it had the good fortune of catching the German army in retreat. Because the German artillery was out of place, the American attack proved successful and increased the status of the US Army in the eyes of its allies. The attack soon faltered, however, because the US food and artillery supplies were left behind because of muddy roads. The attack on Metz was never realized.[987]

Trench Warfare

When people think of World War I they think of trenches and mud. As the map below shows, the German army's advance into France was stopped by the Allied forces at the end of 1914. Both armies dug in across from each other. Trenches protected the soldiers from artillery shells and rifle shots from the enemy. During the war, thousands of miles of front-line trenches, reserve-line trenches, communications trenches, and dummy trenches sprang up on both sides.

Trenches were the most hellish places to live and die. The soldiers lived surrounded by death as men killed by enemy fire were buried in the trench where they fell. Rats proliferated by the millions to feast on the decomposing bodies. The soldiers ate their food cold and intermittently. Water coming up from the ground soaked the men's boots for weeks at a time. All the while, the men were constantly being shot at and shelled. The blank stares of men returning from the front introduced the term "shell shock." The German trenches, it was said, were better made than the Allied ones, but this is understandable. The Allied troops could be pulled from the front and sent to the rear for rest, but the Germans, who were in foreign territory, did not have the luxury of towns filled with friendly faces.

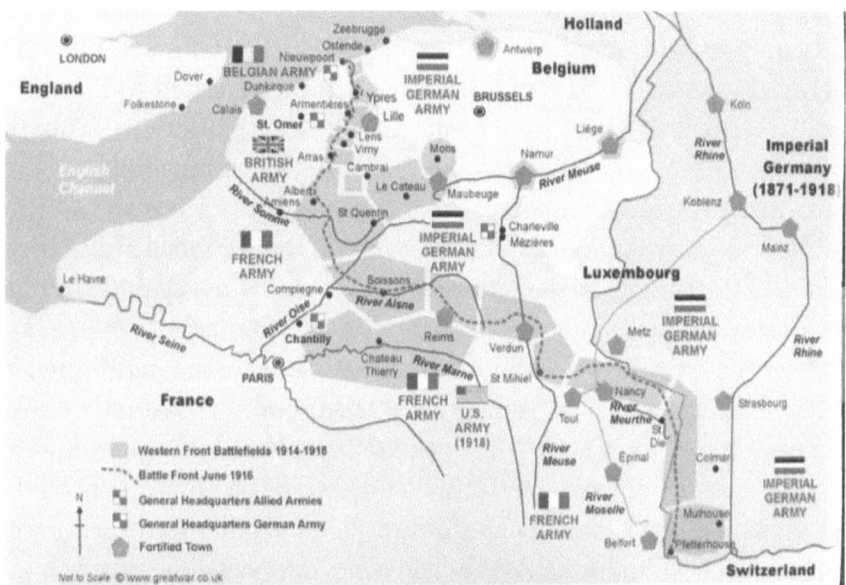

Map 4-14: Trench Warfare in WWI
(Map reproduced by kind permission of www.greatwar.co.uk)

Soldiers in the trenches slept as best as they could. Sometimes an offensive would be called in which a number of men would launch themselves out of the trenches into a No Man's land of mines, barbed wire, and enemy machine gun fire. Mostly these assaults only entailed a few thousand men, but some battles like those at Verdun involved over a million men in the attack.[988]

For nearly four years, the insane, stalemated warfare went on. The casualties mounted into the millions while the front stayed basically the same.

Germany Surrenders

When Germany declared war on the Allied Powers in 1914, the country bristled with new military technology and the people had been whipped into a frenzy of war fever. Kaiser Wilhelm II and his government had promoted policies that had contributed to rising tensions in Europe. German nationalism, militarism, and imperialism, along with the Kaiser's belligerent personality created a mood for war. German industrialists had equipped the army with new weapons: artillery, machine guns, chemical weapons, and flamethrowers and they wanted to see them tested. German admirals were rewarded with new battleships, cruisers, and submarines. The military strategists had drawn up ambitious war plans that promised the conquest of France in just a few weeks. The nationalists exalted about expanding their imperial control over Africa, Asia, and the Middle East. German newspapers ranted against the bullying tactics of the "old empires" of Britain and France.

However, by mid-1916, the German people were feeling the strain of two long years of total war. What was supposed to last only weeks had now lasted for years. The weak German chancellor, Bethmann-Hollweg, was completely ineffectual at meeting the domestic needs of the German people. Food had become difficult to obtain, and bread was being made of wheat husks. As the civilian government dithered, the army took control of domestic policy. Generals Hindenburg and Ludendorff seized control of the press and propaganda, imposed food rationing and ordered compulsory labor for all adult males. They relocated farmers to factories to double munitions production. In July 1917, the Reichstag (Parliament or Congress), responded to the deteriorating situation by passing a resolution calling for peace, but the junta refused to consider this action and forced the chancellor to resign, replacing him with an unimportant puppet. By the winter of 1917, the availability of food in German cities was critically low. The Allied Power's blockade of German ports had all but halted food imports. The local production of food had been drastically cut back by the redeployment of farmers to munitions factories. When the Russians signed a peace treaty with the Germans, this proved to be a shot in the arm and suddenly the war, which seemed like it might drag on for years, now appeared winnable.[989]

But the entry of the Americans into the war squashed this hope. In late 1918, there were food riots in the cities of Germany. In addition, sailors were mutinying and soldiers were deserting by jumping off troop trains. Under these conditions, the civilian politicians found their voice and demanded that the Kaiser abdicate if chaos was to be prevented. The Reichstag went so far as to announce Wilhelm's abdication even before he had agreed to it. The Kaiser complied, however, when the army commanders told him he had also lost their support. On November 10, the deposed emperor took a train across the border into the Netherlands where he bought a manor house in the town of Doorn, and remained there for the remainder of his life.[990] During this time he wrote a self-promoting memoir defending his actions during the war.[991]

The abdication of the emperor dashed all hopes of a German victory. An Armistice was signed two days later ending the fighting on the Western Front. The event is commemorated each year as Armistice Day. The actual signing of the armistice took place on the "eleventh hour of the eleventh day of the eleventh month" of 1918. In the United States this day is remembered as Veterans Day.[992]

Religion and WWI: For God and Country

Sixty million soldiers fought in WWI and when the war ended in 1918, over ten million had died along with seven million civilians. In addition, millions more were permanently maimed and disfigured. The physical deprivation and the emotional strain on the people of Europe was incalculable.

Philip Jenkins, in his book *The Great and Holy War: How World War I Became a Religious Crusade,* tells us that the Christian nations that formed the combatant Powers promoted the war as a "Holy War" to gain the people's support. This was different from the "Just War" of Augustine and Aquinas, who simply believed that a Christian nation could use deadly force against another nation so long as it promoted long-term peace and avert injustice. The idea of a Holy War, by contrast, eliminated the idea of morality all together. Under the ideology of nationalism, the nation's cause became God's cause and the enemy was no longer considered a human being, rather he became a force of evil. It did not matter that he was a fellow Christian. The soldiers of one's own nation were, of course, the instruments of God and if they fell in battle they became holy martyrs. The ruling classes of the so-called Christian nations continue to use religion as a divisive force to this very day.

As we have seen, religion has always been used to promote divisiveness, either directly through its own institutions or indirectly as support of nation-states and their ruling classes. Christians had long been acculturated to fight among themselves in the name of God. And the behavior of Christians in World War I was no different. The Russians denounced Germany's Kaiser Wilhelm as the Antichrist. The Germans equated Britain with the great whore of Babylon described in Revelation. English bishops preached to their countrymen that they were God's "predestined instruments to save the Christian civilization of Europe," while the German Protestant clergy promoted the values of nationalism, militarism, and imperialism because they were directly employed by the state to promote the war.[993]

Unfortunately, the followers of Judaism, Islam, Hinduism, and Buddhism are guilty of the same sin against humanity. Therefore, it was only a small leap forward to believing, as did the Nazis, that white people (Aryans) were created as a superior race by God or that the Russians were "godless Communists, or Muslims are all evil terrorists as the Americans hold.

The Christian religions in WWI provided language, context, and justification for the war. The soldiers and citizens of the warring nations, living in a world gone mad, turned to their religions for something sacred to believe in. What they were offered for their solace was nothing more than a crude group sentiment channeled into the service of their nation-state. Religion had lost all sense of humanity. People should know that it was not God that died, but the religions that marched their Christian soldiers into hell and abandoned them there.

The common people were mollified by preposterous stories of dead soldiers rising to fight again, or rumors of appearances of angels, Jesus or, Mary. Metals of saints were kept as good luck charms along with anything else that made one feel lucky. Some read the Bible or Quran for comfort.

The polarization of the mind that occurs in conditions that demand one to kill or be killed has always indicated a loss of reason and sense of humanity. When such a mind state exists across entire populations, we can say that the world has gone insane. Now people cease to be people and become inert symbols of God or the Devil.

Wartime governments found willing clergies to perpetuate the idea of holy war. Countless sermons and articles reveal just how far the clergy would go to justify earthly warfare. When we examine the assumptions of the mainstream churches at the time, we see how closely the Christian tradition merges in allegiance with the militant state, and how easily such militancy erupts in times of crisis. Nationalism, militarism, and imperialism are encoded in the DNA of the white man's world. This is why our children adapt to it so easily as they grow up. Racism, sexism, religious hatred, and xenophobia are the stock in trade that justifies our encoding. Unfortunately, we can no longer solve the problems that confront humanity today with such a worthless collection of tools.

The Muslims in the War fared no better than those under the sway of Christian churches. World War I led to the final collapse and dismemberment of the Ottoman Empire. With it, came the end of the caliphate and the symbolic and religious center that it represented. This sent Muslims on a quest for a new source of legitimacy and authority—a quest that has not been satisfied to this day. Muslims are still killing Muslims in a manner reminiscent of Christians killing Christians that began in the Middle Ages and has not ceased as we move into the twenty-first century. Christianity and Islam have both been nationalized and divided into competing brands. The religious institutions promote their brand name in order to sell their wares—their language, myths, and dogmas—to the highest authority where they are spun into justifications for political schemes, corporate exploitation, and military aggression.

While Germany, Austria-Hungary, Russia, and the Ottoman Empire lay in ruins, the people in the victorious countries mourned their losses in the name of a "good" cause.[994] The fallen soldiers had performed the "the most glorious form of public service and self-sacrifice."

African Americans in the War

World War I stemmed the flow of European immigrants into the United States at the same time that it increased the need for industrial workers in the Northeast and Midwest. This forced the previously segregated factories to hire African-Americans. Over the course of the war, large numbers of African-Americans moved from the former slave-holding South to the industrial Midwest and Northeast. So many African Americans made the journey north that the entire period is known as The Great Migration.[995]

The migration was a watershed in the history of African Americans. It lessened their overwhelming concentration in the South, opened up industrial jobs to people who had up to then been mostly farmers, and gave the first significant impetus to the full nationalization of the African-American population.

Before 1910, the black population of Chicago was two percent; by 1970 the figure was thirty-three percent. One of the great lasting legacies of World War I is its influence on the racial makeup of the United States.

African-American soldiers had served in the United States Army long before WWI. Free blacks *and* slaves enlisted in state militias and the Continental Army during the American Revolution. So also, many fought in the Civil War and the Spanish-American War. But World War I marked a turning point for black soldiers, both on the battlefield and when they returned home.

Over two hundred thousand African-Americans fought with the American Expeditionary Force (AEF) in France. None of them fought alongside white American troops, however. Instead, fully segregated black units fought within the French Army and took orders from French commanders. This was part of the bargain struck by General Pershing to appease the French, who immediately needed fresh troops in the front lines. Mostly, however, it was a sign of how pervasively racist the United States was. White troops refused to fight alongside black troops, even though they were all fighting on the same side.

One hundred and seventy one African-Americans were awarded the French Legion of Honor for their heroism in battle, and the 369th Infantry, an all-black unit, was one of the most decorated American units of the war. At war's end, over six hundred African-Americans had been commissioned as officers, a rank denied to them before the war. Though still segregated and suffering terrible prejudice, black soldiers proved to the world that they stood as warriors with the best of them.

Even though black soldiers faced German bullets for their country and won decorations for bravery in Europe, back home in the United States, little had changed. Returning black soldiers continued to suffer terrible prejudice, harassment, and death in the South. Even though the National Association for the Advancement of Colored People (NAACP)[996] was quick to rise to the defense of aggrieved veterans, it only met with mixed success.

Angered by the fact that the French had treated blacks in a humane manner during the war, white mobs lynched seventy black veterans, many still in uniform, in the first year after the war. Many Americans of all races were appalled by this grave injustice and the beginning of the Civil Rights Movement was set in motion. The terrible treatment of returning black World War I veterans would profoundly effect race relations in all parts of the country for decades to come.[997]

Women in World War I

The rise of women in the US quickened during the Progressive era when Teddy Roosevelt cut his deal with J. P. Morgan to create a partnership between the monopoly capitalists and the federal government. At this time, women's movements won victories in their efforts to involve the federal government in social services, particularly education, sanitation, health, wages, working conditions, and social welfare.

When the United States entered the war in 1917, women supported the war effort in numerous ways. In addition to continuing their pre-war reform work, women's groups sold war bonds and conserved food. Some groups sent relief supplies to suffering Europeans. Others sent delegations to Europe to provide relief for American soldiers.

The government, realizing that they could not fight without the help of women, established an advisory committee called the Women's Committee of the Council of National Defense. It was headed by suffragist Dr. Anna Shaw with the purpose to coordinate women's war efforts. The Committee had several areas of emphasis: Americanization, Child Welfare, Educational Propaganda, Food Administration, Food Production, Foreign and Allied Relief, Health and Recreation, Registration, Women in Industry, and the Maintenance of Existing Social Agencies. The Woman's Committee struggled with establishing its authority over this work, however, because it lacked clear direction from the federal government.[998]

Total war demanded the mobilization of all the nation's resources for a common goal. Soldiers had to be sent to the front lines. Behind the lines, on the home front, labor power had to be redirected from peace time to war time production. In particular, vast munitions industries had to be built to provide shells, guns, warships, uniforms, airplanes, and a hundred other weapons, both old and new. Agriculture had to be mobilized as well, to provide food for civilians, soldiers and farm animals, including horses that were still being used to move supplies.

During the war, women mobilized to keep the home front operating. They entered the workforce in almost every capacity. Many were recruited into factory jobs vacated by men who had gone to fight in the war.

Fig. 4-36: Woman at Work in a Factory in WWI

The high demand for weapons, for example, resulted in the munitions factories becoming the largest single employer of women during 1918. American women produced eighty percent of the weapons and shells used by the British Army. The TNT (trinitrotoluene) caused the women's skin to turn yellow and they became known as "canaries." The women risked their lives working with poisonous substances without adequate protective clothing or the required safety measures. Nearly four hundred died from overexposure to TNT during WWI.[999]

Women were also recruited by the government to work as railway guards and ticket collectors, bus and tram conductors, postal workers, police, firefighters, and as bank 'tellers' and clerks. Some women also worked with heavy or precision machinery in high-end production.

Some took over the production of farms to keep food on the table for the civilian population and also to send to the troops abroad. Still others were employed as civil service workers. For the first time ever, department stores employed African American women as elevator operators and cafeteria waitresses.[1000]

The women received lower wages for doing the same work as men, and this led to the earliest struggle for equal pay, a fight that exists to this day.

Some women also joined the military and thousands served as nurses abroad. The draft began in the spring of 1917. Four million men and thousands of women joined the Armed Services for the duration of the war.[1001] By the summer of 1918, American soldiers under General Pershing were arriving in France at the rate of ten thousand a day.[1002]

World War I had a profound impact on woman suffrage across the warring countries. Many countries recognized their sacrifices by giving them the vote during or shortly after the war, including the United States, Britain, Canada (except Quebec), Denmark, Austria, the Netherlands, Germany, Russia, Sweden, and Ireland. France almost did, but stopped short. It would not be until World War II, when women could vote in France.

The Economics of World War I

The Powers in 1914 expected a short war; none had stockpiled food or critical raw materials. Everyone believed that the "Boys would be home by Christmas." The main focus of the governments was on mobilization. They wanted to keep up the short-term confidence of the people and maintain the long-term power of the political establishment. The long-term economic health of the nation seemed less a concern as the nations plunged into war.

The Allies spent an estimated one hundred and forty-seven billion dollars on the war and the Central Powers sixty-one billion dollars. When the war ended, the Allies expected Germany to make reparations for their costs.

By 1916, *Britain* was funding most of the Allies war expenditures, including all of Italy's (Italy had abandoned the Central Powers at the start of the war, and joined the Allies later), two thirds of the war costs

Fig 4-37: Navy Recruitment Poster

of France and Russia, and the costs of smaller nations as well. Their gold reserves, overseas investments, and private credit ran out after about a year and forced England to borrow four billion dollars from the US Treasury in 1917–18.[1003] American shipments of raw materials and food allowed Britain to feed itself and its army while maintaining her domestic productivity.

The government had to contend with the spread of revolutionary socialist ideas among the working class. To counter these ideas, the government encouraged trade unions as an alternative. Union membership in England grew from 4.1 million in 1914 to 6.5 million in 1918, and peaked at 8.3 million in 1920 before relapsing to 5.4 million in 1923.

Energy was a critical factor for the British war effort. Most of the energy supplies came from coal mines in Britain, but they also needed oil for ships, trucks and industrial use. Because there were no oil wells in Britain, it had to be imported. In 1917, total British consumption was eight hundred and twenty-seven million barrels, of which eighty-five percent was supplied by the United States, and six percent by Mexico. The biggest concern regarding energy supplies in 1917 was how many tankers would survive the German U-boat attacks. The attacks came to be offset by the creation of convoys and the construction of new tankers.

In *Scotland*, the shipyards increased production by one-third and supplied the transport ships for England as quickly as the Germans could destroy them. Confident of postwar expansion, the companies borrowed heavily to expand their facilities. But after the war, employment tumbled as the yards proved too big, too expensive, and too inefficient. Demand for ships also fell. The most skilled craftsmen were especially hard hit, because there were few alternative uses for their specialized skills.[1004]

Canada was prosperous during the war but ethnic conflict between the English and the French escalated almost out of control.[1005] The war hardly affected the direction or the speed of the overall economy. Business, finance and technology continued at pace. Women temporarily took war jobs, and at the end of the war there was a great deal of unrest among union members and farmers for a few years.[1006]

Australia entered the war to support the mother country and also to improve its economy. The government sought to create new industries, gain control of the German colony of New Guinea, and secure high prices for their exports. While the government aggressively promoted industrial modernization, it was also guilty of exclusion and repression. The war turned a peaceful nation into one that was violent, aggressive, anxious, conflict-ridden, and torn apart by ethnic conflict and socio-economic and political upheaval.[1007]

In 1914 the Australian economy was small, but the population of five million was very nearly the most prosperous in the world per capita. The nation depended on the export of wool, mutton, wheat, and minerals. London provided assurances that it would underwrite the war risk insurance for shipping in order to allow trade amongst the Commonwealth to continue in the face of the German U-boat threat. On the whole, Australian commerce expanded. Australian exports rose almost forty-five per cent, while the number of Australians employed in the manufacturing industry increased over eleven per cent. Unfortunately, because the government wanted to keep the cost of their exports low, the cost of living for many average Australians decreased.

The trade union movement split on the question of conscription, which led to violent opposition. Between 1914 and 1918 there were 1,945 industrial disputes, resulting in 8,533,061 working days lost and £4,785,607 in lost wages.[1008]

This resulted in a 9.5 percent decline in the Gross Domestic Product between 1914 and 1920. Per capita incomes also fell by 16 percent.

South Africa's main economic role was to supply two-thirds of the gold production in the British Empire. When the war began, the Bank of England worked with the government of South Africa to block any gold shipments to Germany and forced the mine owners to sell only to the British Treasury, at prices set by the Treasury. This ensured capital to facilitate the purchases of munitions and food from the US and other neutrals. By 1919, however, London lost control of the mining companies, which were now backed by the South African government. They wanted the higher prices and sales that the New York free market would provide.

The Germans invaded *Belgium* at the start of the war and held the country for the entire war. They stripped it bare in what became known as "*The Rape of Belgium.*"[1009] The German army engaged in systematic atrocities against the civilian population and the mass destruction of property. In 1914 alone, they killed six thousand Belgians and destroyed twenty-five thousand homes in eight hundred and thirty-seven separate communities. Throughout the whole war, the Germans killed almost one hundred thousand people. One and a half million people (twenty percent of the entire population) fled from the invading German army. There was never an armed resistance movement, but there was a large-scale refusal to work for the benefit of Germany. While farm life continued and small shops stayed open, most factories shut down or drastically reduced their output. Intellectuals closed their universities and publishers shut down their newspapers. In 1916, Germany deported one hundred and twenty thousand men and boys to work in Germany. This act outraged neutral countries and they were returned. Germany then stripped the factories of all useful machinery, and used the rest as scrap iron for its steel mills.[1010]

With the German invasion, the National Bank's reserves were transferred to Antwerp and eventually to England where they were deposited at the Bank of England. Throughout the German occupation, there was a shortage of official coins and banknotes in circulation, and about six hundred municipalities, local governments, and companies issued their own unofficial "Necessity Money" to enable the continued functioning of the local economies.

Some businesses collaborated with the Germans, and some women cohabitated with them. They were treated roughly in a wave of popular violence in November and December 1918. The government set up judicial proceedings to punish the collaborators.

Neutral countries led by the United States set up the *Commission for Relief in Belgium*, headed by American engineer Herbert Hoover. It shipped in large quantities of food and medical supplies, which it tried to reserve for civilians and keep out of the hands of the Germans.[1011]

Rubber had long been the main export of the *Belgian Congo*, but during the war, cooper exports soared from nine hundred and ninety-seven tons in 1911 to twenty-seven thousand tons in 1917. Before the war the copper was sold to Germany, but in order to prevent loss of capacity, the British purchased all the Congo's wartime output with the revenues going to the Belgian government in exile. Diamond and gold mining also expanded during the war. The Anglo-Dutch firm Lever Brothers expanded their palm oil business and there was an increased output of cocoa, rice, and cotton. New rail and steamship lines opened to handle the expanded export traffic.[1012]

In *France*, when the Germans invaded the country, they captured forty percent of the country's heavy industry, including steel and coal. France's GDP dropped by twenty-four percent during the war and the people's standard of living fell by fifty percent. Yet, as a testament to human resilience in dire circumstances, thousands of small factories opened up across the country and hired men, women, and teenagers to meet people's basic needs. Algerian and Vietnamese laborers were also brought in to help replace the men who were fighting on the front. Miraculously, with the help of finance and raw materials from Britain and the US, the French produced enough artillery, tanks, and airplanes to equip not only their own army but the United States as well. The network of small plants produced two hundred thousand 75mm shells each day.

After 1917, American loans were used to purchase food and household goods that increased the standard of living. The arrival of over a million American soldiers in 1918 also meant heavy spending on local food and construction materials. Labor shortages were in part alleviated by the use of women, young people, and volunteer workers from the French colonies.[1013]

J. P. Morgan & Co. of New York was the major American financier for the Allies. The war in Europe required England and France to go heavily into debt. When their respective central banks and local merchant banks could no longer meet that need, the beleaguered governments turned to the Americans and selected the House of Morgan, the acting partner of the Rothschilds, to be the sales agent for their bonds. The money raised in this fashion was quickly returned to the House of Morgan to purchase weaponry and war materials. Because Morgan was selected as the US purchase agent for these weapons, etc., a commission was paid on all transactions in both directions—once when the money was borrowed and again when it was spent. It is not surprising that many of the companies that received the production contracts from Morgan were either owned outright by Morgan holding companies or were within his orbit of bank control. Under such an arrangement, it is not surprising to learn that despite the death of millions, including the death of Americans, Morgan was not overly anxious to see World War I come to an end.[1014]

The *Russian* economy was unprepared for a major war. Although the Russian soldiers fought well, the army was poorly organized and lacked weaponry. Casualties were enormous because many soldiers were sent to the front unarmed. They were told to pick up whatever weapons they could find from the battlefield. Such was the disrespect for the common man on the part of the Russian aristocracy before the Revolution.

Italy joined the Allies in 1915, but like Russia, was poorly prepared for war even thought loans from Britain paid for nearly all its war expenses. The Italian army lacked leadership and was short on heavy artillery and machine guns. The industrial base was too small to provide adequate amounts of modern equipment, and the rural base barely produced enough food.

The Italian war effort was also hindered by the socialist working class, who opposed the war. To win converts, the government introduced high wage scales and collective bargaining. The war industry then grew significantly. At Fiat, for example, the workforce grew from four thousand to forty thousand. While inflation doubled the cost of living, the industrial wages kept pace, but the farmers were left out, leading to discontent in the countryside.

Because *Germany* had long prepared for the war, it rapidly mobilized its soldiers, but the conversion of the civilian economy to a wartime economy was more difficult and it was greatly hampered by the British blockade that cut off food supplies, raw materials, and machinery from its allies and colonies.

The War Ministry set up a War Raw Materials Department to keep the civilian economy supplied but greed on the part of the German capitalists in commerce and industry, and complex regulations on the part of the government, made the Department inefficient. This resulted in the creation of two dozen additional agencies to deal with specific products. Cartels were set up by the government for greater ease of central control.

Total spending by the national government reached one hundred and seventy billion marks during the war, of which taxes only covered eight percent. Unlike the French government, which imposed an income tax to pay for the war, the German Emperor and the Reichstag decided to fund the war entirely by borrowing. They believed that the government would be able to pay off the debt by annexing resource-rich industrial territory to the west and east and by imposing massive reparations on the defeated Allies. The strategy backfired catastrophically when Germany lost the war. The new Weimar Republic,[1015] which was the constitutional assembly that replaced the Kaiser after his abnegation, was now saddled with a massive war debt that it could not afford. Because Germany had floated its currency against gold at the beginning of the war, it was now in the position of having to print money with no resources to back it up.[1016] The Treaty of Versailles,[1017] which ended the state of war between Germany and the Allies, set onerous terms of reparation from the Central Powers.

Because the western theatre of warfare during World War I was mostly fought in France and Belgium, Germany came out of the war with most of its industrial infrastructure intact and in a better position to become the dominant economic force on the European continent. However, the

London Schedule of Payments, sometimes called *The London Ultimatum* of May 1921, demanded reparations in gold or foreign currency to be paid in annual installments of two billion gold marks plus twenty-six percent of the value of Germany's exports.

The reparations for the Central Powers was calculated at one hundred and thirty-two billion gold marks. This figure was divided into three series of bonds: "A" and "B" Bonds together had a nominal value of fifty billion gold marks (US $12.5 billion). "C" Bonds, comprised the remainder of the reparation figure, but these bonds were completely fabricated to mislead public opinion "into believing that the one hundred and thirty-two-billion-mark figure was being maintained".[1018] The Allies knew that Germany could not pay one hundred and thirty-two billion marks and that the other Central Powers could pay little. Thus the A and B Bonds, which were genuine, represented the actual Allied assessment of German capacity to pay. Taking into account the sum already paid between 1919 and 1921, Germany's immediate obligation was forty-one billion gold marks.

German currency was relatively stable at about ninety marks per US dollar during the first half of 1921. The first payment was made when it came due in June 1921. Immediately the German currency (mark) began to deteriorate, falling in value to less than one third of a cent by November. Because reparations were required to be repaid in hard currency (gold) which the Germans did not have, the government began the mass printing of paper marks to buy foreign currency, which was in turn used to pay reparations. This greatly exacerbated the inflation rate of the paper mark.

Beginning in August 1921, Germany began to buy foreign currency with marks at any price, but that only increased the speed of breakdown in the value of the mark. The lower the mark sank in international markets, the greater the amount of marks was required to buy the foreign currency demanded by the Reparations Commission.

During the first half of 1922, the mark stabilized at about three hundred and twenty marks per dollar. In January 1923, French and Belgian troops, believing that they would not get paid their due reparations, occupied the Ruhr Valley, the industrial region of Germany. In protest, the German workers in the Ruhr went on a general strike and the government printed more money to pay their wages, in support of their "passive resistance."

By the end of 1923, the mark stood at 4,210,500,000,000 German marks per dollar.[1019] Many of us have seen photographs of German citizens pushing wheel barrels loaded with marks to buy a loaf of bread. This phenomenon became known as "hyper-inflation." It was due to the constant printing of paper money without anything of value to support the money. The mark became worth so little that people used it for wallpaper or burned it in metal barrels to keep warm.

In the *Ottoman Empire*, Turkish nationalists (The Young Turks) seized control of the government and replaced the absolute monarchy with a constitutional government. As part of their new administration, they instituted a policy of ethnic cleansing against the Greeks and Armenian populations inside Turkey that began as removal and confiscation of property and ultimately ended in genocide. The Greek and Armenian populations had been the backbone of the business community and were now replaced by ethnic Turks who were given favorable contracts, but who lacked the international connections, credit sources, and entrepreneurial skills needed for business.[1020] The Armenian homeland was within the borders of the Ottoman empire (Turkey) at the time, so the Armenians had no country to return to as did the Greeks. In response to this situation, the Turks systematically massacred the Armenian population. The number of victims is estimated at between 800,000 to 1.5 million men, women, and children. The massacres began in April 1915, when the authorities rounded up, arrested, and deported some two hundred and fifty Armenian intellectuals and community leaders from Constantinople to Ankara, the majority of whom were eventually murdered. The genocide was carried out during and after World War I. The able-bodied male population was either massacred or subjected to forced labor. The women, children, elderly, and infirm were deported in death marches that led into the Syrian desert. Driven forward by military escorts, the deportees were deprived of food and water and subjected to periodic robbery, rape, and massacre. Most Armenian Diaspora communities around the world came into being as a direct result of the genocide.[1021]

The Ottoman economy, at the time, was based on subsistence agriculture with very little industry. When the war cut off imports, except from Germany, prices quadrupled. The Germans provided loans and supplied the army with hardware captured from the Belgians and Russians. Nonetheless, the soldiers were in rags. Medical services were very bad and illness and death rates were high. Most of the Ottoman soldiers deserted when they had the opportunity, so the size of the army shrank from a peak strength of eight hundred thousand in 1916 to only one hundred thousand in 1918.[1022]

Compared to Germany and Britain, the economy of *Austria-Hungary* lagged behind because industrialization had begun much later there. Even so, the empire built up the fourth-largest machine building industry of the world, after the United States, Germany, and Britain.

By the end of the nineteenth century, economic differences between Austria and Hungary gradually began to even out as the strong agriculture and food industry of the Kingdom of Hungary became dominant within the empire and made up a large proportion of the empire's exports. At the same time, Austria excelled in various manufacturing industries. The division of labor between the east and west worked to both countries advantage.

During the war the national governments in Vienna and Budapest created a highly centralized war economy that essentially became a bureaucratic dictatorship. The Czech region, north of Austria also had an advanced economy, but it was reluctant to support the war. The Czechs wanted nothing to do with Germany, which it saw as a threat to its language and culture. Czech bankers plotted for an early independence. They purchased many securities from the Czech lands, thus ensuring their strong domestic position in what became Czechoslovakia in 1918.

Bulgaria, a poor rural nation of 4.5 million people, at first stayed neutral. In 1915, however, it joined the Central Powers. It mobilized a very large army of eight hundred thousand men, using equipment supplied by Germany. Even so, Bulgaria was unprepared for a long war. The loss of so many men to the military sharply reduced agricultural output, and much of what was harvested was smuggled out of the country to feed black markets that paid a higher price for the food. By 1918, the soldiers were not only short of basic clothing, but also they were being fed mostly on corn bread. The peace treaty with the Allied Powers in 1919 [1023] stripped Bulgaria of its conquest territories, reduced its army to twenty thousand men, and demanded reparations of one hundred million pounds.

When the *United States* entered the war, confusion prevailed. Nobody knew what to do or who was in charge. The federal bureaucracy that Teddy Roosevelt sought to create was still in its infancy and competitive cartels were not willing to coordinate with each other. An example of this can be seen in the coal shortage that hit the country in December 1917. Coal was the major source of energy and heat and while there was plenty of coal being mined, forty-four thousand loaded freight and coal cars were tied up in horrendous traffic jams in the rail yards of the East Coast.[1024] Two hundred ships were waiting in New York harbor for cargo that was delayed by this mass inefficiency. To solve the problem, the government nationalized the coal mines and the railroads for the duration of the war.

When the war began, the US economy was in recession. But the war created a four year economic boom between 1914 and 1918. Initially, the Europeans began purchasing US goods for the war. This caused US manufacturing to grow. It also grew in exactly those industries that would be needed when the US itself entered the war.[1025]

Secondly, when the US did enter the war in 1917, a massive amount of federal spending was unleashed as the economy shifted from the production of civilian goods to war goods. Around three million men and women were added to the military and half a million were added to the government to coordinate the war effort. Unemployment declined from 7.9 percent to 1.4 percent in this period, as the number of workers expanded to take on the new manufacturing jobs, while the military draft removed many young men from the civilian labor force. During the war years, wages rose in the industrial sector by six or seven percent per year. This, plus the fact that finding work was so easy, drew many additional workers into the labor force.[1026]

This is the major reason that the American Federation of Labor (AFL), and nearly all other labor unions strongly supported the war. The war drew the country out of recession and eliminated workers strikes as wages were increased and full employment was reached. President Wilson appointed Samuel Gompers,[1027] the founder and president of the AFL, to the powerful Council of National Defense. The AFL membership soared to 2.4 million in 1917 and the union even encouraged its members to enlist in the military. However, in 1919, after the war, when the capitalists no longer needed the cooperation of labor, wages fell. The Union fought back by calling a series of major strikes in meat, steel, and other industries in order to make their gains permanent, but the strikes failed and the unions were forced back to an even weaker position than they had held prior to the war.[1028]

Not all labor unions were pro-war, however. The socialist Industrial Workers of the World (IWW) remained an anti-capitalist, anti-war union all throughout the war. The union was led by people like Eugene V. Debs[1029] of the Socialist Party and Daniel De Leon of the Socialist Labor Party. Also present were Mother Jones, the "angel of the miners," and Lucy Parsons, whose husband had been executed in the Haymarket affair.[1030] The "Wobblies," as they were called, tried to tell the working class that the war was a "boss's war." Many of its members refused the draft and organized strikes in opposition to the AFL policy. The union has some success in organizing industries critical to the war effort and this led to the arrest of many of its leaders under provisions of the controversial Espionage Act.[1031] The union called its philosophy "revolutionary industrial unionism" and although it never achieved its goals, many of its ideas, like the "sitdown strike," were adopted by the CIO (Congress of Industrial Organizations), which like the Wobblies before them, was made up of unskilled workers. Later the CIO would merge with the AFL.

The total cost of World War I to the United States was approximately thirty-two billion dollars, or fifty-two percent of the gross national product at the time. By contrast, the cost of WWII was three hundred and forty-one billion or forty-two percent of GDP and the War in Iraq, cost two trillion dollars or one percent of GDP.

In terms of the value of the dollar, WWI had an extravagant price tag. How did the US pay for this war, considering that it was in a recession when the war began? Twenty-two percent was raised by taxes, twenty percent by money creation and fifty-eight percent through borrowing. To raise money from taxes, the War Revenue Act of 1917 created a progressive taxation system. Corporations were taxed on profits that exceeded a certain rate of return per industry (twenty to sixty percent) within a base period. The tax on individuals with incomes starting at fifty thousand dollars (one-half of one percent of the population) rose from 1.5 percent in 1914 to more than 18 percent in 1918. The great majority of American workers at the time made between one thousand dollars and four thousand dollars per year.[1032]

Borrowing was facilitated by the peddling of war bonds. Hollywood stars and Boy Scouts were enlisted in the promotion of the bonds. Patriotic themes, like "Liberty bonds" or "Victory bonds" created social pressure to purchase them. The government knew, however, that patriotism was not sufficient to alter the market prices of assets and therefore made the yields on the bonds comparable to any standard municipal bond.[1033]

During the war, the production of bonds now had to go through the hands of the new Federal Reserve Board. The government would sell a bond (IOU) to the newly created Federal Reserve that would create a deposit in the Bank which the government could now draw from to pay its expenses. In the end, the result would be much the same as if the government had simply printed greenbacks, i.e., the government would be paying for the war with newly created money. The difference was that now the Bank got an interest payment from every IOU the government issued.[1034]

There was considerable debate at the time as to whether the war should be funded by raising taxes or borrowing from the public. Most economists at the time believed that raising taxes was best. There was a long tradition that supported this viewpoint. Among the supporting ideas for this tradition was that it would be unfair to draft men into the armed forces and then expect them to come home and pay higher taxes to fund the interest and principal of the war bonds. Treasury Secretary William Gibbs McAdoo thought that financing about fifty percent from taxes and fifty percent from bonds would be about right. He argued that financing more from taxes, especially progressive taxes, would anger the wealthy class and undermine their support for the war. This is an interesting possibility to consider. Would the war have ended sooner and more lives saved if the ruling class had withdrawn its support of the war? Probably not, because the war meant huge profits for the rich, as the example of J. P. Morgan showed. Why would they withdraw their support for the war?

As it was, the bonds were tax-exempt and the wealthy got a great deal by holding them. The socialists criticized the government for imposing "high" taxes on the wealthy while at the same time creating a loophole for them to avoid taxes. The Federal Reserve also bought many of the bonds, which as we have seen allowed it to create new money. Some of this "high powered money" augmented the reserves of the commercial banks, which allowed them to buy bonds or to finance their purchase by private citizens. Thus, directly or indirectly, the bonds were also just another form of money creation for the war rather than savings by the general public. But there was a price for this sleight of hand that later was paid for by the working people in the form of lower wages after the war, poor social services, and, ultimately, the Great Depression.

One of the problems of central banks, like the Fed, is that they can make the fighting of wars extremely easy by increasing the money supply very quickly. The money supply rose from $20.7 billion in 1916 to $35.1 billion in 1920 (about seventy percent). At the same time, however, the price level increased by eighty-five percent. Although money increased quickly, prices rose even faster. This inflation was another real cost to the American people.

The worst cost of WWI to the American people, however, was the loss of life and the destruction of families. Almost one hundred thousand soldiers died in battle or from disease. Another quarter of a million were wounded or handicapped.[1035]

Postwar

It is not facetious to say that the US monopoly capitalists "made a killing" in WWI. After the war, Europe was decimated and the reparations that were imposed on Germany at the Treaty of Versailles were supposed to help rebuild the damage to civilian economies. Not surprisingly, little of the reparation payments were used for this purpose. Germany had to borrow money from American banks to make their reparation payments. In turn, the recipients of the payments had to use the money to pay off their loans to the US bankers. Between 1919 and 1932, Germany paid out nineteen billion gold marks in reparations, and received twenty-seven billion gold marks in loans from New York bankers and others. It took Germany until 2010 to pay back these loans.[1036]

Before entering the war, Americans were indebt $2.2 billion. By 1919, the Americans were *creditors* to the tune of $6.4 billion. Before the war, the center of the world capital market was London and the Bank of England was the world's most important financial institution. After the war, New York became the financial capital of the world and the Federal Reserve Bank became the most important financial institution on the planet.

Another significant change was that the war created an agglomeration of Federal agencies, which now led people to believe that the government could serve a positive role in the economy. While this lesson remained dormant during the roaring 1920s, it resurfaced when the United States stared into the black pit of the Great Depression. In effect, the federal government declared war on the Depression by creating federal agencies to fight it. Many of these agencies and programs reflected precedents set during World War I. The Civilian Conservation Corps attempted to achieve the benefits of military training in a civilian setting. The National Industrial Recovery Act reflected the War Industries Board, and the Agricultural Adjustment Administration hearkened back to the Food Administration. The partnership role of the federal government in the success of state monopoly capitalism in the United States just took another big "Mother may I" step forward.[1037]

The Great Depression

The decade that followed the war is called the "Roaring Twenties." It was a time when Americans were rich and self-confident and for the first time more people lived in cities than in rural areas. The economy boomed as the war debts of other countries were repaid and jobs were created to transition the economy back to civilian life. As the civilian economy expanded, the American *consumer economy* was born. People learned to buy products over time by using "installment plans." They bought refrigerators, cars, etc., with money they did not have. They could simply make a monthly, weekly, or yearly payment on an item that they wanted or needed. This happened until Black Tuesday, 1929 when the stock market crashed. The system of installment buying resulted in millions of people finding themselves in debt. Many also lost their jobs and could not pay the debts they had incurred.[1038] Nonetheless, during the 20s, the expansion of credit and the availability of a wide selection of consumer goods led to a collective exuberance in which a unique American pop culture came into being. Women who lived in the cities and had worked in the factories during the war years now had money of their own, and with this new freedom came a new and vital self-confidence. As Cyndi Lauper said, girls just want to have fun. They began to express themselves in ways they were never able to do before. And as we know, whenever the girls are having fun, the boys are too.

Fig. 4-38: 1920's Flapper

The twenties are famous for vaudeville, flappers, dance halls, movie palaces, start of radio empires, speak easies, and illegal booze. Thanks to the inventions of radio and movies, a single American culture began to ripple across the American continent. People now sang the same songs, did the same dances, and used the same slang. Black Americans experienced their own cultural renaissance. In New York City, Harlem became a cultural center for black writers, artists, musicians, photographers, poets, and scholars.[1039] Harlem gave rise to the jazz age and young white aristocrats rushed into Harlem on the weekends to party, listen to jazz singers, and dance at the Cotton

Club where Duke Ellington, Cab Calloway, and Ethel Waters, among other greats, performed.[1040]

The rapid rise of pop culture, consumer culture, and the increased freedom of expression achieved by women and blacks challenged the established order and created a massive conservative backlash. The same decade that bore witness to urban culture and greater sexual freedom also introduced the authoritarianism of the Ku Klux Klan, Prohibition, nativism (a return to traditional white racist culture), and religious fundamentalism. The conservatives were caught up in a bitter and angry reaction to anything they did not understand and viewed as a challenge to their limited worldview. As is so evident today, while many Americans were looking boldly into the future, many others were looking backward out of fear of losing their power and their cherished traditions. The contradiction between authoritarianism versus freedom occurs whenever large changes happen in society.

What is not generally known is that America entered the 1920s in a short depression that lasted for fourteen months after the end of World War I. It was the time when the war economy ground to a halt, but the civilian economy had not yet started to grow.[1041] Returning soldiers flooded the job market driving down wages. At the same time, businesses continued to charge wartime prices, which the domestic population, many of whom were unemployed, could no longer afford. Fewer sales meant the businesses could not pay their bills and many were forced to close their doors in failure. Conflicting economic theories emerged as to how to solve the problem.

Inflation during the 1920s

Conservatives like to point out how President Harding brought the country out of the depression that occurred at the end of WWI by essentially doing nothing to rectify it except to pay off government debt and keep labor in its place. Harding was certainly a conservative's dream president and his administration is often referred to as an example of a successful conservative strategy for running a government.

Here is the actually story of the activities of Harding's administration. Treasury Secretary Andrew Mellon, one of the original robber barons, began by reducing income taxes that had been raised during the war. He also drastically lowered corporate taxes on profits. The reduction of taxes put more money into circulation.

President Harding also advocated for an increase in tariffs on agricultural goods as a means to protect the American farmer. Additionally, he supported the building of highways, aviation, and radio. Harding's attitude toward business was that government should aid it as much as possible,[1042] and that organized labor was a conspiracy against business.[1043] Lack of support for the working man created strikes in the coal and railroad industries in 1922. In the steel mills, management's policy was to keep men working twelve hour days, seven days a week. Harding supported this policy, but the public was outraged and management, in response, reduced the work day to eight hours. We can see how this scenario concerning the Harding administration would gain admiration from conservatives and big business. What the conservative economists rarely include in their Roaring Twenties scenario is that the policies put in place by Andrew Mellon and President Harding would lead to the Great Depression that occurred at the end of the decade.

President Harding died after suffering a stroke in August 1923, and he was succeeded by Vice President Calvin Coolidge. Mellon enjoyed better relations with President Coolidge than he had with President Harding, and Coolidge and Mellon shared similar views on most major issues, including the necessity for further tax cuts.[1044] After Coolidge's presidency, Mellon went on to serve under Herbert Hoover the next president who was in office from 1929 to 1933, the years of the onset of the Great Depression.

Allen Greenspan, a former Chairman of the Fed and a scholar on post-WWI economics, has a different interpretation than the conservatives on how the Roaring 20s led to the Great Depression. According to Greenspan, the Great War had left Britain a basket case and the US government/Fed decided to help Britain recuperate. This decision led to events that caused the Great Depression. Here is how it happened.

Because countries at the time were on a fixed exchange rate with their currencies tied to gold, if a country's balance of trade with another country was negative, they could be required to ship their gold to that country to create a balance of payments. Britain had been sending gold to the US because of all the assistance it received during the war. Normally, when a country loses its gold, its currency, which is backed by gold, becomes more expensive because it is in shorter supply. Thus, interest rates rise as the competition for the scarce money increases. As it happened, however, the Bank of England did not want to raise interest rates on its money because the country was already in a depression from the war and charging a higher price for money would only make things worse. To assist Britain in its dilemma, Greenspan wrote:

> The reasoning of the authorities involved was as follows: if the Federal Reserve pumped excessive paper reserves into American banks, interest rates in the United States would fall to a level comparable with those in Great Britain; this would act to stop Britain's gold loss and avoid the political embarrassment of having to raise interest rates. The "Fed" succeeded; it stopped the gold loss, but it nearly destroyed the economies of the world, in the process. The excess credit with the Fed pumped into the economy spilled over into the stock market – triggering a fantastic speculative boom.[1045]

This account of events contradicts the official version of history that claims that the Fed and Hoover did not do enough to save the economy and their lack of involvement caused the world to fall into the Great Depression.

The Stock Market Crash of 1929

As American production rapidly increased, due to the infusion of excess cash by the Fed, people bought goods on credit, businesses flourished, and the price of stocks soared. Wall Street gambling on stocks went crazy. Rather than conservatively investing in companies for their long-term growth potential, traders gambled on stocks based upon market fluctuations and the herd instincts of fear and greed. By the latter part of the decade, "buying on margin" had entered the American vocabulary. This allowed more Americans to speculate on the soaring stock market. Buying on margin is essentially borrowing money from a broker to purchase stock. It is basically getting a loan from your broker, which allows you to buy more stock than you would be able to normally. If your stock rises, you then have more shares to sell. After paying your loan to the broker, you walk away with a bigger profit.

Borrowing money is not without its costs, however. To cover himself, the broker requires that you keep a minimum amount of money in your brokerage account to cover your interest payments to him. If you do not do this, the broker will force you to sell some or all of your stock to pay down your loan. This act is called a *margin call*.

You can keep your loan as long as you fulfill your obligations. When you sell the stock in a margin account, the proceeds must first go to your broker against the repayment of the loan until it is fully paid. The interest on your loan increases as your debt increases.[1046]

As the economy grew in the twenties, the stock market soared. Margin buying increased and soon the debt became enormous. Buying on margin increased the value of stocks as it allowed more money to be bet on them, but it also created inflated prices that were no longer in sync with the actual values of the companies represented by the stock. Very few expected the crash that began in 1929, and none suspected it would be so drastic or so prolonged.

As always, stock market crashes reflect changes that are going on within the economy itself. During the twenties, the American people possessed the strongest economy in the world and were certainly the richest people in the world. They thought the economy would keep growing forever. While some people celebrated this newfound freedom, others seethed in anger at the license afforded women, blacks, and liberal Christians. As the benefits of the consumer economy preoccupied peoples' daily lives and fostered their dreams of tomorrow, subtle cracks began to form in the foundation of the American economy. While farms and factories produced a never-ending stream of goods and products, people's wages stayed the same even while the prices for these goods continued to rise. People who lived on farms felt the pressure even more than the city dwellers.

There came a time, when some people could no longer pay for their basic needs, even with the benefit of installment buying. With little or no money, they stopped buying products. For awhile, factories and farms did not notice what was happening and continued to produce their goods at the same rate. When surplus products began to pile up in their bins and warehouses, however, they cut back on production. As they cut production, they laid off workers. This reduced demand for goods even more, and led to more layoffs.

In the summer of 1929, a few stock market investors began to sense the underlying weakness in the economy. They began to sell their stock. They believed that the bull market was ending, and they wanted to sell their stock before they would have to take a loss. Seeing these few investors begin to sell, others soon followed, creating a domino effect. The sudden selling, without buyers, caused stock prices to slide. President Herbert Hoover tried to reassure the investors. He told them that the country's economy was in fine shape and there was no reason to worry. People did not believe him and continued to sell.

Because many investors in the stock market had bought large amounts of stock on margin, the brokers now began to panic and put out margin calls requiring the investors to pay their debts. But they were too late. The investors could not repay their debt and were forced to sell their stocks, causing stock prices to fall even more.

On Tuesday, October 29, 1929, stock prices plummeted because there were no longer any buyers for the stocks offered by the desperate sellers. Forty billion dollars were lost in a single day due to the decrease in stock prices.[1047] By 1930, the value of shares had fallen by ninety percent.[1048]

The Next Three Years

The Stock Market Crash greatly exasperated the downturn of the economy that had already begun. Production continued to slow, unemployment continued to grow, and for those lucky enough to keep their jobs, wages fell and their buying power decreased. Middle class Americans, who had bought household items on credit or took out mortgages on their homes, fell into debt and bank foreclosures and repossessions climbed steadily.

In November 1929, President Herbert Hoover was telling the American people, "Any lack of confidence in the economic future or the basic strength of business in the United States is foolish." Nonetheless, the depression that followed would last for ten years and it would be the deepest and longest-lasting economic crisis in the history of the Western industrialized world.

Despite the President's assurances, matters continued to get worse over the next three years. By 1930, four million Americans were looking for work but could not find jobs. The number rose to six million in 1931. Twenty-five percent of the workforce was idle. The country's industrial production had dropped by half. Bread lines, soup kitchens, and rising numbers of homeless people became a common sight in America's towns and cities. Hundreds of thousands of Americans became homeless, and began congregating in shantytowns—dubbed "Hoovervilles"—that began to appear across the country. In response, President Hoover and Congress approved the Federal Home Loan Bank Act, to spur new home construction, and reduce foreclosures. Hoover also tried to stimulate the economy by passing the Emergency Relief and Construction Act (ERA), but his efforts amounted to too little too late. Farmers (who had been struggling with their own economic depression for much of the 1920s due to drought and falling food prices) now could not afford to harvest their crops. They left them rotting in the fields while people elsewhere starved.

In the fall of 1930, the bank panics began. Bank runs swept the United States as people tried desperately to withdraw their savings from banks but were unable to do so. By early 1933, thousands of banks had closed their doors. In the face of this dire situation, Hoover's administration tried to support these failing banks and other institutions by providing government loans. The idea was that the banks in turn would loan to businesses, which would be able to hire back their employees. His efforts were, however, inadequate for the task.

By now the street corners of New York City and other American cities were filled with people selling apples, pencils, etc., anything to make a few cents for a meal.

In January 1931, a Texas congressman, Wright Patman, introduced legislation authorizing immediate payment of "bonus" funds to World War I veterans. The "bonus" was equal to $1 a day for each day of service in the US, and $1.25 for each day overseas. President Hoover vetoed the bill saying it would cost the Treasury too much money.

"Food riots" began to break out across the country. As a parent in England, Arkansas put it: "Our children are crying for food and we are going to get it. We are not going to let our children starve." The newspapers carried a shocking story about a riot in Minneapolis where several hundred men and women smashed the windows of a grocery store and stole fruit, canned goods, bacon, and ham. The owner pulled out a gun to stop them but looters leapt on him and broke his arm. A hundred police showed up and seven people were arrested.[1049]

In the same year, Ray Wilbur, Secretary of the Interior, made the announcement, "There is no poverty in America," even though thousands of unemployed workers were looting food stores across the country. The food riots became so commonplace that the press stopped reporting on them.

Resentment of "foreign" workers increased. In Los Angeles, California, Mexican Americans were accused of stealing jobs from "real" Americans. In February of 1931 alone, 6,024 Mexican Americans were deported.

In December, New York's Bank of the United States collapsed. With over two hundred million dollars in deposits, it was the largest single bank failure in the nation's history.

The Republicans, including President Hoover, still believed that the worker's struggle for survival was good for them. According to Calvinist-derived capitalist ideology, struggle built strength and self-reliance. By 1932, however, even the Republicans saw that they had to do something quick or face national chaos and perhaps revolution. Hoover's first measure to combat the depression was to appeal to businesses not to reduce their workforce or cut wages. This failed for obvious reasons. His next step was to give money to big businesses, believing that these enterprises would create jobs and that money would begin to trickle down to the average American family. After three years of Depression, Congress passed the *Reconstruction Finance Corporation (RFC) Act*. The RFC lent money to businesses, agricultural organizations, and local governments. Again, the effort was insufficient for the tasks. The unions, which had already lost a third of their membership to unemployment, called the RFC the millionaires' dole.[1050]

Congress also passed the Norris-LaGuardia Anti-Injunction Act, which stopped management from forcing workers to sign anti-union pledges.[1051] It was of little help. In March 1932, three thousand unemployed workers marched on the Ford Motor Company's plant in River Rouge, Michigan. They carried signs that read, "Give Us Work," "We Want Bread Not Crumbs," and "Tax the Rich and Feed the Poor." The march was broken up by the Dearborn police and Ford's private security force. They attacked the workers, killed five and injured sixty more. The event came to be known as the *Ford Massacre*.[1052]

By mid-1932, almost three-quarters of a million people in New York City were dependent upon welfare relief, with an additional one hundred and sixty thousand on a waiting list. Expenditures averaged about $8.20 per month for each person on relief.[1053]

In June, twenty-five thousand WWI veterans, determined to collect a war bonus that had been promised to them by law, set up encampments near the White House and the Capitol in Washington, D.C. This led the House to pass Wright Patman's "bonus bill," but the bill was again defeated, this time by the Senate. The vets vowed to stay camped out until they got their pay. As a sop to the vets, President Hoover signed a one hundred thousand dollar transportation bill to assist the demonstrators in getting home. He set a July 24th deadline for the men to abandon their encampments. On July 28, when the vets resisted being moved from their camps, violence erupted, leading to the deaths of two veterans. Hoover ordered Federal troops, under the command of General Douglas MacArthur, to assist D.C. police in clearing the veterans. One thousand soldiers accompanied by tanks and machine guns came in and destroyed the camps.[1054] This was a great example of how the troops lacked a class consciousness. In a version of Jay Gould's famous quote, the government could hire half the working class to kill the other half.

In November, Franklin Delano Roosevelt was elected president in a landslide over Herbert Hoover. During the campaign, Roosevelt had repeatedly blamed Hoover for the Depression and the worsening economy. With unemployment above twenty percent in 1932, Hoover had little to say in his own defense. Roosevelt promised recovery with a *New Deal* for the American people. His campaign song was "Happy Days Are Here Again."[1055]

Speaking to a large crowd during his inauguration, Roosevelt told the crowd: "The people of the United States have not failed. In their need they have registered a mandate that they want direct, vigorous action. They have asked for discipline and direction under leadership. They have made me the present instrument of their wishes. In the spirit of the gift I take it."[1056]

Roosevelt argued that a fundamental restructuring of the economy would be necessary to end the depression and also to prevent another depression. When he took office, his New Deal strategy used the federal government to develop programs that made concrete connections to the actual lives of everyday citizens.

His New Deal programs sought to stimulate demand by focusing on meeting people's basic needs and to provide work and relief for the impoverished through increased government spending and the institution of financial reforms. In other words, he believed that unadulterated capitalism had caused the depression and would continue to create more depressions in the future if there was not a strong intervention on the part of the federal government to curb its excesses and clean up its mess.

Saving the Banks

FDR got right to work. He announced a four-day "bank holiday" to begin on Monday, March 6, promising that Congress was developing a plan to save the failing banking industry. Across the country, there had been a steady run on banks that had caught the banks unprepared to meet the demand for cash and gold. This happened to most banks because they were only legally responsible to keep ten percent of the people's cash as reserves. Consequently, many banks were forced to close their doors.

Congress passed the Emergency Banking Act of 1933,[1057] in the same month that allowed the twelve Federal Reserve Banks to issue additional currency on good assets so that banks that were still solvent could reopen their doors and be able to pay the people the cash they wanted. By month's end, three-quarters of the nation's banks that had been closed were back in business. What saved the banking system was the fact that the federal government was willing to go into debt without limit in order to get the Fed to supply unlimited amounts of currency to reopened the banks. This act effectively provided a one hundred percent deposit insurance that would lead to the creation of the Federal Deposit Insurance Corporation[1058] as part of the 1933 Banking Act (Glass-Seagall Act)[1059] that was passed later in the year.

Because the government had acted to restore faith in the banking system, as soon as the banks opened for business after the four-day bank holiday, many depositors stood in line to return their cash to neighborhood banks. Within two weeks, Americans had redeposited more than half of the currency they had withdrawn from the banks.

In 1934, Congress passed the Gold Reserve Act that required all gold and gold certificates held by the Federal Reserve Bank to be surrendered to the US Treasury. They were able to accomplish this because the American people were angry and attributed the depression to the mismanagement of monetary policy by the Bank. Roosevelt argued that because there was not enough gold to pay all holders of gold certificates that the federal government should keep all of the gold. The Act made it illegal for citizens to own gold. All confiscated gold was sent to a bullion depository at Fort Knox. The Act also changed the value of gold from $20.67 per troy ounce to $35 in order to give foreign investors an incentive to export their gold to America. These actions resulted in a large accumulation of gold in the US Treasury. This stockpile of gold allowed the government to issue more paper money and reduce the cost of money, thereby stimulating the economy.[1060]

Fireside Chats

FDR made excellent use of the new mass media, radio, to reach out to the people of America. He held thirty different "fireside chats" with millions of Americans between 1933 and 1944. "It was the first time in history that a large segment of the population could listen directly to a chief executive," wrote radio historian John Dunning.[1061] No other president in history had such an intimate relationship with the people. Roosevelt used the simplest words to communicate, while his tone and demeanor also communicated a self-assurance that the people greatly needed during their times of despair and uncertainty. In his first chat, he appealed to the people not to be fearful, promising them that things would be all right. In subsequent chats, he discussed the Emergency Banking Act, the recession, New Deal initiatives, and the course of World War II. By using radio to talk directly to the people, he was able to quell rumors and explain his policies in detail. The capitalists hated Roosevelt and considered him to be "a traitor to his class."[1062]

The Dust Bowl and the Civilian Conservation Corps (CCC)

In order to put American men back to work, Roosevelt instituted the *Civilian Conservation Corps (CCC)*, which was a public work relief program that operated from 1933 to 1942.[1063] As part of the New Deal, the CCC employed young men from seventeen to twenty-three years old in unskilled manual labor jobs related to the conservation and development of natural resources in rural lands owned by federal, state, and local governments. Maximum enrollment at any one time was three hundred thousand, but over nine years three million young men participated in the CCC. The program provided them with shelter, clothing, and food, together with a small wage of thirty dollars (about five hundred and forty-seven dollars in 2015) a month (twenty-five dollars of which had to be sent home to their families).[1064] The American people loved the program. As far as the young men were concerned, the program increased their physical health, improved their morale, and gave them employable skills. The CCC also led to a greater awareness and appreciation of the outdoors and the nation's natural resources. It instilled in them a belief that as a people we must plan a comprehensive approach to the protection and development of natural resources. What added special poignancy to this idea was the fact that destructive agricultural practices in the southwest had turned a large portion of the country into a Dust Bowl.

The Dust Bowl was a period of severe dust storms that greatly damaged the ecology and agriculture of the US prairies during the 1930s. Severe drought and a failure to prevent wind erosion caused the phenomenon. The drought came in three waves, 1934, 1936, and 1939–40, but some regions of the high plains experienced drought conditions for as many as eight years. With insufficient understanding of the ecology of the plains, farmers had been deep plowing the virgin topsoil of the Great Plains for years. This destroyed the native, deep-rooted grasses that normally trapped soil and moisture even during periods of drought and high winds. During the drought of the 1930s, the exposed, unanchored soil turned to dust, which blew away in huge clouds that blackened the sky. The "black blizzards" traveled cross-country, reaching as far as New York City and Washington, D.C. The drought and erosion of the Dust

Bowl affected one hundred million acres (four hundred thousand square kilometers) that centered on the panhandles of Texas and Oklahoma and touched adjacent sections of New Mexico, Colorado, and Kansas.[1065]

During the time of the CCC, young men planted nearly three billion trees to help reforest America, constructed more than eight hundred federal parks nationwide, and upgraded most state parks. They also built a network of service buildings and public roadways in remote areas.[1066] In order to assist farmers with correct knowledge they began to organize farmers into soil conservation districts. The federal government established the Soil Erosion Service to help farmers. It is still active today. When the US government instituted the draft in 1942, however, Congress voted to close the CCC program.

Fig. 4-39: 1930's Dust Bowl

Other Recovery Programs

The Federal Emergency Relief Administration (FERA) was created in May 1933. Its main goal was to alleviate household unemployment by creating new unskilled jobs in local and state government. Jobs were more expensive than direct welfare payments (called "the dole"), but were psychologically more beneficial to the unemployed, who wanted any sort of job for their self-esteem. Men needed to know they could take care of their families. FERA provided work for over twenty million people.[1067]

Faced with continued high unemployment and concerns for public welfare during the coming winter of 1933-34, FERA instituted the Civil Works Administration (CWA) as a four hundred million dollars short-term measure to get people to work. It was terminated in 1935 and its work taken over by two entirely new federal agencies, the Works Progress Administration (WPA) and the Social Security Administration (SSA). When the Great Depression began, the United States was the only industrialized country in the world without some form of unemployment insurance or social security. In 1935, Congress passed the Social Security Act, which for the first time provided Americans with unemployment, disability, and pensions for old age.[1068]

FERA operated a wide variety of work relief projects, including construction, projects for artists and projects for the production of consumer goods.

FERA created an adult education program in 1933. It employed two thousand teachers and reached at least one million workers nationwide until it was ended in World War II.

Some five hundred thousand women also worked for FERA projects doing sanitation surveys, highway and park beautification, public building renovation, public records surveys, and museum development. Most were unemployed white-collar clerical workers.

During the summer of 1933, the Agricultural Adjustment Administration was created to reduce agricultural production by paying farmers subsidies not to plant on part of their land and to kill off excess livestock in order to maintain adequate food prices.[1069] Their artificial scarcity strategy led to food crops being plowed up or left to rot and six million pigs being killed and discarded in the first year of operation. While the farmers had surplus food that was driving prices down, the poor were without food. The public outcry over the waste of food led to the establishment of the Federal Surplus Relief Corporation (FSRC), which aimed to provide surplus food such as apples, beans, canned beef ,and cotton to local relief organizations.[1070] In December 1933, the agency distributed three million tons of coal to the unemployed of Wisconsin, Minnesota, Michigan, North Dakota, South Dakota, and Iowa [1071] and in September 1934, shipped 692,228,274 pounds of foodstuffs to the unemployed in thirty US states.[1072] The FSRC became the forerunner of the school lunch program, Food Stamps and the direct provision of food to Food Pantries.

In 1933, the Roosevelt administration also set up the National Recovery Administration (NRA).[1073] The goal of this agency was to eliminate the "cut-throat competition" that had characterized the dealings of the monopoly capitalists during the Progressive Era and throughout the war and into the roaring twenties. The NRA brought industry, labor, and government together to create codes of "fair practices" and to set prices. The codes were also intended to help workers by setting minimum wages and maximum weekly hours.

What an excellent idea! Yet this provided too much support for the American people and the capitalists bristled under its directives. In 1935, they convinced the U.S. Supreme Court that the NRA law was unconstitutional, ruling that it infringed on the separation of powers under the United States Constitution. In other words, they argued that the President was asserting too much power and thereby diminishing the role of the legislative and judicial branches of government. The NRA was forced to stop its efforts to create a greater balance of power within the economy, although some of its labor provisions reappeared in the National Labor Relations Act (Wagner Act), passed later the same year. The long-term result, much to the capitalists' dismay, was a surge in the growth and power of unions. These unions became a core group in the coalition that dominated national politics for the next three decades.

The Tennessee Valley Authority

Also in 1933, the Roosevelt administration created The Tennessee Valley Authority (TVA). It was the first great experiment in American social planning and it remains successful to this day.[1074] The capitalists called it "communistic to its core." Yet the TVA did what no cartel of capitalists would consider doing because there was no profit in it for them. At the time, thirty percent of the population was sick with malaria and the average income was only six hundred and thirty-nine dollars per year.

Some families were surviving on as little as one hundred dollars per year. Much of the land had been farmed too hard for too long and the soil was eroded and depleted. Crop yields had fallen along with farm incomes. The best timber had been cut, with another ten percent of forests being burnt each year.[1075]

The TVA was designed to bring the region out of abject poverty by using experts across a range of disciplines and by developing electricity to combat human and economic problems. To help the farmers, the TVA developed fertilizers, taught farmers how to improve their crop yields, helped replant forests, controlled forest fires, and improved the habitat for fish and wildlife. The most dramatic change in Valley life came, however, when the TVA began to generate its own electricity from hydro-electric plants. Electric lights and modern home appliances made life easier and farms more productive. The availability of affordable electricity also drew industries into the region, providing desperately needed jobs.

Today the service area of the TVA covers most of Tennessee, portions of Alabama, Mississippi, and Kentucky, and small slices of Georgia, North Carolina, and Virginia. Under the leadership of David Lilienthal ("Mr. T.V.A."),[1076] the T.V.A. also became a model for helping third world countries modernize their agricultural base.[1077]

It was during the 1920s that Americans began to support the idea of publicly-owned utilities. While controversial even today, many believe that privately owned power companies charge too much for power, employ unfair operating practices, and have no accountability to the local people. By forming utility holding companies, the monopoly capitalists (private sector) had already controlled ninety-four percent of power generation by 1921. They were essentially unregulated. Because everybody depends upon power for personal and business needs, Roosevelt held firm to the belief that the American people should not be held hostage to the decisions of unknown power elites.

Today regional consumers continue to benefit from lower-cost electricity supplied from TVA's network of twenty-nine power-producing hydropower facilities. Federal taxpayers save millions of dollars annually because the government no longer subsidizes the TVA production of power. While the capitalists raged against this "socialist" project and barraged the people with decades of negative public relations concerning the agency, the TVA remains overwhelmingly popular in Tennessee among liberals and conservatives alike. Barry Goldwater discovered this in 1964 when he proposed selling the agency to a private corporation. The people turned against him and he lost the state to the Democrats.[1078]

In local discussion concerning the privatization of the TVA, people soon realized that while privatization may reduce costs, it would not reduce the prices for electricity. Rather, people understood that layoffs would happen, costs would be cut, and then prices would begin to rise. The profit would leave the area according to the dictates of the big shareholders. That's how it works under capitalism. It is how it is designed to work.[1079]

The TVA was not an easy project to put on the ground. Many local landowners were suspicious of government agencies. And while the creation of dams displaced families, and farmers were hesitant to take advice from experts in suits and ties, the agency was able to successfully introduce new agricultural methods by finding community leaders and convincing them that crop rotation and the application of fertilizers would restore soil fertility. Once they had convinced the leaders, the rest followed.

The Authority also hired the local unemployed to conduct conservation, economic development, and social programs, such as a library service that operated for the surrounding area. While the workers were categorized by the usual racial and gender biases of the day, the TVA hired a few African Americans for janitorial or other low-level positions. It also recognized labor unions, allowing skilled and semi-skilled blue collar employees to unionize. This was a breakthrough in an area because the capitalists had suppressed union efforts by miners and textile workers. Women were excluded from construction work, but the TVA's cheap electricity attracted textile mills to the area, and these hired mostly women as workers.[1080]

Many of the federal agencies created by the Roosevelt administration to pull the country out of depression and provide jobs and security to the American people still exist today. It can safely be said that without such programs the American people would be greatly suffering today. Imagine the United States without unemployment compensation, food stamps, social security, emergency relief, disability insurance, early education, job training, etc. Despite a relentless campaign by the capitalists and their political talking heads to discredit such programs in an attempt to end financing for them, the people continue to need such programs in order to survive in the capitalist system. Such aid to the people remains necessary as the capitalist system continues to lay off workers, transfer jobs overseas where labor is cheapest, reduce wages, etc. The money spent on such relief programs remains insignificant compared to the wealth that the capitalists exploit from the people. The proof of this is that a few thousand people in the capitalist class controls outright fifty percent of the wealth of America. If such wealth was redistributed in a more equitable manner, as the Roosevelt administration attempted to do, the economy would prosper and people's standard of living would greatly improve. Monopoly Capitalism does not work for most of the people in America. It never did, and it never will.

By 1936, the main economic indicators had regained the levels of the late 1920s, except for unemployment, which remained high at eleven percent, although this was considerably lower than the twenty-five percent unemployment rate seen in 1933. Thinking that the country had turned a corner, in mid-1937 the Roosevelt administration cut spending for social programs and increased taxation in an attempt to balance the federal budget. The American economy immediately took a sharp downturn that lasted through most of 1938. Unemployment jumped from 14.3 percent in May, 1937 to 19 percent in June 1938, rising from five million to more than twelve million.[1081] As unemployment rose, consumers' expenditures declined, leading to further cutbacks in production. Industrial production fell thirty-seven percent.[1082] By May 1938, however, the economy started to turn around. Retail sales began to increase, employment improved, and industrial production turned up after June 1938. After the recovery from the recession, the capitalists were able to form a bipartisan conservative coalition to stop further expansion of the New Deal and, when unemployment dropped to two percent in the early 1940s, they abolished the work programs, including the Civilian Conservation Corp. Social Security, however, remained in place.

The Global Impact of the Great Depression

The adherence to the gold standard, which joined countries around the world in a fixed currency exchange, helped spread the Depression from the United States throughout the world, especially in Europe.

The majority of countries were forced to set up relief programs and most underwent some sort of political upheaval. Many countries in Europe and Latin America that had democratic forms of government were overthrown by dictatorships or authoritarian rule. Germany, Italy, and Spain in Europe are examples of this political change.

Australia was hard hit by the great depression. Its economy was largely built on exports of wool and wheat to the British Empire. When exports flattened due to the collapse of international demand, the Australians suffered years of high unemployment, poverty, and plunging incomes. Civil unrest occurred, but while extremist movements on the left and right were active, they remained on the periphery of Australian politics. The United Australia Party, which was fiscally conservative, provided political stability during the 1930s, although unlike other capitalist countries, it did not embark on a program of spending to recover from the Depression. As the economies of the countries in the British Empire began to improve, so also did the export economy of Australia.

Canada was affected by the slow down in the global economy and also by the Dust Bowl. By 1932, its industrial production had fallen forty-two percent. Total national income fell to fifty-six percent of the 1929 level and, by 1933, unemployment had reached twenty-seven percent. The Great Depression left millions of Canadians unemployed, hungry, and homeless. Few countries were affected as severely as Canada during what became known as the Dirty Thirties. Like in the US, the widespread losses of jobs and savings triggered the birth of social welfare, populist political movements, and a more activist role for government in the economy.[1083]

Latin America was strongly tied to the US through investments in their raw material export industries. Thus, these countries were also severely damaged by the Depression. Chile, Bolivia, and Peru were particularly hard hit as the prices for wheat, coffee, and copper plunged. Exports fell by over two-thirds by 1933. Fascism began to rise in some countries, especially in Brazil.[1084] On the other hand, following the example of the

New Deal, some governments began to develop new local industries and expand local consumption and production. They approved regulations and created welfare institutions that helped millions of new industrial workers to achieve a better standard of living. This served Latin American countries in the long run.

When the Great Depression struck *England*, it was still recovering from the impact of WWI on its economy. When the demand for industrial goods collapsed in the wake of the war, Britain's industrial areas in the north were devastated. By the end of 1930, twenty percent of the workforce had lost their jobs and the value of exports had fallen by fifty percent. In some towns and cities in the northeast, unemployment reached as high as seventy percent as shipbuilding fell ninety percent.[1085]

A series of National Hunger Marches occurred over the decade. Work camps were started that served two hundred thousand unemployed men. The camps continued until 1939 when England entered WWII. In the less industrial Midlands and Southern England, the effects of the depression did not last as long. Growth in the light manufacture of electrical goods, agriculture, and the manufacture of automobiles began to speed up thanks to a growing population and an expanding middle class.

The depression caused Great Britain to abandon the gold standard in 1931. This allowed them to print money beyond the value of the gold that it held.

Ireland was a largely agrarian economy, trading almost exclusively with the UK, at the time of the Great Depression. Beef and dairy products comprised the bulk of exports, and Ireland fared well relative to many other commodity producers, particularly in the early years of the depression.

Sweden was the first country worldwide to recover completely from the Great Depression. By 1938, *Life magazine* reported that Sweden had the "world's highest standard of living." Its government was run by social democrats after 1932. They intervened strongly to assist the people and created many welfare policies that saw them prosper through the years of the depression. The Social Democrat party remained in power until 1976, making them the most successful political party in the history of Western democracy.

The crisis in *France* was relatively mild because of its high degree of self-sufficiency that was built during the war years. Unemployment peaked below five percent, the fall in production was at most twenty percent below the 1929 output level, and there was no banking crisis. Nonetheless, social turmoil resulted from the changes and polarized the country politically between extreme liberal and conservative positions. Both the socialists and the ultra-nationalists saw an increase in popularity. Even so, democracy prevailed in France throughout the depression and WWII.

The Great Depression hit *Germany* very hard. The impact of the Wall Street Crash forced American banks to stop the loans that had been used to fund its war reparation payments. In 1932, ninety percent of German reparation payments were cancelled. Widespread unemployment reached twenty-five percent as every sector was hurt. The government was unable to spend money on social programs because they were afraid that a high-spending policy would lead to a return of the hyperinflation that had affected the country in 1923.

By 1932, the unemployment rate reached nearly thirty percent. This bolstered public support for extremist movements like the Nazi (NSDAP) and Communist (KPD) parties. Economic pressures and political extremists eventually collapsed the centrist coalition under President Hindenburg. Hitler ran for the Presidency in 1932, and while he lost to the incumbent Hindenberg in the election, the Nazi Party and the Communist parties became the Reichstag majority following the presidential election.

From roughly 1931 to 1937, the *Netherlands* had a rough go of it. Because they had remained neutral during WWI, they did not suffer the economic damage and loss of human life that affected other European combatants. Nonetheless, they were a small country that was tied to the global economy. Political instability and riots gave rise to the ultra nationalist Dutch national-socialist party (NSB). The government had maintained the gold standard until 1936, which severely hurt any effort to rebuild its domestic economy. Consequently, it did not recuperate until after World War II.

Spain had a relatively isolated economy with high protective tariffs, and was not one of the main countries affected by the Depression. The banking system held up well, as did agriculture. Nonetheless, it was during the years of the Great Depression that political turmoil in Spain led to the Spanish Civil War. On July 18, 1936, right-wing Spanish military officers (ultra-nationalists) created a revolt against the leftist government in Spanish Morocco that soon spread to mainland Spain. General Francisco Franco, leader of the fascists, broadcasted a message calling for the army to join the uprising and overthrow Spain's leftist Republican government. During the war, the Republicans and the Nationalists secured their respective territories by executing thousands of suspected political opponents. Franco eventually won the war with the help of fascist Germany and Italy. Aside from the thousands killed, the countries industrial infrastructure was also destroyed. Many talented workers were forced into permanent exile. By staying neutral in the Second World War, and selling goods and materials to both sides, the economy avoided further disasters.

During the Depression, *Portugal* was under the rule of a dictatorial junta, the Ditadura Nacional. Although the country squirmed under the thumb of a fascist dictatorship that imposed harsh measures on the people, its economic policies of self-reliance and a balanced budget created economic stability and eventually economic growth.

The Great Depression hit *Italy* very hard. As industries began to fail due to the Depression, they were bought up by the banks. But the assets used to buy the companies were largely worthless. The banks lacked the capital to reorganize and reopen the companies and this created a financial crisis that peaked in 1932, leading to a major government intervention. Under the fascist dictatorship of Benito Mussolini, the Industrial Reconstruction Institute (IRI) was formed in January 1933 and took control of the bank-owned companies. This decisive action gave Italy the largest state-owned industrial sector in Europe (excluding the USSR). IRI proved to be successful in its efforts to restructure and modernize industry.

The reverberations of the Great Depression hit *Greece* in 1932. Because the Greek drachma was pegged to the US dollar, it had no option but to shrink its economy because it had a large trade deficit with the US. The deflationary efforts failed and the country's gold reserves were almost totally wiped out by the end of 1932. The value of the drachma plummeted. Greece went off the gold standard in April 1932 and declared a moratorium on all interest payments. The country also created import quotas. These protectionist policies allowed Greek industry to grow during the Great Depression. The dictatorial regime of Ioannis Metaxas took control of the Greek government in 1936, and economic growth remained strong in the years leading up to the Second World War.

Hungary's economy was dependent upon grain exports and when the stock market crashed in the US, the economy buckled as world grain prices plummeted. With the drop in the volume of grain sales, tax revenues dropped, foreign sources of credit dried up and loans were called in. Hungary asked the new League of Nations for help but the institution's demand for rigid belt tightening only increased unemployment. The peasants reverted to subsistence living. Industrial production dropped and businesses went bankrupt. Government workers lost their jobs or had their paychecks cut. By 1933 unemployment stood at thirty-six percent and eighteen percent of the population lived in abject poverty. The mood of the country shifted to the right and anti-Semitism created national turmoil. A reactionary demagogue, Gyula Gombos, came to power, but fortunately he was forced to compromise with moderate political forces to maintain his government.

At the time of the stock market crash, *Poland* was eighty percent agrarian and only twenty percent industrial. Agriculture provided sixty percent of the jobs in the country. As the global economic crisis spread, foreign investment stopped. As the urban industrial workers in the economy faced increased unemployment, they purchased less food and the farmers found themselves with overproduction. This caused them to reduce the price of food, but this meant that they now they had to sell more food to meet their own basic needs and pay taxes. In time, this situation led to a great imbalance between food that was cheap and industrial goods that were expensive. In the cities, the industrial slowdown reduced competition and led to the creation of monopolies that charged higher prices. By 1932, unemployment stood at forty-four percent.

The Polish government was slow to respond to the crisis. They kept the price of the currency high, which led to restricted access to credit, reduced investment in production and budget cuts. These, in turn, led to a lower standard of living for the people. Finally, toward the end of 1932, the government stepped in. It increased the price of food and lowered the price of industrial goods. It also set up work projects and made loans to businesses. The number of strikes eventually decreased, but many businesses were unable to pay their loans so they became public corporations.

Because the *Soviet Union* was the only communist state in the world, its economy was not tied to the global capitalist system and was only slightly affected by the Great Depression. But the Soviet Union had its own problems. The communist party was attempting to transform its subsistence rural economy, dominated by petty aristocrats and serfs, to an industrial society. While it succeeded in building up heavy industry, it did so at the cost of millions of lives in rural Russia and Ukraine.

This "apparent" economic success of the Soviet Union, at a time when the capitalist world was in crisis, led many Western intellectuals to view the Soviet system favorably. Jennifer Burns wrote, "As the Great Depression ground on and unemployment soared, intellectuals began unfavorably comparing their faltering capitalist economy to Russian Communism...."[1086] A *New York Times* reporter, Walter Duranty, who was a fan of Stalin, vigorously debunked accounts of the Ukraine famine that Stalin precipitated.[1087] Stalin eliminated approximately seven million persons in the Ukraine, the breadbasket of Europe, because the people sought independence from his rule. [1088] He deprived the people of the food they had grown with their own hands.

As world trade slumped, demand for *South African* agricultural and mineral exports fell drastically. The Carnegie Commission on Poor Whites had concluded in 1931 that nearly one third of Afrikaners lived as paupers. The social turmoil caused by the Depression gave rise to ultra-nationalist sentiments and political splits developed in the white political parties. The system of apartheid was enforced and blacks were sequestered onto thirteen percent of the land base. Black leaders did not contest this, but encouraged the black people to better themselves and obey their tribal leaders. In 1935, however, some black leaders, dissatisfied with this approach, allied with representatives of Indian and colored political organizations, met, and formed the All-African Convention (AAC) to protest the proposed new laws as well as segregation in general. But even this organization, composed largely of members of the black professional class, along with church leaders and students, avoided a confrontational approach. Violence against the apartheid system did not begin until the 1950s.

New Zealand relied almost totally on agricultural exports to the United Kingdom for its economy. The drop in exports led to destitution among farm families who were the mainstay of the local economy. Jobs disappeared and wages plummeted, leaving people desperate and charities unable to meet people's basic needs. The government set up work relief programs for the unemployed who made up thirty percent of the workforce. In 1932, riots occurred among the unemployed in three of the country's main cities Auckland, Dunedin, and Wellington.[1089]

The Great Depression did not strongly affect *Japan*. Even though the Japanese economy shrank by eight percent during 1929–31, the Japan's Finance Minister, Takahashi Korekiyo, acted quickly to ward off disaster. He was the first to implement what has come to be identified as Keynesian economic policy. As in the US, he stimulated the economy by deficit spending and by devaluing the currency. Basically, the government went into debt to create the necessary cash to stimulate the Japanese economy. The Finance Minister used the Bank of Japan to "sterilize" the deficit spending and minimize inflationary pressures. His strategy proved effective in keeping Japan out of a prolonged and deep depression.

Spending went into the purchase of munitions for the armed forces. By devaluing the currency, exports increased because other countries were able to buy Japanese goods at a cheaper cost. An immediate effect was that Japanese textiles began to displace British textiles in export markets. By 1933, Japan was already out of the depression. By 1934, the economy was in danger of overheating, and to avoid inflation, Korekiyo moved to reduce the deficit spending that went towards armaments and munitions. This resulted, however, in a strong and swift negative reaction from ultra-nationalists, especially those in the army. He was assassinated for his efforts. This had a chilling effect on all civilian bureaucrats in the Japanese government. From 1934, the military began to dominate the government. Instead of reducing deficit spending, the military introduced price controls and rationing schemes that reduced, but did not eliminate, a persistent inflation that remained problematic until the end of World War II.

In *Thailand*, then known as the Kingdom of Siam, the Great Depression led to the Siamese revolution of 1932 and the overthrow of the monarchy of King Rama VII. When the king tried to institute policies to help the poor, the aristocracy, who sought to apply the principles of Western colonialism to their own people, objected and plotted his overthrow.[1090]

China was initially unaffected by the Depression, because the Chinese had for centuries used silver for money.[1091] As such, their economy was not affected by the rules of the gold standard. However, in 1934, the United States passed the Silver Purchase Act in an attempt to support its own currency. As a result, the demand for China's silver coins all but eliminated Chinese money, so they had to abandon silver and create a fiat currency. The Chinese people became dependent on the new "legal notes" issued by the four biggest banks in China. This stabilized prices and raised revenues for the government. The British colony of Hong Kong followed suit in September 1935. With available cash due to deficit spending, the Nationalist Government, under the control of Generalissimo Chiang Kai-shek, acted quickly to modernize the country's finances. They amortized debt, stabilized prices, and enacted banking and currency reforms. The government also employed workers to build railroads and highways, improve public health facilities, and augment industrial and agricultural production.[1092]

Women in the Great Depression

Women were primarily housewives. When the money dried up, they needed to ensure that their families still had enough food and other essentials. Birthrates fell everywhere because families could not support more children. The average birthrate for fourteen major countries fell twelve percent from 1930 to 1935.[1093] In predominantly Catholic countries, the women defied Church teachings and used contraception to postpone births.

There was a widespread demand to limit families to one paid job, so that a wife often lost her job if their husband was employed. Women who sought paid employment were often scorned for taking jobs and money away from more deserving men. When Norman Cousins realized that the number of gainfully employed women in 1939 roughly equaled the national unemployment total, he offered this flippant remedy: "Simply fire the women, who should not be working anyway, and hire the men. Presto! No unemployment. No relief rolls. No depression."[1094]

Yet, many women had no choice but to work. Many, especially young women, were single or supported families without husbands. Despite traditional gender stereotypes in the workplace, businessmen would often rather hire a woman than a man because they were able to pay her less for a comparable job. Often it was also impossible for men to take women's jobs. Laid off coalminers or steel workers could not easily become nursemaids, cleaning women, or do clerical jobs.

One-quarter of National Recovery Administration jobs set lower minimum wages for women than men. New Deal agencies like the Civil Works Administration and Civilian Conservation Corps gave jobs almost exclusively to men. The Social Security Act and the Fair Labor Standards Acts did not initially cover areas of women's employment such as agricultural work or domestic service. Social security benefits were based on the traditional model of a male breadwinner and dependent female housewife, which implied that women deserved economic rights only in relation to men. The Wagner Act of 1935 fueled a dramatic growth in organized labor, and woman workers participated in major CIO strikes and union organizing drives, but few women held leadership positions.

Women who were on their own were largely invisible. The iconic image of the Depression is "The Forgotten Man": the newly poor, downwardly mobile, unemployed worker, often standing in a breadline or selling apples on a street corner. Women who found themselves in similar dire straits rarely turned up in public spaces like breadlines or street corners; instead they often tried to cope quietly on their own. "I've lived in cities for many months broke, without help, too timid to get in breadlines," remembered the writer Meridel LeSueur. "I've known many women to live like this until they simply faint on the street from privations, without saying a word to anyone. A woman will shut herself up in a room until it is taken away from her, and eat a cracker a day and be as quiet as a mouse."[1095]

Men and women experienced the Depression differently. Men were socialized to think of themselves as breadwinner so when they lost their jobs or got a pay cut, they felt like failures because they could not take care of their families. Their feelings of inadequacy became even worse when their life savings were used up and they had to endure the humiliating experience of applying for relief. Unemployed men often found themselves hanging around their homes, irritating their wives. Quarrels became more frequent between husbands and wives. Domestic violence increased. Many men withdrew emotionally and even physically from their families and friends. Some took up drinking. Others went off on long trips, looking for employment in other cities. Some deserted their wives and families altogether.

Women, on the other hand, saw their roles in the household enhanced as they struggled to make ends meet. According to sociologists Robert and Helen Lynd, in a study of Muncie, Indiana, published in 1937:

> The men, cut adrift from their usual routine, lost much of their sense of time and dawdled helplessly and dully about the streets; while in the homes the women's world remained largely intact and the round of cooking, housecleaning, and mending became if anything more absorbing.[1096]

In other words, no housewife lost her job in the Depression. In rural and small-town areas, where only one home in ten had electricity, women grew as much food as they could. They raised poultry for meat and eggs and made practical items like quilts. They taught each other the skill. Quilts had a practical use, were made from inexpensive materials and promoted camaraderie and personal fulfillment.

Housewives in the cities made cheap meals like soups or beans and noodles. They purchased the cheapest cuts of meat. The women sewed and patched clothing, traded with their neighbors for outgrown items, and adjusted to colder homes. Many women also worked outside the home, took on boarders, did laundry for trade or cash, or sewed for neighbors in exchange for something they could offer. Extended families helped each other with extra food, spare rooms, repair-work, or gave cash loans to help their relatives.[1097]

As today, many families lived close to the edge and prayed that no catastrophic accident or illness would swamp their tight budgets. "We had no choice," remembered one housewife. "We just did what had to be done one day at a time."

Hard times did not alleviate traditional gender stereotypes, instead they exaggerated them. If it were not for an informal network of women in Roosevelt's administration, women might have been completely left out in the cold. Secretary of Labor Frances Perkins, the first woman in the Cabinet, oversaw many of the social welfare initiatives and Ellen Sullivan Woodward supervised women's relief projects for the Works Progress Administration. Molly Dewson promoted women's perspective from her position at the Democratic National Committee. Their effectiveness was dramatically enhanced by access to Eleanor Roosevelt, who used her position as First Lady to advance the causes of women, blacks, and other marginalized groups. She was a strong woman who stood for women empowerment and also served as the conscience of the New Deal.[1098]

Even so, the Depression left a scar on those who lived through it, but in the struggle, women in America grew stronger and more resilient. Their iron resolve carried them through WWI and when the war was over, laid the foundations for the women's revolution that began in the 1950s with the publication of Betty Freidan's *The Feminine Mystique*. In her book, Friedan addressed what she called "the problem that has no name." It was the widespread unhappiness of women in the 1950s and early 1960s. Women, for the first time, were able to see that they were not alone in their suffering due to their restrictive role as a mindless appendage to her husband, locked in the domestic role of a housewife.[1099] Women wanted to be strong heroines like their grandmothers who lived through the Great Depression. They wanted to be themselves.

Because the Great Depression was worldwide, women in every country suffered according to the disposition of their patriarchal governments. In Japan, for example, the government launched a nationwide campaign to induce households to reduce their consumption by focusing on housewives spending.[1100] In Germany, the Nazi government began a Four-Year Plan in 1936 to achieve German economic self-sufficiency and prepare for the coming war. Nazi women's organization promoted the values of thrift and healthy living.[1101]

Lessons Learned from the Great Depression

There are lessons to be learned at the federal level and at the household level. Let us begin at the macro-level.

At the Government Level

When the Depression hit, most countries tried to protect their domestic economies by creating higher taxes on foreign goods (tariffs). The idea was to get people in the home country to buy local goods instead of importing them as a way to strengthen the local economy. In the United States, the Smoot-Hawley tariff was imposed. But this only led other countries to retaliate in-kind and this squeezed global trade. When the stock market crashed this added to the stagnation of local economies within the US.

The Fed's creation of a surplus money supply in the US economy to pay for WWI and bail out Britain after the war created a massive imbalance in the domestic and global economy. In the US, the supply of cash (credit) was not easily absorbed by the working class, while the availability of credit for the upper classes exceeded their demand for it. This created an imbalanced in the domestic economy and resulted in the surplus cash being used to gamble on the stock market. The economy began to slow when the working people could no longer afford to pay rising prices for basic goods. This eventually reduced the production of these goods, weakened the economy, and devalued corporate stocks. When stock traders got wind of this, they began to sell their stocks and this caused a panic that crashed the market.

Another lesson is that the gold standard had traditionally worked well as a mechanism to maintain a balance of payments in international trade, but failed miserably when the Fed began to inject massive amounts of cash independent of the gold standard into the United States during World War I. While the Fed supplied artificial credit to unleash the great demand of warfare production, it also created a great imbalance in the accounts of countries that traded with the United States. In the process, most countries, which tried to maintain the gold standard, while the Fed was creating cash out of nothing, became in debt to the Fed. When they attempted to pay their debt by sending gold to the US, this greatly dragged down the availability of local credit and created high interest rates on local currencies. This further slowed production in those countries. As long as a country maintained its link with the gold standard, their only options was to continue to shrink their economies through monetary policies and protectionism as a means to stay solvent.[1102] In such circumstances, by trying to maintain their currencies on a fixed ratio to gold, these countries sunk further into depression. Countries, like Germany and Austria, who followed the Fed example and floated their currencies in relation to gold, began to recover first. During the Depression, the Fed continued to float its currency. In this way, it continued to turn other countries into beggars. This is how the American depression turned into the Great Depression following the Great War.

At the Family and Community Level

The Great Depression impoverished the nation yet people made it through, even as many people today continue to make it through despite incredible hardships. It is not the loss of a job that ultimately threatens a family; it is their inability to meet their basic needs in a sustainable manner. These basic needs include food, clothing, shelter, health care, and education. Certainly, having a job creates the money necessary to purchase these goods and services, but the Great Depression proved that people could also meet their needs through direct action. They grew their own food, extended the life of their clothing, and traded with neighbors. They used home remedies to care for their children.

There is little doubt among people who watch the trends of the present economy that we are heading into Great Depression II. All the signs are there, including social unrest, political extremism, jobs that do not pay a living wage, environmental problems, foreign wars, financial stress, etc. Each of us needs to think how we can protect our families and ourselves through an era of destitution. Many people have already become "survivalists" because they know that the government, which is dangerously insolvent, will not be able to cope with large-scale unemployment and increasing environmental disasters beyond what it is presently doing. In

Book III of this trilogy we will discuss what families and communities can do to meet their basic needs through direct action. More than this, we will discuss how people working together at the local level can create a long-term, healthy economy that meets people's basic needs without destroying the environment.

Recovery

Despite the artificial stimulus of the economy by the government, unemployment in the United States remained an intractable problem. People had no money so there was no demand for goods and services. Thus, production remained stagnant and no jobs were created. The money that the government used to stimulate the economy was basically used to keep the unemployed population on the dole. While work projects like the creation of parks and the building of infrastructure created work, they did not create long-term jobs. In April 1838, FDR asked Congress to authorize another $3.75 billion in federal spending to stimulate the sagging economy. Still, unemployment remained high and was predicted to stay that way for some time.

There is no question that employment began to increase with the onset of WWII. The rearmament policies leading up to World War II had helped to stimulate the economies of Europe beginning in 1937 and when the war began in September 1939, unemployment in Europe ended.

When the US entered the war in 1941, unemployment dropped to ten percent from a high of twenty-five percent. The domestic capitalists ignored the mounting federal debt and higher taxes and focused instead on taking advantage of huge government contracts. The massive government spending doubled the economic growth rate of the country. It is interesting that the same government, having the same fiscal and monetary tools, was able to double the size of the economy going into a war while it was unable to do so in a war on domestic poverty. Why was that? Well, certainly a survival instinct kicked in for everyone in the country, not just the poor and unemployed. But at a deeper level, we can understand that the working of the economy is determined by the will of the capitalist class. If these people want to enlarge the economy they can. If they want to shrink the economy, they can. They can do this despite the fact that we think living in a democracy gives us control over our lives. We may live in a *political democracy*, in which we may have some impact on who becomes our political leader, but we do not live in an *economic democracy* in which we can control access to our own basic necessities. Thus we can easily be manipulated at every turn. We need to remember this going forward.

In 1940, Roosevelt was elected to an unprecedented third term as president, indicating that the American people supported his socialist economic policies.

When WWII began, the president lost little time in lobbying Congress to pass the Lend-Lease Act, which provided military aid to Britain and "any country whose defense the president deems vital to the defense of the United States."

The hardships of the Great Depression had fueled the rise of extremist political movements in various European countries, most notably that of Adolf Hitler's Nazi regime in Germany. The Nazi invasion of Czechoslovakia in 1939 created war in Europe. In response, the US government immediately restructured the Work Projects Administration (WPA) to build the military infrastructure of the United States, even as the country maintained its neutrality. With Roosevelt's decision to support Britain and France in the struggle against Germany and its allies (the Axis Powers), defense manufacturing geared up. In 1941, the same year that the Lend Lease law was passed, Japanese planes bombed Pearl Harbor destroying most of the ships in the US navy in one fell swoop. The attack led to an American declaration of war. Money was instantly found and factories went back into full production. Industrial production and the draft reduced the unemployment rate to below pre-Depression levels.

World War II

While the Great Depression preoccupied the United States during the 1930s, its impact on Europe was even more devastating. Europe had barely begun to rebuild its infrastructure after World War I when the Depression struck. Suffering from lack of industrial production and faced with wide scale unemployment, tensions between countries and within countries mounted anew. It was a time of extreme political polarization as ideologues and demagogues on the left and the right fought for attention. It was a time of the rise of fascists and communists who vied for control of the countries of Europe, which, at the time, were still governed by the ideas of nationalism, militarism, and imperialism.

As early as November 1923, Adoph Hitler had attempted to overthrow the German government by force in what became known as the *Beer Hall Putsch*. Hitler's Nazi party, along with other ultra-nationalist groups, marched two thousand men to the center of Munich, where they confronted the police. The police put down the marchers and Hitler was arrested and charged with treason. According to Hitler, this event had three advantages. First, it created headlines around the world and the trial provided a platform for him to present his ultra-nationalist view. Secondly, he used his imprisonment of nine months to write *Mein Kampf*, which became the Nazi bible. Thirdly, Hitler realized that, under the circumstances, when the government was stronger, it was better to seek power through legitimate means rather than force. This led Hitler to concentrate on developing Nazi propaganda.[1103] Hitler continued to do so throughout the remainder of the 1920s.

In September 1931, the Japanese army invaded Manchuria in China and set up a puppet state. This was a shock to the Japanese people because these actions were not ordered by the civilian government. The government, however, was powerless to do anything about it because the constitution required Army and Navy members to form any government cabinets. Without military support, the government would collapse.[1104]

In Germany, during the April 1932 election for the President of the Weimar Republic, Paul von Hindenburg, running for a second term defeated his opponent Adolph Hitler. Hindenburg deeply distrusted and personally detested Hitler. Nevertheless, subsequent Reichstag elections propelled Hitler's anti-democratic Nazi party to hold the majority of seats. Having no choice, Hindenburg reluctantly appointed Hitler as Chancellor of Germany in January 1933.[1105] The Chancellor (Reichskanzler) was appointed by the President and was responsible to the Reichstag. At the time, the position was not that powerful. The

Chancellor served as the chairman of the cabinet and decisions were made by a majority vote. Hitler changed all that.

Two months earlier, on February 27, 1933, the German parliament (*Reichstag*) building burned down due to arson. Hitler had falsely charged that the Communists had committed this act in an effort to overthrow the state. Hitler used this event to push Hindenburg to declare a state of emergency. Limits were set on what the press could report and gave the police the authority to break up political meetings and marches. This effectively stopped electoral campaigning. New regulations also suspended the right to assembly, freedom of speech, freedom of the press, and other constitutional protections, including all restraints on police investigations.[1106]

Upon taking office, Hitler pushed through the Enabling Act, which gave him full legislative powers for the next four years. Now he could introduce any legislation that he wanted without consulting the Parliament. When Hindenburg died, Hitler combined the offices of the President with that of the Chancellor into a new office, *der Führer*.

These actions occurred at the same time that Franklin D. Roosevelt was elected president of the United States and began his New Deal program. The contrast could not have been greater.

In March of 1933, Hitler ordered the German people to boycott Jewish goods. A month later the Gestapo, Hitler's secret police, was established. In May, Hitler outlawed trade unions and banned all other parties in Germany. By November, the homeless and unemployed were rounded up and sent to concentration camps to become slave labor.

In Austria, February 1934, a struggle between socialists and fascists for control of the government led to street fighting in major cities that went on for several days. The fascists gained control of the country when the army threatened to use artillery fire in the cities.[1107]

In April, Hitler assassinated all of his potential rivals in what becomes known as the Night of the Long Knives. In August, the German people were made to swear allegiance to Hitler instead of the German constitution.

In September, as the New Deal was in full gear, Hitler's Germany passed the Nuremberg laws against the Jews. The laws excluded Jews from German citizenship and prohibited them from marrying or having sexual relations with persons of "German or related blood." Additional ordinances took away the Jewish peoples' right to vote and deprived them of most political rights.

The Nuremberg Laws did not define a "Jew" as someone with particular religious beliefs, but anyone who had three or four Jewish grandparents. Many Germans who had never practiced Judaism found themselves rounded up in a Nazi terror campaign.[1108]

In March 1936, Germany began to remilitarize in violation of the Treaty of Versailles. Hitler's military was funded by big banks and corporations, many of them American.

In July, the Spanish civil war began between the socialist Republicans, who were loyal to the democratic, Second Spanish Republic, and the Nationalists, a fascist group led by General Francisco Franco. The fascists ultimately won the three-year war and Franco ruled Spain for the next thirty-six years, until his death in 1975.[1109]

At the same time, Stalin began his two-year Great Purge in the Soviet Union. During this time, Stalin purged the Communist Party, government officials, and the Red Army. He also repressed the peasants who bristled under their forced collectivization. It was a time of widespread surveillance by Stalin's secret police (NKVD). Imprisonment and arbitrary executions became the order of the day. It has been estimated that the Soviet Government murdered between nine hundred and fifty thousand and twelve hundred thousand people. The loss of leadership handicapped Russia going into World War II.[1110]

In November, Hitler sends airplanes to help the fascists in the Spanish Civil War. In the same month he signs a pact with Japan that if one of them is attacked by the Soviet Union, the other will go to war as well. In December, Hitler mandates that all German boys between ten and eighteen must join the Hitler Youth, a paramilitary organization.

During these years, a civil war in China was being fought between the communists and forces loyal to the Kuomintang government. The war began in August 1927, when Generalissimo Chiang Kai-Shek led his army north to destroy the legitimate government in Beijing. Having succeeded, a constitutional government was set up, but it was undermined by strong personal and factional ties. Overall, the government was extremely corrupt, incompetent, and tyrannical. Chiang Kai-Shek purged his army of Communists, which ultimately led to the Civil War between his army and the communists. The civil war continued intermittently until late 1936, when the two parties came together to form the Second United Front to counter any further incursions into the country by Japan. The civil war did not resume until 1945 after Japan was defeated to end World War II. Three years later, the civil war came to an end with the communists establishing the People's Republic of China on the mainland of China, while the nationalists were restricted to Taiwan and a few other outlying islands.[1111]

As tensions mount and civil wars ravage major countries, in October 1937, Roosevelt moves away from the US position of neutrality. He gives a speech calling for the quarantine of all aggressors. The speech intensifies America's isolationist mood and causes protests from non-interventionists. While not mentioning any countries by name, people knew that he was referring to Japan, Italy, and Germany. Roosevelt did not call for war but economic pressure.[1112]

In November, 1937, Italy joins the pact between Japan and Germany to form the *Anti-Comintern* pact. It becomes a pact between fascist governments to fight socialism and communism.

In December, 1937, the Japanese attacked China and destroyed the capital city of Nanking. The event becomes known as the Rape of Nanking. Over a six-week period, the Japanese army went berserk, killing an estimated three hundred thousand Chinese while raping women and looting the city. The event is still a sore point affecting Chinese and Japanese relations to this day.

Japan's army penetrated deep into the heartland of China, but it was never able to force the Chinese army to capitulate. When the Japanese attacked Pearl Harbor in 1941, the United States began to airlift military equipment to the Chinese. The war between China and Japan went back and forth, but despite Japan occupying much of China's territory, its defeat in WWII forced them to abandon their occupation.[1113]

In March 1938, Germany annexed Austria in a bloodless coup. It remained part of Germany until after World War II when the Allies granted independence to the Austrian people.[1114]

Fate of Jewish Refugees

Between the Nazi rise to power in 1933 and Nazi Germany's surrender in 1945, more than three hundred and forty thousand Jews emigrated from Germany and Austria. Nearly one hundred thousand of them found refuge in countries that were subsequently conquered by Germany. German authorities would deport them to be exterminated.

After the *Kristalnacht* pogroms in November 1938, nations in Western Europe and the Americas feared an influx of refugees. About eighty-five thousand Jewish refugees reached the United States between March 1938 and September 1939, but this level of immigration was far below the number seeking refuge. By late in 1938, one hundred and twenty-five thousand applicants lined up outside US consulates hoping to obtain twenty-seven thousand visas under the existing immigration quota. By June 1939, the number of applicants had increased to over three hundred thousand but most visa applicants were unsuccessful.

In a highly publicized event during this month, the United States refused to admit over nine hundred Jewish refugees who had sailed on the *Saint Louis* from Hamburg, Germany. Denied permission to land in the United States, the ship was forced to return to Europe. The governments of Great Britain, France, the Netherlands, and Belgium each agreed to accept some of the passengers as refugees. Of the *St. Louis* passengers who returned to Europe, two hundred and fifty-four are known to have died in the Holocaust. Two hundred and eighty-eight passengers found refuge in Britain. And of the six hundred and twenty who returned to the continent, only three hundred and sixty-six are known to have survived the war.[1115]

A British White Paper in May 1939, approved by the British Parliament, contained measures that severely limited Jewish entry into Palestine. As the number of hospitable destinations dwindled, tens of thousands of German, Austrian, and Polish Jews immigrated to Shanghai, one destination that did not require a visa. Shanghai's International Settlements quarter, effectively under Japanese control, admitted seventeen thousand Jews.

During the second half of 1941, even as reports of the mass murder perpetrated by the Nazis filtered to the West, the US Department of State placed even stricter limits on immigration based on national security concerns. Great Britain itself limited its own intake of immigrants in 1938–1939, though the British government did permit the entry of some ten thousand Jewish children in a special program.

At a conference in April 1943, held in Bermuda, on the topic of Jewish refugees, the only agreement made was that the war against the Nazis must be won. US immigration quotas were not raised nor was the British prohibition on Jews seeking refuge in the British Mandate of Palestine lifted. The Allies offered no concrete proposals for rescue.[1116]

Other countries in Europe that were not conquered by the Axis Powers took in some Jews but much larger numbers were refused entrance. After the war, hundreds of thousands of survivors found shelter as displaced persons in camps administered by the western Allies in Germany, Austria, and Italy. Immigration to Palestine remained severely limited until the establishment of the State of Israel in May 1948, at which time Jewish refugees began streaming into that new sovereign state. Some one hundred and forty thousand Holocaust survivors entered Israel during the next few years. The United States admitted four hundred thousand displaced persons between 1945 and 1952. Approximately eighty thousand (roughly twenty-four percent) of them were Jews who had survived the Holocaust.[1117]

1938 Developments Continued

In July 1938, a series of border skirmishes began between Japan and the Soviet Union over a common borderline with Manchuria that Japan now occupied. The Japanese were beaten back.

In September the infamous *Munich Agreement* is signed between Germany, Italy, France, and Great Britain that allows Hitler to annex the Czech Sudetenland in exchange for peace. Following the annexation of Austria, the conquest of Czechoslovakia became Hitler's next ambition. The incorporation of the Sudetenland, which formed a large region in the northwest of the country, left Czechoslovakia weak and powerless to resist the subsequent occupation. Six months later, on March 15, 1939, the German war machine (Wehrmacht) moved into the remainder of Czechoslovakia. The occupation did not end until the surrender of Germany following World War II.

In January 1939, the Americans split the atom at Columbia University.

During this same month, Hitler orders the expansion of the German navy to be able to defeat the UK's royal navy.

In March, Hitler dissolves Czechoslovakia and forms the puppet government of the Slovak Republic. Its president was Father Jozef Tiso, a Catholic priest. He met with Hitler to create anti-Semitic legislation. In the new state of the Slovak Republic, Jews could not own real estate or luxury goods. They were excluded from public office and could not participate in sports or cultural events. They were banned from high schools and colleges. In public, they were forced to wear the Star of David on their clothing. Later, Father Tiso deported Jews to Germany for extermination.[1118]

In the same month that Hitler dissolved Czechoslovakia, he demanded that Lithuania surrender its Klaipeda region to Germany. Before WWI, the area was the most northern part of the German province of East Prussia. The land was inhabited by Germans and Slavs and since the end of WWI was overseen by the League of Nations until a democratic election could be held to determine if the people wanted to return to Germany or not. Rather than go to war, the people acquiesced to being annexed to Germany.[1119] When this happened, Great Britain and France assured Poland that they would fight for its continued independence.

During the month of April 1939, the pace of conflict quickened. Franco won the Spanish Civil War. Italy invaded Albania. The Soviet Union proposed a pact with the UK and France but it is rejected. Roosevelt sent his second letter to Hitler seeking peace.

In May, Japan attacks the Soviet border again, but is rebuffed once more. The Swedes, Norwegians, and Finns reject an offer of a non-aggression pact with Germany. Hitler convinces Mussolini in Italy to sign a military alliance pact with him.

In August, Hitler and Stalin sign a non-aggression pact with secret plans to divide up Eastern Europe between them. This ruse by Hitler removes the threat of Soviet intervention as he plans his next step to invade Poland. Upon getting the Soviet's promise of non-intervention, Hitler demands that Poland give up the Polish corridor and free city of Danzig (Gdansk) that separates Germany from East Prussia. Poland did not respond.

In September, Hitler invades Poland. Britain and France, bound by their commitment to aid Poland, entered the fight to stop Hitler. WWII has begun.

How Hitler Built the Wehrmacht with Money from US Corporations

When Adolf Hitler rose to power in 1933, he cancelled all war reparations payments. While American investors lost a lot of money because of this, there was a silver lining for the bankers and big business. They believed that Hitler had the capacity to make them a lot of money and they were right, but war profiteers are a particularly loathsome group. While people are being killed and their families submitted to the worst atrocities imaginable, and while decent people struggle to end the nightmare, others justify their role in advancing human and environmental destruction. These people are the true enemies of humanity. The thought that many US companies supported the most deadly regime in the world and went on to become famous brand-name fixtures in our daily lives is loathsome. It remains a bitter reality to this day.

Here is a sample of the US corporations that supported Adolph Hitler and made fortunes on his fascist regime, even as he made war on America and our allies.

The Banks

Most of the big US Banks helped the Nazis during World War II. Of these, Chase Manhattan Bank,[1120][1121] J. P. Morgan,[1122][1123] Guaranty Trust Co. of New York,[1124] American Express,[1125] Bank of the City of New York,[1126] Brown Brothers Harriman,[1127] and Citibank[1128] all handed over information to the Nazis concerning their Jewish customers. They also gladly handed over accounts information regarding the Jews to make it easier for the Nazis to exterminate the Jewish people. These bankers then kept the money that was in these people's bank accounts.[1129]

But the bankers' betrayal of the American people and the democracies in Europe goes much deeper than this. Files from the US National Archives reveal that Prescott Bush, father to H. W. Bush, and grandfather of George W. Bush, profited directly from financial dealings with the Nazis. Prescott Bush worked for Brown Brothers Harriman, which acted as a US base for the German industrialist, Fritz Thyssen, who was the main financier of Hitler in the 1930s. Bush was also the director and founding member of the Union Banking Corporation (UBC) that was set up by Harriman and Thyssen. The UBC became a pillar in the financial architecture of Nazi Germany. Thyssen, at the time, owned the largest steel and coal company in Germany and grew rich from Hitler's efforts to re-arm the German military between the two world wars.[1130] By the late 1930s, UBC had bought and shipped millions of dollars of gold, fuel, steel, coal, and US treasury bonds to Germany, both feeding and financing Hitler's build-up to war.[1131]

While our "customer-friendly" banks financed both sides of the war, Bush and a secret cabal of other bankers and corporate executives, angry and frightened by Roosevelt's socialist policies, decided that he must be stopped. They plotted a coup against President Roosevelt with the intent of establishing fascism in America based on the model of Nazi Germany.

The British Broadcasting Corporation (BBC) reported that Prescott Bush, in 1933, was involved in a plot to overthrow the US government and replace it with a fascist dictatorship and that he was acting on a consensus among the Wall Street capitalists. Here is what happened.

In the early days of the Great Depression, as we previously discussed, thousands of veterans of World War I were camped in Washington DC in an effort to secure their promised bonus checks from the US army. At the time, the vets were among the ranks of the twelve million unemployed. Washington newspapers and politicians referred to the men as "bums, drifters, riff raff, and trouble makers". It was at this low point that the head of the Veterans of Foreign Wars, James Van Zandt, called on his friend, Major General Smedley Butler to invite him to Washington to boost the moral of the troops. Many of the men had fought under Butler in different campaigns. All the veterans knew him as a man who stood up for his troops. He had even run for a senate position on the Bonus Bill issue. When the general stood to address the men encamped along the Anacostia River, he was greeted with a roar that echoed through Washington like thunder. Butler told the men, "If you don't hang together you aren't worth a damn!" "They may call you tramps now," he continued, "but in 1917 they didn't call you bums! ... You are the best-behaved group of men in this country today. I consider it an honor to be asked to speak to you." Butler told the vets that when they went home, they should go to the polls and throw out those politicians who stood against them. When his speech was over, the men mobbed him as their savior. He stayed all night and listened to their stories about lost jobs, families in distress, and old wounds.[1132]

After this event, all of America knew that Butler was the man most revered by the half a million US veterans in the country. As the fascist bankers plotted their coup in their private, wood paneled clubs in New York City, their thoughts turned to General Butler. Others involved in the plots included GM, Goodyear, Standard Oil, the DuPont family, the owners of Heinz, Birds Eye, and Maxwell House coffee, the KKK and the American Liberty League.[1133] [1134] [1135]

If the fascists could only get the general on their side, they could realize their ambitions. They hatched a plan to enlist the revered Major General Smedley Butler, believing that he had the power to call an army of veterans to Washington to demand FDR's resignation. The plotters wanted to turn this army into brown shirts and promised Butler that he would become the first dictator of America, a Caesar. They told Butler that when FDR would refuse to step down, they would give him a post that would have no authority. The plotters would then, with the help of Butler, establish a new government as a capitalist dictatorship modeled on Nazi Germany.[1136]

Certainly, General Butler was popular enough to pull off such an event and the fascists' plan was almost flawless. As they wooed the general; they told him that the American people would accept the new government because they controlled the newspapers. By God's Grace, Butler was loyal to the government and secretly collected evidence against the conspirators and took it to Congress.

We may ask ourselves, if such an outrageous event happened, as can be corroborated by US government archival files, why is so little known about the biggest coup ever hatched against the United States government? Essentially, the capitalists were too powerful to be taken down on the word of one general. Business as usual prevailed and the

American people were kept in the dark by the mainstream press who passed it off as a hoax.

Fig. 4-40: General Butler Testifying Before the HUAC

General Butler testified before the McCormack-Dickstein Committee in 1933, which became known as the House Committee on Un-American Activities (HUAC). (See photo above). In his testimony Butler stated that a group of men, representing mainly Wall-Street Banking interests, had approached him to help lead a plot to overthrow Roosevelt in a fascist military coup. In their final report, the Congressional committee supported General Butler's claims on the existence of the plot, but no prosecutions or further investigations followed, and the matter was mostly forgotten. To access the entire "Public Statement on Preliminary Findings of HUAC, November 24, 1934," see footnote 1135.[1137]

In specific language, the Congressional Committee final report said:

> In the last few weeks of the committee's official life it received evidence showing that certain persons had made an attempt to establish a fascist organization in this country. No evidence was presented and this committee had none to show a connection between this effort and any fascist activity of any European country. There is no question that these attempts were discussed, were planned,

and might have been placed in execution when and if the financial backers deemed it expedient.

A *New York Times* editorial dismissed Butler's story as "a gigantic hoax" and a "bald and unconvincing narrative."[1138] J. P. Morgan called it "perfect moonshine."[1139] General Douglas MacArthur, alleged to be the back-up leader of the putsch if Butler declined, referred to it as "the best laugh story of the year." It was MacArthur that was called in shortly after Butler's speech to the veterans to destroy their encampment. *Time* magazine and other publications also scoffed at the allegations. This is not surprising since the capitalists controlled the press, as they had told Butler.

Even despite the ridicule heaped on General Butler, the capitalist-fascist cabal remained a serious threat to American democracy. In 1936, we have a statement made by William Dodd, the U.S. Ambassador to Germany, in a letter to President Roosevelt:

> A clique of U.S. industrialists is hell-bent to bring a fascist state to supplant our democratic government and is working closely with the fascist regime in Germany and Italy. I have had plenty of opportunity in my post in Berlin to witness how close some of our American ruling families are to the Nazi regime.... A prominent executive of one of the largest corporations, told me point blank that he would be ready to take definite action to bring fascism into America if President Roosevelt continued his progressive policies. Certain American industrialists had a great deal to do with bringing fascist regimes into being in both Germany and Italy. They extended aid to help Fascism occupy the seat of power, and they are helping to keep it there. Propagandists for fascist groups try to dismiss the fascist scare. We should be aware of the symptoms. When industrialists ignore laws designed for social and economic progress they will seek recourse to a fascist state when the institutions of our government compel them to comply with the provisions.[1140]

The War Effort

While the big capitalists have a slight setback in their attempted coup, they were not exposed for who they were. They had succeeded in covering up their plot through manipulation of the media and by pressuring the House Committee on Un-American Activities not to mention publicly the names given to them by General Butler, or to investigate any of Butler's accusations. The news eventually died and the incident was forgotten. The capitalists were able to continue their business as usual. Many US corporations continued to provide the Nazis with resources and thereby profit from this effort. This occurred all the while that the Nazis were slaughtering American soldiers and destroying American families. The corporations not only continued to be traitors to the American people, but also to our allies who supported democracy around the world. As the people of the world were dying in the millions, these corporate parasites were playing one side against the other and profiting from both sides.

It is worth remembering now, as we continue to experience global chaos and environmental disaster, that someone is benefitting financially from this destruction. WWII was fought by the parents of the Baby Boomer generation and the grandparents of the Millenials. These people are us. They are out families. The big banks and companies that betrayed us are still alive and well today, working even harder to assert their self-interest against the welfare of the American people? Many of us are forced to work for them to earn our daily bread and support our families. Those people, who do, consider themselves fortunate to have a job compared to the millions of Americans who are unemployed. We discussed the bankers anti-American behavior, but let us now take a look at some of the other large American corporations that collaborated with Hitler's Nazi Germany.

IBM

Perhaps the most odious of US corporations at the time of the war against the fascists was IBM that helped the Nazis identify Jews in Europe for extermination. When Hitler came to power in 1933, his desire for the genocide of European Jewry was so ambitious he required the resources of a computer. But in 1933, no computer existed. What did exist was the Hollerith punch-card system. An American in Buffalo, New York had invented it for the Census Bureau. This punch-card system could store all the information about individuals, places, products, inventories, and schedules in the holes that were punched or not punched in columns and rows.[1141]

The Hollerith system reduced everything to number code. Over time, the IBM alphabetizers could convert this code to alphabetical information. As Hitler invaded more countries more machines were required and IBM created them for their Nazi client.

On September 13, 1939, The *New York Times* headlined the fact that three million Jews were going to be "immediately removed" from Poland, and that they were targeted for "physical extermination." On September 9, the German managers of IBM Berlin sent a letter to the CEO of IBM, Thomas Watson, saying that, due to the "situation," they needed high-speed alphabetizing equipment. Since IBM wanted no paper trail, an oral agreement was made and passed from New York to Geneva to Berlin. Watson personally approved those alphabetizers before the end of the month.

That month he also approved the opening of a new Europe-wide school for Hollerith technicians in Berlin to produce some fifteen million punch cards to help the Nazis create a database of the Jews. When the Nazis invaded Holland in 1940, they built another punch card factory in that country. They also sent another one hundred and thirty-two million punch cards from New York to help the Nazis identify Jews among the Dutch population. Holland had the highest rate of Jewish extermination of all of Europe. Of the Jews in Holland, seventy-two percent were exterminated using the punch cards. When Germany invaded France, IBM built two more factories there to supply the Nazis with more punch cards. These punch card machines did not work as well as those in Holland so only twenty-four percent of the Jewish were identified for exterminated.[1142]

When the US entered the war after Pearl Harbor, and regulations concerning trading with the enemy were put in force, Watson sent a cable to his European subsidiaries telling them not to tell him what they were doing and not to ask any questions. It is clear that he did not say, do not send machines to concentration camps, or stop what you are doing.

To distance himself from his European subsidiaries in case of public scrutiny, Watson split the company and created a management center in Geneva. So now all communication concerning European activities went from Switzerland to New York instead of directly from Germany. As the war proceeded, a Hollerith department was set up in every Nazi concentration camp. The original Auschwitz tattoo was an IBM number.

Standard Oil

The Nazi air force (*Luftwaffe*) needed tetraethyl lead gas in order to get their planes off the ground. Standard Oil sold tetraethyl to the Nazis. Britain was incensed by this action and complained to the US government. To avoid censure, Standard changed the registration of their entire fleet to Panama to avoid British search or seizure. These ships continued to carry oil to the Nazis. In time, Standard Oil built an oil refinery in Germany to supply Hitler's war machine with fuel.[1143]

Ford

Ford made cars for the Nazis. When the war broke out, Ford continued to do business with Nazi Germany, including the manufacture of war material. Beginning in 1940, with the requisitioning of between one hundred and two hundred French POWs to work as slave laborers, Ford-Werke contravened Article 31 of the 1929 Geneva Convention. At that time, which was before the US entered the War and still had full diplomatic relations with Nazi Germany, Ford-Werke was under the control of the Ford Motor Company. The number of slave laborers grew as the war expanded.

Wikipedia also points out that Henry Ford was one of the world's biggest anti-Semites ... inspiring Hitler, Himmler, and other high-level Nazis.[1144]

In Germany, Ford's anti-Semitic articles from The Dearborn Independent were issued in four volumes, cumulatively titled, "The International Jew, the World's Foremost Problem." In a letter written in

1924, Heinrich Himmler described Ford as "one of our most valuable, important, and witty fighters." Ford is the only American mentioned in *Mein Kampf*. Speaking in 1931 to a Detroit News reporter, Hitler said he regarded Ford as his "inspiration," explaining his reason for keeping Ford's life-size portrait next to his desk. Steven Watts wrote that Hitler "revered" Ford, proclaiming that, "I shall do my best to put his theories into practice in Germany," and by modeling the Volkswagen, the people's car, on the Model T, Henry Ford had the Grand Cross of the German Eagle award bestowed on him by Nazi Germany. See photo below.

Fig 4-41: Henry Ford Receiving the Grand Cross of the German Eagle Award

At the time of Hitler's rise to power, Ford and GM controlled seventy percent of Germany's car market. At the outbreak of the war, they rapidly retooled to supply war materials and military vehicles for the Nazi army. As these companies stepped up their production of war materials for Germany, they resisted Roosevelt's call to convert their American plants to US war production.

The Washington Post reported:

> "General Motors was far more important to the Nazi war machine than Switzerland," said Bradford Snell, who has spent two decades researching a history of the world's largest automaker. "Switzerland was just a repository of looted funds. GM was an integral part of

the German war effort. The Nazis could have invaded Poland and Russia without Switzerland. They could not have done so without GM."[1145]

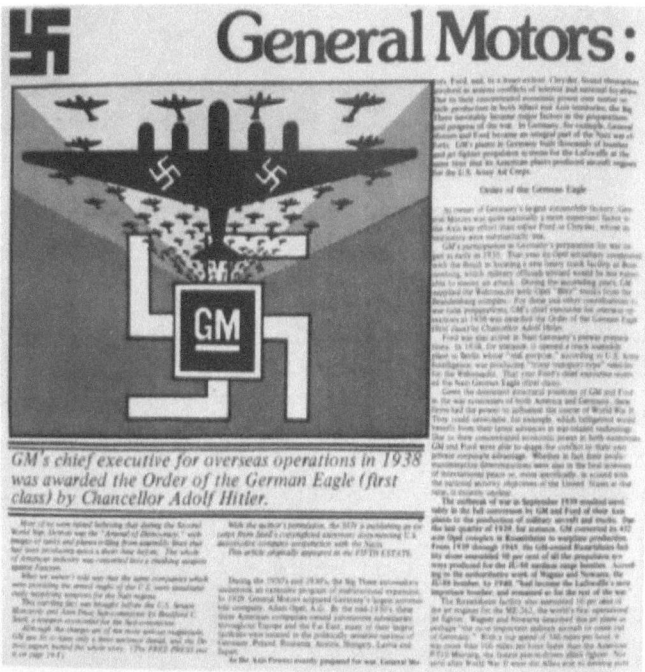

Fig. 4-42: Washington Post Story on GM's contribution to the German War Effort

When American GIs invaded Europe in June 1944, they did so in jeeps, trucks, and tanks manufactured by the Big Three motor companies. They were shocked to see that the Nazi vehicles were produced by the same corporations. Author Snell says that Nazi armaments chief Albert Speer told him in 1977 that Hitler "would never have considered invading Poland" without synthetic fuel technology provided by General Motors.[1146]

Documents show that the parent companies followed a conscious strategy of continuing to do business with the Nazi regime, rather than divest themselves of their German assets. Less than three weeks after the Nazi occupation of Czechoslovakia in March 1939, GM Chairman Alfred P. Sloan defended this strategy as sound business practice, given the fact that the company's German operations were "highly profitable."[1147]

The real moral corruption of the Ford and IBM capitalists is that they not only profited from slave labor supplied by the Nazis, but they also demanded and received compensation from the US taxpayer for damages done by the US army to their plants in Germany. General Motors alone received thrity-two million dollars in compensation from the US government.

Kodak

During World War Two, Kodak's German branch also used slave laborers from concentration camps.[1148] Several of their other European branches did heavy business with the Nazi government. Wilhelm Keppler, one of Hitler's economic advisers advised Kodak to fire all of their Jewish employees if they wished to do business with the Nazis. They complied.[1149]

Coca Cola

While Coke profited from the American troops they also supplied the Nazis with their soft drinks. In 1941, the German branch of Coke ran out of syrup, and could not get any from America because of wartime restrictions. So, Coke invented a new drink, specifically for the Nazis: A fruit-flavored soda called Fanta.[1150]

Other Corporations

Hugo Boss made Nazi uniforms for the storm troopers and SS, as well as the Hitler Youth organization. Porsche, was in business deals with Hitler to create the Volkswagen. Hitler told them to make a people's car that looked like a "beetle." Bayer was a division of IG Farben that manufactured the gas used in the concentration camp to kill millions of people. Ironically, Arthur Eichengrun, a Jewish employee, invented the aspirin, the mainstay of the company. Bayer did not want to admit this fact. To this day, Bayer officially gives credit to Felix Hoffman, a nice Aryan man, for inventing the aspirin.[1151]

Siemens, a German company with a US subsidiary that is still active, used slave labor to construct the gas chambers that would eventually kill them and their families. In 2001, Siemens tried to trademark the word

"Zyklon" to become the name of a new line of products ... including a line of gas ovens. Zyklon was the name of the poison gas used in their gas chambers during the Holocaust.[1152] Random House's parent company, Bertelsmann A.G., worked for the Nazis by publishing Hitler's propaganda. They also published "Sterilization and Euthanasia: A Contribution to Applied Christian Ethics."[1153]

Hollywood studios also collaborated with the Nazis. The Nazi Party was active in Hollywood spreading hatred against the Jews and advocating that the studios present a positive image of Hitler and the Nazis. Jews were fired from studios and the film industry's content monitor, the Production Code Administration (PCA), issued a ban on anti-Nazi "propaganda" in films.[1154] As Nazi pressure increased, Universal and MGM opened their studios to Nazis and allowed them to view their films and suggest revisions.[1155]

Dow Chemical was one of the companies that provided the Nazis with raw materials and also American technological innovations in regards to oil refinery. These contributions allowed the Nazis to achieve a massive armament build up in a short time. They sold huge quantities of magnesium to the Nazis for the making of incendiary bombs [1156]that obliterated London.

Fig. 4-43: Woolworth Receives the German Designation "Adefa Zeichen"
(Source: : Getty Images; Henry Guttmann Collection)

Woolworth provided legitimacy to Nazi racism by firing all of its Jewish employees in Germany. This won them the designation "Adefa Zeichen," an award reserved for companies that were "pure Aryan." Today Woolworth does not advertise their products with this seal of approval.

Alcoa, in 1941, had a monopoly on aluminum, in addition to owning a large percentage of America's electricity production and other minerals. Before America declared war on Germany, it sent so much of its aluminum to Germany that the country made upwards of sixty percent more aluminum products than America. When the US involvement in the war began, there was a massive aluminum production shortage in America due to this act on Alcoa's part. Alcoa essentially sold the Axis powers much of the material to build their war machines while the American army suffered.

Eugenics

Aside from war profiteering by corporate fascists, the Nazi's eugenic program that justified the myth of Aryan superiority as well as the Nazis racist and anti-Semitic social policies was also created by Americans corporate foundations. The concept of a white, blond-haired, blue-eyed master race did not originate with Hitler but was created in the United States decades before Hitler came to power.

Eugenics was the pseudoscience aimed at "improving" the human race. In practice, this meant wiping away all human beings deemed "unfit" and preserving only those who conformed to a Nordic stereotype. It is cause for reflection that elements of this philosophy were enshrined as national policy by forced sterilization and segregation laws, as well as marriage restrictions, enacted in twenty-seven states. In 1909, California became the third state to adopt such laws. Ultimately, eugenics practitioners coercively sterilized some sixty thousand Americans, barred the marriage of thousands, forcibly segregated thousands in "colonies," and persecuted untold numbers in ways we are just learning about. This is an example of American racism that is little known, but which helps us understand the racist programming in this country.

Eugenics would have been little more than drunken racist ridicule if it had not been for extensive financing by corporate philanthropies like the Carnegie Institution, the Rockefeller Foundation, and the Harriman Brothers. They were all in league with some of America's most respected scientists from Stanford, Yale, Harvard, and Princeton. These academicians espoused race theory and race science, and then faked and twisted data to serve their racist aims.[1157]

Under Nazi eugenics policies, state-operated institutions began to systematically identify those people who were "unworthy of life." These included, not only Jews, but also prisoners, dissidents, the mentally ill, homosexuals, the weak, and the idle. They were all targeted to be eliminated from the chain of heredity. More than four hundred thousand people were sterilized against their will, while more than three hundred thousand were killed under Action T4, a euthanasia program.[1158] Eugenic research will later be called "genetic" research in an effort to sanitize the research and mask its original intentions.

The Course of the War

As human beings became more integrated as a result of imperialism and world trade, more people become involved in the political, economic, and military actions of the world's greater powers. As such, WWII, as initiated by the world's power elite, was the greatest human disaster that humanity had ever faced.

The war pitted three global groups against each other. These were the fascists (Germany, Italy, Ukraine, Japan, and other ultra-nationalist dictators), vs. the social democrats (Great Britain and the United States) and the communists (USSR and their puppet governments).

As in all previous wars, when people are afraid for their lives, society polarizes into extreme left and the right positions. The left looks forward to changing a system that they believe causes human misery. The right looks back in nostalgia to a time when they felt safe and, having lost this feeling, become fearful and angry, desiring to destroy any who oppose their return to the past. The right takes the form of ultra-nationalism. Women, minorities, and any political opponents are targeted. The left either opts for social democracy or a left-wing dictatorship.

In time the dogs of war are released, insanity and depravity sweep away human values, and divisive feelings lead to rape, torture, and killing.

During WWII, the fascists were the most brutal and animalistic. The communists under Stalin easily countenanced mass exterminations, and of all the combatants, the United States and Britain governments were the most humane. The racist tensions that continued to build below the surface of European society—occasionally spilling over into pogroms and murder of Jews—finally vented in a mass effort to completely exterminate an entire people. It is sad to know that while the fascists were busy exterminating the Jews, the other Christians in Europe did little to stop it. The Christian churches offered no resistance other than a few hollow condemnations. Even Britain and the United States closed their borders to Jews quite early in the war. This is not to deny that a few brave individuals stood their moral ground.

It can be said that at the time the Jews were a nonviolent people. They had no homeland to which to escape. These factors made them easy prey for massacre and every vile perversion that so-called Sunday Christians could dream up in their darkest moments. The Jews will never make the mistake of being homeless and nonviolent again.

World War II resulted in a staggering loss of human life and natural resources. Many cities in Europe, Africa, and the Far East were razed to the ground by constant aerial bombardment. Millions of noncombatants were killed regardless of their support, opposition, or indifference to the war.

World War II clearly reflected the flaws inherent in a social outlook based upon nationalism, imperialism, and militarism. It showed what could happen when people fail to use their rationality and lack a universal worldview. Land-based sentiments like nationalism as well as sentiments based on social groupism like self-serving religions, have left us with little option to improve our human condition. Consequently, the same sentiments continue to rule us today. The same dynamics are occurring again as people become more insecure economically and lose hope for the future. This is why it is so important to know our history, have a universal value system and know how to prevent social disintegration.

The following section takes us through the prominent military developments that ultimately engulfed the entire world in a raging conflagration.

1939

The Invasion of Poland[1159] by Nazi Germany begins on September 1, 1939 at 4:45 a.m., with the Luftwaffe attacking the cities of Krakow, Lodz, and Warsaw. Within five minutes of the Luftwaffe attacks, the Nazi Battleship Schleswig-Holstein opens fire on the Polish military base at Westerplatte in the Free City of Danzig on the Baltic Sea. By 8:00 a.m., troops of the German Army launch an attack near the Polish town of Mokra. War has not been declared.[1160] Upon hearing the news, Estonia, Finland, Latvia, Lithuania, Norway, and Switzerland declare their neutrality, while Britain declares a general mobilization of its armed forces and begins evacuation plans in preparation for German air attacks. The United Kingdom and France issue a joint ultimatum to Germany, requiring German troops to evacuate Polish territory. Italian dictator Benito Mussolini declares the neutrality of his nation. President Douglas Hyde of the Republic of Ireland declares the neutrality of his nation. The Swiss government orders a general mobilization of its forces. When Germany fails to respond to the British and French ultimatum, Britain and France declare war on Germany. Australia, India, and New Zealand also declare war on Germany.

Within hours of the British declaration of War, the SS Athenia, a British cruise ship en route from Scotland to Canada is torpedoed by a German U-boat killing one hundrded and twelve passengers and crew members. The "Battle of the Atlantic" begins.[1161] The effort to dominate the trade routes of the Atlantic Ocean lasts throughout the entire war and pits Nazi submarines (U-boats) and warships, along with its aircraft against the Royal Canadian Navy, the British Royal Navy, Allied merchant shipping, and eventually the United States Navy. The German strategy is to prevent supplies from getting to France and England. The Allies intent is to prevent supplies from reaching Germany.

Japan announced its neutrality. The British Admiralty announced the beginning of a naval blockade on Germany, one of a range of measures by which the British would wage economic warfare on the Axis Powers. President Franklin D. Roosevelt declares United States' neutrality on September 5, and declares the formation of a *Neutrality Patrol* to survey developments in the Atlantic.[1162]

South Africa and Canada declared war on Germany. The Soviet Union invaded Poland from the east, occupying the territory east of the Curzon line as well as Białystok and Eastern Galicia. The German and Soviet armies linked up near Brest Litovsk.

The Imperial Japanese Army launched attacks on the Chinese city of Changsha. In the fighting, the Japanese attack the Chinese National Revolutionary Army using poison gas during the battle.

In the first offensive operations by the German Army in Western Europe, guns on the Siegfried Line opened up on villages behind the French Maginot line in France. The United States issued the *Declaration of Panama* establishing a neutrality zone of some three hundred miles in breadth to be patrolled by the U.S. Navy.[1163]

Estonia, Latvia, Lithuania, and Finland were pressured by the Soviet Union to allow them to put military bases in their countries. The Finns cut off relations with Russia which then accused the Finns of killing Soviet soldiers and attacked them in what became known as the *Winter War*. Norway, Sweden, and Denmark proclaimed their neutrality in the Russo-Finnish quarrel.

Britain moved its forces to the Belgian border anticipating a German invasion in the West.

In one week after being attacked, the Polish resistance collapsed. Russia and Germany divided the country. Hitler spoke before the Reichstag, declaring a desire for peace with Britain and France. British Prime Minister Chamberlain and French Premier Édouard Daladier declined Hitler's offer of peace. Two days later, Hitler issued orders to prepare for the invasion of Belgium, France, Luxembourg, and the Netherlands.

On September 12, Adolf Eichmann begins deporting Jews from Austria and Czechoslovakia into Poland. The first Jewish ghetto is established at Lublin and Polish Jews are ordered to wear Star of David armbands.

Belgium announces that it is neutral in the present conflict.

At the end of September, the British government releases a report that concentration camps are being built in Europe for Jews and anti-Nazis.

Neither the French nor the British come to the aid of Poland as promised. England sends air force bombers to target Nazi ships in the Atlantic.

The British belief that "the bombers will always get through" is proven wrong as Germany defeats Britain in the Battle of the Heligoland Bight.[1164]

As the year ends, the Finns hold back the Soviet invaders, capturing many men and vehicles.

1940

Rationing of basic foodstuffs begins in the UK.

Reinhard Heydrich is appointed by Göring to develop the *Final Solution to the Jewish Question*.[1165]

Germany makes final plans for the invasion of Denmark and Norway. Britain and France intervene in Norway to cut off German access to iron in anticipation of an expected German occupation. Within a month, Germans land in several Norwegian ports and take Oslo. Denmark surrenders and the Germans set up a Norwegian government under Vidkun Quisling, former minister of defense. "Quisling" becomes another word for traitor in the English language. The British begin their *Norwegian Campaign*[1166] with a surprise attack against a larger German naval force. British and French troops land on the Danish Faroe Islands and Norwegian towns along the coast. Within a month, they decide to end their invasion. Meanwhile, Finland is forced to sign a peace treaty with the Soviet Union after one hundred and five days of conflict, giving up significant territory in exchange for peace.

The Soviet Communists express the same values of nationalism, militarism, and imperialism as the western capitalist countries. They want territory. Molotov speaks to the Supreme Soviet, about "an unsettled dispute" with *Romanian Bessarabia*, which had previously been the country of Moldavia until the Romanians occupied it in 1918.[1167]

Japan establishes a puppet regime in Nanking, China.

Britain begins secret reconnaissance flights to photograph targets inside the Soviet Union in preparation for Operation Pike, the code name for a strategic bombing plan. The plan is designed to destroy the Soviet oil industry, to cause the collapse of the Soviet economy, and to deprive Nazi Germany of Soviet resources.[1168]

In April 1940, the Soviets massacre twenty-two thousand Polish officers, policemen, and others who are considered a threat to their occupation.

Winston Churchill becomes Minister for the Coordination of Defense in England as Germany begins a massive offensive against the Western Front, including attacks on Belgium, France, Luxembourg, and the Netherlands.[1169] Luxembourg is immediately occupied by the Nazis. The Belgians blow up their bridges across the Meuse River to stop the German advance but are unsuccessful. The Germans occupy Brussels and Antwerp. In the Netherlands, Rotterdam is carpet-bombed by the Luftwaffe forcing the Dutch to surrender, with the exception of Zeeland where Dutch resisters aided by the French are quickly routed after eight days.[1170]

Unlike the United States where identified fascists are ignored, England jails the leader of the British Union of Fascists, Sir Oswald Ernald Mosley, 6th Baronet. He and his wife are released in 1943.[1171]

In May 1940, during the Battle of France, the British Expeditionary Force in France is cut off from the rest of the French Army by the German advance. Encircled by the Germans, four hundred thousand men retreat to the area around the northern port of Dunkirk. The German land forces can easily destroy the British Expeditionary Force that, in their haste to withdraw, leave behind their heavy equipment. The German general Gerd von Rundstedt, for unknown reasons, orders the German army to halt. The lull in the action gives the British a few days to evacuate by sea. Winston Churchill orders any ship or boat available, large or small, to pick up the stranded soldiers. The rescue effort evacuates 338,226 men (including 123,000 French soldiers). Churchill thereafter refers to this evacuation as the miracle of Dunkirk. Over nine hundred ships participate in the event. More than forty thousand vehicles, as well as massive amounts of other military equipment and supplies, are left behind.[1172]

Boulogne-sur-Mer and Calais, two French towns, surrender to the Nazis. Within a couple of weeks the Germans occupy Paris.

Belgium surrenders.

The Japanese heavily bomb the Nationalist capital Chungking, on the upper Yangtse River.

The Soviet Union prepares for a total takeover of the Baltic States. It accuses Lithuania of kidnapping Soviet soldiers and gives them eight hours to surrender. At the same time, it sets up a total naval blockade of the Baltic States. The Red Army along the Baltic borders is prepared to organize communist coups in all the Baltic States. Soviet troops enter Lithuania and attack Latvian border guards.

Italy declares war on France and the United Kingdom. Norway surrenders.

The Soviet Union gives an eight-hour ultimatum to Latvia and Estonia to surrender. After eight hours, the Soviets occupy these two countries along with Lithuania.

Meanwhile the Germans had been sinking British ships in the Atlantic with virtual impunity because they sorely lack air cover. In June 1940, The Germans sink the *RMS Lancastria* off the French coast. The ship was being used as a British troopship and three thousand men are killed in the attack. Soviet troops enter Latvia and Estonia.

On June 22, 1940, France signed an armistice with Germany. The agreement established a German occupation zone in Northern and Western France that encompassed all of the English Channel and Atlantic Ocean ports. It left the remainder of France "free" to be governed by the French.[1173]

Operation Ariel evacuated another 191,870 allied soldiers, airmen, and some civilians from France.[1174]

The Soviet Union sent an ultimatum demanding that Romania surrender Bessarabia and Northern Bukovina or face war. The Red Army occupied these territories.

Germany invades the islands in the English Channel and occupies them.

The Italian Royal Air Force started bombing the British Mandate of Palestine while Hitler prepares plans for an invasion of Britain, code named *Operation Sea Lion*. The English closed Brighton Beach to the public. Mines, barbed wire, and other defenses were put in place. The Luftwaffe bombed Cardiff, the capital of Wales.

The British bomb the French navy on the coast of French Algeria, fearing it will be taken over by the Nazis because a collaborationist French government in Vichy now controls the French navy. The attack results in the deaths of 1,297 French servicemen, the sinking of a battleship, and the damaging of five other ships.[1175]

The combined air-and-sea attack is conducted by the Royal Navy as a direct response to the Franco-German armistice of June 22, which replaces Britain's sole continental ally with a collaborationist, pro-Nazi government administrated from Vichy. In response to the attack of the French navy, the Vichy French government bombs British held Gibraltar.

The *Battle of Britain* begins in July 1940 with Luftwaffe raids on channel shipping. President Roosevelt asks Congress for huge increases in military preparations. The Luftwaffe bombs targets in Wales, Scotland, and Northern Ireland.

The Soviet Union organizes rigged elections in the Baltic States. Their parliaments are now under the control of the soviets. These soviets request membership in the USSR.

The United States of America activates the General Headquarters of the United States Army to organize and train army field forces within the continental United States.

The Italian Royal Navy establishes its submarine base in Bordeaux and joins the "Battle of the Atlantic." Under General Guglielmo Nasi, it invades and occupies British Somaliland during the East African Campaign.

The USSR annexes Bessarabia and Northern Bukovina and also Lithuania.

Hermann Göring starts a two-week assault on British airfields in preparation for invasion. The RAF begins to win some victories over the Luftwaffe along the East coast. British fighter aircraft production is accelerated. Germans are hampered by poor aircraft range and British extensive use of radar. Radar makes use of radio waves that are reflected by metallic objects. Radar systems produce short pulses of radio energy on an oscilloscope. With this device, the range of a target can be determined while the direction of the antenna reveals its angular location. The two, combined, produce a "fix" on the target.[1176] Germans begin to suffer severe losses on bomber formations. Göring calls his fighter pilots cowards and orders them to closely guard the bombers. This, however, only restricts their capabilities.

Italy announces a blockade of British ports in the Mediterranean area. Churchill gives his "Never was so much owed by so many to so few" speech in the House of Commons praising the efforts of the Royal Air Force in its defense of the British homeland.[1177]

Chinese Communists launch the *Hundred Regiments Offensive* against the Japanese in North China. In 1939 and 1940, the Japanese occupiers had launched more than one hundred and nine small campaigns (one thousand combatants) and ten large campaigns (ten thousand combatants) to wipe out Communist guerrillas. In addition, Wang Jingwei's anti-Communist puppet government conducted its own offensive against the CCP guerrillas. There was also a general belief among the anti-Japanese resistance forces, particularly the Nationalist Kuomintang, that the Communists were not contributing enough to the war effort, and were only interested in expanding their power base. These circumstances initiated the Communists' great offensive.[1178]

The Germans are now shelling Dover England and the nearby coastal area with long-range artillery. They bomb a church in Cripplegate. In retaliation, Churchill orders the bombing of Berlin. In return, Hitler begins the "the London Blitz."[1179]

The *Destroyers for Bases Agreement* is completed between the US and Britain. Britain receives fifty destroyers in exchange for giving the United States land grants in various British possessions in the Bahamas, Antigua, St. Lucia, Trinidad, Jamaica, and British Guiana to establish naval and air bases.[1180]

In one of the major mistakes of the war, the Luftwaffe shifts its focus to London, away from the RAF airfields. While two thousand civilians were killed, the RAF remained the most powerful weapon against German expansion. It stopped Operation Sea Lion in its tracks.

The Japanese occupy French Indochina (Vietnam). Local authorities become figureheads.

Germany invades Romania to block the Soviet Army and get access to valuable oil fields.

The Royal Navy clashes with and defeats several Italian ships, which attacked them after a convoy mission to Malta.

Mussolini decides to invade Greece. On July 28, the Italian ambassador to Greece issues an ultimatum to Greece to surrender. Greek Prime Minister Metaxas replies: "So it is war." The Italian Royal Army launches attacks into Greece from Italian-held Albania and begins the Greco-Italian War. The Greek army counter-attacks and forces the Italians to retreat. By mid-December, the Greeks occupied nearly a quarter of

Albania, tying down five hundred and thirty thousand Italian troops. In March 1941, an Italian counter-offensive fails and on April 6, 1941, Nazi Germany intervenes by invading Greece through Bulgaria and Yugoslavia. This begins the Battle of Greece. [1181]

President Roosevelt wins a third term and the British are hopeful that the US will continue to send supplies.

British naval forces launch an attack against the Italian navy at Taranto, a coastal town in southern Italy. The British damage three battleships, two cruisers, and multiple auxiliary craft. The success of this attack augurs the ascendancy of naval aviation over the big guns of battleships. The event secures British supply lines in the Mediterranean. The British strategy will be studied by the Japanese military, already preparing for an attack on Pearl Harbor.[1182]

Molotov meets Hitler in Berlin to discuss the new world order. Molotov tells Hitler he wants Finland, Bulgaria, Romania, Dardanelles, and Bosporus for the Soviet Union, but Hitler talks broader lines of worldwide spheres of influence between Russia, Germany, Italy and Japan. Molotov meets Hitler a second time asking acceptance to "liquidate" Finland. Hitler demurs. Because he wants Finland's nickel and lumber, he does not want any new conflict in the Baltic Sea where shipping still remains open to Germany.[1183] Hitler from now on resists every attempt of Soviet expansion in Europe. He believes Britain is already defeated and offers India to the Soviet Union.[1184]

Hungary, Romania, and the Slovak Republic sign the Tripartite Pact and join the Axis Powers.

By December 1940, the Axis powers have greatly expanded in Europe and Northern Africa. Britain and Germany continue their massive bombing raids on each other's cities. Joseph P. Kennedy, the US Ambassador to the United Kingdom is asked to resign by President Roosevelt after giving a newspaper interview in which he states that, "Democracy is finished in England."

Hitler issues a directive to begin planning *Operation Barbarossa*, the German invasion of the Soviet Union. The operation is driven by Adolf Hitler's desire to conquer Soviet territory as outlined in *Mein Kampf*. Over the course of the operation, about three million soldiers of the Axis powers invade the Soviet Union along a eighteen hundred-mile front, the largest invasion force in the history of warfare. In addition, the Germans employ some six hundred thousand motor vehicles and six hundred thousand horses. It leads to some of the bloodiest and cruelest battles in history.[1185]

1941

As part of *Operation Compass*, Australian troops of XIII Corps capture Italian-held fortifications in Barida, Libya and take forty-five thousand Italian prisoners.[1186]

Lend-Lease is introduced into the U.S. Congress.

By the beginning of the year, Germany has complete command of the air space over the Mediterranean.

In London, fifty-seven people are killed and sixty-nine injured when a German bomb lands outside the Bank of England, demolishing the Underground station below and leaving a one hundred and twenty foot crater. Bombings of London are now carried out almost daily.

Britain begins its East African counter-offensive against Italian-held Ethiopia.

The *Battle of Ko Chang* ends in a decisive victory for the Vichy French naval forces against Thailand (Siam) in a war over French Indochina (Vietnam, Cambodia and Kwangtung Province in southern China).[1187]

The 4th and 5th Indian Divisions continue the British offensive in East Africa, attacking Italian-held Eritrea.[1188] Hitler and Mussolini meet several times during 1941 and Hitler agrees to provide aid to the Italians in North Africa as the war there continues to spread.

Reports surface that Romanian Fascists ("Iron Guards") are executing Jews in Bucharest. The Iron Guard is an ultra-nationalist, anti-Semitic, anti-communist, anti-capitalist organization that promotes the Orthodox Christian faith. Its members are also called "Greenshirts" because of the green uniforms they wear.[1189]

Charles Lindbergh testifies before the US Congress and recommends that the United States negotiate a neutrality pact with Adolf Hitler. Lindbergh has achieved rock star status for his solo nonstop flight from New York to Paris, a distance of nearly thirty-six hundred miles in a single-seat, single-engine, monoplane, the *Spirit of St. Louis*. Lindbergh had been accused of being a fascist sympathizer. He supported the isolationist *America First* movement. This conflicted with the Roosevelt administration's official policy, which sought to protect Britain from a German takeover. In his later years, Lindbergh became a prolific prize-winning author, international explorer, inventor, and environmentalist.[1190]

In February, Lieutenant-General Erwin Rommel is appointed head of German Army troops in Africa. This unit is later to be officially designated as the "Afrika Korps."

After several days of desperate fighting, the Australians cut off the retreating Italian 10th Army during the Battle of Beda Fomm. The Italians are unable to break through a small blocking force and nearly one hundred and thirty thousand Italians surrender.[1191]

Rommel arrives in Tripoli. The Afrika Korps starts to move eastward towards British positions at El Agheila, a coastal city in far western Libya. German and English troops confront each other. Rommel takes the city and the British retreat. In three weeks, the British are driven back to Egypt. German Panzer tanks arrive in North Africa providing heavy armor for the first major German offensive.

The deportation of Austrian Jews to ghettos in Poland begins. Hitler gives orders for the expansion of Auschwitz prison camps to be run by Commandant Rudolf Höss.

The German U-boat offensive in the Atlantic is increasingly successful. Huge convoy losses hurt the Allies.

In an effort to prevent Britain from bombing the Romanian oilfields from which the Nazis obtained most of their oil, Hitler turns his attention to the Baltic States. He gains agreements from Hungary, Romania, and Bulgaria to join the Axis Powers. He pressures Yugoslavia to do the same. The Regent, Prince Paul of Yugoslavia and his cabinet, succumb to the pressure, but the move is rejected by the Serb-dominated officer corps of the military and some segments of the public, including a large part of the Serbian population, liberals, and communists. A coup d'état is launched on March 27, 1941 by mainly Serb military officers, and Prince Paul is dethroned.

On the same day as the coup, Hitler issues Führer Directive 25, which calls for Yugoslavia to be treated as a hostile state. Hitler considers the coup to be a personal insult and is determined "to destroy Yugoslavia militarily and as a state." Hitler invades Yugoslavia.[1192] A result of this decision is a critical time delay in Hitler's invasion of the Soviet Union.

Buckingham Palace in London is bombed. Across England and Wales cities are mercilessly bombed. Liverpool is bombed over two hundred times.

Japanese spy Takeo Yoshikawa arrives in Honolulu, Hawaii and begins to study the United States fleet at Pearl Harbor.

In Iraq, pro-German Rashid Ali and four influential army officers known as the "Golden Square" stage a military coup d'état and overthrow the regime of the pro-British Regent 'Abd al-Ilah. Rashid Ali names himself Chief of a "National Defense Government." The leaders of the coup will be defeated when British troops later entered Baghdad.[1193]

An Atlantic convoy suffers almost fifty percent losses to a U-boat attack.

German, Hungarian, and Italian troops initiate invasions of Yugoslavia and Greece.

Rommel moves through North Africa with little resistance. The Germans take Salonika, Greece.

Greenland is occupied by the United States with the approval of a "free Denmark" in order to build naval and air bases to counter the German U-boat submarines.

The Kingdom of Yugoslavia is split up by Germany and Italy. They create the *Independent State of Croatia* in an area, which includes modern-day Croatia and Bosnia and Herzegovina, together with some parts of modern-day Serbia. Hitler appoints Ante Pavelić, a Croatian fascist dictator to lead the government. His ultra-nationalist Ustasha organization will murder hundreds of thousands of Serbs, Jews, Roma (Gypsies), and dissident Croats in Yugoslavia during World War II.

Japan and the Soviet Union sign a neutrality pact two years after the Soviet–Japanese Border War (1939)[1194]

British destroyers intercept an Afrika Korps convoy and sink all five transports and three Italian destroyers.

The Germans continue their invasion of Yugoslavia and cut off the Greek army in Albania, which has had notable success against the Italians in January. Yugoslavia surrenders. The Greek Prime Minister Alexandros Koryzis commits suicide. The British evacuate Greece. With their retreat cut off by the German advance, two hundred and twenty-three thousand Greek soldiers in Albania surrender. In April, Athens is occupied by German troops. Greece surrenders.

In North Africa, Rommel attacks the Gazala defense line and crosses into Egypt. The Allied forces in Tobruk, Libya continue to hold out.

The British capture a Nazi U-boat (*U-110*) and discover a copy of the "Enigma" machine which produces code for the German army by which it coordinates military operations. Alan Turing, who is considered today to be the father of theoretical computer science and artificial intelligence, and his team working at the Government Code and Cypher School at Bletchley Park, break the code. Turing plays a pivotal role in enabling the Allies to defeat the Nazis in many crucial engagements, including the Battle of the Atlantic. It is estimated that this work shortened the war in Europe by as many as four years. Despite his service, the country punishes him for being a homosexual. He accepts a treatment of chemical castration as an alternative to prison.[1195]

Rudolf Hess, one time cellmate and homosexual lover[1196] of Adolph Hitler, is captured in Scotland after bailing out of his plane. His self-appointed mission is to make peace with the United Kingdom.

The United Kingdom's House of Commons is damaged by the Luftwaffe in an air raid. Hull, Liverpool, Belfast, and the shipbuilding area of the River Clyde in Scotland are also heavily bombed. It is near the end of the Blitz, as Germany shifts its focus toward Soviet Union and the East.

A Civilian Public Service camp opens for conscientious objectors in the United States.

Adolf Hitler issues "Fuhrer Directive No. 30" in support of "The Arab Freedom Movement in the Middle East," his "natural ally against England." On May, 27, 1941, British forces advance on Baghdad. Members of the German military mission flee Iraq along with Rashid Ali and his supporters. The Mayor of Baghdad surrenders the city to British forces and the Anglo-Iraqi War ends.

Rationing of clothes begins in the United Kingdom.

Stalin begins deporting Lithuanians to prison camps in Siberia.

Deportations continue for five days and total thirty-five thousand Lithuanians, among them seven thousand Jews.[1197] They also deport ten thousand Estonians and fifteen thousand Latvians.

On June 22, Germany invades the Soviet Union under *Operation Barbarossa*, a three-pronged operation aimed at Leningrad, Moscow, and the southern oil fields of the Caucasus, in violation of the German-Soviet non-aggression pact. Romania invades southwestern border areas of the Soviet Union as part of the German initiative.

The *June Uprising* begins against the Soviet Union in Lithuania. Lithuanian ultra-nationalists, who fought against the Russian occupation, go on a killing spree against Jews when the Nazi "liberators" enter Vilnius, the capital city. Hundreds of Jews in Vilnius are taken to Soviet-dug fuel tank pits near the Ponary suburb of Vilnius, where they are shot or buried alive. Reports by witnesses are dismissed as hallucinations. *Nuremberg Laws* are imposed on Jews. The mass deportations and shooting of Jews continues until 1943.[1198]

Hungary, Slovakia, and Italian-occupied Albania declare war on the Soviet Union. Malta, a small group of islands in the Mediterranean Sea between Sicily and North Africa, is attacked by the Germans.

Stalin announces a "scorched earth policy."

On July 4th, German troops mass murder Polish intellectuals when they captured the Polish city of Lwow.

The German armies isolate Leningrad from the rest of Soviet Union. Britain and the USSR sign a mutual defense agreement, promising not to sign any separate peace agreement with Germany. Nazi Panzers take Minsk, the capital of Belarus. The Germans advance farther into the Ukraine. Units of the Italian Expeditionary Corps in Russia begin to arrive. A legion from the Independent State of Croatia is part of the Italian corps. On the 15th, the Red Army starts a counter-attack against the Nazi Wehrmacht (war machine) near Leningrad.

Heinrich Himmler visits Soviet POWs near Minsk and Lublin, a city in Poland, and decides to build a concentration camp near Lublin that becomes known as Majdanek concentration camp. The camp will be used to kill people on an industrial scale during Operation Reinhard, the German plan to murder all Jews within occupied Poland.[1199] As many as two million Jews were sent to extermination camps in Poland to be put to death in gas chambers built for that purpose. The mass killing facilities use Zyklon B a deadly gas supplied by the Siemens Corporation. Majdanek was the first concentration camp discovered by Allied forces, because the Nazis evacuated the site before they could destroy the camp and burn all evidence.[1200]

Japanese troops occupy southern French Indochina. The Vichy French colonial government is allowed by the Japanese to continue to administer Vietnam. French repression of the Vietnamese people continues. The Vichy French in return allow the Japanese to set up bases in Indochina.

German armies take the Russian city of Smolensk, trapping three hundred thousand soldiers. Smolensk is three hundred and sixty miles south of Moscow.

The German armies continue to solidify their occupation in the Baltic States where native Jewish populations are now being exterminated.

SS Commander Hans Krueger orders the *registration* of hundreds of intellectuals in Stanislawow, Poland who are subsequently tortured and murdered. The Nazi SS is now following the armies, killing all the Jews in their wakes. Their method of assassination is based upon the principle of "one bullet one Jew" in order to save ammunition.[1201]

Franklin D. Roosevelt and Winston Churchill meet in Newfoundland where they create the *Atlantic Charter*. It defines the Allied goals for the war and post-war world: no territorial aggrandizement; no territorial changes made against the wishes of the people, self-determination; restoration of self-government to those deprived of it; reduction of trade restrictions; global cooperation to secure better economic and social conditions for all; freedom from fear and want; freedom of the seas; and abandonment of the use of force, as well as disarmament of aggressor nations. The adherents of the Atlantic Charter will also sign the *Declaration by United Nations* on January 1, 1942. It will become the basis for the modern United Nations.[1202]

Adolf Hitler orders a temporary halt to Germany's systematic euthanasia of mentally ill and handicapped people due to world protests. However, graduates of the *Action T4* program are then transferred to concentration camps where they continued in their deadly trade. Under the Action T4 program, German physicians are directed to declare patients "incurably sick, by critical medical examination" and then administer to them a "mercy death." Adolf Hitler signed a "euthanasia decree" that authorized Philipp Bouhler, the chief of his Chancellery and Dr. Karl Brandt, his personal physician, to carry out the program.[1203]

Fascist volunteers from Spain join the German infantry and are sent to Poland.

German forces close in on Leningrad.

British and Soviet troops invade Iran to take control of the Abadan oilfields and the important railway routes to the Soviet Union for the supply of war materials.

On August 30, German forces stage a false attack on their soldiers by Jews, in Vilnius, Lithuania, leading to a retaliatory mass arrest of the residents of the old Jewish quarter. Almost ten thousand Jews are murdered three days later. The event becomes known as The *Great Provocation*.[1204]

The Siege of Leningrad begins as German forces surround the Soviet Union's second-largest city. German armies also surround Kiev another Russian city.

Orders are given by the United States Navy to shoot on sight if any ship or convoy is threatened.

Reza Pahlavi, the Shah of Iran, who had conducted a coup d'etat against the British in 1921 is forced to resign by the invading British and Soviet forces. They place his son Mohammad Reza Pahlavi on the throne and he becomes a puppet of the British Government. The new Shah of Iran remains in power until the Iranian Revolution in February 1979. The Shah, a man who loves titles, refers to himself as Shāhanshāh, "King of Kings" or Āryāmehr "Light of the Aryans." Before his puppet government was established, the Iranian oil industry was nationalized, under the democratically elected Prime Minister Mohammad Mosaddegh. Mosaddegh was a democrat and constitutionalist. After the war, he was overthrown by a US and UK-backed coup d'état. US and UK oil firms were able to seize control of Iran's oil until the revolution in 1979.[1205]

On September 19, the Germans capture Kiev and SS troops kill thirty thousand Jews at Babi Yar on the outskirts of the city.

The National Liberation Front (EAM) is founded in Greece. It became the main movement of the Greek Resistance during the Axis occupation. Its main driving force is the Communist Party of Greece (KKE), but its membership includes several other leftist and republican groups. The EAM becomes the first mass social movement in modern Greek history.[1206]

German forces begin an all-out offensive against Moscow, code named *Operation Typhoon*.[1207]

Mahatma Gandhi urges his followers to begin a passive resistance against British rule in India.

The German invasion of Russia is beginning to bog down as rainy weather creates muddy roads for both tanks and men. German armies encircle about six hundred and sixty thousand Red Army troops near the town of Vyasma (east of Smolensk). It is a great loss and some predict this will be the end of the war.

Germans attempt another drive toward Moscow when the once muddy ground hardens. By the 14th of October, however, temperatures drop on the Moscow front. Heavy snows follow and immobilize German tanks. Meanwhile, the citizens of Moscow frantically build tank traps and other fortifications for the coming siege. An official "state of siege" is announced in Moscow and the city is placed under martial law. Red Army troops arrive in Moscow from Siberia; Stalin is assured that the Japanese will not attack the USSR from the East.

On November 18 General Hideki Tōjō becomes the 40th Prime Minister of Japan.

On the 22nd, the *Odessa Massacre* begins and continues for two days. Twenty-five thousand to thrity-four thousand Jews are led in a long procession and are shot and killed in an antitank ditch, or burnt alive after being crowded into four buildings. At the same time, thirty-five thousasnd Jews are expelled to the Slobodka Ghetto in Lithuania and are left in freezing conditions for ten days. Many perish in the cold. In the Vilna Ghetto, fifty-five hundred Jews, including one hundred and forty old or paralyzed people, are exterminated.[1208]

The Battle of Moscow begins. Temperatures around Moscow drop to minus 12 °C (ten degrees Fahrenheit). The Soviet Union launches ski troops against the freezing German forces near the city.

On the 17th of November, Joseph Grew, the United States ambassador to Japan, cables the State Department that Japan has plans to launch an attack against Pearl Harbor. His cable is ignored. Many historians had suspected that Roosevelt had pre-knowledge of the attack on Pearl Harbor. A later review of information from the National Archives proves them correct. Between November 17 and the 25th, the Japanese Admiral

Yamamoto consistently sent radio messages to his warships headed toward Pearl Harbor. The United States Navy intercepted eighty-three of these messages. Part of the November 25 message read: " . . . the task force, keeping its movements strictly secret and maintaining close guard against submarines and aircraft, shall advance into Hawaiian waters, and upon the very opening of hostilities shall attack the main force of the United States fleet in Hawaii and deal it a mortal blow. . . ." [1209]

If the Roosevelt administration knew about the impending attack why did they let it happen? Why did they not act to save the US navy ships and the thousands of lives of military personnel and civilians? The answer is that, at this time, Roosevelt and his military advisers believed that a victory of the Axis Powers would be a long-term threat to the national security of the United States and they were probably correct. We could all be living in a totally fascist world today if the United States had not entered the war. Because eighty to ninety percent of the American people at the time were against getting involved in "Europe's war," Roosevelt decided to hide the information of a Japanese invasion on Pearl Harbor. He believed that America needed a call to action and the assault on December 7 galvanized the country to war.

German Panzers arrive on the outskirts of Moscow. The temperature on the Moscow front falls to −31 °F. The USSR counter-attacks during a heavy blizzard

Conscription in the United Kingdom now includes all men between eighteen and fifty. Women are recruited to work in fire brigades to minimize the damage of incendiary bombings, and to work in women's auxiliary groups.

On December 7, 1941, Japan declares war on the United States and the United Kingdom and launches the attack on Pearl Harbor. It also invades Thailand, Burma, and British Malaya. It also launches aerial attacks against Guam, Hong Kong, the Philippines, Shanghai, Singapore, and Wake Island. The United States, Britain, the Netherlands, New Zealand, Canada, and Australia declare war on Japan.

Japanese forces take the Gilbert Islands. In a bombing of Clark Field in the Philippines, many American aircraft are destroyed on the ground.

Germany and Italy declare war on the United States. The United States reciprocates and declares war on Germany and Italy.

The United States and the United Kingdom declare war on Romania and Bulgaria after they declare war on them. India declares war on Japan. Hungary declares war on the United States and the United Kingdom; the United States and the United Kingdom reciprocate and declare war on Hungary. The hell fires of war spread around the globe.

Japan invades Borneo and Hong Kong Island.

The German offensive around Moscow is now at a complete halt.

Battle of Sevastopol begins. The Axis powers of Germany, Romania, and Italy battle the Soviet Union for control of Sevastopol, a port in the Crimea on the Black Sea.[1210] The suffering of besieged Leningrad continues. About three thousand are dying each day of starvation and various diseases.

Forty thousand prisoners in the Nazi Bogdanovka concentration camp in Romania are massacred after a few people get typhus, even though the typhus vaccine has existed since 1930. Thousands of disabled and ill inmates are forced into two locked stables, which are doused with kerosene and set ablaze, burning alive all those inside. Other inmates were led in groups to a ravine in a nearby forest and shot in their necks. The remaining Jews dig pits with their bare hands in the bitter cold, and packed them with frozen corpses. Thousands of Jews freeze to death. A break is made for Christmas, but the killing is resumed on December 28. By December 31, over forty thousand Jews had been killed.[1211]

Hong Kong surrenders to Japan.

1942

A secret meeting called the Arcadia Conference is held in Washington DC to plan Allied strategy.[1212] As part of the conference a Declaration by United Nations is drafted. By 1945, twenty-six Allied countries sign the Declaration.

Japanese forces capture Manila, the capital city of the Philippines.

The Soviet Winter counter-offensive comes to a halt, after having pushed the exhausted and freezing German Army back over sixty miles from Moscow. *Operation Barbarossa* has failed.

Nazis at the Wannsee Conference, held in a suburb of Berlin, decide that the "final solution to the Jewish problem" is relocation and extermination.[1213] All military efforts are coordinated to achieve this genocide.

In February, Singapore surrenders to Japanese forces, arguably the most devastating loss in British military history. On the 22nd, President Roosevelt orders General MacArthur to evacuate the Philippines as American defense of the nation collapses.

The United States begins to intern Japanese-American citizens on US soil as fears of invasion increase. The Japanese army continues its conquest of islands in the Pacific.

In March, Britain raises the conscription age to forty-five. It institutes rationing of electricity, coal, and gas. Clothing is rationed as well.

Jews in Berlin must now clearly identify their houses.

The RAF bombs Lübeck, a port city in Germany noted for its medieval architecture. Thirty percent of the city is destroyed. The Fuhrer is outraged and begins bombing English tourist towns.

Japanese forces begin an all-out assault on United States and Filipino troops in Bataan. Bataan falls to the Japanese. The "Bataan Death March" begins, as seventy-six thousand Filipino and American prisoners are forced to march sixty-five miles and then loaded on boxcars to be taken to prisoner-of-war camps. Sixty-six thousand Filipinos and ten thousand Americans die enroute. The reported death tolls vary, especially among Filipino POWs, because historians cannot determine how many prisoners blended in with the civilian population and escaped. On the march, the men are subject to severe physical abuse.[1214] Corregidor, in the middle of Manila Bay, remains a final point of resistance.

The Japanese sustain air attacks on Mandalay in Burma.

Adolf Hitler issues Directive No. 41, outlining his plans for the coming summer offensive in Russia. The object is to seize the Russian oil fields in the Caucasus. A second thrust will be to capture Stalingrad and protect the flank of the main advance.

The RAF bombs Hamburg.

Malta, in the Mediterranean is awarded the George Cross by English King George VI for "heroism and devotion" after sustaining over one thousand air raid attacks.

In April, the United States Navy begins blackouts along the East Coast. This deprives U-boat commanders of background illumination, but provides very little relief from U-boat attacks. As the nights grow shorter more U-boat attacks are occurring in daylight hours.

In May, a US bill creates the Women's Auxiliary Army Corps (WAAC) and is signed into law.

In Russia, General Paulus's (German) 6th Army is forging toward Stalingrad. At Kharkov, the German armies under Paulus and Kleist execute a pincher attack on the Soviets' 6th and 9th armies.

The Japanese conquest of Burma is complete. It is considered to be a "military catastrophe" by Allied forces.

Mexico declares war on the Axis Powers.

In Belgium and France, it becomes compulsory for the Jews to wear the Star of David.

"The Thousand Bomber Raid" on Cologne begins. A mass bombing by one thousand aircraft is meant to stun the Germans and demoralize them. The mass bombing raids become a new strategy.[1215]

In June, The Japanese launch air raids against Alaska. Britain nationalizes the coal industry. The Battle of Midway begins and the American navy inflicts devastating damage on the Japanese fleet that proves irreparable. The battle is viewed as a turning point in the Pacific war. It is believed by many historians to be "the most stunning and decisive blow in the history of naval warfare." Four Japanese carriers and one cruiser are sunk.[1216]

Japanese forces invade and occupy Attu and Kiska off the coast of Alaska. This is the first invasion of American soil in one hundred and twenty-eight years.

The United States opens its Office of War Information, a center for production of propaganda.

In North Africa, during the first battle between the Nazis and British troops in Africa, Rommel destroys large amounts of British armored equipment and threatens to envelop the 50th Division and 1st South African Division at the Battle of Gazala. The British refer to the event as "Black Saturday."[1217]

On June 18th, the Manhattan Project is started in the US. It is the beginning of a scientific approach to nuclear weapons.

General Dwight D. Eisenhower arrives in London ready to assume the post of Commander of American forces in Europe.

Sevastopol falls to the Germans, ending any Red Army resistance in the Crimea.

Guadalcanal is now firmly in the hands of the Japanese.

On July 4th, the American Air Force in Europe begins its first missions.

It is now clear that Stalingrad in Russia will be the largest challenge to the Nazi invaders.

On order from the fascist Vichy France government, French police officers arrest 13,152 Jews and hold them at the Winter Velodrome, an indoor sports arena, not far from the Eiffel Tower. The Jewish people are deported to Auschwitz.

The systematic deportation of Jews from the Warsaw Ghetto begins as Treblinka II, "a model" extermination camp, is opened in Poland.

The Red Army is in a general retreat along the Don River.

The British RAF conducts heavy incendiary attacks on Hamburg.

On the 5th of August, Janusz Korczak, a pediatrician, and two hundred children at his orphanage in Warsaw are led to the Treblinka II death camp and exterminated.

Operation Watchtower begins the Guadalcanal Campaign as American forces invade Gavutu, Tulagi, Tanambogo, and Guadalcanal in the Solomon Islands.

Riots in favor of independence begin in India; Mahatma Gandhi is arrested.

Fighting increases as the Germans approach Stalingrad.

Brazil declares war on the Axis countries, in response to numerous riots caused by the sinking of Brazilian ships by the Nazis.

Mordechai Goldstein, the head of the Jewish Council, a Nazi-imposed administrative structure in all the ghettos, is publicly hanged in Stanislau, Ukraine, along with twenty of the Jewish police. Jewish girls are raped before being shot at the Gestapo headquarters, and one thousand Jews are shot and killed.[1218]

Germany conducts a massive air raid on Stalingrad.

Incendiary bombs from a Japanese seaplane cause a forest fire in Oregon.

Luxembourg is formally annexed to the German Reich. The people call a general strike against conscription.

On September 3rd, the Battle of Stalingrad begins. Every man and boy in the city is conscripted by the Red Army to assist in its defense.

The battle consists of direct assaults on civilians by air raids. The city becomes a jagged landscape of building rubble in which fighting goes on hand to hand and house to house under conditions of starvation and freezing cold. Nearly 2.2 million people are killed or wounded. The heavy losses inflicted on the German Wehrmacht make it arguably the most decisive battle of the whole war. German forces never regain the initiative in the East and are forced to withdraw a vast military force from the West to replace their losses.[1219]

Australian and US forces defeat Japanese forces at Milne Bay, Papua, the first outright defeat for Japanese land forces in the Pacific War. The consequent Japanese evacuation and their failure to establish an airbase lessen the threat to Australia.

SS commander Brandt orders three thousand to four thousand Stanislau Jews deported to the Belzec death camp on Rosh Hashana, the Jewish New Year holiday, where they are killed on that day.

The *Greek Pan-Hellenic Union of Fighting Youths* blow up the offices of the pro-Nazi National-Socialist Patriotic Organization in central Athens, thwarting attempts to raise a Greek fascist volunteer legion for the Eastern Front.[1220]

The Germans test launch the A4-rocket. It flies nintey-one miles (one hundred and forty-seven kilometers) and reaches a height of fifty-three miles (84.5 kilometers), becoming the first man-made object reaching space.

The French resistance creates a coup in Algiers. Four hundred fighters neutralize the Vichy XIXth Army Corps. In violation of a 1940 armistice, Germany invades Vichy France, responding to the fact that French Admiral François Darlan signed an armistice with the Allies in North Africa.

The war in Africa continues to rage on with American and Australian troops joining British forces there. In the Pacific, the Americans and the Japanese are engaged in the Battle for Guadalcanal. At Stalingrad, the Soviet Union launches *Operation Uranus* aimed at encircling the German armies in the city.[1221] The operation is successful and General Paulus sends Adolf Hitler a telegram saying that the German 6th Army is surrounded. Hitler orders Paulus not to surrender.

Below the football field bleachers at the University of Chicago, a team led by Enrico Fermi creates the first nuclear chain reaction. It releases several million times more energy per reaction than any chemical reaction, paving the way for the creation of the first nuclear bomb.[1222]

In an operation named *Operation Winter Storm*, the Germans attempt to break through to aid their forces trapped in Stalingrad. Germany is, however, on the ropes and cannot offer much assistance to its 6th army. The Luftwaffe flies in meager supplies to the beleaguered Stalingrad troops. In the Caucasus, the Germans begin a retreat. The winter in Russia is too punishing for the Nazi troops who are not dressed for the temperature.

As the year draws to a close, things look much brighter for the Allies than they did a few months earlier: Rommel is trapped in Tunisia, the Germans are encircled at Stalingrad, and the Japanese appear ready to abandon Guadalcanal.

1943

On the 14th of January, the *Casablanca Conference* begins. Winston Churchill and Franklin D. Roosevelt discuss the invasion of mainland Europe, the impending invasion of Sicily and Italy, and the wisdom of the principle of "unconditional surrender".[1223]

Jews in Poland rise up in the *Warsaw Ghetto Uprising*. It begins when the Ghetto refuses to surrender to the SS police commander, who then orders the burning of the Ghetto, block by block. A total of thirteen thousand Jews died, about half of them burned alive or suffocated. Another forty thousand are immediately sent to the death camp at Treblinka. German casualties are not known, but they were not more than three hundred.[1224]

The last airfield at Stalingrad is taken by Red forces, preventing the Luftwaffe from further supplying the German troops. Hitler still demands that General Paulus, commander of the 6th army, continue the fight. Paulus surrenders by the end of the month to the Soviet forces. Out of an army of two hundred and eighty-five thousand men, only six thousand remain alive. The German public is informed of the disaster. It is the first time the Nazi government has acknowledged a failure in the war effort.[1225]

On January 28th, Hitler introduces a new conscription law: men between sixteen and sixty-five and women between seventeen and fifty are open to mobilization.

Guadalcanal is secured; it is the first major achievement of the American offensive in the Pacific war.

Major German cities continue to be bombed, including Berlin.

Fig. 4-44: Jews Being Rounded Up by the Nazis

On Feb. 26th, six Norwegians, led by Joachim Ronneberg, successfully attack the heavy water plant Vemork. This greatly delays the Nazi attempt to build a nuclear bomb.

As the month of March begins, the US and Australian naval forces sink eight Japanese troop transports near New Guinea in the *Battle of the Bismarck Sea*.[1226]

On March 13, German forces "liquidate" the Krakow ghetto in Poland. During the operation, the SS kills approximately two thousand Jews and transfers another two thousand Jews to Plaszow, another concentration camp. Another three thousand Jewish people are sent to Auschwitz-Birkenau, where the camp authorities select four hundred and ninety-nine men and fifty women for forced labor. The rest are murdered in the gas chambers.[1227]

The first reports of the *Katyn Massacre* in Poland seep into the West. This time, Polish people are massacred by the Soviet secret police (NKVD) on approval from Stalin. The victims are executed in the Katyn Forest in Russia and other prison camps. Twenty-two thousand people are killed. About eight thousand are officers who were imprisoned during the 1939 Soviet invasion of Poland, another six thousand are police officers, and the rest are arrested Polish intelligentsia, including business men, lawyers, officials, and priests who the Soviets deem a threat to their occupation.[1228]

Fig. 4-45: Jews Humiliated and Murdered by Germans in WWII

On April 19th, the *Bermuda Conference* begins in which UK and US leaders finally discuss the imprisonment and massacres of European Jews. The topic of discussion is what to do with the Jewish refugees who have been liberated by Allied forces as well as those who still remain in Nazi-occupied Europe. The only agreement made was that the war must be won against the Nazis. US immigration quotas are not raised, nor are the British prohibition on Jewish refugees seeking refuge in the British Mandate of Palestine lifted.[1229]

On May 8th, the Japanese begin a three-day massacre and rape of civilians in the city of Changjiao, in the Hunan province of China. About thirty thousand Chinese are killed.[1230]

On May 13th, the remaining German Afrika Korps and Italian troops in North Africa surrender to Allied forces. The Allies take over two hundred and fifty thousand prisoners.

Allies bomb Sicily and Sardinia, both possible landing sites for an invasion of Italy.

The German Admiral Karl Dönitz orders the majority of U-boats to withdraw from the Atlantic because of heavy losses due to new Allied anti-sub tactics. The Nazis call it "Black May." It signals a turn in the war of the Atlantic.[1231]

Josef Mengele becomes Chief Medical Officer in Auschwitz. He is notorious for his torture and deadly human experiments on prisoners.[1232]

The ultra-nationalist Ukrainian Insurgent Army (UPA) begins an ethnic cleansing operation in Nazi-occupied Poland beginning in March 1943 and lasts until the end of 1944. Most of the victims are women and children. The actions of the UPA result in thirty-five to forty thousand Polish deaths in Volhynia and twenty-five to thirty thousand in Eastern Galicia.[1233] Under the Ukrainian fascists, Jews are humiliated and murdered one by one. Many of them are forced to stand in front of mass graves and shot dead. Women are stripped naked and beaten in the streets during "organized riots."

On July 12, the *Battle of Prokhorovka* begins. It is the largest tank battle in human history. Five hundred Soviet tanks faced three hundred German tanks as part of the Nazi's *Operation Citadel*. The battle was inconclusive. While the Germans destroyed more Soviet tanks, the battle stopped the German advance.

U.S. forces under Patton capture Palermo, Sicily.

Hamburg is heavily bombed in Operation Gomorrah by UK and US forces. It is the heaviest assault in the history of aviation. A giant firestorm kills forty-two thousand and six hundred civilians and wounds thirty-seven thousand more. The assault virtually destroys the city.[1234] In Italy, Mussolini is arrested and relieved of his office.

In early August 1943, General Patton slaps two United States Army soldiers under his command during the Sicily Campaign. The men were suffering from post-traumatic stress disorder (PTSD). Patton berates the soldiers after discovering they were patients at evacuation hospitals away from the front lines.[1235]

German and Italian forces begin to evacuate Sicily.

The Bialystok Ghetto uprising begins, led by the Jewish Anti-Fascist Military Organization, a branch of the Warsaw Anti-Fascist Bloc. The revolt begins when the Germans announce a mass deportation from the Ghetto. The main objective of the uprising is to break the German siege and allow the maximum number of Jews to escape into the neighboring Knyszyn Forest. A group of about three hundred to five hundred insurgents armed with only twenty-five rifles, one hundred pistols, and some homemade Molotov cocktails attack the overwhelming German force with a great loss of life. Leaders of the uprising commit suicide when their ammunition runs out. About one hundred and fifty combatants manage to break through and run into the Knyszyn Forest where they join other guerrilla groups.[1236]

A British Ministry of Labor report, issued in early September, states that 22,750,000 British men and women are either in the services or Civil Defense or doing essential war work.

With Mussolini gone, Italy drops out of the war.

Nazi Germany begins the evacuation of civilians from Berlin.

The Soviet Union declares war on Bulgaria.

German troops begin the *Holocaust of Viannos* in Crete, killing citizens and burning villages in retaliation for their support of war resisters. Over five hundred people are killed.

Neapolitans complete their uprising and free Naples from German military occupation.

Italy declares war on Germany.

The US air force suffers a horrendous loss to German anti-aircraft artillery in its attempt to bomb factories that produce ball bearings in Schweinfurt. Of two hundred and ninety-one B-17 "Flying Fortresses" sent on the mission, sixty were shot out of the sky and another seventeen were damaged so heavily that they had to be scrapped. Another one hundred and twenty-one had varying degrees of battle damage. The US air force loses air superiority over Germany.

Members of the Sobibor extermination camp, led by Polish-Jewish prisoner Leon Feldhendler and Soviet-Jewish POW Alexander Pechersky, succeed in covertly killing eleven German SS officers and a number of camp guards. Although their plan was to kill all the SS and walk out of the main gate of the camp, the killings are discovered and only about three hundred of the six hundred conspirators manage to escape into the surrounding forest under heavy gun fire. It is estimated that a minimum of two hundred and fifty thousand Jews were murdered at this camp in Poland. After the revolt, the Germans closed the camp, bulldozed the earth, and planted it over with pine trees to conceal its location. Today, the site is occupied by the Sobibór Museum, which displays a pyramid of ashes and crushed bones of the victims, collected from the cremation pits. [1237]

On October 1st, *Operation Goodtime* begins. The United States Marines land on Bougainville in the Solomon Islands. The fighting on this island will continue to the end of the war.

German SS leader Heinrich Himmler orders that Gypsies and "part-Gypsies" are to be put "on the same level as Jews and placed in concentration camps."

The Tehran Conference brings together Roosevelt, Churchill, and Stalin to discuss opening a Middle Eastern front against the Nazis. During the meeting, the leaders agree to grant Iran independence.[1238]

On the 19th, prisoners of the Janowska concentration camp in German-occupied Poland stage a mass escape when they are ordered to cover up evidence of a mass-murder. Most are rounded up and killed. According to Soviet prosecutor at the Nuremberg Trials, Janowska was an extermination camp where up to two hundred thousand people perished.[1239]

The *Cairo Conference* is held in which Roosevelt, Churchill, and Chiang Kai-Shek meet to discuss strategies to defeat Japan.

Heavy bombing of Berlin continues with huge civilian losses.

In December, resistance leader Marshal Josip Broz Tito proclaims a provisional democratic Yugoslav government in-exile.

1944

On January 20th, the Royal Air Force drops two thousand three hundred tons of bombs on Berlin.

In early February, Germans defeat American troops in the Battle of Cisterna near Anzio in the battle for control of Italy.

On the 14th, the Supreme Headquarters Allied Expeditionary Force headquarters are established in Britain by US General Dwight D. Eisenhower in anticipation of an invasion of mainland Europe.

From February 20 to 25, the US and UK launch the *Big Week*, a bombing campaign of German cities and air force bases, in an attempt to lure the Luftwaffe into a decisive battle and secure air superiority over Europe.[1240] The American P-51 Mustang fighter with its long range proves invaluable in protecting American bombers over Germany.

On March 7, the Japanese invade India, starting a four-month battle around Imphal, the capital of the Indian state of Manipur.

The Allies bomb Vienna, Austria. Frankfurt, Germany is also bombed with heavy civilian losses. Other German cities at strategic locations are bombed for twenty-four hours straight. The RAF suffers grievous losses in an air raid on Nuremberg.

Allied bombers hit Budapest, Hungary, now occupied by the Germans, and Bucharest, Romania, ahead of the advancing Red Army.

General Charles de Gaulle takes command of all Free French forces. Soviet forces enter Odessa, Ukraine, and Kerch in Crimea.

On April 19, Japanese launch *Operation Ichi-Go* (Operation Number One) with over four hundred thousand men in central China. The objectives are to open a land route to French Indochina, and capture air bases in southeast China from which American bombers are attacking the Japanese homeland and shipping.[1241]

Vast preparations for D-Day are going on all over southern England.

An Allied air raid on Paris kills a large number of civilians. Increased Allied bombing of targets in France are made in preparation for D-Day.

On the 31st, the Japanese retreat from Imphal (India) with heavy losses; their invasion of India is over.

Allied troops enter Rome in early June while the German troops fall back to the Trasimene Line, so-named for Lake Trasimene, to keep Allies from moving further north in Italy.

On June 5, *Operation Overlord* begins as more than one thousand British bombers drop five thousand tons of bombs on German gun batteries on the Normandy coast of France in preparation for D-Day. The first Allied troops land in Normandy, France. Paratroopers are scattered from Caen southward. D-Day begins on the 6th with the landing of one hundred and fifty-five thousand Allied troops on the beaches of Normandy. The Allied soldiers quickly break through the Atlantic Wall and push inland. It is the largest sea-born military operation in history.

Joseph Stalin launches an offensive against Finland with the intent of occupying Finland before pushing on to Berlin.

On the 13th, Germany launches a V1 Flying Bomb attack on England in revenge for the D-Day invasion. The V1 are early cruise missiles, called buzz bombs that are fired from launch facilities along the French and Dutch coasts. At its peak, more than one hundred V-1s a day are fired at southeast England; 9,521 bombs are launched in total. Like the bombing of German cities, these terror bombings are used to destroy the morale of the people.[1242] Hitler believes his V1 attacks will win him the war. The bombing of London continues with horrifying losses.

The *Battle of the Philippine Sea*, nicknamed by the Americans as the "Great Marianas Turkey Shoot," begins. The United States Fifth Fleet wins a decisive naval battle over the Imperial Japanese Navy shooting down three hundred Japanese planes while only losing one hundred and thirty to enemy action.[1243]

Soviet troops attack the German forces in Belarus and destroy the German Army Group Centre, the headquarter for all German armies fighting on the Eastern front. This was possibly the greatest defeat of the Wehrmacht during World War II.

The Allies find themselves being easily ambushed in the "battle of the hedgerows," stymied by the agricultural hedges in Western France which army intelligence had not properly evaluated.

On the 6th of July, in the largest Banzai charge of the war, forty-three hundred Japanese troops are slaughtered on Saipan, one of the Northern Mariana Islands. A banzai attack is typically the outcome of an operational failure, and becomes the final effort to turn the tide of battle, or die in the attempt.

If the Japanese run out of ammunition or fail to overrun the enemy, they make a suicidal charge. The soldiers are indoctrinated that, in the event of a Banzai charge, they are to kill themselves to avoid capture, if their attack fails. Their suicide prevents them from being interrogated and forced into giving information to the enemy.

After the failure of the Banzai charge, Saipan is soon declared secure. The Japanese lose over thirty thousand men, many of whom, including civilians, committed suicide.

On July 18, General Hideki Tojo resigns as chief minister of the Japanese government as the defeats of the Japanese military continue to mount.

On the 20, the *July 20 Plot* is carried out by Colonel Claus von Stauffenberg. It is a failed attempt to assassinate Hitler. Hitler was inside his Wolf's Lair field headquarters near Rastenburg, East Prussia when a bomb explodes. A furious Hitler retaliates. More than 7,000 people are arrested and 4,980 are executed. Not all of them are connected with the plot. The Gestapo used the occasion to settle scores with many other people suspected of opposition sympathies. The overwhelming response of the German people was to punish the conspirators. It was a time in which the people were losing the war, their cities were being destroyed, and they believed that only a strong man like Hitler could save them.[1244] The plotters were hanged and their bodies hung on meat hooks. Reprisals against their families continued.

The Poles rise up against the Germans in the *Lwow Uprising*. The Soviet Union is now in control of several large cities in Poland, including Lublin.

From July 27 to August 10, 1944, battles between the Soviet and Nazi forces are fought on the Tannenberg Line in Estonia. The strategic aim of the Soviets is to reoccupy Estonia as a favorable base for the invasions of Finland and East Prussia. Roughly half of its infantry consists of local Estonian conscripts who fight to regain Estonian independence rather than support the Nazis. The German force of 22,250 men holds off 136,830 Soviet and Estonian troops. The deaths from the battles can only be estimated, because no records were kept by either side.[1245] The battles delay the Soviet Baltic Offensive for a month and a half.

On August 1, the Polish Home Army begins the *Warsaw Uprising*. The Poles expect aid from the approaching Soviet Union armies, but it never comes. Polish Boy Scouts play a big role in the uprising. Germans round up young men in Krakow to stop a potential Kraków Uprising.

By August 10, Guam is liberated by American troops. All of the Marianas are now in American hands. The islands will be turned into a major air and naval center against the Japanese homeland.

A clash between Italian POWs and American servicemen ends in the Fort Lawton Riot in Seattle, Washington. After the riot, prisoner

Guglielmo Olivotto is found dead. This leads to the court-martial of forty-three soldiers, all of them African Americans. Later the US Army Board for Correction of Military Records finds that the prosecutor Leon Jaworski had committed an "egregious error," and that all convictions should be reversed. President George W. Bush signed legislation allowing the Army to disburse back pay to the defendants or their survivors.[1246]

The Nazis continue to lose ground in Europe. They are driven to their last strategic position in North Italy, while Allied forces land in southern France. In Belgium, Nazi collaborationists are being killed by paramilitary resisters. In Paris, the French Resistance begins an uprising in the city.

Fig. 4-46: Warsaw Uprising

On August 21, the *Dumbarton Oaks Conference* begins to set up the basic structure of the United Nations. The conference is attended by delegations from the Republic of China, the Soviet Union, the United Kingdom, and the United States in an effort to establish an organization to maintain peace and security in the world.[1247]

Romania breaks with the Axis Powers, surrenders to the Soviet Union, and joins the Allies.

On August 25, Paris is liberated; Charles De Gaulle and Free France parade triumphantly down the Champs-Élysées. The German military disobeys Hitler's orders to burn the city. Soon, the Germans surrender at Toulon and Marseilles, in southern France. Patton's tanks cross the Marne. The Allies enter Rouen in northwestern France.

On the 29th, the anti-German Slovak National Uprising starts in Slovakia, while the Soviet army enters Bucharest, Romania.

In Western Europe, the Allies liberate one city after another. Governments that have been in exile during the war, begin to reorganize and return to their homelands.

Sensing victory, Dutch railway workers in the German-occupied Netherlands go on strike. In retaliation, the Germans blockade food and fuel shipments from farm areas. Some 4.5 million are affected and survive because of soup kitchens. As many as twenty-two thousand are estimated to have died by starvation.[1248]

On the 13th, American troops reach the Siegfried Line, the west wall of Germany's defense system.

The Soviet army begins its Baltic offensive against the German army to the East one day later. The result of a series of battles is the encirclement of the Army Group North and the Soviet re-occupation of the Baltic States.[1249]

The Nazis offer strong resistance to British troops in Arnhem and the British are forced to pull out of the city. Over six thousand Allied paratroopers are captured and hopes of an early end to the war quickly fade.

In October, the Soviet army moves rapidly through the Baltics. They are now in Poland, Latvia, Hungary, Yugoslavia, Prussia, Romania, and Slovakia. In the *Moscow Conference* (1944), Churchill and Stalin discuss spheres of influence in the postwar Balkans.

American troops are now in a full-scale attack on the German "West Wall." Allied forces land on Crete and take control of Greece. British troops enter Athens.

US Navy carriers attack the Japanese in Formosa (Taiwan).

Field Marshal Rommel, under suspicion as one of the "bomb plotters," voluntarily commits suicide to save his family. He is later buried with full military honors.

US forces land on Leyte, Philippines. MacArthur announces: "I have returned." The United States Third Fleet and the Seventh Fleet win a decisive naval battle over the Imperial Japanese Navy in the Philippine Islands.

The U.S. First Army occupies Aachen. It is the first major German city to be captured.

Canadian troops take Zeebrugge in Belgium; Belgium is now entirely liberated.

US planes bomb Singapore under Japanese control.

Zionist terrorists assassinate the British government representative in the Middle East.

Franklin Delano Roosevelt wins a fourth term as US president.

V-2 rockets continue to hit Britain, at the rate of about eight a day. The V-2 is a "Retribution Weapon" designed to attack Allied cities in retaliation for the bombing of German cities. The V-2 is the world's first long-range guided ballistic missile. Beginning in September 1944, over three thousand V-2s are launched by the German Wehrmacht against Allied cities, first London and later Antwerp and Liège. According to a 2011 BBC documentary, the attacks resulted in the deaths of an estimated nine thousand civilians and military personnel, while twelve thousand forced laborers and concentration camp prisoners died producing the weapons, having been worked to death.[1250]

The Japanese air force begins suicidal Kamakaze raids on US ships by crashing their planes into the ships. Many American ships are heavily damaged. About 3,860 kamikaze pilots die, and about nineteen percent of kamikaze attacks manage to hit a ship.[1251]

On the 17th, local partisans force the Germans out of Tirana, Albania.

On the 25th, the Japanese take Nanning in south China, as the war in that theatre continues.

Sensing the end, Heinrich Himmler orders the crematoriums and gas chambers of Auschwitz II-Birkenau dismantled and blown up.

On November 30, the Thiaroye Massacre begins in French West Africa, a federation of eight French colonial territories including Mauritania, Senegal, French Sudan, Mali, French Guinea, Ivory Coast, Burkina Faso, Benin, and Niger. About thirteen hundred black conscripts in the French army, the *Senegalese Tirailleurs*, mutiny because of poor conditions and inadequate pay at the French Thiaroye camp, on the outskirts of Dakar, Senegal. All the men were former prisoners of war and had been repatriated to West Africa and placed in a holding camp awaiting discharge. When their demonstration began the white French soldiers guarding the camp opened fire killing thirty-five and wounding seventy African soldiers. The "mutiny" is seen as an indictment of the colonial system and constitutes a watershed for the nationalist movement.[1252]

On the 3rd of December, the British army and the police shoot unarmed protestors in Athens Greece. The crowd carried Greek, American, British, and Soviet flags, and chanted: "Viva Churchill, Viva Roosevelt, Viva Stalin'" The crowd consised of supporters of the leftist National Liberation Front which was not backed by the British government.

The bombardment of Iwo Jima begins. In the Philippines, the Japanese army kills over one hundred American POW's in the Palawan Massacre.[1253]

On the 16, the *Battle of the Bulge* begins as German forces counter attack against the Allied forces in Europe. The surprise attack catches the Allied forces completely off guard. United States forces bear the brunt of the attack and incur their highest casualties for any operation during the war. The battle also severely depletes Germany's personnel, armored forces and later Luftwaffe aircraft.

On December 17, Typhoon Cobra hits the Third Fleet of Admiral Halsey destroying three destroyers. Almost eight hundred lives are lost. Racial tensions within the US military boil over into the Agana race riot on Guam. After defeating the Japanese, the Allies develop Guam for use as an air force base. Racial tensions begin in late August when the all-black Marine 25th Depot Company arrives to begin loading operations at the newly constructed Naval Supply Depot. Whites of the 3rd Marines Division, some new to the area, try to prevent black marines from visiting the city and its women.

A black Marine stationed on the island compares the military community to "a city deep down in the South" commenting, "Where there are women and white and Negro men, you will find discrimination in large quantities."

Discrimination against blacks involves whites shouting racial slurs, throwing rocks, and occasionally smoke grenades from passing trucks into the camp for black sailors.

Map 4-15: Battle of the Bulge, 1944

The pervasive pattern of discrimination causes tensions to rise between the two groups. A white sailor shoots and kills a "black Marine of the 25th Depot Company in a quarrel over a woman. A black sentry from the 27th Marine Depot Company reacts to harassment by fatally wounding his tormentor, a white Marine. A race riot erupts on Christmas Eve 1944.[1254]

1945

The Luftwaffe launches its last major air offensive of the war in the West. The Battle of the Bulge rages on.

American troops kill dozens of German POWs at Chenogne in revenge for German killings of American soldiers in the Malmedy massacre.

On January 13, the Red Army begins its *East Prussian Offensive*. There is heavy fighting in Poland and Russia.

Hitler is now firmly ensconced in his bunker in Berlin with his companion Eva Braun.

The British commander in Athens accepts a request for a ceasefire from the Greek People's Liberation Army. This results in a defeat for the Greek Left.

Red Army troops enter Warsaw and, against the wishes of the people, set up a puppet government.

The American navy bombards Iwo Jima in preparation for an invasion.

The Red Army crosses the Oder River into Germany and is now less than fifty miles from Berlin.

The Battle of Manila (1945) begins, with US and Philippine militia fighting the occupying Japanese army. The Japanese troops take out their anger and frustration on the civilians in the city. Violent mutilations, rapes, and massacres occur in schools, hospitals, and convents. The Bayview Hotel is used as a "rape center." The Japanese massacre from one hundred thousand to five hundred thousand civilians.[1255]

At the *Yalta Conference*, Roosevelt, Winston Churchill, and Joseph Stalin meet to discuss postwar spheres of influence.

Dresden is firebombed by Allied air forces and large parts of the historic city are destroyed.

The Americans bomb Prague by mistake.

American naval vessels bombard Tokyo and Yokohama, while US Marines invade Iwo Jima. On February 23 the Marines raise the American flag on Mount Suribachi.

Approximately nine thousand bombers are now bombing German cities.

On March 3, Manila is fully liberated.

The allies attempt to bomb V-2s missiles positioned near The Hague ,but mistakenly destroy a Dutch neighborhood killing five hundred and eleven civilians.

By now Allied troops are invading Germany and occupying cities. Germany is being attacked from all sides. The Western Allies slow their advance and allow the Red Army to take Berlin.

The US firebombs a number of cities in Japan, including Tokyo, with heavy civilian casualties.

Iwo Jima is finally secured after a month's fighting. The battle is the only time that the number of American casualties is larger than that of the Japanese. Sporadic fighting will continue as isolated Japanese fighters emerge from caves and tunnels.

The Red Army approaches Danzig (postwar Gdańsk).

At the end of March, General Eisenhower broadcasts a demand for the Germans to surrender.

On April 1, the Battle of Okinawa begins.

The Allied forces begin to liberate concentration camps.

On April 12, President Franklin D. Roosevelt dies suddenly and Harry S. Truman becomes president of the United States.

On April 20, Hitler celebrates his fifty-sixth birthday in the bunker in Berlin. He is nervous, and depressed. The next day, the Soviets launch the Battle of Berlin.

Hermann Göring sends a radiogram to Hitler's bunker, asking to be declared Hitler's successor. He proclaims that if he gets no response by 10:00 p.m., he will assume Hitler is incapacitated and assume leadership of the Reich. Furious, Hitler strips him of all his offices and expels him from the Nazi Party. On the 25th, the Soviet and American troops link up for the first time at the river Elbe, near Torgau in Germany.

Mussolini, heavily disguised, is captured in northern Italy while trying to escape. He and his mistress Clara Petacci, are shot and hanged in Milan the next day. Italian partisans execute other members of his puppet government and their bodies are put on display in Milan. All forces in Italy officially surrender and a ceasefire is declared.

Hitler and Eva Braun commit suicide. He dies by a combination of poison and a gunshot. Before he dies, he dictates his last will and testament. In it Joseph Goebbels is appointed Reich Chancellor and Grand Admiral Karl Dönitz is appointed Reich President.

On May 1, Goebbels and his wife kill their children and commit suicide.

Soviet forces capture the Reichstag building and install the Soviet flag.

Karl Dönitz orders all U-boats to cease operations.

Formal negotiations for Germany's surrender begin at Reims, France.

Czech resistance fighters begin the *Prague Uprising* against the Nazis.

The Soviets begin the Prague Offensive to drive the Germans out of Czechoslovakia. The Germans still have over one million men in the area.

Japanese fire balloons claim their first and only lives from a Sunday school group in Bly, Oregon.

On the 7th of May, Germany surrenders unconditionally to the Allies at the Western Allied Headquarters in Rheims, France. The 8th is declared *Victory in Europe Day*.

In order to disarm the Japanese in Vietnam, the Allies divide the country in half at the sixteenth parallel. Chinese Nationalists will move in and disarm the Japanese from the north while the British will move in and do the same in the south. During the conference, representatives from France request the return of all French pre-war colonies in Indochina. Their request is granted.

Fighting in the southern Philippines continues.

Heinrich Himmler, head of the notorious SS, dies of suicide via cyanide pill.

Fighting breaks out in Syria and Lebanon, as nationalists demand freedom from French control.

On June 5, the Allies agree to divide Germany into four areas of control (American, British, French, and Soviet).

By mid-month, the Japanese are in a general retreat in central China. They are completely defeated on Okinawa.

On the 26th, the United Nations Charter is signed in San Francisco.

On July 5, General Douglas MacArthur announces that the Philippines have been liberated.

On the 17th, the *Potsdam Conference* begins. Churchill, Stalin, and Truman insist upon the unconditional surrender of Japan. Truman hints at the conference that the United States has nuclear weapons.

The US is now heavily bombing Japanese cities.

On August 6, the B-29 bomber *Enola Gay* drops the first atomic bomb "Little Boy" on Hiroshima. Three days latter, the B-29 bomber *Bockscar* drops the second atomic bomb "Fat Man" on Nagasaki. On the 15th, Emperor Hirohito issues a radio broadcast announcing the Surrender of Japan. The real mortality of the atomic bombs that were dropped will never be known because the destruction and overwhelming chaos made orderly counting impossible. Conservative estimates are that one hundred and fifty thousand people were killed and wounded in Hiroshima while seventy-five thousand were killed or wounded in Nagasaki.[1256]

Victory over Japan Day is celebrated.

At a spontaneous, non-communist meeting in Hanoi, Ho Chi Minh and the Viet Minh assume a leading role in the movement to wrest power from the French. Later, Ho Chi Minh's guerrillas occupy Hanoi and proclaim a provisional government. Ho Chi Minh issues his Proclamation of Independence, drawing heavily upon the American Declaration of Independence. Ho declares himself president of the Democratic Republic of Vietnam and pursues American recognition but is repeatedly ignored by President Truman. One hundred and eighty thousand Chinese Nationalist soldiers, mainly poor peasants, arrive in Hanoi to disarm the Viet Minh army and accept their surrender north of the line. After having looted Vietnamese villages during their entire march down from China, they then proceed to loot Hanoi.

Hostilities between Chinese Nationalists and Chinese Communists break out.

General MacArthur takes over command of the Japanese government in Tokyo.

British forces arrive in Saigon to disarm and accept the surrender of the Japanese Occupation Forces in Vietnam south of the sixteenth parallel.

The Japanese garrison in Hong Kong officially signs the instrument of surrender.

The British rearm fourteen hundred French soldiers from Japanese internment camps around Saigon. On the night of September 24th, a mob composed of Viet-Minh militants and sympathizers attacks the French colonial administration and kills around one hundred and fifty people. An estimated twenty thousand French civilians live in Saigon. In southern Vietnam, the British and French recognize the French administration in the southern zone. In North Vietnam, Chinese troops go on a "rampage." Ho Chi Minh and the Viet Minh are hopelessly ill-equipped to deal with it.

The Japanese turn over Taiwan to the Chinese Nationalists (Kuomintang). The island becomes Taiwan Province under the Republic of China.

In November, the prohibition against marriage between GIs and Austrian women is rescinded. Later it will be rescinded for German women too. Black soldiers serving in the army are not allowed to marry white women. In 1948, however, the prohibition against interracial marriages is removed.

In March 1946, Ho Chi Minh accepts an Allied offer of fifteen thousand French troops to rid the North of Chinese Nationalists. The Nationalist troops flee to Taiwan, looting as they depart. As World War II ends, starvation kills up to two million Vietnamese.[1257] The conflict between the French and the Viet Minh continues.

Hermann Göring commits suicide.

In February 1947, the U.S. signs peace treaties with Italy, Bulgaria, Finland, Hungary, and Romania.

It takes until October 1951 for peace between the US and Germany to be realized because the US wanted to keep an occupying force inside Western Germany. The US does not withdraw from West Germany until 1955. East Germany remains annexed by the Soviet Union.

It is not until the end of 1990 when the United States, USSR, Britain, and France, together with the governments of East and West Germany, sign the *Treaty on the Final Settlement with Respect to Germany*. This treaty paves the way for German reunification. The Four Powers renounce all rights they formerly held in Germany, including those regarding the city of Berlin. In March of 1991, German sovereignty is restored.

Women in World War II

As America mobilized for war and men joined the armed forces, women stepped up to fill the vacuum left by men. They took over their husbands' roles and jobs and supported their communities. Many entered the industrial job market, which was now being transformed into war production. The women worked in munitions and weapons plants as well as every other industry. In the military, they served as nurses and clerical help, but some also became pilots and operated anti-aircraft gunnery on the front. In countries that were invaded by the Nazis or ruled over by fascist administrations, many women joined the resistance in great numbers. They fought side by side with men, conducted espionage operations, and served in every capacity. World War II proved beyond a shadow of a doubt that women could serve in any capacity on an equal footing with men. There was nothing that women could not do, if they were not suppressed by men. Still the values of patriarchy kept its control over women. They were paid less than men for comparable jobs, they were not provided military benefits, and when the war ended, they were sent back to their homes. In this way, the patriarchal status quo reconstituted after the war and the contribution of women was largely forgotten by society. Baby boomers forgot what their parents went through and millennials never knew what their grandparents lived through. However, many women who lived through World War II did not forget what had happened and even though the majority of women remained thoroughly indoctrinated by the rules of patriarchy and remained submissive in their inferior positions, a few realized that something was wrong and they could not forget it. Suppressed attitudes and feelings eventually erupted during the women's revolution of the 1960s and the struggle continues until this day.

After the Japanese attack on Pearl Harbor, the United States committed itself to *total war*. This effort included utilizing all of America's resources, including its greatest resource—women. When the war began, young people married in great numbers before the men were sent overseas. Women remained on the *Home Front* to perform the physical work of running the country. In their homes, women "became proficient cooks and housekeepers, managed the finances, learned to fix the car, worked in a defense plant, and wrote letters to their soldier husbands that were consistently upbeat."[1258] Women did anything required to keep the economy running.

Rosie the Riveter helped assure that the Allies would have the war materials needed to defeat the Axis.[1259] The *Rosie the Riveter* campaign inspired by Norman Rockwell's Saturday Evening Post cover, along with a myriad of movies, newspapers, posters, photographs, and articles, stressed the patriotic need for women to enter the work force. Women were now encouraged to do "man's work" and they responded in huge numbers even though their pay rarely earned more than fifty percent of "man's" wages.

Fig 4-47: Poster Campaign Encouraging Women to Enter the Workforce

In addition, nearly three hundred and fifty thousand American women served in the armed forces, volunteering for the newly formed Women's Army Corps (WACS), the Navy Women's Reserve (WAVES), the Marine Corps Women's Reserve (MCWR), the Coast Guard Women's Reserve (SPARS), the Women Airforce Service Pilots (WASPS). They also served in the Army Nurses Corps, and the Navy Nurse Corps. General Eisenhower knew that he could not win the war without the aid of the women in uniform. "The contribution of the women of America, whether on the farm or in the factory or in uniform, to D-Day was a sine qua non of the invasion effort."[1260]

The women in uniform took office and clerical jobs in order to free men to fight. They drove trucks, repaired airplanes, worked as laboratory technicians, rigged parachutes, served as radio operators, analyzed photographs, flew military aircraft across the country, test-flew newly repaired planes, and even trained anti-aircraft artillery gunners by acting as flying targets. Some women served near the front lines in the Army Nurse Corps.

Fig. 4-48: Female Pilots During WWII

More than sixteen hundred nurses were decorated for bravery under fire and meritorious service, and five hundred and sixty-five WACs in the Pacific Theater won combat decorations. Nurses were in Normandy on D-plus-four where they served within the Rescue Flotilla to save the soldiers who were shot or injured in the water during the landing at Normandy. During the invasion, the flotilla rescued fourteen hundred and thirty-eight men from the English Channel. Three months later, these small cutters were still picking up survivors out of the cold, stormy waters bringing the total number of survivors to over two thousand.[1261]

In the United States, almost one hundred and twenty thousand Japanese-Americans and resident Japanese aliens on the West Coast were put into internment camps to await the end of the war. Those interned included women and children. In addition, at least ten thousand nine hundred and five German citizens were held in internment sites throughout the United States and Hawaii. Italian nationals in the United States during World War II were classified as "enemy aliens" and some were detained by the Department of Justice under the Alien and Sedition Act. In 1942, there were six hundred and ninety-five thousand Italian enemy aliens in the United States.

Some Asian-American women were trained as military translators and worked in Army Intelligence to interpret captured Japanese documents.[1262]

At the war's end, women were forced out of their jobs by men returning home and by the downturn in demand for war materials. Women veterans faced roadblocks when they tried to receive army benefits, like the G.I. Bill, which provided education and training for returning soldiers.[1263] The nation that needed their help in a time of crisis, it seems, was not yet ready for greater social equality.[1264]

In other Allied countries, including Canada, Australia, India, and Britain, women essentially served in the same capacity as women in the United States. In Canada, they became "lumberjills", shipbuilders, scientists, and munition workers.[1265]

In France, Italy, and Poland women joined the resistant movements and fought in battles.

Other women, euphemistically called *comfort women*, were forced into sexual slavery by the Imperial Japanese Army before and during World War II. Women were rounded up in occupied countries, including Korea, China, the Philippines, Burma, Thailand, Vietnam, Malaysia, Taiwan, Indonesia, and East Timor and taken to military "comfort stations" to be raped.[1266]

Approximately two million Jewish women in the Holocaust were killed by Nazis and their racist surrogates. The Nazis also killed women with disabilities and Roma women.

In Germany, most of the women worked on small farms. As Germany required labor for its war effort, it paid high wages that attracted women and freed up men for military duty. Germany then began to use Jews and prisoners of war to work the farms, freeing up more women to work in munitions and other war industries. The Third Reich used women in combat roles. All women were under the control of the Nazi SS (Schutzstaffel "Protective Squad"), which was originally set up to be the armed wing of the Nazi Party. Its members could only be Aryan men. Even though it grew in size to thirty-eight divisions, Hitler kept the SS separate from the main army because he intended to use it as a police force after the war. It was the SS that ran the concentration camps and organized slave labor. It was the SS that exterminated two million Jewish women, murdered women with disabilities, murdered partisan women as well as tortured women by sexual harassment, beatings, and rape. Many other women were used in human genetic experiments.[1267]

A half million German women also served in the Nazi armed forces and another four hundred thousand as nurses. Many of these women were forced to look the other way as their patients were murdered in cold blood.[1268]

In Italy, many women joined the anti-fascist resistance, others served in Mussolini's fascist army. Some all-female organizations engaged in civilian and political action. The Germans aggressively tried to suppress them, sending five thousand to prison and deporting three thousand to Germany. On a much larger scale, non-military auxiliaries of the Catholic Centro Italiano Femminile (CIF) and the leftist Unione Donne Italiane (UDI) were new organizations that gave women political legitimacy after the war.[1269] Mostly, however, women's main role was to serve as "birthing machines" and as noncombatants in paramilitary units and police formations (Servizio Ausiliario Femminile). Today in Germany and Japan reference to women as birthing machines is still being used.[1270][1271]

In occupied Poland, as elsewhere, women played an important role in the resistance movement, putting them on the front lines. During the Warsaw Rising of 1944, female members of the Home Army were couriers and medics, but many carried weapons and took part in the fighting. Among the more notable women of the Home Army was Wanda Gertz who created and commanded the DYSK (Women's sabotage unit). For her bravery in these activities and later in the Warsaw Uprising, she was awarded Poland's highest awards—Virtuti Militari and Polonia Restituta.[1272]

Romanian women were pilots in the Royal Romanian Air Force that fought along side the German Luftwaffe. After the war and the Communist seizure of power in Romania, women aviators were largely ignored and their service faded into obscurity.[1273] However, since the Romanian Revolution of 1989, in which the people overthrew the brutal Communist dictator Nicolae Ceaușescu and ended forty-two years of Communist rule, there has been a new wave of recognition of female aviators, as exemplified by Mariana Drăgescu's promotion to the rank of Commander (Comandor) in 2013.[1274]

In Russia, women were mobilized as part of the war effort. About eight hundred thousand women served in the military, of these three hundred thousand served in anti-aircraft units and performed all functions in the batteries, including the use of weaponry. A small number were combat flyers in the Air Force. The photo below is of Klavdiya Kalugina, one of the youngest female Soviet snipers, who was seventeen at the start of her military service in 1943).[1275]

Despite being largely unrecognized for their wartime efforts in the armed forces, the participation of women in World War II allowed for the founding of permanent women's forces in many countries.[1276]

Fig. 4-49: Photo of Klavdiya Kalugina, Young Female Soviet Sniper

Religion in World War II

During the greatest devastation ever experienced by humanity, at the time when horrific torture, rape, and massacre, of not just millions of Jews, but tens of millions of men, women, and children blighted the planet, creating untold suffering and death; at a time when humanity created a hell on earth more awful than at any time during its violent history, why were the voices of Christian leaders not heard in opposition to it. Why is it that we never heard a note of protest from them during this cataclysmic human catastrophe? What were the Catholic and Protestant leaders thinking while all this was going on around them? The awesome human holocaust of World War II was, after all, generated in the heart of the Christian empire, an empire that had long controlled the hearts and minds of the European people. How was it that the average German and Italian Christian, as well as fascist Christians in Serbia and other countries, became so complicit in the greatest evil ever experienced by humanity?

From our review of history, we have learned something about European Christians. For one thing, they have always been racist regarding the Jews. The anti-Semitism of Hitler and the Nazis did not come from some new ideology invented in Mein Kampf. Rather, the hatred that Christians held for Jews and disbelievers of any type was a main course in the people's religious diet for centuries. The Catholic Church had conditioned the tribes of Europe to hate any who were not Christians or who in any way challenged the hegemony of the Catholic priest class. We need only remember the Crusades, the Inquisitions, and the Witch Hunts to substantiate this truth. The hatred of the "other" was always sanctioned by the Christian god, whether it was pronounced from the pulpits of Catholic or Protestant churches. Wars and pogroms were always conducted in his name and so the priests and ministers had disciplined Christians to believe that they could participate in the death and torture of others in an honorable and morally acceptable manner. Hitler, himself was born a Catholic and raised in a Protestant environment where he was conditioned to such beliefs, as were the generations that preceded him and who were his peers and members of his army. Hitler's imperialist cause and his psychopathic obsession to rid the world of Jews once and for all, was a cause long considered to be godly and indeed, blessed by god. Hitler had only to appeal to his fellow German Christians to put him in power and he would help them accomplish their long-cherished dream. The justification for atrocious acts committed by Christians and priests during WWII could only have come from their own beliefs and faiths.

The charge of accountability for the war crimes committed by the Nazis and other fascist states must be made against the long line of Christian leaders who had created the social conditioning of the European people for over a millennium. People were just acting according to their beliefs, the very beliefs that they had been taught as children and which they in turn taught their children; the same beliefs that had been preached from pulpits as they sat and listened in their Sunday clothes; the same beliefs spouted by their politicians who had been indoctrinated in the same beliefs as the people.

In other words, Jewish persecutions, the banning of Jews from working for public office, the enforcement of wearing yellow badges, the Jewish ghettos, the burning of synagogues, and the extermination of millions of Jewish people derive from the practices of Catholicism, centuries before Hitler came into power.[1277]

The seeds of Christian hatred for Jews began with St Paul's epistle to the Thessalonians (2:14-15) in which he wrote, "the Jews who both killed the Lord Jesus, and their own prophets. . . ." The Gospel of John even has Jesus telling the Jews that their Father is the devil (8:44). Many prominent priests and ministers used these statements as a Biblical justification for Jewish persecution. They forget that Jesus and all his apostles, his mother Mary, and even Paul were Jews.

The early Christian fathers also picked up the theme of anti-Semitism, including Barnabas, Justin the Martyr, Tertullian, Oregin, and John Chrysostom. Origen had written, "The blood of Jesus falls not only on the Jews of that time, but on all generations of Jews up to the end of the world." John Chrysostom wrote, "The Synagogue is a brothel, a den of robbers, a lodging for filthy wild beasts. . . ." In comparing Jews to filthy wild beasts, John continued, "Although such beasts are unfit for work, they are fit for killing. And this is what happened to the Jews: while they were making themselves unfit for work, they grew fit for slaughter."[1278]

As soon as Constantine sanctioned Christianity as the state religion, the Church began to persecute the Jews. Constantine imposed heavy penalties on anyone who visited a pagan temple or converted to Judaism. Mixed marriages between Jews and Christians were punished by death. Justinian legalized the burning and pillaging of Jewish synagogues by Christian bishops and monks, many of whom were later made saints for their efforts. In the *Codex Theodosianus* of Theodosis II (AD 408-450), it forbade Jews to hold any public office. Thomas Aquinas, in the treatise *De regimine Judaeorum ad Ducissam Brabantae*, made it acceptable for popes and kings to dispose of property belonging to the Jews.[1279]

When the Fourth Lateran Council of 1215 set up the Inquisition, they required that Jews wear a yellow spot on their clothes and a horned cap (*pileum cornutum*) to mark them as the murderers of Christ and descendants of the devil. During the Black Death plague which ravaged Europe in the fourteenth century, the Catholic clergy aimed its blame at the Jews, claiming they worked for the Devil and had poisoned the wells and springs. During these years in which the Church ruled with an iron hand, many Jews were tortured, killed, and their property inherited by the Church. Hitler was just following the example of his ancestors. He prided himself on fulfilling their dreams.

Popes had a long history of supporting anti-Semitism. Hitler did not invent propaganda; it was an invention of the Church. Pope Gregory XV in the seventeenth century had created the *Sacra Congregatio de Propaganda Fide* (an office created by the pope to promote Church propaganda and counter non-Catholic expressions of faith).

In the 1930s, as Church leaders, along with the German people, listened to Hitler's anti-Semitic rhetoric his speeches only collaborated and justified the Church's long history of Jewish hatred. Hitler reiterated this fact when he met with Bishop Berning and Monsignor Steinmann on April 26, 1933. The Church was concerned about its future under the Nazis. Hitler assures them that Christianity was indispensable in personal and in public life. Germany needs Christianity to serve as a moral foundation for the Third Reich. He reminded the priests that the Catholic Church regarded the Jews as parasites for fifteen hundred years. As a consequence, the Church had forced them into ghettos and had denied them civil and human rights. His intention to drive them out of German society was nothing more or less than an attempt to fulfill what the Church had failed to accomplish:

> "I am moving back toward the time in which a fifteen-hundred-year-long tradition was implemented. I do not set race over religion, but I recognize the represen-

tatives of this race as pestilent for the state and for the Church, and perhaps I am thereby doing Christianity a great service by pushing them out of schools and public functions."[1280]

There was exceedingly few times before or during Hitler's rise to power that the Catholic Church spoke up or denied his racist rants and when protests did occur they were usually in the form of private letters with no follow up. Except for a handful of brave Catholics, the Catholic Church as an institution remained silent about Hitler's intended genocide of the Jews.[1281] The Vatican's only objective was to maintain its own power structure in Germany. In order to do so, it became complicit in the massacre of tens of million of human beings and, in particular, the death, rape, and extermination of millions of Jews.

In Italy, the Holy See had already signed a pact with the fascist dictator Mussolini in February 1929, known as the *Lateran Treaty*, which gave the Church certain benefits in relation to the state. In return, the Vatican encouraged priests to support the Fascists and the Pope spoke of Mussolini as "a man sent by Providence."[1282] The Church had a history of agreements with criminal states regardless of the slavery, inhumanity, or torture they may have delivered upon fellow human beings. Thus, their pact with Mussolini was nothing new. Even the dictator's attack on Ethiopia, on October 3, 1935, was not condemned by the Holy See. Nor did Pius XI restrain the Italian hierarchy from war enthusiasm. "O Duce!," declared the bishop of Terracina, "today Italy is Fascist and the hearts of all Italians beat together with yours."[1283]

Hitler had taken note of the Lateran Treaty and hoped for an identical agreement for his future regime.[1284] In 1933, the Catholic Church signed the *Reich Concordat* with Hitler which begins:

> His Holiness Pope Pius XI and the President of the German Reich, moved by the common desire to consolidate and promote the friendly relations existing between the Holy See and the German Reich, and wishing to regulate lastingly, in a manner satisfying to both parties, the relations between the Catholic Church and the State for

the entire territory of the German Reich, have decided to conclude a solemn agreement. . . .[1285]

Dancing with the Devil

The Reich Concordat declared in so many words that the Church had sold its soul to the devil. It had been corrupt for so long, however, that it did not even notice that it had done so. Hitler now had the authority of the Catholic Church behind him in his efforts to exterminate the Jewish people. It was all that he needed.

The Church argued that it had signed this agreement with the Nazis to protect German Catholics. If Hitler were to close down the Church for any reason, the priests would not be able to administer the sacraments, and the people would be hindered in their quest for salvation. The Concordat gave the papacy what it wanted, a guarantee of its inviolable rights as a religious institution. It was also promised money from Hitler to run its schools and to make German public schools open to Church religious dogma.

Nonetheless, the cost to the Church was the profound loss of its spiritual authority even as it maintained its religious authority.

Many political commentators, journalists and historians viewed the agreement as a manifestation of the pope's underlying motives, which included his preference for dictatorships over democracies, his readiness to use Nazi Germany as a bulwark against the spread into Europe of Stalin's Communism and his utter disregard for the fate of German Jews.

The Concordat of 1933 gave the papacy what it wanted, but it also required it to commit mortal sins. These included forcing Catholic clergy and laity to surrender their spiritual integrity by forbidding them to speak out against the Nazis actions, or to contest political offices. In addition, Catholic bishops were required to swear an oath of loyalty to the Reich and its government. By agreeing to these stipulations, the Church signed away the civil and human rights and obligations of twenty million German Catholics. In doing so, the Papacy demoralized the millions of German Catholics, who had stood with their bishops against the Nazis all during the 1920s and early 1930s. When the news of the Reich Concordat reached the German clergy, they were forced to rescind their bans against Catholics becoming members in the Nazi Party. Because the Concordat did not protect individual parishes and diocese, however, local priests, their congregations and publications were left vulnerable to the state's suppression if they were to raise a voice against Nazi fascism, especially its murder, rape, torture, and attempted extermination of an entire people.

It should not, however, be interpreted that German Catholics, were on the whole against Nazism. Thousands of Catholic priests across Germany immediately put themselves in service to the Reich by participating in an anti-Semitic attestation bureaucracy, in which they supplied details of blood purity through marriage and baptism registries in accordance with the Nazi Nuremberg laws. Catholic compliance in the process would continue throughout the period of the Nazi regime. Any efforts on the part of a few heroic Catholics to help the Jews in their awful desperation must be weighed against the millions who died in the death camps as an indirect result of the official actions of the Catholic papacy and its army of "good Catholics."

Kristallnacht, the night in which the Nazis attacked and burnt Jewish businesses and synagogues, raised nearly a peep of condemnation from the Catholic Church. On March 12, 1939, Cardinal Pacelli, the man who had drafted and arranged for the signing of the Reich Concordat, became Pope Pius XII. The new pope made it clear that he would handle all German affairs personally. He proposed the following affirmation of Hitler:

> To the Illustrious Herr Adolf Hitler, Fuhrer and Chancellor of the German Reich! Here at the beginning of Our Pontificate We wish to assure you that We remain devoted to the spiritual welfare of the German people entrusted to your leadership.... During the many years we spent in Germany, We did all in Our power to establish harmonious relations between Church and State. Now that the responsibilities of Our pastoral function have increased Our opportunities, how much more ardently do We pray to reach that goal. May the prosperity of the German people and their progress in every domain come, with God's help, to fruition![1286]

Let it be accepted that during the reign of the new pope, the Catholic Church did everything it could to promote and assist the Nazi cause.

The Protestant Churches in Germany

Protestantism constituted the major religion in Germany during the early 1930s. Until Hitler attempted to establish a German Reich Church, there existed no such thing as an official German Protestant Church. The Nazi party made a call for all German Protestants to unite in the hour of national need.[1287]

Most German Protestants at the time of Hitler were Lutherans. Early in his life, Luther had argued that the Jews had been prevented from converting to Christianity because the Catholic Church had delivered the wrong message to the Jews. He believed they would respond favorably to his evangelical message if it were presented to them gently. Luther expressed sympathy for the Jews who lived in ghetto slums and accused anyone who denied that Jesus was born a Jew of committing heresy.[1288]

In 1519, Luther challenged the doctrine *Servitus Judaeorum* ("Servitude of the Jews"). He criticized those theologians who hated the Jews and asked what Jew would consent to become Christians when they were treated so badly by Christians.

Luther makes another reference to Jews in his commentary on the *Magnificat*, a Christian hymn in which Elizabeth, who is carrying John the Baptist in her womb, praises Mary for her faith in God. In this commentary, Luther criticizes Jews for placing too much emphasis on the Torah (Old Testament) instead of the New Testament, which accounts the life of Jesus Christ. He stated that the Jews "undertook to keep the law by their own strength, and failed to learn from it their needy and cursed state."[1289] Yet, he concludes that God's grace will continue for Jews as Abraham's descendants, since they may always become Christians. "We ought ... not to treat the Jews in so unkindly a spirit, for there are future Christians among them."

In his essay *That Jesus Christ Was Born a Jew*, written in 1523, Luther condemned the inhuman treatment of the Jews and urged Christians to treat them kindly. He argued:

If I had been a Jew and had seen such dolts and blockheads govern and teach the Christian faith, I would sooner have become a hog than a Christian. They have dealt with the Jews as if they were dogs rather than human beings; they have done little else than deride them and seize their property. When they baptize them they show them nothing of Christian doctrine or life, but only subject them to popishness and monkery... If the apostles, who also were Jews, had dealt with us Gentiles as we Gentiles deal with the Jews, there would never have been a Christian among the Gentiles ... When we are inclined to boast of our position [as Christians] we should remember that we are but Gentiles, while the Jews are of the lineage of Christ. We are aliens and in-laws; they are blood relatives, cousins, and brothers of our Lord. Therefore, if one is to boast of flesh and blood the Jews are actually nearer to Christ than we are ... If we really want to help them, we must be guided in our dealings with them not by papal law but by the law of Christian love. We must receive them cordially, and permit them to trade and work with us, that they may have occasion and opportunity to associate with us, hear our Christian teaching, and witness our Christian life. If some of them should prove stiff-necked, what of it? After all, we ourselves are not all good Christians either.[1290]

By August 1536, however, Luther was angry with the Jews because they would not convert to his brand of Christianity and he turned on them. Luther's prince, the Elector of Saxony John Frederick, had issued a mandate that prohibited Jews from inhabiting, engaging in business, or passing through his realm. Rabbi Josel of Rosheim approached Luther in order to obtain an audience with the prince, but Luther refused, saying, "I would willingly do my best for your people but I will not contribute to your [Jewish] obstinacy by my own kind actions. You must find another intermediary with my good lord."[1291]

A year later, Luther got Jews expelled from Saxony, and in the 1540s he drove them from many German towns.

For Luther, salvation depended on the belief that Jesus was the Son of God, a belief that adherents of Judaism did not share. As time went on, his anger against the Jews increased. In 1543, Luther wrote his *On the Jews and Their Lies*, a sixty-five thousand word anti-Semitic treatise.[1292]

It was a vicious attack, filled with venom, against a people that would not bend to his interpretation of the will of God. In the treatise, Luther describes Jews as a "base, whoring people, that is, no people of God, and their boast of lineage, circumcision, and law must be accounted as filth." Luther wrote that the Jews were "full of the devil's feces... which they wallow in like swine." He called the synagogue an "incorrigible whore and an evil slut".

To destroy this evil in their midst, Luther recommended that good Christians follow his remedy:

1. to burn down Jewish synagogues and schools and warn people against them;
2. to refuse to let Jews own houses among Christians;
3. to destroy Jewish religious writings;
4. to forbid rabbis to preach;
5. to offer no protection to Jews on highways;
6. to prohibit the charging of interest on loans (usury)
7. to take away all the Jew's money and put it aside until they convert to Christianity; and
8. to enslave young strong Jews and make them do physical labor.

And so it came to pass that Germany under Hitler and the Nazi fascists came to carry out the wishes of the greatest Christian holy men in the realm and the people gladly followed their god-given leaders.

While the Catholics in Germany were united in one church, Germany's forty-five million Protestants were not. They were either members of the Lutheran, Reformed, or United Churches. They differed not only in their religious practices but also in their political views. A few openly opposed the Nazis, while others saw themselves as neutral. Still others actively supported Nazism, calling themselves "storm troopers of Jesus Christ." As a result, as Protestant churches responded to National Socialism, some struggled to preserve the independence of their churches from politics and government, while others sought to claim a central place for Christianity in Nazi Germany.

Fig. 4-50: Illustration of Christians Bowing to the Will of the German Leaders

Propaganda posters read, "Hitler's fight and Luther's teaching are the best defense for the German people."

In time, the Nazi government made key changes to the Protestant churches in Germany. The Nazi leadership supported the German Christian movement, a group of Protestants who wanted to combine Christianity and National Socialism into a movement "that would exclude all those deemed impure and embrace all 'true Germans' in a spiritual homeland for the Third Reich."

Secondly, the Nazi leadership urged Protestants to unite all regional churches into a national church under the centralized leadership of Ludwig Müller, a well-known pastor and Nazi Party member, who was appointed as Reich bishop. Many German Protestants embraced these changes. By supporting the German Christian movement and Müller, they could continue to practice their faith and at the same time show support for Hitler. In a national vote by Protestants taken in July 1933, the German Christians were supported by two-thirds of voters, and Müller won the national election to lead them.

Instead of classifying people as Christians or Jews based on their faith, as the Protestants had always done, German Christians began to classify people by racial heritage, as the Nazis did. Therefore, church leaders, whose parents or grandparents had converted from Judaism to Christianity, were still considered Jewish and, according to the 1933 civil service law, no longer officially permitted to serve in those positions.

A public appeal released by German Christian leaders claimed that: "the eternal God created for our nation a law that is peculiar to its own kind. It took shape in the Leader Adolf Hitler, and in the National Socialist state created by him. This law speaks to us from the history of our people.... It is loyalty to this law which demands of us the battle for honor and freedom ... One Nation! One God! One Reich! One Church!"[1293]

As with the Catholics, there were a few brave Protestants who fought against expropriation of the Protestant Churches by the Nazis. They formed the "Confessing Church" and their slogan was "Church must remain church." Not all Protestants in Germany agreed with the German Christian movement and the changes it instituted.

Early on, Confessing Church member Martin Niemöller and two Protestant bishops met with Hitler and his top aides. The religious leaders reaffirmed their support for Hitler's domestic and foreign policies and asked only for the right to disagree on religious matters. Hitler did not compromise, and after the meeting both bishops signed a statement of unconditional loyalty to Hitler; Niemöller did not. As a result, Niemöller was increasingly targeted by the Nazis and was eventually imprisoned for seven years in concentration camps.

Another member of the Confessing Church, Dietrich Bonhoeffer, also resisted the actions of the Nazis. In April 1933, he professed sympathy for Jewish victims of Nazism and argued that National Socialism and Christianity were incompatible. He later became an important symbol of resistance to Nazi Germany and was executed for his role in a plot to assassinate Hitler in 1945. As a disciple of Jesus Christ, he gave his life for true Christianity.

The only Protestant denomination that stood against Hitler was the tiny Jehovah's Witnesses. For their Christian integrity, the Nazis destroyed their national headquarters, outlawed their church, and sent many thousands to concentration camps or prisons, where more than one thousand were killed.

We must remember that many of the German police battalions and SS troopers, who so zealously enslaved, tortured, and executed Jewish men, women, and children, were recruited straight from the German populace who grew up in traditional Christian homes. In the end, neither the official Protestant nor Catholic churches tried to stem the tide of anti-Semitic measures taken by the Nazis.

The Church in the Immediate Aftermath of Germany's Surrender

With the defeat of the Nazis, the German government collapsed, leaving the Catholic and Protestant churches with largely undamaged organizational structures, with branches in every village. The churches, even though they had been complicit in Hitler's evil actions, even though they had sent obsequious communication to Hitler praising his vision and his actions in the name of Christianity, even though its priests and ministers had delivered countless sermons in support of Nazi atrocities, when the Allies moved into Germany, the Churches acted as if they were on the side of the victors. They promoted themselves as being attacked by Hitler for their beliefs and their actions and had stood tall against the atrocities of the German Reich. Their arguments were more or less accepted by the Allies whose troops were also members of the Catholic and Protestant denominations.

The Allies treated all the churches and their representatives, especially the bishops, as if they had all been victims of the Nazis, without any check on the behavior of individual clerics. When honest people began to point their fingers at notorious Nazi sympathizers, the churches treated these people as mavericks and withdrew them from public functions. Forgotten was the pernicious racism on the part of many clergy who supported the actions of Hitler, including torture, rape, and genocide, because they believed he was their defender against the Jewish Bolsheviks, Socialists, and "Jewish" Liberals. Those few Christian heroes who spoke out against the Nazis or who tried to help the Jews were used to prove that church resistance to the Nazis had been general and total. This mythology became a story of a battle between the "cross and swastika," God and Satan, good and evil. This myth took its place along side other authoritative Church doctrine with the publishing of a book by bishop Johann Neuhäusler, entitled the *Cross and the Swastika: the Battle of National Socialism against the Catholic Church and the Church Resistance*, published in 1946, a year after the war ended.[1294]

Lessons Learned

How can we come to terms with the powerful and oppressive hierarchy of religious institutions that deny their participation in crime and evil? Here we speak of evil as knowing that you are doing something terribly wrong to others and you do it anyway because you profit in some way by your actions.

How are the churches consistently able to hide their self-serving intentions behind the veil of protecting their flocks? Certainly, the calculating and backstabbing behavior of the Christian church hierarchies do not reflect the intentions of Jesus Christ who stood for the spiritual truth that, in order to know God, we must love our neighbors and serve our neighbors with every thought, word, and deed. While it cannot be denied that Jesus opposed the oppressive, materialistic Jewish priest class of his day, his condemnation of their hypocrisy does not imply that he hated Jews for being Jews or that all Jews were bad people or that they should be systematically liquidated. True spiritual Christians today, those who follow the teachings of Christ, may oppose the oppressive and materialist Christian priest classes just as Jesus had done with his own religious leaders. But this does not mean that they condemn all Christians for the action of their leaders, nor seek to liquidate all Christians.

Throughout the history of the Catholic Church and its Protestant spin-offs, we have witnessed a long collaboration with evil. The priests and ministers who abandon their moral integrity and their role as spiritual guides are not worthy of our fellowship. They do not deserve our respect, much less our blind faith in their counsel. People of every religion are faced with similar circumstances when their religion is complicit with evil. Why then, as human beings, do we continue to empower those organized religions that continue to lead us to slaughter and to sin against our humanity without so much as a peep against them?

In simple terms, the churches live much longer than an average person. As such, they can disguise their actions and rewrite history according to their needs. The next generation will see only the humble community priests and ministers giving their sermons on Sunday morning. The children will once again listen to the sweet Catholic nuns and gentle teachers in their classes and Sunday school programs. The children will attend their local church services and a new generation will fall victim again to the deceit and lies of organized religion.

The churches demand "blind faith" in their leadership. We are taught that only by blind faith in our religious leaders can a simple person like oneself come to know God. New priests and ministers will arise and with them another generation of Christians will be indoctrinated into a philosophy of "blind faith." Once again, the faith will not be in the person of Jesus or the potentiality that he opens within us, but in the words that the priests and preachers tell us about Jesus. Unfortunately, their interpretation of "what would Jesus do" seldom reaches the universal message of Jesus's life. Under periods of peace, the priests and ministers easily preach feel good religious platitudes, but under periods of stress, their subconscious programming regarding race, gender, ultra-nationalism, xenophobia, and antipathy to other religious faiths rise to the fore. We have seen it happen whenever people are worried about survival. We have seen these same negative sentiments arise in the people before every war. This was certainly true in WWI and WWII and is once again arising in the minds of human beings as the "War on Terrorism" rages on without end.

Under normal conditions, Christian people are attracted to the Church because they are captivated by the idea of Jesus Christ, a man-God, who discovered the secret of God-realization, and who loved all people despite their personal weaknesses as human beings. Christians are no different from other people. We all need hope in our lives—something greater to believe in than the pain and drudgery of our difficult lives. More than this, hope lies at the core of our human nature. It reflects our essential *thirst for unlimited happiness*. As a species, we always hope to

With each succeeding generation, the same moral platitudes are repeated and the same religious services are indulged in that have nothing to do wth the past sins of the Church. There is no discussion allowed. There is no apology. The Church never makes a good act of contrition for its sins. Becauses of this cover up, the racists, sexists, child molesters, and other sinners in the Church are also absolved of their sins. We are led to believe that because they have faith, they hold a respected place in the congregation of God-loving men and women. Those who challenge this counterfeit reality are kicked out of the Church. In this way, the Church washes itself clean from every act of evil—like a man after showering, shaving, and putting on a clean shirt steps out into the dawn of a new day, his sins, committed in the dark of night, forever forgotten.

There is only one way to come to terms wth the evils inherent in organized religions and that is to clearly understand the different between mysticism (spirituality) and religion. We define mysticism here as the personal quest to reduce the distance between one's individual consciousness and God consciousness (Absolute Consciousness in and out of form). Religion, on the other hand, is a collective effort, led by a priest class, to establish a political institution to share a common set of beliefs and values. While religions may serve to awaken a love of the Divine in its members, by demanding that their definition of the Divine is the only definition that is true, religions are by their very nature divisive forces within human society. While mysticism introduces us to the idea of Supreme Oneness and encourages us to promote unity and care of all, religions tear us apart.

A mystic may or may not worship in a religion. He or she may worship in any religion. These things do not matter. What matters is that the mystic has dedicated his or her life in service to the Supreme Oneness and becomes a force to create unity within human society and unity among all of life. Spiritual progress is realized by moving in a path toward oneness. Everything finds its oneness in being a manifestation of Absolute Consciousness. As such, by serving one's neighbor and the created universal we serve the Divine Consciousness.

If a mystic is a member of an organized religion, he or she has the responsibility to ensure his or her religion acts for the welfare of those most in need of help to move forward. It is not sufficient, regardless of what religious leaders say, to follow blindly what we are told to believe. Rather, as human beings we must exercise our rational minds. Does what we are asked to believe lead us toward the Divine Oneness, and love of creation, or does it lead us toward a divisive and self-serving path of manipulation, bigotry, and hatred of others. As with every institution in which we willingly or unwillingly participate, we must see our religion for what it truly is, warts and all, and if we decide to stay in it, we then have the spiritual responsibility to speak out against its evils whenever they arise, even at the cost of self-sacrifice. Jesus was willing to die for love. This was his example to Christians.

A righteous voice of dissent is required to keep any human organization spiritually pure and moving in the right direction. Without a strong voice of dissent, the organization stagnates, becomes corrupt, causes great pain, and then dies an ignoble death. The path to Divine Oneness begins inside each of us, not in religious myths and dogmas. The truth remains, as Jesus and other spiritual masters have told us, that the kingdom of God is within you. Often in this life we are tested in our relationship with God. Fighting evil, is the only way to become spiritually strong. It is the only way to prove our love of the Divine and gain His/Her gratitude in return.

Appendix A: Significant Artists of the Italian Renaissance

Giotto di Bondone (1266-1337) was an Italian painter and architect from Florence in the late Middle Ages. He is generally considered the first of the great artists who contributed to the Renaissance. Giotto's masterwork is the decoration of the Scrovegni Chapel in Padua. This fresco cycle depicts the life of the Virgin and the life of Christ in thirty-seven scenes. Giotto pioneered three-dimensional figures that had faces and gestures that were based on close observation and garments that hung naturally with form and weight. He also introduced characters who faced inwards with their backs or profiles towards the observer, creating the illusion of space.

Fra Angelico (1395 -1455) was an Italian monk, whose name means "Angelic Friar." He worked on altar pieces and frescoes but he also contributed to the process of humanizing the figures in sacred art giving them a "mystical" quality. In his works, people and saints are placed on the same level as the Virgin Mary or Jesus, instead of being below them. Fra Angelico is known for his clear bright pastel colors, the careful arrangement of a few significant figures, and the skillful use of expression, motion, and gesture. He set the stage for artists like Giovanni Bellini, Perugino, and Raphael.

Masaccio (1401-1428) was a Florentine painter who continued to experiment with moving the human form beyond the flatness of fresco images and portrayed the human form more realistically. Masaccio was considered to be the best painter of his generation because of his skill at recreating lifelike figures and movements as well as a convincing sense of three-dimensionality.

Piero della Francesca (1415-1492) was a mathematician who worked in the field of geometry. He is also appreciated for his paintings, which were characterized by their serene humanity and by the use of geometric forms and perspective. His greatest work is considered to be *Virgin and Child Enthroned With Four Angels*.

Giovanni Bellini (1430 -1516) was a Venetian painter who is considered to have revolutionized Venetian painting, moving it towards a more sensuous and coloristic style. Through the use of clear, slow-drying oil paints, Giovanni created deep, rich tints and detailed shadings. He was a teacher to Giorgione and Titian. His *Self Portrait*, *Christ Blessing*, and *Madonna and Child* are among his great works.

Andrea di Michele di Francesco de' Cioni (1435 -1488) was an Italian painter, sculptor, and goldsmith who was the master of an important studio in Florence. He became known by his nickname "Verrocchio" which in Italian means "true eye," a tribute given to him for his artistic achievement. His pupils included Leonardo da Vinci, Pietro Perugino, and Lorenzo di Credi. His greatest achievement was as a sculptor and his last work, the *Equestrian statue of Bartolomeo Colleoni* in Venice, is generally accepted as a masterpiece.

Sandro Botticelli (1445 –1510) was an Italian painter who belonged to the Florentine School under the patronage of Lorenzo de' Medici. Among Botticelli's best-known works are *The Birth of Venus* and *Primavera*.

Michelangelo (1475 - 1564) (see section on Sculpture in text).

Leonardo Da Vinci (1452 - 1519) was a true Renaissance man of "unquenchable curiosity" and "feverishly inventive imagination" whose areas of interest included painting, sculpting, architecture, invention, science, music, mathematics, engineering, literature, anatomy, geology, astronomy, botany, writing, history, and cartography. He has also been called the father of paleontology, ichnology, and architecture. He is widely considered to be one of the greatest painters of all time. His greatest works are the *Mona Lisa* and *The Last Supper*.

Raphael (1483 – 1520) was an Italian painter and architect of the High Renaissance. His work is admired for its clarity of form, ease of composition, harmony, and serenity. Together with Michelangelo and Leonardo da Vinci, he forms the traditional trinity of great masters of that period. Raphael eventually had a studio in which he taught fifty pupils and assistants, many of whom later became significant artists in their own right.

Titian (1490 -1576) was the most important member of the Sixteenth Century Venetian school. Recognized by his contemporaries as "The Sun Amidst Small Stars," Titian was one of the most versatile of Italian painters, adept at portraits, landscape backgrounds, and mythological and religious subjects. His application and use of color profoundly influenced not only painters of the Italian Renaissance, but all future generations of Western art.

As the Italian Renaissance flourished, another movement called the Northern Renaissance was born. Within this movement another great school of painting developed throughout Germany, the Netherlands, and Belgium. Great artists of the north include:

Jan van Eyck (1390 – 1441) produced paintings for private clients in addition to his work at the court. The private works tend to be donor portraits, in which Mary, the mother of Jesus, is presented as an apparition before the donor kneeling in prayer. Mary was viewed as an intercessor between the Divine and members of the Church, so that prayers to Mary were customary in the day. The object of such prayer was to reduce the time one spent in purgatory before getting to heaven. Van Eyck was considered revolutionary in his lifetime and his designs and methods were heavily copied and reproduced.

Hieronymus Bosch (1450 – 1516) was an early painter in the Netherlands. His work is known for its fantastic imagery, detailed landscapes, and illustrations of religious concepts, especially his macabre and nightmarish depictions of hell. The triptych altarpieces, entitled the *Garden of Earthly Delights*, is arguably his greatest masterpiece.

Albrecht Dürer (1471 - 1528) was a German painter and printmaker, especially known for his high-quality woodcut prints which revolutionized the potential of that medium. He was in contact with the major Italian artists of his time, including Raphael, Giovanni Bellini, and Leonardo da Vinci, which allowed him to introduce the classical motifs into Northern art. From 1512, the Emperor Maximilian I became his patron. His well-known engravings include the *Knight, Death, and the Devil* (1513), *Saint Jerome in his Study* (1514), and *Melencolia I* (1514), which has been the subject of extensive analysis and interpretation.

Dürer wrote a theoretical treatise on art that addressed principles of mathematics, perspective, and ideal proportions.

Pieter Bruegel (1525 – 1569) was a Netherland Renaissance painter and printmaker known for his landscapes and peasant scenes. He made the life and manners of peasants the main focus of his work, which was rare in painting in Bruegel's time and he was a pioneer of the genre painting. His earthy, unsentimental but vivid depiction of the rituals of village life are unique windows on a vanished folk culture. His most famous paintings are *Flemish Proverbs*, *Children's Games*, and *The Hunters in the Snow*.

Hendrick Goltzius (1558 - 617) was a Dutch printmaker, draftsman, and painter. He was the leading Dutch engraver of the early Baroque period known for his sophisticated technique and the "exuberance" of his compositions. Goltzius "was the last professional engraver who drew with the authority of a good painter and the last who invented many pictures for others to copy." In his middle age, he also began to produce paintings.

Rembrandt van Rijn (1606 -1669) is considered to be one of the greatest painters and printmakers in European art and the most important in Dutch history. He produced nearly three hundred paintings and three hundred etchings. His contributions to art came in a period of great wealth and cultural achievement that historians call the Dutch Golden Age, which gave rise to important new genres in painting. Among the more prominent characteristics of Rembrandt's work are his theatrical use of light and shadow. His presentation of subjects is devoid of the rigid formality displayed by his contemporaries. Rembrandt felt a deep compassion for mankind, irrespective of wealth, gender, or age. His immediate family often figured prominently in his paintings, many of which had mythical, biblical, or historical themes. *Self-Portrait with Beret and Turned-Up Collar*, T*he Storm on the Sea of Galilee*, and the *Night Watch* are considered among his masterpieces.

Other great painters among the Northern Renaissance artists include Joachim Wtewael, Jan Mabuse, Maarten van Heemskerck, Frans Floris, Joachim Patinir, Pieter Aertsien, Joachim Beuckelaer, and Anthonis Mor.

In France, important Renaissance painters included Simon Marmion (1425 – 1489), Jehan Bellegambe (1470 - 1536), Jean Clouet (1480 -1541);

Nicolas Dipre (1495 - 1532), Jean Cousin (1500 - 1593), François Clouet (1510 - 572); Jean Cousin the Younger (1522 - 1595); and Didier Barra (1590 – 1656).

Appendix B: Significant Musicians of the Renaissance

Johannes Ockeghem (1410 -1497) was the most famous composer of the Franco-Flemish School in the last half of the fifteenth century. In addition to being a renowned composer, he was also an honored singer, choirmaster, and teacher.[1295]

Josquin des Prez (1450 - 1521) is widely considered by music scholars to be the first master of the high Renaissance style of polyphonic vocal music that was emerging during his lifetime. He was praised for both his supreme melodic gift and his use of ingenious technical devices.[1296]

Giovanni Pierluigi da Palestrina (1525 - 1594) was a composer of sacred music and the best-known sixteenth century representative of the Roman School of musical composition. He had a lasting influence on the development of church music and his work has often been seen as the culmination of Renaissance polyphony.[1297]

Orlande de Lassus (1532 - 1594) was a Franco-Flemish composer considered to be the chief representative of the mature polyphonic style of the Franco-Flemish school and one of the most famous and influential musicians in Europe at the end of the sixteenth century.[1298]

William Byrd (1543 – 1623) wrote in many of the forms current in England at the time, including the keyboard and instrumental ensembles. He produced various types of sacred and secular polyphony. While, he produced sacred music for use in Anglican services, he himself became a Roman Catholic in later life and wrote Catholic sacred music as well.[1299]

Giovanni Gabrieli (1557 - 1612) was an Italian composer and organist. He represented the culmination of the style of the Venetian School, at the time of the shift from Renaissance to Baroque idioms.[1300]

Thomas Campion 1567 - 1620) was an English composer, poet, and physician. He wrote over a hundred lute songs, masques for dancing, and an authoritative technical treatise on music.[1301]

Notes

1   Mark A. Peterson, *Galileo's Muse: Renaissance Mathematics and the Arts* (Cambridge: Harvard University Press, 2011), 128.
2   Dr. Jeremy Brotton, "The Myth of the Renaissance in Europe," BBC, last updated February 17, 2011, http://www.bbc.co.uk/history/british/tudors/renaissance_europe_01.shtml.
3   Nathan Nunn and Nancy Qian, "The Columbian Exchange: A History of Disease, Food, and Ideas," *Journal of Economic Perspectives 24*, no. 2: 163–188, https://en.wikipedia.org/wiki/Columbian_Exchange.
4   Wikipedia, "Early Modern Period," last edited on October 26, 2019, https://en.wikipedia.org/wiki/Early_modern_period.
5   Marvin Perry, J. Wayne Baker, Pamela Pfeiffer Hollinger, *The Humanities in the Western Tradition: Ideas and Aesthetic* (New York: Houghton Mifflin, 2003), Chap. 13. Referenced at https://en.wikipedia.org/wiki/Renaissance#cite_note-perry-humanities-17.
6   "Leonardo's Vitruvian Man," History, accessed June 30, 2018, http://leonardodavinci.stanford.edu/submissions/clabaugh/history/leonardo.html.
7   Joseph Gwilt, The Encyclopedia of Architecture. Referenced at Wikipedia, "Classical Order," last edited September 15, 2019, https://en.wikipedia.org/wiki/Classical_order#cite_note-1.
8   Wikipedia, "Renaissance," last edited October 27, 2019, https://en.wikipedia.org/wiki/Renaissance.
9   Wikipedia, "Erasmus," last edited October 21, 2019, https://en.wikipedia.org/wiki/Desiderius_Erasmus.
10   Wikipedia, "Philip Melanchthon," last edited October 15, 2019, https://en.wikipedia.org/wiki/Philip_Melanchthon.
11   Wikipedia, "Erasmus," last edited October 21, 2019.
12   Wikipedia, "Jacques Lefèvre d'Étaples," last edited January 3, 2019, https://en.wikipedia.org/wiki/Jacques_Lef%C3%A8vre_d'%C3%89taples.
13   Wikipedia, "Nicola Pisano," last edited October 25, 2019, https://en.wikipedia.org/wiki/Nicola_Pisano.
14   Anthony Hughes and Caroline Elam, "Michelangelo," Oxford Art Online, last edited October 24, 2019, https://en.wikipedia.org/wiki/Michelangelo.

15   Wikipedia, "Polyphony," last edited September 23, 2019, https://en.wikipedia.org/wiki/Polyphony.
16   Wikipedia, "Polyphony," last edited September 23, 2019.
17   Wikipedia, "Origins of Opera," last edited May 4, 2019, https://en.wikipedia.org/wiki/Origins_of_opera.
18   Wikipedia, "English Renaissance Theater," last edited October 15, 2019, https://en.wikipedia.org/wiki/English_Renaissance_theatre.
19   Kate O'Connor, "Ben Jonson: Renaissance Playwright, Renaissance Man," accessed October 28, 2019, http://writersinspire.org/content/ben-jonson-renaissance-playwright-renaissance-man.
20   Wikipedia, "Masque," last edited October 17, 2019, https://en.wikipedia.org/wiki/Masque.
21   Wikipedia, "History of Science in the Renaissance," last edited October 15, 2019, https://en.wikipedia.org/wiki/History_of_science_in_the_Renaissance.
22   Wikipedia, "History of Science in the Renaissance," last edited October 15, 2019.
23   Wikipedia, "Alchemy," last edited October 24, 2019, https://en.wikipedia.org/wiki/Alchemy#Renaissance_and_early_modern_Europe.
24   Steph Solis, "Copenicus and the Church: What the History Books Don't Say," February 19, 2013, http://www.csmonitor.com/Technology/2013/0219/Copernicus-and-the-Church-What-the-history-books-don-t-say.
25   Wikipedia, "Johannes Kepler," last edited October 18, 2019, https://en.wikipedia.org/wiki/Johannes_Kepler.
26   Maurice Finocchiaro, Defending Copernicus and Galileo: Critical Reasoning in the two Affairs, 2010, Referenced in Wikipedia, "Galileo Galilei," last edited October 15, 2019, https://en.wikipedia.org/wiki/Galileo_Galilei.
27   Wikipedia, "Union of Lublin," last edited September 25, 2019, https://en.wikipedia.org/wiki/Union_of_Lublin.
28   Grażyna Urban-Godziek, ed., "Renaissance and Humanism from the Central-East European Point of View," Columbian University Press, November 2015,http://cup.columbia.edu/book/renaissance-and-humanism-from-the-central-east-european-point-of-view/9788323337416.
29   Wikipedia, "Renaissance in Poland," last edited September 24,

2019, https://en.wikipedia.org/wiki/Renaissance_in_Poland.
30   Michael J. Mikoś, ed., *Polish Renaissance Literature: An Anthology* (Columbus, Ohio: Slavica Publishers, 1995).
31   Wikipedia, "Schweipolt Fiol," last edited March 7, 2019, https://en.wikipedia.org/wiki/Schweipolt_Fiol.
32   Wikipedia, "Ideal City," accessed April 13, 2018, https://en.wikipedia.org/wiki/Ideal_city.
33   Wikipedia, "Renaissance in Poland," last edited September 24, 2019.
34   Wikipedia, "Renaissance Architecture," last edited October 28, 2019, https://en.wikipedia.org/wiki/Renaissance_architecture.
35   Wikipedia, "The Baroque in Poland," last edited September 13, 2019, https://en.wikipedia.org/wiki/Baroque_in_Poland.
36   Wikipedia, "John Hunyadi," last edited September 21, 2019, https://en.wikipedia.org/wiki/John_Hunyadi.
37   Lorant Czigany, "The Renaissance in Hungary," *A History of Hungarian Literarture: Frm the Earliest Times to the Mid-1970s*, http://mek.oszk.hu/02000/02042/html/5.html.
38   Wikipedia, "Primatial Basilica of the Blessed Virgin Mary Assumed Into Heaven and St Adalbert," last edited October 10, 2019, https://en.wikipedia.org/wiki/Primatial_Basilica_of_the_Blessed_Virgin_Mary_Assumed_Into_Heaven_and_St_Adalbert.
39   Wikipedia, "Matthias Church," last edited October 12, 2019, https://en.wikipedia.org/wiki/Matthias_Church.
40   Wikipedia, "Buda Castle," last edited October 25, 2019, https://en.wikipedia.org/wiki/Buda_Castle.
41   Wikipedia, "Visegrád," last edited August 25, 2019, https://en.wikipedia.org/wiki/Visegr%C3%A1d.
42   Wikipedia, "Dormition Cathedral, Moscow," last edited June 9, 2019, https://en.wikipedia.org/wiki/Dormition_Cathedral,_Moscow.
43   Wikipedia, "Renaissance Architecture in Central and Eastern Europe," last edited October 24, 2019, https://en.wikipedia.org/wiki/Renaissance_architecture_in_Eastern_Europe.
44   "Bibliotheca Corviniana Online," Medieval Hungary, accessed October 28, 2019, http://jekely.blogspot.com/p/bibliotheca-corviniana.html.
45   Lorant Czigany, "The Renaissance in Hungary," *A History of Hungarian Literarture: Frm the Earliest Times to the Mid-1970s*.

46   Lorant Czigany, "The Renaissance in Hungary," *A History of Hungarian Literarture: Frm the Earliest Times to the Mid-1970s.*
47   Wikipedia, "Battle of Mohács," last edited October 23, 2019, https://en.wikipedia.org/wiki/Battle_of_Moh%C3%A1cs.
48   Wikipedia, "John Zápolya," last edited September 7, 2019, https://en.wikipedia.org/wiki/John_Z%C3%A1polya.
49   Stephen R. Burant, ed. *Hungary: A Country Study* (Washington: GPO for the Library of Congress, 1989), Hungary-Renaissance and Reformation," accessed October 28, 2019..
50   Szaboics Varga, "The Kingdom of Hungary," Oxford Bibliographies, June 29, 2011, http://www.oxfordbibliographies.com/view/document/obo-9780195399301/obo-9780195399301-0145.xml.
51   "The Cathedral of St. James in Šibenik," UNESCO World Heritage Centre, last edited October 28, 2019, http://whc.unesco.org/en/list/963.
52   Wikipedia, "Trogir Cathedral," last edited August 15, 2019, https://en.wikipedia.org/wiki/Trogir_Cathedral.
53   "Croatian Art," Revolvy, accessed October 28, 2019, http://www.revolvy.com/main/index.php?s=Croatian%20art.
54   Wikipedia, "Giorgio da Sebenico," last edited June 3, 2019, https://en.wikipedia.org/wiki/Giorgio_da_Sebenico.
55   Wikipedia, "Lovro Dobričević," last edited September 21, 2019, https://en.wikipedia.org/wiki/Lovro_Dobri%C4%8Devi%C4%87.
56   Wikipedia, "Mihajlo Hamzic," last edited July 11, 2019, https://hr.wikipedia.org/wiki/Mihajlo_Hamzi%C4%87.
57   Wikipedia, "Nikola Božidarević," last edited September 21, 2019, https://en.wikipedia.org/wiki/Nikola_Božidarević.
58   Wikipedia, "John of Kastav," last edited April 29, 2019, https://en.wikipedia.org/wiki/John_of_Kastav.
59   Wikipedia, "Karlovac," last edited October 24, 2019, https://en.wikipedia.org/wiki/Karlovac.
60   Wikipedia, "Veliki Tabor Castle," last edited October 7, 2019, https://en.wikipedia.org/wiki/Veliki_Tabor_Castle.
61   Wikipedia, "Marko Marulić," last edited June 18, 2019, https://en.wikipedia.org/wiki/Marko_Maruli%C4%87.
62   Wikipedia, Jeronim Vidulić," last edited December 21, 2018, https://en.wikipedia.org/wiki/Jeronim_Viduli%C4%87.
63   Wikipedia, "Hanibal Lucić," last edited October 27, 2019,

https://en.wikipedia.org/wiki/Hanibal_Luci%C4%87.
64   Wikipedia, "Juraj Šižgorić," last edited September 9, 2019, https://en.wikipedia.org/wiki/Juraj_%C5%A0i%C5%BEgori%C4%87.
65   Wikipedia, "Janus Pannonius," last edited October 25, 2019, https://en.wikipedia.org/wiki/Janus_Pannonius.
66   Wikipedia, "Petar Hektorović," last edited October 27, 2019, https://en.wikipedia.org/wiki/Petar_Hektorovi%C4%87.
67   Wikipedia, "Marin Držić," last edited October 11, 2019, https://en.wikipedia.org/wiki/Marin_Dr%C5%BEi%C4%87.
68   Wikipedia, "Petar Zoranić," last edited October 24, 2019, https://en.wikipedia.org/wiki/Petar_Zorani%C4%87.
69   Wikipedia, "Brne Karnarutić," last edited September 1, 2019, https://en.wikipedia.org/wiki/Brne_Karnaruti%C4%87.
70   Wikipedia, "Dinko Zlatarić," last edited October 14, 2019, https://en.wikipedia.org/wiki/Dinko_Zlatari%C4%87.
71   Wikipedia, "Renaissance in Croatia," last edited October 12, 2019, https://en.wikipedia.org/wiki/Renaissance_in_Croatia.
72   Connor Cole, "Russia During the Renaissance," *Prezi*, December 4, 2013, https://prezi.com/v16wenyzwcdo/russia-during-the-renaissance/.
73   Wikipedia, "Bogdan Saltanov," last edited October 22, 2019, https://en.wikipedia.org/wiki/Bogdan_Saltanov.
74   Wikipedia, "Simon Ushakov," last edited July 2, 2017, https://en.wikipedia.org/wiki/Simon_Ushakov.
75   Wikipedia, "Gury Nikitin," last edited October 16, 2019, https://en.wikipedia.org/wiki/Gury_Nikitin.
76   Wikipedia, "Karp Zolotaryov," last edited April 29, 2018, https://en.wikipedia.org/wiki/Karp_Zolotaryov.
77   Wikipedia, "Renaissance Architecture in Central and Eastern Europe," last edited October 24, 2019, https://en.wikipedia.org/wiki/Renaissance_architecture_in_Eastern_Europe.
78   Wikipedia, "Terem Palace," last edited September 29, 2019, https://en.wikipedia.org/wiki/Terem_Palace.
79   Wikipedia, "Palace of Facets," last edited October 4, 2019, https://en.wikipedia.org/wiki/Palace_of_Facets.
80   Wikipedia, "Cathedral of the Archangel," last edited October 13, 2019, https://en.wikipedia.org/wiki/Cathedral_of_the_Archangel.
81   Wikipedia, "Saint Peter of Moscow," last edited June 28, 2018,

https://en.wikipedia.org/wiki/Peter_of_Moscow.
82   Connor Cole, "Russia During the Renaissance" *Prezi*, December 3, 2013.
83   Wikipedia, "Isidore (inventor)," last edited September 23, 2019, https://en.wikipedia.org/wiki/Isidore_%28inventor%29.
84   Connor Cole, "Russia During the Renaissance," *Prezi*, December 3, 2013
85   Wikipedia, "Renaissance," last edited October 27, 2019, https://n.wikipedia.org/wiki/Renaissance#Russia.
86   John M. Najemy, ed., *Italy in the Age of the Renaissance:1300-1550* (Oxford: Oxford University Press, 2004), 86.
87   Wikipedia, "Monte delle doti," last edited September 8, 2019, https://en.wikipedia.org/wiki/Monte_delle_doti.
88   Wikipedia, "Monte delle doti," last edited September 8, 2019.
89   Wikipedia, "Alessandra Scala," last edited July 26, 2019, https://en.wikipedia.org/wiki/Alessandra_Scala.
90   Wikipedia, "Lucrezia Tornabuoni," last edited June 23, 2019, https://en.wikipedia.org/wiki/Lucrezia_Tornabuoni.
91   Wikipedia, "Marguerite de Navarre," last edited September 20, 2019, https://en.wikipedia.org/wiki/Marguerite_de_Navarre.
92   Wikipedia, "Lousie Labé," last edited Septemer 29, 2019, https://en.wikipedia.org/wiki/Louise_Lab%C3%A9.
93   Wikipedia, "Vittoria Colonna," last edited October 25, 2019, https://en.wikipedia.org/wiki/Vittoria_Colonna.
94   Wikipedia, "Lucrezia Borgia," last edited October 27, 2019, https://en.wikipedia.org/wiki/Lucrezia_Borgia
95   Wikipedia, "Artemisia Gentileschi," last edited October 17, 2019, 2018, https://en.wikipedia.org/wiki/Artemisia_Gentileschi.
96   Wikipedia, "Sofonisba Anguissola," last edited October 21, 2019, https://en.wikipedia.org/wiki/Sofonisba_Anguissola.
97   Wikipedia, "Levina Teerlinc," last edited September 3, 2019, https://en.wikipedia.org/wiki/Levina_Teerlinc.
98   Wikipedia, "Catharina van Hemessen," last modified Oct. 10, 2018, https://en.wikipedia.org/wiki/Catharina_van_Hemessen.
99   Wikipedia, "Mary Beale, last edited August 20, 2019, https://en.wikipedia.org/wiki/Mary_Beale.
100 Wikipedia, "Fede Galizia," last edited March 3, 2019, https://en.wikipedia.org/wiki/Fede_Galizia.

101   Wikipedia, "Lavinia Fontana," last edited September 9, 2019, https://en.wikipedia.org/wiki/Lavinia_Fontana.
102   Frima Fox Hofrichter, *Judith Leyster: A Woman Painter in Holland's Golden Age* (Doornspijk, Netherlands: Davaco Publishers, 1989), 32.
103   George S. Keyes, *Masters of Dutch Painting* (1st ed.) (Detroit: Detroit Institute of Arts, 2004), 212–214.
104   George R. Marek, T*he Bed and the Throne: The Life of Isabella d'Este* (New York: Harper and Row Publishers, 1976), ix.
105   Wikipedia, "Catherine dé Medici," last edited October 11, 2019, https://en.wikipedia.org/wiki/Catherine_de'_Medici.
106   Wikipedia, "Mary I of England," last edited October 23, 2019, https://en.wikipedia.org/wiki/Mary_I_of_England.
107   Wikipedia, "Mary, Queen of Scots," last edited October 23, 2019, https://en.wikipedia.org/wiki/Mary,_Queen_of_Scots.
108   Elizabethi, "Queen Elizabeth I," last edited October 28, 2019, http://www.elizabethi.org/.
109   John Knox, "The First Blast of the Trumpet Against the Monstrous Regiment of Women," available to http://www.gutenberg.org/files/9660/9660-h/9660-h.htm.
110   Leon Battista Alberti, "The Family in Renaissance Florence," cited in *The Civilization of the Italian Renaissance: A Sourcebook*, 2nd Edition, ed. Kenneth Bartlett. https://books.google.com/books?id=vu-JICgAAQBAJ&pg=PT256&lpg=PT256&dq=I+often+used+to+-express+my+disapproval+of+bold+and+forward+females&-source=bl&ots=xNkG5r8Dcx&sig=zF7zCGAi0cHWNudlNf-HIx56kVIg&hl=en&sa=X&ved=2ahUKEwiwms3u_ZXeAhUwrYM-KHQuhB70Q6AEwAHoECAkQAQ#v=onepage&q=I%20often%20used%20to%20express%20my%20disapproval%20of%20bold%20and%20forward%20females&f=false.
111   Wikipedia, "Chronological List of Saints and Bessed's in the 14th Century," https://en.wikipedia.org/wiki/Chronological_list_of_saints_and_blesseds_in_the_14th_century; and Wikipedia, "Chronological List of Saints and Bessed's in the 15th Century, https://en.wikipedia.org/wiki/Chronological_list_of_saints_and_blesseds_in_the_15th_century, both accessed October 29, 2019.
112   Wikipedia, "Spice Trade," http://web.clark.edu/afisher/HIST252/lectures_text/women_%20Renaissance.pdf, October 24,

2019, https://en.wikipedia.org/wiki/Spice_trade.
113   Patricia O'Neill, "Christopher Columbus' Discoveries: History & Summary," Study.com, accessed October 29, 2019, http://study.com/academy/lesson/christoper-columbuss-discoveries-history-summary-quiz.html.
114   Wikipedia Commons, "File: Republik Venedig Handelswege01.png," https://commons.wikimedia.org/wiki/File:Republik_Venedig_Handelswege01.png.
115   Wikipedia, "Dutch Colonizations of the Americas," last edited September 24, 2019, https://en.wikipedia.org/wiki/Dutch_colonization_of_the_Americas.
116   Wikipedia, "John Wycliffe," last edited October 26, 2019, https://en.wikipedia.org/wiki/John_Wycliffe.
117   Editors of the Encyclopedia Britannica, "Lollard: English Religious History," Encyclopedia Britannica, accessed October 29, 2019, http://www.britannica.com/topic/Lollards.
118   Wikipedia, "Jan Hus," last edited October 28, 2019, https://en.wikipedia.org/wiki/Jan_Hus.
119   "Wycliff Trialogus," Cambridge University Press, accessed October 29, 2019, http://www.cambridge.org/us/academic/subjects/religion/church-history/wyclif-trialogus.
120   Wikipedia, "Hussite Wars," last edited October 29, 2019, https://en.wikipedia.org/wiki/Hussite_Wars.
121   Wikipedia, "Huldrych Zwingli," last edited October 11, 2019, https://en.wikipedia.org/wiki/Huldrych_Zwingli.
122   Carter Lindberg, *The European Reformations* (Hoboken, New Jersey: John Wiley and Sons, 2009), 161.
123   Wikipedia, "Martin Luther," last edited October 24, 2019, https://en.wikipedia.org/wiki/Martin_Luther.
124   Wikipedia, "Indulgence," last edited October 7, 2019, https://en.wikipedia.org/wiki/Indulgence.
125   Wikipedia, "Martin Luther," last edited October 24, 2019.
126   Wikipedia, "Justification (theology)," last edited October 11, 2019, http://en.wikipedia.org/wiki/Justification_%28theology%29.
127   Wikipedia, "Thomas More," last edited October 28, 2019, https://en.wikipedia.org/wiki/Thomas_More.
128   "England in the Age of Discovery," United States History, accessed October 29, 2019, http://www.u-s-history.com/pages/h1130.html.

129 This interpretation of the main points of Calvin is taken from Reverend Barry Gritters, *The Five Points of Calvinism*, available at http://www.prca.org/pamphlets/pamphlet_41.html
130 R. H. Tawney, *Religion and the Rise of Capitalism* (New York: . Pelican Books, NY 1926), 93.
131 Paul Guichonnet and Maurice Cranston, "Geneva Switzerland," Encyclopedia Britiannica, accessed October 29, 2019, http://www.britannica.com/EBchecked/topic/229000/Geneva/26294/John-Calvin.
132 John Calvin, *Institutes of the Christian Religion*, accessed October 29, 2019, http://www.a-voice.org/tidbits/calvinp.htm.
133 John Calvin, *Defense of Orthodox Faith against the Prodigious Errors of the Spaniard Michael Servetus*, written in 1554; cited in Philip Schaff, *History of the Reformation* [New York, 1892], vol. 2, 791.
134 A Voice in the Wilderness, "Calvin and Persecution," accessed Oct 29, 2019, http://www.a-voice.org/tidbits/calvinp.htm.
135 Philip Schaff. *History of the Christian Church in 8 Volumes* (Pea ody, Massachusetts: Hendrickson Publishers, 1996), Vol. 8.
136 "John Calvin: Journalist, Theologian (1509-1564), Biography," last edited August 13, 2019, http://www.biography.com/people/john-calvin-9235788#leading-figure-of-reformation.
137 Gerald Strauss ed., trans., *Manifestations of Discontent in Germany on the Eve of the Reformation*, "Von der gult: Hie kompt ein Beuerlein zu einem reichen Burger …" (Bloomington, IN: Indiana University Press, 1971), 109-110.
138 Gerald Strauss ed., trans., Manifestations of Discontent in Germany on the Eve of the Reformation, 109-110.
139 Gerald Strauss ed., trans., *Manifestations of Discontent in Germany on the Eve of the Reformation*, 100-101.
140 Literally, "city dweller" the term refers to the rising merchant class during the sixteenth century. It was still used by Marx in the nineteenth century and is often used by communist ideologues today.
141 Working class.
142 R. H. Tawney, *Religion and the Rise of Capitalism* (New York: Penguin Books, 1926), 99.
143 Wikipedia, "Protestant Work Ethic," last edited October 24, 2019, https://en.wikipedia.org/wiki/Protestant_work_ethic.
144 Wikipedia, "Protestant Work Ethic," last edited October 24, 2019.

145   Wikipedia, "Separation of Powers," last edited October 25, 2019, http://en.wikipedia.org/wiki/Separation_of_powers.
146   Clifton E. Olmstead, *History of Religion in America* (Englewood Cliffs, New Jersey: Prentice-Hall, Inc., 1960), 74–76, 99–117.
147   Wikipedia, "Counter-Reformation," last edited October 17, 2019, https://en.wikipedia.org/wiki/Counter-Reformation.
148   Wikipedia, "Roman Inquisition," last edited October 22, 2019, https://en.wikipedia.org/wiki/Roman_Inquisition.
149   Wikipedia, "Fifth Council of the Lateran," last edited September, 2019, https://en.wikipedia.org/wiki/Fifth_Council_of_the_Lateran.
150   Congregation For The Doctrine Of The Faith, "Responses To Some Questions Regarding Certain Aspects Of The Doctrine On The Church," last edited October 29, 2019, http://www.vatican.va/roman_curia/congregations/cfaith/documents/rc_con_cfaith_doc_20070629_responsa-quaestiones_en.html.
151   Wikipedia, "Breviary," last edited September 30, 2019, https://en.wikipedia.org/wiki/Breviary.
152   Wikipedia, "Council of Trent," last edited October 14, 2019, https://en.wikipedia.org/wiki/Council_of_Trent.
153   Wikipedia, "Counter-Reformation," last edited October 17, 2019, 2018, https://en.wikipedia.org/wiki/Counter-Reformation.
154   Wikipedia, "Battle of Lepanto," last edited October 17, 2019, https://en.wikipedia.org/wiki/Battle_of_Lepanto.
155   Wikipedia, "History of the Catholic Church," last edited December 12, 2019, https://en.wikipedia.org/wiki/History_of_the_Catholic_Church.
156   Wikipedia, "Colloquium Marianum," last edited October 6, 2019, https://en.wikipedia.org/wiki/Colloquium_Marianum.
157   Wikipedia, "Sodality of Our Lady," last edited July 20, 2019, https://en.wikipedia.org/wiki/Sodality_of_Our_Lady.
158   Wikipedia, "Seven Deadly Sins," last edited October 7, 2019, https://en.wikipedia.org/wiki/Seven_deadly_sins.
159   Wikipedia, "Peace of Augsburg," last edited September 22, 2019, https://en.wikipedia.org/wiki/Peace_of_Augsburg.
160   Wikipedia, "Spanish Armada," last edited October 19, 2019, https://en.wikipedia.org/wiki/Spanish_Armada.
161   Wikipedia, "Thirty Years' War," last edited October 28, 2019, https://en.wikipedia.org/wiki/Thirty_Years'_War.

162   The House of Hapsburg, a Germany dynasty, controlled the throne of the Holy Roman Empire between 1438 and 1740.
163   Wikipedia, "Defenestrations of Prague," last edited October 7, 2019, https://en.wikipedia.org/wiki/Defenestrations_of_Prague.
164   Wikipedia, "Peace of Westphalia," last edited October 28, 2019, https://en.wikipedia.org/wiki/Peace_of_Westphalia.
165   Henry Kissinger, "Introduction and Chap 1," (Penguin Kindle Books, 2014.) Referenced in Wikipedia, "Peace of Westphalia, last edited October 28, 2019, https://en.wikipedia.org/wiki/Peace_of_Westphalia.
166   *The Chronicle of the Hutterian Brethren, Known as Das grosse Geschichtbuch der Hutterischen Brüder* (Rifton, New York: Plough Pub. House. 1987), 45.
167   *The Chronicle of the Hutterian Brethren, Known as Das grosse Geschichtbuch der Hutterischen Brüder*, 45.
168   Wikipedia, "Magisterial Reformation," last edited December 2, 2019, https://en.wikipedia.org/wiki/Magisterial_Reformation.
169   Wikipedia, "History of the Episcopal Church (United States)," last edited September 22, 2019, http://en.wikipedia.org/wiki/History_of_the_Episcopal_Church_%28United_States%29.
170   Got Questions, "What is the Anglican Church, and what do Anglicans believe?" accessed Oct. 29, 2019, http://www.gotquestions.org/Anglicans.html.
171   Wikipedia, "Restoration (1660)," last edited October 23, 2019, https://en.wikipedia.org/wiki/Restoration_(1660).
172   Wikipedia, "History of the Puritans in North America," last edited September 30, 2019, https://en.wikipedia.org/wiki/History_of_the_Puritans_in_North_America.
173   Ira Stoll, *Samuel Adams: A Life* (New York: Simon and Schuster, Inc, 2008), 258.
174   Randall Balmer, *The Encyclopedia of Evangelicalism* (Westminster: John Knox Press, 2002), vii–viii.
175   J. William T. Youngs, *The Congregationalists: Denominations in America*. 4 (Student ed.) (Westport, Connecticut: Praeger, 1998), 8.
176   Wikipedia, "Pietism," last edited October 3, 2019, http://en.wikipedia.org/wiki/Pietism.
177   Wikipedia, "Women in the Protestant Reformation," last edited October 10, 2019, https://en.wikipedia.org/wiki/Women_in_the_

Protestant_Reformation.

178 Louis Grijp and Louis and Hermina Jolderma, (eds and trans.), "Elisabeth's Manly Courage: Testimonials and Songs of Martyred Anabaptist Women in the Low Countries." Referenced at Wikipedia, "Women in the Protestant Reformation," last edited October 10, 2019.

179 Martin Luther, "Lectures on Genesis 3:11." Referenced in Wikipedia, "Women in the Protestant Reformation," accessed September 8, 2018.

180 John Calvin, "A Sermon of M. Iohn Caluine upon the Epistle of Saint Paul, to Titus." Referenced in Wikipedia, "Women in the Protestant Reformation," last edited October 10, 2019.

181 "1 Corinthians 14:34," John Gill's Exposition of the Bible, accessed October 28, 2019, last edited http://www.biblestudytools.com/commentaries/gills-exposition-of-the-bible/1-corinthians-14-34.html.

182 "1 Corinthians 14 Bible Commentary: John Wesley's Explanatory Nnotes," on the Bible, 1 Cor. 14:34,35Christianity.com, https://www.christianity.com/bible/commentary.php?com=wes&b=46&c=14.

183 "1 Corinthians 14:34," *Bible Hub*, accessed October 28, 2019, https://biblehub.com/commentaries/1_corinthians/14-34.htm

184 "Bible Versions and Translations," Our Library. Referenced at Wikipedia, "Women in the Protestant Reformation," last edited October 10, 2019, https://en.wikipedia.org/wiki/Women_in_the_Protestant_Reformation#cite_note-11.

185 A. Hastings Boss, "The silence of women in the churches — objections considered," Article viii; *Bibliotheca Sacra And Theological Review*, Volume 27 (1870), 739-763.

186 "1 Corinthians 14:34," *John Gill's Exposition of the Bible*, accessed October 29, 2019, http://www.biblestudytools.com/commentaries/gills-exposition-of-the-bible/1-corinthians-14-34.html.

187 "Women in the C church," The Presbyterian Quarterly 3, Volume 3, No. 8 (April, 1889), 166-179.

188 Tracey R. Rich, "Role of Women, Judaism 101, accessed October 29, 2019, http://www.jewfaq.org/women.htm.

189 "Protestant Reformation," Theopedia, accessed Oct 29, 2019, http://www.theopedia.com/protestant-reformation.

190 Wikipedia, "Reformation," last edited October 17, 2019, https://en.wikipedia.org/wiki/Reformation.

191   Wikipedia, "Gallicanism," last edited September 20, 2019, https://en.wikipedia.org/wiki/Gallicanism.
192   Wikipedia, "Conciliarism," last edited September 17, 2019, https://en.wikipedia.org/wiki/Conciliarism.
193   Wikipedia, "Jansenism," last edited September 21, 2019, https://en.wikipedia.org/wiki/Jansenism.
194   Arturo Ortiz, "Heresies in the Modern World," Walking in the Desert: Defending and Living the Catholic Faith, July 16, 2014, http://walkinginthedesert.com/2014/07/16/heresies-in-the-modern-world/.
195   Edward Norman, *The Roman Catholic Church, An Illustrated History* (Oakland, California, University of California Press, 2007), 37, https://en.wikipedia.org/wiki/History_of_the_Catholic_Church#cite_note-166.
196   Edward Norman, *The Roman Catholic Church, An Illustrated History*, 328.
197   Wikipedia, "History of the Catholic Church," last edited October 21, 2019, https://en.wikipedia.org/wiki/History_of_the_Catholic_Church.
198   Editors of the Encyclopaedia Britannica, "Intendant," Encyclopedia Brittanica, accessed October 29, 2019, http://www.britannica.com/topic/intendant-French-official.
199   Wikipedia, "Cardinal Mazarin," last edited September 30, 2019, https://en.wikipedia.org/wiki/Cardinal_Mazarin.
200   Wikipedia, "Fronde," last edited September 25, 2019, https://en.wikipedia.org/wiki/Fronde.
201   Wikipedia, "Persecution of Huguenots under Louis XV," last edited October 8, 2019, https://en.wikipedia.org/wiki/Persecution_of_Huguenots_under_Louis_XV.
202   John Butler, Flow of History, Computer application, Oct 29, 2014, Version 3.0.
203   Wikipedia, "Estates-General of 1789," last edited October 19, 2019, https://en.wikipedia.org/wiki/Estates-General_of_1789.
204   Wikipedia, "What is the Third Estate?" last edited October 16, 2019, https://en.wikipedia.org/wiki/What_Is_the_Third_Estate%3F.
205   Wikipedia, "Great Fear," last edited October 25, 2019, https://en.wikipedia.org/wiki/Great_Fear.
206   Wikipedia, "September Massacres," last edited October 20, 2019, https://en.wikipedia.org/wiki/September_Massacres.
207   Wikipedia, "Jacobin (politics)," last edited October 7, 2019,

https://en.wikipedia.org/wiki/Jacobin_%28politics%29.
208   Wikipedia, "Reign of Terror," last edited October 21, 2019, https://en.wikipedia.org/wiki/Reign_of_Terror.https://en.wikipedia.org/wiki/Reign_of_Terror.
209   Wikipedia, "Maximilien Robespierre," last edited October 29, 2019, https://en.wikipedia.org/wiki/Maximilien_Robespierre.
210   Wikipedia, "Oliver Cromwell," last edited October 25, 2019, https://en.wikipedia.org/wiki/Oliver_Cromwell.
211   Wikipedia, "Oliver Cromwell," last edited October 25, 2019.
212   Wikipedia, "James II of England," last edited October 29, 2019, https://en.wikipedia.org/wiki/James_II_of_England.
213   Wikipedia, "Bank of England," last edited October 27, 2019, https://en.wikipedia.org/wiki/Bank_of_England.
214   Wikipedia, "Battle of Vienna," last edited October 22, 2019, https://en.wikipedia.org/wiki/Battle_of_Vienna.
215   Ágoston Gábor, "Treaty of Karlowitz," *Encyclopedia of the Ottoman Empire* (New York: Infobase Publishing, 2010), 309–10, https://en.wikipedia.org/wiki/Treaty_of_Karlowitz.
216   John Butler, Flow of History, Computer application, Oct 29, 2014, Version 3.0.
217   Wikipedia, "Ivan the Terrible," last edited October 21, 2019, https://en.wikipedia.org/wiki/Ivan_the_Terrible.
218   Shannon Lindon, "Peter the Great and Ivan the Terrible," Prezi, November 14, 2012, https://prezi.com/w1cqoqs31jje/peter-the-great-and-ivan-the-terrible/.
219   Shannon Lindon, "Peter the Great and Ivan the Terrible," Prezi, November 14, 2012.
220   Wikipedia, "Catherine the Great," last edited October 29, 2019, https://en.wikipedia.org/wiki/Catherine_the_Great.
221   Wikipedia, "Crimean Khanate," last edited October 27, 2019, https://en.wikipedia.org/wiki/Crimean_Khanate.
222   Wikipedia, "Pugachev's Rebellion," last edited October 9, 2019, https://en.wikipedia.org/wiki/Pugachev's_Rebellion.
223   Wikipedia, "Catherine the Great," last edited October 29, 2019.
224   Wikipedia, "Crimean War," last edited October 25, 2019, https://en.wikipedia.org/wiki/Crimean_War.
225   Alexis Troubetzkoy,. *A Brief History of the Crimean War* (London: Constable & Robinson, 2006), 208.

226   Michael Lynch, "The Emancipation of the Russian Serfs, 1861: A Charter of Freedom or an Act of Betrayal?" History Today, http://www.historytoday.com/michael-lynch/emancipation-russian-serfs-1861-charter-freedom-or-act-betrayal.
227   Michael Lynch, "The Emancipation of the Russian Serfs, 1861," accessed October 29, 2019.
228   Michael Lynch, "The Emancipation of the Russian Serfs, 1861," accessed October 29, 2019.
229   Wikipedia, "Public Sphere," last edited October 23, 2019, https://en.wikipedia.org/wiki/Public_sphere.
230   Gerard A Hauser, *Vernacular Voices: The Rhetoric of Publics and Public Spheres* (Columbia: University of South Carolina Press, 1999), 61.
231   Wikipedia, "Age of Enlightenment," last edited October 29, 2019, https://en.wikipedia.org/wiki/Age_of_Enlightenment#cite_note-109.
232   Wikipedia, "Age of Enlightenment," last edited October 29, 2019.
233   Wikipedia, "Age of Enlightenment," last edited October 29, 2019.
234   Wikipedia, "Age of Enlightenment," last edited October 29, 2019,
235   Wikipedia, "Salon (gathering)," last edited October 25, 2019, https://en.wikipedia.org/wiki/Salon_%28gathering%29.
236   Evelyn Gordon Bode, "Salonnières and the Bluestockings: Educated Obsolescence and Germinating feminism," *Feminist Studies* 3, no.3/4 (Spring-Summer, 1976): 186.
237   Wikipedia, "Hôtel de Rambouillet," last edited September 27, 2019, https://en.wikipedia.org/wiki/H%C3%B4tel_de_Rambouillet.
238   Wikipedia, "Madeleine de Scudéry," last edited September 26, 2019, https://en.wikipedia.org/wiki/Madeleine_de_Scud%C3%A9ry.
239   Wikipedia, "Salon (gathering)," last edited October 25, 2019.
240   Jim Edwards, "This Is the First Ever Ad For Coffee, From 1652," July 23, 2012, http://www.businessinsider.com/this-is-the-first-ever-ad-for-coffee-from-1652-2012-7.
241   Maria Lobiondo, "Culture of Coffee, "syrup of soot," Princeton Weekly Bulletin, April 5, 1999, https://www.princeton.edu/pr/pwb/99/0405/coffee.htm.
242   "London's Coffee Houses," History, accesssed October 29, 2019, https://www.history.co.uk/history-of-london/londons-coffee-houses.
243   "Primary Source 9.6 The Coffee Houses (1673 and 1675)," http://media.bloomsbury.com/rep/files/Primary%20Source%20

9.6%20-%20Coffeehouses.pdf.
244   "London's Coffee Houses," History, accessed October 29, 2019.
245   Wikipedia, "Republic of Letters," last edited September 1, 2019, https://en.wikipedia.org/wiki/Republic_of_Letters.
246   Wikipedia, "Republic of Letters," last edited September 1, 2019.
247   Sassystephb, "The Enlightenment and the Creation of Feminism," November 3, 2010, https://sassystephb.wordpress.com/2010/11/03/the-enlightenment-and-the-creation-of-feminism/.
248   Carol Blum, "Rousseau and Feminist Revision," *Eighteenth-Century Life* 34 no. 3 (Fall), 51-54, Duke University Press. https://muse.jhu.edu/journals/ecl/summary/v034/34.3.blum.html.
249   Shmoop, "Jean-Jacques Rousseau: Unfair Thinker," accessed October 29, 2019, http://www.shmoop.com/a-vindication-of-the-rights-of-woman/jean-jacques-rousseau.html.
250   "Society of Revolutionary Republican Women (Société des républicaines révolutionnaires) (1793)," Towards Emancipation? accessed October 29, 2019, http://hist259.web.unc.edu/societyrepublicanwomen/.
251   Wikipedia, "Marianne," last edited October 26, 2019, https://en.wikipedia.org/wiki/Marianne.
252   "The Plight of Women's Work in the Early Industrial Revolution in England and Wales," Classroom Lessons Series, http://www.womeninworldhistory.com/lesson7.html.
253   Lyn Reese, "Textile Workers Industrial Revolution," Lessons – More Info, accessed October 29, 2019, http://www.womeninworldhistory.com/textile.html.
254   "Children in Mines," National Museum Wales, accessed October 29, 2019, https://museum.wales/articles/2011-04-11/Children-in-Mines/.
255   "Lest we Forget – The Miner's Bond," Durham Records Online, accessed October 29, 2019, https://www.durhamrecordsonline.com/literature/miners_lives.php.
256   Lyn Reese, "The Coal Mines: Industrial Revolution," Lessons – More Info, accessed October 29, 2019, http://www.womeninworldhistory.com/coalMine.html.
257   "Living Conditions in the Industrial Revolution," History Crunch, accessed October 29, 2019, https://www.historycrunch.com/

living-conditions-in-industrial-towns.html#/.
258   "The Glorious Revolution of 1688," SkyMinds, accessed Oct 20, 2018, https://www.skyminds.net/the-glorious-revolution-of-1688/.
259   John B. Cobb Jr. "To Whom Can We Go? I. Jesus' Call for Progressive Protestants," Religion Online, http://www.religion-online.org/article/to-whom-can-we-go-i-jesus-call-for-progressive-protestants/.
260   Wikipedia, "Religious Liberalism," last edited August 10, 2019, http://en.wikipedia.org/wiki/Religious_liberalism.
261   Wikipedia, "Religious Liberalism," last edited August 10, 2019.
262   "Theological liberalism," Encyclopedia Britannica, accessed October 29, 2019, http://www.britannica.com/EBchecked/topic/590847/theological-liberalism.
263   Wikipedia, "Friedrich Schleiermacher," last edited October 22, 2019, https://en.wikipedia.org/wiki/Friedrich_Schleiermacher.
264   Religion online, http://www.religion-online.org/showarticle.asp?title=3470.
265   Wikipedia, "Francis Bacon," last edited October 29, 2019, http://en.wikipedia.org/wiki/Francis_Bacon.
266   Wikipedia, "Scientific method," last edited October 29, 2019, https://en.wikipedia.org/wiki/Scientific_method.
267   Wikipedia, "Empiricism," last edited October 25, 2019, http://en.wikipedia.org/wiki/Empiricism.
268   "Privi Council Documents: Introduction," New Foundland and Labrador Heritage Website, 2013, http://www.heritage.nf.ca/law/lab4/labvol4_1701.html.
269   "In the Matter of the Boundary Between the Dominion of Canada and the Colony of New Foundland in the Labrador Peninsula," http://www.heritage.nf.ca/articles/politics/pdf/labrador-boundary-dispute-documents.pdf.
270   "From Thomas Jefferson to John Trumbull, 15 February 1789," Founders Online, National Archives, https://founders.archives.gov/Jefferson/01-14-02-0321
271   "The Ancient and Mystical Order Rosae Crucis," AMORC, https://www.rosicrucian.org/history.
272   Sharon A. Lloyd and Susanne Sreedhar, "Hobbes Moral and Political Philosophy," *Stanford Encyclopedia of Philosophy*, February 12, 2012. Retrieved February 25, 2014. Referenced in Wikipedia, "Thomas Hobbes," accessed October 29, 2019, http://en.wikipedia.org/wiki/

Thomas_Hobbes.
273   Wikipedia, "Social Contract," last edited October 16, 2019, http://en.wikipedia.org/wiki/Social_contract.
274   Wikipedia, "Thomas Hobbes," last edited October 28, 2019, http://en.wikipedia.org/wiki/Thomas_Hobbes.
275   Wikipedia, "English Civil War," last edited September 30, 2019, http://en.wikipedia.org/wiki/English_Civil_War.
276   Wikipedia, "De Cive," last edited September 15, 2019, http://en.wikipedia.org/wiki/De_Cive.
277   Thomas Hobbes, *Leviathan* XIII, 9, modified by Noel Malcolm (London: Oxford University Press. 2012).
278   Wikipedia, "Leviathan (Hobbes book)," last edited Octobers 16, 2019, https://en.wikipedia.org/wiki/Leviathan_(Hobbes_book)#cite_ref-6.
279   Wikipedia, "Leviathan (Hobbes book)," last edited October 16, 2019.
280   Wikipedia, "Leviathan (Hobbes book)," last edited October 16, 2019.
281   Wikipedia, "Leviathan (Hobbes book)," last edited October 16, 2019.
282   Wikipedia, "Leviathan (Hobbes book)," last edited October 16 2019.
283   Wikipedia, "Thomas Hobbes," last edited October 30, 2019.
284   Wikipedia, "René Descartes," last edited October 29, 2019, http://en.wikipedia.org/wiki/Ren%C3%A9_Descartes.
285   Wikipedia, "Wax Argument," last edited July 30, 2019, http://en.wikipedia.org/wiki/Wax_argument.
286   John Veitch (trans.), "Selections From The Principles Of Philosophy Of Rene Descartes (1596-1650)," The Classical Library, 2002, accessed October 30, 2019, http://www.classicallibrary.org/descartes/principles/preface.htm.
287   Wikipedia, "Trademark argument," last edited September 10, 2019, http://en.wikipedia.org/wiki/Trademark_argument.
288   Wikipedia, "Biblical criticism," last edited September 20, 2019, http://en.wikipedia.org/wiki/Biblical_criticism.
289   Wikipedia, "Biblical criticism," last edited September 20, 2019.
290   "Baruch Spinoza," National Liberty Alliance, https://www.nationallibertyalliance.org/baruch-spinoza.

291   Jeremy Waldron, *God, Locke, and Equality: Christian Foundations in Locke's Political Thought* (Cambridge: Cambridge University Press, 2002), 217.
292   Wikipedia, "Cosmological argument," last edited October 21, 2019, http://en.wikipedia.org/wiki/Cosmological_argument.
293   Jeremy Waldron, *God, Locke, and Equality: Christian Foundations in Locke's Political Thought*, 142.
294   Wikipedia, "John Locke," last edited October 26, 2019, http://en.wikipedia.org/wiki/John_locke.
295   Wikipedia, "John Locke," last edited October 26, 2019.
296   Wikipedia, "Civil liberties," last edited October 10, 2019, http://en.wikipedia.org/wiki/Civil_liberties.
297   Wikipedia, "John Locke," last edited October 26, 2019.
298   Martin Cohen, *Philosophical Tales* (Malden, Massachusetts: Blackwell Publishing, 2008), 101.
299   Wikipedia, "John Locke," last edited October 26, 2019.
300   "Gottfried Wilhelm Leibniz," *Stanford Encyclopedia of Philosophy*, rev. July 24, 2013, http://plato.stanford.edu/entries/leibniz/.
301   "Gottfried Wilhelm Leibniz," *Stanford Encyclopedia of Philosophy*, rev. July 24, 2013.
302   "Montesquieu Biography," Encyclopedia of World Biography, accessed October 30, 2019, https://www.notablebiographies.com/Mo-Ni/Montesquieu.html.
303   "Montesquieu Biography," Encyclopedia of World Biography, accessed October 30, 2019.
304   Baron de Montesquieu, Charles-Louis de Secondat, *Stanford Encyclopedia of Philosophy*, rev. April 2, 2014, accessed October 30, 2019, http://plato.stanford.edu/entries/montesquieu/.
305   "Burns Night: 35 great quotes about Scotland and the Scots," The Telegraph, January 25, 2018, https://www.telegraph.co.uk/books/authors/35-great-quotes-about-scotland-and-the-scots/35-great-quotes-about-scotland-and-the-scots20/.
306   Bruce Lenman, "Scotland, the Caribbean and the Atlantic world, 1750-1820," *Journal of Imperial and Commonwealth History*, Sept. 2006. 439-441.
307   "Innate Ideas," *Columbia Electronic Encyclopedia*, 6th edition (2012), accessed October 30, 2019, http://www.infoplease.com/encyclopedia/society/innate-ideas.html.

308   Wikipedia, "David Hume," last edited October 29, 2019, https://en.wikipedia.org/wiki/David_Hume.
309   Wikipedia, "Jean-Jacques Rousseau," last edited October 28, 2019, https://en.wikipedia.org/wiki/Jean-Jacques_Rousseau.
310   Wikipedia, "Jean-Jacques Rousseau," last edited October 28, 2019.
311   Wikipedia, "Unitarianism," last edited October 27, 2019, http://en.wikipedia.org/wiki/Unitarianism.
312   Peter Gay, *The Enlightenment, The Science of Freedom* (New York: W. W. Norton, 1996), 72.
313   Wikipedia, "Jean-Jacques Rousseau," last edited October 28, 2019, http://en.wikipedia.org/wiki/Jean-Jacques_Rousseau.
314   "Jean Jacques Rousseau, *Stanford Encyclopedia of Philosophy*, rev May 26, 2017, http://plato.stanford.edu/entries/rousseau/.
315   Marie Bussing-Burks, *Influential Economists* (Minneapolis: Oliver Press, 2003), 39.
316   Mark Skousen, *The Making of Modern Economics: The Lives and Ideas of Great Thinkers* (Armonk, New York: M.E. Sharpe, 2001), 32. https://en.wikipedia.org/wiki/Adam_Smith#cite_note-5.
317   Wikipedia, "Adam Smith," last edited October 29, 2019, https://en.wikipedia.org/wiki/Adam_Smith.
318   Wikipedia, "Adam Smith," last edited October 29, 2019.
319   Wikipedia, "Adam Smith," last edited October 29, 2019.
320   Rohlf, Michael, "Immanuel Kant," *The Stanford Encyclopedia of Philosophy Archive* (Summer 2014 Edition), Edward N. Zalta (ed.), http://plato.stanford.edu/archives/sum2014/entries/kant/.
321   "Idealism," Philosophy Pages, http://www.philosophypages.com/dy/i.htm#idlm.
322   Immanuel Kant, *Critique of Pure Reason* [1781], trans. Norman Kemp Smith (NY: St. Martins, 1965), A 51/B 75.
323   Immanuel Kant, *Critique of Pure Reason*, eds. Paul Guyer and Allen W. Wood (Cambridge: Cambridge University Press, 1998), 248.
324   Immanuel Kant, *Critique of Pure Reason* [1781], trans. Norman Kemp Smith, A801.
325   Kant, Immanuel. "Perpetual Peace: A Philosophical Essay," p. 125. Available at https://www.gutenberg.org/files/50922/50922-h/50922-h.htm.
326   Wikipedia, "Immanuel Kant," last edited October 26, 2019,

http://en.wikipedia.org/wiki/Immanuel_Kant.
327   Wikipedia, "Transcendental idealism," last edited October 27, 2019, http://en.wikipedia.org/wiki/Transcendental_idealism.
328   B. A. Gerrish, *A Prince of the Church: Schleiermacher and the Beginnings of Modern Theology* (Philadelphia, PA: Fortress Press, 1984), 25.
329   Wikipedia, "Friedrich Schleiermacher," last edited October 22, 2019, https://en.wikipedia.org/wiki/Friedrich_Schleiermacher.
330   Wikipedia, "Prussian Union of Churches," last edited October 24, 2019, https://en.wikipedia.org/wiki/Prussian_Union_of_churches.
331   Wikipedia, "Georg Wilhelm Friedrich Hegel," last edited October 26, 2019, https://en.wikipedia.org/wiki/Georg_Wilhelm_Friedrich_Hegel.
332   Wikipedia, "Georg_Wilhelm_Friedrich_Hegel," last edited October 26, 2019.
333   Wikipedia, "Georg_Wilhelm_Friedrich_Hegel," last edited October 26, 2019.
334   Wikipedia, "Ontology," last edited October 20, 2019, http://en.wikipedia.org/wiki/Ontology.
335   Wikipedia, "Monism," last edited September 21, 2019 , http://en.wikipedia.org/wiki/Monism.
336   Wikipedia, "Hegelianism," last edited June 15, 2019 , http://en.wikipedia.org/wiki/Hegelianism.
337   Wikipedia, "Absolute idealism," last edited October 2, 2019, http://en.wikipedia.org/wiki/Absolute_idealism.
338   Wikipedia, "Jacob Bohme," last edited October 23, 2019, http://en.wikipedia.org/wiki/Jakob_ Böhme.
339   Stefan Gruner: "Hegel's Aether Doctrine", VDM Publ., 2010, ISBN 978-3-639-28451-5, http://www.stefan-gruner.de/PREPRINT-AETHER.pdf.
340   "The Development of Absolute Idealism," accessed October 30, 2019, http://www.philosophypages.com/hy/5k.htm#abso.
341   "Georg Wilhelm Friedrich Hegel," New World Encyclopedia, accessed October 30, 2019, http://www.newworldencyclopedia.org/entry/Georg_Wilhelm_Friedrich_Hegel.
342   Arthur Schopenhauer, *The World as Will and Representation*, Vol. 1, trans. E. Payne (New York: Dover Publishing Inc., 1969), 3.
343   David A. Leeming, Kathryn Madden, Stanton Marlan, eds.

(2009), Encyclopedia of Psychology and Religion, Volume 2, Springer. p. 824. A more accurate statement might be that for a German – rather than a French or British writer of that time – Schopenhauer was an honest and open atheist.

344   Wikipedia, "Johann Gottlieb Fichte," last edited October 28, 2019, http://en.wikipedia.org/wiki/Johann_Gottlieb_Fichte.

345   "The reality is what Schopenhauer calls the Will, the Will to Live." Letter to Richard C. Lyon, 1 August 1949, George Santayana, *The Letters of George Santayana* (New York: Scribner's, New York, 1955).

346   *The Oxford Encyclopedic English Dictionary*, "Schopenhauer" (Oxford: Oxford University Press, 1991), 1298.

347   Arthur Schopenhauer, *On the Fourfold Root of the Principle of Sufficient Reason* (Chicago: Open Court Publishing. 1974), 212.

348   On the Fourfold Root of the Principle of Sufficient Reason, 49.

349   Arthur Schopenhauer, *The World as Will and Representation*, Vol. I, 62.

350   Arthur Schopenhauer, *The World as Will and Representation*, Vol. II, Ch. XLVII.

351   Arthur Schopenhauer, Author's preface to "On The Fourfold Root of the Principle of Sufficient Reason," 1.

352   Arthur Schopenhauer, "Parerga and Paralipomena," Volume II, Section 92.

353   Arthur Schopenhauer, "Parerga and Paralipomena," "On Ethics," Sec. 5.

354   Wikipedia, "Arthur Schopenhauer," last edited October 9, 2019, https://en.wikipedia.org/wiki/Arthur_Schopenhauer#cite_note-57.

355   Arthur Schopenhauer, "On the basis of morality," 19, https://en.wikipedia.org/wiki/Arthur_Schopenhauer#Animal_welfare.

356   Clarke, John James, *Oriental enlightenment* (London: Routledge, 1997), 68.

357   Wikipedia, "Upanishads," last edited October 2, 2019, http://en.wikipedia.org/wiki/Upanishads.

358   "The Noble Truths of Buddhism," Learn Religions, accessed October 30, 2019, http://buddhism.about.com/od/thefournobletruths/a/fournobletruths.htm.

359   "Arthur Schopenhauer," *Stanford Encyclopedia of Philosophy*, May 11, 2017, http://plato.stanford.edu/entries/schopenhauer/.

360   Wikipedia, "Arthur Schopenhauer," last edited October 9, 2019.

361   "John Stuart Mill," https://plato.stanford.edu/entries/mill/, last edited October 27, 2019.
362   Wikipedia, "John Stuart Mill," last edited October 27, 2019, http://en.wikipedia.org/wiki/John_Stuart_Mill.
363   "John Stuart Mills," last edited October 30, 2019, http://www.biography.com/people/john-stuart-mill-9408210#select-major-works.
364   Alina Bradford, "What is Science," Live Science, August 4, 2017, https://www.livescience.com/20896-science-scientific-method.html.
365   "Steps of the Scientific Method," Science Buddies, accessed October 30, 2019, http://www.sciencebuddies.org/science-fair-projects/project_scientific_method.shtml.
366   Halevy, Elie, *The Growth of Philosophic Radicalism* (Boston, Massachusetts: Beacon Press, 1966), 282–284.
367   Wikipedia, "John Stuart Mills," last edited October 27, 2019, http://en.wikipedia.org/wiki/John_Stuart_Mill.
368   Wikipedia, "John Stuart Mills," last edited October 27, 2019.
369   Wikipedia, "Jean-Francois Marmontel," last edited July 25, 2019, http://en.wikipedia.org/wiki/Jean-Fran%C3%A7ois_Marmontel.
370   Wikipedia, "William Wordsworth," last edited October 14, 2019, https://en.wikipedia.org/wiki/William_Wordsworth.
371   Wikipedia, "Single Transferable Vote," last edited October 22, 2019, https://en.wikipedia.org/wiki/Single_transferable_vote.
372   Linda C. Raeder, "Spirit of the Age," *John Stuart Mill and the Religion of Humanity* (Columbia, Missouri: University of Missouri Press, 2002), 65. Comte welcomed the prospect of being attacked publicly for his irreligion, he said, as this would permit him to clarify the non-atheistic nature of his and Mill's "atheism."
373   Wikipedia, "On Liberty," last edited October 28, 2019, https://en.wikipedia.org/wiki/On_Liberty.
374   Mill, John Stuart, "On Liberty," (London: Penguin Classics, 2006), 10–11.
375   *John Stuart Mill and Jeremy Bentham, Utilitarianism and other essays*, ed. Alan Ryan (London: Penguin Books, 2004), 11.
376   John Stuart Mill, ed. Stephen Nathanson, *Principles of Political Economy with some of their Applications to Social Philosophy*, IV.7.6. p. 199 http://www.untag-smd.ac.id/files/Perpustakaan_Digital_2/POLITICAL%20ECONOMY%20John%20Stuart%20Mill%20%20prin-

ciples%20of%20political%20economy%20with%20applications%20to%20social%20p.pdf .

377   John Stuart Mill, ed. Stephen Nathanson, *Principles of Political Economy with some of their Applications to Social Philosophy*, IV, VI, 191.

378   Nicholas Capaldi, *John Stuart Mill: A Biography* (Cambridge: Cambridge University Press, 2004), 41.

379   Wikipedia, "Classical economics," last edited August 7, 2019, https://en.wikipedia.org/wiki/Classical_economics.

380   Wikipedia, "James Mill," last edited October 26, 2019, http://en.wikipedia.org/wiki/James_Mill.

381   Wikipedia, "James Mill," last edited October 26, 2019.

382   Wikipedia, "Chartered company," last edited October 19, 2019, https://en.wikipedia.org/wiki/Chartered_company.

383   Jennie Cohen, "Native Americans Hailed From Siberian Highlands, DNA Reveals," accessed October 30, 2019, https://www.history.com/news/native-americans-hailed-from-siberian-highlands-dna-reveals.

384   Jennie Cohen, "Native Americans Hailed From Siberian Highlands, DNA Reveals," accessed October 30,2019.

385   Wikipedia, "Altai people," last edited October 29, 2019, https://en.wikipedia.org/wiki/Altai_people.

386   Ker Than, "On Way to New World, First Americans Made a 10,000-Year Pit Stop," National Geographic, February 27, 2014, https://news.nationalgeographic.com/news/2014/04/140227-native-americans-beringia-bering-strait-pit-stop/.

387   Wikipedia, "Algonquian peoples," last edited October 23, 2019, https://en.wikipedia.org/wiki/Algonquian_peoples.

388   "Algonquin," New World Encyclopedia, accessed October 30, 2019, http://www.newworldencyclopedia.org/entry/Algonquin.

389   "Algonquin," New Work Encyclopedia, accessed October 30, 2019.

390   "The Algonquins," United States History, accessed October 30, 2019, https://www.u-s-history.com/pages/h560.html.

391   Wikipedia, "New France," last edited October 22, 2019, https://en.wikipedia.org/wiki/New_France.

392   Wikipedia, "David Kirke," last edited October 18, 2019, https://en.wikipedia.org/wiki/David_Kirke.

393   Wikipedia, "Pontiac's War," last edited October 21, 2019,

https://en.wikipedia.org/wiki/Pontiac's_War.
394   "Algonquin," New World Encyclopedia, accessed October 30, 2019.
395   Wikipedia, "Powhatan," last edited October 20, 2019, https://en.wikipedia.org/wiki/Powhatan.
396   Wikipedia, "Powhatan," last edited October 20, 2019.
397   Wikipedia, "First Families of Virginia," last edited September 20, 2019, https://en.wikipedia.org/wiki/First_Families_of_Virginia.
398   See letter written by the Virginia Council on Indians at https://web.archive.org/web/20120224023658/http://indians.vipnet.org/resources/writersGuide.pdf.
399   Margaret Odrowaz-Sypniewska, B.F.A, "The Haudenosaunee (Iroquois) and Feminism" Indigenous Americans: Their Genealogy, History and Heraldry," accessed October 30, 2019, http://www.angelfire.com/mi4/polcrt/matrilineal.html.
400   Wikipedia, "Great Peacemaker," last edited October 4, 2019, https://en.wikipedia.org/wiki/Great_Peacemaker.
401   "History of the Mohawk Valley: Gateway to the West 1614-1925," Chapter 9: "Dekanawida and Hiawatha," last updated June 10, 2018,   https://www.schenectadyhistory.org/resources/mvgw/history/009.html.
402   Wikipedia, "Jogonhsasee," last edited April 6, 2019, https://en.wikipedia.org/wiki/Jigonhsasee.
403   Gerald Murphy, "About the Iroquois Constitution," Modern History Sourcebook: The Constitution of the Iroquois Confederacy, accessed October 30, 2019, https://sourcebooks.fordham.edu/mod/iroquois.asp.
404   Loretta Hall, "Iroquois confederation," Countries and Their Cultures, accssed October 30, 2019, http://www.everyculture.com/multi/Ha-La/Iroquois-Confederacy.html.
405   Loretta Hall, "Iroquois confederation," Countries and Their Cultures, accessed October 30, 2019.
406   Loretta Hall, "Iroquois confederation," Countries and Their Cultures, accessed October 30, 2019.
407   Margaret Odrowaz-Sypniewska, B.F.A, "The Haudenosaunee (Iroquois) and Feminism," Indigenous Americans: Their Genealogy, History and Heraldry, accessed October 30, 2019.
408   Loretta Hall, "Iroquois confederation," Countries and Their

Cultures, accessed October 30, 2019.

409   Wikipedia, "Kateri Tekakwitha," last edited October 30, 2019, https://en.wikipedia.org/wiki/Kateri_Tekakwitha.

410   Daniel Sargent, *Catherine Tekakwitha* (New York: Longmans, Green & Co., 1936), 164.

411   Wikipedia, "Kateri Tekakwitha," last edited October 30, 2019.

412   See Thomas Jefferson's letter to Handsome Lake. "Jefferson's Indian Addresses, To Brother Handsome Lake, Washington, November 3, 1802," The Avalon Project, Yale Law School, http://avalon.law.yale.edu/19th_century/jeffind2.asp.

413   Loretta Hall, "Iroquois Confederacy," Encyclopedia.com, last edited October 1, 2019, http://www.encyclopedia.com/topic/Iroquois_Confederacy.aspx.

414   Loretta Hall, "Iroquois Confederacy," Encyclopedia.com, last edited October 1, 2019.

415   Loretta Hall, "Iroquois Confederacy," Encyclopedia.com, last edited October 1, 2019.

416   Jazmin Kay, "The Roles of Iroquois Women in the Iroquois Tribe," feminist.com, accessed October 30, 2019, http://www.feminist.com/resources/artspeech/girls/iroquoiswomen.html.

417   Margaret Odrowaz-Sypniewska, B.F.A, "The Haudenosaunee (Iroquois) and Feminism" Indigenous Americans: Their Genealogy, History and Heraldry, accessed October 30, 2019.

418   Loretta Hall, "Iroquois Confederacy," Encyclopedia.com.

419   "Colonial Hunts: South America" excerpt from Secret History of the Witches, © 2000, Max Dashu, http://www.suppressedhistories.net/secrethistory/colhuntsouth.html.

420   Loretta Hall, "Iroquois confederation," Countries and Their Cultures.

421   Wikipedia, "Tuscarora War," last modified June 30, 2018, https://en.wikipedia.org/wiki/Tuscarora_War.

422   Wikipedia, "Iroquois," last modified Oct. 24, 2018, https://en.wikipedia.org/wiki/Iroquois#American_Revolution.

423   Loretta Hall, "Iroquois confederation," Countries and Their Cultures, accessed October 30, 2019.

424   Loretta Hall, "Iroquois confederation," Countries and Their Cultures, accessed October 30, 2019.

425   Wikipedia, "Cherokee society," last edited September 16, 2019,

https://en.wikipedia.org/wiki/Cherokee_society.
426   Wikipedia, "Cherokee history," last edited September 16, 2019, https://en.wikipedia.org/wiki/Cherokee_history.
427   Wikipedia, "Cherokee society," last edited September 26, 2019.
428   Wikipedia, "Cherokee history," last edited September 16, 2019.
429   Wikipedia, "Cherokee society," last edited September 26, 2019.
430   Indian Country Today, "The Power of Cherokee Women," accessed October 30, 2019, https://newsmaven.io/indiancountry-today/archive/the-power-of-cherokee-women-cguyNX91RE6asAy-IQwYheg/.
431   "Women's Rights in Cherokee Society," Feminists, Native American Women, Cherokee Women's Rights, accessed October 30, 2019, http://www.womenhistoryblog.com/2008/12/cherokee-womens-rights.html.
432   Indian Country Today, "The Power of Cherokee Women," accessed October 30, 2019.
433   Barbara Sproul, *Primal Myths* (New York: HarperOne, Harper Collins Publishers, 1979), 254-255.
434   Wikipedia, "Great Spirit," last edited October 2, 2019, https://en.wikipedia.org/wiki/Great_Spirit.
435   Wikipedia, "Cherokee mythology," last edited September 30, https://en.wikipedia.org/wiki/Cherokee_mythology.
436   Wikipedia, "Cherokee mythology," last edited September 30, 2019.
437   "Cherokee Heritage Center - Ancient Village," accessed October 30, 2019, http://wsharing.com/WSphotosTahlequahAV.htm.
438   Wikipedia, "Cherokee clans," last edited September 6, 2019, https://en.wikipedia.org/wiki/Cherokee_clans.
439   "Cherokee Marriage Customs: Cherokee Marriage Customs Between the Clans," Cherokee, accessed October 30, 2019, https://www.aaanativearts.com/cherokee/cherokee-marriage-customs.htm.
440   Wikipedia, "Cherokee clans," last edited September 16, 2019, https://en.wikipedia.org/wiki/Cherokee_clans.
441   Jacob Broadley, "Cherokee Hunting Traditions," Sciencing, accessed October 30, 2019, https://sciencing.com/cherokee-hunting-traditions-8801.html.
442   "Southeast Cherokee Indians Food and Clothing," Daily Life in Olden Times for Kids, accessed October 30, 2019, https://nativeamer-

icans.mrdonn.org/southeast/cherokee/food-clothing.html.
443   "Cherokee Festivals," Cherokee Nations, http://www.cherokee.org/about-the-nation/culture.
444   Wikipedia, "Five Civilized Tribes," last edited October 21, 2019, https://en.wikipedia.org/wiki/Five_Civilized_Tribes.
445   Charles Hudson, *Knights of Spain, Warriors of the Sun: Hernando de Soto and the South's Ancient Chiefdoms* (Athens, Georgia: University of Georgia Press, 1998), 190–199.
446   Sarah H. Hill, *Weaving New Worlds: Southeastern Cherokee Women and Their Basketry* (Chapel Hill: University of North Carolina Press, 1997), 65.
447   Wikipedia, "Cherokee history," last edited September 16, 2019.
448   James Mooney, *Myths of the Cherokee* (Mineola NY: Dover Publications, 1995), 32.
449   Wikipedia, "Charleston, South Carolina," last edited October 25, 2019, https://en.wikipedia.org/wiki/Charleston,_South_Carolina.
450   Wikipedia, "Charleston, South Carolina," last edited October 25, 2019.
451   Wikipedia, "Yamasee War," last edited October 23, 2019, https://en.wikipedia.org/wiki/Yamasee_War.
452   Wikipedia, "Battle of Taliwa," last edited May 30, 2019 https://en.wikipedia.org/wiki/Battle_of_Taliwa   https://en.wikipedia.org/wiki/Anglo-Cherokee_War.
453   "Beloved Woman of the Cherokee - Nancy Ward," Women's Circle, accessed October 30, 2019, https://www.manataka.org/page1163.html.
454   Wikipedia, "Anglo-Cherokee War," last edited October 23, 2019, https://en.wikipedia.org/wiki/Anglo-Cherokee_War.
455   Wikipedia, "Royal Proclamation of 1763," last edited October 29, 2019, https://en.wikipedia.org/wiki/Royal_Proclamation_of_1763.
456   Hester A. Davis, "Indians in Arkansas: The Cherokee," accessed October 30, 2019, http://archeology.uark.edu/wp-content/uploads/2015/06/Cherokee-Indians-in-Arkansas.pdf.
457   "A Brief History of the Trail of Tears," Cherokee Nation, http://www.cherokee.org/AboutTheNation/History/TrailofTears/ABriefHistoryoftheTrailofTears.aspx.
458   Wikipedia, "Trail of Tears," last edited October 23, 2019, https://en.wikipedia.org/wiki/Trail_of_Tears.

459   Wikipedia, "Slavery among Native Americans in the United States," last edited October 24, 2019, https://en.wikipedia.org/wiki/Slavery_among_Native_Americans_in_the_United_States.
460   Wikipedia, "1842 Slave Revolt in the Cherokee Nation," last edited September 4, 2019, https://en.wikipedia.org/wiki/1842_Slave_Revolt_in_the_Cherokee_Nation.
461   Wikipedia, "1842 Slave Revolt in the Cherokee Nation," last edited September 4, 2019.
462   Wikipedia, "Dutch colonization of the Americas," last edited September 4, 2019, https://en.wikipedia.org/wiki/Dutch_colonization_of_the_Americas.
463   Wikipedia, "New Netherland," last edited October 22, 2019, https://en.wikipedia.org/wiki/New_Netherland.
464   Wikipedia, "Spanish conquest of Guatemala," last edited September 25, 2019, https://en.wikipedia.org/wiki/Spanish_conquest_of_Guatemala.
465   Wikipedia, "Mexican War of Independence," last edited October 26, 2019, https://en.wikipedia.org/wiki/Mexican_War_of_Independence.
466   Wikipedia, "Mexican secularization act of 1833," last edited October 28, 2019, https://en.wikipedia.org/wiki/Mexican_secularization_act_of_1833.
467   Wikipedia, "Florida," last edited October 30, 2019, https://en.wikipedia.org/wiki/Florida.
468   Wikipedia, "Fort Mose Historic State Park," last edited October 27, 2019, https://en.wikipedia.org/wiki/Fort_Mose_Historic_State_Park.
469   Wikipedia, "Fort Mose Historic State Park," last edited October 27, 2019.
470   Wikipedia, "French colonization of the Americas," last edited October 15, 2019, https://en.wikipedia.org/wiki/French_colonization_of_the_Americas.
471   "The Original 13 Colonies," accessed October 31, 2019, http://www.landofthebrave.info/american-history-of-13-colonies.htm.
472   Wikipedia, "Seven Years' War," last edited October 30, 2019, https://en.wikipedia.org/wiki/Seven_Years'_War.
473   John Ferling, *A Leap in the Dark: The Struggle to Create the American Republic* (Oxford: Oxford University Press, 2003), 2.
474   John Ferling, *A Leap in the Dark: The Struggle to Create the*

American Republic, 5-6.

475   John Ferling, *A Leap in the Dark: The Struggle to Create the American Republic*, 7.

476   "French and Indian War/Seven Years' War, 1754–63," Office of the Historian, Bureau of Public Affairs, United States Department of State, accessed October 31, 2019, https://history.state.gov/milestones/1750-775/french-indian-war.

477   "Louisbourg," United States History, accesssed October 31, 2019, http://www.u-s-history.com/pages/h556.html.

478   Wikipedia, "Battle of Fort Frontenac," last edited September 8, 2019, https://en.wikipedia.org/wiki/Battle_of_Fort_Frontenac.

479   Wikipedia, "Battle of the Plains of Abraham," last edited October 30, 2019, https://en.wikipedia.org/wiki/Battle_of_the_Plains_of_Abraham.

480   "Treaty of Paris, 1763," Office of the Historian, Bureau of Public Affairs, United States Department of State, accessed October 31, 2019, https://history.state.gov/milestones/1750-1775/treaty-of-paris, Office of the Historian, Bureau of Public Affairs, United States Department of State.

481   Wikipedia, "Treaty of Fort Stanwix," last edited January 23, 2019, https://en.wikipedia.org/wiki/Treaty_of_Fort_Stanwix.

482   Marshall Trimble, "What is the Treaty of Hard Labor," February 12, 2013, https://truewestmagazine.com/what-is-the-treaty-of-hard-labor/.

483   "Treaty of Lochaber," last modified Nov 5, 2010, https://www.wvencyclopedia.org/articles/773.

484   Mark Puls, *Samuel Adams: Father of the American Revolution* (New York: Palgrave Macmillan, 2006,) references throughout.

485   Mark Puls, *Samuel Adams: Father of the American Revolution*.

486   Wikipedia, "Massachusetts Charter," last edited September 4, 2019, https://en.wikipedia.org/wiki/Massachusetts_Charter.

487   Wikipedia, "Samuel Adams," last edited October 16, 2019, https://en.wikipedia.org/wiki/Samuel_Adams.

488   Wikipedia, "Sugar Act," last edited September 21, 2019, https://en.wikipedia.org/wiki/Sugar_Act.

489   Mark Puls, *Samuel Adams: Father of the American Revolution*, 37-38.

490   Mark Puls, *Samuel Adams: Father of the American Revolution*, 39.

491   William M. Fowler and Lillian M. Fowler, *Samuel Adams: Radical Puritan* (New York: Longman, 1997), 190.
492   Wikipedia, "Samuel Adams," last edited October 16, 2019.
493   Mark Puls, *Samuel Adams: Father of the American Revolution*, 40-43.
494   Mark Puls, *Samuel Adams: Father of the American Revolution*, 48-49.
495   Mark Puls, *Samuel Adams: Father of the American Revolution*, 49.
496   Mark Puls, *Samuel Adams: Father of the American Revolution*, 51-52.
497   Mark Puls, *Samuel Adams: Father of the American Revolution*, 55.
498   Mark Puls, *Samuel Adams: Father of the American Revolution*, 57.
499   William V. Wells, *The Life and Public Service of Samuel Adams: Being a Narrative of His Acts and Opinions, And His Agency in Forwarding and Producing the American Revolution*, Vol. 1 (Boston: Little, Brown & Co., 1865), 76.
500   "George Bancroft, *History of the United States from the Discovery of the American Continent,* Vol. 5 (London: Little, Brown and Co., 1852), 349,
501   William V. Wells, *The Life and Public Service of Samuel Adams: Being a Narrative of His Acts and Opinions, And His Agency in Forwarding and Producing the American Revolution*, Vol. 1, 81.
502   "Adam Smith, An Inquiry into the Nature and Cause of the Wealth of Nations. Chapter VII Of Colonies," On-line at https://www.gutenberg.org/files/3300/3300-h/3300-h.htm#link2HCH0027.
503   "The World Famous Orations, America: I," (1761-1837), 1906, I. His Examination Before the House of Commons, Benjamin Franklin (1706-90) 1766," accessed October 31, 2019, https://www.bartleby.com/268/8/10.html.
504   Mark Puls, *Samuel Adams: Father of the American Revolution*, 62.
505   Mark Puls, *Samuel Adams: Father of the American Revolution*, 62-63.
506   "George Bancroft, *History of the United States from the Discovery of the American Continent*, Vol. 3, 236, 238.
507   Mark Puls, *Samuel Adams: Father of the American Revolution*, 72.
508   Mark Puls, *Samuel Adams: Father of the American Revolution*, 83.
509   Mercy Otis Warren. The American Revolution. CD-Rom edition. Vol. 1, Chapter 6.

510   Mark Puls, *Samuel Adams: Father of the American Revolution*, 105.
511   Sam Adams, "The Writings of Sam Adams," Vol 2, Article in the *Boston Gazette*, December 10, 1770.
512   Richard D. Brown, *Revolutionary Politics in Massachusetts: The Boston Committee of Correspondence and the Towns, 1772-1774* (Cambridge: Harvard University Press, 1970), 56-57.
513   Ira Stoll, *Samuel Adams: A Life* (New York: Free Press, 2008), 97-98.
514   Ira Stoll, *Samuel Adams: A Life*, 88.
515   Sam Adams, "The Writings of Sam Adams," Vol 2, 422-423.
516   Andrew M. Allison, *The Real Benjamin Franklin* (Malta, IN: Freeman Institute and National Center for Constitutional Studies, 1982), 161.
517   George Bancroft, *History of the United States from the Discovery of the American Continent*, Vol. 3, 236, 238.
518   Mark Puls, *Samuel Adams: Father of the American Revolution*, 133-134.
519   William V. Wells, *The Life and Public Service of Samuel Adams: Being a Narrative of His Acts and Opinions, And His Agency in Forwarding and Producing the American Revolution*, Vol. 2, 25.
520   William V. Wells, *The Life and Public Service of Samuel Adams: Being a Narrative of His Acts and Opinions, And His Agency in Forwarding and Producing the American Revolution*, Vol. 2, 25.
521   Samuel Adams. "The Writings of Samuel Adams," Vol. 2, Document of March 2, 1773; quoted in Mark Puls, S*amuel Adams: Father of the American Revolution*, 135-137.
522   George Bancroft. *History of the United States from the Discovery of the American Continent*, Vol. 3, 440.
523   Mark Puls, *Samuel Adams: Father of the American Revolution*, 138.
524   Samuel Adams, "Writings of Samuel Adams," Vol. 2, article in *Boston Gazette*, September 27, 1773; quoted in Mark Puls, *Samuel Adams: Father of the American Revolution*, 139.
525   Benjamin Woods Larabee, *The Boston Tea Party* (Boston: North University Press, 1979), 104.
526   Benjamin Woods Larabee, *The Boston Tea Party*, 141.
527   Ira Stoll, *Samuel Adams: A Life*, 153.
528   Mark Puls, *Samuel Adams: Father of the American Revolution*, 160.
529   William Jackman, *History of the American Nation*, Vol. 8 (Chi-

cago: K. Gaynor, 1911), 2389-2390.
530   "Samuel Adams to Elizabeth Adams," The Letters of Delegates to Congress, Vol. 2. p. 217, quoted in Mark Puls, *Samuel Adams: Father of the American Revolution*, 178.
531   Mark Puls, S*amuel Adams: Father of the American Revolution*, 188.
532   John Ferling, *A Leap in the Dark: The Struggle to Create the American Republic*, 183.
533   "General Washington's Battle Engagements in 1776," Varsity Tutors, https://www.varsitytutors.com/earlyamerica/maps/maps/general-washingtons-battle-engagements-1776.
534   L. H. Butterfield, et. al., eds. *The Diary and Autobiography of John Adams*, Vol 3 (Cambridge: Harvard University Press, 1961), 441-42.
535   John Ferling, *A Leap in the Dark: The Struggle to Create the American Republic*, 88-89.
536   Wikipedia, "New Jersey in the American Revolution," last edited September 27, 2019, https://en.wikipedia.org/wiki/New_Jersey_in_the_American_Revolution.
537   "Jefferson and Hamilton, Political Rivals in Washington's Cabinet," George Washington's Mount Vernon, accessed October 31, 2019, https://www.mountvernon.org/george-washington/the-first-president/washingtons-presidential-cabinet/jefferson-and-hamilton-political-rivals/.
538   "A Biography of Alexander Hamilton (1755-1804), Aide-de-camp to Washington (1777-1781)," American History from Revolution to Reconstruction, accessed October 31, 2019, http://www.let.rug.nl/usa/biographies/alexander-hamilton/aide-de-camp-to-washington-(1777-1781).php.
539   John Ferling, *A Leap in the Dark: The Struggle to Create the American Republic*, 318.
540   John Ferling, *A Leap in the Dark: The Struggle to Create the American Republic*, 318.
541   Wikipedia, "First Report on the Public Credit," last edited August 29, 2019, https://en.wikipedia.org/wiki/First_Report_on_the_Public_Credit.
542   Wikipedia, "First Report on the Public Credit," last edited August 29, 2019.
543   John Ferling, *A Leap in the Dark: The Struggle to Create the*

American Republic, 318-319.
544   "Hamiltonianism," Merriam-Webster, accessed October 31, 2019, http://www.merriam-webster.com/dictionary/Hamiltonianism.
545   Gordon S. Wood, *The Radicalism of the American Revolution* (New York: Vintage Books, 1991), 326.
546   Wikipedia, "Alexander Hamilton," last edited October 6, 2019, https://en.wikipedia.org/wiki/Alexander_Hamilton.
547   Andrew Burstein and Nancy Isenberg, *Madison and Jefferson* (New York: Random House, 2010), 218.
548   X. Jefferson's Account of the Bargain of the Assusmption and Residence Bills," National Archives, Founders Online, accessed October 31, 2019, https://en.wikipedia.org/wiki/Compromise_of_1790; https://founders.archives.gov/domuments/Jefferson/01-17-02-0018-0012.
549   John Ferling, *A Leap in the Dark: The Struggle to Create the American Republic*, 327.
550   Wikipedia, "Funding Act of 1790," last edited October 30, 2019, https://en.wikipedia.org/wiki/Funding_Act_of_1790.
551   Wikipedia, "Funding Act of 1790," last edited October 30, 2019.
552   Wikipedia, "Bank Bill of 1791," last edited October 6, 2019, https://en.wikipedia.org/wiki/Bank_Bill_of_1791.
553   "Democracy and the Federal Constitution: Notes from the Constitutional Convention, May-Sept., 1787," accessed October 31, 2019, https://userpages.umbc.edu/~bouton/History101/ConstitutionalConvention.htm.
554   John Ferling, *A Leap in the Dark: The Struggle to Create the American Republic*, 338.
555   "About National gazette. (Philadelphia [Pa.]) 1791-1793," National Endowment of the Humanities, accessed October 31,2019, dhttps://chroniclingamerica.loc.gov/lccn/sn83025887/.
556   John Ferling, *A Leap in the Dark: The Struggle to Create the American Republic*, 341.
557   John Ferling, *A Leap in the Dark: The Struggle to Create the American Republic*, 340.
558   Thomas Paine, "The American Crisis," Originally published as a series of pamphlets between 1776 – 1783 (New York: Barnes and Noble, 2002), ix.
559   Thomas Paine, *The Writings of Thomas Paine, Collected and*

Edited by Moncure Daniel Conway (New York: G. P. Putnam's Sons, 1894), Volume 2, XIII, "Rights of Man," 258, http://oll.libertyfund.org/titles/paine-the-writings-of-thomas-paine-vol-ii-1779-1792.

560   Thomas Paine, T*he Writings of Thomas Paine, Collected and Edited by Moncure Daniel Conway.*

561   William T. Hutchinson, et, al., eds., *The Papers of James Madison* (Chicago: University of Chicago Press, 1962), 14:370-372.

562   Mark Puls, *Samuel Adams: Father of the American Revolution*, 228.

563   "Jeffersonian Ideology," accessed October 31, 2019, http://www.ushistory.org/us/20b.asp.

564   "Jeffersonian Ideology," accessed October 31, 2019.

565   John Adams, 3 June 1776, in *Papers of John Adams*, 11 vols., ed. Robert Joseph Taylor (Cambridge: Harvard University Press, 1979), 4:235; John Adams to Abigail Adams, 14 April 1776, Adams Family Correspondence, 1:382. Cited in Gary B. Nash, *The Unknown American Revolution: The Unruly Birth of Democracy and the Struggle to Create America* (New York: Viking Press, 2005), 203.

566   Gary B. Nash, *The Unknown American Revolution: The Unruly Birth of Democracy and the Struggle to Create America*, 203.

567   Gary B. Nash, *The Unknown American Revolution: The Unruly Birth of Democracy and the Struggle to Create America*, 204.

568   Gary B. Nash, *The Unknown American Revolution: The Unruly Birth of Democracy and the Struggle to Create America*, 204-205.

569   "Women's Rights After the American Revolution," History of American Women, acessed October 31, 2019, http://www.womenhistoryblog.com/2013/06/womens-rights-after-american-revolution.html.

570   John Schutz and Douglas Adair, eds., *Spur of Fame: Dialogues of John Adams and Benjamin Rush, 1805-1813* (San Marino, California: The Huntington Library, 1966), 170, cited in Gary B. Nash, T*he Unknown American Revolution: The Unruly Birth of Democracy and the Struggle to Create America*, 450.

571   Gary B. Nash, *The Unknown American Revolution: The Unruly Birth of Democracy and the Struggle to Create America*, 206

572   Wikipedia, "Republican motherhood," last edited June 5, 2019, https://en.wikipedia.org/wiki/Republican_motherhood.

573   "Women's Rights After the American Revolution," History of American Women, acessed October 31, 2019.

574   "Women's Rights After the American Revolution," History of American Women, acessed October 31, 2019.
575   Wikipedia, "Nineteenth Amendment to the Constitution," accessed October 31, 2019, https://en.wikipedia.org/wiki/Nineteenth_Amendment_to_the_United_States_Constitution.
576   "Declaration of Rights of the Women of the United States by the National Woman Suffrage Association, July 4th, 1876," The Elizabeth Cady Stanton and Susan B. Anthony Papers Project, http://ecssba.rutgers.edu/docs/decl.html.
577   Wikipedia, "Andrew Jackson," last edited October 30, 2019, https://en.wikipedia.org/wiki/Andrew_Jackson.
578   H. W. Brands, *Andrew Jackson: His Life and Times* (New York: Doubleday, 2005), 26.
579   H. W. Brands, *Andrew Jackson: His Life and Times*, 31.
580   Wikipedia, "War of 1812," last edited October 29, 2019, https://en.wikipedia.org/wiki/War_of_1812.
581   Wikipedia, "Chesapeake-Leopard affair," last edited September 4, 2019, https://en.wikipedia.org/wiki/Chesapeake%E2%80%93Leopard_affair.
582   Wikipedia, "War of 1812," last edited October 29, 2019
583   Wikipedia, "Battle of New Orleans," last edited October 31, 2019, 2018, https://en.wikipedia.org/wiki/Battle_of_New_Orleans.
584   H. W. Brands, *Andrew Jackson: His Life and Times*, 257.
585   H. W. Brands, *Andrew Jackson: His Life and Times*, 260.
586   Wikipedia, "Siege of Pensacola (1707)," last edited August 20, 2019, https://en.wikipedia.org/wiki/Siege_of_Pensacola_%281707%29.
587   H. W. Brands, *Andrew Jackson: His Life and Times*, 261-262.
588   Wikipedia, "Lake Borgne," last edited October 9, 2019, https://en.wikipedia.org/wiki/Lake_Borgne.
589   H. W. Brands, *Andrew Jackson: His Life and Times*, 266 – 267.
590   Wikipedia, "Treaty of Ghent," last edited October 21, 2019, https://en.wikipedia.org/wiki/Treaty_of_Ghent.
591   Wikipedia, "Battle of New Orleans," last edited October 31, 2019 https://en.wikipedia.org/wiki/Battle_of_New_Orleans.
592   Wikipedia, "History of the United States Democratic Party," last edited October 25, 2019, https://en.wikipedia.org/wiki/History_of_the_United_States_Democratic_Party.

593   Wikipedia, "Manifest destiny," last edited October 30, 2019, https://en.wikipedia.org/wiki/Manifest_destiny.
594   Wikipedia, "John Quincy Adams," last edited October 30, 2019, https://en.wikipedia.org/wiki/John_Quincy_Adams.
595   H. W. Brands, *Andrew Jackson: His Life and Times*, 408.
596   H. W. Brands, *Andrew Jackson: His Life and Times*, 412-413.
597   Wikipedia, "Spoils system," last edited October 5, 2019, https://en.wikipedia.org/wiki/Spoils_system.
598   Daniel W. Howe, *What hath God Wrought, The Transformation of America, 1815-1848* (Oxford: Oxford University Press, Inc., 2007), 334.
599   Wikipedia, "Tariff of Abominations," last edited October 25, 2019, https://en.wikipedia.org/wiki/Tariff_of_Abominations.
600   Wikipedia, "Nullification Crisis," last edited October 20, 2019, https://en.wikipedia.org/wiki/Nullification_Crisis.
601   Sean Wilentz, *The Rise of American Democracy: Jefferson to Lincoln* (New York: W. W. Norton Co. Inc., 2005), 388.
602   Wikipedia, "First Bank of the United States," last modified Oct. 21, 2018, https://en.wikipedia.org/wiki/First_Bank_of_the_United_States.
603   Wikipedia, "Second Bank of the United States," last edited November 4, 2019, https://en.wikipedia.org/wiki/Second_Bank_of_the_United_States.
604   Bray Hammond, *Banks and Politics in America, from the Revolution to the Civil War* (Princeton: Princeton University Press, 1957), 102.
605   History.com editors, "Whig Party," accessed October 31, 2019, http://www.history.com/topics/whig-party.Hisotry.com.
606   Wikipedia, "Panic of 1819," accessed October 17, 2019, https://en.wikipedia.org/wiki/Panic_of_1819.
607   Wikipedia, "Panic of 1819," accessed October 17, 2019
608   Wikipedia, "Panic of 1819, accessed October 17, 2019.
609   Wikipedia, "Jacksonian democracy," accessed October 28, 2019, https://en.wikipedia.org/wiki/Jacksonian_democracy.
610   Wikipedia, "Bank War," last edited December 25, 2019, https://en.wikipedia.org/wiki/Bank_War.
611   Robert V. Remini, *Andrew Jackson and the Course of American Freedom, 1822–1832* (New York: NY: Harper & Row Publishers, Inc., 1981), 342-343.
612   H. W. Brands, *Andrew Jackson: His Life and Times*, 498.

613   H. W. Brands, *Andrew Jackson: His Life and Times*, 498.
614   David M. Kennedy and Bailey Cohen. *The American Pageant*, 13th edition (Boston: Houghton Mifflin Company, 2006), 256–265.
615   Wikipedia, "Panic of 1837," last modified Oct. 27, 2018, https://en.wikipedia.org/wiki/Panic_of_1837.
616   "Andrew Jackson's Enslaved Laborers," Andrew Jackson Hermitage, accessed October 31, 2019, http://thehermitage.com/learn/mansion-grounds/slavery/.
617   H. W. Brand, *Andrew Jackson: His Life and Times*, 148.
618   H. W. Brand, *Andrew Jackson: His Life and Times*, 147.
619   Amargi, "Newt Gingrich, Andrew Jackson & the Metaphysics of (Neo)Indian-Hating," Unsettling America, accessed October 31, 2019, https://unsettlingamerica.wordpress.com/2012/01/21/newt-gingrich-andrew-jackson-the-metaphysics-of-neoindian-hating/.
620   Wikipedia, "Creek War," accessed September 16, 2019, https://en.wikipedia.org/wiki/Creek_War.
621   Wikipedia, "Indian Removal Act," accessed October 23, 2019, https://en.wikipedia.org/wiki/Indian_Removal_Act.
622   History.com editors, "Trail of Tears," History, accessed October 31, 2019, https://www.history.com/topics/native-american-history/trail-of-tears.
623   Wikipedia, "Indian removal," accessed October 7, 2019, https://en.wikipedia.org/wiki/Indian_Removal.
624   Wikipedia, "Johnson v. M'Intosh," accessed May 7, 2019, https://en.wikipedia.org/wiki/Johnson_v._M'Intosh.
625   Daniel Feller, "Andrew Jackson: Domestic Affairs," UVA/Miller Center, accessed October 31, 2019, http://millercenter.org/president/biography/jackson-domestic-affairs.
626   Catherine Allgor, "Female Trouble: Andrew Jackson versus the Ladies of Washington," History Now, accessed October 31, 2019, http://mrtomecko.weebly.com/uploads/1/3/2/9/13292665/femaletrbl.pdf.
627   Catherine Allgor, "Female Trouble: Andrew Jackson versus the Ladies of Washington."
628   Catherine Allgor, "Female Trouble: Andrew Jackson versus the Ladies of Washington."
629   Catherine Allgor, "Female Trouble: Andrew Jackson versus the Ladies of Washington."

630   Wikipedia, "History of slavery," accessed October 29, 2019, https://en.wikipedia.org/wiki/History_of_slavery.
631   David P. Forsythe, *Encyclopedia of Human Rights*, Volume 1 (Oxford: Oxford University Press, 2009), 399.
632   "Human Trafficking," Polaris, accessed October 31, 2019, https://polarisproject.org/human-trafficking.
633   "Slavery in America," History, accessed October 31, 2019, http://www.history.com/topics/black-history/slavery.
634   Sven Beckert, "Slavery and Capitalism," The Chronicle of Higher Education, accessed November 1, 2019, http://chronicle.com/article/SlaveryCapitalism/150787/.
635   "How Slavery Led To Modern Capitalism," Bloomberg View," accessed November 1, 2019, http://www.huffingtonpost.com/2014/02/24/slavery_n_4847105.html."
636   "How Slavery Led To Modern Capitalism," Bloomberg View, accessed November 1, 2019.
637   Sven Beckert, "Slavery and Capitalism," The Chronicle of Higher Education.
638   Sven Beckert, "Slavery and Capitalism," The Chronicle of Higher Education.
639   Wikipedia, "Cabot Family," last edited October 27, 2019, https://en.wikipedia.org/wiki/Cabot_family.
640   Wikipedia, "Boston Brahmin," last modified Oct. 28, 2018, https://en.wikipedia.org/wiki/Boston_Brahmin.
641   Wikipedia, "Lowell family," last edited April 14, 2019, https://en.wikipedia.org/wiki/Lowell_family.
642   Wikipedia, "Samuel Slater," last edited October 30, 2019, https://en.wikipedia.org/wiki/Samuel_Slater.
643   How Slavery Shaped America's Oldest and Most Elite Colleges," NPR, September 17, 2013, http://www.npr.org/sections/codeswitch/2013/09/17/223420533/how-slavery-shaped-americas-oldest-and-most-elite-colleges.
644   Susan Svrluga, "The Harvard Law shield tied to slavery is already disappearing, after corporation vote," The Washington Post, March 15, 2019, https://www.washingtonpost.com/news/grade-point/wp/2016/03/15/the-harvard-law-shield-tied-to-slavery-is-already-disappearing-after-corporation-vote/.
645   Nathan Giannini, "MAP: where every US president was born,"

Yahoo News, accessed November 1, 2019, https://www.yahoo.com/news/map-where-every-us-president-was-born-120535059.html.

646   "Democratic Party," accessed November 1, 2019, http://www.britannica.com/topic/Democratic-Party.

647   "Democratic Party," accessed November 1, 2019, http://www.britannica.com/topic/Democratic-Party.

648   "The Transatlantic Slave Trade," accessed November 1, 2019, http://www.inmotionaame.org/print.cfm;jessionid=f8302854001572602056791?migration=1&bhcp=1.

649   Dr. Hakin Adi, "Africa and the Transatlantic Slave Trade," accessed November 1, 2019, http://www.bbc.co.uk/history/british/abolition/africa_article_01.shtml. http://theculturetrip.com/africa/ghana/articles/ghana-s-slave-castles-the-shocking-story-of-the-ghanaian-cape-coast/.

650   Lilian Diarra, "Ghana's Slave Castles: The Shocking Story of the Ghanaian Cape Coast," Culture Trip, accessed November 1, 2019, https://theculturetrip.com/africa/ghana/articles/ghana-s-slave-castles-the-shocking-story-of-the-ghanaian-cape-coast/.

652   Robert Walsh, "Notices of Brazil in 1828 and 1829," (1831), accessed November 1, 2019, https://archive.org/details/noticesofbrazili02wals/page/486.

653   "Resistance on Board the Ships," The Abolition Project, accessed November 1, 2019, http://abolition.e2bn.org/resistance_63.html.

654   "Resistance on Board the Ships," The Abolition Project accessed November 1, 2019.

655   Wikipedia, "Afonso I of Kongo," last edited May 15, 2019, https://en.wikipedia.org/wiki/Afonso_I_of_Kongo.

656   Wikipedia, "Nanny of the Maroons," last edited October 23, 2019, https://en.wikipedia.org/wiki/Nanny_of_the_Maroons.

657   Wikipedia, "Cudjoe," last edited August 2, 2019, https://en.wikipedia.org/wiki/Cudjoe.

658   Wikipedia, "Cuffy (Guyanese rebel)," last edited My 21, 2019, https://en.wikipedia.org/wiki/Cuffy_%28Guyanese_rebel%29.

659   Wikipedia, "Quamina," last edited October 1, 2019, https://en.wikipedia.org/wiki/Quamina.

660   Wikipedia, "Bussa's rebellion," last edited September 15, 2019, https://en.wikipedia.org/wiki/Bussa's_rebellion.

661   Wikipedia, "Richard Allen (bishop)", last edited Sepember 27,

2019, https://en.wikipedia.org/wiki/Richard_Allen_%28bishop%29.
662   Wikipedia, "Mary Ann Shadd," last edited September 19, 2019, https://en.wikipedia.org/wiki/Mary_Ann_Shadd.
663   Wikipedia, "Maria Weston Chapman," last edited October 20, 2019, https://en.wikipedia.org/wiki/Maria_Weston_Chapman.
664   Wikipedia, "Joseph Cinque," last edited October 3, 2019, https://en.wikipedia.org/wiki/Joseph_Cinque.
665   Wikipedia, "Samuel Cornish," last edited September 17, 2019, https://en.wikipedia.org/wiki/Samuel_Cornish.
666   Wikipedia, "Frederick Douglass," last edited October 24, 2019, https://en.wikipedia.org/wiki/Frederick_Douglass.
667   Wikipedia, "Sojourner Truth," last edited October 31, 2019, https://en.wikipedia.org/wiki/Sojourner_Truth.
668   Wikipedia, "Harriet Tubman," last edited October 28, 2019, https://en.wikipedia.org/wiki/Harriet_Tubman.
669   Wikipedia, "Haitian Revolution," last edited October 31, 2019, https://en.wikipedia.org/wiki/Haitian_Revolution.
670   Wikipedia, "Haitian Revolution," last edited October 31, 2019.
671   Ed Vulliamy, "The 10 best revolutionaries," The Guardian, August 28, 2019, https://www.theguardian.com/culture/2015/aug/28/10-best-revolutionaries-che-guevara-mahatma-gandhi-leon-trotsky.
672   Philip James Kaisary, "The Literary Impact of the Haitian Revolution," Ph.D. dissertation, (University of Warwick. 2008,) 8–10. accessed November 1, 2019, https://drive.google.com/file/d/0B_q6VhhkczIYWmthRC1STHVDWWs/view.
673   "Haiti, the Price of Revolution," Jan.1, 2017, Telesur, accessed November 1, 2019, https://www.telesurenglish.net/analysis/Haiti-The-Price-of-Liberation-20141231-0006.html,
674   Wikipedia, "Gabriel Prosser," last edited October 24, 2019, https://en.wikipedia.org/wiki/Gabriel_Prosser.
675   Wikipedia, "Denmark Vesey," last edited October 21, 2019, https://en.wikipedia.org/wiki/Denmark_Vesey.
676   Wikipedia, "Nat Turner," last edited October 31, 2019, https://en.wikipedia.org/wiki/Nat_Turner.
677   Adam Kloppe, "The Louisiana Purchase and the Haitian Revolution," March 5, 2015, Missouri Historical Society, accessed November 1, 2019, http://mohistory.org/blog/the-louisiana-pur-

chase-and-the-haitian-revolution/.

678   Katérina Stenou, ed. Struggles against slavery: International Year to Commemorate the Struggle against Slavery and its Abolition. "The Influences of the Haitian Revolution in the Caribbean and the Americas" Oruno D. Lara. p. 55. UNESCO, 2004, http://www.unesco.org//culture/slaveroute/flippdf/struggles_against-slaverye/files/struggles_against%20slaverye.pdf.

679   Wikipedia, "Encomienda," last edited October 27, 2019, https://en.wikipedia.org/wiki/Encomienda.

680   Wikipedia, "Repartimiento," last edited February 26, 2019, https://en.wikipedia.org/wiki/Repartimiento.

681   Katerina Stenou, "Struggles against slavery," UNESCO, 49.

682   "From Indentured Servitude to Racial Slavery," accessed November 1, 2019, http://www.pbs.org/wgbh/aia/part1/1narr3.html.

683   "From Indentured Servitude to Racial Slavery," accessed November 1, 2019.

684   "From Indentured Servitude to Racial Slavery," accessed November 1, 2019.

685   "Virginia's Slave Codes," Virginia General Assembly declaration, 1705," accessed November 1, 2019, https://www.pbs.org/wgbh/aia/part1/1p268.html.

686   Augustine of Hippo, *City of God*, quoted by Elaine Pagels, *Adam, Eve, and the Serpent* (New York: Vintage Books, 1988), 114.

687   Wikipedia, "Slavery and religion," last edited October 24, 2019, https://en.wikipedia.org/wiki/Slavery_and_religion.

688   "Christianity and Slavery," World Future Fund, accessed November 1, 2019, http://www.worldfuturefund.org/wffmaster/Reading/Religion/slavery.htm.

689   "Church apologizes for slave trade," accessed Nov. 1, 2019, BBC, http://news.bbc.co.uk/2/hi/uk_news/4694896.stm.

690   Wikipedia, "Codrington Plantations," last edited October 3, 2019, https://en.wikipedia.org/wiki/Codrington_Plantations.

691   Wikipedia, "George Whitefield," last edited October 11, 2019, https://en.wikipedia.org/wiki/George_Whitefield.

692   Thomas S. Kidd, "George Whitefield's troubled relationship to race and slavery," January 6, 2015, The Christian Century, accessed November 1, 2019, https://www.christiancentury.org/blogs/archive/2015-01/george-whitefield-s-troubled-relationship-race-and-

slavery.
693   T. W. Hoit, "The right of American slavery," Making of America accessed November 1, 2019, https://quod.lib.umich.edu/cgi/t/text/text-idx?c=moa;idno=ABJ1322.
694   T. W. Hoit, "The right of American slavery," Making of America, accessed November 1, 2019.
695   Wikipedia, "Slavery and religion," last edited October 24, 2019.
696   Wikipedia, "Sierra Leone," last edited October 25, 2019, https://en.wikipedia.org/wiki/Sierra_Leone.
697   "The Black Poor," Black Presence, accessed November 1, 2019, http://www.nationalarchives.gov.uk/pathways/blackhistory/work_community/poor.htm.
698   "Society for Effecting the Abolition of the Slave Trade," last edited September 30, 2019, https://en.wikipedia.org/wiki/Society_for_Effecting_the_Abolition_of_the_Slave_Trade.
699   Wikipedia, "Slave Trade Act 1807," last edited September 29, 2019, https://en.wikipedia.org/wiki/Slave_Trade_Act_1807.
700   Wikipedia, "Slavery Abolition Act 1833," last edited October 28, 2019, https://en.wikipedia.org/wiki/Slavery_Abolition_Act_1833.
701   "The African-American Mosaic: Colonization," Library of Congress, accessed November 1, 2019, https://www.loc.gov/exhibits/african/afam002.html.
702   Wikipedia, "American Colonization Society," last edited November 1, 2019, https://en.wikipedia.org/wiki/American_Colonization_Society.
703   Wikipedia, "Slavery and religion," last edited October 24, 2019.
704   Wikipedia, "Christian Identity," last edited October 28, 2019, https://en.wikipedia.org/wiki/Christian_Identity.
705   Wikipedia, "Ku Klux Klan," last edited October 30, 2019, https://en.wikipedia.org/wiki/Ku_Klux_Klan.
706   The Knights Party, The Premier Voice of America's White Resistance," accessed November 1, 2019, http://www.kkk.com/
707   Wikipedia, "Underground Railroad," last edited October 30, 2019, https://en.wikipedia.org/wiki/Underground_Railroad.
708   Lisa Vox, "3 Major Ways Slaves Showed Resistance to Slavery," ThoughtCo, accessed November 1, 2019, https://www.thoughtco.com/

ways-slaves-showed-resistance-to-slavery-45401.
709   Wikipedia, "City upon a Hill," last edited October 15, 2019, https://en.wikipedia.org/wiki/City_upon_a_Hill.
710   Frank Lambert, "The Founding Fathers and the Place of Religion in America" (Princeton NJ: Princeton University Press, 2006), accessed November 2, 2019, http://press.princeton.edu/titles/7500.html.
711   Wikipedia, "First Great Awakening," last edited October 10, 2019, https://en.wikipedia.org/wiki/First_Great_Awakening.
712   "Bill of Rights in Action," Constitutional Rights Foundation, http://www.crf-usa.org/bill-of-rights-in-action/bria-20-4-a-jonathan-edwards-and-the-great-awakening-in-colonial-america.
713   "Religious Affiliation of the Delegates to the Constitutional Convention of 1787, including the Signers of the Constitution of the United States of America," accessed November 2, 2019, http://www.adherents.com/gov/Founding_Fathers_Religion.html#Constitution
714   Natalie Alonso, "Why Did Samuel Adams Not Attend the Constitutional Convention," Classroom, accessed November 2, 2019, http://classroom.synonym.com/did-samuel-adams-not-attend-constitutional-convention-22713.html.
715   Ira Stoll, *Samuel Adams: A Life*, 16.
716   Wikipedia, "Treaty of Tripoli," last edited October 10, 2019, http://en.wikipedia.org/wiki/Treaty_of_Tripoli.
717   Wikipedia, "Calvinistic Methodists," last edited September 21, 2019, https://en.wikipedia.org/wiki/Calvinistic_Methodists.
718   Wikipedia, "Methodism," last edited October 10, 2019, http://en.wikipedia.org/wiki/Methodism.
719   U.S. Bureau of the Census, "Historical Statistics of the United States: From: the Colonial Times to the Present," 1976, 8, 392.
720   Wikipedia, "Baptists," last edited November 1, 2019, http://en.wikipedia.org/wiki/Baptists.
721   Bill J Leonard, *Baptist Ways: A History* (Valley Forge, Pennsylvania: Judson Press, 2003), 24.
722   Wikipedia, "Baptists," last edited November 1, 2019.
723   Wikipedia, "Baptists," last edited November 1, 2019.
724   "The Slave Experience: Religion," Thirteen, accessed November 2, 2019, http://www.pbs.org/wnet/slavery/experience/religion/history2.html.

755	Wikipedia, "Timeline of events leading to the American Civil War," last edited September 25, 2019, https://en.wikipedia.org/wiki/Timeline_of_events_leading_to_the_American_Civil_War.
756	Wikipedia, "John Randolph of Roanoke," last edited October 15, 2019, https://en.wikipedia.org/wiki/John_Randolph_of_Roanoke.
757	Wikipedia, "Timeline of events leading to the American Civil War," last edited September 25, 2019.
758	"Missouri Compromise," History, last edited October 27, 2019, http://www.history.com/topics/missouri-compromise.
759	Wikipedia, "Parallel 36o30'north," last edited September 10, 2019, https://en.wikipedia.org/wiki/Parallel_36%C2%B030%E2%80%B2_north.
760	"The Kansas-Nebraska Act," US History Online Textbook, 2018, accessed Nov. 3, 2019, http://www.ushistory.org/us/31a.asp.
761	Wikipedia, "Bleeding Kansas," last edited November 3, 2019, https://en.wikipedia.org/wiki/Bleeding_Kansas.
762	James M. McPherson, James K. Hogue, *Ordeal By Fire: The Civil War and Reconstruction* (Boston: McGraw Hill, 1982), 92.
763	Wikipedia, "Topeka Constitution," last edited September 26, 2019, https://en.wikipedia.org/wiki/Topeka_Constitution.
764	Wikipedia, "John Brown (Abolutionist)," last edited October 28, 2019, https://en.wikipedia.org/wiki/John_Brown_%28abolitionist%29.
765	Wikipedia, "Doughface," last edited September 28, 2019, https://en.wikipedia.org/wiki/Doughface.
766	Wikipedia, "James Buchanan," last edited October 31, 2019, https://en.wikipedia.org/wiki/James_Buchanan.
767	Wikipedia, "Provisional Constitution of the Confederate States," last edited October 14, 2019, https://en.wikipedia.org/wiki/Provisional_Constitution_of_the_Confederate_States.
768	Wikipedia, "Confederate States of America," last edited November 2, 2019, https://en.wikipedia.org/wiki/Confederate_States_of_America.
769	Wikipedia, "Confederate States of America," last edited November 2, 2019.
770	Wikipedia, "Jefferson Davis," last edited October 30, 2019, https://en.wikipedia.org/wiki/Jefferson_Davis.
771	Wikipedia, "Fort Sumter," last edited October 31, 2019, https://en.wikipedia.org/wiki/Fort_Sumter.

772 Wikipedia, "Timeline of events leading to the American Civil War," last edited September 25, 2019.
773 Wikipedia, "Union (American Civil War)," last edited October 22, 2019, https://en.wikipedia.org/wiki/Union_%28American_Civil_War%29.
774 "The Emancipation Proclamation," National Archives, accessed November 3, 2019, https://www.archives.gov/exhibits/featured_documents/emancipation_proclamation/.
775 Wikipedia, "Emancipation Proclamation," last edited October 25, 2019, https://en.wikipedia.org/wiki/Emancipation_Proclamation.
776 Wikipedia, "Sherman's March to the Sea," last edited October 20, 2019, https://en.wikipedia.org/wiki/Sherman's_March_to_the_Sea.
777 Wikipedia, "Sherman's March to the Sea," last edited October 20, 2019.
778 Wikipedia, "Confederate States of America," last edited November 2, 2019.
779 "Homestead Act," Primary Documents in American History, accessed November 3, 2019, https://www.loc.gov/rr/program/bib/ourdocs/Homestead.html.
780 Charles Hooper, "List of Political Factors During the Civil War," The Classroom, accessed November 3, 2019, http://classroom.synonym.com/list-political-factors-during-civil-war-5337.html.
781 Charles Hooper, "List of Political Factors During the Civil War," The Classroom, accessed November 3, 2019.
782 Roger L. Ransom, "The Economics of the Civil War," EH.net, accessed November 3, 2019, https://eh.net/encyclopedia/the-economics-of-the-civil-war/.
783 Roger L. Ransom, "The Economics of the Civil War," EH.net, accessed November 3, 2019.
784 Wikipedia, "Pacific Railroad Acts," last edited October 8, 2019, https://en.wikipedia.org/wiki/Pacific_Railroad_Acts.
785 Claudia Goldin and Frank Lewis, "The Economic Costs of the American Civil War: Estimates and Implications," *Journal of Economic History*, 35 (1975), 299-326.
786 Williamson, Jeffrey. "Watersheds and Turning Points: Conjectures on the Long-Term Impact of Civil War Financing," *Journal of Economic History*, 34 (1974), 636-661.
787 John James, "Public Debt Management and Nineteenth-Cen-

tury American Economic Growth," *Explorations in Economic History* 21 (1984), 192-217.
788   Wikipedia, "Independent Treasury," last edited October 15, 2019, https://en.wikipedia.org/wiki/Independent_Treasury.
789   "In His Own Words: Abraham Lincoln on Banking," Office of the Comptroller of the Currency, accessed November 3, 2019, http://www.occ.treas.gov/about/what-we-do/history/lincoln-his-own-words-on-banking.html.
790   "Collected Works of Abraham Lincoln," (CWAL), Volume 1, 61 – 69, The Abraham Lincoln Association, accessed November 3, 2019, http://quod.lib.umich.edu/l/lincoln/.
791   Wikipedia, "National Bank Act," last edited October 10, 2019, https://en.wikipedia.org/wiki/National_Bank_Act.
792   "Collected Works of Abraham Lincoln," (CWAL), Volume 8, 143 – 44.
793   "The History of Money Part 2," XAT3, accessed November 3, 2019, http://www.xat.org/xat/usury.html.
794   "The History of Money Part 2," XAT3, accessed November 3, 2019.
795   "The Mysterious Col. Edmund D. Taylor: Father of the Greenback," accessed November 3, 2019, http://www.heritech.com/pridger/lincoln/taylor.htm.
796   "The History of Money Part 2," XAT3, accessed November 3, 2019.
797   "The History of Money Part 2," XAT3, accessed November 3, 2019.
798   Dean Henderson. "The Federal Reserve Cartel: Freemasons and The House of Rothschild," Global Research, June 8, 2011, https://www.globalresearch.ca/the-federal-reserve-cartel-freemasons-and-the-house-of-rothschild/25179.
799   Senator Daniel of Virginia, May 22, 1890, from a speech in Congress, to be found in the Congressional Record, p. 5128, quoting from the Bankers Magazine of August, 1873, quoted in "The History of Money Part 2," XAT3.
800   James A. Garfield quotes, Goodreads, accessed November 3,2019,   https://www.goodreads.com/quotes/288058-whoever-controls-the-volume-of-money-in-our-country-is.
801   From a circular issued by authority of the Associated Bankers

of New York, Philadelphia, and Boston signed by one James Buel, secretary, sent out from 247 Broadway, New York in 1877, to the bankers in all of the States, quoted in "The History of Money Part 2," XAT3.

802   Nicholas Kristof, "An Idiot's Guide to Inequality," July 23, 2014, retrieved Nov. 4, 2018, The New York Times, https://www.nytimes.com/2014/07/24/opinion/nicholas-kristof-idiots-guide-to-inequality-piketty-capital.html.

803   Claudia Goldin and Frank Lewis, "The Economic Costs of the American Civil War: Estimates and Implications." *Journal of Economic History,* 35 (1975), 299-326.

804   Roger L. Ransom, "The Economics of the Civil War," EH.net, accessed November 3, 2019.

805   Roger L. Ransom and Richard Sutch, "Growth and Welfare in the American South in the Nineteenth Century," *Explorations in Economic History,* 16 (19790, 207-235.

806   Roger L. Ransom, "The Economics of the Civil War," EH.net, accessed November 3, 2019.

807   "14th Amendment to the U.S. Constitution," Primary Documents in American History, Library of Congress, https://www.loc.gov/rr/program/bib/ourdocs/14thamendment.html.

808   "15th Amendment to the U.S. Constitution," Primary Documents in American History, Library of Congress, https://loc.gov/rr/program/bib/ourdocs/15thamendment.html.

809   "Reconstruction: Lincoln's Plan," Infoplease, accessed November 3, 2019, http://www.infoplease.com/encyclopedia/history/reconstruction-lincoln-plan.html.

810   Wikipedia, "Black Codes (United States)," last edited November 1, 2019. https://en.wikipedia.org/wiki/Black_Codes_%28United_States%29.

811   Wikipedia, "Carl Schurz," last edited October 20, 2019, https://en.wikipedia.org/wiki/Carl_Schurz.

812   Carl Schurz, "Report on the Condition of the South", December 1865 (U.S. Senate Exec. Doc. No. 2, 39th Congress, 1st session) Cited in https://en.wikipedia.org/wiki/Reconstruction_Era.

813   Wikipedia, "Reconstruction era," last edited October 30, 2019, https://en.wikipedia.org/wiki/Reconstruction_era.

814   Jacqueline Jones, *Labor of Love, Labor of Sorrow: Black Women, Work, and the Family, from Slavery to the Present* (New York: Basic

Books, 2010), 70.
815   Wikipedia, "Wade-Davis Bill," last edited May 8, 2019, https://en.wikipedia.org/wiki/Wade%E2%80%93Davis_Bill.
816   Wikipedia, "Civil Rights Act of 1866," last edited October 9, 2019, https://en.wikipedia.org/wiki/Civil_Rights_Act_of_1866.
817   Wikipedia, "Freedmen's Bureau," last edited October 16, 2019, https://en.wikipedia.org/wiki/Freedmen's_Bureau.
818   Wikipedia, "Carpetbaggers," last edited November 2, 2019, https://en.wikipedia.org/wiki/Carpetbagger.
819   History.com Editors, "Black Leaders During Reconstruction," last edited August 24, 2019, https://www.history.com/topics/american-civil-war/black-leaders-during-reconstruction.
820   Wikipedia, "1876 United States presidential election, 1876," last edited October 27, 2019, https://en.wikipedia.org/wiki/United_States_presidential_election,_1876.
821   Wikipedia, "Compromise of 1877," last edited October 25, 2019, https://en.wikipedia.org/wiki/Compromise_of_1877.
822   Wikipedia, "Redeemers," last edited October 13, 2019, https://en.wikipedia.org/wiki/Redeemers.
823   Wikipedia, "White League," last edited October 9, 2019, https://en.wikipedia.org/wiki/White_League.
824   Wikipedia, "Red Shirts (United States)," last edited September 23, 2019, https://en.wikipedia.org/wiki/Red_Shirts_%28Southern_United_States%29.
825   Wikipedia, "Ku Klux Klan," last edited October 30, 2019, https://en.wikipedia.org/wiki/Ku_Klux_Klan.
826   Wikipedia, "Coushatta massacre," last edited September 17, 2019, https://en.wikipedia.org/wiki/Coushatta_massacre.
827   Wikipedia, "Reconstruction era," last edited October 30, 2019.
828   Nicholas Lemann, *Redemption: The Last Battle of the Civil War* (New York: Farrar, Straus & Giroux, 2007), 76.
829   Wikipedia, "Wade Hampton III," last edited October 3, 2019, https://en.wikipedia.org/wiki/Wade_Hampton_III.
830   "Georgia Democrats in state House of Representatives move to expel blacks from the State Legislature," The History Engine, accessed November 3, https://historyengine.richmond.edu/episodes/view/818.
831   Wikipedia, "W. E. B. Du Bois," last edited November 1, 2019, https://en.wikipedia.org/wiki/W._E._B._Du_Bois

832   J. Bradford DeLong, "Robber Barons," January 1, 1998, http://www.j-brsadford-delong.net/Econ_Articles/Carnegie/DeLong_Moscon_paper2.html.
833   "'Let them eat cake': The GOP and its attacks on the middle class," http://m.dailykos.com/stories/1345709.
834   Jay Gould, The Quotations Page, Quote 33148, accessed November 3, 2019, http://www.quotationpage.com/quote/33148.html.
835   "John D. Rockefeller Quotes," Successories, http://www.successories.com/iquote/author/1285/john-d-rockefeller-quotes/41.
836   Wikipedia, "Robber baron (industrialist)," last edited October 23, 2019, http://en.wikipedia.org/wiki/Robber_baron_(industrialist).
837   "Thomas Gibbons, (1757 – 1826)," http://www.nysl.nysed.gov/mssc/steamboats/player_gibbons.htm.
838   Wikipedia, "Steamboat," last edited October 24, 2019, https://en.wikipedia.org/wiki/Steamboat.
839   .The Constitution of New York: April 20, 1777," Yale Law School, Lillian Goldman Law Library, https://avalon.law.yale.edu/18th_century/ny01.asp.
840   Wikipedia, "Aaron Ogden," last edited September 22, 2019, https://en.wikipedia.org/wiki/Aaron_Ogden.
841   Wikipedia, "Gibbons v. Ogden," last edited Nov. 1, 2018, https://en.wikipedia.org/wiki/Gibbons_v._Ogden.
842   Wikipedia, "California Gold Rush," last edited October 18, 2019, https://en.wikipedia.org/wiki/California_Gold_Rush.
843   Wikipedia, "Timeline of United States railway history," last edited October 13, 2019, https://en.wikipedia.org/wiki/Timeline_of_United_States_railway_history.
844   History.com Editors, "Cornelius Vanderbilt," History, last edited September 9, 2019, http://www.history.com/topics/cornelius-vanderbilt.
845   Wikipedia, "New York, Providence and Boston Railroad," last edited October 11, 2019, https://en.wikipedia.org/wiki/New_York,_Providence_and_Boston_Railroad.
846   Wikipedia, "Livingston Avenue Bridge," last edited September 25, 2019, https://en.wikipedia.org/wiki/Livingston_Avenue_Bridge#History.
847   Wikipedia, "Lake Shore and Michigan Southern Railway," last edited July 18, 2018, https://en.wikipedia.org/wiki/Lake_Shore_and_Michigan_Southern_Railway.

848   Wikipedia, "James Fisk (financier)," last edited October 16, 2019, https://en.wikipedia.org/wiki/James_Fisk_%28financier%29.
849   "Jay Gould: Financier in the Age of Robber Barons," United States History, accessed November 3, 2019, http://www.u-s-history.com/pages/h866.html.
850   "The Tweed Ring," United States History, accessed November 3, 2019, http://www.u-s-history.com/pages/h703.html.
851   "The Erie War: Corporate Conflict in the Gilded Age," United States History, accessed November 3, 2019, http://www.u-s-history.com/pages/h874.html.
852   "The Erie War: Corporate Conflict in the Gilded Age," United States History, accessed November 3, 2019.
853   Spelman College, http://www.spelman.edu/.
854   "John D. Rockefeller and the Standard Oil Company," 6.4 Alliances with the railroads, http://www.micheloud.com/fxm/so/alliance.htm.
855   "The Congregationalists and John D. Rockefeller," The Sacred Heart Review, Vol. 33, No. 14, 1 April, 1905, Boston College Libraries, http://newspapers.bc.edu/cgi-bin/bostonsh?a=d&d=BOSTONSH19050401-01.2.7.
856   Wikipedia, "Seven Sisters (Oil Companies)," ast edited October 17, 2019, https://en.wikipedia.org/wiki/Seven_Sisters_%28oil_companies%29.
857   Wikipedia, "John D. Rockefeller," last edited October 10, 2019, https://en.wikipedia.org/wiki/John_D._Rockefeller.
858   "John D. Rockefeller: Robber Baron," https://prezi.com/d1amzt0k6wla/john-d-rockefeller-robber-baron/.
859   "Biography: Andrew Carnegie," American Experience, PBS, http://www.pbs.org/wgbh/amex/carnegie/peopleevents/pande01.html.
860   Wikipedia, "Adams Express Company," last edited November 24, 2019, https://en.wikipedia.org/wiki/Adams_Express_Company.
861   Wikipedia, "Theodore Tuttle Woodruff," last edited March 5, 2019, https://en.wikipedia.org/wiki/Theodore_Tuttle_Woodruff.
862   Wikipedia, "Keystone Bridge Company," last edited October 31, 2019, https://en.wikipedia.org/wiki/Keystone_Bridge_Company.
863   "Andrew Carnegie Becomes a Capitalist, 1856," EyeWitness to History, (2007) http://www.eyewitnesstohistory.com/carnegie.htm.
864   Wikipedia, "Pinkerton (detective agency)," last edited October 26, 2019, https://en.wikipedia.org/wiki/Pinkerton_%28detective_

agency%29.

865 Wikipedia, "Ludlow Massacre," ast edited October 31, 2019, https://en.wikipedia.org/wiki/Ludlow_Massacre.

866 Wikipedia, "Battle of Blair Mountain," last edited October 7, 2019, https://en.wikipedia.org/wiki/Battle_of_Blair_Mountain.

867 Wikipedia, "Homestead Strike," last edited October 31, 2019, https://en.wikipedia.org/wiki/Homestead_Strike.

868 "Biography: Andrew Carnegie," American Experience, PBS, accessed November 4, 2019, https://www.pbs.ordg/wgbh/americanexperience/features/carnegie-biography.

869 Wikipedia, "Andrew Carnegie," last edited October 12, 2019, https://en.wikipedia.org/wiki/Andrew_Carnegie.

870 Wikipedia, "The Gospel of Wealth," last edited October 14, 2019, https://en.wikipedia.org/wiki/The_Gospel_of_Wealth.

871 The Editors of Encyclopedia Britannica, "Andrew Carnegie: American Industrialist and Philanthropist," Encyclopedia Britannica, http://www.britannica.com/biography/Andrew-Carnegie.

872 Wikipedia, "Permanent Court of Arbitration," last edited October 9, 2019, https://en.wikipedia.org/wiki/Permanent_Court_of_Arbitration.

873 Wikipedia, "International Court of Justice," last edited October 16, 2019, https://en.wikipedia.org/wiki/International_Court_of_Justice.

874 Wikipedia, "Peace Palace," last edited November 3, 2019, https://en.wikipedia.org/wiki/Peace_Palace.

875 "Biography: Andrew Carnegie," American Experience, PBS.

876 History.com Editors, "J. P. Morgan," last edited June 7, 2019, http://www.history.com/topics/john-pierpont-morgan.

877 Ron Chernow, *The House of Morgan: An American Banking Dynasty and the Rise of Modern Finance* (London: Atlantic Books, 2003), 31.

878 The Editors of Encyclopedia Britannica, "J. P. Morgan: American Financier," Encyclopedia Britannica, http://www.britannica.com/EBchecked/topic/392225/John-Pierpont-Morgan.

879 Ron Chernow, *The House of Morgan: An American Banking Dynasty and the Rise of Modern Finance*, 67.

880 Wikipedia, "Anthony Joseph Drexel," last edited September 7, 2019, https://en.wikipedia.org/wiki/Anthony_Joseph_Drexel.

881 Ron Chernow, *The House of Morgan: An American Banking*

Dynasty and the Rise of Modern Finance, 34

882   "Two Wall Street banks dominated deal making in 2015," Business Insider, January 4, 2016, http://www.businessinsider.com/goldman-sachs-jpmorgan-lead-fee-rankings-2016-01.

883   Wikipedia, "Jay Cooke," last edited September 23, 2019, https://en.wikipedia.org/wiki/Jay_Cooke.

884   Ron Chernow, *The House of Morgan: An American Banking Dynasty and the Rise of Modern Finance*, 35

885   Wikipedia, "Northern Pacific Railway," last edited October 30, 2019, https://en.wikipedia.org/wiki/Northern_Pacific_Railway.

886   History.com Editors, "Credit Mobilier," last edited June 10, 2019, History.com, https://www.history.com/topics/19th-century/credit-mobilier.

887   Ron Chernow, *Titan: the life of John D. Rockefeller, Sr* (New York: Random House, 1998), 160.

888   Wikipedia, "Jay Gould," last edited October 30, 2019, http://en.wikipedia.org/wiki/Jay_Gould.

889   Ron Chernow, *The House of Morgan: An American Banking Dynasty and the Rise of Modern Finance*, 83.

890   "Morgan helps end the Panic of 1893," J. P. Morgan, accessed November 4, 2019, https://www.jpmorgan.com/country/US/en/jpmorgan/about/history/month/feb.

891   "Testimony of Deadria C. Farmer-Paellmann, Chicago City Council Hearing On J. P. Morgan Chase Manhattan Bank Merger, March 5, 2004," http://academic.udayton.edu/race/02rights/repara30.htm.

892   Ron Chernow, *The House of Morgan: An American Banking Dynasty and the Rise of Modern Finance*, 108.

893   Ron Chernow, *The House of Morgan: An American Banking Dynasty and the Rise of Modern Finance*, 114.

894   Ron Chernow, *The House of Morgan: An American Banking Dynasty and the Rise of Modern Finance*, 50.

895   Ron Chernow, *The House of Morgan: An American Banking Dynasty and the Rise of Modern Finance*, 90.

896   Wikipedia, "Kuhn, Loeb and Co.," last edited September 3, 2019, https://en.wikipedia.org/wiki/Kuhn,_Loeb_%26_Co.

897   Ron Chernow, *The House of Morgan: An American Banking Dynasty and the Rise of Modern Finance*, 88.

898   Wikipedia, "James J. Hill," last edited October 10, 2019, https://

en.wikipedia.org/wiki/James_J._Hill.

899   "Harriman vs. Hill: Wall Street's Great Railroad War," EH.net, accessed November 3, 2019, http://eh.net/book_reviews/harriman-vs-hill-wall-streets-great-railroad-war/

900   "Jacob Henry Schiff Facts," Your Dictionary, accessed November 4, 2019, http://biography.yourdictionary.com/jacob-henry-schiff.

901   Ron Chernow, *The House of Morgan: An American Banking Dynasty and the Rise of Modern Finance*, 93.

902   Wikipedia, "Panic of 1901," last edited June 27, 2019, https://en.wikipedia.org/wiki/Panic_of_1901.

903   Ron Chernow, *The House of Morgan: An American Banking Dynasty and the Rise of Modern Finance*, 94.

904   Henry F. Pringle, T*heodore Roosevelt*, Reprint edition (Old Saybrook, Connecticut: Konecky & Konecky, 2003), 256.

905   Ron Chernow, T*he House of Morgan: An American Banking Dynasty and the Rise of Modern Finance*, 108.

906   "Financing the Panama Canal," J. P. Morgan, accessed November 4, 2019, https://www.jpmorgan.com/pages/jpmorgan/about/history/month/may.

907   Wikipedia, "History of Panama (1821-1903)," last edited August 25, 2019, http://en.wikipedia.org/wiki/History_of_Panama_%281821%E2%80%931903%29.

908   "Building the Panama Canal, (1903-1914)," Department of State, Office of the Historian, https://history.state.gov/milestones/1899-1913/panama-canal.

909   Ron Chernow, *The House of Morgan: An American Banking Dynasty and the Rise of Modern Finance*, 109.

910   Morgan has previously been approached by Roosevelt to help him broker a wage increase for railroad workers which Morgan obliged. Roosevelt was gushy in his praise for Morgan, and Pierce knew how to use this event as a public relations victory.

911   John Garraty, *Right-Hand Man: The Life of George W. Perkins* (New York: J. P. Lippincott, 1964), 219.

912   Ron Chernow, The House of Morgan: An American Banking Dynasty and the Rise of Modern Finance, 110.

913   Joseph R. Stromberg, "The Role of State Monopoly Capitalism in the American Empire," *Journal of Libertarian Studies*, Vol. 15, No. 3 (Summer, 2001), 57-93, https://mises-media.s3.amazonaws.

com/15_3_3.pdf?file=1&type=document.
914   Ron Chernow, *The House of Morgan: An American Banking Dynasty and the Rise of Modern Finance*, 108.
915   Jonathon Trugman, "America's 'recovery' is baloney – we're actually broke," New York Post, May 28, 2016, http://nypost.com/2016/05/28/americas-recovery-is-baloney-were-actually-broke/.
916   Joseph R. Stromberg, "The Role of State Monopoly Capitalism in the American Empire," *Journal of Libertarian Studies* Volume 15, no. 3 (Summer 2001), 57-93. Available online at http://www.mises.org/journals/jls/15_3/15_3_3.pdf, p. 64.
917   Kevin A. Carson. "Austrian And Marxist Theories Of Monopoly-Capital: A Mutualist Synthesis," http://mutualist.org/id10.html.
918   Wikipedia, "Anti-establishment," last edited September 12, 2019, https://en.wikipedia.org/wiki/Anti-establishment.
919   Howard Zinn. "The Seventies: Under Control?" History Is A Weapon. The People's History of the United States, accessed November 4, 2019, http://www.historyisaweapon.com/defcon1/zinnseven20.html.
920   Murray Rothbard, "War Collectivism in World War I," in Murray Rothbard and Ronald Radosh, eds., *A New History of Leviathan: Essays on the Rise of the American Corporate State* (New York: E. P. Dutton & Co., Inc., 1972), 66-67.
921   Kevin A. Carson. "Austrian And Marxist Theories Of Monopoly-Capital: A Mutualist Synthesis," 4.
922   The New Left opposed what it saw as the prevailing authority structures in society, which it termed "The Establishment", and those who rejected this authority became known as "anti-Establishment". The New Left did not seek to recruit industrial workers, but rather concentrated on a social activist approach to organization, convinced that they could be the source for a better kind of social revolution. See http://en.wikipedia.org/wiki/New_Left.
923   Wikipedia, "Noam Chomsky," last edited November 2, 2019, https://en.wikipedia.org/wiki/Noam_Chomsky.
924   Wikipedia, "Paul Sweezy," last edited August 31, 2019, https://en.wikipedia.org/wiki/Paul_Sweezy.
925   Wikipedia, "James Weinstein (author)," last edited February 5, 2019, https://en.wikipedia.org/wiki/James_Weinstein_%28author%29.
926   Wikipedia, "Gabriel Kolko," last edited September 16, 2019,

https://en.wikipedia.org/wiki/Gabriel_Kolko.
927   Wikipedia, "William Appleman Williams," last edited October 17, 2019, https://en.wikipedia.org/wiki/William_Appleman_Williams.
928   Kevin A. Carson. "Austrian And Marxist Theories Of Monopoly-Capital: A Mutualist Synthesis," 3.
929   Robert Rives La Monte, "You and Your Vote," *International Socialist Review* XIII, No. 2 (August 1912); "Editorial," *International Socialist Review* XIII, No. 6 (December 1912).
930   Wikipedia, "Ingsoc," last edited October 26, 2019, https://en.wikipedia.org/wiki/Ingsoc.
931   George Orwell, *1984*, *Signet Classics* reprint (New York: Harcourt Brace Jovanovich, 1949), 169.
932   Kevin A. Carson. *Austrian And Marxist Theories Of Monopoly-Capital: A Mutualist Synthesis*. References throughout.
933   Edward A. Ross. *Social Control: A Survey of the Foundations of Order* (New York: The Macmillan Company, 1901), Reprinted 2009 by Transaction Publishers, New Jersey.
934   The Rockefeller General Education Board, Occasional Letter No.1, 1906, accessed November 4, 2019, available at http://www.zhibit.org/diemythographer/die-mythographer-die/occasional-letter-number-one-2006.
935   Woodrow Wilson, 28th President of the United States, in a speech to businessmen, and from an address to The New York City High School Teachers Association, Jan. 9th, 1909, accessed November 4, 2019, available at http://www.zhibit.org/diemythographer/die-mythographer-die/occasional-letter-number-one-2006.
936   Ellwood P. Cubberley, Stanford's Dean of Education, Public School Administration, 1929, 338, available at https://archive.org/details/publicschooladmi1922cubb.
937   Ivan Illich, *Deschooling Society*, (New York: Harper and Row, 1971), 1-3.
938   William Appleman Williams, *The Contours of American History* (Cleveland and New York: The World Publishing Company, 1961), 382.
939   Harry Braverman, *Labor and Monopoly Capital: The Degradation of Work in the Twentieth Century*, 25th Anniversary Edition (New York: Monthly Review Press, 1998), 107-117.
940   Hilaire Belloc, *The Servile State* (Indianapolis: Liberty Classics, 1913, 1977), 146-147.

941   Wikipedia, "Eugenics," last edited November 1, 2019, https://en.wikipedia.org/wiki/Eugenics.
942   William E. Seidelman MD, "Science and Inhumanity: The Kaiser-Wilhelm/Max Planck Society," research archive (eugenics_transhumanism), accessed November 4, 2019, https://ce399eugenics.wordpress.com/2011/09/08/science-and-inhumanity-the-kaiser-wilhelmmax-planck-society/.
943   Wikipedia, "Kaiser Wilhelm Society," last edited October 26, 2019, https://en.wikipedia.org/wiki/Kaiser_Wilhelm_Society#Kaiser_Wilhelm_Institutes.
944   Wikipedia, "Panic of 1907," last edited October 30, 2019, https://en.wikipedia.org/wiki/Panic_of_1907.
945   Tyler E. Bagwell, "The Jekyll Island duck hunt that created the Federal Reserve," Jekyll Island History, accessed November 4, 2019, http://www.jekyllislandhistory.com/federalreserve.shtml.
946   Tyler E. Bagwell, "The Jekyll Island duck hunt that created the Federal Reserve," Jekyll Island History, accessed November 4, 2019.
947   Wikipedia, "Triple Alliance (1882)," last edited September 3, 2019, https://en.wikipedia.org/wiki/Triple_Alliance_%281882%29.
948   Wikipedia, "Allies of World War I," last edited November 4, 2019, https://en.wikipedia.org/wiki/Allies_of_World_War_I.
949   James E. Kitchen, "Colonial Empire," International Encyclopedia of the First World War, accessed November 4, 2019, https://encyclopedia.1914-1918-online.net/article/colonial_empires_after_the_wardecolonization.
950   Wikipedia, "Austria-Hungary," last edited October 31, 2019, https://en.wikipedia.org/wiki/Austria-Hungary.
951   Wikipedia, "Austria-Hungary," last edited October 31, 2019.
952   Wikipedia, "Austria-Hungary," last edited October 31, 2019.
953   Wikipedia, "Austria-Hungary," last edited October 31, 2019.
954   Wikipedia, "Austro-Hungarian rule in Bosnia and Herzegovina," last edited September 18, 2019, https://en.wikipedia.org/wiki/Austro-Hungarian_rule_in_Bosnia_and_Herzegovina.
955   Wikipedia, "Bosnian crisis," last edited October 6, 2019, https://en.wikipedia.org/wiki/Bosnian_crisis.
956   Wikipedia, "Pan-Slavism," last edited October 16, 2019, https://en.wikipedia.org/wiki/Pan-Slavism.
957   Wikipedia, "Russo-Japanese War," last edited October 28,

2019, https://en.wikipedia.org/wiki/Russo-Japanese_War.

958   History.com Editors, "Austria-Hungary annexes Bosnia-Herzegovina," last edited July 28, 2019, https://www.history.com/this-day-in-history/austria-hungary-annexes-bosnia-herzegovina.   .

959   Wikipedia, "Balkan League," last edited October 31, 2019, hytps://en.wikipedia.org/wiki/Balkan_League.

960   Wikipedia, "Treaty of London (1913)," last edited August 30, 2019, https://en.wikipedia.org/wiki/Treaty_of_London_%281913%29.

961   Wikipedia, "Second Balkan War," last edited November 1, 2019, https://en.wikipedia.org/wiki/Second_Balkan_War.

962   Wikipedia, "Treaty of Bucharest (1913)," last edited October 14, 2019, https://en.wikipedia.org/wiki/Treaty_of_Bucharest_%281913%29.

963   Wikipedia, "Black Hand (Serbia)," last edited October 28, 2019, https://en.wikipedia.org/wiki/Black_Hand_%28Serbia%29.

964   Wikipedia, "Black Hand (Serbia)," last edited October 28, 2019.

965   Wikipedia, "Franco-Russian Alliance," last edited October 25, 2019, https://en.wikipedia.org/wiki/Franco-Russian_Alliance.

966   "The July Crisis," Firstworldwar.com, accessed November 4, 2019, http://firstworldwar.com/origins/julycrisis.htm.

967   "Austria-Hungary declares war on Servia," History, accessed November 4, 2019, http://www.history.com/this-day-in-history/austria-hungary-declares-war-on-serbia.

968   "Working and Living Conditions," The Industrial revolution, accessed Novemer 4, 2019, https://firstindustrialrevolution.weebly.com/working-and-living-conditions.html..

969   Wikipedia, "Anti-Socialist Laws," last edited October 14, 2019, See https://en.wikipedia.org/wiki/Anti-Socialist_Laws.

970   Wikipedia, "Anti-Socialist Laws," last edited October 14, 2019.

971   Wikipedia, "Iskra," last edited July 29, 2019 https://en.wikipedia.org/wiki/Iskra.

972   The Editors of Encyclopedia Britannica, "Bolshevik: Russian Political Faction," accessed November 4, 2019, http://www.britannica.com/topic/Bolshevik.

973   "World War I Timeline," accessed November 4, 2019, https://shmoop.com/wwi/timeline.html.

974   Wikipedia, "Russian Civil War," last edited October 26, 2019, https://en.wikipedia.org/wiki/Russian_Civil_War.

975	Wikipedia, "Russian Revolution," last edited October 17, 2019, https://en.wikipedia.org/wiki/Russian_Revolution.
976	The Editors of the Encyclopedia Britannica, "Russian Civil War," accessed November 4, 2019, http://www.britannica.com/event/Russian-Civil-War.
977	Wikipedia, "Russian Civil War," last edited October 26, 2019.
978	Elisabeth Gaynor Ellis; Anthony Esler, "Revolution and Civil War in Russia," *World History; The Modern Era* (Boston: Pearson Prentice Hall, 2007) 483.
979	Dell Markey, "The Spread of Marxism and Its Influence on Russian Communism," the classroom, accessed November 4, 2019, http://classroom.synonym.com/spread-marxism-its-influence-russian-communism-8058.html.
980	History.com Editors, "Germans introduce poison gas," last edited July 28, 2019, http://www.history.com/this-day-in-history/germans-introduce-poison-gas.
981	"Topics in Chronicling America – Sinking the Lusitania," Library of Congress, Newspaper and Periodical Reading Room, accessed November 4, 2019, https://www.loc.gov/rr/news/topics/lusitania.html.
982	Wikipedia, "Battle of the Somme," last edited November 4, 2019, https://en.wikipedia.org/wiki/Battle_of_the_Somme.
983	Wikipedia, "Zimmermann Telegram," last edited November 4, 2019, https://en.wikipedia.org/wiki/Zimmermann_Telegram.
984	Wikipedia, "Battle of Cantigny," last edited September 18, 2019, https://en.wikipedia.org/wiki/Battle_of_Cantigny.
985	Wikipedia, "3rd Infantry Division (United States)," last edited October 21, 2019, https://en.wikipedia.org/wiki/3rd_Infantry_Division_%28United_States%29#World_War_I.
986	Wikipedia, "Battle of Belleau Wood," last edited October 11, 2019, https://en.wikipedia.org/wiki/Battle_of_Belleau_Wood.
987	Wikipedia, "Battle of Saint-Mihiel," last edited September 13, 2019, https://en.wikipedia.org/wiki/Battle_of_Saint-Mihiel.
988	"War in World War I," accessed November 4, 2019, https://shmoop.com/wwi/war.html.
989	"World War I and Germany," Alpha History: Weimar Republic," accessed November 4, 2019, http://alphahistory.com/weimarrepublic/world-war-i/.
990	History.com Editors, "Kaiser Wilhelm II," last edited August 1,

2019, http://www.history.com/topics/world-war-i/kaiser-wilhelm-ii.
991   "World War I Timeline," accessed November 4, 2019, https://shmoop.com/wwi/timeline.html.
992   Wikipedia, "Armistice Day," last edited October 19, 2019, https://en.wikipedia.org/wiki/Armistice_Day.
993   Robert Tracy McKenzie, "The Forgotten Side of the First World War," June 27, 2014, http://www.christianitytoday.com/ct/2014/june/wwi-philip-jenkins-great-and-holy-war-review.html.
994   Richard Gamble, "Was World War I the Last Crusade?" The American Conservative, June 24, 2014, http://www.theamericanconservative.com/articles/was-world-war-i-the-last-crusade/.
995   "The Great Migration," accessed November 5, 2019, http://www.inmotionaame.org/migrations/topic.cfm?migration=8&topic=1.
996   "The NAACP and World War I," The Walter White Project, accessed November 5, 2019, http://scalar.usc.edu/nehvectors/stakeman/the-naacp-and-world-war-i.
997   Shmoop Editorial Team, "Race in World War I," Shmoop University, Inc., last modified November 11, 2008, https://shmoop.com/wwi/race.html.
998   Shanna Stevenson, "Women's Committee of the Council of National Defense," Washington State Historical Society, accessed November 5, 2019, http://www.washingtonhistory.org/research/whc/milestones/aftersuffrage/minutewomen/wccnd/.
999   "World War I: 1914-1918," Striking Women, Women and Work, accessed November 5, 2019, http://www.striking-women.org/module/women-and-work/world-war-i-1914-1918.
1000   Wikipedia, "Economic history of World War I," last edited September 5, 2019, https://en.wikipedia.org/wiki/Economic_history_of_World_War_I.
1001   John W. Chambers, T*o Raise an Army: The Draft Comes to Modern America* (New York: Free Press, 1987).
1002   "American soldiers arrive in France," The First World War East Sussex, accessed November 5, 2019, http://www.eastsussexww1.org.uk/american-soldiers-arrive-france/index.html.
1003   Steven Lobell, "The Political Economy of War Mobilization: From Britain's Limited Liability to a Continental Commitment," *International Politics* (2006) Vol 43, Issue 3 pp 283–304.
1004   Lewis Johnman and Hugh Murphy, "An Overview of the Eco-

nomic and Social Effects of the Interwar Depression on Clydeside Shipbuilding Communities," *International Journal of Maritime History*, (2006), Vol.18, Issue 1 pp 227–254.
1005   Wikipedia, "Conscription Crisis of 1917," last edited October 29, 2019, https://en.wikipedia.org/wiki/Conscription_Crisis_of_1917.
1006   Douglas McCalla, "The Economic Impact of the Great War," in *Canada and the First World War*, ed., David MacKenzie (Toronto: University of Toronto Press, 2005), 138–153.
1007   Gerhard Fischer, "'Negative integration' and an Australian road to modernity: Interpreting the Australian homefront experience in World War I," *Australian Historical Studies*, (April 1995) Vol. 26, Issue 104, 452-76, https://www.tandfonline.com/toc/rahs20/26/104?nav=tocList.
1008   Gerhard Fischer, "'Negative integration' and an Australian road to modernity: Interpreting the Australian homefront experience in World War I," accessed November 5, 2019.
1009   Wikipedia, "The Rape of Belgium," last edited October 6, 2019, https://en.wikipedia.org/wiki/Rape_of_Belgium.
1010   Wikipedia, "The Rape of Belgium," last edited October 6, 2019.
1011   Wikipedia, "Commission for Relief in Belgium," last edited October 7, 2019, https://en.wikipedia.org/wiki/Commission_for_Relief_in_Belgium.
1012   "Belgian Congo (addition)," Internet Archive Wayback Machine, accessed November 5, 2019, https://web.archive.org/web/20080220101851/http://www.1911encyclopedia.org/Belgian_Congo_%28addition%29.
1013   Pierre Chancerel, "Labour (France)," International Encyclopedia of the First World War, last edited May 19, 2015, 2019, https://encyclopedia.1914-1918-online.net/article/labour_france.
1014   Peter Palms' Blog, "The Role of J. P. Morgan In Providing Loans to England and France in World War I," Seeking Alpha, November 16, 2015, https://seekingalpha.com/instablog/25783813-peter-palms/4550806-role-j-p-morgan-providing-loans-england-france-world-war-souring-loans-became-apparent.
1015   Wikipedia, "Weimar Republic," last edited November 4, 2019, https://en.wikipedia.org/wiki/Weimar_Republic.
1016   Richard J. Evans, *The Coming of the Third Reich* (New York City: Penguin Press, 2003), 103.
1017   Wikipedia, "Treaty of Versailles," last edited November 3,

2019, https://en.wikipedia.org/wiki/Treaty_of_Versailles.
1018   Wikipedia, "World War I reparations," last edited November 1, 2019, https://en.wikipedia.org/wiki/World_War_I_reparations.
1019   Wikipedia, "Hyperinflation in the Weimar Republic," last edited November 4, 2019, https://en.wikipedia.org/wiki/Hyperinflation_in_the_Weimar_Republic.
1020   Erik J. Zürcher, Turkey: *A Modern History*, Revised Edition (New York: Palgrave Macmillan, 2004), 126.
1021   Martin W. Lewis, "The Many Armenian Diasporas, Then and Now," GeoCurrents, February 6, 2012, http://www.geocurrents.info/place/russia-ukraine-and-caucasus/caucasus-series/the-many-armenian-diasporas-then-and-now.
1022   Erik J. Zürcher, Turkey: *A Modern History*, Revised Edition, 122-131.
1023   Wikipedia, "Treaty of Neuilly-sur-Seine," last edited October 14, 2019, https://en.wikipedia.org/wiki/Treaty_of_Neuilly-sur-Seine.
1024   David M. Kennedy, *Over Here: The First World War and American Society* (Oxford: Oxford University Press, 2004), 113-125.
1025   "The Economics of World War I," the National Bureau of Economic Research, accessed November 5, 2019, http://www.nber.org/digest/jan05/w10580.html.
1026   Hugh Rockoff, "U.S. Economy in World War I," EH.net, accessed November 5, 2019, http://eh.net/encyclopedia/u-s-economy-in-world-war-i/.
1027   Wikipedia, "Samuel Gompers," last edited October 28, 2019, https://en.wikipedia.org/wiki/Samuel_Gompers.
1028   1026 Wikipedia, "Economic history of World War I," last edited September 5, 2019, https://en.wikipedia.org/wiki/Economic_history_of_World_War_I.
1029   Wikipedia, "Eugene V. Debs," last edited November 4, 2019, https://en.wikipedia.org/wiki/Eugene_V._Debs.
1030   "Industrial Workers of the World," United States History, accessed November 5, 2019, http://www.u-s-history.com/pages/h1050.html.
1031   Wikipedia, "Espionage Act of 1917," last edited October 31, 2019, https://en.wikipedia.org/wiki/Espionage_Act_of_1917.
1032   "Statistics of Income: Compiled from the Returns for 1917," Treasury Department, United States Internal Revenue, accessed November 5, 2019, https://www.irs.gov/pub/irs-soi/17soirepar.pdf.

1033   "The Economics of World War I," the National Bureau of Economic Research accessed November 5, 2019.
1034   Hugh Rockoff, "U.S. Economy in World War I," EH.net, accessed November 5, 2019.
1035   Hugh Rockoff, "U.S. Economy in World War I," EH.net, accessed November 5, 2019.
1036   Claire Suddath, "Why Did World War I Just End?" *Time Magazine*, Oct. 4, 2010, http://content.time.com/time/world/article/0,8599,2023140,00.html.
1037   Hugh Rockoff, "U.S. Economy in World War I," EH.net, accessed November 5, 2019.
1038   "Causes of the Depression," The Educational Forum of Mr. Michelot, accessed November 5, 2019, https://sites.google.com/site/tourogmichelot/social-studies-page/the-great-economic-depression-of-the-1930-s/what-is-buying-on-margin.
1039   "The Harlem Renaissance (1917-1935)," The Rise and Fall of Jim Crow, accessed November 5, 2019, https://www.thirteen.org/wnet/jimcrow/stories_events_harlem.html.
1040   "Cotton Club of Harlem (1923 -)," African American History, accessed November 5, 2019, http://www.blackpast.org/aah/cotton-club-harlem-1923.
1041   Wikipedia, "Depression of 1920-21," last edited September 19, 2019, https://en.wikipedia.org/wiki/Depression_of_1920%E2%80%9321.
1042   Eugene P. Trani, David L. Wilson, *The Presidency of Warren G. Harding. American Presidency* (Lawrence, Kansas: The Regents Press of Kansas, 1977), 83.
1043   Andrew Sinclair, *The Available Man: The Life behind the Masks of Warren Gamaliel Harding* (New York: Quadrangle Books, 1969), 253-254.
1044   David Cannadine, *Mellon: An American Life* (New York: Alfred A. Knopf, 2006), 311-315.
1045   Peter Schiff, *The Real Crash: How To Save Yourself And Your Country* (New York: St. Martin's Press, 2014), 35.
1046   Investopedia Staff, "Margin Trading: What is Buying on Margin?" Investopedia, last edited June 25, 2019, http://www.investopedia.com/university/margin/margin1.asp.
1047   Tejvan Pettinger, "What Caused the Wall Street Crash of 1929?"

(2017), Economics Help, accessed November 5, 2019, http://www.economicshelp.org/blog/76/economics/wall-street-crash-1929/.
1048   Tejvan Pettinger, "What Caused the Wall Street Crash of 1929?" (2017), Economics Help, accessed November 5, 2019.
1049   midtowng, "Hunger on the March," Feb. 25, 2008, http://www.progressivehistorians.com/2008/02/hunger-on-march.html.
1050   "The Stock Market Crash of 1929," U.S. History, Ebrary.net, accessed November 5, 2019, http://academlib.com/11427/history/stock_market_crash_1929.
1051   "The Stock Market Crash of 1929," U.S. History, Ebrary.net, accessed November 5, 2019.
1052   Wikipedia, "Ford Hunger March," last edited October 14, 2019, https://en.wikipedia.org/wiki/Ford_Hunger_March.
1053   Barbara Blumberg, *The New Deal and the Unemployed: The View From New York City* (Lewisburg, PA: Bucknell University Press, 1979), 27.
1054   Terence McArdle, "The veterans were desperate. Gen. MacArthur ordered U.S. troops to attack them," July 28, 2017, *The Washington Post*, https://www.washingtonpost.com/news/retropolix/wp/2017/07/28/the-veterans-were-desperate-gen-macarthur-ordered-u-s-troops-to-attack-them/.
1055   Wikipedia, "United States presidential election, 1932," last edited October 29, 2019, https://en.wikipedia.org/wiki/1932_United_States_presidential_election.
1056   "The only thing we have to fear is fear itself," Franklin D. Roosevelt's inauguration speech, Mar. 4, 1933, *The Guardian*, April 24, 2007, https://www.theguardian.com/theguardian/2007/apr/25/greatspeeches.
1057   Wikipedia, "Emergency Banking Act," last edited October 20, 2019, https://en.wikipedia.org/wiki/Emergency_Banking_Act.
1058   Wikipedia, "Federal Deposit Insurance Corporation," last edited October 28, 2019, https://en.wikipedia.org/wiki/Federal_Deposit_Insurance_Corporation.
1059   Wikipedia, "1933 Banking Act," last edited October 25, 2019, https://en.wikipedia.org/wiki/1933_Banking_Act.
1060   Wikipedia, "Gold Reserve Act," last edited November 1, 2019, https://en.m.wikipedia.org/wiki/Gold_Reserve_Act.
1061   Wikipedia, "Fireside chats," last edited September 28, 2019, https://en.wikipedia.org/wiki/Fireside_chats.

1062   "Traitor to His Class: the Privileged Life and Radical Presidency of Franklin Delano Roosevelt," *The Christian Science Monitor*, November 13, 2008, http://www.csmonitor.com/Books/Book-Reviews/2008/1113/traitor-to-his-class.
1063   Wikipedia, "Civilian Conservation Corps," last edited October 30, 2019, https://en.wikipedia.org/wiki/Civilian_Conservation_Corps.
1064   John A. Salmond, *The Civilian Conservation Corps CCC 1933-1942: a New Deal case study,* Chapter 1 (Durham, NC: Duke University Press, 1967), https://www.nps.gov/parkhistory/online_books/ccc/salmond/contents.htm.
1065   Wikipedia, "Dust Bowl," last edited October 15, 2019, https://en.wikipedia.org/wiki/Dust_Bowl.
1066   "CCC Brief History," Civilian Conservation Corps Legacy, accessed November 5, 2019, http://www.ccclegacy.org/CCC_Brief_History.html.
1067   Wikipedia, "Federal Emergency Relief Administration," last edited October 10, 2019, https://en.wikipedia.org/wiki/Federal_Emergency_Relief_Administration.
1068   "Social Security Act (1935)," accessed November 5, 2019, https://www.ourdocuments.gov/doc.php?flash=true&doc=68.
1069   "Agricultural Adjustment Act," United States History, accessed November 5, 2019, https://www.u-s-history.com/pages/h1639.html.
1070   "Federal Surplus Relief Corporation," last modified Nov. 7, 2016, https://ipfs.io/ipfs/QmXoypizjW3WknFiJnKLwHCnL72vedxjQkDDP-1mXWo6uco/wiki/Federal_Surplus_Relief_Corporation.html.
1071   Wikipedia, "Federal Surplus Relief Corporation," accessed November 5, 2019,https://en.wikipedia.org/wiki/Federal_Surplus_Relief_Corporation.
1072   Wikipedia, "Federal Surplus Relief Corporation," accessed November 5, 2019.
1073   "National Recovery Administration," Social Welfare History Project, Virginia Commonwealth University, accessed November 5, 2019, https://socialwelfare.library.vcu.edu/eras/great-depression/u-s-national-recovery-administration/.
1074   "Our History," Tennessee Valley Authority, accessed November 5, 2019, https://www.tva.com/About-TVA/Our-History.
1075   Preston J. Hubbard, *Origins of the TVA: The Muscle Shoals*

Controversy, 1920-1932 (Nashville: Vanderbilt University Press, 1961). References throughout.

1076 Wikipedia, "David E. Lilienthal," last edited September 18, 2019, https://en.wikipedia.org/wiki/David_E._Lilienthal.

1077 "International Visitors Seek TVA's Secret to Success," Tennessee Valley Authority, October 18, 2014, https://www.tva.com/Newsroom/International-Visitors-Seek-TVAs-Secret-to-Success.

1078 "Why Barry Goldwater Lost Tennessee," Unintentional Irony, Feb. 20, 2007, http://unintentional-irony.blogspot.com/2007/02/why-barry-goldwater-lost-tennessee.html.

1079 "Why Barry Goldwater Lost Tennessee," Unintentional Irony, Feb. 20, 2007.

1080 Jennifer Long, "Government Job Creation Programs- Lessons from the 1930s and 1940s," *Journal of Economic Issues*, Vol. 33, 1999, Issue 4, 903-918, https://www.tandfonline.com/doi/abs/10.1080/00213624.1999.11506220.

1081 Maurice W. Lee, *Economic Fluctuations* (Homewood, IL: R.D. Irwin, Inc., 1955), 236.

1082 James Arthur Estey, *Business Cycles* (West Lafayette, IN: Purdue University, Prentice-Hall, 1950), 22-23 chart.

1083 James Struthers, "Great Depression," July 11, 2013, last edited September 16, 2019, The Canadian Encyclopedia, http://www.thecanadianencyclopedia.ca/en/article/great-depression/.

1084 Wikipedia, "Great Depression in Latin America," last edited September 16, 2019, https://en.wikipedia.org/wiki/Great_Depression_in_Latin_America.

1085 Wikipedia, "Great Depression in the United Kingdom," last edited October 9, 2019, https://en.wikipedia.org/wiki/Great_Depression_in-the-United_Kingdom.

1086 Jennifer Burns, *Goddess of the Market: Ayn Rand and the American Right* (Oxford: Oxford University Press, 2009), 34.

1087 Wikipedia, "Walter Duranty," last edited October 29, 2019, https://en.wikipedia.org/wiki/Walter_Duranty.

1088 "Genocide in the 20th Century," The History Place, accessed November 5, 2019, http://www.historyplace.com/worldhistory/genocide/stalin.htm.

1089 "Unemployed Disturbances in Dunedin," April 9, 1932, New Zealand History, accessed November 5, 2019, https://nzhistory.govt.

nz/unemployed-disturbances-in-dunedin.
1090   Wikipedia, "Siamese revolution of 1932," last edited October 29, 2019, https://en.wikipedia.org/wiki/Siamese_revolution_of_1932.
1091   Wikipedia, "Silver standard," last edited October 24, 2019, https://en.wikipedia.org/wiki/Silver_standard.
1092   Wikipedia, "Great Depression," last edited October 27, 2019, https://en.wikipedia.org/wiki/Great_Depression.
1093   W.S. and E.S. Woytinsky, *World population and production: trends and outlook* (New York: The 20th Century Fund, 1953), 148.
1094   Cheyenne Blumberg, "Rosie the Riveter," The History of the U.S. Working Class, May 20, 2013, http://historyoftheusworkingclass.blogspot.com/2013/05/blumberg-rosie-riveter.html.
1095   Meridel LeSueur, "Women on the Breadlines (1932)," http://historymuse.net/readings/womenonbreadline.html.
1096   Robert S. and Helen Lynd, Middletown in Transition: *A Study in Cultural Conflicts* (New York: Harcourt Brace and Company, 1937), 179.
1097   Denyse Baillargeon, *Making Do: Women, Family and Home in Montreal during the Great Depression*, trans. Yvonne Klein (Ontario: Wilfrid Laurier University Press, 1999), 70, 108, 136–38, 159.
1098   History.com Editors, "Eleanor Roosevelt," History, last edited May 16, 2019, https://www.history.com/topics/first-ladies/eleanor-roosevelt.
1099   Wikipedia, "The Feminine Mystique," last edited September 26, 2019, https://en.wikipedia.org/wiki/The_Feminine_Mystique.
1100   Mark Metzler, "Woman's Place in Japan's Great Depression: Reflections on the Moral Economy of Deflation," *Journal of Japanese Studies* (2004) Volume 30, Issue 2, 315–352.
1101   N. R. Reagin, "Marktordnung and Autarkic Housekeeping: Housewives and Private Consumption under the Four-Year Plan, 1936–1939," *German History* (2001), Vol 19, Issue 2, 162–184.
1102   C.R., "What can we learn from the Depression, The economist, November 8, 2013, https://economist.com/free-exchange/2013/11/08/what-can-we-learn-from-the-depression.
1103   Wikipedia, "Beer Hall Putsch," last edited November 5, 2019, https://en.wikipedia.org/wiki/Beer_Hall_Putsch
1104   Wikipedia, "Japanese invasion of Manchuria," last edited October 24, 2019, https://en.wikipedia.org/wiki/Japanese_invasion_of_

Manchuria.

1105   Wikipedia, "German presidential election, 1932, last edited November 5, 2019, https://en.wikipedia.org/wiki/German_presidential_election,_1932.

1106   "The Reichstag Fire," Holocaust Encyclopedia, accessed November 5, 2019, https://www.ushmm.org/wlc/en/article.php?ModuleId=10007657.

1107   Wikipedia, "Austrian Civil War," last edited October 217 2019, https://en.wikipedia.org/wiki/Austrian_Civil_War.

1108   "The Nuremberg Race Laws," Holocaust Encyclopedia, United States Holocaust Memorial Museum, accessed November 5, 2019, https://www.ushmm.org/outreach/en/article.php?ModuleId=10007695.

1109   Wikipedia, "Spanish Civil War," last edited November 4, 2019, https://en.wikipedia.org/wiki/Spanish_Civil_War.

1110   Wikipedia, "Great Purge," last edited November 2, 2019, https://en.wikipedia.org/wiki/Great_Purge.

1111   Wikipedia, "Chinese Civil War," last edited November 1, 2019, https://en.wikipedia,org/wiki/Chinese_Civil_War.

1112   Wikipedia, "Quarantine Speech," last edited October 26, 20198, https://en.wikipedia.org/wiki/Quarantine_Speech.

1113   Wikipedia, "Second Sino-Japanese War," last edited November 4, 2019, https://en.wikipedia.org/wiki/Second_Sino-Japanese_War.

1114   History.com Editors, "Germany annexes Austria," last edited July 28, 2019, http://www.history.com/this-day-in-history/germany-annexes-austria.

1115   "Refugees," Holocaust Encyclopedia, accessed November 6, 2019, https://www.ushmm.org/wlc/en/article.php?ModuleId=10005139.

1116   Wikipedia, "Bermuda Conference," last edited August 28, 2019, https://en.wikipedia.org/wiki/Bermuda_Conference.

1117   "How did the United States government and American people respond to Nazism?" Holocaust Encyclopedia, United States Holocaust Memorial Museum, accessed November 6, 2019,https://encyclopedia.ushmm.org/content/en/question/how-did-the-united-states-government-and-american-people-respond-to-nazism.

1118   Wikipedia, "Jozef Tiso," last edited September 21, 2019, https://en.wikipedia.org/wiki/Jozef_Tiso

1119   Wikipedia, "1939 German ultimatum to Lithuania," last edited October 6, 2019, https://en.wikipedia.org/wiki/1939_German_ultimatum_to_Lithuania.
1120   Wikipedia, "Chase Bank," last edited November 5, 2019. https://en.wikipedia.org/wiki/Chase_Bank.
1121   Paul Beckett, "Chase Manhattan Bank Uncovers Deal That Aided Nazi Germany," The Wall Street Journal, February 23, 2001, https://www.wsj.com/articles/SB951271524654360876.
1122   Joseph P. Fried, "Chase and Morgan Sued Over Jewish Assets," Dec. 4, 1998, New York Times, https://www.nytimes.com/1998/12/24/business/chase-and-morgan-sued-over-jewish-assets.html.
1123   Yuri Rubtsov, "History of World War II: Nazi Germany was Financed by the Federal Reserve and the Bank of England," Global Research, May 14, 2016, https://www.globalresearch.ca/history-of-world-war-ii-nazi-germany-was-financed-by-the-federal-reserve-and-the-bank-of-england/5530318.
1124   US Banks Turned Over Jewish Accounts to Nazis, Panel Reports," Chicago Tribune, February 3, 1999, https://www.chicagotribune.com/news/ct-xpm-1999-02-03-9902030269-story.html.
1125   US Banks Turned Over Jewish Accounts to Nazis, Panel Reports," Chicago Tribune, February 3, 1999.
1126   US Banks Turned Over Jewish Accounts to Nazis, Panel Reports," Chicago Tribune, February 3, 1999.
1127   "How Bush's grandfather helped Hitler's rise to power," September. 25, 2004, The Guardian, https://www.theguardian.com/world/2004/sep/25/usa.secondworldwar.
1128   Glen Yeadon, "The Nazi Hydra in America" (Progressive Press, San Diego ,CA, 2008), 341-343. "Wall Street and the Rise of Hitler-the history of banks who funded Nazis," July, 2013. Also Basta Balkana Magazine, accessed November 6, 2019, http:www.bastabalkana.com/2013,07/wall-street-and-the-rise-of-hitler-the-history-of-banks-who-funded-nazis/.
1129   Timothy L. O'Brien, "Chase Reviews Nazi-Era Role," Nov. 7, 1998, The New York Times, http://www.nytimes.com/1998/11/07/world/chase-reviews-nazi-era-role.html.
1130   "How Bush's grandfather helped Hitler's rise to power," Sept. 25, 2004, The Guardian.
1131   Washington Blog. "American Banks Funded the Nazis,"

Global Research, July 19, 2012, https"//globalresearch.ca/american-banks-funded-the-nazis/31983..

1132   Jules Archer, *The White House: The Shocking True Story of the Conspiracy to Overthrow FDR* (New York: Hawthorne Books, Inc., 1973), 3-5.

1133   Mike Thompson, "The Whitehouse Coup," July 23, 2007, BBC Radio, http://www.bbc.co.uk/radio4/history/document/document_20070723.shtml.

1134   Jules Archer, *The White House: The Shocking True Story of the Conspiracy to Overthrow FDR*. References throughout.

1135   Wikipedia, "Business Plot," last modified Nov. 3, 2018, https://en.wikipedia.org/wiki/Business_Plot.

1136   Wikipedia, "Business Plot," last modified Nov. 3, 2018.

1137   Wikipedia, "McCormack-Dickstein Committee," accessed November 6, 2019, https://en.wikisource.org/wiki/McCormack-Dickstein_Committee.

1138   "Credulity Unlimited," Nov. 22, 1934, The New York Times, https://www.nytimes.com/1934/11/22/archives/credulity-unlimited.html.

1139   Hans Schmidt, *Maverick Marine: General Smedley D. Butler and the Contradictions of American Military History* (reprint) (Lexington: University Press of Kentucky, 1998), 224.

1140   Gary G. Kohls, "Contrasting the Foiled American Fascist Coup Plot of 1934 With the Successful Brazilian Fascist Coup Plot of 2016," Sept 29, 2016, Duluth Reader, accessed November 6, 2019, http://duluthreader.com/articles/2016/09/28/8032_contrasting_the_foiled_american_fascist_coup_plot.

1141   Wikipedia, "IBM and the Holocaust," last edited November 2, 2019, https://en.wikipedia.org/wiki/IBM_and_the_Holocaust.

1142   "Secret History: The U.S. Supported and Inspired the Nazis," March 26, 2018, Global Research, http://www.globalresearch.ca/secret-history-the-u-s-supported-and-inspired-the-nazis/5439236.

1143   The American Chronicle, "The Treason Of Rockefeller Standard Oil (Exxon) During World War II," Feb. 4, 2012. https://archive.org/stream/pdfy-eQ-GW5bGFH1vHYJH/The%20Treason%20Of%20Rockefeller%20Standard%20Oil%20%28Exxon%29%20During%20World%20War%20II_djvu.txt.

1144   Wikipedia, "Henry Ford," last edited December 30, 2019,

https://en.wikipedia.org./wiki/Henry_Ford.
1145   Michael Dobbs, "Ford and GM Scrutinized for Alleged Nazi Collaboration," Nov. 30, 1998, Washington Post, accessed November 6, 2019, http://www.washingtonpost.com/wp-srv/national/daily/nov98/nazicars30.htm.1146   "Secret History: The U.S. Supported and Inspired the Nazis," Global Research, March 26, 2018, accessed November 6, 2019.
1147   Edwin Black, "The Nazi Party: General Motors and the Third Reich," Jewish Virtual Library, accessed November 6, 2019, http://www.jewishvirtuallibrary.org/jsource/Holocaust/gm.html.
1148   John S. Friedman, "Kodak's Nazi Connections," March 8, 2001, The Nation, http://www.thenation.com/issue/march-26-2001/.
1149   John S. Friedman, "Kodak's Nazi Connections," March 8, 2001, The Nation.
1150   Sam Greenspan, "11 Companies That Surprisingly Collaborated with the Nazis," Feb. 24, 2018, http://www.11points.com/11-companies-surprisingly-collaborated-nazis/.
1151   "Wikipedia, "Arthur Eichengrun," last edited October 15, 2019, https://en.wikipedia.org/wiki/Arthur_Eichengr%C3%BCn..
1152   "Siemens retreats over Nazi name," Sept. 5, 2002, BBC News, accessed November 6, 2019, http://news.bbc.co.uk/2/hi/business/2233890.stm.
1153   Elizabeth Manus, "Bertelsmann's Nazi Past Gets Ho-Hummed in U.S.," Observer, Jan. 18, 1999, http://observer.com/1999/01/bertelsmanns-nazi-past-gets-hohummed-in-us/.
1154   "Warner Bros. Fight Fascism," History Detectives Special Investigations, accessed November 6, 2019, http://www.pbs.org/opb/historydetectives/feature/warner-bros-fight-facism/.
1155   Steven J. Ross, "When Hitler's Henchmen Called the Shots in Hollywood," Dec. 3. 2017, Daily Beast, https://www.thedailybeast.com/when-hitlers-henchman-called-the-shots-in-hollywood.
1156   Dusty Sklar, "Doing Business with Hitler," Feb. 11, 2016, Jewish Currents, accessed November 6, 2019, https://jewishcurrents.org/editor/doing-business-with-hitler/.
1157   Edwin Black, "Eugenics and the Nazis—the California Connection," Nov. 9, 2003, SFGate, http://www.sfgate.com/opinion/article/Eugenics-and-the-Nazis-the-California-2549771.php.
1158   Wikipedia, "Nazi eugenics," last edited October 10, 2019,

https://en.wikipedia.org/wiki/Nazi_eugenics#cite_note-USHMM-2.
1159 Wikipedia, "Invasion of Poland," last edited November 2, 2019, https://en.wikipedia.org/wiki/Invasion_of_Poland.
1160 Wikipedia, "Timeline of World War II (1939)," last edited October 4, 2019, https://en.wikipedia.org/wiki/Timeline_of_World_War_II_(1939)
1161 Wikipedia, "Battle of the Atlantic," last edited November 6, 2019, https://en.wikipedia.org/wiki/Battle_of_the_Atlantic.
1162 Wikipedia, "Neutrality Patrol," last edited September 7, 2019, https://en.wikipedia.org/wiki/Neutrality_Patrol.
1163 Wikipedia, "Pan-American Security Zone," last edited November 20, 2019, https://en.wikipedia.org/wiki/Pan-American_Security_Zone.
1164 Wikipedia, "Battle of the Heligoland Bight, (1939)," last edited August 30, 2019, https://en.wikipedia.org/wiki/Battle_of_the_Heligoland_Bight_%281939%29.
1165 Wikipedia, "Reinhard Heydrich," last edited October 28, 2019, https://en.wikipedia.org/wiki/Reinhard_Heydrich.
1166 Wikipedia, "Battles of Narvik," last edited November 6, 2019, https://en.wikipedia.org/wiki/Battles_of_Narvik#First_Naval_Battle_of_Narvik.
1167 Wikipedia, "Bessarabia," last edited September 8, 2019, https://en.wikipedia.org/wiki/Bessarabia.
1168 Wikipedia, "Operation Pike," last edited October 30, 2019, https://en.wikipedia.org/wiki/Operation_Pike.
1169 Wikipedia, "Western Front (World War II)," last edited October 25, 2019, https://en.wikipedia.org/wiki/Western_Front_(World_War_II).
1170 Wikipedia, "Battle of Zeeland," last edited September 1, 2019, https://en.wikipedia.org/wiki/Battle_of_Zeeland.
1171 Wikipedia, "Oswald Mosley," last edited October 28, 2019, https://en.wikipedia.org/wiki/Oswald_Mosley.
1172 Wikipedia, "Dunkirk," last edited October 15, 2019, https://en.wikipedia.org/wiki/Dunkirk.
1173 Wikipedia, "Armistice of 22 June 1940," last edited October 25, 2019, https://en.wikipedia.org/wiki/Armistice_of_22_June_1940.
1174 Wikipedia, "Operation Aerial," last edited October 24, 2019, https://en.wikipedia.org/wiki/Operation_Aerial.

1175   Wikipedia, "Attack on Mers-el-Kébir," last edited November 6, 2019, https://en.wikipedia.org/wiki/Attack_on_Mers-el-K%C3%A9bir.
1176   Wikipedia, "History of radar," last edited October 16, 2019, https://en.wikipedia.org/wiki/History_of_radar.
1177   Wikipedia, "Never was so much owed by so many to so few," last edited October 14, 2019, https://en.wikipedia.org/wiki/Never_was_so_much_owed_by_so_many_to_so_few.
1178   Wikipedia, "Hundred Regiments Offensive," last edited October 5, 2019, https://en.wikipedia.org/wiki/Hundred_Regiments_Offensive.
1179   "The London Blitz," Eye Witness to History, accessed November 6, 2019, http://www.eyewitnesstohistory.com/blitz.htm.
1180   "Fact File: Destroyers-for-bases Agreement," September 2, 1940, , WW2 People's War, BBC, accessed November 6, 2019 http://www.bbc.co.uk/history/ww2peopleswar/timeline/factfiles/nonflash/a1138420.shtml.
1181   Wikipedia, "Battle of Greece," last edited November 3, 2019, https://en.wikipedia.org/wiki/Battle-of-Greece.
1182   Wikipedia, "Battle of Taranto," last edited October 29, 2019, https://en.wikipedia.org/wiki/Battle_of_Taranto.
1183   "Memorandum of the Conversation Between the Führer and the Chairman of the Council of People's Commissars Molotov in the Presence of the Reich Foreign Minuter and the Deputy People's Commissar for Foreign Affairs, Dekanosov, as Well as of Counselor of Embassy Hilger and Herr Pavlov, Who Acted as Interpreters, in Berlin on November 13, 1940," Nazi-Soviet relations 1939-1941. Documents from the Archives of The German Foreign Office. Washington, Department of State, publication 3023, 1948., http://www.histdoc.net/history/NaSo1940-11-13.html.
1184   Wikipedia, "Timeline of World War II (1940)," last edited September 30, 2019.
1185   Wikipedia, "Operation Barbarossa," last edited November 6, 2019, https://en.wikipedia.org/wiki/Operation_Barbarossa.
1186   Wikipedia, "Bardia," last edited November 22, 2019, https://en.wikipedia.org/wiki/Bardia.
1187   Wikipedia, "Franco-Thai War," last edited November 6, 2019, https://en.wikipedia.org/wiki/Franco-Thai_War.
1188   "East African Campaign (World War II)," last edited No-

vember 4, 2019, https://en.wikipedia.org/wiki/East_African_Campaign_%28World_War_II%29#Allied_counter-offensive.
1189   Wikipedia, "Iron Guard," last edited November 2, 2019, https://en.wikipedia.org/wiki/Iron_Guard.
1190   Wikipedia, "Charles Lindberg," last edited November 2, 2019, hhttps://en.wikipedia.org/wiki/Charles_Lindbergh.
1191   Wikipedia, "Battle of Beda Fomm," last edited August 9, 2019, https://en.wikipedia.org/wiki/Battle-of-Fomm.
1192   Wikipedia, "Invasion of Yugoslavia," last edited October 29, 2019, https://en.wikipedia.org/wiki/Invasion_of_Yugoslavia.
1193   Wikipedia, "Golden Square (Iraq)," last edited October 10, 2019, https://en.wikipedia.org/wiki/Golden_Square_%28Iraq%29.
1194   Wikipedia, Soviet-Japanese Neutrality Pact," last edited June 7, 2019, https://en.wikipedia.org/wiki/Soviet%E2%80%93Japanese_Neutrality_Pact.
1195   Wikipedia, "Alan Turing," last edited November 7, 2019, https://en.wikipedia.org/wiki/Alan_Turing.
1196   Siobhan Pat Mulcahy "The Peculiar Sex Life of Adolf Hitler' offers insight into the dictator's gay partners," April 7, 2016, http://www.irishexaminer.com/lifestyle/features/the-peculiar-sex-life-of-adolf-hitler-offers-insight-into-the-dictators-gay-partners-391500.html.
1197   Wikipedia, "Timeline of World War II (1941), last edited September 25, 2019, https://en.wikipedia.org/wiki/Timeline_of_World_War_II_(1941).
1198   Will Stewart, "Blood oozed through the soil at grave sites. You could see the pits move, some of them were still alive," Aug. 24, 2015, Daily Mail, http://www.dailymail.co.uk/news/article-3205754/Blood-oozed-soil-grave-sites-pits-alive-secrets-Ukraine-s-shameful-Holocaust-Bullets-killing-centre-1-6million-Jews-executed.html.
1199   Wikipedia, "Operation Reinhard," last edited October 6, 2019, https://en.wikipedia.org/wiki/Operation_Reinhard.
1200   Wikipedia, "Majdanek concentration camp," last edited October 6, 2019, https://en.wikipedia.org/wiki/Majdanek_concentration_camp.
1201   Wikipedia, "Timeline of World War II (1941)," last edited September 25, 2019.
1202   Wikipedia, "Atlantic Charter," last edited October 21, 2019, https://en.wikipedia.org/wiki/Atlantic_Charter.

1203   Wikipedia, "Aktion T4," last edited November 7, 2019, https://en.wikipedia.org/wiki/Aktion_T4.
1204   Wikipedia, "Vilna Ghetto," last edited October 17, 2019, https://en.wikipedia.org/wiki/Vilna_Ghetto#Establishment.
1205   Wikipedia, "Mohammad Mosaddegh," last edited October 29, 2019, https://en.wikipedia.org/wiki/Mohammad_Mosaddegh.
1206   Wikipedia, "National Liberation Front (Greece)," last edited November 7, 2019, https://en.wikipedia.org/wiki/National_Liberation_Front_%28Greece%29.
1207   Wikipedia, "Battle of Moscow," last edited November 3, 2019, https://en.wikipedia.org/wiki/Battle_of_Moscow.
1208   Wikipedia, "1941 Odessa massacre," last edited October 25, 2019, https://en.wikipedia.org/wiki/1941_Odessa_massacre.
1209   Robert B. Stinnett and Douglas Cirignano, "Do Freedom of Information Act Files Prove FDR Had Foreknowledge of Pearl Harbor?," Independent Institute, accessed November 7, 2019, http://www.independent.org/newsroom/article.asp?id=408.
1210   Wikipedia, "Siege of Sevastopol (1941-42)," last edited October 11, 2019, https://en.wikipedia.org/wiki/Siege_of_Sevastopol_(1941%E2%80%9342).
1211   Wikipedia, "Bogdanovka," last edited October 16, 2019, https://en.wikipedia.org/wiki/Bogdanovka.
1212   Wikipedia, "Arcadia Conference," last edited May 7, 2019, https://en.wikipedia.org/wiki/Arcadia_Conference.
1213   Wikipedia, "Wannsee Conference," last edited October 31, 2019, https://en.wikipedia.org/wiki/Wannsee_Conference.
1214   Wikipedia, "Bataan Death March," last edited October 29, 2019, https://en.wikipedia.org/wiki/Bataan_Death_March.
1215   Wikipedia, "Bombing of Cologne in World War II," last edited October 29, 2019, https://en.wikipedia.org/wiki/Bombing_of_Cologne_in_World_War_II.
1216   Wikipedia, "Battle of Midway," last edited November 5, 2019, https://en.wikipedia.org/wiki/Battle_of_Midway.
1217   "Black Saturday for the British Eighth Army," World War II Today, accessed November 7, 2019, http://ww2today.com/13th-june-1942-black-saturday-for-the-british-eighth-army.
1218   Wikipedia, "Stanislawow Ghetto," last edited November 6, 2019, http://www.yadvashem.org/yv/en/exhibitions/vilna/during/ak-

tions_oct_dec1941.asp.

1219   Wikipedia, "Battle of Stalingrad," last edited November 5, 2019, https://en.wikipedia.org/wiki/Battle_of_Stalingrad.

1220   Wikipedia, "Panhellenic Union of Fighting Youths," last edited October 16, 2019, https://en.wikipedia.org/wiki/Panhellenic_Union_of_Fighting_Youths.

1221   Wikipedia, "Operation Uranus," last edited November 7, 2019, https://en.wikipedia.org/wiki/Operation_Uranus.

1222   Wikipedia, "Nuclear chain reaction," last edited July 2, 2019, https://en.wikipedia.org/wiki/Nuclear_chain_reaction.

1223   Wikipedia, "Casablanca Conference," last edited November 5, 2019, https://en.wikipedia.org/wiki/Casablanca_Conference.

1224   Wikipedia, "Warsaw Ghetto Uprising," last edited November 6, 2019, https://en.wikipedia.org/wiki/Warsaw_Ghetto_Uprising.

1225   Wikipedia, "Battle of Stalingrad" last edited November 5, 2019, https://en.wikipedia.org/wiki/Battle_of_Stalingrad.

1226   Wikipedia, "Battle of the Bismarck Sea," last edited October 6, 2019, https://en.wikipedia.org/wiki/Battle_of_the_Bismarck_Sea.

1227   "Liquidation of the Krakow Ghetto," United States Holocaust Memorial Museum, accessed November 7, 2019, https://www.ushmm.org/learn/timeline-of-events/1942-1945/liquidation-of-the-krakow-ghetto.

1228   Wikipedia, "Katyn massacre," last edited October 29, 2019, https://en.wikipedia.org/wiki/Katyn_massacre.

1229   Wikipedia, "Bermuda Conference," last edited August 28, 2019, https://en.wikipedia.org/wiki/Bermuda_Conference.

1230   "Japanese Massacre Thousands of Chinese at Changjiao," World War II Today, accessed November 7, 2019, http://ww2today.com/8th-may-1943-japanese-massacre-thousands-of-chinese-at-changjiao.

1231   Wikipedia, "Black May (1943)," last edited June 9, 2019, https://en.wikipedia.org/wiki/Black_May_%281943%29.

1232   Wikipedia, "Josef Mengele," last edited October 15, 2019, https://en.wikipedia.org/wiki/Josef_Mengele.

1233   Wikipedia, "Massacres of Poles in Volhynia and Eastern Galicia," last edited September 21, 2019, https://en.wikipedia.org/wiki/Massacres_of_Poles_in_Volhynia_and_Eastern_Galicia.

1234   Wikipedia, "Bombing of Hamburg in World War II," last edited September 29, 2019, https://en.wikipedia.org/wiki/Bombing_of_

Hamburg_in_World_War_II.

1235 Wikipedia, "George S. Patton slapping incidents," last edited August 7, 2019, https://en.wikipedia.org/wiki/George_S._Patton_slapping_incidents.

1236 Wikipedia, "Bialystok Ghetto uprising," last edited July 28, 2019, https://en.wikipedia.org/wiki/Bia%C5%82ystok_Ghetto_uprising.

1237 Wikipedia, "Sobibor extermination camp," last edited November 7, 2019, https://en.wikipedia.org/wiki/Sobib%C3%B3r_extermination_camp.

1238 Wikipedia, "Tehran Conference," last edited November 7, 2019, https://en.wikipedia.org/wiki/Tehran_Conference.

1239 Wikipedia, "Janowska concentration camp," last edited November 4, 2019, https://en.wikipedia.org/wiki/Janowska_concentration_camp.

1240 "Big Week - WW2 Timeline (February 20th - 25th, 1944)," Second World War History, accessed November 7, 2019, https://www.secondworldwarhistory.com/big-week-bombing-campaign.php.

1241 "Operation Ichi-Go," World War II Database, accessed November 7, 2019, https://ww2db.com/battle_spec.php?battle_id=144.

1242 Wikipedia, "V-1 Flying Bomb" last edited November 6, 2019, https://en.wikipedia.org/wiki/Strategic_bombing#Terror_bombing.

1243 "Battle of the Philippine Sea," Encyclopedia Britannica, accessed November 7, 2019, https://www.britannica.com/event/Battle-of-the-Philippine-Sea.

1244 Wikipedia, "20 July Plot," last edited November 4, 2019, https://en.wikipedia.org/wiki/20_July_plot.

1245 Wikipedia, "Battle of Tannenberg Line," last edited October 27, 2019, https://en.wikipedia.org/wiki/Battle_of_Tannenberg_Line.

1246 Wikipedia, "Fort Lawton Riot," last edited September 4, 2019, https://en.wikipedia.org/wiki/Fort_Lawton_Riot.

1247 Wikipedia, "Dumbarton Oaks Conference," last edited November 5, 2019, https://en.wikipedia.org/wiki/Dumbarton_Oaks_Conference.

1248 Wikipedia, "Dutch famine of 1944-45," last edited November 6, 2019, https://en.wikipedia.org/wiki/Dutch_famine_of_1944%E2%80%9345.

1249 Wikipedia, "Baltic Offensive," last edited November 3, 2019, https://en.wikipedia.org/wiki/Baltic_Offensive.

1250   Wikipedia, "V-2 rocket," last edited October 28, 2019, https://en.wikipedia.org/wiki/V-2_rocket.
1251   Wikipedia, "Kamikaze," last edited November 7, 2019. https://en.wikipedia.org/wiki/Kamikaze.
1252   Wikipedia, "Thiaroye Massacre," last edited August 13, 2019, https://en.wikipedia.org/wiki/Thiaroye_Massacre.
1253   Wikipedia, "Palawan massacre," last edited September 23, 2019, https://en.wikipedia.org/wiki/Palawan_massacre.
1254   Wikipedia, "Agana race riot," last edited September 27, 2019, https://en.wikipedia.org/wiki/Agana_race_riot.
1255   Wikipedia, "Manilla massacre," last edited September 18, 2019, https://en.wikipedia.org/wiki/Manila_massacre.
1256   "Hiroshima and Nagasaki Death Toll," Children of the Atomic Bomb, accessed November 7, 2019, http://www.aasc.ucla.edu/cab/200708230009.html.
1257   Geoffrey Gunn, "The Great Vietnamese Famine of 1944-45 Revisited," The Asia-Pacific Journal, accessed November 7, 2019, https://apjjf.org/2011/9/5/Geoffrey-Gunn/3483/article.html.
1258   Steven E. Ambrose, *D-Day, June 6, 1944: The Climactic Battle of World War II* (New York: Simon and Schuster, 1994), 489
1259   Sarah Pruitt, "Uncovering the Secret Identity of Rosie the Riveter," History, accessed November 7, 2019, https://www.history.com/news/rosie-the-riveter-inspiration.
1260   Steven E. Ambrose, *D-Day, June 6, 1944: The Climactic Battle of World War II*, 498.
1261   "D-Day June 6, 1944 Plus Four," accessed November 7, 2019, http://www.usmilitariaforum.com/forums/index.php?/topic/268463-d-day-june-6-1944-plus-four/.
1262   Wikipedia, "American women in World War II," last edited October 3, 2019, https://en.wikipedia.org/wiki/American_women_in_World_War_II.
1263   "Education and Training," US Department of Veterans Affairs, accessed November 7, 2019, http://benefits.va.gov/gibill/.
1264   "History at a Glance: Women in World War II," The National World War II Musuem, accessed November 7, 2019, http://www.nationalww2museum.org/learn/education/for-students/ww2-history/at-a-glance/women-in-ww2.html.
1265   Wikipedia, "Canadian women in the World Wars," last edited

September 24, 2019 https://en.wikipedia.org/wiki/Canadian_women_in_the_World_Wars.
1266   Wikipedia, "Women in World War II," last edited October 31, 2019, https://en.wikipedia.org/wiki/Women_in_World_War_II.
1267   Wikipedia, "Waffen-SS," last edited November 7, 2019, https://en.wikipedia.org/wiki/Waffen-SS.
1268   Wikipedia, "Women in World War II," last modified Nov. 8, 2018.
1269   Dan A. D'Amelio, "Italian Women In The Resistance, World War II," *Italian Americana*, Vol.19, Issue 2, (2001), 127-141.
1270   "Japanese minister wants 'birth-giving machines,' aka women, to have more babies," The Guardian, https://www.theguardian.com/world/2007/jan/29/japan.justinmccurry
1271   German Bishop Slammed For Calling Women "Birthing Machines," D.W.com, http://www.dw.com/en/german-bishop-slammed-for-calling-women-birthing-machines/a-2362515.
1272   Wikipedia, "Wanda Gertz," last edited July 30, 2019, https://en.wikipedia.org/wiki/Wanda_Gertz.
1273   Wikipedia, "Women in World War II," last edited October 31 2019.
1274   WikiVisual, "Mariana Dragescu," accessed November 7, 2019, https://wikivisually.com/wiki/Mariana_Dr%C4%83gescu.
1275   Wikipedia, "Women in World War II," last edited October 31 2019.
1276   Wikipedia, "Women in World War II," last edited October 31 2019.
1277   Jim Walker, "Christianity in Europe during World War II," accessed November 7, 2019, http://www.nobeliefs.com/ChurchesWWII.htm.
1278   John Chrysostom, "Against the Jews. Homily 1," http://www.tertullian.org/fathers/chrysostom_adversus_judaeos_01_homily1.htm.
1279   Jim Walker, "Christianity in Europe during World War II," accessed November 7, 2019.
1280   Austin Cline, "Bishop Berning and Monsignor Steinmann Meet Hitler, Concerned about Catholic Groups Under Nazis," http://skepticism.org/timeline/april-history/5174-bishop-berning-and-monsignor-steinmann-meet-hitler-concerned-about-catholic-groups-under-nazis.html.
1281   Wikipedia, "Catholic Church and Nazi Germany during World War II," last edited November 3, 2019, https://en.wikipedia.org/wiki/Catholic_Church_and_Nazi_Germany_during_World_War_II.
1282   Wikipedia, "Propaganda of Fascist Italy," last edited October 16, 2019, https://en.wikipedia.org/wiki/Propagands_of_Fascist_Italy.

1283   John Cornwell, *Hitler's Pope: The Secret History of Pius XII* (New York: Viking Press, 1999), 175.
1284   John Cornwell, *Hitler's Pope: The Secret History of Pius XII*, 175.
1285   "Reich Concordat between the Holy See and the German Reich (July 20, 1933)," GHDI, accessed November 7, 2019, http://ghdi.ghi-dc.org/sub_document.cfm?document_id=1570.
1286   Jim Walker, "Christianity in Europe during World War II," accessed November 7, 2019.
1287   John B. Hold, *Under the Swastika* (Chapel Hill: The University of North Carolina Press, 1936), 168-169.
1288   Wikipedia, "On the Jews and Their Lies," last edited October 22, 2019, https://en.wikipedia.org/wiki/On_the_Jews_and_Their_Lies.
1289   Wikipedia, "On the Jews and Their Lies," last edited October 22, 2019.
1290   "MARTIN LUTHER, "That Jesus Christ Was Born a Jew (1523), excerpts," Primary Texts on History of Relations, http://www.ccjr.us/dialogika-resources/primary-texts-from-the-history-of-the-relationship/272-luther-1523.
1291   Wikipedia, "On the Jews and Their Lies," last edited October 22, 2019.
1292   "MARTIN LUTHER, "On the Jews and Their Lies (1543), excerpts," Primary Texts on History of Relations., http://www.ccjr.us/dialogika-resources/primary-texts-from-the-history-of-the-relationship/273-luther-1543.
1293   "Protestant Churches and the Nazi State," Facing History and Ourselves, accessed November 7, 2019, https://www.facinghistory.org/holocaust-and-human-behavior/chapter-5/protestant-churches-and-nazi-state.
1294   "The German churches before and after 1945," original source: Johannes Neumann, "Die Kirchen in Deutschland,1945: Vorher und nachher, Versuch einer Bilanz", First delivered as a lecture at the University of Tübingen in 1995, the full-length German original — with footnotes — can be found at http://www.ibka.org/artikel/ag98/1945.html. Translated and edited by Muriel Fraser, with the kind permission of Dr. Neumann, http://www.concordatwatch.eu/kb-36941.934.
1295   Wikipedia, "Johannes Ockeghem," last edited July 23, 2019, https://en.wikipedia.org/wiki/Johannes_Ockeghem.
1296   Wikipedia, "Josquin des Prez," last edited December 17, 2019,

https://en.wikipedia.org/wiki/Josquin_des_Prez.

1297   Wikipedia, "Giovanni Pierluigi da Palestrina," last edited December 3, 2019, https://en.wikipedia.org/wiki/Giovanni_Pierluigi_da_Palestrina.

1298   Wikipedia, "Orlande de Lassus," last edited October 27, 2019, https://en.wikipedia.org/wiki/Orlande_de_Lassus.

1299   Wikipedia, "William Byrd," last edited November 19, 2019, https://en.wikipedia.org/wiki/William_Byrd.

1300   Wikipedia, "Giovanni Gabrieli," last edited December 17, 2019, https://en.wikipedia.org/wiki/Giovanni_Gabrieli.

1301   Wikipedia, "Thomas Campion," last edited November 8, 2019, https://en.wikipedia.org/wiki/Thomas_Campion.

Illustration Credits

The authors have made every effort to contact the owners of illustrations reproduced in this book. In the few cases where they have been unsuccessful they invite copyright holders to contact them at cpaprocki@gmail.com

Cover Photo: J. P, Morgan
Author: JohPierpontMOrgan.jpg; derivative work: Beao
Date: January 29, 2010
Source: JohnPierpontMorgan.jpg
Photo from Images of American Political in the public domain

Fig. 4-1: DaVinci's Vitruvian MAN
Photo from www.lucnix.be. 2007-09-08 (photograph)
This work is in the public domain in its country of origin and other countries and areas where the copyright term is the author's life plus 100 years or fewer.
U.S. work public domain in the U.S. for unspecified reason but presumably because it was published in the U.S. before 1924.

Fig. 4-2: Fig. 4-2: Nicolas Pisano's The Baptistery of Pisa
Author: Yellow Cat from Roma, Italy
This file is licensed under the Creative Commons Attribution 2.0 Generic license.

Fig. 4-3: Michelangelo's Ceiling of the Sistine Chapel
Source: Own work Antoine Taveneaux Taken on 14 June 2014
I, the copyright holder of this work, hereby publish it under the following license: This file is licensed under the Creative Commons Attribution-Share Alike 3.0 Unported license.

Fig. 4-4: Michelangelo's Pieta
Author: Stanislav Traykov, Niabot
I, the copyright holder of this work, hereby publish it under the following

licenses: Permission is granted to copy, distribute and/or modify this document under the terms of the GNU Free Documentation License, Version 1.2 or any later version published by the Free Software Foundation; with no Invariant Sections, no Front-Cover and no Back-Cover Texts. A copy of the license is included in the section entitled GNU Free Documentation License.

Fig. 4-5: Michelangelo's David
Author: Jorg Bittner Unna
I, the copyright holder of this work, hereby publish it under the following license: This file is licensed under the Creative Commons Attribution 3.0 Unported license.

Fig. 4-6: Gentilischi's Self-Portrait as a Lute Player
Source: http://www.thehistoryblog.com/wp-content/uploads/2014/03/Artemisia-Gentileschi-Self-Portrait-as-a-Lute-Player-c.-1616–18
This is a faithful photographic reproduction of a two-dimensional, public domain work of art. The work of art itself is in the public domain for the following reason: This work is in the public domain in its country of origin and other countries and areas where the copyright term is the author's life plus 100 years or fewer.

Fig. 4-7: Gentilischi's Judith Slaying Holofernes
Source: Uffizi
This is a faithful photographic reproduction of a two-dimensional, public domain work of art. The work of art itself is in the public domain for the following reason: This work is in the public domain in its country of origin and other countries and areas where the copyright term is the author's life plus 100 years or fewer.

Fig. 4-8: Anguissola's Self-Portrait at Easel
Source: Selected work 4 from Anthony Bond, Joanna Woodall (2005). Self Portrait: Renaissance to Contemporary.
This is a faithful photographic reproduction of a two-dimensional, public domain work of art. The work of art itself is in the public domain for the following reason: This work is in the public domain in its country of origin and other countries and areas where the copyright term is the author's life plus 100 years or fewer.

Fig. 4-9: Anguissola's Portrait of the Artist's Family
Source: http://www.the-athenaeum.org/art/detail.php?ID=110190
This is a faithful photographic reproduction of a two-dimensional, public domain work of art. The work of art itself is in the public domain for the following reason: This work is in the public domain in its country of origin and other countries and areas where the copyright term is the author's life plus 100 years or fewer.

Fig. 4-10: van Hemessen's Self-Portrait
Source: Öffentliche Kunstsammlung, Kunstmuseum, Basel. Dépôt de l'Institut Professeurs Bachofen et J.J. Burckhardt, 1921
This is a faithful photographic reproduction of a two-dimensional, public domain work of art. The work of art itself is in the public domain for the following reason: This work is in the public domain in its country of origin and other countries and areas where the copyright term is the author's life plus 100 years or fewer.

Fig. 4-11: Beale's Self-Portrait
Source: St Edmundsbury Borough Council - Moyse's Hall Museum, Bury St Edmunds.
This file is licensed under the Creative Commons Attribution-Share Alike 2.5 Generic license.
Attribution: St Edmundsbury Borough Council - Moyse's Hall Museum.

Fig. 4-12: Galizia's Still Life
Source :http://www.bluffton.edu/.../galiziaporcelain.jpg.
This image is in the public domain in the United States. In most cases, this means that it was first published prior to January 1, 1924 (see the template documentation for more cases). Other jurisdictions may have other rules, and this image might not be in the public domain outside the United States. See Wikipedia:Public domain and Wikipedia:Copyrights for more details.

Fig. 4-13: Galizia's Judith with Head of Holofernes
Source: Fede Galizia
This is a faithful photographic reproduction of a two-dimensional, public

domain work of art. The work of art itself is in the public domain for the following reason: This photographic reproduction is therefore also considered to be in the public domain in the United States. In other jurisdictions, re-use of this content may be restricted; see Reuse of PD-Art photographs for details.

Fig. 4-14: Fontana's Portrait of a Lady with a Dog
Source: hgHdLNktbrMoDg at Google Cultural Institute
This is a faithful photographic reproduction of a two-dimensional, public domain work of art. The work of art itself is in the public domain for the following reason: This work is in the public domain in the United States because it was published (or registered with the U.S. Copyright Office) before January 1, 1924.

Fig. 4-15: Fontana's Minerva Dressing
Source: Web Gallery of Art
This is a faithful photographic reproduction of a two-dimensional, public domain work of art. The work of art itself is in the public domain for the following reason:This work is in the public domain in the United States because it was published (or registered with the U.S. Copyright Office before January 1, 1924.

Fig. 4-16: Leyster's Game of Cards
Source: Own work, uploader: Rlbberlin
This is a faithful photographic reproduction of a two-dimensional, public domain work of art. The work of art itself is in the public domain for the following reason: This work is in the public domain in its country of origin and other countries and areas where the copyright term is the author's life plus 100 years or fewer.

Fig. 4-17: Leyster's Serenade
Source: http://www.vlinder-01.dds.nl/cdr/paintings/judith_leyster4.htm. This work is in the public domain in its country of origin and other countries and areas where the copyright term is the author's life plus 70 years or fewer. You must also include a United States public domain tag to indicate why this work is in the public domain in the United States.{{PD-US}} – U.S. work public domain in the U.S. for unspecified

reason but presumably because it was published in the U.S. before 1924
.

Fig. 4-18: Ruysch's Flowers on Stone Slab
Source: http://www.kunstkopie.de/a/Kunstkopie/&wid=1123584644853043&mpos=1001 (transfered from de.wiki: http://de.wikipedia.org/w/index.php?title=Datei:Blumenstilleben.jpg&filetimestamp=20081129184048).
This work is in the public domain in its country of origin and other countries and areas where the copyright term is the author's life plus 100 years or fewer. This image is in the public domain in the United States. In most cases, this means that it was first published prior to January 1, 1924.

Fig. 4-19: Ruysch's Still Life with FlowersTitle: Flower-piece
Source: LSH 86742 (hm_dig4506_3718)
This work is in the public domain in the United States because it meets three requirements: it was first published outside the United States (and not published in the U.S. within 30 days); it was first published before 1 March 1989 without copyright notice or before 1964 without copyright renewal or before the source country established copyright relations with the United States; it was in the public domain in its home country on the URAA date (January 1, 1996 for most countries).

Fig. 4-20: Cantino planisphere
Source: Biblioteca Estense Universitaria, Modena, Italy
Author: anonymous Portuguese (1502)
This image is in the public domain because it is a mere mechanical scan or photocopy of a public domain original, or—from the available evidence—is so similar to such a scan or photocopy that no copyright protection can be expected to arise. The original itself is in the public domain for the following reason: This work is in the public domain in its country of origin and other countries and areas where the copyright term is the author's life plus 100 years or fewer. {PD-US}} – U.S. work public domain in the U.S. for unspecified reason but presumably because it was published in the U.S. before 1924.

Map 4-1: Map of New Russia
Title: Map of what was called New Russia during the Russian Empire (now southern Ukraine).
Author: Dim Grits
Source: Own work
Date: 30 July 2011
I, the copyright holder of this work, hereby publish it under the following license: This file is licensed under the Creative Commons Attribution-Share Alike 3.0 Unported license.

Fig. 4-21: Woman Lowering Children Down into a Coal Mine
All of Esther M. Zimmer Lederberg's photographs and other material used on this website are copyright protected as prescribed by the U.S. Copyright Office. Use of these images is available without fee, with the sole requirement that each image carry a clear attribution to Esther M. Zimmer Lederberg and this memorial website (Esther M. Zimmer Lederberg Memorial Website.

Fig. 4-22: Woman Pulling Coal Tub
Source : From www.victorianweb.org/history/ashley.html, a educational site offering free info on the victorian age. Image is a copy of one from an official report of a parliamentary commission done in the mid 18th century. Transferred from en.wikipedia to Commons. Second time from Commons as a GIF which I converted to PNG.
This work created by the United Kingdom Government is in the public domain. This is because it is one of the following: It is a photograph taken prior to 1 June 1957; or It was published prior to 1969; or It is an artistic work other than a photograph or engraving (e.g. a painting) which was created prior to 1969. HMSO has declared that the expiry of Crown Copyrights applies worldwide (ref: HMSO Email Reply)

Fig. 4-23: The British East India Company
East India House," by Thomas Malton the Younger (1748-1804), watercolour over etched outline. 8 1/2 in. x 11 15/16 in. (21.6 cm x 30.3 cm). Courtesy of the Paul Mellon Collection, Yale Center for British Art, Yale

University, New Haven, Connecticut
This is a faithful photographic reproduction of a two-dimensional, public domain work of art. The work of art itself is in the public domain for the following reason: This work is in the public domain in its country of origin and other countries and areas where the copyright term is the author's life plus 100 years or fewer. {{PD-US}} – U.S. work public domain in the U.S. for unspecified reason but presumably because it was published in the U.S. before 1924.

Map 4-2: Native Languages of North America
Title: Distribution of North American language families north of Mexico. Vector image recreated from File:Langs N.Amer.png.
Date: 31 May 2019
This file is licensed under the Creative Commons Attribution-Share Alike 4.0 International license.

Map 4-3: Land of Beringia
Printed with permission from: Jeffrey Bond, MSc Head, Surficial Geology, Yukon Geological Survey.

Fig 4-24: Iroquois Cradleboard
Wrote to Smithsonian and they requested additional information which I sent but never heard back from them. Contacted them again and no response was received. I assumed that the information I sent was sufficient.

Fig. 4-25 & Fig. 4-26: Traditional Iroquois Dress.
Photos found on Iroquois website (https://iroquoisgroup24.weebly.com/clothing.html) under the subheading clothing.

Fig. 4-27: Traditional Cherokee House
The source of this photo was from the AAANATIVEARTS.COM website under Cherokee Houses – Dwellings – Lodges (https://www.aaanativearts.com/cherokee/cherokee-houses.htm).

Map 4-4: Fork of the Ohio River
Title: Self-made map of the Forks of the Ohio (Monongahela, Allegheny

and Ohio rivers).
Author: en:User:Tomcool
Date: 22 March 2009 (original upload date)
Tomcool, the copyright holder of this work, hereby publishes it under the following licenses: This file is licensed under the Creative Commons Attribution-Share Alike 3.0 Unported license.

Fig. 4-28: 1772 Portrait of Sam Adams Pointing to the Massachusetts Charter
Artist: John Singleton Copley (1738-1815)
Source: Humanitiesweb.org
This is a faithful photographic reproduction of a two-dimensional, public domain work of art. The work of art itself is in the public domain for the following reason: This work is in the public domain in its country of origin and other countries and areas where the copyright term is the author's life plus 100 years or fewer. {{PD-US}} – U.S. work public domain in the U.S. for unspecified reason but presumably because it was published in the U.S. before 1924.

Map 4-5: Battle of Long Island
Description: Map of the New York-New Jersey Campaign during the American Revolution
Author: NY-NJ-retreat-1776.jpg: Red4tribe
I, the copyright holder of this work, hereby publish it under the following license: I, the copyright holder of this work, release this work into the public domain. This applies worldwide. In some countries this may not be legally possible; if so: I grant anyone the right to use this work for any purpose, without any conditions, unless such conditions are required by law.

Fig. 4-29: Alexander Hamilton
Reference: Smithsonian Art Inventory Catalog, IAP 08930129
Source/Photographer: dwEqB1Eg2s_kpw at Google Cultural Institute
The author died in 1843, so this work is in the public domain in its country of origin and other countries and areas where the copyright term is the author's life plus 100 years or fewer. This work is in the public domain in

the United States because it was published (or registered with the U.S. Copyright Office) before January 1, 1924.

Fig. 4-30: James Madison
References: https://www.whitehousehistory.org/photos/james-madison
Source/Photographer: The White House Historical Association
This work is in the public domain in its country of origin and other countries and areas where the copyright term is the author's life plus 100 years or fewer. {{PD-US}} – U.S. work public domain in the U.S. for unspecified reason but presumably because it was published in the U.S. before 1924.

Fig. 4-31: Thomas Jefferson
Source/Photographer: Extracted from PDF version of Keeping the Seal in Good Hands poster, part of a U.S. Diplomacy Center (State Department) exhibition on the 225th anniversary of the Great Seal. Direct PDF URL [1]
The U.S. Diplomacy Center exhibition page states All materials in this exhibition are in the public domain and can be reproduced without permission. Citation of this source is appreciated.

Map 4-6: Louisiana Purchase
Map 4-7: United States in 1830
Source: wpclipart.com.
These images are public domain (PD), and that means they can be used and edited for whatever purpose you wish, personal or commercial. No attribution or linking is required.

Fig. 4-32: Interior Hold of a Slave Ship
Description: Stowage of the British slave ship Brookes under the regulated slave trade act of 1788.
Source: This image is available from the United States Library of Congress's Prints and Photographs division under the digital ID cph.3a34658.Author: Plymouth Chapter of the Society for Effecting the Abolition of the Slave Trade.
This work is in the public domain in its country of origin and other countries and areas where the copyright term is the author's life plus

100 years or fewer. This work is in the public domain in the United States because it was published (or registered with the U.S. Copyright Office) before January 1, 1924.

Map 4-8: Louisiana Purchase
Source: United States Geological Survey (USGS)
This image is in the public domain in the United States because it only contains materials that originally came from the United States Geological Survey, an agency of the United States Department of the Interior.

Map 4-9 Slave Trade Routes from Africa to the Americas
Source: 20130530-DSC_8800.
Author: jbdodane
This file is licensed under the Creative Commons Attribution 2.0 Generic license.

Map 4-10: Northwest Territory
Northwest-territory-usa-1787
Permission is granted to copy, distribute and/or modify this document under the terms of the GNU Free Documentation License, Version 1.2 or any later version published by the Free Software Foundation; with no Invariant Sections, no Front-Cover Texts, and no Back-Cover Texts. A copy of the license is included in the section entitled GNU Free Documentation License. Subject to disclaimers.This file is licensed under the Creative Commons Attribution-Share Alike 3.0 Unported.

Map 4-11: Louisiana Purchase
Source: Sources: Natural Earth and Portland State University (https://gist.github.com/wboykinm/05756ac2e625bae9ed81.
Author: William Morris
This file is licensed under the Creative Commons Attribution-Share Alike 4.0 International license.

Fig. 4-33: Value of the Stock of Slaves in the US, 1805-1860
Chart was found at The Economics of the Civil War, by Roger L. Ransom, University of California, Riverside

https://eh.net/encyclopedia/the-economics-of-the-civil-war/.
Contacted the website where chart was located and received the following response: On Wed, Nov 20, 2019 at 1:50 PM Admin at EH.net <admin@eh.net> wrote: You may use the chart as long as you provide the appropriate citation. Lana Sooter, Administrative Coordinator, Economic History Association

Fig. 4-34: Revenues of the US Government, 1861-1865
Source: US Census Bureau (1975)
Chart was found at The Economics of the Civil War by Roger L. Ransom, University of California, Riverside
https://eh.net/encyclopedia/the-economics-of-the-civil-war/.
Fig. 4-35: Robber Barons
This photo appears on multiple sites and is assumed to be in the public domain.

Map 4-12: WWI Military Alliances in 1914
Description: Map of military alliances of Europe in 1914. (Russian)
Source: Translated in Russian from Map_Europe_alliances_1914 en.svg
Author: historicair (French original).
Date: 18 November 2010
I, the copyright holder of this work, hereby publish it under the following license:This file is licensed under the Creative Commons Attribution-Share Alike 2.5 Generic, 2.0 Generic and 1.0 Generic license.

Map 4-13: Treaty of Bucharest, 1913
Description: Geographical region of Macedonia 1913
This image is a work of a Central Intelligence Agency employee, taken or made as part of that person's official duties. As a Work of the United States Government, this image or media is in the public domain in the United States.

Map 4-14: Trench Warfare in WWI
Author: Joanna Legg
Map reproduced by kind permission of www.greatwar.co.uk
Copyright © www.greatwar.co.uk All rights reserved.

Author was contacted and stated. "I first drew this map in the 1990s. You may reproduce the map with pleasure."

Fig. 4-36: Women at Work in a Factory in WWI
Title: Lancashire women at work in a factory during World War I, between 1914-1916.
Source: The Illustrated war news
Author: London Illustrated London News and Sketch, Photo. by Illustrations Bureau.
This media file is in the public domain in the United States. This applies to U.S. works where the copyright has expired, often because its first publication occurred prior to January 1, 1924, and if not then due to lack of notice or renewal.

Fig. 4-37: Navy Recruitment Poster
Naval Historical Foundation
Source: World War I Navy Recruiting Poster by artist Howard Chandler Christy, 1917 NH 81543-KN (Color)
All images are believed to be in the Public Domain and are subsequently free to download.

Fig. 4-38: 1920's FlapperPicture was found at the website: Flappers: The Mothers of the Modern Woman. at
https://flappernhd.weebly.com/appearance.html
Attempt was made to contact them but no contact information could be found.

Fig. 4-39: 1930's Dust Bowl
Description: Farmer and sons walking in the face of a dust storm. Cimarron County, Oklahoma, USA
Date: April, 1936
Author: Arthur Rothstein, for the Farm Security Administration
This image is a work of an employee of the United States Farm Security Administration or Office of War Information domestic photographic units, taken as part of that person's official duties. As a work of the U.S. federal government, the image is in the public domain in the United States.

Fig. 4-40: General Butler Testifying Before the HUAC
Description: Gen. Smedley Butler describes an alleged political conspiracy to overthrow President Franklin D. Roosevelt in 1933.Date: December 28, 1935
Source: Universal Studios; Universal City Studios donated their newsreel collection into the public domain, and gave film materials to the National Archives in 1976.

Fig. 4-41 Henry Ford Receiving the Grand Cross of the German Eagle Award
Source: AP photograph: German diplomats award Henry Ford, center, with their nation's highest decoration for foreigners, the Grand Cross of the German Eagle, in July 1938.
http://www.washingtonpost.com/wp-srv/national/daily/nov98/nazi-cars30.htm.
Photo appears on multiple sites and is assumed to be in the public domain.

Fig. 4-42: Washington Post Story on GM's Contribution to the German War Effort
This photo appears on multiple sites and is assumed to be in the public domain.

Fig. 4-43: Woolworth Receives the German Designation "Adefa Zeichen"
Title: NAZI GERMANY, 1933: BACK TO THE FUTURE
Date: May 31, 2012
Source: whatwouldjackdo.net/2012/05/nazi-germany-1933-back-to-the-future.html.
Second Source: Getty Images; Henry Guttmann Collection.
Source was contacted and the responses from whatwouldjackso: "I have no problem with you using the photo, though I'd suggest making an effort to credit the source."

Fig. 4-44: Jews Being Rounded Up by the Nazis
Description: Stroop Report - Warsaw Ghetto Uprising 06b.jpg; Polish Jews captured by Germans during the suppression of the Warsaw Ghetto

Uprising (Poland)
Source: Image:Warsaw-Ghetto-Josef-Bloesche-HRedit.jpg uploaded by United States Holocaust Museum.
This work is in the public domain in the United States because it meets three requirements: it was first published outside the United States (and not published in the U.S. within 30 days); it was first published before 1 March 1989 without copyright notice or before 1964 without copyright renewal or before the source country established copyright relations with the United States;it was in the public domain in its home country (Poland) on the URAA date (1 January 1996).

Fig. 4-45: Jews Humiliated and Murdered by Germans in WWII
This picture appears on multiple sites and is assumed to be in the public domain.

Fig. 4-46: Warsaw Uprising
Description: Warsaw Uprising: Soldiers from the "Radosław Regiment" after several hours marching through sewers from Krasiński Square to Warecka Street in the Śródmieście district, early morning on September 2, 1944.
Author: Jerzy Tomaszewski (1924-2016)
Date: September 2, 1944
This work is in the public domain in the United States because it meets three requirements: it was first published outside the United States (and not published in the U.S. within 30 days); it was first published before 1 March 1989 without copyright notice or before 1964 without copyright renewal or before the source country established copyright relations with the United States; it was in the public domain in its home country (Poland) on the URAA date (1 January 1996).

Map 4-15: Battle of the Bulge, 1944
Map was found at a site entitled Battle of The Bulge
Facts, information and articles about Battle Of The Bulge, a battle of World War II
https://www.historynet.com/battle-of-the-bulge
Contacted the source of the photo Petro Carthography at https://www.pethocarto.com/contact/ to request permission. Received no response.

Fig. 4-47: Poster Campaign Encouraging women to Enter the Workforce
Title: We Can Do ItAuthor: J. Howard Miller; Restored by Adam Cuerden
Date: between circa 1942 and circa 1943
Source: U.S. National Archives and Records Administration
Work is in the public domain in the United States because it was published in the United States between 1924 and 1977 without a copyright notice.

Fig. 4-48: Female Pilots During WWII
Description: These four female pilots leaving their ship, Pistol Packin' Mama, at the four engine school at Lockbourne AAF, Ohio, are members of a group of Women Airforce Service Pilots (WASPS) who have been trained to ferry the B-17 Flying Fortresses. L to R are Frances Green, Margaret (Peg) Kirchner, Ann Waldner and Blanche Osborn.
Author: U.S. Air Force photo
Date: circa 1944
Source:http://www.302aw.afrc.af.mil/news/story.asp?id=123117795
This image or file is a work of a U.S. Air Force Airman or employee, taken or made as part of that person's official duties. As a work of the U.S. federal government, the image or file is in the public domain in the United States.

Fig. 4-49: Photo of Klavdiya Kalugina, Young Female Soviet Sniper
Source: peoples.ru
Author: Unknown
This work is in the public domain in the United States because it meets three requirements: it was first published outside the United States (and not published in the U.S. within 30 days); it was first published before 1 March 1989 without copyright notice or before 1964 without copyright renewal or before the source country established copyright relations with the United States; it was in the public domain in its home country on the URAA date (January 1, 1996 for most countries).

Fig. 4-50: Illustration of Christians Bowing to the Will of the German Leaders
Contacted Contacted Conccordatwatch.eu (http://www.concordatwatch.eu/list_KBheaders.php?org_id=858) for permission on November 9–no response was received.

Index

95 Theses 48, 66, 160

A

Abenaki 200
Abigail Adams 306, 637
Abraham Martin 241
Absalom Jones 355
Absolute Consciousness 4, 5, 184
A Chaste Maid in Cheapside 18
Adam Clarke 81
Admiral Yamamoto 548
Adolf Eichmann 534
A. D. Williams 356
Afrika Korps 542, 543, 557
ageism 5
Agricultural Adjustment Administration 477, 491
Alan Turing 544, 678
A Larum for London 18
Albert I 446
Albert Speer 527
Alchemy 19, 604
Alcoa 530
Alessandra Scala 31, 608
Alexander Bettis 356, 647
Alexander II 95
Alexander Mack 77
Alexandra Mavrokordatou 101
Alfred Ploetz 434
Alfred P. Sloan 527
Algonquin 200, 201, 204, 626, 627
All-African Convention 501
Allied Powers 439, 452, 455, 472
Almagest 19, 20
Alonso González de Berruguete 12

Altaian 197, 198
American Express 518
American Liberty League 520
Amerigo Vespucci 42, 43
Amish 73
Anabaptist 73, 80, 614
Andrew Mellon 479, 480
Andrzej Frycz Modrzewski 22, 24
Anglican 36, 63, 73, 74, 77, 84, 92, 125, 127, 341, 347, 348, 351, 601, 613
Anishinaabe 200
Anna Shaw 461
Anne Boleyn 50, 51
Ante Pavelić 543
Antonio the negro 337
Apalachee 231
Apalachicola 231
Apostolic Christian Church 73
Arapaho 201, 411
Arcadia Conference 550, 679
Archduke Franz Ferdinand 439, 444
Archive for Racial and Social Biology 434
Ariosto 36
Aristotile Fioravanti 25
Armada 37, 70, 612
Arnolfo di Cambio 12
Artamène 100
Artemisia Gentilischi 31
Arthur Shelton 437
Arthur Zimmerman 453
Astronomia nova 20
Astronomy 19, 20, 31
A System of Logic 186

Atikamekw 200
Atlantic Charter 546, 678
Atlantic slave trade 322, 335, 363
A Treatise of Human Nature 153
Auschwitz-Birkenau 556
A Vindication of the Rights of Women 105
Aztecs 236

B

Baccio da Montelupo 12
Bacon 121, 124, 125, 126, 135, 160, 418, 420, 619
Bakócz Chapel 25
Bakongo 231
Baldassare Castiglione 30
Balkan League 441, 442, 443, 662
Baptist 80, 121, 341, 344, 346, 348, 351, 352, 354, 355, 356, 358, 586, 646, 647
Bartholomew Fair 18
Bartolomeo Bellano 12
Bartolomeu Dias 41, 43
Bartolommeo Berecci 22
Bataan Death March 551, 679
Battle of Blair Mountain 407, 656
Battle of Britain 538
Battle of Cantigny 453, 663
Battle of Manila 569
Battle of Midway 552, 679
Battle of Stalingrad 553, 680
Battle of the Bismarck Sea 556, 680
Battle of the Bulge 567, 568, 699
Battle of the Heligoland Bight 535, 676
Battle of the Philippine Sea 562, 681
Bayer 528
Beatrix of Aragon 25
Beer Hall Putsch 511, 671
Belleau Wood 453, 663
Belzec 554

Benedict Arnold 277
Benedict XIII 69
Benedict XIV 69
Ben Jonson 18
Beringia 198, 692
Berkeley 126, 162
Bermuda Conference 557, 672, 680
Bernardo Morando 22
Bernard Wapowski 22
Bethmann-Hollweg 456
Betsiamites 200
Betty Freidan 506
Bible 11, 46, 47, 49, 56, 58, 67, 72, 78, 79, 81, 82, 83, 117, 118, 119, 120, 121, 132, 133, 140, 141, 161, 170, 339, 344, 350, 352, 458, 614
Big Week 560, 681
Black Codes 385, 652
Blackfoot 201
Bluestone Church 354
Bockscar 571
Bogdanovka 550, 679
Bogdan Saltanov 28, 607
Bolsheviks 449, 591
Bosnian Crisis 440
Boss Tweed 400
Boston Massacre 246, 263, 277
Boston Tea Party 246, 272, 634
Braddock 241
Brne Karnarutić 28, 607
Brown Brothers Harriman 518, 519
Bruderhof 73
Buchanan 366, 394, 649
Buda Castle 25, 605
Bussa 332, 642

C

Cab Calloway 479
Cairo Conference 560

Calvin 3, 11, 38, 47, 48, 50, 51, 52, 53, 54, 55, 56, 57, 58, 59, 60, 61, 62, 63, 69, 73, 75, 80, 82, 83, 119, 121, 125, 159, 358, 415, 480, 611, 614
Calvinism 3, 51, 54, 55, 56, 69, 74, 75, 77, 86, 155, 156, 358, 611
Cantino planisphere 42, 690
Cape Fear 231
capital 8, 22, 24, 25, 26, 30, 86, 92, 109, 159, 160, 182, 186, 191, 192, 217, 228, 287, 307, 310, 319, 323, 325, 383, 386, 405, 406, 408, 409, 410, 412, 414, 424, 429, 443, 466, 477, 499, 514, 536, 537, 545, 550, 561, 652
capitalists 1, 60, 63, 71, 75, 114, 115, 143, 148, 159, 160, 285, 286, 287, 290, 310, 313, 322, 323, 325, 333, 358, 376, 379, 382, 392, 393, 395, 396, 401, 406, 408, 413, 415, 416, 419, 424, 425, 426, 427, 433, 437, 438, 446, 447, 448, 449, 450, 461, 469, 474, 476, 488, 492, 493, 495, 509, 519, 520, 522, 523, 528, 590
Carnegie 392, 394, 395, 396, 403, 404, 405, 406, 407, 408, 414, 501, 531, 654, 655, 656
Catawba 231
Catharina van Hemessen 33, 608
Cathedral of St James 27
Cathedral of the Archangel 28, 607
Cathedral of the Dormition 25, 28
Catherine de Medici 36
Catherine of Aragon 50
Catherine the Great 93, 616
Catholic Church 2, 3, 11, 20, 30, 36, 46, 47, 48, 49, 51, 52, 54, 55, 60, 67, 68, 69, 71, 73, 74, 80, 83, 84, 91, 120, 125, 133, 137, 160, 211, 218, 341, 351, 580, 582, 583, 585, 586, 592, 612, 615, 683

Cayuga 206, 220
Central Pacific 397
Central Powers 439, 444, 463, 469, 470, 472
Chapel of Blessed John 27
Charles de Condren 65
Charles De Gaulle 565
Charles Fox Parham 357, 647
Charles I 18, 91, 128
Charles II 75, 91, 103, 128, 231
Charles III 66
Charles Lindbergh 541
Charles V 50, 69
Charles Wesley 348
Charles W. Morris 435
Charlotte Corday 107
Charlotte Schimmelman 101
Chase Manhattan Bank 518, 657, 673
Château-Thierry 453
cheque 7
Cheraw 231
Cherokee 200, 206, 207, 220, 221, 222, 223, 224, 225, 226, 227, 228, 229, 230, 231, 232, 233, 234, 316, 629, 630, 631, 692
Cheyenne 201, 411, 671
Chiang Kai-shek 503
Chicago, Burlington, and Quincy railroad (CB&Q) 417
Chickahominy 201
Chickasaw 231, 234, 317
Chief Ross 233
Choctaw 234, 317
Christine Sophie Holstein 101
Christopher Columbus 8, 41, 43, 610
Churchill 536, 538, 539, 546, 555, 560, 565, 569, 571
Citibank 323, 518
Civilian Conservation Corps 477,

489, 504, 669
Civil Works Administration 491, 504
Claudius Ptolemy 19
Claus von Stauffenberg 563
Clement XI 68
Coca Cola 528
Codex Theodosianus 581
Coercive Acts 247, 274, 275
Colloquium Marianum 68, 612
colonization 8, 41, 44, 45, 71, 196, 197, 232, 234, 610, 631
Coluccio Salutati 11
Columbian Exchange 8, 603
Committee of Correspondence 246, 267, 634
common sense 208
Communist Manifesto 448
Compromise of 1790 289
Compromise of 1877 389, 653
Concerning the Form and Principles of the Sensible and Intelligible World 161
Congaree 231
Congregationalist 77, 81, 402
Conrad Grebel 72
Considerations on Representative Government 188, 191
Constance Trotti 101
constitutional democracy 4
Consumerism 86
continental congress 274
Coolidge 480
Copernicus 20, 22, 24, 604
Cornwallis 282, 283
Coronation Church of Buda 25
Corvina Library 25
Cotton Club 478, 667
Councilarism 85
Council of Trent 66, 68, 612

Credit Mobilier 412, 657
Cree 201
Creek 126, 231, 232, 233, 234, 283, 304, 316, 317, 640
Critique of Pure Reason 161, 162, 177, 622
Croatia 21, 27, 440, 543, 545, 607
Cudjoe 332, 642
Cuffy 332, 642

D

Dalmatia 27, 440
Daniel Drew 394, 399
Das Kapital 448
David 13, 14
David Kirke 204, 626
David Lilienthal 493
David Rockefeller 428
Deacon Adams 244, 245
De Architectura 10
Declaration of Panama 534
Declaration of Rights of the Women of the United States 299, 638
Declaration of Sentiments 298
Declaration of the Rights of Woman 107
Defenestrations of Prague 70, 613
Defense of Orthodox Faith against Prodigious Errors of the Spaniard Michael Servetus 57
Deganawidah 206, 207
Denis Diderot 105
Denmark Vesey 334, 643
De regimine Judaeorum ad Ducissam Brabantae 582
De revolutionibus orbium coelestium 20, 22
Descartes 117, 122, 124, 125, 134, 135, 136, 137, 138, 139, 143, 152, 620

Destroyers for Bases Agreement 539
Dialogue Concerning the Two Chief World Systems 20
Dick Taylor 377
Dietrich Bonhoeffer 590
Disruption of 1843 75
Dissonance 16
Dmitry Donskoy 29
Dominko "Dinko" Zlatarić 28
Donatella 12
Dow Chemical 529
Dragutin Dimitrijević 444
Dr. Faustus 18
Duchess Sieniawska 101
Duke Ellington 479
Dumbarton Oaks Conference 564, 681
DuPont 520
Dust Bowl 489, 490, 496, 669, 697
Dutch 34, 35, 41, 44, 45, 50, 64, 70, 71, 87, 91, 121, 125, 134, 138, 151, 200, 203, 207, 219, 235, 236, 239, 287, 321, 342, 346, 347, 395, 467, 498, 524, 536, 562, 565, 569, 599, 609, 610, 631, 681

E

Earnest Desire for a Reform of the True Evangelical Church 78
East Prussian Offensive 569
economic liberalism 4
Edict of Fontainebleau 86
Edward A. Ross 431, 660
Edward II 18
Edward VI 36, 51
Eisenhower 552, 560, 570, 575
Eleanor Roosevelt 506, 671
Elisabetta Gonzaga 100
Elizabeth Cady Stanton 217, 298, 299, 638

Elizabeth I 37, 70, 73, 609
Elizabeth Montagu 101
Ellwood Cubberley 432
Emancipation Proclamation 327, 368, 650
Emergency Banking Act of 1933 487
Emergency Relief and Construction Act 484
Emile 105, 156, 157
Emily Donelson 320
encomienda 335
Engels 179, 447
Enola Gay 571
Episcopalian 356
Epitome of Copernican Astronomy 20
Epitome of the Almagest 20
Erasmus 11, 12, 23, 48, 603
Erie Railroad 399, 410, 413
Espionage Act 474, 666
Estates General 90, 106
Ethan Allen 277
Ethel Waters 479
Eugene V. Debs 474, 666
Eugenics 434, 435, 530, 661, 675
Eva Braun 569, 570
Evangelical 78, 79, 343, 346

F

Famous Chronicle of King Edward the First 18
Fat Man 571
Fede Galizia 34, 608, 688
Federal Emergency Relief Administration (FERA) 490
Federal Home Loan Bank Act 484
Federal Reserve Bank 314, 360, 409, 424, 425, 427, 429, 435, 437, 438, 477, 488

Federal Surplus Relief Corporation (FSRC) 491
Ferdinand I of Hapsburg 26
Feuerbach 179
Fibonacci 7
Fifth Council of the Lateran 64, 65, 612
finance 7, 8, 241, 287, 290, 360, 369, 375, 376, 377, 394, 395, 398, 400, 409, 410, 411, 413, 414, 422, 465, 467, 476
Fishing and Fishermen's Talk 28
Fisk 394, 399, 400, 655
Flagellation of Christ 27
Floride Calhoun 320
Ford 485, 486, 525, 526, 528, 668, 675, 698
Ford Massacre 486
Fort Le Boeuf 239, 241
Four Plays in One 18
Fox 122, 201, 357, 609, 647
Francesco Fiorentino 22
Francesco II Gonzaga 36
Frances Perkins 506
Francisco Franco 499, 513
Francis de Sales 65
Frank A. Vanderlip 437
Franklin 124, 207, 243, 251, 252, 259, 268, 269, 271, 279, 347, 361, 486, 512, 533, 546, 555, 566, 570, 633, 634, 668, 697
Franklin Delano Roosevelt 486, 566, 669
Frederick Douglas 332
French and Indian War 220, 232, 238, 241, 243, 247, 250, 252, 277, 632
Friend of the People 107
Fritz Thyssen 519
Fronde 88, 615

G

Gabriel Bethlen 26
Gabriel Kolko 430, 660
Gabriel Princip 439
Gabriel Prosser 334, 643
Galileo 20, 603, 604
Gallicanism 85, 87, 615
Garfield 381, 651
Gaspar Corte-Real 42, 43
Gdansk 23, 517
General Paulus 552, 554, 555
General Pershing 453, 454, 460, 463
George Blaurock 72
George III 232, 242, 253, 259, 280
George Liele 355, 647
George Orwell 431, 660
George Peele 18
George Perkins 415, 427
George Whitefield 341, 348, 350, 644
Georg Purbach 19
Gerd von Rundstedt 536
Ghana 327, 642
Gibbons v. Ogden 397, 654
Giovan Francesco Rustici 12
Giovanni Battista di Quadro 22
Giovanni da Verrazzano 44, 201
Giovanni Pisano 12
Glass-Seagall Act 487
Glorious Revolution 92, 619
GM 520, 526, 527, 675, 698
Gold Reserve Act 488, 668
Goodyear 520
Gorbachev 450
Gottlieb Priber 232
Gould 393, 394, 399, 400, 413, 414, 486, 654, 655, 657
Gracia Real de Santa Teresa de Mose 237

Grant 369, 377, 384, 389
Great Awakening 333, 341, 346, 349, 350, 351, 352, 357, 358, 646
Great Northern 417, 419
Great Purge 513, 672
Gregory XVI 87
Grieselda 38
Guaranty Trust Co. of New York 518
Gury Nikitin 28, 607
Gutenberg press 16
Gyula Gombos 500

H

Hail Mary 69
Hamilton 142, 243, 278, 284, 285, 287, 289, 291, 292, 293, 295, 296, 309, 325, 347, 361, 396, 446, 635, 636, 693
Hamiltonianism 287, 289, 291, 325, 636
Hamlet 18
Handbook of a Christian Knight 11
Handsome Lake 211, 628
Hanibal Lucić 27, 28, 606
Hans Dürer 23
Hans Holbein 33
Hans von Kulmbach 23
Hapsburgs 27, 88, 92
Harmonices Mundi 20
Harmony 16
Harriet Tubman 332, 344, 643
Harriman 323, 394, 417, 418, 419, 421, 518, 519, 531, 658
Hastings Boss 81, 614
Hazard Circular 379
Hedonism 86
Hegel 119, 122, 124, 162, 171, 172, 173, 174, 175, 176, 177, 178, 179, 180, 181, 182, 623
Heinrich Himmler 545, 560, 566, 571
Henriette Herz 101
Henry Bessemer 406
Henry Clay 310, 312, 365, 394
Henry Frick 406
Henry II 36, 37
Henry III 36
Henry IV 47
Henry P. Davidson 437
Henry V 18
Henry VIII 18, 32, 36, 37, 44, 47, 50, 51, 73, 121
Hermann Göring 538, 570, 573
Hiawatha 206, 627
Hideki Tōjō 548
Hilaire Belloc 434, 660
Hindenburg 456, 498, 511, 512
Hiroshima 571, 682
Hitler 435, 498, 510, 511, 512, 513, 516, 517, 518, 519, 523, 524, 525, 526, 527, 528, 529, 530, 534, 537, 539, 540, 541, 542, 543, 544, 546, 551, 554, 555, 562, 563, 565, 569, 570, 577, 580, 581, 582, 583, 584, 585, 586, 588, 589, 590, 591, 673, 675, 678, 683, 684
Hobbes 122, 124, 125, 126, 127, 128, 129, 130, 132, 133, 134, 138, 141, 152, 619, 620
Ho Chi Minh 572
Hollerith punch-card system 524
Holocaust of Viannos 559
Homestead Act 369, 371, 650
Homestead Strike 407, 656
Hoover 467, 480, 481, 483, 484, 485, 486
Hoovervilles 484
House Committee on Un-American Activities (HUAC) 521
Hudson River Railroad 399
Hudson's Bay Company 197
Hugo Boss 528

Huldrych Zwingli 48, 610
humanism 10, 11, 26, 31, 116, 188, 195, 604
Hume 119, 122, 124, 126, 137, 151, 152, 153, 154, 156, 157, 161, 162, 622
Hundred Regiments Offensive 539, 677
Hutcheson 152, 158
Hutchinson 253, 254, 257, 264, 266, 268, 270, 272, 273, 637
Hutterites 73

I

IBM 523, 524, 525, 528, 674
Ignatius of Loyola 65
Illini 201
Immaculate Conception 68
Indian Removal Act 233, 317, 640
indulgences 49, 68
Institutes of the Christian Religion 52, 56, 611
intellectual 1, 2, 11, 19, 78, 104, 105, 107, 119, 120, 152, 162, 183, 350, 428, 432, 434, 450
International Court of Justice 408, 656
Invasion of Poland 533, 676
Iron Guards 541
Iroquois 199, 200, 203, 204, 205, 206, 207, 208, 209, 210, 211, 212, 213, 214, 215, 216, 217, 218, 219, 220, 221, 233, 627, 692
Isabella D'Este 35
Isidore 29, 608
Iskra 448, 662
Italian Renaissance 1, 7, 16, 17, 21, 25, 34, 596, 598, 609
Ivan the Terrible 93, 616
Izabela Czartoryska 101

J

Jackson 233, 294, 300, 301, 302, 303, 304, 306, 307, 308, 309, 310, 312, 313, 315, 316, 317, 319, 320, 325, 364, 372, 375, 376, 380, 437, 638, 639, 640
Jacksonian Democrats 311
Jacopo Sansovino 12
Jacques Lefevre 11
Jakob Böhme 176
James Buel 381, 652
James I 18, 91, 270
James Otis 253, 263, 297
James Van Zandt 519
James Weinstein 430, 659
Jane Seymour 51
Jan Kochanowski 23
Jan Łaski 24
Janos (John) Hunyadi 24, 605
János Szapolyai 26
Jansenism 85, 86, 615
Janus Pannonius 28, 607
Jan Zamoyski 23
Jay Cooke 394, 411, 412, 413, 657
Jean Eudes 65
Jean-Jacques Olier 65
Jean-Paul Marat 107
Jefferson 107, 124, 126, 142, 211, 233, 243, 268, 278, 279, 284, 285, 287, 288, 289, 290, 292, 293, 294, 295, 303, 305, 316, 317, 325, 334, 347, 361, 362, 363, 364, 367, 437, 628, 635, 636, 639, 649, 694
Jefferson Davis 326, 367, 649
Jehovah's Witnesses 358, 590, 648
Jekyll Island Club 438
Jeremy Bentham 186, 625
Jeronim Vidulić 27, 606
Jigonhasasee 206

John Brown 324, 344, 366, 649
John Cabot 43, 44
John C. Frémont 366
John Chrysostom 341, 581, 683
John Cotton 76, 122
John Fletcher 18
John Gill 80, 81, 614
John Hancock 260, 261, 263, 267, 279
John Howard Payne 221
John Huss 47
John Knox 38, 75, 121, 609, 613
John of Kastav 27, 606
John Owen 76
John Punch 337
John Randolph 363, 649
John Spilsbury 351
John Wesley 77, 79, 81, 119, 122, 343, 348, 356, 614
John Winthrop 345
John Wycliffe 46, 121, 610
Jonas Clarke 277
Joseph Cinque 332, 643
Joseph Goebbels 570
Joseph Grew 548
Joseph P. Kennedy 540
Józef Struś 24
Jozef Tiso 517, 672
Judita 28
Judith Jans Leyster 34
Julie 156
Julius III 67
July 20 Plot 563
June Uprising 545
Junípero Serra 87
Juraj Dalmatinac 27
Juraj Šižgorić 28, 607

K

Kaiser Wilhelm 435, 452, 453, 455, 458, 661, 664
Kansas-Nebraska Act 365, 649
Kant 119, 122, 124, 127, 160, 161, 162, 163, 164, 165, 166, 167, 168, 169, 174, 175, 177, 180, 181, 622
Karl Brandt 547
Karp Zolotaryov 28, 607
Katherine Bora 82
Katyn Massacre 556
Kepler 20, 604
Khruschev 450
Kickapoo 201
Kierkegaard 179
King Charles IX 36
Kingdom of Naples 9
King Francis I 44
King Lear 18
King Matthias I 25
King Rama VII 503
King Ulászló II 25
Kiowa 411
Klavdiya Kalugina 579, 700
Kodak 528, 675
Krakow Academy 22
Kristalnacht 515
Kuhn Loeb 417, 418

L

Lady Mary Wortley Montagu 105
Lavinia Fontana 34, 609
Leif Ericson 41
Le Marais 100
Lend Lease 510
Lenin 448, 449, 450, 453
Leon Alberti 38
Leonardo Da Vinci 19, 35, 597
Leon Feldhendler 559
Leon Jaworski 564

Les Femmes Illustres 101
Leviathan 127, 128, 129, 130, 134, 620, 659
Levina Teerlinc 32, 608
Liber abbaci 7
Liebniz 122, 124, 143, 144, 145
Lincoln 326, 364, 366, 367, 368, 372, 375, 376, 377, 378, 379, 380, 382, 384, 385, 387, 411, 436, 437, 639, 651, 652
Locke 117, 122, 124, 126, 127, 140, 141, 142, 143, 154, 621
Lollards 47, 610
Lorenzo Ghiberti 12
Louise Labe 31
Louisiana Purchase 303, 334, 363, 364, 365, 643, 648, 694, 695
Louis XIII 88
Louis XIV 86, 88, 91, 241
Louis XV 90, 187, 615
Louis XVI 90, 106, 146
Lovro Marinov Dobričević 27
lubok printing 29
Lucas Cranach 23
Lucretia Mott 217
Lucrezia Borgia 31, 608
Lucrezia Tornabuoni 31, 608
Ludendorff 456
Ludlow Massacre 407, 656
Ludwig von Mises 429
Luftwaffe 525, 533, 536, 537, 538, 539, 544, 555, 561, 567, 568, 578
Lukács 179
Lusitania 452, 663
Luther 11, 48, 49, 50, 51, 65, 66, 80, 82, 83, 118, 119, 121, 160, 176, 356, 384, 586, 587, 588, 589, 610, 614
Lwow Uprising 563

M

MacArthur 486, 522, 551, 565, 571, 572, 668
Macbeth 18
Maciej of Miechów 22, 24
Madame Condorcet 105
Madame du Chatelet 105
Madeleine de Scudéry 100, 617
Madison 142, 154, 285, 288, 289, 290, 291, 292, 294, 302, 305, 309, 325, 347, 364, 636, 637, 694
Magnificat 586
Mahatma Gandhi 548, 553
Majdanek 545, 678
Malinke 231
Maliseet 200
Mannerism 13, 24
Marcin Kromer 22, 24
Margaret Eaton 319, 321
Marguerite de Navarre 31, 608
Maria Cayetana de Silva 101
Mariana Drăgescu 578
Maria Weston Chapman 332, 643
Marie Gouze 107
Marie-Jean Caritat 107
Marie-Jeanne Roland 108
Marin Držić 28, 607
Mariquita Sánchez 101
Marko Marulić 27, 28, 606
Marlowe 18
Marquis de Condorcet 105, 107
Marquise de Rambouillet 100
Martin Niemöller 590
Marx 63, 123, 124, 178, 179, 180, 192, 194, 294, 447, 611
Mary Ann Shadd Carey 332
Mary Astell 105
Mary Beale 33, 608

Mary I 36, 37, 51, 609
Mary Queen of Scots 37
Mary Wollstonecraft 105
Massachusetts 64, 77, 197, 235, 238, 241, 245, 248, 250, 251, 252, 253, 255, 256, 257, 258, 262, 263, 264, 265, 266, 268, 269, 274, 275, 276, 277, 278, 279, 291, 323, 345, 365, 611, 621, 625, 632, 634, 693
Massachusetts Bay Colony 64, 270
Massachusetts Bay Company 197
Massachusetts Resolves 257
Mateo Gucci 22
Materiae Medicae 21
Materialism 86
Matilda Joslyn Gage 217, 299
Matteo Bandello 36
Matthew Henry 81
Matthew Moore 355
Matthew Poole 81
Matthias 24, 25, 26, 605
Maximilian Colt 12
Max Planck Society 435, 661
Mazarin 88, 615
Mbundu 231
McKinley 418, 420, 428, 429
Mein Kampf 511, 526, 540, 580
Melanchthon 11, 23, 603
Melodies for the Polish Psalter 23
Mende 231
Mennonites 73
Menominee 201
mercantilism 7
merchant 1, 2, 3, 7, 8, 9, 16, 22, 30, 40, 44, 59, 60, 61, 71, 75, 86, 89, 90, 91, 99, 106, 110, 159, 173, 195, 258, 263, 302, 401, 468, 533, 611
merchant class 3, 8, 9, 16, 30, 59, 75, 89, 90, 91, 99, 106, 159, 195, 611

merchants 1, 3, 7, 8, 9, 40, 44, 46, 47, 55, 59, 60, 61, 62, 69, 89, 90, 98, 99, 102, 180, 248, 250, 251, 252, 258, 259, 260, 264, 287, 308
Meridel LeSueur 504, 671
Metaphysical Foundations of Natural Science 162
Metaxas 500, 539
Metropolitan Peter Cathedral 28
Miami 201
Michael Servetus 56, 57, 611
Michelangelo 12, 13, 24, 32, 597, 603, 686, 687
Michelozzo 12
Michigan Southern Railway 399, 654
Miguel Hidalgo 236
Mihajlo Hamzic 27, 606
Mi'kmaq 200
Mikołaj Gomółka 23
Mikolaj Rej 22
Mill 123, 185, 186, 187, 188, 190, 191, 192, 193, 194, 625, 626
Minutes Book of the Geneva City Council 57
Modernism 86
Mohammad Mosaddegh 547, 679
Mohawk 206, 208, 210, 211, 212, 220, 275, 627
Mohegan 200
Molly Dewson 506
Molotov 535, 540, 559, 677
monophony 16
Montagnais/Naskapi 200
Monte Delle Doti 30
Montesquieu 122, 124, 146, 147, 148, 149, 150, 151, 621
Mordechai Goldstein 553
Morgan 323, 392, 394, 395, 396, 404,

407, 409, 410, 412, 413, 414, 415, 416, 417, 418, 419, 420, 421, 422, 423, 424, 427, 428, 429, 430, 436, 437, 448, 461, 468, 475, 518, 522, 656, 657, 658, 659, 665, 673, 686
Mount Suribachi 569
multinational corporations 2, 159
Munich Agreement 516
Muscogee 231, 232
Muslim 7, 321, 415, 441
Mussolini 499, 517, 533, 539, 541, 558, 559, 570, 578, 583

N

NAACP 460, 664
Nagasaki 571, 682
Nanny 332, 642
Nanticoke 201
Nan'yehi 232
Napoleon Bonaparte 91
Narragansett 200
National Bank Act 376, 380, 651
National City Bank 417, 436, 437
National Industrial Recovery Act 477
nationalism 5, 178, 391, 438, 455, 457, 458, 511, 531, 532, 535, 593
National Recovery Administration 492, 504, 669
Nat Turner 334, 354, 643
Nelson Aldrich 437
New Deal 429, 430, 486, 487, 488, 489, 495, 497, 504, 506, 512, 668, 669
New France 204, 626
New System of Nature 143
New York Central 399, 400, 409
New York & Harlem Railroad 398
Niccolò da Correggio 36
Nicholas Biddle 310, 375
Nicola Pisano 12, 603

Nicolas Cracoviensis 23
Night of the Long Knives 512
Nikola Božidarević 27, 606
Nipmuck 200
Noam Chomsky 430, 659
Norman Cousins 503
Norris-LaGuardia Anti-Injunction Act 485
Northern Pacific 410, 411, 412, 413, 416, 417, 418, 419, 420, 421, 657
Northwest Ordinance 247, 362, 363, 648
Nzinga Mbemba 332

O

Odessa Massacre 548
Of Proficience and Advancement of Learning Divine and Human 160
Of the Social Contract, Principles of Political Right 156
Ojibwe/Chippewa 201
Oliver Cromwell 91, 128, 231, 616
On Civility in Children 11
Oneida 206, 220
On Free Will 11
On Liberty 188, 625
Onondaga 206, 220
On the Jews and Their Lies 588, 684
On the Motion of the Heart and Blood in Animals 21
Operation Barbarossa 540, 545, 550, 677
Operation Gomorrah 558
Operation Goodtime 560
Operation Ichi-Go 561, 681
Operation Overlord 561
Operation Reinhard 545, 678
Operation Sea Lion 537, 539

Operation Typhoon 548
Operation Uranus 554, 680
Ordinance of Nullification 309
Oswald Ernald Mosley 536
Othello 18
Ottawa 201, 205
Otto Heinze 435, 436
Ottoman Empire 19, 24, 66, 88, 94, 95, 238, 440, 441, 442, 459, 471, 616
Otto of Freising 9

P

Paine 124, 207, 243, 284, 292, 293, 347, 636
Palace of Facets 28, 607
Panama 43, 397, 421, 422, 525, 534, 658
Panic of 1819 311, 639
Panic of 1873 412
Panic of 1901 419, 658
panic of 1907 436
Pan-Slavism 440, 441, 661
Papal States 9
Passamaquoddy 200
Patrick Henry 250, 268, 276, 277
Paul III 67
Paul Revere 276, 278
Paul Sweezy 430, 659
Paul W. Warburg 437
Peace of Augsburg 69, 612
Peace Palace 408, 656
Pedro Fernandes de Queiros 45
Pee Dee 231
Pennacook 200
Pennsylvania and Ohio 409
Pequot 200
Perle Mesta 101
Permanent Court of Arbitration 408, 656

Petar Hektorović 28, 607
Petar Zoranić 28, 607
Peter I 93
Peter Minuit 45
Petrarch 11
Pharmacopoeiae 21
Phenomenology of Spirit 173, 174, 175
Philipp Bouhler 546
Philipp Jakob Spener 77
Phillip II 69
philosophy 1, 7, 9, 10, 11, 12, 56, 84, 98, 99, 116, 118, 119, 123, 124, 126, 127, 134, 135, 137, 138, 143, 144, 145, 146, 152, 154, 155, 156, 157, 158, 160, 161, 162, 163, 164, 165, 166, 167, 168, 169, 170, 171, 173, 174, 176, 177, 179, 180, 181, 184, 185, 190, 195, 423, 434, 446, 474, 530, 593
Philosophy of Right 173, 174, 177
Piatt Andrew 437
Pierre de Berulle 65
Pieta 13, 15, 686
Pietist 77, 78, 79, 118, 119, 161
Piotr Skarga 24
Pius IV 67
Planine 28
Plaszow 556
Plautus 17
Plymouth Colony 64, 77
Plymouth Company 196
Pocahontas 205
Pocumtuc 200
Poggio Bracciolini 11
polyphony 16, 601
Ponce de Leon 43, 237
Pope Clement VII 50
Pope John XXII 16
Pope John XXIII 66

Pope Pius XII 585
Potawatomi 201
Potsdam Conference 571
Powhatan 205, 627
Prague Uprising 570
Premier Édouard Daladier 534
Prescott Bush 519
Prime Minister Chamberlain 534
Prince Henry the Navigator 41
Prince Ivan III 28
Principles of Political Economy 190, 191, 625, 626
Proclamation of Amnesty and Reconstruction 385, 387
profit 7, 8, 291, 342, 406, 423, 425, 482, 492, 494, 523, 592
Protestant 2, 3, 11, 20, 24, 26, 36, 38, 46, 47, 48, 49, 51, 52, 53, 54, 55, 56, 62, 64, 65, 66, 69, 70, 71, 72, 73, 74, 80, 82, 83, 84, 85, 86, 89, 91, 118, 120, 123, 125, 128, 135, 151, 155, 160, 169, 171, 172, 211, 346, 347, 348, 351, 358, 415, 446, 458, 580, 586, 589, 591, 592, 611, 613, 614, 648, 684
Ptolemy 7, 19, 22
public sphere 98, 99, 104
Pugachev's Rebellion 95, 616
Puritan 59, 75, 77, 81, 91, 122, 205, 244, 345, 348, 633

Q

Quamina Gladstone 332
Queen Elizabeth 18, 73, 126, 609
Quinnipiac 200

R

Rachel Jackson 319
Rachel Ruysch 35
racism 5, 87, 143, 194, 233, 316, 327, 339, 342, 344, 359, 387, 391, 420, 530, 591
Rahel Varnhagen 101
Rakoczi Castle 26
Rape of Belgium 466, 665
Rape of Nanking 514
Rashid Ali 543, 544
Ray Wilbur 485
Reconstruction 326, 356, 384, 385, 387, 388, 389, 485, 499, 635, 649, 652, 653
Reconstruction Finance Corporation (RFC) Act 485
Reich Concordat 583, 585, 684
Reign of Terror 91, 616
Reinhard Heydrich 535, 676
religious exclusivism 5
Religious Liberalism 116, 619
Renaissance 1, 7, 9, 10, 11, 12, 13, 15, 16, 17, 18, 19, 21, 22, 23, 24, 25, 26, 27, 28, 29, 30, 31, 32, 34, 35, 38, 39, 50, 56, 66, 68, 84, 99, 100, 101, 120, 195, 596, 597, 598, 599, 601, 603, 604, 605, 606, 607, 608, 609, 667, 687
repartimiento 335
Republican Motherhood 298
Republic of Florence 9
Republic of Letters 104, 618
Restoration of 1660 75
Reza Pahlavi 547
Ricardo 187, 192
Richard Allen 332, 355, 642
Richard III 18
Richelieu 88, 100
RMS Lancastria 537
Robert Dinwiddie 239
Robert E. Lee 369
Robert R. Livingston 396
Robinja 28

Rockefeller 392, 393, 394, 395, 396, 401, 402, 403, 404, 405, 411, 417, 428, 431, 434, 435, 531, 654, 655, 657, 660, 674
Roger Williams 64, 351
Rolfe 205
Rommel 542, 543, 552, 555, 565
Rosie the Riveter 575, 671, 682
Rousseau 105, 122, 124, 127, 154, 155, 156, 157, 173, 178, 618, 622
Royal Society 104
Rudolf Hess 544
ruling class 1, 3, 74, 92, 95, 96, 97, 155, 180, 246, 415, 449, 451, 475
Russia 21, 23, 28, 29, 44, 87, 92, 93, 94, 95, 96, 97, 160, 194, 198, 439, 440, 441, 443, 445, 448, 449, 450, 459, 463, 468, 501, 513, 527, 534, 540, 545, 548, 551, 552, 553, 555, 556, 569, 578, 607, 608, 663, 690
Rutherford B. Hayes 385, 388
Ruth Logan Roberts 101
Rutledge 207

S

Sacra Congregatio de Propaganda Fide 582
Salmon P. Chase 376
Sam Adams 243, 246, 248, 251, 253, 256, 260, 263, 264, 265, 266, 268, 269, 276, 285, 291, 293, 294, 296, 347, 361, 634, 693
Samuel Adams 75, 124, 243, 245, 246, 255, 260, 276, 613, 632, 633, 634, 635, 637, 646, 648
Samuel Clarke 117
Samuel Cornish 332, 643
Samuel Courtauld 111
Samuel Gompers 473, 666

Samuel Huntington 428
Santi Gucci 22
Sauk 201
Saybrook Platform 77
Schleiermacher 119, 122, 123, 169, 170, 171, 181, 619, 623
scholasticism 10
Schopenhauer 122, 124, 180, 181, 182, 183, 184, 185, 623, 624
Schwarzenau Brethren 73
science 1, 8, 9, 12, 19, 20, 40, 84, 98, 99, 104, 121, 123, 124, 125, 135, 136, 137, 138, 140, 145, 152, 153, 160, 163, 166, 174, 185, 195, 420, 432, 435, 531, 544, 604, 625, 661
Science of Logic 173, 174
scientific method 125, 152, 170, 186, 192
Second Great Awakening 333, 350, 352, 357
Second Vatican Council 66
Secularism 86
Seminole 234, 237, 317
Seneca 17, 206, 208, 211, 212, 217, 218, 220, 298
Servitus Judaeorum 586
Seven Years War 204, 238, 241
sexism 5, 80, 297, 459
Shakespeare 18, 37, 38
Shawnee 201, 231, 233
Sherman 368, 403, 650
Sherman Antitrust Act 403
Siege of Leningrad 547
Siemens 528, 546, 675
Simon Bolivar 333
Simon Ushakov 28, 607
Sir Francis Drake 70
Sir Isaac Newton 103, 104, 135
Sir John Oldcastle 47
Sistine Chapel 13, 14, 686

Slave Codes of 1705 338
Slavery 234, 314, 321, 322, 324, 325, 331, 337, 338, 339, 341, 343, 362, 631, 641, 644, 645, 647, 648, 653
Smedley Butler 519, 520, 697
Smith 115, 122, 124, 152, 158, 159, 160, 187, 191, 192, 249, 258, 622, 633
Smoot-Hawley 507
social psychology 1, 2, 4
Social Security Administration (SSA) 491
Society of Revolutionary Republican Women 108, 618
Sodality of Our Lady 68, 612
Sofonisba Anguissola 32, 608
Sojourner Truth 332, 344, 643
sola scriptura 118
Sons of Liberty 254, 272, 277
Sophia Elisabet Brenner 101
Sorkočević's villa 27
Southern Pacific 417
Spanish 7, 18, 37, 40, 41, 42, 44, 45, 56, 64, 69, 71, 87, 217, 218, 230, 234, 235, 236, 237, 239, 304, 321, 333, 335, 353, 460, 499, 513, 517, 612, 631, 672
Specie Circular 314
Spinoza 117, 122, 124, 138, 139, 143
Spoils System 307
SS SAthenia 533
Stalin 450, 501, 513, 517, 532, 544, 545, 548, 556, 560, 562, 565, 567, 569, 571, 584
Stamp Act 246, 251, 253, 255, 256, 257, 258, 259, 260
Standard Oil 401, 402, 403, 404, 520, 525, 655, 674
Stanislaw August Poniatowski 94
State Monopoly Capitalism 419, 426, 427, 434, 658

States Rights 308
Stephen A. Douglas 326
Sterilization and Euthanasia: A Contribution to Applied Christian Ethics 529
St. John of the Cross 64
St. Mihiel 454
Stonington Railroad 398
St. Teresa of Avila 39
Sugar Act 246, 247, 248, 250, 251, 260, 632
Susan B. Anthony 217, 299, 638
Szwajpolt Fiol 23

T

Tadadaho 206
Takahashi Korekiyo 502
Takeo Yoshikawa 543
Taming of the Shrew 38
Tarleton 300
Tehran Conference 560, 681
Tekakwitha 210, 211, 628
Tennessee Valley Authority 492, 669
Terem Palace 28, 607
Terence 17
That Jesus Christ Was Born a Jew 586, 684
The Courtier 30
The Devil is an Ass 18
The Elements of Law, Natural and Politic 128
The First Blast of the Trumpet Against the Monstrous Regiment of Women 38, 609
The Great Provocation 547
The Jew of Malta 18
The Last Judgment 13
The New Atlantis 126
Theodore Roosevelt 419, 420, 427,

429, 430, 436, 658
Theoricae novae planetarum 20
The Praise of Folly 11
The Right of American Slavery 341
The Rights of the British Colonies Asserted and Proved 297
The Shoemaker's Holiday 18
The Spanish Tragedy 18
The Spirit of the Laws 146
The Subjection of Women 190
The Theory of Moral Sentiments 159
The Wealth of Nations 159, 192
The World as Will and Representation 180, 181, 623, 624
Third Great Awakening 350
thirst for limitlessness 2, 4, 185
Thirty Years War 23, 64, 70, 85, 86, 87, 88, 91, 143
Thomas Aquinas 341, 581
Thomas A. Scott 404
Thomas Dekker 18
Thomas Gibbons 396, 654
Thomas Hooker 64
Thomas Kyd 18
Thomas Middleton 18
Thomas More 23, 31, 51, 610
Thomas Watson 524
Thousand Bomber Raid 552
Tony Drexel 410
Topeka Constitution 365, 649
Toussaint L'Ouverture 333
Townshend Acts 261, 262
Tractatus de duabus Sarmatis 22
trade 2, 8, 26, 27, 40, 41, 42, 44, 50, 55, 60, 87, 93, 103, 111, 113, 138, 142, 150, 154, 158, 160, 196, 197, 201, 204, 218, 231, 235, 249, 252, 258, 276, 285, 290, 295, 306, 316, 322, 323, 324, 326, 327, 328, 335, 336, 339, 343, 362, 364, 369, 379, 397, 403, 408, 415, 418, 429, 431, 449, 459, 464, 465, 480, 499, 501, 505, 507, 512, 531, 533, 546, 587, 610, 644, 694
Trail of Tears 233, 318, 630, 640
Treaties of Westphalia 71
Treaty of Fort Stanwix 242, 632
Treaty of Hard Labor 242, 632
Treaty of Karlowitz 92, 616
Treaty of Lochaber 242, 632
Treaty of Versailles 469, 476, 513, 666
Treaty on the Final Settlement with Respect to Germany 573
Treblinka II 553
Trialogus 47, 610
Trilateral Commission 428
Trotsky 448, 450
Tunxis 200
T. W. Hoit 341, 645

U

U-boats 533, 558, 570
Union Banking Corporation 519
Union of Lublin 22, 604
Union Pacific 397, 412, 417
United States Steel Corporation 414
universal morality 4, 5, 194
University of Pozsony 26
Upanishads 184, 624
Ustasha 543
utilitarianism 142, 152, 186, 187

V

V1 562
V-2 566, 682
Vanderbilt 392, 393, 394, 395, 396, 397, 398, 399, 400, 402, 404, 405, 654, 670

Vasco da Gama 41
Veliki Tabor 27, 606
Veterans Day 457
Virginia Company 196
Virgin Mary 68, 83, 605
Visegrád Palace 25
Vitruvian Man 10, 603
Vittoria Colonna 31, 608
Volpone 18
Voltaire 124, 152
voting trust 414

W

Wacław Szamotulski 24
Wade-Davis Bill 387, 653
Wade Hampton 390, 653
Walsh 328, 330, 642
Wampanoag 200
Wampanoags 205
Wanda Gertz 578, 683
Wannsee Conference 550, 679
War of 1812 302, 308, 309, 310, 367, 638
warrior 1, 2, 199, 221, 235, 301, 450
Warsaw Uprising 563, 564, 578, 699
Washington 233, 239, 240, 243, 246, 275, 278, 280, 281, 282, 283, 284, 288, 290, 293, 294, 295, 306, 307, 317, 319, 320, 325, 333, 347, 355, 361, 395, 402, 411, 425, 433, 452, 486, 489, 519, 520, 526, 527, 550, 563, 606, 628, 635, 640, 641, 664, 668, 674, 675, 677, 698
Washington Gladden 402
Wawrzyniec Grzymała Goślicki 24
Waxhaw 231
W. E. B. Du Bois, 390, 653
What is Enlightenment 124
Wicocomico 201
Willem Janszoon 45

William Appleman Williams 430, 660
William Byrd 354, 601, 685
William Dodd 522
William Gibbs McAdoo 475
William Harvey 21
William Lloyd Garrison 344
William Penn 64, 257
William Reublin 72
William Rockefeller 417
William Seymour 357
William Wilberforce 343
Wilson 114, 347, 420, 432, 453, 473, 660, 667
Wolof 231
Women's Auxiliary Army Corps (WAAC) 552
Woodrow Wilson 420, 432, 660
Woolworth 529, 530, 698
Works Progress Administration (WPA) 491
World War I 93, 360, 408, 429, 438, 439, 441, 444, 445, 446, 449, 452, 454, 457, 458, 459, 460, 461, 463, 468, 469, 471, 474, 477, 479, 484, 507, 510, 519, 659, 661, 662, 664, 665, 666, 667
World War II 463, 488, 491, 498, 502, 509, 510, 513, 514, 516, 518, 532, 543, 562, 573, 574, 576, 577, 579, 673, 674, 676, 677, 678, 679, 680, 681, 682, 683, 699
Wright Patman 484, 486

Y

Yalta Conference 569
Yamasee 231, 232, 630
Yamasee War 231, 232, 630
Yuchi 231

Z

Zamosc 23
Zofia Lubomirska 101

About the Authors

Charles Paprocki has spent many years working with troubled teenagers, prison inmates, welfare recipients, and migrant workers in the human services system. He also owned a graphics and advertising agency in New York City where he combined his skill and knowledge to create social marketing campaigns. He was one of the core leaders to create the Universal Pre-K program in New York State and the local food movement in Illinois. His last work was to manage an organic farm in southern Illinois. He has consulted with international NGO's on management strategies and participated in the Earth Summit in Brazil and the Social Summit in Denmark. He is now retired and living in Carbondale, Illinois.

Tom Paprocki has worked several years in social services, including starting a preschool and daycare center in rural southern Illinois and serving as an administrator for a drug education and crisis center. After receiving a Masters in Public Administration, he was hired by the NASA Goddard Space Flight Center as a Presidential Management Intern. He served thirty years at Goddard, which included positions as head of Personnel, Procurement, and Institutional Resources. He spent the last seven years as Director of Management Operations, which included facilities, acquisitions, environmental and health services, security, and logistics for the research and launch facilities at Greenbelt, Maryland and Wallops Island, Virginia. He is now retired and living in Dunkirk Maryland.

www.ingramcontent.com/pod-product-compliance
Lightning Source LLC
Chambersburg PA
CBHW021136080526
44588CB00008B/84